CHINA REVIEW OF
MARITIME AND COMMERCIAL ARBITRATION (VOL. 2)

中国海事商事仲裁评论

(第二辑)

国际仲裁的区域协同和实践发展

李虎 主编

Regional Coordination and Practical Development of
International Arbitration

图书在版编目（CIP）数据

中国海事商事仲裁评论. 第二辑，国际仲裁的区域协同和实践发展 / 李虎主编. -- 北京：北京大学出版社，2024.12. -- ISBN 978-7-301-35895-5

Ⅰ. D925.7-53

中国国家版本馆 CIP 数据核字第 2024P9A600 号

书　　　名	中国海事商事仲裁评论（第二辑）：国际仲裁的区域协同和实践发展 ZHONGGUO HAISHI SHANGSHI ZHONGCAI PINGLUN（DI-ER JI）：GUOJI ZHONGCAI DE QUYU XIETONG HE SHIJIAN FAZHAN
著作责任者	李　虎　主编
责 任 编 辑	周子琳　王建君
标 准 书 号	ISBN 978-7-301-35895-5
出 版 发 行	北京大学出版社
地　　　址	北京市海淀区成府路 205 号　100871
网　　　址	http://www.pup.cn　http://www.yandayuanzhao.com
电 子 邮 箱	编辑部 yandayuanzhao@163.com　总编室 zpup@pup.cn
新 浪 微 博	@北京大学出版社　@北大出版社燕大元照法律图书
电　　　话	邮购部 010-62752015　发行部 010-62750672 编辑部 010-62117788
印 刷 者	大厂回族自治县彩虹印刷有限公司
经 销 者	新华书店
	650 毫米 × 980 毫米　16 开本　32.5 印张　468 千字 2024 年 12 月第 1 版　2024 年 12 月第 1 次印刷
定　　　价	88.00 元

未经许可，不得以任何方式复制或抄袭本书之部分或全部内容。
版权所有，侵权必究
举报电话：010-62752024　电子邮箱：fd@pup.cn
图书如有印装质量问题，请与出版部联系，电话：010-62756370

编委会成员名单

主　任　于健龙
副主任　张月姣　沈四宝　张永坚　刘晓红　李　虎
委　员　(按姓氏笔画排序)
　　　　王承杰　王彦君　王雪华　牛　磊　刘亚军
　　　　刘敬东　关正义　杜焕芳　杨国华　肖永平
　　　　宋迪煌　张文广　张晓君　陈云东　郑　蕾
　　　　赵　云　郭　雳　黄　巍　蒋　弘　韩立新
　　　　覃华平　蔡晨风　薛　虹　薛　源

编辑部成员名单

主　编　李　虎
副主编　黄　巍　杨　帆　齐　骥
编　辑　刘　颖　徐　飞　黄晨亮　洪慧敏　郑秋钰
　　　　贾云鹏　周　昕　莫之颖　耿　迪　张傲霜
　　　　唐嘉玮　肖　鹏　郭晓霞　陈　迅　王　辰
　　　　陈末末　付　慈　曲扬波　张琳雪　杨意茹
　　　　赵亭轩　王鸣杰

前　言

时光如白驹过隙,转瞬之间,中国仲裁事业的发展已经迈入第 66 个年头。为更好地满足国内外仲裁专家、学者、从业人士交流学习的需求,推动中国海事商事仲裁事业的高质量发展,在业内同仁的大力支持下,中国海事仲裁委员会(以下简称"中国海仲")经过一年多的筹备,正式推出《中国海事商事仲裁评论》(以下简称《评论》)系列丛书。

出版专业文集,以承载业务宣传、理念交流、文化培育等功能,是国际领先仲裁机构的通行做法。2021 年以来,中国海仲贯彻中共中央办公厅、国务院办公厅《关于完善仲裁制度提高仲裁公信力的若干意见》,围绕"服务航运贸易实务,促进仲裁研讨交流"这一宗旨,精心筹划,聚焦理论研究、热点追踪、案例分析、法律解读等内容,依托行业资源,主动向具有权威性、代表性的国内外专家约稿,通过"海仲杯"中国海事商事仲裁征文大赛向青年仲裁从业者征集文章,力求《评论》在体现前瞻性强、参考价值高、影响力大的权威专家观点的同时,为新时期的涉外法律人才培养交流提供平台。总体而言,《评论》呈现出以下亮点:

一是立足中国仲裁发展实际,充分展现中国仲裁的实践优势和理论特色。自中国国际贸易促进委员会的涉外仲裁肇始,历经半个多世纪的风风雨雨,仲裁早已深深植根于社会主义市场经济的土壤,在改革开放的春风中绽放出无数绚烂的花朵。《评论》所辑录之作着眼于中国仲裁的特有实践,深度剖析中国仲裁变革发展所回应的现实关切,精心提炼、传播、弘扬中国仲裁在服务大局、普惠民生、传播法治文化等方面所形成的"东方经验",同时亦体现反思意识,倡导不忘初心、正本清源、去芜存菁,以批判的眼光直面当前仲裁实践中存在的问题,以坚定的立场毫不动摇地推进中国仲裁在曲折中前进。

二是探讨国际仲裁的发展趋势和创新成果,为中国仲裁的进步提供参考思路。"以我为主,为我所用"是涉外法律工作者需要一贯坚持的原则,对于我们前方道路的选择至关重要。《评论》鼓励国际视野,努力汇集各方声音,及时追踪、观察、评析国际仲裁中的最新实践,力求以域外经验推动中国仲裁顶层设计、理论和实操层面的不断完善;同时注重兼顾当下国情,强调从当前中国仲裁的实际需求出发,辩证地看待各类解决方案。

《评论》将认真贯彻习近平法治思想,在借鉴国际先进经验的基础上,力争为探索适合中国国情的仲裁发展道路贡献力量。希望理论界、实务界同仁积极支持、踊跃投稿,同时也希望读者多多提出宝贵的意见和建议。未来,我们将全力把《评论》办好、办精,努力将其打造为中国仲裁法律领域的代表性文集,切实服务于中国仲裁事业的发展。

《中国海事商事仲裁评论》编委会

2022年9月1日

目　　录

粤港澳大湾区民商事多元纠纷解决机制相关问题研究 …………001
　　一、非诉讼方面 ………………………………………………003
　　二、诉讼方面 …………………………………………………009

《仲裁法》修订前沿问题探析 ……………………………………013
　　一、临时仲裁制度尚存客观瓶颈待突破 ……………………015
　　二、仲裁庭自裁管辖权制度修订细节待商榷 ………………022
　　三、临时措施决定的执行效力问题有待解决 ………………025
　　四、仲裁司法审查机制有待完善 ……………………………032
　　结　语 …………………………………………………………039

仲裁司法审查中的价值选择问题探析 ……………………………040
　　一、问题的提出 ………………………………………………040
　　二、仲裁协议效力司法审查的价值选择 ……………………042
　　三、仲裁裁决司法审查的价值选择 …………………………053
　　四、仲裁司法审查价值选择对有效衔接与协调多元化纠纷解决
　　　　机制的实际功用 …………………………………………058
　　结　语 …………………………………………………………060

最密切联系原则纳入仲裁协议法律适用之证成 …………………061
　　一、最密切联系原则与涉外仲裁协议法律适用之渊源 ……063
　　二、"隐名"适用有效性原则下最密切联系原则之新解 …065
　　三、必要性：作为法律选择理由的最密切联系原则 ………068
　　四、可行性：最密切联系原则与有效性原则"互动"之可能 …072
　　结　语 …………………………………………………………074

第三方资助国际商事仲裁法律问题研究 ································· 075
引　言 ··· 075
一、第三方资助国际商事仲裁的内涵与发展 ························· 076
二、规制第三方资助国际商事仲裁的必要性 ························· 078
三、第三方资助国际商事仲裁的国际规制经验探究 ················· 082
四、第三方资助国际商事仲裁在中国的发展路径 ···················· 085
结　论 ··· 091

东北亚仲裁发展观察 ·· 092
中国篇 ·· 092
一、扬帆四海 ·· 093
二、改弦更张 ·· 093
三、创新与展望 ··· 095

俄罗斯篇 ··· 095
一、悠久的商事仲裁传统 ······································ 096
二、2015年仲裁改革的背景 ··································· 097
三、现行俄罗斯仲裁法的主要特点 ··························· 098
四、俄罗斯目前主要的商事仲裁机构 ························ 103
五、俄罗斯商事仲裁实践中需要注意的几个问题 ·········· 105

蒙古国篇 ··· 110
一、介绍 ·· 110
二、现代蒙古国仲裁法与法律规制解决 ····················· 113
三、修订后的仲裁法 ·· 114
结　语 ·· 118

朝鲜篇 ·· 119
一、立法背景 ·· 120
二、主要内容 ·· 121
三、对于朝鲜仲裁管辖权的思考 ······························ 127
四、《朝鲜涉外经济仲裁法》存在的一些问题 ············· 131
结　语 ·· 133

韩国篇……………………………………………………………135
  一、韩国仲裁产业政策导向及现状………………………………135
  二、仲裁产业化导向下韩国仲裁法制建设………………………140
  结　语………………………………………………………………149

日本篇……………………………………………………………150
  引　言………………………………………………………………150
  一、日本司法机关对仲裁裁决进行司法审查的制度概要………153
  二、日本司法机关对仲裁裁决进行司法审查的判例运用………161
  结　语………………………………………………………………165

试论以集团公司名义订立仲裁协议的效力扩张 ………………166
  一、基本案情………………………………………………………166
  二、问题的提出……………………………………………………167
  三、以集团公司名义订立仲裁协议效力扩张的理论适用分析…169
  四、我国以集团公司订立仲裁协议效力扩张的法律制度完善…180
  结　论………………………………………………………………184

商事仲裁中逾期提交证据涉及的若干法律问题研究 …………185
  一、研究逾期提交证据具有重要意义……………………………186
  二、"逾期提交证据"与"违反仲裁规则"的关系…………………188
  三、逾期提交证据与证据持有人故意隐瞒证据（及撤销裁决
     之间）的关联性…………………………………………………193
  四、对于仲裁庭擅自接受一方当事人逾期提交的证据，对方
     当事人如何正确应对？…………………………………………195
  五、关于逾期提交证据的立法建议………………………………196

CONTENTS

Studies About Issues Related to the ADR Mechanism on Civil and Commercial Disputes in the Guangdong-Hongkong-Macao Greater Bay Area ·············201
    I. Non-litigation ·············204
    II. Litigation ·············215

An Analysis of Frontier Issues in the Amendment of Arbitration Law ······220
    I. There are Objective Bottlenecks in the Ad Hoc Arbitration System to be Broken Through ·············223
    II. The Details of the Revision of Competence-Competence Need to be Discussed ·············235
    III. Unresolved Issue of Effectiveness of the Enforcement of Decisions on Interim Measures ·············239
    IV. The Judicial Review Mechanism for Arbitration Needs to be Improved ·············250
    Conclusion ·············261

The Analysis of the Value Option for Judicial Review for Arbitration ······262
    I. Formulation of the Question ·············263
    II. Value Options for Judicial Review of the Validity of Arbitration Agreements ·············265
    III. Value Options for Judicial Review of Arbitral Awards ·············284
    IV. Practical Utility of the Value Choice of Judicial Review of Arbitration for the Effective Articulation and Coordination of Diversified Dispute Resolution Mechanisms ·············293

  Conclusion 296

The Choice of Law of the Arbitration Agreement: New Approach Towards
  the Application of the Closest Connection Principle 297
  I. The Closest Connection Principle as a Source of Choice of
   Law for Foreign-related Arbitration Agreements 300
  II. Noval Framework for Application of the Closest Connection
   Principle Under the Hidden Pro-validation Approach 304
  III. Necessity: the Closest Connection Principle as Basis for Choice
   of Laws 308
  IV. Feasibility: Bridging the Validation Principle with the Closest
   Connection Principle 314
  Conclusion 317

Study on the Legal Issues of the Third Party Funding for International
  Commercial Arbitration 318
  Introduction 318
  I. The Connotation and Development of Third Party Funding for
   International Commercial Arbitration 319
  II. Necessity of Regulating Third Party Funding for International
   Commercial Arbitration 323
  III. Exploration of International Regulation Experience of Third
   Party Funding for International Commercial Arbitration 328
  IV. Development Path of Third Party Funded International
   Commercial Arbitration in China 333
  Conclusion 342

Observations on the Developments of Arbitration in Northeast Asia 344
China 345
  I. Worldwide Routes 345
  II. Setting the Sails 346
  III. Innovation and Outlook 348
Russia 348

    I. A Long Tradition of Commercial Arbitration ·················349
    II. Background of the 2015 Arbitration Reform ···············351
    III. Features of the Arbitration Law of Russian·················353
    IV. Current Main Commercial Arbitration Institutions in Russia ······359
    V. Issues to be Noticed in the Practice of Commercial Arbitration
       in Russia ···363
Mongolia ··369
    Introduction ··369
    I. Modern Mongolian Arbitration Law and Legal Regulation
       Settlement ··375
    II. The Revised Arbitration Law ································376
    Conclusion··382
Democratic People's Republic of Korea·····························383
    I. Legislation Background ······································384
    II. Main Contents ··385
    III. Reflections on the DPRK Jurisdiction of Arbitration ··············396
    IV. Problems of the Foreign Economic Arbitration Law of the
       DPRK ···402
    Conclusion··405
Republic of Korea ··407
    I. Industrial Policy Orientation and Current Status of the Arbitration
       of Republic of Korea ···407
    II. Legal System Construction of Arbitration of Republic of Korea
       Under the Orientation of Arbitration Industrialization ··············414
    Conclusion··429
Japan ··430
    Introduction ··430
    I. Summary of the Judicial Review System of Arbitral Awards by
       Japanese Judicial Organs ····································434
    II. The Application of Judicial Review in the Judicial Precedents
       of Arbitral Awards by Japanese Judicial Organs ···············447

Conclusion ···453
Study on the Expansion of the Validity of Arbitration Agreements
　　Concluded in the Name of a Group Company ·······························455
　　　I. Basic Facts ···456
　　　II. Problems Raised ··457
　　　III. Analysis of the Application of Theory to the Expansion of the
　　　　　Validity of Arbitration Agreements Concluded in the Name of
　　　　　a Group Company ···459
　　　IV. Improvement of the Legal System for the Expansion of the
　　　　　Validity of Arbitration Agreements Concluded by Group
　　　　　Company in China ··477
　　　Conclusion ··483
Studies on the Production of Evidence After the Expiry of the Time Period
　　in Commercial Arbitration ···484
　　　I. Significance of Studies on Production of Evidence After the
　　　　　Expiry of the Time Period ···485
　　　II. The Relationship Between "Producing Evidence After the Expiry
　　　　　of the Time Period" and " Violation of Arbitration Rules" ··········489
　　　III. The Connection Between the Evidence Produced After the Expiry
　　　　　of the Time Period and the Deliberate Concealment of Evidence
　　　　　by the Holder (and Setting Aside the Arbitration Award) ············497
　　　IV. How to Correctly Deal with the Arbitral Tribunal's Arbitrary
　　　　　Admission to the Evidence Produced by the Other Party After
　　　　　the Specified Time Period ···499
　　　V. Legislative Proposals on Legal Issues concerning Evidence
　　　　　Produced After the Expiry of the Time Period ······················501

粤港澳大湾区民商事多元纠纷解决机制相关问题研究

李 虎*

摘要：民商事多元纠纷解决是粤港澳大湾区融合发展的重要事项。粤港澳分别实行不同的法律制度，区际法律冲突客观存在。本文从实务角度对推动构建并完善粤港澳大湾区民商事多元纠纷解决机制所涉及的相关问题进行了梳理研究。这些问题主要包括非诉讼和诉讼两个方面的七个问题。非诉讼方面涉及的问题有三地仲裁规则与调解规则的衔接、仲裁员与调解员的资格标准和操守准则、仲裁裁决与和解协议的认可和执行，以及专业服务机构的准入；诉讼方面涉及的问题则包括诉讼、仲裁和调解的衔接机制与平台建设，大湾区商事和解协议、仲裁裁决和法院判决的转化与跨境执行，以及信息化平台建设。建立和完善大湾区民商事多元化纠纷解决机制是一个系统工程，需要把握两个基本原则：一是要有国际化的视野，二是要确立并恪守国际争端解决中"争议解决地"的理念。

关键词：大湾区；民商事多元纠纷解决机制；诉讼；仲裁；调解

2021年9月，中共中央、国务院印发《全面深化前海深港现代服务业合作区改革开放方案》（以下简称《前海深港方案》）及《横琴粤澳深度合作区建设总体方案》（以下简称《横琴粤澳方案》）。《前海深港

---

* 中国海事仲裁委员会副主任兼秘书长。本文的撰写得到了中国海事仲裁委员会案件管理处处长齐骥和监督协调处案件经办人莫之颖的大力支持与协助，特此致谢。

方案》提出要建设高水平对外开放门户枢纽,要求提升法律事务对外开放水平,在前海合作区内建设国际法律服务中心和国际商事争议解决中心,探索不同法系、跨境法律规则的衔接,建设诉讼、调解、仲裁既相互独立又衔接配合的国际区际商事争议争端解决平台。《横琴粤澳方案》要求强化法治保障,加强粤澳司法交流协作,建立完善国际商事审判、仲裁、调解等多元化商事纠纷解决机制。2022年6月,国务院印发《广州南沙深化面向世界的粤港澳全面合作总体方案》(以下简称《南沙粤港澳方案》),提出要打造规则衔接机制对接高地,要求打造国际一流营商环境,健全多元化纠纷解决机制,搭建一站式民商事纠纷解决系统平台,促进诉讼与仲裁、调解等多元化纠纷解决方式信息互通、有机衔接。上述三个方案对粤港澳大湾区民商事多元纠纷解决机制建设提出了明确要求。

民商事多元纠纷解决机制作为现代高端法律服务模式,是粤港澳大湾区全面合作中的重要事项,对大湾区深度融合发展具有重要意义。因粤港澳分别实行不同的法律制度,区际法律冲突客观存在,在我们推动构建完善粤港澳大湾区民商事多元纠纷解决机制的过程中,对相关问题需要深入研究和妥善处理。结合上述三个方案的相关要求,这些问题主要包括非诉讼和诉讼两个方面的七个问题。非诉讼方面涉及的问题有三地仲裁规则与调解规则的衔接、仲裁员与调解员的资格标准和操守准则、仲裁裁决与和解协议的认可和执行,以及专业服务机构的准入;诉讼方面涉及的问题则包括诉讼、仲裁和调解的衔接机制与平台建设,大湾区商事和解协议、仲裁裁决和法院判决的转化与跨境执行,以及信息化平台建设。

中国海事仲裁委员会(以下简称"中国海仲")2014年在中国香港特别行政区(以下简称"香港特区")设立香港仲裁中心;2023年在广州设立大湾区仲裁中心(华南分会),为粤港澳大湾区当事人就近提供仲裁服务;2017年与广州海事法院签署合作备忘录,建立案件委托调解工作机制;2020年分别与香港特区一邦国际网上仲调中心和澳门特别行政区(以下简称"澳门特区")的澳门世界贸易中心仲裁中心签署合作协议,深化合作交流,积极参与粤港澳大湾区民商事多元纠纷解决机制建设,积累了一些成功经验,取得了一定的成绩。

一、非诉讼方面

(一)关于争议解决规则衔接

1. 仲裁规则

在国际仲裁中,仲裁适用仲裁地法。当事人对仲裁地有约定的,从其约定,没有约定的,则由仲裁庭决定,一般为机构所在地。三地机构仲裁规则的制定不能违背各自仲裁法的强制性规定。三地仲裁法规定的不同导致仲裁规则和实践的差异,从而会产生规则之间的衔接问题。这些问题主要体现在以下几个方面:

第一,谁决定仲裁案件管辖权?

在内地,依法由仲裁机构决定案件管辖权;而在港澳地区,则是根据国际仲裁中的"自裁管辖理论"由仲裁庭决定案件的管辖权。

第二,谁决定仲裁员是否回避?

在内地,由仲裁机构(仲裁委员会主任)就仲裁员是否回避作出决定;在港澳地区,仲裁员是否回避可由仲裁庭决定,法院拥有最终决定权。

第三,谁决定保全以及临时措施?

在内地,保全由有管辖权的人民法院决定;在香港特区,保全和临时措施由仲裁庭决定,直接针对第三人的保全和临时措施则由法院决定;在澳门特区,保全由法院决定,而临时措施则由仲裁庭决定。

第四,谁决定仲裁地、仲裁语言等重要程序事项?

内地多规定由仲裁机构决定,而港澳地区均规定由仲裁庭决定。

第五,机构案件经办人可否担任仲裁庭秘书?

依国际仲裁通例,仲裁机构为仲裁等争议解决活动提供管理服务,其本身并不解决争议,仲裁庭是审理裁决案件的主体,对案件的程序和实体负责。机构可以指定其工作人员作为案件经办人,代表机构管理案件,但不得指定案件经办人担任仲裁庭秘书,仲裁庭可以指定专业人员担任仲裁庭秘书,为其审理裁决提供专业协助。仲裁庭秘书为仲裁庭服务,职责由仲裁庭确定。在内地,仲裁机构的案件经办人在仲裁庭组成后实际同时担任仲裁庭秘书;而在香港特区,仲裁机构的工作人员可以被仲裁庭指定担任秘书,但不得担任同一个案件的案件经办人。

第六,仲裁员可否在案件中担任调解员?

在内地和港澳地区,仲裁员依法均可以在仲裁程序中作为调解员对案件进行调解(仲裁与调解相结合),但对调解中获取的实质性或保密性案情,调解失败恢复仲裁程序后,三地仲裁法规定的披露要求不同。①

对于三地仲裁规则的差异,一是可以借助《仲裁法》修订的契机,加强顶层设计,整体解决问题,诸如仲裁管辖权决定、临时保全措施决定,以及仲裁员回避决定等问题。二是引导内地仲裁机构通过及时修订仲裁规则,加强衔接对接,与国际做法接轨。《中国海事仲裁委员会仲裁规则(2021)》(以下简称 2021 年《仲裁规则》)即已规定,案件管辖权决定由中国海仲作出,但如有必要,中国海仲可以授权仲裁庭作出管辖权决定。这既符合现行《仲裁法》的规定,又与国际通行做法保持基本一致。2021 年《仲裁规则》进一步明确,由仲裁庭决定仲裁地、仲裁语言等重要程序事项。仲裁庭可以指定中国海仲的工作人员担任仲裁庭秘书,但该人不得是同一个仲裁案件的案件经办人。三是对发端于内地的"仲裁与调解相结合"等实践中行之有效的做法,可以扩大宣传,大力弘扬,增进理解,求同存异,发挥优势。

2. 调解规则

相对于仲裁而言,调解程序更为灵活简便。调解不是由调解员作

---

① 根据香港特区《仲裁条例》第 33 条的规定,如果"仲裁员在由他以调解员身分进行的调解程序中,从一方取得机密资料","该调解程序在没有达成各方接受的和解下终止,则该仲裁员在恢复进行仲裁程序之前,须向所有其他各方尽量披露该等资料中他认为对仲裁程序具关键性的资料"。澳门特区《仲裁法》第 55 条第 4 款规定:"如调停程序终止时仍未就争议的解决达成约定,仲裁员应披露关于程序属重要的保密资料。"内地《仲裁法》第 51 条对仲裁中的调解作出规定,但并未明确仲裁员在调解程序中获知的当事人重要资料信息的处理问题。实践中,多由仲裁机构在仲裁规则中予以规定。2021 年《仲裁规则》第 56 条第 9 款规定:"如果调解不成功,任何一方当事人均不得在其后的仲裁程序、司法程序和其他任何程序中援引对方当事人或仲裁庭在调解过程中曾发表的意见、提出的观点、作出的陈述、表示认同或否定的建议或主张作为其请求、答辩或反请求的依据。"

裁断,而主要是由调解员主持斡旋、调停,引导争议双方厘清争议,明了责任,互谅互让,促成双方当事人达成和解,签署和解协议,落实执行。就粤港澳法律传统而言,内地和澳门特区遵从大陆法传统,而香港特区则遵从普通法传统。大陆法传统下的调解,对应的英文词汇应该是conciliation,调解员在调解中更为积极主动,可以提出调解方案建议,供争议双方参考。而普通法传统下的调解,对应的英文词汇则更接近于mediation,调解员在调解中主要是促成争议双方达成和解。

香港特区制定了《调解条例》,内地和澳门特区目前尚无专门的"商事调解法"。调解机构在不违背所在地相关法律强制性规定的前提下,各自制定自己的调解规则。虽然各地调解机构和调解员在调解程序中的职能作用有所不同,但其最终目的与结果都是促成当事人和解,签署和解协议。粤港澳调解规则在衔接上没有实质性障碍,所在湾区调解机构可以加强协同,促进调解应用,丰富调解实践。

(二)关于仲裁员与调解员资格标准和操守准则

1. 仲裁员

一方面,在国际范围内,相关国际公约和内国仲裁法对仲裁员的资格均有实质性要求,即"独立公正",而较少有其他形式要求。比如,《瑞典仲裁法》[Swedish Arbitration Act of 1999(SFS 1999: 116)]明确规定,仲裁员必须独立公正。包括国际商会国际仲裁院(The ICC International Court of Arbitration)、斯德哥尔摩商会仲裁院(Arbitration Institute of the Stockholm Chamber of Commerce)、伦敦国际仲裁院(London Court of International Arbitration, LCIA)等诸多知名仲裁机构均不设仲裁员名册,其他仲裁机构比如新加坡国际仲裁中心(Singapore International Arbitration Centre, SIAC)等虽然设有仲裁员名册,但名册多为推荐性的。另一方面,国际上大量的海事商事争议是通过无须机构管理的临时仲裁解决的。潜在的专业人士通过参加公信力较高的第三方专业协会[比如皇家特许仲裁员协会(Chartered Institute of Arbitrators, CIArb)]等机构组织的仲裁员培训,取得认证证书,从而增加其在具体仲裁案件中获得当事人或仲裁机构指定担任仲裁员的机会。专业协会［比如国际律师协会（International Bar Association, IBA）］也会制定发布示范性的仲裁员操守准则，供具体案件中的当事人约定适用或仲裁庭决定适用。

香港特区仲裁市场非常成熟，专业人士一般是通过参加皇家特许仲裁员协会东亚分会等机构的培训获取资格认证，辅之以专业经历，申请成为仲裁机构的仲裁员，或接受临时仲裁当事人指定，审理裁决案件。香港特区本土机构香港国际仲裁中心（Hong Kong International Arbitration Centre, HKIAC）也提供仲裁员培训，但对仲裁员是否具有培训认证则没有强制要求。实务中，相应的培训认证对能否成为其仲裁员实际上是有很大影响的。该中心仲裁员名册是推荐性的，供当事人参考，选择指定仲裁员，机构也制定有仲裁员操守准则。[①] 在澳门特区，民商事争议传统上多通过诉讼解决，商事仲裁发展相对滞后。在回归之前，澳门特区民事诉讼法中有对仲裁的专门规定，回归之后，澳门特区2020年5月实施《仲裁法》，仲裁处于发展过程中。澳门特区于2014年成立澳门仲裁协会，提供有关仲裁研讨培训等服务。在内地，除"公道正派"的实质性要求外，《仲裁法》对仲裁员有"三八两高"的法定标准要求，各仲裁机构按照法定标准外加本机构要求选聘仲裁员，制定仲裁员守则和行为规范，对其在册仲裁员进行培训管理，绝大多数仲裁机构规定当事人只能在其名册中指定仲裁员[②]。在中国仲裁协会筹组过程中，内地目前尚无具备较高公信力的第三方培训认证机构。各机构仲裁员选聘标准和操守准则也不尽相同。

比较可见，粤港澳在仲裁员资格标准及操守准则方面实际差异较

---

① 《香港国际仲裁中心道德行为规范》适用于该中心在册仲裁员，其明确指出，仲裁员也要同时遵守其初始专业组织有关会员实践或行为规范。参见香港国际仲裁中心网站（www.hkiac.org/arbitration/arbitrators/code-of-ethical-conduct），访问日期：2022年7月24日。

② 2021年《仲裁规则》首次明确中国海仲仲裁员名册属于推荐性的。根据该规则第30条的规定，"当事人可以从仲裁委员会仲裁员名册中选定仲裁员，也可以在仲裁委员会仲裁员名册外选定仲裁员；除非仲裁委员会另有决定，首席仲裁员和独任仲裁员应从仲裁委员会仲裁员名册中产生"，"当事人在仲裁委员会仲裁员名册外选定仲裁员，应当符合仲裁地法律的规定"。

大。考虑到内地仲裁市场持续开放,临时仲裁逐步落地①,内地需要加快筹组中国仲裁协会,就仲裁员的培训认证和操守准则进行统一的行业规范。粤港澳可加强协同合作,对公信力较高的第三方培训认证机构进行评估认证,由其提供粤港澳大湾区仲裁员培训认证,提高仲裁员的业务水平和职业素养,提升仲裁公信力。

2. 调解员

粤港澳调解员资格标准和操守准则情形与上述仲裁员情形相似。香港特区已有成熟的第三方培训认证机构。内地尚无有关调解员的统一资格标准和操守准则要求,第三方认证机构缺乏,实践中由各商事调解机构(比如中国国际贸易促进委员会调解中心)自行规范。同样,粤港澳可加强合作,由相互认可的第三方认证机构对粤港澳大湾区调解员进行认证培训,促进调解健康发展。

(三)关于仲裁裁决与和解协议的认可与执行

1. 仲裁裁决

在裁决的认可和执行方面,粤港澳之间的相关机制已经相当完善。首先,我国于1986年决定加入《承认及执行外国仲裁裁决公约》(又称《纽约公约》),该公约于1987年对我国生效。目前该公约成员已达170个。凡在我国(包括港澳地区)作出的仲裁裁决,均可以在公约其他成员方法院得到承认和执行。其次,1999年最高人民法院与香港特区签署《最高人民法院关于内地与香港特别行政区相互执行仲裁裁决的安排》,2007年最高人民法院与澳门特区签署《最高人民法院关于内地与澳门特别行政区相互认可和执行仲裁裁决的安排》,2013年港澳地区之间签署《关于澳门特别行政区与香港特别行政区相互认可和执行仲裁裁决的安排》。三个安排的有关内容,尤其是关于拒绝认可和执行裁决的事由与《纽约公约》相同,粤港澳裁决得以相互认

---

① 国际上具有示范意义的临时仲裁规则一般均由海事仲裁员协会等商协会制定发布。2022年3月18日,中国海商法协会遵循国际惯例首次在国内制定并发布《中国海商法协会临时仲裁规则》,中国海仲同步配套制定并发布《中国海事仲裁委员会临时仲裁服务规则》,两者相互衔接,有机结合,在国内首创性地共同开展临时仲裁服务。参见中国海事仲裁委员会网站(www.cmac.org.cn/index.php?id=606),访问日期:2022年7月24日。

可和执行顺畅。司法机关可加强有关安排适用方面的协同,进一步统筹司法裁判幅度与标准,提高粤港澳裁决相互认可和执行的质效。

2. 和解协议

在和解协议的相互认可和执行方面,内地和港澳地区之间尚无机制性安排。

调解是由调解员促成双方当事人解决纠纷,达成和解协议。和解协议是当事人之间一个新的合同,主要靠双方当事人自动履行。因为和解协议不具备法律上的可强制执行性,除非法律有明确规定,和解协议也就无法如同判决或裁决一样由法院直接予以强制执行。在这方面,2018年《联合国关于调解所产生的国际和解协议公约》(又称《新加坡调解公约》)已就此作出明确规定。根据《新加坡调解公约》,基于国际商事调解而达成的国际和解协议,依循《新加坡调解公约》可以在公约成员方法院得到承认和执行,这就解决了基于国际商事调解而达成的和解协议在法律上的可执行性问题。

我国已于2019年签署《新加坡调解公约》,公约对我国生效后,我国(包括港澳地区)调解机构经过调解所形成的国际商事和解协议可以根据公约在公约其他成员得到承认和执行,除非和解协议具有公约规定的不予承认和执行的法定事由。对于粤港澳而言,一方面可以加强协同合作,改善法治环境,加快诚信体系建设,有效提高经由调解而达成的和解协议的自动履行率;另一方面,可考虑借鉴《新加坡调解公约》,在条件成熟时,由内地司法机构分别与港澳地区以及港澳地区之间签署相互认可和执行和解协议的安排,以制度化解决三地和解协议的认可和执行问题。

(四)关于专业服务机构的准入

首先,仲裁和调解作为法院诉讼之外的争议解决服务,均遵循"当事人意思自治原则",由当事人通过仲裁协议或调解协议自愿约定选择。在国际仲裁中,相对于仲裁机构的选择,仲裁地的选择更为重要。在当事人没有约定的情况下,仲裁程序适用仲裁地法律,仲裁地法律决定了对仲裁予以支持和进行监督的法院,也决定了裁决的籍属(裁决视为在仲裁地作出），进而决定了裁决执行的法律依据（依据裁决地法律还是区际安排或者国际公约）。除当事人另有约定外，仲裁庭也往往根据国际私法冲突规范决定解决争议的实体法为仲裁地法律。粤港澳可协同推进，努力提高多元争议解决服务的国际公信力，吸引粤港澳大湾区内外当事人更多地选择将其作为争议解决的目的地。

其次，就专业服务机构的准入来说，港澳地区均持开放态度。中国海仲2014年已在香港特区设立香港仲裁中心，和香港特区本土机构香港国际仲裁中心一样，是依据香港特区法律登记注册的担保有限责任公司，属于非营利法人。根据澳门特区第36/2019号行政法规《仲裁机构的设立与运作制度》的规定，内地仲裁机构凡满足其规定要求的，即可在澳门特区设立分支机构。内地对港澳地区及外国仲裁机构在内地设立分支机构事宜尚无统一规定。实践中，上海和北京已经先行出台政策，支持港澳地区及外国仲裁机构在京沪设立办事机构和业务机构。《前海深港方案》已明确规定，"允许境外知名仲裁等争议解决机构经广东省政府司法行政部门登记并报国务院司法行政部门备案，在前海合作区设立业务机构，就涉外商事、海事、投资等领域发生的民商事争议开展仲裁业务"。湾区内的广东省亦可积极考虑。2021年《仲裁法（修订）（征求意见稿）》规定，外国仲裁机构在内地设立机构的，应经省级司法行政部门登记，报国务院司法行政部门备案。实际上，除内地仲裁外，由《仲裁法》对港澳特区仲裁机构、外国仲裁机构及国际仲裁机构在我国领域内进行的所有仲裁活动进行统一的规范调整，是理想选择。

二、诉讼方面

（一）关于诉讼、仲裁和调解的衔接机制与平台建设

从法院诉讼角度看，关于粤港澳大湾区多元纠纷解决的衔接机制，笔者认为最高人民法院有关"一站式"纠纷解决机制和平台建设实践可资借鉴。

最高人民法院通过设立国际商事法庭，制定规则规范，构建"一站

式"纠纷解决机制和平台,吸纳特定的内地及港澳地区仲裁机构和调解机构,使诉讼、仲裁和调解有机衔接,提供一揽子争议解决服务。对于相关国际商事争议,当事人愿意通过仲裁或调解解决的,法庭引导当事人选择纳入机制的仲裁机构进行仲裁或调解机构进行调解,同时,法庭对仲裁和调解直接给予支持,确认仲裁协议效力、提供财产或证据保全,进行司法监督审查,对和解协议进行司法确认等。

大湾区涉及粤港澳不同的法律制度和司法体系,可联合建立粤港澳大湾区"一站式"民商事纠纷解决机制和平台,建立相应的工作制度和运行规范。明确参与该机制的各地法院层级,商定纳入该机制的仲裁机构和调解机构名单,由各地法院依规则引导粤港澳大湾区内外当事人通过诉讼、仲裁和调解解决争议,根据争议解决地的不同依据、各地相应的法律规定,以及内地和港澳地区有关区际安排①提供更为便捷的支持,方便当事人一揽子解决争议。

(二)关于大湾区商事和解协议、仲裁裁决和法院判决的转化与跨境执行

鉴于目前经由调解而形成的和解协议不具有法律上的可强制执行的效力,和解协议无法直接由法院予以执行。在内地,和解协议可以三种方式转化为其他法律文书得以执行:一是当事人双方在和解协议中订入仲裁条款,按约定将和解协议提交仲裁机构,由仲裁机构根据其仲裁规则组成独任仲裁庭,以快捷方式审理确认后,按照和解协议内容作出仲裁裁决②,由法院依法执行;二是按规定将和解协议提交

---

① 如前所述,内地与港澳地区相互之间有关仲裁安排已经相当完善。2024年1月29日,《最高人民法院关于内地与香港特别行政区法院相互认可和执行民商事案件判决的安排》已经正式施行。如果内地与港澳地区之间有关基于民商事调解而达成的和解协议的认可和执行安排能够在近年内达成实施的话,内地与港澳地区相互之间有关诉讼、仲裁和调解的区际安排将会更加完整健全,这将会实质性地促进粤港澳大湾区民商事多元纠纷解决机制的建立和完善。

② 2021年《仲裁规则》第56条第10款规定:"当事人在仲裁程序开始之前自行达成或经调解达成和解协议的,可以依据由仲裁委员会仲裁的仲裁协议及其和解协议,请求仲裁委员会组成仲裁庭,按照和解协议的内容作出仲裁裁决。除非当事人另有约定,仲裁委员会主任指定一名独任仲裁员成立仲裁庭,由仲裁庭按照其认为适当的程序进行审理并作出裁决。具体程序和期限,不受本规则其他条款关于程序和期限的限制。"

给有管辖权的人民法院进行司法审查确认,转化为法院裁定,依法执行;三是将和解协议提交给公证机构进行公证确认后,转化为公证文书,由法院依规执行。在港澳地区法律框架下,亦不禁止将经单独调解而形成的和解协议通过仲裁审理审查转化为仲裁裁决予以执行。

如上所述,内地与港澳地区仲裁裁决的互相认可和执行机制健全,运行良好。从粤港澳大湾区多元争议解决机制角度看,可以提倡鼓励当事人约定将所涉和解协议转化为仲裁裁决,依循彼此之间签署的相互执行裁决的安排在粤港澳予以认可执行。此外,此类裁决亦可根据《纽约公约》在外国寻求承认与执行。也可以鼓励当事人将和解协议转化为法院裁定,依据内地和香港特区有关相互认可和执行民商事案件判决的安排在内地和香港特区予以认可执行。鉴于内地和澳门特区法院裁定的相互认可执行尚缺乏"安排"基础,以及粤港澳民商事判决在外国法院的承认执行,目前仍需要通过国际司法互助得以进行,难度较大,周期较长。因此,在内地与港澳地区之间尚未就直接认可执行和解协议作出安排的情况下,将和解协议转化为仲裁裁决予以执行,是目前较为理想现实的选项。

(三)关于信息化平台建设

粤港澳可以合作建立粤港澳大湾区民商事多元纠纷解决信息平台,作为民商事多元纠纷解决机制的载体,宣传推介诉讼及非诉讼争议解决服务,以及相应的多元解纷机制和配套服务及衍生服务,供粤港澳大湾区内外当事人选择,同时提供相关法律法规数据库及信息资讯,全面服务于粤港澳大湾区融合发展。

在推动建立和完善粤港澳大湾区民商事多元纠纷解决机制过程中需要把握两个基本原则:一是要有国际化的视野和格局,与国际规则和国际惯例接轨,将整个机制安排放在区域乃至国际范围内统筹考量;二是要确立并恪守国际争端解决中"争议解决地"的理念,无论粤港澳大湾区内外当事人选择何等机构、通过何等方式解决争议,都要根据所选定或确定的争议解决地,由相应的粤港澳的法律对争议解决活动进行相应的规范调整。

建立和完善粤港澳大湾区民商事多元纠纷解决机制是一个系统工程,需要深入贯彻落实相关粤港澳大湾区建设三个方案的精神,凝聚共识、加强统筹、相互协同、系统推进、善作善成、久久为功。

(王鸣杰　审校)

《仲裁法》修订前沿问题探析

崔 强[*]

摘要: 现行《仲裁法》通过于1994年,与国际惯例存在较大差距。在学界和实务界普遍认为需修订的背景下,司法部于2021年公布了《仲裁法(修订)(征求意见稿)》。笔者对此次修订中的重要议题进行了研究,在分析相关制度改革亮点的基础上,提出改进和完善建议。笔者认为,临时仲裁制度在我国落地存在的客观瓶颈待突破,尚需发挥自贸区先行先试及机构仲裁引领带动的作用;仲裁庭自裁管辖权因与法院事前审查机制存在潜在冲突,其修订细节尚待商榷;紧急仲裁员程序及临时措施的适用还需克服执行效力等问题;仲裁司法审查机制则有必要从改进撤销仲裁裁决制度及废除不予执行仲裁裁决制度两方面进行完善。

关键词: 临时仲裁;仲裁庭自裁管辖权;紧急仲裁员;临时措施;仲裁司法审查

作为一项社会化的纠纷解决机制,仲裁制度在服务商事关系方面具有不可否认的价值。我国的商事仲裁制度最早可以追溯到中华人民共和国成立初期。改革开放以来,为适应全球经济一体化、国家治理现代化的现实需求,仲裁制度也在关注国际经验和本土国情的道路上推陈出新。现行《仲裁法》自1995年9月1日起施行,结束了当

---

[*] 北京大学法学学士,美国宾夕法尼亚大学法学硕士,北京市通商律师事务所合伙人,中国海事仲裁委员会、中国国际经济贸易仲裁委员会仲裁员。

时我国各类仲裁实行行政管理体制、仲裁机构多附属于行政主管机关的局面[1],并将仲裁制度提升到了国家基本法律的地位。然而,1995年《仲裁法》虽然在制定过程中参考借鉴了《联合国国际贸易法委员会国际商事仲裁示范法》(以下简称《示范法》)[2],但与《示范法》的建议条款仍存在重大差异,较大程度上体现了转轨时期的过渡色彩,故施行后不久学界即开始关注修法问题。后续全国人大常委会分别于2009年、2017年对《仲裁法》进行过两次修正[3],但这两次修正主要的目的是解决因《民事诉讼法》修正造成的条款援引错位问题,以及适应国家法律职业资格制度的改革,不涉及实质性的条款变动。

随着时间的推移,实务界、学术界关于《仲裁法》立法滞后、亟待修订的讨论逐渐形成了一股不小的声量。与之呼应的是,十三届全国人大常委会于2018年9月7日公布立法规划,将"仲裁法(修改)"列为47件第二类立法项目之一,即"需要抓紧工作、条件成熟时提请审议的法律草案"[4]。2021年7月30日,司法部公布《仲裁法(修订)(征求意见稿)》[5],时隔26年对《仲裁法》进行了大刀阔斧的修改。该征求意见稿较为全面地考虑了现行《仲裁法》与国际惯例之间的差距,作出了许多根本性的改变和尝试,公布后迅速引发了仲裁实务界和学术界热烈而广泛的讨论。就此次修订涉及的众多前沿问题,笔者从自身经验出发,重点关注临时仲裁、仲裁庭自裁管辖权、紧急仲裁员程序及

---

[1] 国务院于1983年发布的《经济合同仲裁条例》(已失效)第2条规定:"经济合同仲裁机关是国家工商行政管理局和地方各级工商行政管理局设立的经济合同仲裁委员会。"

[2] 例如,现行《仲裁法》第19条第1款"仲裁协议独立存在,合同的变更、解除、终止或者无效,不影响仲裁协议的效力"的规定就在一定程度上参考了《示范法》第16条第1款"为此目的,构成合同的一部分的仲裁条款应视为独立于其他合同条款以外的一项协议。仲裁庭作出的关于合同无效的决定,不应在法律上导致仲裁条款的无效"的规定。

[3] 现行《仲裁法》施行后,经《全国人民代表大会常务委员会关于修改部分法律的决定》(2009年8月27日发布,2009年8月27日实施)、《全国人民代表大会常务委员会关于修改〈中华人民共和国法官法〉等八部法律的决定》(2017年9月1日发布,2018年1月1日实施)两次修正。

[4] 《十三届全国人大常委会立法规划》,载中国政府网(https://www.gov.cn/xinwen/2018-09/08/content_5320252.htm),访问日期:2023年6月2日。

[5] 参见《司法部关于〈中华人民共和国仲裁法(修订)(征求意见稿)〉公开征求意见的通知》,载中国法制信息网(http://www.moj.gov.cn/pub/sfbgw/lfyjzj/lflfyjzj/202107/t20210730_432967.html),访问日期:2023年6月2日。

临时措施、仲裁司法审查机制改革等议题。

一、临时仲裁制度尚存客观瓶颈待突破

(一)现行法对临时仲裁制度从体系性的否认到有限定的接纳

在国际商事仲裁法和实践中,仲裁的概念包括机构仲裁和临时仲裁(或称非机构仲裁)。其中,机构仲裁,顾名思义,是指由专门的常设仲裁机构根据自己颁布的仲裁规则对仲裁程序进行管理的仲裁;临时仲裁则与之相对,是指当事人依仲裁协议进行而无须仲裁机构来管理或监督其仲裁程序的仲裁。[1] 虽然临时仲裁对我国从业者来说可能是更为陌生的概念与形式,但从国际角度来看,临时仲裁的历史甚至可以追溯到古希腊时期[2],并实际上构成了国际仲裁制度的传统基因与制度内核[3]。而机构仲裁则被广泛认为是仲裁制度现代化的产物,世界上大多数主要的仲裁机构都是在18世纪末至20世纪末才建立起来的[4]。

我国现行《仲裁法》以一种相对含蓄的方式对临时仲裁制度作出了体系性的否认。具体而言,现行《仲裁法》规定,只有双方当事人之间存在明确的仲裁协议,才能申请仲裁,而一份有效的仲裁协议必须满足以下四个基本要件:以书面方式订立、具有请求仲裁的意思表示、具有明确的仲裁事项、具有选定的仲裁委员会。[5] 其中,当事人可以就仲裁事项或者仲裁委员会没有约定或者约定不明确的部分签订补充

---

[1] 参见杨良宜:《国际商务仲裁》,中国政法大学出版社1997年版,第136页。
[2] See Henry T. King Jr., Marc A. LeForestier: Arbitration in Ancient Greece, 49 Disp. Resol. J. 33(1994).
[3] 参见李建忠:《临时仲裁的中国尝试:制度困境与现实路径——以中国自贸试验区为视角》,载《法治研究》2020年第2期。
[4] 据不完全统计,世界上主要的仲裁机构成立时间为:伦敦国际仲裁院(LCIA)成立于1892年;国际商会国际仲裁院成立于1923年;美国仲裁协会(AAA)成立于1926年;斯德哥尔摩商会仲裁院成立于1917年;中国国际经济贸易仲裁委员会(CIETAC)成立于1956年;香港国际仲裁中心(HKIAC)成立于1985年;新加坡国际仲裁中心(SIAC)成立于1991年。
[5] 《仲裁法》第16条规定:"仲裁协议包括合同中订立的仲裁条款和以其他书面方式在纠纷发生前或者纠纷发生后达成的请求仲裁的协议。仲裁协议应当具有下列内容:(一)请求仲裁的意思表示;(二)仲裁事项;(三)选定的仲裁委员会。"

协议,但若未达成补充协议,则该仲裁协议将被认定为无效。① 根据上述规定,作为一种非常设仲裁机构管理的仲裁,临时仲裁并不满足"具有选定的仲裁委员会"这一仲裁协议生效要件,其效力原则上不被现行《仲裁法》所承认。对此,全国人大常委会法工委的解释是,中国历史上只有机构仲裁没有临时仲裁,缺乏支持有效临时仲裁的经验。②

2016年12月30日,《最高人民法院关于为自由贸易试验区建设提供司法保障的意见》(以下简称《自贸区试点意见》)发布,在承认临时仲裁协议效力方面取得了重大突破。该意见第9条第3段对于未明确约定仲裁机构的仲裁协议采取了宽容和支持的态度,虽然前提是满足"三个特定"的限制,并仅适用于在自由贸易试验区(以下简称"自贸区")内注册的企业。③ 随后不久,与该意见配套的《横琴自由贸易试验区临时仲裁规则》(以下简称《横琴规则》)于2017年3月18日由广东自贸试验区横琴新区管委会和珠海仲裁委员会联合发布。无独有偶,中国互联网仲裁联盟于同年9月也发布了《中国互联网仲裁联盟临时仲裁与机构仲裁对接规则》。前述系列举措开启了我国临时仲裁制度在特定地区与领域的有限度的尝试,并被学术界和实务界人士认为有望成为推动现行《仲裁法》修订的契机。

作为前述尝试的延续,司法部于2021年7月发布的《仲裁法(修订)(征求意见稿)》首次从立法层面松动了现行《仲裁法》拒绝承认临时仲裁协议效力的原则性立场,拟将临时仲裁制度纳入我国仲裁法律体系之中,并确定了相关具体规则。

一方面,《仲裁法(修订)(征求意见稿)》变更了现行《仲裁法》第16条规定的仲裁协议生效要件,体现在该征求意见稿第21条,即有效的仲裁协议仅需满足"书面方式"与"具有请求仲裁的意思表示"这

---

① 《仲裁法》第18条规定:"仲裁协议对仲裁事项或者仲裁委员会没有约定或者约定不明确的,当事人可以补充协议;达不成补充协议的,仲裁协议无效。"

② 参见江伟、肖建国主编:《仲裁法》(第3版),中国人民大学出版社2016年版,第22页。

③ 《自贸区试点意见》第9条第3段规定:"在自贸试验区内注册的企业相互之间约定在内地特定地点、按照特定仲裁规则、由特定人员对有关争议进行仲裁的,可以认定该仲裁协议有效。人民法院认为该仲裁协议无效的,应报请上一级法院进行审查。上级法院同意下级法院意见的,应将其审查意见层报最高人民法院,待最高人民法院答复后作出裁定。"

两个要件即可,不再要求具有"明确的仲裁事项"和"选定的仲裁委员会"。① 也就是说,该征求意见稿对约定明确的仲裁机构不再作硬性要求,从而为临时仲裁的适用提供了空间,顺应了国际商事仲裁领域尊重当事人意思自治的趋势。

另一方面,结合我国具体国情,临时仲裁的范围仅限于"涉外商事纠纷",国内仲裁仍执行机构仲裁方式,当事人并无约定临时仲裁的权利。《仲裁法(修订)(征求意见稿)》在第七章"涉外仲裁的特别规定"中引入了"专设仲裁庭"的概念,并通过第91条至第93条明确了适用涉外仲裁规定的条件,对临时仲裁的组庭、回避等核心程序进行了必要的规范。

(二)临时仲裁在我国落地的客观阻碍及未来展望

1. 客观阻碍

在当前竞争性国际纠纷解决格局日益凸显的背景下,临时仲裁制度的引入,充分体现了我国仲裁立法对当事人意思自治的重视,更是对我国商事仲裁国际化所面临的现实需求作出的积极回应。但不容忽视的是,我国现阶段引入临时仲裁制度仍存在如下客观阻碍。

第一,临时仲裁制度的程序优势与我国当前仲裁事业发展不完全匹配,可能出现"橘生淮北则为枳"的后果。

一般认为在国际仲裁实务中,机构仲裁的价值在于可预测性,而临时仲裁的价值在于灵活性,对不同价值的偏好决定了当事人选择的仲裁形式。② 然而,临时仲裁制度灵活性目标的实现依赖于精心设计的临时仲裁协议、经验丰富的仲裁员,以及当事人、律师及仲裁员之间的良好合作。如果缺乏仲裁方面的技能、经验以及合作意识,则各方

---

① 《仲裁法(修订)(征求意见稿)》第21条规定:"仲裁协议包括合同中订立的仲裁条款和以其他书面方式在纠纷发生前或者纠纷发生后达成的具有请求仲裁的意思表示的协议。一方当事人在仲裁中主张有仲裁协议,其他当事人不予否认的,视为当事人之间存在仲裁协议。"

② See Namrata Shah, Niyati Gandhi, Arbitration: One Size Does Not Fit All: Necessity of Developing Institutional Arbitration in Developing Countries, 6 Journal of International Commercial Law and Technology 4 (2011).

追求的灵活性将被扭曲成一种任意性,进而脱离最初的仲裁目标,导向不可预测的结果。

在我国机构仲裁的实践中,仲裁机构长期负责委任仲裁员、确定并收取仲裁费、处理仲裁员回避申请、指定开庭地点、保存文件并向当事人送达、召开专家论证会、推动仲裁程序的进行等一系列事务性工作,仲裁员并不直接应对和负责上述程序问题。并且,双方当事人及其代理律师几乎不会就程序事项进行任何面对面的直接交流。

引入临时仲裁制度后,专设仲裁庭将在尊重当事人意思自治的基础上,负责处理全部的程序问题,这对于各方理解程序规则、合作推进各项安排的业务能力提出了很高的要求。虽然临时仲裁的当事人也会共同选定需遵循的程序规则,但这不一定能经得起各类突发事件的考验。一旦仲裁庭在与当事人进行协商沟通、组织和推进仲裁程序管理的过程中处理欠妥,不仅会造成仲裁程序的延迟、仲裁花费的增加,甚至可能导致仲裁裁决被撤销,而立法却未对可能出现的相关问题给出进一步的解决方案。相比之下,机构仲裁对于仲裁程序有清晰、明确且可预见的管理,至少能保证仲裁的推进和成本是可控的。

第二,临时仲裁缺乏有效的外部监督。在仲裁机构缺位的情况下,《仲裁法(修订)(征求意见稿)》第93条所规定的临时仲裁裁决书备案制度能起到的司法监督作用有限。

在机构仲裁制度下,仲裁机构作为一种他律机制,能够对仲裁员的执业道德与纪律加以有效约束,而当事人自行组建的临时仲裁庭并不存在这种监督机制。甚至可以说,在临时仲裁中,当事人的权利义务是否能够得到恰当妥善的保护完全依赖于仲裁员自身的职业素质、法律及专业素养。临时仲裁没有确定的仲裁员名册,理论上,任何人都可以组成仲裁庭,签署仲裁裁决,因此,也无法排除不法分子利用虚假仲裁规避外汇监管政策等风险。国际仲裁中十分常见以从事仲裁员工作为专职的独立仲裁员,但是,我国的仲裁员绝大部分属于兼职而非专职,即我国尚未形成独立专业的仲裁员群体。仲裁的质量和公信力最终取决于仲裁员的专业水平和职业操守,而在目前缺乏仲裁员自律机制的环境下,临时仲裁庭究竟能否合理发挥立法赋予其作为

"裁判者"的作用,令人存疑。

机构仲裁制度的另一个优点是仲裁机构对仲裁裁决的监督,即仲裁裁决核稿制度。该制度起源于国际商会1975年版的调解与仲裁规则,国际商会要求仲裁庭在签署裁决前将裁决草案提交仲裁院核阅,以确保裁决有质量地覆盖仲裁庭需要回应的全部问题。[①]我国现行《仲裁法》未对仲裁裁决核阅制度作出明确规定,但中国国际经济贸易仲裁委员会在其1995年的仲裁规则中,率先规定裁决草案应提交仲裁委员会核阅。[②]随后,我国多数仲裁机构也都因袭了这一做法,并在其仲裁规则中作出了明文规定。北京仲裁委员会的仲裁规则虽然没有此类规定,但由其处理的案件实际上也都有核稿的流程。尽管核稿人不会在实质上修改仲裁员的观点,但是这种监督可以给仲裁员施加压力,增加当事人对仲裁程序的信任。临时仲裁缺乏相应的核稿机制,而在我国暂未形成独立的仲裁员群体及竞争性的仲裁员市场的情况下,声誉监督机制亦无从发挥作用,临时仲裁裁决的质量难以得到切实保障。

《仲裁法(修订)(征求意见稿)》第93条第3款规定:"仲裁庭应当将裁决书送达当事人,并将送达记录和裁决书原件在送达之日起三十日内提交仲裁地的中级人民法院备案。"该条款的设置在某种程度上是为了解决上述临时仲裁制度缺乏监督机制的问题,但是《仲裁法(修订)(征求意见稿)》缺乏对该备案制度与裁决效力或裁决执行间存在何种关联的有效解释,因此,反而可能会给仲裁庭和法院增添负担。

一方面,临时仲裁的核心价值在于对当事人意思自治的尊重和保护,这也是合同、契约普遍适用的原则。商事仲裁的裁决结果由争议当事人自觉履行,而非必须通过法院强制执行。如果是双方当事人认

---

① Article 21 of ICC Rules of Conciliation and Arbitration (1975): Before signing an award, whether partial or definitive, the arbitrator shall submit it in draft page "163" form to the Court. The Court may lay down modifications as to the form of the award and, without affecting the arbitrator's liberty of decision, may also draw his attention to points of substance. No award shall be signed until it has been approved by the Court as to its form.

② 《中国国际经济贸易仲裁委员会仲裁规则(1995)》第56条第2款规定:"仲裁员应在签署裁决前将裁决书草案提交仲裁委员会。在不影响仲裁员独立裁决的情况下,仲裁委员会可以就裁决书的形式问题提请仲裁员注意。"

可仲裁结果并且自愿履行裁决的情形,那么裁决送达的第二天就有可能已经得到履行;如果是需要向法院申请强制执行裁决的情形,则需要在境外强制执行的涉外仲裁裁决,并无必要向中国法院备案,而需要在境内承认及执行仲裁裁决的当事人,自然会向中国法院披露相关裁决书,法院将会依照审查机构仲裁裁决的标准,审查临时仲裁裁决并作出裁定,实无备案的必要。因此,强制备案要求在某种程度上是对临时仲裁制度尊重当事人意思自治的立法原意的颠覆,实践中存在与仲裁保密性相冲突、引起当事人顾虑进而影响到制度本身适用的风险。

另一方面,在比较法的视角下,《承认及执行外国仲裁裁决公约》(又称《纽约公约》)和《示范法》均没有对临时仲裁裁决提出在法院备案的要求,《仲裁法(修订)(征求意见稿)》第93条的备案规定缺乏合理的参照对象。

第三,经过多年的仲裁实践,我国当事人对机构仲裁存在路径依赖,而对临时仲裁认可度较低。

我国作为《纽约公约》的缔约成员,根据《纽约公约》的相关规定,中国对在另一缔约成员境内作出的仲裁裁决的承认和执行,不仅针对机构仲裁裁决,也包括临时仲裁裁决。因此,对我国不承认境内作出的临时仲裁裁决的一项最大的诟病是其事实上造成了对外国人的"超国民待遇"。[①] 然而,此种理解是不准确的,因为这种"超然"的待遇与案涉当事人的国籍无关,而是附属于仲裁裁决的国籍,我国当事人在境外取得的临时仲裁裁决同样可以在我国得到承认和执行。而境外临时仲裁裁决之所以能在我国取得与机构仲裁裁决同等的待遇,从根本上归因于对境外临时仲裁裁决质量的认可。因此,临时仲裁制度能否在我国落地,取决于我国的临时仲裁能否作出不逊于机构仲裁质量的裁决,而非不顾实际地追求所谓"平等"。

另外,根据笔者多年在仲裁领域的观察和实践,虽然境外作出的

---

① 参见刘敬东、刘艳:《临时仲裁制度及司法审查相关问题研究》,载李虎主编:《中国海事商事仲裁评论(2021):新时代中国海事商事仲裁的创新发展》,北京大学出版社2022年版,第28页。

临时仲裁裁决在我国也能获得承认与执行,但参与国际商事活动的我国企业在绝大部分情况下都会选择机构仲裁,也即当事人在制度选择上对机构仲裁表现出较为强烈的倾向性。在可预见的一定时期内,临时仲裁尚不能完全获得我国当事人在文化上的认同,仲裁从业者在我国推广临时仲裁制度的主观信心和客观环境还有所欠缺。

2. 未来展望

自现行《仲裁法》颁布并默认临时仲裁制度缺位以来,学术界关于是否要引入临时仲裁制度的讨论不绝于耳,绝大多数学者持支持态度,只是在引入时机上存在分歧。笔者认为,从完善商事争议解决机制、促进我国商事仲裁与国际商事仲裁接轨的角度看,引入临时仲裁制度确实有其必要性,尤其是在海事、航空等特殊领域。但考虑到前述客观阻碍的存在,引入步伐不宜过急。未来一段时间内,应继续推进临时仲裁制度在特定领域及区域的先行先试,并鼓励仲裁机构积极参与临时仲裁协助工作,以机构仲裁带动临时仲裁。对此,笔者也尝试给出如下建议,以期临时仲裁制度最终能在我国稳步落地。

第一,明确自贸区临时仲裁制度的适用范围,并对自贸区临时仲裁的司法审查权限进行统一配置。

《自贸区试点意见》允许自贸区注册企业之间有条件地选择临时仲裁。所谓自贸区,是指我国依法设立的以贸易自由化为目标的多功能经济特区,同时也是法治试验区。自 2013 年 8 月中国(上海)自由贸易试验区经国务院批准设立以来,我国已在多个省市设立了自贸区。但需要指出的是,不同自贸区的发展水平并不一致,司法管辖模式也各异,这导致了临时仲裁制度在各自贸区推行的复杂性和差异性。[1]此外,《自贸区试点意见》为临时仲裁的适用设定了"三个特定"的前提,但相关表述过于模糊,难以判断其具体内涵,此种不确定性势必将部分潜在临时仲裁用户阻挡在外。有鉴于此,建议最高人民法院针对临时仲裁制度在自贸区的推行出台进一步的意见,明确临时仲裁制度的适用范围,并对临时仲裁的司法审查权限进行统一配置,比如,

---

[1] See Liu Ying, Zhang Weijia, Establishment of Ad hoc Arbitration System in China, 10 J. WTO & CHINA 68 (2020).

可规定由最高人民法院第一巡回法庭对广东、海南等地自贸区的临时仲裁承担司法监督责任。

第二，在有效发挥机构仲裁对临时仲裁带动作用的同时，为仲裁机构对临时仲裁的参与划定界限。

一方面，在国际临时仲裁的实践中，当事人即使选择临时仲裁，也不排斥由仲裁机构提供行政服务。我国现阶段要推行临时仲裁制度，显然也需要从机构仲裁中汲取养分。具体而言，仲裁机构可以协助提供可资适用的程序规则、必要的程序服务，也可以对仲裁员进行监督，保障临时仲裁决定及裁决的执行，这将显著降低当事人约定临时仲裁面临的不确定性，帮助没有经验的当事人和仲裁员持续、有效地推进仲裁程序进行。而且，仲裁机构是现阶段与仲裁员联系最为紧密的主体，也是最能胜任临时仲裁仲裁员的引导和培训工作的主体。

另一方面，我国已形成庞杂的临时仲裁机构市场，各自贸区所在地的仲裁机构也都有兴趣抓住新兴的临时仲裁市场，珠海仲裁委员会出台《横琴规则》显然也有此意。但是，由仲裁机构制定临时仲裁的规则将在很大程度上混淆机构仲裁和临时仲裁的界限，在国际上也少有先例。[1] 为遏制各仲裁机构各自为营、竞相制定临时仲裁规则的局面，并降低临时仲裁规则的地域色彩，建议由全国性的协会统一制定能够普适于各自贸区的临时仲裁规则。近期，由中国海商法协会发布的《中国海商法协会临时仲裁规则》、中国海事仲裁委员会发布的《中国海事仲裁委员会临时仲裁服务规则》可资借鉴。

二、仲裁庭自裁管辖权制度修订细节待商榷

（一）《仲裁法》修订拟打破"诉仲自择、法院优先"的管辖权限划分

现行法律框架下，关于确认仲裁协议效力的管辖职责分工主要规

---

[1] 伦敦大学玛丽王后学院和伟凯律师事务所发布的《2021年国际仲裁调查报告》显示，最受欢迎的临时仲裁规则为《联合国国际贸易法委员会仲裁规则》，该临时仲裁规则由联合国国际贸易法委员会制定。

定在《仲裁法》《最高人民法院关于适用〈中华人民共和国仲裁法〉若干问题的解释》以及《最高人民法院关于确认仲裁协议效力几个问题的批复》等规定中,综合相关规定可知,如一方当事人向仲裁机构申请确认仲裁协议效力,而另一方向法院申请,原则上由法院作出决定,除非仲裁机构已经作出了正式的决定,仲裁机构就仲裁协议效力作出决定后,法院可在当事人申请撤销仲裁裁决及不予执行仲裁裁决的案件中就仲裁协议效力重新作出认定,即法院掌握着对仲裁协议效力最终的决定权。现行法虽然赋予了当事人自择管辖机构的权利,但客观上容易导致程序冲突及司法资源浪费。

尤其是当仲裁程序涉及多个被申请人主体时,甚至会出现多个被申请人依次、轮流提起仲裁协议效力确认程序,干扰仲裁程序正常推进的情况。以广东省佛山市中级人民法院审理的一起确认仲裁协议效力案件为例,某公司向佛山仲裁委员会提起金融借款合同纠纷的仲裁申请,在佛山仲裁委员会受理后,相关借款人及保证人反复向法院申请确认仲裁协议无效,导致仲裁程序被多次中止,无奈之下,某公司只能反过来针对全部仲裁被申请人提起确认仲裁协议有效的申请。[①]与之类似,在笔者近期代理的一起股东协议纠纷中,被申请人也同样采取了反复提起确认仲裁协议效力之诉的方式来拖延仲裁程序。[②]

与现行法律框架不同,《仲裁法(修订)(征求意见稿)》赋予了仲裁庭自裁管辖权。[③]具体而言,当事人对仲裁协议效力、仲裁管辖权有异议时不再具有选择权,而是只能向仲裁庭提出异议申请。如果此时

---

① 参见广东省佛山市中级人民法院(2021)粤06民特113号民事裁定书。
② 参见北京市第四中级人民法院(2022)京04民特207号民事裁定书;北京市第四中级人民法院(2022)京04民特261号民事裁定书;北京市第四中级人民法院(2022)京04民特486号民事裁定书;北京金融法院(2022)京74民特59号民事裁定书。
③ 《仲裁法(修订)(征求意见稿)》第28条规定:"当事人对仲裁协议是否存在、有效等效力问题或者仲裁案件的管辖权有异议的,应当在仲裁规则规定的答辩期限内提出,由仲裁庭作出决定。仲裁庭组成前,仲裁机构可以根据表面证据决定仲裁程序是否继续进行。当事人未经前款规定程序直接向人民法院提出异议的,人民法院不予受理。当事人对仲裁协议效力或者管辖权决定有异议的,应当自收到决定之日起十日内,提请仲裁地的中级人民法院审查。当事人对仲裁协议无效或者仲裁案件无管辖权的裁定不服的,可以自裁定送达之日起十日内向上一级人民法院申请复议。人民法院应当在受理复议申请之日起一个月内作出裁定。人民法院的审查不影响仲裁程序的进行。"

仲裁庭尚未组建,则由仲裁机构先根据表面证据决定是否继续进行仲裁程序。此外,未经过仲裁庭的审查,当事人无权直接向法院提出异议,只有仲裁庭作出决定后,其才具有诉诸法院的权利,且法院的审查不再影响仲裁程序的继续进行。

对于上述引入仲裁庭自裁管辖权的变革,立法用意是简化仲裁协议效力司法审查程序,避免一方当事人恶意拖延而造成另一方当事人权利受损,从而更好地发挥仲裁独立、高效的制度优势,同时也是为了与拟设的临时仲裁相适应。

(二)仲裁庭自裁管辖权与法院事前审查机制存在潜在冲突

《仲裁法(修订)(征求意见稿)》对仲裁庭自裁管辖权的确立顺应了国际商事仲裁尊重仲裁独立性的趋势,但仲裁庭自裁成为法院审理的前置程序,可能造成新的程序拖延,对仲裁效率目标的实现无益。

具体而言,《仲裁法(修订)(征求意见稿)》第 28 条第 3 款、第 4 款规定法院仍保有对仲裁庭管辖权决定的事前监督职能。如果当事人对管辖权决定有异议,则无须等到裁决后再通过申请撤销仲裁裁决及不予执行仲裁裁决来挑战仲裁协议的效力,而是可以直接要求法院对管辖权决定进行司法审查。

尽管《仲裁法(修订)(征求意见稿)》第 28 条第 5 款拟规定法院的审查不影响仲裁程序的进行,但是在实践中,仲裁庭很可能为避免出现推进程序甚至作出裁决后又被法院认定为没有管辖权的尴尬局面,而选择拒绝推进仲裁程序、等待法院最终确认管辖权决定效力。另外,如果仲裁庭先行作出裁决,而后法院又推翻了仲裁庭对仲裁协议效力的认定,那么不仅当事人和仲裁庭因为审理案件所产生的成本将被浪费,而且仲裁裁决究竟是自动无效还是需另行申请撤销也会变成一个有待解决的问题。如果仲裁裁决并不自动无效,那么为了中止仲裁裁决的执行,当事人需要另行向法院提起撤销仲裁裁决之诉,同时,还可申请对管辖权决定进行司法审查,这实际上是司法救济程序重叠。

由此可见,仲裁庭自裁管辖权作为司法审查的前置程序极可能不仅不会减轻程序拖延的问题,反而可能会带来当事人重复异议、法院重复审查等问题,甚至可能出现前后审查程序结论不一的情况,司法效率和权威也将被极大贬损。

一般来说,已确立"自裁管辖权"原则的司法管辖通常都采事后审查的方式[①],即不在仲裁程序中进行事先的司法审查,而是在当事人后续提起的仲裁裁决异议程序中,再度审视仲裁协议的效力问题。综上,此次《仲裁法》修订确立仲裁庭自裁管辖权的立法用意本身值得肯定,但具体制度细节还有待进一步叩问,尤其需要重点关注和解决仲裁庭自裁管辖权与确认仲裁协议效力的司法审查制度之间的潜在冲突问题。

三、临时措施决定的执行效力问题有待解决

(一)紧急仲裁员程序在我国的引入尝试及制度困境

在仲裁程序中,如果一方当事人故意采取措施逃避其义务,例如,挥霍资产、处置争议标的物或销毁对案件结果至关重要的证据,则另一方当事人将可能由此遭受不可弥补的损害。仲裁作为一种争议解决方式,其有效性在某些情况下将取决于仲裁庭是否有权采取临时措施及时保护当事人的合法利益。然而,考虑到寻求临时措施的关键时点往往是当事人纠纷的开端,而仲裁员的选任及组庭的完成可能需要数周甚至数月的时间,为免此种固有的限制挫败仲裁提供有效救济的能力,许多仲裁机构在其规则中规定了紧急仲裁员制度以填补这一空白。

紧急仲裁员制度最早可追溯到国际商会于1990年推出的《仲裁前公断程序规则》(Rules for a Pre Arbitral Referee Procedure),由于仲裁前裁判程序是任择性质的,当事人可以自由选择是否加入,因此,该程序在实践中很少被应用。[②] 2006年,美国仲裁协会(American Arbitration Association)的国际分支机构国际争议解决中心

---

① See William W. Park, Determining Arbitral Jurisdiction: Allocation of Tasks Between Courts and Arbitrators, 8 Am. Rev. Int'l Arb. 133 (1997).

② See ICC Arbitration and ADR Commission Report on Emergency Arbitrator Proceedings, https://iccwbo.org/news-publications/arbitration-adr-rules-and-tools/emergency-arbitrator-proceedings-icc-arbitration-and-adr-commission-report/, accessed June 6, 2023.

（International Centre for Dispute Resolution, ICDR）首次在其仲裁规则中引入"紧急仲裁员"一词，随后世界上大多数主要的仲裁机构都采取了类似的规则。

正如国际商会仲裁和替代性争议解决委员会（the ICC Commission on Arbitration and ADR）于2019年发布的《紧急仲裁员程序》中所述："虽然获取紧急临时救济的程序和条件在不同规则中可能有所不同，但各仲裁机构似乎已经确定，紧急仲裁员程序填补了一项公认的空白并满足了仲裁用户的需求。"①

通过数十年的应用实践，紧急仲裁员程序的制度优势主要表现在以下四方面：

第一，拥有仲裁程序通常具备的众多优势，包括保密性、中立性、高效性、独立性、专业性、尊重当事人意思自治等。除此之外，紧急性/高效性是紧急仲裁员程序最突出的特征，体现在紧急仲裁员的指定、紧急仲裁程序的推进、紧急仲裁员作出决定的期限等多个环节。第二，紧急仲裁员决定是否提供临时救济的标准更为灵活，并且不强制要求提供担保。第三，可以避免向法院寻求保护性救济的诉累，并规避可能出现的地方保护倾向。第四，紧急仲裁员决定的承受与执行不受仲裁地所在法域的法律限制，并且可以消除当事人需在多个不同法域获得临时救济的困难。

虽然紧急仲裁员程序在我国现行立法中尚属空白，但考虑到我国在紧急仲裁员制度设计上的缺失无法适应国际仲裁发展的趋势，难以满足仲裁当事人寻求有效救济的正当需求，国内主流仲裁机构当前均已将紧急仲裁员程序纳入仲裁规则，如上海国际经济贸易仲裁委员会《中国（上海）自由贸易试验区仲裁规则（2015）》第21条、《中国国际经济贸易仲裁委员会仲裁规则（2015）》第23条及第77条、《北京仲裁委员会仲裁规则（2022）》第63条等。

此外，尽管紧急仲裁员制度在我国仲裁实务界已经得到了广泛的

---

① "Although the procedure and conditions for obtaining emergency interim relief may vary somewhat between different rules, many institutions seem to have determined that EA proceedings fill a perceived void and satisfy a demand from users."

应用,但在实践中仍面临着许多问题,其中,最显著的便是紧急仲裁员临时措施决定的执行问题。具体而言,根据现行《民事诉讼法》第84条、第103条、第104条,以及《仲裁法》第28条、第46条的相关规定,我国立法者选择采用法院独占临时救济权力的"单轨制"立法和运作模式,也即法律仅授权法院发布保全措施,并未授权紧急仲裁员发布临时措施。紧急仲裁员作出的临时措施决定在现行法上找不到依据,故现阶段由仲裁庭或紧急仲裁员作出的临时措施难以申请法院强制执行,制度的有效性主要依赖于当事人的主动履行。在笔者代理过的某件适用紧急仲裁员程序的案件中,银行书面确认会执行仲裁委员会发出的禁止根据案涉保函付款的指令,这才避免了临时措施决定作出后无法执行的风险。

  实践中,当事人也确实可能愿意主动履行,但究其原因,很大程度上是出于对仲裁庭自由裁量权的忌惮,担心无正当理由不配合可能被作出不利推定,进而影响实体审理结果。此外,当事人也可能会担心仲裁庭在分配仲裁费用时,因己方拒绝执行临时措施、违背仲裁约定而作出对己方不利的调整。但如上所述,紧急仲裁员制度仅在提起仲裁后、仲裁庭组建前发挥作用,且除当事人另有约定外,紧急仲裁员一般不得参与后续组庭,因此,前述对当事人自愿履行的"软性约束"的实际作用有限,而且仲裁庭能否仅仅因为一方当事人对临时措施决定的不合作态度而作出对该当事人方不利的推定,这也是具有不确定性的,至少目前没有明确的制度支持。另外,如果违反临时措施决定的收益远大于成本,则一方当事人仍可能选择无视决定、不顾潜在的不利仲裁结果。①

  《仲裁法(修订)(征求意见稿)》第49条第2款正式引入了国际商事仲裁的通行做法——紧急仲裁员程序,从而有望在法律层面上赋予这一制度以合法性。②需指出的是,该条款仅仅概括地规定了当事人

---

① See Mika Savola, Access to Arbitral Justice: Time Aspects of Access to Arbitral Justice: Interim Measures and Emergency Arbitrator Proceedings, 23 Croat. Arbit. Yearb. 73 (2016).

② 《仲裁法(修订)(征求意见稿)》第49条第2款规定:"仲裁庭组成前,当事人需要指定紧急仲裁员采取临时措施的,可以依照仲裁规则向仲裁机构申请指定紧急仲裁员。紧急仲裁员的权力保留至仲裁庭组成为止。"

申请启动紧急仲裁员程序的权利，但是并没有触碰紧急仲裁员的临时措施决定的执行问题，而能否获得执行效力是决定紧急仲裁员制度能否发挥其价值的关键，目前仍有一些基本问题亟待完善。例如，紧急仲裁员的定位并不明确，而这一问题关系着紧急仲裁员的临时措施决定是否具有执行力。鉴于仲裁员可被定义为由当事人选定的听取各方争论并据此作出有约束力裁决的个人[1]，而紧急仲裁员所作出的临时措施决定确实解决了当事人的争议，且对仲裁各方当事人都具有拘束力，建议立法明确紧急仲裁员也属于仲裁员的范畴，从而赋予其所作出的决定具有法律层面上的合法性与可执行性。部分国家和地区的仲裁规则/立法对此进行了明确，例如，我国台湾地区仲裁协会于2017年制定的《仲裁规则》及新加坡于2012年修订的《1994年国际仲裁法》（International Arbitration Act 1994，以下简称《新加坡国际仲裁法》）。

（二）《仲裁法》修订对临时措施决定权及其执行效力问题的初步摸索

1. 临时措施决定权重新配置的必要性

临时措施是指仲裁的一方当事人在仲裁庭就是非曲直作出决定之前提供的对权利或财产的直接和临时保护措施。[2] 前文已经初步介绍紧急仲裁员作出的临时措施，参考境内外主要仲裁机构的仲裁规则及相应实践，临时措施也可在组庭后由仲裁庭作出。尽管在不同的司法区域，根据不同国家的法律规定，临时措施的名称略有不同[3]，但是都具有相同或相似的功能。例如，《示范法》第17条第（2）款列举了临时措施的四项功能，即"维持争议原状""保护仲裁程序""保全资

---

[1] See Arbitrator, Black's Law Dictionary, 2nd Ed., https://thelawdictionary.org/arbitrator/, accessed June 8, 2023.

[2] See Marianne Roth, Interim Measures, in: Marianne Roth, Michael Geistlinger(ed.), Yearbook on International Arbitration Vol. 3, 2014, p. 141.

[3] 根据《示范法》以及《联合国国际贸易法委员会仲裁规则》，临时救济措施被称为临时措施（interim measures）和初步命令（preliminary order）；根据《新加坡国际仲裁中心仲裁规则》的规定，临时救济措施被称为临时救济（interim reliefs）；根据《香港国际仲裁中心仲裁规则》的规定，其被称为临时保护措施。

产"及"保全证据"。①

在我国以往的立法中,临时措施的决定权与执行权均由法院掌握,而仲裁庭只能发挥转递申请材料的"二传手"作用。②《仲裁法(修订)(征求意见稿)》对此作出了极大突破,在第四章"仲裁程序"中专"设临时措施"一节,对仲裁庭临时措施的决定与执行程序进行了详细的规定。

具体而言,《仲裁法(修订)(征求意见稿)》突破了现行法所采纳的法院专属权力模式,采取了法院与仲裁庭权力并存模式,赋予了仲裁庭发布包括财产保全措施、证据保全措施、行为保全措施和其他有必要的短期措施的权力。当事人在提起仲裁后,可以根据自身需要向相关法院或者仲裁庭申请临时措施。③ 就临时措施决定发布权的立法模式而言,除《仲裁法(修订)(征求意见稿)》采取的"自由选择模式"外,还存在英国等国家采取的"法院辅助模式",即原则上以仲裁庭作为临时措施决定的发布主体,法院只能在特定情况下介入。④ 从世界范围来看,两种立法模式各有市场,可能"自由选择模式"稍占上风。在《示范法》修订过程中,对于是否要继续采取法院与仲裁庭权力并存的模式,也存在过争论,最终工作组出于维护临时措施双重可获得

---

① 《示范法》第17条第(2)款规定:"临时措施是以裁决书为形式的或另一种形式的任何短期措施,仲裁庭在发出最后裁定争议的裁决书之前任何时候,以这种措施责令一方当事人实施以下任何行为:(a)在争议得以裁定之前维持现状或恢复原状;(b)采取行动防止目前或即将对仲裁程序发生的危害或损害,或不采取可能造成这种危害或损害的行动;(c)提供一种保全资产以执行后继裁决的手段;或(d)保全对解决争议可能具有相关性和重要性的证据。"

② 参见刘晓红主编:《国际商事仲裁专题研究》,法律出版社2009年版,第343页。

③ 《仲裁法(修订)(征求意见稿)》第43条规定:"当事人在仲裁程序进行前或者进行期间,为了保障仲裁程序的进行、查明争议事实或者裁决执行,可以请求人民法院或者仲裁庭采取与争议标的相关的临时性、紧急性措施。临时措施包括财产保全、证据保全、行为保全和仲裁庭认为有必要的其他短期措施。"

《仲裁法(修订)(征求意见稿)》第46条第2款规定:"当事人提起仲裁后申请保全措施的,可以直接向被保全财产所在地、证据所在地、行为履行地、被申请人所在地或者仲裁地的人民法院提出;也可以向仲裁庭提出。"

④ See William Wang, International Arbitration: The Need for Uniform Interim Measures of Relief, 28 Brooklyn J. Int'l L. 1059.

性的目的保留了原有模式。①

综合来看,法律授权仲裁庭作出临时措施决定的必要性可以归纳为以下几方面:

第一,体现了对当事人程序选择权利的尊重与保障。法律既已允许当事人选择以仲裁方式解决争议,由仲裁庭行使管辖权,就意味着认可法院基于当事人的程序选择权利,放弃对部分特定纠纷的管辖权。在此基础上,将临时措施的决定权与实体争议问题的裁决权一并交由仲裁庭是对尊重当事人意思自治的立法趋势的一种延续。

第二,有利于节约司法资源,提高争议解决效率。仲裁庭得益于其对实体争议的全面审查权,能够更准确地评估当事人在实际争议中取得胜诉的可能性,以及保全措施对仲裁程序及当事人的影响。此外,仲裁庭还能更加敏锐地识别当事人滥用保全措施的请求及背后的策略意图。相较于诉诸法院,仲裁庭决定临时措施的机制能够有效避免引发不必要的拖延和高昂的成本。

第三,决定权不等于执行权,不影响法院在执行阶段实施司法监督及必要的司法审查。具体而言,可以通过区分仲裁中临时措施的决定权与执行权,在将部分决定权配置给仲裁庭的同时,将执行权保留在法院来发挥法院对仲裁的司法审查作用。但法院对仲裁庭临时措施决定的审查,应以对程序的监督审查为限,而不能涉及实体事项。

第四,仲裁庭行使决定权的弊端可以通过制度设计予以解决。由仲裁庭行使临时措施的决定权有两个比较显著的障碍:一是组庭前临时措施的决定与发布;二是仲裁庭临时措施决定的执行问题。然而这些弊端均可以通过合理的制度设计予以解决,比如,引入紧急仲裁员程序、完善仲裁庭决定权与法院执行权之间的衔接机制等。

第五,符合国际商事仲裁的实践趋势。随着仲裁在解决国际经济贸易问题中的裁断力逐步加强,仲裁独立的观念得到了较为广泛的认可,仲裁庭享有临时措施的决定权也被越来越广泛地接受,并体现在《示范法》及诸多主流国际仲裁机构的仲裁规则中。另据学者的整理

---

① See Report of the Working Group on Arbitration on the Work of Its 32nd Session (Vienna, 20-31 March 2000), https://digitallibrary.un.org/record/413924, accessed June 10, 2023.

调查,英国、瑞典、德国、美国、新加坡、日本等许多国际商事交易发达的国家,也都赋予了仲裁庭下达临时措施决定的合法性。①

2. 临时措施决定的可执行性问题

与法院下达的临时措施决定相比,紧急仲裁员/仲裁庭下达的临时措施决定的主要缺点之一就是缺乏可执行性。临时措施决定的执行大致有以下三个问题:一是境内临时措施决定在境内的执行问题;二是境内临时措施决定在境外的执行问题;三是境外临时措施决定在境内的执行问题。

首先,在此次《仲裁法》的拟议修订中,当事人可就仲裁庭作出的临时措施决定向有管辖权的法院申请执行,初步解决了境内作出的临时措施决定在境内的执行问题。②当然,《仲裁法(修订)(征求意见稿)》尚未明确法院的审查标准、执行程序等制度细节,相关机制能否以及如何落地运转还有待进一步观察。

其次,在《仲裁法(修订)(征求意见稿)》的语境下,当事人亦有权向境外法院申请执行临时措施决定,而在境外的主要执行机制是我国参与缔结的《纽约公约》及执行地的国内法等。

具体而言,《纽约公约》第3条要求每个缔约国均应承认仲裁裁决具有约束力并予以执行,但本身并未以明确包含或排除临时措施决定的方式描述可执行裁决的含义,这导致临时措施决定在公约下可执行性的支持者与反对者均无法互相说服。从各国法院处理此类问题的情况来看,《纽约公约》的语焉不详确实给临时措施决定基于公约的执行留下了解释的空间,但未能直接促使此种基于公约的执行得到广泛实现。在颇有影响力的1993年"国际度假公寓案"中,澳大利亚昆士兰州最高法院裁定临时裁决不具备《纽约公约》下的执行力。该案涉及美国申请人和澳大利亚被申请人之间的纠纷,仲裁员发布了一项临时裁决,要求被申请人在仲裁期间履行协议。然而,法院认为临时裁

---

① 参见张圣翠:《论我国仲裁保全措施制度的重构》,载《上海财经大学学报》2016年第2期。

② 《仲裁法(修订)(征求意见稿)》第47条第2款规定:"当事人向仲裁庭申请保全措施的,仲裁庭应当及时作出决定,并要求当事人提供担保。保全决定经由当事人或者仲裁机构提交有管辖权的人民法院后,人民法院应当根据相关法律规定及时执行。"

决在之后的仲裁程序中可能被撤销、中止或修改,不具有"最终性"的法律效力,所以不满足《纽约公约》对仲裁裁决具有"约束力"的要求。

为扩大法院对仲裁庭临时措施决定的执行,已有部分国家及地区采取了积极的做法,主要分为两类:一类是扩大《纽约公约》中"仲裁裁决"定义的涵射范围,以包括仲裁庭作出的临时措施决定,例如,《新加坡国际仲裁法》[1]和《荷兰仲裁法》(Dutch Arbitration Act)[2]。另一类是直接在立法中颁布允许法院执行仲裁庭临时措施决定的制度,例如,我国香港特别行政区《仲裁条例》[3]和《德国民事诉讼法》(German Code of Civil Procedure)[4]。

最后,关于境外作出的临时措施决定在境内的执行问题,《仲裁法(修订)(征求意见稿)》未予明确。考虑到国际经贸活动规模不断扩大,而纠纷解决能力日益成为各个国家或地区参与国际竞争的关键,笔者建议就境外临时措施决定的承认和执行单独作出规定,在原则上允许法院承认和执行境外临时措施决定的基础上,明确不予承认和执行的例外情形,比如和本国公共政策相抵触等。

四、仲裁司法审查机制有待完善

仲裁司法审查机制是法院依法对仲裁活动进行审查与监督的机

---

[1] See Section 27(1) of the Singapore International Arbitration Act: "Arbitral award" has the meaning given by the Convention, but also includes an order or a direction made or given by an arbitral tribunal in the course of an arbitrations in respect of any of the matters set out in section 12(1)(c) to (j).

[2] See Article 1043b(4) of Dutch Arbitration Act: Unless the arbitral tribunal determines otherwise, a decision by the arbitral tribunal, upon request for an interim measure, is considered to be an arbitral award, to which the provisions of Section Three to Five inclusive of this Title shall be applicable.

[3] 香港特别行政区《仲裁条例》第45条第(2)款规定:"原讼法庭可应任何一方的申请,就已在或将会在香港或香港以外地方展开的任何仲裁程序,批给临时措施。"

[4] See Section 1041(2) of the German Code of Civil Procedure: Upon a party having filed a corresponding petition, the court may permit the enforcement of a measure pursuant to subsection (1), unless a corresponding measure of temporary relief has already been petitioned with a court. It may issue a differently worded order if this is required for the enforcement of the measure.

制。我国对仲裁的司法审查主要有仲裁协议、仲裁裁决两个维度。在本次《仲裁法》修订拟引入仲裁庭自裁管辖权的背景下,面向仲裁协议效力的事前审查机制实际上已无必要。至于仲裁裁决的事后审查机制,主要体现为《仲裁法》第58条及第63条的当事人申请撤销及不予执行仲裁裁决制度,近些年来也逐渐出现与商事仲裁发展趋势不符的现象。有鉴于此,《仲裁法(修订)(征求意见稿)》有所呼应地提出了关于仲裁裁决作出后司法审查机制的改革方案,具体分为两方面:第一,完善撤销仲裁裁决制度;第二,废除不予执行仲裁裁决制度。笔者将围绕这两部分的改革亮点进行介绍和分析,并提出相应的立法完善建议。

(一)完善撤销仲裁裁决制度

1. 建议仅因程序事由才能撤销仲裁裁决

在我国,当事人申请撤销仲裁裁决的法定事由主要规定于现行《仲裁法》第58条[①]。该条采用了类似于《纽约公约》第5条的立法结构,对法院审查仲裁裁决依据的事由进行了列举,并借鉴了第5条规定中"不存在有效仲裁协议""违反正当程序""超越协议范围"等不予执行裁决的事由,但除此之外,还纳入了两项实体审查事由,即第1款第(四)项"伪造证据"、第(五)项"隐瞒证据"。过往的司法实践中,对这两项撤裁事由存在较为严重的误用、滥用问题,部分裁定书甚至通过这两项事由介入仲裁事实认定,并据此撤销仲裁裁决。

例如,有裁定书以合同在形式上不完整且没有其他证据证明合同的真实性为由,认定仲裁庭裁决合同有效不合法。[②] 然而,仲裁庭对证据的证明效力有决定权,瑕疵证据也不一定均是伪造的,并不必然构成撤裁事由。再比如,有裁定书以仲裁申请人提出的仲裁请求金额没

---

① 《仲裁法》第58条规定:"当事人提出证据证明裁决有下列情形之一的,可以向仲裁委员会所在地的中级人民法院申请撤销裁决:(一)没有仲裁协议的;(二)裁决的事项不属于仲裁协议的范围或者仲裁委员会无权仲裁的;(三)仲裁庭的组成或者仲裁的程序违反法定程序的;(四)裁决所根据的证据是伪造的;(五)对方当事人隐瞒了足以影响公正裁决的证据的;(六)仲裁员在仲裁该案时有索贿受贿,徇私舞弊,枉法裁决行为的。人民法院经组成合议庭审查核实裁决有前款规定情形之一的,应当裁定撤销。人民法院认定该裁决违背社会公共利益的,应当裁定撤销。"

② 参见山东省德州市中级人民法院(2017)鲁14民特12号民事裁定书。

有扣减已经支付的款项为由,认定仲裁申请人隐瞒了足以影响公正裁决的证据。[①]在裁定书说理部分,法院关于仲裁被申请人"不应当承担因未披露已返还 3 万元而使仲裁裁决不公导致的不利后果"实际上相当于越过仲裁庭重新分配了举证责任,违反了仲裁司法审查机制的初衷。不可否认,实现仲裁结果实质公正是仲裁司法审查机制追求的内在价值,但不应以突破当事人对实体管辖权的约定为代价。

《仲裁法(修订)(征求意见稿)》第 77 条对上述两项实体审查事由进行了整合修订,将"伪造证据"事由拓展为"裁决因恶意串通、伪造证据等欺诈行为取得的",并删除了"隐瞒证据"事由。[②]本次《仲裁法》修订对撤裁法定事由的限缩显然有助于限制法院对仲裁实体问题的介入,但当前列出的审查事由仍然同时涉及程序和实体两方面,建议彻底删除"伪造证据"和"隐瞒证据"两项实体审查事由。

首先,司法监督的有限原则应得到尊重和遵循。既然当事人举证和质证的权利在仲裁程序中已经能够充分得到保护,那么法院在司法审查中没有必要再对案件本身进行实体审查。我国民商事诉讼与仲裁制度采用"谁主张、谁举证"的原则,任何一方当事人没有义务主动证明对自己不利的事实。即便相关证据由对方掌握,当事人也可以在案件审理过程中,对证据的出示提出请求(包括申请调查取证、申请采取证据保全措施等),而非在案后再主张对方隐瞒证据。并且,双方当事人理应在案件审理过程中完成对证据真实性的主张或抗辩,而不应在仲裁审理结束后又以对方"伪造证据"为由主张撤销仲裁裁决。

另外,排除法院的实体审查也符合"禁反言原则"。"禁反言原则"虽未明文规定于我国法律中,但并不影响该法理在司法实践中的普适性。当事人在仲裁程序中认可证据真实性,但之后又以该证据系伪造

---

① 参见山东省东营市中级人民法院(2016)鲁 05 民特 21 号民事裁定书。
② 《仲裁法(修订)(征求意见稿)》第 77 条第 1 款规定:"当事人提出证据证明裁决有下列情形之一的,可以向仲裁地的中级人民法院申请撤销裁决:(一)没有仲裁协议或者仲裁协议无效的;(二)裁决的事项不属于仲裁协议的范围或者超出本法规定的仲裁范围的;(三)被申请人没有得到指定仲裁员或者进行仲裁程序的通知,或者其他不属于被申请人负责的原因未能陈述意见的;(四)仲裁庭的组成或者仲裁的程序违反法定程序或者当事人约定,以致于严重损害当事人权利的;(五)裁决因恶意串通、伪造证据等欺诈行为取得的;(六)仲裁员在仲裁该案时有索贿受贿,徇私舞弊,枉法裁决行为的。"

为由提出撤销仲裁裁决的,违反"禁反言原则",法院对该主张应当不予支持。①

其次,国际通行的立法均未规定仲裁当事人可以对仲裁裁决的实体内容申请审查。②例如,《示范法》第 34 条明确规定法院对撤销仲裁裁决的审查限于程序审查。北京市高级人民法院在其发布的《北京市高级人民法院国内商事仲裁裁决司法审查工作要点》第 1 条中亦明确规定:"法院不得以仲裁裁决实体错误作为撤销理由,不得针对仲裁裁决关于举证责任分配、证据的认证、事实的认定等实体处理内容进行审查。"建议本次《仲裁法》修订吸纳这一观点,将仲裁司法审查意识和对案件进行实体判决的意识相分离,将法院审查限制在程序事项的范围内,而不再包括任何实体争议。③

2. 赋予当事人复议权或上诉权

根据我国现行法律的规定,当事人对于撤销仲裁裁决的裁定没有上诉权,亦不得申请再审,也即当事人不具有程序上的救济权利。为了在全国范围内统一司法审查的适用标准,曾出台《最高人民法院关于仲裁司法审查案件报核问题的有关规定》(以下简称《报核规定》),确立了仲裁司法审查案件的报核制度,以此监督下级人民法院对仲裁裁决的司法审查。该报核制度要求:如果下级人民法院裁定撤销仲裁裁决,必须向辖区内高级人民法院报核;其中,涉外涉港澳台的撤裁案件、以"违背社会公共利益"作为撤裁事由的案件,必须逐级上报至最高人民法院。

这一规定无疑有助于统一司法审查尺度、促进仲裁事业发展、维护当事人的合法权益,但其未能妥善兼顾司法审查效率的要求。具体而言,现行《仲裁法》第 60 条规定申请撤销仲裁裁决案件的审限为 2 个月,而报核制度导致很多撤裁案件的办理时间长达 4 至 6 个月。④

---

① 参见北京市第四中级人民法院(2018)京 04 民特 326 号民事裁定书。
② 参见孔德越:《撤销或不予执行仲裁裁决之实证研究——以 103 份民事裁定书为分析样本》,载《商事仲裁与调解》2021 年第 2 期。
③ 参见沈伟:《我国仲裁司法审查制度的规范分析——缘起、演进、机理和缺陷》,载《法学论坛》2019 年第 1 期。
④ 参见《明辨理念 梳理规则 提升审查工作质效——陕西高院关于仲裁司法审查报核案件审查情况的调研报告》,载《人民法院报》2020 年 10 月 22 日,第 8 版。

而且,上级人民法院对于上报的案件以复函形式作出答复,当事人在报核程序中缺位,此种职权主义的审查模式过分强调法院的主导作用,忽略了当事人在冲突中的作用。

《仲裁法(修订)(征求意见稿)》注意到了上述问题,在第81条中赋予了当事人对撤销仲裁裁决裁定的复议权。① 该条款有助于提高仲裁司法监督的透明度和当事人的参与度,体现了立法在实现当事人权利保护与司法审查效率之间的平衡所作出的努力。

更进一步地,申请撤销仲裁裁决的程序存在对立当事人,其审理事项涉及当事人的重大程序利益甚至实体利益,具有明显的争讼性质。而争讼的基本要求是法官中立、法官亲历、程序透明和双方平等。现行的报核制度采书面审查模式,双方当事人无法接触到法官并发表己方观点和意见。相比之下,本次《仲裁法》修订拟赋予当事人复议权,更符合"人本位"的现代司法理念,能够最大程度地尊重与保护当事人的合法权益。

引入当事人复议权后,报核制度将无适用的必要。但《报核规定》的层级设置有其特殊的公共政策考虑,为与该等层级设置相适用,可以相应调整撤裁案件的级别管辖。另外,按照现行《报核规定》的要求,特殊撤裁案件应层报高级人民法院、最高人民法院,形成了事实上的"三审终审"效果,与我国《民事诉讼法》规定的两审终审制不符。有鉴于此,笔者建议规定一般撤裁案件由中级人民法院负责一审,由高级人民法院负责二审。对于涉外涉港澳台、涉及公共利益的特殊撤裁案件,可参照《报核规定》的精神,交由高级人民法院一审,最高人民法院终审。

3. 提高申请成本

根据《诉讼费用交纳办法》的相关规定,申请撤销仲裁裁决的案件,每件仅需交纳400元。② 因此,很多当事人会在没有正当理由的情况下申请撤裁,以非常低的成本拖延履行裁决的时间。如果再考虑到

---

① 《仲裁法(修订)(征求意见稿)》第81条规定:"当事人对撤销裁决的裁定不服的,可以自收到裁定之日起十日内向上一级人民法院申请复议。人民法院应当在受理复议申请之日起一个月内作出裁定。"

② 《诉讼费用交纳办法》第14条规定:"申请费分别按照下列标准交纳:……(五)申请撤销仲裁裁决或者认定仲裁协议效力的,每件交纳400元。"

申请不予执行仲裁裁决(部分法院参照申请撤裁案件的标准收取申请费)可以拖延的2至3个月的时间①,则仲裁败诉方能够以极低的成本拖延履行仲裁裁决近半年,不利于维护仲裁制度的高效性、便捷性。有鉴于此,有必要提高申请撤销仲裁裁决案件的申请费,以使仲裁败诉方审慎运用将仲裁裁决诉诸司法审查的权利。

(二)废除不予执行仲裁裁决制度

根据现行法律的规定②,当事人基于相同的理由,既可以请求撤销仲裁裁决,也可以请求不予执行仲裁裁决,即我国对仲裁裁决采双重监督模式。在此前多年的发展中,立法也曾尝试厘清撤销与不予执行仲裁裁决两种司法监督制度之间的关系,并取得了一些成果③,但均未能从根本上解决问题。笔者认为,双重监督模式实无必要,并存在诸多弊端。

第一,两制度法律效果相同,重复使用造成了司法资源的浪费。根据《民事诉讼法》第248条第5款的规定,不予执行足以使仲裁裁决丧失执行力和既判力,在法律效果上等同于撤销仲裁裁决,此种双重监督在一定程度上导致了审判权与执行权行使的混同。

第二,两制度并用将进一步造成程序拖延,有损仲裁制度的高效

---

① 《最高人民法院关于人民法院办理仲裁裁决执行案件若干问题的规定》第12条规定:"人民法院对不予执行仲裁裁决案件的审查,应当在立案之日起两个月内审查完毕并作出裁定;有特殊情况需要延长的,经本院院长批准,可以延长一个月。"

② 《民事诉讼法》第248条规定:"对依法设立的仲裁机构的裁决,一方当事人不履行的,对方当事人可以向有管辖权的人民法院申请执行。受申请的人民法院应当执行。被申请人提出证据证明仲裁裁决有下列情形之一的,经人民法院组成合议庭审查核实,裁定不予执行:(一)当事人在合同中没有订有仲裁条款或者事后没有达成书面仲裁协议的;(二)裁决的事项不属于仲裁协议的范围或者仲裁机构无权仲裁的;(三)仲裁庭的组成或者仲裁的程序违反法定程序的;(四)裁决所根据的证据是伪造的;(五)对方当事人向仲裁机构隐瞒了足以影响公正裁决的证据的;(六)仲裁员在仲裁该案时有贪污受贿,徇私舞弊,枉法裁决行为的。人民法院认定执行该裁决违背社会公共利益的,裁定不予执行。裁定书应当送达双方当事人和仲裁机构。仲裁裁决被人民法院裁定不予执行的,当事人可以根据双方达成的书面仲裁协议重新申请仲裁,也可以向人民法院起诉。"

③ 2006年发布的《最高人民法院关于适用〈中华人民共和国仲裁法〉若干问题的解释》第26条规定,撤销仲裁裁决的申请被驳回后,当事人不能再以相同理由申请不予执行;2018年发布的《最高人民法院关于人民法院办理仲裁裁决执行案件若干问题的规定》第20条在肯定前述司法解释的基础上,完善了裁决撤销与不予执行的衔接机制,明确两者之间应以撤销仲裁裁决的审查优先。

性和便捷性。根据《仲裁法》第 59 条的规定,申请撤销仲裁裁决的法定期限为收到裁决书之日起 6 个月①,本身就长于域外通行的申请撤裁期限(通常为 3 个月)②。除此之外,当事人还有权在执行程序开始后、终结前随时提出不予执行仲裁裁决的申请,导致仲裁裁决的效力在执行终结前始终处于不安定的状态之中。仲裁的快速性决定了仲裁司法审查程序必须是迅速高效的③,现阶段两项仲裁司法审查制度叠加使用,不利于仲裁事业的发展。

第三,不予执行仲裁裁决的制度可能涉及地方保护的问题。根据《最高人民法院关于人民法院办理仲裁裁决执行案件若干问题的规定》第 2 条第 3 款以及《仲裁法》第 58 条第 1 款的规定④,仲裁裁决的不予执行由执行法院(被执行人 / 被执行财产所在地法院)管辖,容易滋生地方保护主义。而仲裁裁决的撤销则由仲裁机构所在地的法院管辖,更有利于维护当事人的权利。

有鉴于此,《仲裁法(修订)(征求意见稿)》第 82 条拟废除不予执行仲裁裁决制度,同时规定法院有权主动审查仲裁裁决是否符合社会公共利益。⑤这一创新之举值得肯定,也符合国际通行做法。仲裁虽然具有一

---

① 《仲裁法》第 59 条规定:"当事人申请撤销裁决的,应当自收到裁决书之日起六个月内提出。"
《最高人民法院关于适用〈中华人民共和国民事诉讼法〉的解释》第 479 条规定:"当事人请求不予执行仲裁裁决或者公证债权文书的,应当在执行终结前向执行法院提出。"
② 《示范法》第 34 条第(3)款规定:"当事人在收到裁决书之日起三个月后不得申请撤销仲裁裁决;已根据第 33 条提出请求的,从该请求被仲裁庭处理完毕之日起三个月后不得申请撤销。"
③ 参见姜霞:《仲裁司法审查程序要论》,湘潭大学出版社 2009 年版,第 48 页。
④ 《最高人民法院关于人民法院办理仲裁裁决执行案件若干问题的规定》第 2 条第 3 款规定:"被执行人、案外人对仲裁裁决执行案件申请不予执行,负责执行的中级人民法院应当另行立案审查处理;执行案件已指定基层人民法院管辖的,应当于收到不予执行申请后三日内移送原执行法院另行立案审查处理。"
《仲裁法》第 58 条第 1 款规定:"当事人提出证据证明裁决有下列情形之一的,可以向仲裁委员会所在地的中级人民法院申请撤销裁决:……"
⑤ 《仲裁法(修订)(征求意见稿)》第 82 条规定:"当事人应当履行裁决。一方当事人不履行的,对方当事人可以向有管辖权的中级人民法院申请执行。人民法院经审查认定执行该裁决不违背社会公共利益的,应当裁定确认执行;否则,裁定不予确认执行。裁定书应当送达当事人和仲裁机构。裁决被人民法院裁定不予确认执行的,当事人就该纠纷可以根据重新达成的仲裁协议申请仲裁,也可以向人民法院起诉。"

定的准司法性质,但仍属民间性的纠纷解决方式,得到司法机关的确认并赋予执行力后才能被强制执行。[①] 将法院在仲裁裁决执行程序中所发挥的监督作用由经申请裁定不予执行变为主动审查确认,同时严格限定审查范围是否违反公共利益的范畴,有利于在维护法院对仲裁的审查监督作用的前提下,解决好当前双重监督机制下的冲突问题。

结语

作为司法部对实务界与学界关于仲裁法修改呼声的回应,本次征求意见稿一方面顺应了国际商事仲裁制度的发展趋势,另一方面更是立足于我国国情的量体裁衣式的创举。尽管当前的草案还存在一些语焉不详之处,但笔者相信在未来的演进和变革中,这些问题将被逐步解决,同时也期待新《仲裁法》在未来商事仲裁的舞台上发挥更大的作用,焕发新的活力。

(王鸣杰　审校)

[①] 参见张卫平:《现行仲裁执行司法监督制度结构的反思与调整——兼论仲裁裁决不予执行制度》,载《现代法学》2020年第1期。

仲裁司法审查中的价值选择问题探析

张丝路*

摘要：我国法院对于仲裁协议效力司法审查的价值取向，明显从重规范仲裁协议转变为最大限度支持当事人选择仲裁的合意。然而在审查仲裁裁决时，我国法院的价值取向是保证仲裁裁决的公正性，只在适当程度上，即对于当事人可以自行决定的事项，尊重当事人关于仲裁程序的合意。前述价值选择体现了法院对仲裁的支持与监督，但这只是我国仲裁事业提升国际化竞争力的一个方面，也只是推进多元化纠纷解决机制中司法与仲裁的有效衔接和协调的一环。有效衔接与协调多元化纠纷解决机制中的司法与仲裁，更有赖于通过仲裁法的顶层设计，实现法院在仲裁司法审查中秉持的价值选择、仲裁机构自身的规范化运行，以及司法审查程序的优化这三方面的同步推进。

关键词：仲裁协议效力；仲裁裁决司法审查；多元化纠纷解决机制；价值选择

一、问题的提出

根据《最高人民法院关于审理仲裁司法审查案件若干问题的规定》(以下简称《仲裁司法审查规定》)第 1 条[①]的规定，仲裁司法审查

---

* 西北政法大学国际法学院讲师，法学博士，博士后，最高人民法院第五批实践锻炼青年学者。

① 《仲裁司法审查规定》第 1 条规定："本规定所称仲裁司法审查案件，包括下列案件：(一)申请确认仲裁协议效力案件；(二)申请执行我国内地仲裁机构的仲裁裁决案件；(三)申请撤销我国内地仲裁机构的仲裁裁决案件；(四)申请认可和执行香港特别行政区、澳门特别行政区、台湾地区仲裁裁决案件；(五)申请承认和执行外国仲裁裁决案件；(六)其他仲裁司法审查案件。"

主要包含两方面的内容:其一,审查仲裁协议的效力;其二,审查仲裁裁决是否存在法定的撤销或不予承认和执行的事由。仲裁司法审查对于仲裁和司法都具有重要的意义。一方面,经过司法审查,仲裁协议的效力得到了法院的最终确认,从而为仲裁庭开展后续仲裁程序奠定了良好的基础。同时,经过司法审查,仲裁裁决的效力得到了法院的认可,进而可以通过法院执行程序实现仲裁裁决的内容。这为当事人通过仲裁维护自身权益提供了有力保障。另一方面,有效的仲裁协议能够为法院分流大量的商事案件,缓解法院面对的案多人少问题。同时,通过仲裁司法审查,法院纠正了损害仲裁当事人合法权益的仲裁裁决,能够促进仲裁的良性发展,是司法支持与监督仲裁的重要体现。

据此,有效衔接与协调多元化纠纷解决机制中的司法与仲裁,有赖于健全的仲裁司法审查制度。我国学者关于仲裁司法审查制度的研究,有的基于比较法的立场,提出完善仲裁裁决撤销制度的建议[1];有的从实证研究的角度出发,考察撤销仲裁裁决之具体事由的适用问题[2];有的分析我国目前仲裁司法审查制度的问题,并提出相应的完善建议[3]。但尚缺乏对于法官在认定仲裁协议是否有效、仲裁裁决是否应予撤销或不予承认和执行时,所采用的价值选择的考察。

法官在解释现行司法审查规定或处理现行司法审查规定未涉及的问题时,需要以价值选择作为支撑,为其作出最终的是非判断提供衡量标准。因此,在仲裁司法审查的过程中,当法官审查仲裁协议效力与审查仲裁裁决效力时,应看是否具有相同的价值取向;如果没有,则需考虑审查仲裁协议效力与审查仲裁裁决各自遵循的价值取向是什么。前述价值取向是否能够有效提升我国仲裁制度的国际竞争力,是否能够有效实现司法对仲裁的支持与监督,从而推进多元化纠纷解决机制中司法与仲裁的有效衔接和协调,是本文考察的问题。

---

[1] 参见张圣翠:《论我国仲裁裁决撤销制度的完善》,载《上海财经大学学报》2012年第1期。

[2] 参见章杰超:《论仲裁司法审查理念之变迁——以N市中院申请撤销国内仲裁裁定为基础》,载《当代法学》2015年第4期。

[3] 参见姜建新、陈立伟:《关于仲裁裁决司法审查的调查与思考——对不予执行及申请撤销仲裁审查的实证分析》,载《法律适用》2013年第10期。

二、仲裁协议效力司法审查的价值选择

根据《最高人民法院关于适用〈中华人民共和国仲裁法〉若干问题的解释》(以下简称《仲裁法司法解释》)第27条第2款的规定,法院而非仲裁机构才是仲裁协议效力的最终认定主体;而根据该条第1款的规定,当事人一旦在仲裁程序中,不对仲裁协议提出异议,即便当事人之间不存在仲裁协议,仲裁程序也不能被认为是违法的。这一规定体现的精神是,当事人之间是否存在仲裁合意是审查仲裁协议效力的首要问题,而前述合意不仅体现为仲裁协议,也体现为申请或参加仲裁程序的行为。因此,法院在司法审查仲裁协议时的价值选择应是尊重当事人的仲裁合意,而仲裁协议效力司法审查从根本上讲是司法对当事人仲裁合意的认定与规范。

据此,仲裁协议效力司法审查价值选择的核心问题是,尊重当事人的仲裁合意,在多大程度上要受到司法对仲裁合意认定与规范的限制。根据2021年《全国法院涉外商事海事审判工作座谈会会议纪要》(以下简称《会议纪要》)第90条的规定,仲裁协议司法审查包括对仲裁协议是否成立、生效、失效,以及是否约束特定当事人等问题的审查。而在这些问题中,仲裁协议是否约束第三人、先裁后诉条款效力的认定,以及仲裁机构唯一性的认定,是在尊重当事人的仲裁合意与司法对仲裁合意认定与规范之间冲突最为明显的三个问题。因此,本文拟从前述三个问题入手,分别考察仲裁协议效力司法审查价值选择的核心问题。

(一)仲裁协议是否能够约束第三人

仲裁协议归根结底体现的是当事人将有关争议交由仲裁裁决的合意。[①] 从合同相对性的角度看,仲裁协议不能够约束第三人,除非第三人明确表示受仲裁协议的约束。因此,仲裁协议是否能够约束第三人的核心问题在于,法律在何种情况下可以推定第三人同意受他人之

---

① 参见赵秀文:《国际商事仲裁法》(第3版),中国人民大学出版社2012年版,第55页。

间达成的仲裁协议的约束,以及如此推定的合理性基础。①《仲裁法司法解释》第 8 条和第 9 条规定了在合同主体变更和债权让与这两种情况下,第三人是否受他人之间达成的仲裁协议之约束。在司法实践中,仍然存在争议的是,保险人是否受被保险人与第三人之间达成的仲裁协议的约束;债权人行使代位求偿权时,是否受债务人与次债务人之间达成的仲裁协议的约束。

1. 保险人是否受被保险人与第三人之间达成的仲裁协议的约束

对于保险人是否受被保险人与第三人之间达成的仲裁协议的约束,2019 年《全国法院民商事审判工作会议纪要》第 98 条明确规定,被保险人和第三者在保险事故发生前达成的仲裁协议,对保险人具有约束力。与此同时,该条将涉外民商事案件中,保险人是否受被保险人与第三人之间达成的仲裁协议的约束排除在前述规定之外。就该问题,最高人民法院在复函中体现的一贯意见是,保险人不受前述合同中仲裁协议的约束,除非有相反证据证明保险人明知并同意接受该仲裁协议。比如,〔2005〕民四他字第 29 号复函就明确指出:"由于保险人不是协商订立仲裁条款的当事人,仲裁条款并非保险人的意思表示,除非保险人明确表示接受,否则提单仲裁条款对保险人不具有约束力。"②

在涉外案件中,保险人不受被保险人与第三人之间达成的仲裁协议约束的根本原因在于,在海事海商案件中,特别是在班轮运输合同案件中,我国保险人赔偿后,对承运人行使代位求偿权往往面对的是提单中的伦敦仲裁协议。最高人民法院通过否定提单中仲裁协议对我国保险人的约束力,维护我国保险人的利益。严格来讲,这是法政策的体现,而不是理论上自洽的结论。更准确地说,在此种情况下,我国法院的价值取向更偏向于规范仲裁合意。而从理论上讲,判断保险人行使代位求偿权时,是否受被保险人与第三人之间达成的仲裁协议

---

① 参见宋连斌、罗星语:《仲裁协议对保险代位权人的效力》,载《国际法学刊》2021 年第 1 期。

② 《最高人民法院关于中国人民财产保险股份有限公司深圳市分公司诉广州远洋运输公司海上货物运输合同货损纠纷一案仲裁条款效力问题的请示的复函》(2005 年 10 月 9 日,〔2005〕民四他字第 29 号)。对最高人民法院就涉外民商事案件中,保险人是否受被保险人与第三人之间达成的仲裁协议约束的意见,详参此复函。

约束,需要明确仲裁协议与主合同权利义务的关系,以便明确仲裁协议在主合同权利义务转让时,是否应当自动转让。

尽管仲裁协议独立于主合同而存在,但该协议应被认为是附属于主合同中权利义务的程序义务。质言之,仲裁协议实际限制了当事人的诉权,使得当事人有义务通过仲裁程序解决争议。[①]同时,仲裁的基础是当事人之间的合意。从这个角度讲,固然现代仲裁法不再坚持仲裁的人身性,但当事人选择仲裁时,就特定争议与特定当事人进行仲裁的相对性仍应得到尊重。[②]换言之,仲裁协议不仅仅是附随于主合同权利义务的程序义务,而且是具有相对性的程序义务。基于以上分析,保险人行使代位求偿权时,是否受被保险人与第三人之间达成的仲裁协议约束的核心的问题是,仲裁协议这种附属于主合同的相对性程序义务约束保险人是否具有合理性。为明确该问题,可以将保险人的代位求偿权与债权让与进行对比。

《仲裁法司法解释》第9条规定债权转让时,仲裁协议自动转让,除非当事人另有约定、在受让债权债务时受让人明确反对或者不知有单独仲裁协议。由于但书的存在,该条规定实际上没有认可仲裁协议这种附属于主合同的相对性程序义务,在债权让与时,随主债权必然转让。原因在于债权让与对债权同一性的突破。债权让与实际违背了债权的同一性,但立法偏向了债权的财产权属性,故而允许债权作为一种财产自由流通。因此,与其说受让人受让的是转让人与债务人之间的债权,不如说其受让的是一种与前述债权给付内容一致的独立债权。[③]因此,附属于转让人与债务人之间原始债权的程序义务,必然不随着主债权的转让而转让。故而,《仲裁法司法解释》第9条的基本理念是正确的,但该条的问题在于,忽视了仲裁协议还具有相对性。在意定债权让与时,债务人没有反对让与的权利,只要接到了债权人

[①] 参见侯登华:《当事人合意对司法管辖权的效力问题——以仲裁协议为研究对象》,载《河北学刊》2014年第6期。

[②] 参见姚宇:《仲裁协议随债权转让的价值平衡方法——对债务人保护的再审视》,载《中国政法大学学报》2022年第3期。

[③] 参见庄加园:《〈合同法〉第79条(债权让与)评注》,载《法学家》2017年第3期。

的通知,债权让与对债务人就产生效力。但这针对的是实体权利,对于仲裁协议,其本质并不是可以流通的财产权利,而是当事人之间关于争议解决程序的合意。故而,从 2015 年出台一直延续到 2022 年新修订的《最高人民法院关于适用〈中华人民共和国民事诉讼法〉的解释》,关于法院选择协议在债权转让时的但书,也即转让协议另有约定且原合同相对人同意的除外,才是更适当的规范方式。也就是说,需要在债权让与时,赋予受让人和债务人否定仲裁协议拘束力的权利。

保险人代位求偿权被我国学者普遍理解为一种法定的债权让与[1],如果按照上述思路,则保险人和第三人当然也应有反对仲裁协议拘束力的权利。然而,保险人代位求偿权和意定债权让与在制度初衷方面迥然不同,这导致两者在仲裁协议是否自动转让方面也是不同的。保险人代位求偿权源于保险法的填补损害原则,主要的制度价值是使得被保险人快速获得理赔,并避免被保险人获得超过实际损失的赔偿。[2] 因此,保险人代位求偿权侧重于填补损失,而意定债权让与侧重于财产流通。在保险人赔付被保险人后,获得了法定的向第三人求偿的权利。而根据保险法中"赔偿金额范围内代位行使被保险人对第三者请求赔偿的权利"的规定,保险人实际是在被保险人和第三人之间产生了实际损失的法律关系中向第三人求偿。因此,保险人代位求偿权更类似于强制的债权债务概括让与。在此种情况下,不管是保险人还是第三人,当然都需要受到被保险人和第三人之间仲裁协议的约束。

2. 债权人行使代位权时,是否受债务人与次债务人之间达成的仲裁协议的约束

债权人的代位权是指,债权人为保全自己的债权,以自己的名义行使属于债务人权利的权利。[3] 虽然债权人代位权也以代位冠名,但

---

[1] 参见温世扬、武亦文:《论保险代位权的法理基础及其适用范围》,载《清华法学》2010 年第 4 期。

[2] 参见温世扬、武亦文:《论保险代位权的法理基础及其适用范围》,载《清华法学》2010 年第 4 期。

[3] 参见韩世远:《合同法总论》(第 4 版),法律出版社 2018 年版,第 433 页。

与保险人代位求偿权有着根本的不同。后者是一种法定的债权让与，而前者属于债权的对外效力。因此，债权人代位权是债权人对债务人所享有的债权的从权利，是一种法律规定的债权"保全"权利，而非来自债务人的债权让与。① 因此，《民法典》将债权人的代位权规定在合同编的合同保全部分中。从这个角度理解债权人代位权，债权人行使代位权时当然不受债务人与次债务人之间仲裁协议的约束，而应当按照法律规定的代位权制度行使代位权。

在实践中产生争议的是，《民法典》第535条"可以向人民法院请求"的措辞。既然可以向法院请求，当然也可以向仲裁机构请求。然而，从司法实践来看，以最典型的实际施工人代位转包人或者违法分包人向发包人求偿的案件为例，我国法院不支持实际施工人受转包人或者违法分包人与发包人之间仲裁协议的约束。比如，在（2020）最高法民终479号案②中，最高人民法院指出，该案系债权人弈成公司以债务人东泰公司怠于行使其对次债务人湘电公司的到期债权，对弈成公司造成损害，弈成公司以自己的名义代位行使东泰公司对湘电公司的债权而引起的诉讼，并非因债权转让而引起的诉讼。在此基础上，最高人民法院认为，虽然湘电公司主张其与东泰公司所签订的合同明确约定了仲裁条款，该案应由湘潭仲裁委员会审理，但由于弈成公司既非该仲裁条款所涉合同的一方当事人，亦非该仲裁条款所涉合同权利义务的受让人，且该约定管辖与《最高人民法院关于适用〈中华人民共和国合同法〉若干问题的解释（一）》第14条规定的债权人代位权诉讼特殊地域管辖规定相冲突，故原审裁定认定弈成公司不受该仲裁条款的约束，于法有据。

从该案中最高人民法院的认定可以看出：第一，最高人民法院所理解的可以向人民法院请求，是对债权人权利的规定，而不是对债权人行使权利方式的规定；第二，债权人行使代位权时，并不是进入到债

---

① 参见高印立：《实际施工人的代位权若干问题研究》，载《商事仲裁与调解》2021年第2期。
② 参见弈成新材料科技（上海）有限公司、湘电风能有限公司债权人代位权纠纷二审民事判决书。

务人与次债务人之间的法律关系,也不是债务人让与债权。因此,债权人行使代位权,与保险人代位求偿权、债权让与皆不相同,需要按照法定的债权人代位权行使方式——诉讼,实现对自身债权的保全。

据此,分析仲裁协议是否能够约束第三人,要以仲裁协议是附属于主合同且具有相对性的程序义务为出发点。从这个角度看,我国法院在判断仲裁协议是否约束第三人时,其基本的价值选择是尊重当事人的仲裁合意,也尊重第三人选择仲裁的权利。而当第三人完全加入他人之间的法律关系时,除非存在法政策缘由,第三人应受他人之间仲裁协议的约束。

(二) 先裁后诉条款效力的认定

先裁后诉条款的特点是,当事人在约定仲裁之后,又约定可以向法院诉讼。而与或裁或审条款不同的是,先裁后诉条款在仲裁与诉讼之间往往加入了诸如"仲裁不成""对仲裁结果不满意"等表示仲裁与诉讼先后顺序的措辞。对于先裁后诉条款的核心争议是,该类条款是否应被归为或裁或审条款,进而依据《仲裁法司法解释》第7条的规定否定其效力。

在(2013)民二终字第81号案[①]中,当事人约定的仲裁条款为:"解决合同纠纷的方式为:若因合同产生纠纷,合同双方协商解决,协商不成,可向协议签订地所在仲裁委员会提出仲裁,任意一方对仲裁结果提出异议的,可向合同签订地法院提出起诉。"对于该条款,最高人民法院认为,"本案双方当事人虽然约定了任何一方可向协议签订地所在仲裁委员会提出仲裁,但同时又约定任意一方对仲裁结果提出异议的,可向合同签订地法院提出起诉。这样的约定不符合《中华人民共和国仲裁法》第九条第一款关于'仲裁实行一裁终局'的规定,违反了仲裁排除法院管辖的基本原则"。显然,最高人民法院的态度是明确的,先裁后诉条款应被认为是一种特殊类型的或裁或审条款,是无效的。

---

① 参见内蒙古吉祥煤业有限公司与天津冶金集团贸易有限公司买卖合同纠纷管辖权异议上诉案二审民事裁定书。

然而,《会议纪要》第94条却明确规定:"当事人在仲裁协议中约定争议发生后'先仲裁、后诉讼'的,不属于仲裁法司法解释第七条规定的仲裁协议无效的情形。"显然,最高人民法院对于先裁后诉条款的态度有了重大转变,从否定其效力,转变为认可其效力。支撑这种态度变化的价值取向,应是尊重当事人的仲裁合意。而实现这种支持的方式是,根据《仲裁法》第9条第1款关于仲裁裁决作出后当事人不得就同一纠纷向人民法院起诉的规定,"先仲裁、后诉讼"关于诉讼的约定无效,但不影响仲裁协议的效力。这种论证路径的基础是《民法典》第156条,认定后诉部分违反法律规定的同时,将先裁部分与后诉部分进行区分。在此基础上,进一步单独判断先裁部分的效力。

这种论证路径需要进一步回答两方面的潜在问题。其一,如果先裁后审条款的仲裁部分无效,那么后诉部分是否可以是有效的法院选择协议。既然可以选择尊重当事人选择仲裁的合意,那么在此种合意无效且条款本身规定了管辖法院的前提下,后诉部分是否可以构成有效的法院选择合意;如果可以构成,照此推论,任何或裁或审条款只要仲裁部分无效,是否都可以认为是有效的法院选择条款。这是需要最高人民法院明确的问题。其二,先裁后审条款的后审部分无效的原因是约定违反了一裁终局原则,如果当事人没有约定后审,而是约定了其他事项,是否也可以运用部分有效、部分无效的方式论证先裁部分的效力。也就是说,法院需要在个案中不断认定当事人仲裁合意之后的部分是否违反了《仲裁法》的强制规定。而此种规定必须构成效力性强制规定,才能否定仲裁合意之后部分的效力。这种论证必然陷入《仲裁法》哪些规定是效力性强制性规定的讨论,这显然是一个没有必然结论的问题。支持仲裁合意的初衷导致了仲裁司法审查标准的随意性,此种支持是否有其必要性和合理性,是值得商榷的问题。

(三)仲裁机构唯一性的认定

我国现行《仲裁法》并不允许临时仲裁。尽管《最高人民法院关于为自由贸易试验区建设提供司法保障的意见》为临时仲裁在自由贸易试验区打开了政策窗口，允许符合"三特定"原则①的临时仲裁，但目前司法实践中尚未出现自由贸易试验区临时仲裁的案例。而从立法趋势来看，2021年司法部公开征求意见的《仲裁法（修订）（征求意见稿）》第25条关于仲裁协议效力的规定，已经明确取消了仲裁协议约定唯一仲裁机构的要求。而《仲裁法（修订）（征求意见稿）》第35条第2款和第3款，对于没有明确约定唯一仲裁机构的仲裁协议作出了补充规定，规定了如何处理仲裁机构约定不明确和没有约定仲裁机构的情况。

从总体趋势来看，仲裁法未来的修改趋势应是纳入临时仲裁。由于该趋势，我国法院近几年在认定仲裁机构唯一性时的价值取向，倾向于尊重当事人的仲裁合意，结合案件事实和仲裁协议的约定，尽可能推定出唯一的仲裁机构。《会议纪要》第93条针对《仲裁法司法解释》第3条的规定，更进一步明确了"应当按照有利于仲裁协议有效的原则予以认定"，就是对前述价值选择的最好说明。比如，在（2019）最高法知民终338号案②中，最高人民法院认为，合同约定的仲裁条款是"在北京市仲裁委员会仲裁"，虽然北京市的仲裁委员会有北京仲裁委员会、中国国际经济贸易仲裁委员会、中国海事仲裁委员会三家，但从案涉仲裁条款的字面意思来看，其与北京市现有的三家仲裁机构中的"北京仲裁委员会"最为接近，仅有一字之差。考虑到双方并非法律或者纠纷解决专业人士，对其在约定仲裁机构时，不应苛以过高标准。因此，案涉仲裁条款应认为约定了唯一的仲裁机构。如果仅从文

---

① 《最高人民法院关于为自由贸易试验区建设提供司法保障的意见》第9条第3款规定："在自贸试验区内注册的企业相互之间约定在内地特定地点、按照特定仲裁规则、由特定人员对有关争议进行仲裁的，可以认定该仲裁协议有效。人民法院认为该仲裁协议无效的，应请报上一级法院进行审查。上级法院同意下级法院意见的，应将其审查意见层报最高人民法院，待最高人民法院答复后作出裁定。"需要说明的是，此后最高人民法院针对自贸区出台的司法保障意见，不再提及需要最高人民法院答复的程序，比如《最高人民法院关于人民法院为北京市国家服务业扩大开放综合示范区、中国（北京）自由贸易试验区建设提供司法服务和保障的意见》第19条规定："……支持在自由贸易试验区内注册的企业之间约定在特定地点、按照特定仲裁规则、由特定人员对相关争议进行仲裁……"

② 参见互商网（上海）网络技术有限公司与北京米花时代科技有限公司计算机软件开发合同纠纷上诉案二审民事裁定书。

字出发,案涉仲裁协议约定的仲裁机构是不明确的。因此,最高人民法院在该案中,实际是在推定当事人约定仲裁协议时的意思表示,而且这种推定是以尽可能使得仲裁协议有效,而不是以规范不准确的仲裁协议为价值取向。

当事人申请法院确认仲裁协议效力,究其实质,乃是双方当事人对于仲裁协议的效力存在争议,更准确地讲,是一方认为仲裁协议存在效力瑕疵,而另一方不认为仲裁协议存在效力瑕疵。[①]因此,在仲裁协议效力司法审查程序中,法院无法就仲裁协议的本意询问当事人的真实意思。因而,法院在判断仲裁协议效力时,严格来讲,是在推定当事人的意思表示。正如上举案例,最高人民法院的结论实际是说,当事人在订立仲裁协议时,表达的意思应该是选择北京仲裁委员会作为指定仲裁机构。

按照上述方法,法院在认定仲裁机构唯一性时,当然不能以订立仲裁协议后的事实为准,而应判断当事人之间的约定,在达成仲裁协议时,是否指向了唯一的仲裁机构。然而,在(2019)最高法民终1500号案[②]中,最高人民法院认为,双方订立仲裁条款的本意为发生纠纷时选择用仲裁的方式解决纠纷,且选择工程所在地的仲裁委员会为仲裁机构,当中电港航公司于2019年2月向福建省高级人民法院提起诉讼时,工程所在地仲裁委员会,即海峡两岸仲裁中心依法成立,仲裁条款的不确定性已经消除,应当认定仲裁条款有效。显然,这是以订立仲裁协议后发生事实溯及既往地论证仲裁协议的效力。这种认定方式是存在瑕疵的,如果要为此种认定方式背书,唯一的理由只能是充分尊重当事人的仲裁合意。

除《仲裁法司法解释》第3条外,该司法解释第6条也规定了如何认定仲裁机构唯一性。按照尊重当事人选择仲裁合意的价值取向,司法实践对第6条的认定标准也是逐渐放宽。比如,在(2019)陕01

---

① 参见谢石松主编:《商事仲裁法学》(第2版),高等教育出版社2022年版,第331—332页。

② 参见中国电建集团港航建设有限公司、平潭综合实验区土地储备中心建设工程施工合同纠纷案二审民事裁定书。

民特351号案①中,双方当事人在案涉合同中约定的仲裁机构为"工程所在地仲裁委员会"。而案涉工程所在地位于陕西省杨凌示范区,但杨凌示范区内没有仲裁委员会。西安市中级人民法院认为,因杨凌示范区属于陕西省直管行政区域,而陕西省范围内有多家仲裁委员会,故双方约定的工程所在地的仲裁委员会无法对应具体的仲裁委员会。根据《仲裁法司法解释》第6条的规定,案涉仲裁协议无效。由于此案判决是在2020年作出的,按照当时尚未修改的《最高人民法院关于仲裁司法审查案件报核问题的有关规定》(以下简称《报核规定》)第3条的规定②,该案否定仲裁协议的效力且当事人住所地跨省,故需要向最高人民法院报核。该案的认定实际反映了最高人民法院的审核意见。因此,可以看出,最高人民法院对于《仲裁法司法解释》第6条规定的"某地"作出了延伸性的认定。对于该条中的"某地"的理解,不能仅仅止于特定地点,而是需要从行政辖区的角度判断某地的上一级行政辖区是否有唯一的仲裁机构;如有,则仲裁协议同样可以认定为有效。

又如,在(2019)陕01民特37号案③中,案涉仲裁协议约定为,将争议"提交诉讼发生方所在地仲裁委员会仲裁"。该条款显然不仅涉及是否构成或裁或审条款的认定,也涉及诉讼发生方所在地这个不唯一的地点是否可以推定出唯一仲裁机构的认定。西安市中级人民法院审查后认为,因合同当事人的住所地分别位于陕西省西安市和湖北省十堰市,而上述两地均仅有一个仲裁机构,故任一合同当事人申请仲裁时,仲裁机构都是明确的。因此,按照《仲裁法司法解释》第6条的规定,

---

① 参见西安方洲建筑劳务有限公司与江苏南通三建集团股份有限公司申请确认仲裁协议效力特殊程序民事裁定书。
② 《最高人民法院关于仲裁司法审查案件报核问题的有关规定》第3条规定:"本规定第二条第二款规定的非涉外涉港澳台仲裁司法审查案件,高级人民法院经审查拟同意中级人民法院或者专门人民法院认定仲裁协议无效,不予执行或者撤销我国内地仲裁机构的仲裁裁决,在下列情形下,应当向最高人民法院报核,待最高人民法院审核后,方可依最高人民法院的审核意见作出裁定:(一)仲裁司法审查案件当事人住所地跨省级行政区域;(二)以违背社会公共利益为由不予执行或者撤销我国内地仲裁机构的仲裁裁决。"需要说明的是,2021年修改《报核规定》后,第3条第(一)项被删除。
③ 参见李振清与华昌达智能装备集团股份有限公司申请确认仲裁协议效力特殊程序民事裁定书。

仲裁申请人所在地的仲裁委员会应视为约定的仲裁机构。如果严格按照《仲裁法司法解释》第6条和第7条的规定,该案应当否定该仲裁协议的效力,不仅是因为仲裁协议中既出现了诉讼,又出现了仲裁,更因为诉讼发生方所在地这个地点是不唯一的。由于该案裁定是2019年作出的,根据当时尚未修改的《报核规定》,该案需要向最高人民法院报核。该案最终的认定实际也是最高人民法院的审核意见。因此,从最终结论来看,最高人民法院对于《仲裁法司法解释》第6条规定的"某地"作出了更进一步的延伸性认定,即"某地"是对特定当事人的某地,而不是对仲裁协议所有当事人的某地。而由于该案结论不涉及《仲裁法司法解释》第7条,可以推论的是,正如(2019)最高法知民终338号案中最高人民法院的判断,仲裁协议中措辞的不严谨不会对仲裁协议的效力产生重大影响,除非这种不严谨的程度明确地表示出当事人试图既通过诉讼,又通过仲裁解决争议的意思,进而构成或裁或审条款。

据此,在我国立法纳入临时仲裁的脚步越来越快的前提下,我国法院越加不倾向于以当事人约定的仲裁机构不具有唯一性,否定仲裁协议的效力,除非结合案件事实和仲裁条款完全无法确定唯一的仲裁机构。这显然是尊重当事人仲裁合意的重要体现。然而,这种尊重并不是没有代价的,其必然后果是法院需要更加详尽地进行事实调查。不管是对于行政辖区内的仲裁机构,还是对于不同当事人住所地的仲裁机构,在以往的仲裁协议司法审查中显然都是不需要法院调查的,但延伸性认定"某地"后,这种事实调查在所难免。当然,如果未来仲裁法采纳临时仲裁,法院当然不需要进行以上事实调查。但在当下,这种放任当事人随意约定仲裁协议,而加重法院负担的做法是否有其必要性;在法院如此深入地进行事实调查后,认定的仲裁协议约定内容,是否可以被认为是当事人制定仲裁协议时真实意思表示,都是值得商榷的。

综上,不考虑法院在审查先裁后审类型仲裁协议效力时以及认定仲裁机构唯一性时,采用路径之适当性的前提下,笔者的观点是,以2019年4月《中共中央办公厅、国务院办公厅关于完善仲裁制度提高仲裁公信力的若干意见》为界限,为充分贯彻2019年习近平总书记在中央政法工作会议上作出的重要指示,"把非诉讼纠纷解决机制挺在前面",法院对于仲裁协议效力司法审查的取向,明显是从重规范当事人的仲裁合意转变为最大程度支持当事人的仲裁合意,以往许多司法实践中被认定为无效的仲裁协议,比如,先裁后审类型的仲裁协议,都得到了司法的支持。

三、仲裁裁决司法审查的价值选择

根据《仲裁法司法解释》第 17 条的规定,仲裁裁决的司法审查程序,更类似于审判监督程序,是对于已经生效的仲裁裁决的有限度的事由审查。理论上,一般将撤销或不予承认和执行仲裁裁决的事由,分为针对仲裁庭管辖权的事由,包括不存在仲裁协议、可仲裁性及超裁;程序性审查事由,即违反法定或约定的仲裁程序;实体性审查事由。① 由于可仲裁性是一个纯粹的立法选择问题,与司法审查中的价值选择无涉,而超裁问题究其根本是仲裁庭裁决了其本不具有管辖权的实体法律关系,故本文在实体性审查事由部分,考察认定超裁时的价值选择。据此,以下将分别从程序性审查事由和实体性审查事由入手,探讨法院在司法审查仲裁裁决时的价值选择。

(一)审查程序性事由的价值选择

仲裁裁决作出后,当事人以违反法定或约定仲裁程序为由提出异议,主要有两种情况:其一,仲裁程序本身存在瑕疵且仲裁庭没有在仲裁程序中有效处理该瑕疵;其二,当事人对仲裁结果不满意,试图以违反法定或约定程序为由,否定仲裁裁决的效力。第一种情况涉及当事人的异议权;第二种情况的核心问题是,如何认定违反法定或约定仲裁程序达到了可能影响案件公正裁决的程度。

1. 当事人的异议权

尊重当事人的仲裁合意,除了尊重当事人选择仲裁的合意,还有

---

① See Nigel Blackaby et al., Redfern and Hunter on International Arbitration, Oxford University Press, 2015, p.581.

一层含义是,当事人可以根据自身需要就仲裁程序作出特别约定。这种特别约定不仅可以体现在仲裁协议中,也可以通过放弃异议权实现。也就是说,即便仲裁程序违反仲裁规则或当事人关于仲裁程序的特别约定,只要当事人放弃异议,实际等同于当事人通过行为变更了仲裁规则或关于仲裁程序特别约定的合意。因此,在仲裁裁决司法审查程序中,当事人如再就已经放弃异议的程序瑕疵提出抗辩,则必然违反诚实信用原则。

《最高人民法院关于人民法院办理仲裁裁决执行案件若干问题的规定》(以下简称《执行规定》)第14条第3款从司法解释的层面就仲裁程序放弃异议权作出了规定。该条就仲裁程序放弃异议权规定了三个必须同时满足的条件:(1)经特别提示,一方当事人知道或理应知道仲裁程序瑕疵;(2)该方当事人参加仲裁程序或继续进行仲裁程序;(3)该方当事人未提出异议。前述条件也可在撤销仲裁裁决司法审查中,用以判断当事人是否行使了仲裁程序放弃异议权。

实践中,多数情况下,仲裁庭在首次开庭时会询问当事人是否对已经进行的仲裁程序有异议。可以看出,《执行规定》对仲裁程序放弃异议权的规定是从仲裁实践出发,且没有对当事人异议的方式提出过高要求。如果在前述情况下,当事人表示无异议,则在后续的司法审查程序中,法院通常不支持当事人就仲裁程序瑕疵提出的撤销或不予承认和执行仲裁裁决事由;如果当事人表示异议,则仲裁庭必须解决当事人提出的仲裁程序瑕疵,否则法院必然以违反法定或约定仲裁程序为由,撤销或不予承认和执行仲裁裁决。毋庸置疑,在涉及当事人的异议权时,法院关于是否撤销或不予承认和执行仲裁裁决的价值选择是尊重当事人的仲裁合意。

需要补充说明两点:其一,我国几大仲裁机构制定的仲裁规则中都有放弃异议权的规定。比如,2022年修正的《深圳国际仲裁院仲裁规则》第69条、2021年《广州仲裁委员会仲裁规则》第13条、2021年修订的《中国海事仲裁委员会仲裁规则》第10条、2015年《中国国际经济贸易仲裁委员会仲裁规则》第10条等。这些规则的内容基本相同,就放弃异议权提出三项必须同时满足的要求:(1)一方当事人知道或理应知道仲裁程序瑕疵;(2)该方当事人仍参加仲裁程序或继续进行仲裁程序;(3)该方当事人未及时、书面异议。就提出异议的方式,前述仲裁规则的要求高于《执行规定》第14条第3款的规定,但前述仲裁规则并没有规定特别提示当事人的要求。

其二,放弃异议权还有一个层面的问题是,司法审查阶段的放弃异议权。从当事人的角度看,这涉及当事人是否可以对司法审查事由进行特别约定或特别放弃[1];从法院的角度看,这涉及当事人是否必须在撤销仲裁裁决程序中,一次性提出所有的异议,否则就丧失了在执行仲裁裁决中提出异议的权利。遗憾的是,《仲裁法司法解释》第26条仅规定了当事人不能在撤销程序和执行程序中提出同一事由,而没有涉及仲裁司法审查阶段的放弃异议权。由于目前没有明确的立法规定,也尚未有司法实践涉及仲裁司法审查阶段的放弃异议权,故本文不再进一步讨论司法审查阶段的放弃异议权。

2. 可能影响案件公正裁决的认定

根据《仲裁法司法解释》第20条的规定,违反法定或约定程序只有达到可能影响案件正确裁决的程度时,才可能导致仲裁裁决被撤销。而《执行规定》第14条第1款,以及《会议纪要》第101条关于违反法定或约定程序事由,使用的措辞是"可能影响案件公正裁决"。从这一措辞的变化不难看出,司法审查违反法定或约定程序的理念从确保仲裁裁决的正确性,转变为保障仲裁裁决的公正性。尽管不正确的仲裁裁决一定是不公正的,但是违反了程序正义的仲裁裁决即便实体上是正确的,也是不公正的仲裁裁决。显然,措辞的变化标志着司法审查理念的进步。

从《仲裁法司法解释》第20条、《执行规定》第14条第1款,以及《会议纪要》第101条使用的"可能影响"这一措辞可以看出,违反法定或约定程序与不公正的仲裁裁决之间必然隐含着对因果关系的认定。如果这种因果关系是直接的,比如,仲裁裁决是在未适当通知一方当事人的情况下作出的,显然是满足"可能影响"要求的。因此,

---

[1] 参见李红建:《仲裁司法审查的困境及其应对》,载《法律适用》2021年第8期。

间接因果关系是否也可以满足"可能影响"要求,是需要考察的问题。比如,在(2021)陕01民特170号案①中,仲裁庭主要依据其向造价专业机构咨询的计算方法并综合考虑相关定额,对案涉人工费调差数额造价作出了认定。根据《西安仲裁委员会仲裁规则》第31条第2款"仲裁庭收集的证据,应当组织当事人进行质证"的规定,西安市中级人民法院认为,"仲裁庭在对该造价计算方法未组织双方当事人进行质证的情况下,即将该计算方法作为主要定案依据,显属仲裁程序违法的情形",据此撤销了案涉仲裁裁决。该案的核心判断是,存在程序瑕疵的是定案证据的认定过程,而被撤销的是依据定案证据作出的仲裁裁决,法院显然是用间接因果关系认定程序瑕疵对仲裁裁决结果的影响。

"可能影响"这一措辞本身并没有完全排除间接因果关系,但其范围完全由法院自由裁量。因此,判断违反法定或约定仲裁程序的核心要件实际是公正裁决。显然,在这个判断过程中,法院的价值选择是实现当事人之间的公正。因此,以公正裁决作为审查标准,实际意味着法院可以一定程度上对仲裁裁决进行实体性判断。如果仲裁裁决没有公正裁断当事人之间的争议,则法院需要进一步判断当事人提出的撤销或不予承认和执行仲裁裁决的程序瑕疵是否能够与仲裁结果建立因果关系。如果答案都是肯定的,则案涉仲裁裁决就会因违反法定或约定仲裁程序而被撤销或被不予承认和执行。

综上,司法审查程序性事由时,法院的价值选择是在尊重当事人的仲裁合意与保证仲裁裁决公正性之间进行平衡。由于当事人对于仲裁程序具有最终决定权,因而,法院首先需要判断当事人是否通过行使仲裁程序放弃异议权,实质上改变了仲裁程序规则;如果不存在这种情况,保证仲裁裁决公正性就成为了法院作出是否认定仲裁裁决违反法定或约定仲裁程序时的价值选择。在这种价值选择之下,法院一旦通过事实查明,建立起程序瑕疵与不公正仲裁裁决之间的因果关系,就会对仲裁裁决作出违反程序性司法审查事由的肯定性判断。

---

① 参见西安电子科技大学与咸阳第一建筑工程有限公司申请撤销仲裁裁决特殊程序:其他民事特殊程序民事裁定书。

(二)审查实体性事由的价值选择

我国现行仲裁法及其司法解释对国内仲裁裁决规定的实体性审查事由,包括超裁、伪造或隐瞒证据、损害第三人合法权益,以及违背社会公共利益。从理论层面来看,超裁和伪造或隐瞒证据体现了法院保证仲裁裁决公正性的价值选择。超裁是为了解决仲裁庭就无权裁定的法律关系作出认定的问题,伪造或隐瞒证据是为了解决仲裁裁决裁定之法律关系所基于的事实不正确的问题。这些认定都是为了保证仲裁裁决对当事人之间法律关系的认定是公正的。

损害第三人合法权益以及违背社会公共利益的审查事由,分别是为了解决仲裁裁决损害了特定第三人或不特定第三人合法权益的问题。从表面看,这并不是保证仲裁裁决公正性这一价值选择的体现。但如果将仲裁裁决理解为当事人之间的合同,则损害第三人合法权益以及违背社会公共利益的审查事由,实际是为了解决该合同的负外部性问题。而一旦解决了这种负外部性,也就反向地实现了当事人之间的公正。因此,如同尊重当事人仲裁的合意有两层含义,保证仲裁裁决公正性也有正反两面。正面是仲裁裁决公正裁断当事人之间的争议;反面是克服不公正仲裁裁决的负外部性。这两面分别体现于不同的实体性审查事由中。

从司法层面论证法院审查实体性事由时的价值选择是否为了保证仲裁裁决的公正性,需要考察一种仲裁法及其司法解释没有规定的实体性审查事由——新证据。由于仲裁一裁终局的特性,如果仲裁裁决作出后,出现了能够推翻仲裁裁决的新证据,除非当事人同意重新仲裁,否则不管是仲裁庭、仲裁机构或者法院都没有适当的理由推翻已经生效的仲裁裁决。这实际是尊重当事人选择仲裁合意的一种极端情况,即当事人选择了仲裁作为争议解决方式,就必须承担一裁终局可能带来的弊端。因此,在新证据类型的案件中,法院实际面临着尊重当事人仲裁合意与保证仲裁裁决公正性之间的剧烈冲突。法院如何处理这种冲突,既能够有效说明法院审查实体性事由时的价值选择,也能有效说明法院在仲裁裁决司法审查中是以何种价值选择为优先考量。在(2020)辽02执异267号案①中,案涉仲裁裁决认可了申请执行人通过两份证据证明的损失,但被申请人在执行程序中使用新证据证明申请人的该损失并不存在。该案最终以隐瞒证据为由不予执行案涉仲裁裁决,但该案并不严格符合《执行规定》第16条第1款第(三)项"要求对方当事人出示或者请求仲裁庭责令其提交"的要求。法院最终的认定路径实际是,被申请人提供的证据足以证明申请人在仲裁过程中存在隐瞒证据的可能,而被隐瞒的证据显然导致了不公正的仲裁裁决。不难看出,这种论证路径与认定违反法定或约定仲裁程序可能影响公正裁决的论证路径是一致的。尽管该案不能被认为是我国法院司法审查实体性事由的典型情况,但足以说明法院在面对不公正的仲裁裁决时,会通过解释方法,尽可能将案件事实涵摄于法定的司法审查事由,进而撤销或不予承认和执行不公正的仲裁裁决。

据此,笔者认为,在审查仲裁裁决时,法院更关心仲裁裁决的公正性,只在适当程度上,即对于当事人可以自行决定的事项,尊重当事人的仲裁合意。究其原因,司法审查仲裁裁决的根本目的是纠正仲裁制度本身缺乏事后监督机制,以及由此可能导致的仲裁结果不公正问题。因此,司法审查仲裁裁决是一种有限度的审查,只要仲裁裁决能够公正裁断当事人之间的争议,法院就不会介入。②

四、仲裁司法审查价值选择对有效衔接与协调多元化纠纷解决机制的实际功用

我国法院在司法审查仲裁协议效力时的价值选择是尊重当事人选择仲裁的合意,而在司法审查仲裁裁决时的价值选择是保证仲裁裁决的公正性。在此基础上,笔者试图回答第一部分提出的两个问题。

第一,上述价值选择是否能够有效提升我国仲裁制度的国际竞争

---

① 参见顾某某防腐工程有限公司、上海中芬新能源投资有限公司合同纠纷执行审查类执行裁定书。

② See Hossein Abedian, Judicial Review of Arbitral Awards in International Arbitration–A Case for an Efficient System of Judicial Review, Journal of International Arbitration, 2011, Vol. 28 Issue 6, p.555.

力? 党的十八大以来,我国仲裁事业突飞猛进。2018 年全国仲裁机构受案数量和标的额,相当于《仲裁法》实施前 15 年的总和。① 从法院的角度看,尊重当事人的仲裁合意能够有效分流商事案件,为本已高速发展的我国仲裁事业再添薪柴。从仲裁机构的角度看,大量案件进入仲裁程序后,必然以规范化运行仲裁程序为根本依托,否则一旦出现存在质量问题的仲裁裁决,法院从保证仲裁裁决公正性的角度,必然需要撤销或不予承认和执行这些有瑕疵的仲裁裁决。这不仅浪费了仲裁资源,也降低了当事人选择仲裁的信心。显然,我国法院在仲裁司法审查中所秉持的价值选择只是我国仲裁事业提升国际竞争力的一个方面,更重要的是仲裁机构自身通过规范化发展,提升仲裁公信力。

第二,这种价值选择是否能够有效实现司法对仲裁的支持与监督,从而推进多元化纠纷解决机制中司法与仲裁的有效衔接和协调? 毋庸置疑的是,我国法院在司法审查仲裁协议效力时的价值选择——尊重当事人选择仲裁的合意,是对仲裁事业最重要的支持,法院谦抑地解释自己的管辖权,支持当事人通过仲裁这种自治性的争议解决方式化解纠纷;因为仲裁裁决不能公正裁断当事人之间的争议,而否定仲裁裁决的效力,表面上是对仲裁的阻却,但实际上,不仅可以警示仲裁人员谨慎用权,保障仲裁业健康发展,而且有利于保障仲裁裁决的正当性和公信力。② 因此,我国法院在仲裁司法审查中秉持的价值选择,能够有效实现司法对仲裁的支持与监督。

在推进多元化纠纷解决机制中,司法与仲裁的有效衔接和协调是一个三位一体的工程。其一是法院在仲裁司法审查中秉持的价值选择。尊重当事人的仲裁合意,促进更多商事案件通过仲裁解决;纠正损害当事人合法权益的仲裁裁决,维护当事人之间的公平并消解此类仲裁裁决的负外部性。其二是仲裁机构自身的规范化运行。提升仲

---

① 参见最高人民法院民事审判第四庭编:《最高人民法院商事仲裁司法审查年度报告(2019)》,人民法院出版社 2021 年版,第 17 页。
② 参见朱科:《试论国际商事仲裁司法审查的基本原则》,载《河南社会科学》2016 年第 11 期。

裁裁决的质量,增强仲裁这种争议解决方式本身的竞争力。其三是司法审查制度的程序优化。① 提高司法审查程序的透明度、当事人参与度及程序效率。从有效衔接与协调多元化纠纷解决机制的角度看,以上三点必须同步进行,共同推进。因此,更能根本性地有效衔接和协调多元化纠纷解决机制中司法与仲裁的方式是,贯彻多元化纠纷解决理念,修改现行仲裁法,统筹推进以上三位一体的工程。单纯依赖法院在仲裁司法审查过程中的价值选择,既解决不了目前司法审查本身存在的程序问题,更解决不了仲裁机构运作不规范问题。

结语

仲裁司法审查中的价值选择对解释现行立法规定以及处理边缘案件具有重要的意义。为充分发挥仲裁在多元化纠纷解决机制中的作用,人民法院在审查仲裁协议时所采取的价值选择从规范仲裁合意转向了尽可能使得仲裁合意有效。《会议纪要》体现了我国法院在判断仲裁协议效力时,价值选择的重大转变。而在审查仲裁裁决时,法院一定程度上介入了对仲裁裁决实体结果的审查,以保证仲裁裁决的公正性,这似乎背离了仲裁司法审查只进行程序性审查的一般原则。然而,在我国仲裁机构如雨后春笋般设立并且蓬勃发展的当下,为了提升仲裁公信力,这种背离在一定程度上是适当的。

(陈末末　审校)

---

① 关于现行仲裁司法审查制度的程序优化,参见沈伟:《我国仲裁司法审查制度的规范分析——缘起、演进、机理和缺陷》,载《法学论坛》2019 年第 1 期。

最密切联系原则纳入仲裁协议法律适用之证成

张文楷*

摘要：在现行立法框架下，有效性原则只能在仲裁协议第三层次的法律适用中以"隐名"的方式存在，英国法院将最密切联系原则作为法律选择解释原则的做法值得我们参考。在必要性上，仲裁协议冲突规范的特殊形式强化了说理的重要性，而"隐名"的有效性原则难以完成说理的任务，将最密切联系原则作为法律选择解释原则的同时与《涉外民事关系法律适用法》的规定相契合。在可行性上，"隐名"的有效性原则弥补了最密切联系原则自由裁量权过大的缺陷，最密切联系原则的结果考量使得有关连结点具有被解释为最密切联系之可能。因此，应当在"隐名"适用有效性原则的基础上纳入最密切联系原则作为法律选择解释原则，保证仲裁协议法律适用形式和实质上的正当性和可接受性。

关键词：仲裁协议；法律适用；最密切联系原则；有效性原则

　　涉外仲裁协议的法律适用问题直接决定了应当选择何种准据法判断仲裁协议的效力，进而决定了当事人的仲裁合意能否实现，仲裁庭对案涉争议是否具有管辖权，以及仲裁裁决是否能够被承认与执行等事项，对于国际商事仲裁具有重要的意义。受西方国家立法和司法实践的影响，我国越来越多的学者主张，应当在立法上为仲裁协议

---

* 中山大学法学院硕士研究生。

的冲突规范规定尽可能多的连结点,并遵循"有利于仲裁协议有效"的原则(以下简称"有效性原则")进行仲裁协议准据法的选择[①],这种理念被《最高人民法院关于审理仲裁司法审查案件若干问题的规定》(以下简称《仲裁司法审查规定》)第14条所部分采纳。但遗憾的是,2021年7月公布的《仲裁法(修订)(征求意见稿)》虽然在诸多方面有所创新,却并未延续《仲裁司法审查规定》第14条的做法,在第90条中将有效性原则以立法的形式固定下来。对此,有学者认为,修改后的《仲裁法》应当重新引入有效性原则,以保障当事人的合理预期,提升我国仲裁机构在国际市场上的竞争力。[②]然而,立法者既然在《仲裁法(修订)(征求意见稿)》第90条中保留了《涉外民事关系法律适用法》第18条的基本框架,甚至在第二层次的法律适用范围中删除了"仲裁机构所在地"这一连结点,这或许表明了许多学者所期待的参考瑞士等国的立法的观点,即以类似于《涉外民事关系法律适用法》第22条、第32条"满足其一即有效"的形式,"显名"地引入有效性原则的可能性已然较小。在保持《仲裁法(修订)(征求意见稿)》第90条基本内容的情况下,有效性原则只能在第三层次的法律适用中作为法官进行法律选择的考量因素,以"隐名"的方式存在。[③]此时,参考同样采用"隐名"适用有效性原则的英国的实践经验,引入最密切联系原则,为法官在有效性原则支配下选择法律提供理由和解释方法具有重要的意义。下文中,笔者拟从有效性原则的两种适用模式出发,从必要性和可行性两方面对最密切联系原则纳入仲裁协议法律适用进行证成。

[①] 参见黄进、宋连斌:《〈中华人民共和国仲裁法〉(建议修改稿)》,载梁慧星主编:《民商法论丛》(第28卷),法律出版社2003年版;文稳、陈卫佐:《仲裁协议实质有效性准据法的确定:新方法的视角》,载《青海社会科学》2018年第3期;单晓慧:《国际商事仲裁协议效力准据法的新确定方法》,载《仲裁研究》2020年第2期;陈挚:《论主合同准据法对仲裁条款的可适用性——以有效性原则为视角》,载《仲裁研究》2019年第2期。

[②] 参见聂羽欣:《国际商事仲裁协议准据法的确定——英国法和中国法比较考察》,载《商事仲裁与调解》2022年第3期。

[③] 参见马一飞:《涉外仲裁协议的法律适用——〈涉外民事关系法律适用法〉第18条理解与适用》,载《学术交流》2013年第8期。

一、最密切联系原则与涉外仲裁协议法律适用之渊源

最密切联系原则是在当事人没有约定法律适用时,确定国际民商事合同准据法最为广泛和普遍的方法。对于仲裁协议而言,一方面,无论认定其为实体法契约、程序法契约抑或混合型契约,均无法否定其作为私法契约的本质[①];另一方面,包括我国在内的世界各国国际私法立法,均未将国际民商事合同限定为仅规定当事人实体权利义务关系的合同,而将仲裁协议排除在外。[②] 因此,最密切联系原则就不可能不对仲裁协议的法律适用产生深远的影响[③],"没有任何理由否定可以依照最密切联系原则确定仲裁协议应当适用的准据法"[④]。事实上,世界各国在早期的立法和司法实践中,普遍将仲裁协议等同于普通的民商事合同,以"当事人意思自治—最密切联系原则"的方法确定其法律适用。[⑤] 譬如,《美国第二次冲突法重述》[Restatement(Second) of Conflict of Laws]第218条将普通的合同的冲突规则应用于仲裁协议,规定在当事人没有选择法律的情况下,应当适用与仲裁协议具有最密切联系的法律,来确定其有效性。

然而,最密切联系原则天然地赋予法官宽泛的自由裁量权而难以保障当事人合理预期。有鉴于此,为了保证仲裁协议法律适用的统一,越来越多的国家和国际条约抛弃了允许法官根据最密切联系原则选择准据法的做法,转而选择了一般意义上被认为与仲裁协议具有最密切联系的仲裁地法律作为仲裁协议法律适用的连结点加以规定。[⑥]《纽约公约》第5条第1款规定,在当事人未进行法律选择时,如果仲裁协议依仲裁地法律无效,则缔约国可以拒绝承认与执行根据该仲裁

---

① 参见王兰:《仲裁协议法律适用的基本理论及立法诠释》,载《甘肃理论学刊》2013年第5期。
② 参见朱克鹏:《国际商事仲裁的法律适用》,法律出版社1999年版,第59页。
③ 参见李双元主编:《国际经济贸易法律与实务新论》,湖南大学出版社1996年版,第401页。
④ 朱克鹏:《国际商事仲裁的法律适用》,法律出版社1999年版,第59页。
⑤ 参见黄进、陈卫佐:《国际商事仲裁的法律适用》,载《法学评论》1993年第4期。
⑥ 参见马一飞:《涉外商事合同准据法对仲裁条款的适用——以仲裁条款独立性为视角》,载《商事仲裁与调解》2021年第1期。

协议作出的仲裁裁决。嗣后的评注和司法实践一致认为,该项规定实际上表明了《纽约公约》将仲裁地法律作为在当事人未进行法律选择时仲裁协议的准据法的态度。① 在我国,从《最高人民法院关于适用〈中华人民共和国仲裁法〉若干问题的解释》(以下简称《仲裁法司法解释》)到《涉外民事关系法律适用法》及其司法解释,再到《仲裁法(修订)(征求意见稿)》,均将仲裁地这一最密切联系原则的外化作为仲裁协议法律适用的连结点加以规定,只不过由于我国对机构仲裁的"趋之若鹜",上述部分法律将仲裁机构所在地也纳入了仲裁协议法律适用的连结点中。②

在晚近西方国家的立法和司法中,有效性原则得到了显著发展和普遍接受。其中,瑞士和西班牙等国的立法采取了"显名"规定有效性原则的模式,在仲裁协议的冲突规范中设置了尽可能多的连结点,并规定仲裁协议的实质要件只要满足任一连结点所指向的法律即为有效,这种立法模式与我国《涉外民事关系法律适用法》第22条、第32条的规定较为类似。③ 受此影响,我国理论界开始试图将有效性原则以"显名"的形式纳入仲裁协议的冲突规范之中,在这些学者的立法建议中,最密切联系地往往作为待选连结点的其中一个出现。在武汉大学国际法研究所草拟的《仲裁法(建议修改稿)》中,"与仲裁协议有最密切联系的法律"与"仲裁地法""主合同准据法""国际仲裁协议有效性的一般原则"并列作为有效性原则下,法官潜在的准据法选项。④ 文稳、陈卫佐和单晓慧等学者则将"与仲裁协议有最密切联系的法律"与"仲裁地法""仲裁机构所在地法""法院地

---

① See Gary B. Born, International Commercial Arbitration, Third Edition, Kluwer Law International, 2021, p. 529.
② 参见吴俞阳:《仲裁机构所在地法作为仲裁协议准据法的研究》,载北京仲裁委员会/北京国际仲裁中心组编:《北京仲裁》(第114辑),中国法制出版社2021年版,第154页。
③ 此类冲突规范又被称为"法官被动选择的冲突规范",一般反映的是立法者尽可能维护法律关系有效性的取向。参见肖永平、丁汉韬:《论〈法律适用法〉中无条件选择性冲突规范的适用》,载《法律科学(西北政法大学学报)》2017年第4期。
④ 参见黄进、宋连斌:《〈中华人民共和国仲裁法〉(建议修改稿)》,载梁慧星主编:《民商法论丛》(第28卷),法律出版社2003年版。

法"相并列。①然而，虽然自《仲裁法》出台以来，我国理论界要求"显名"规定有效性原则的立法建议不绝如缕，但立法者的态度却并未发生太多变化，2021年公布的《仲裁法（修订）（征求意见稿）》第90条总体上仍然保持了2006年公布的《仲裁法司法解释》第16条的结构。

可以说，最密切联系原则在涉外仲裁协议法律适用中的地位经历了由"盛"转"衰"的过程。"显名"适用有效性原则的立法模式虽然使理论界重新拾起了最密切联系原则，但是仍然将其淹没于备选的众多连结点之中。那么，在不对现行法律进行大幅度修改的情况下，以"隐名"的形式适用有效性原则的模式中，最密切联系原则是否具有更为特殊的地位和作用？对此，有必要对"隐名"适用有效性原则的代表——英国的司法实践进行考察。

二、"隐名"适用有效性原则下最密切联系原则之新解

有效性原则在英国司法实践中的适用最早可以追溯至19世纪英国上议院对Hamlyn & Co v. Talisker Distillery案作出的裁判，但真正将该原则发扬光大的是英国上诉法院在2013年处理的Sulamérica v. Enesa案（以下简称"Sulamérica案"）。在该案中，上诉法院的法官创立了对仲裁协议法律适用问题的"三步分析法"：首先审查当事人对于仲裁协议的准据法是否具有明示的选择；若无，则其次审查当事人对于仲裁协议的准据法是否具有默示的选择；若仍然不能得到答案，则最后适用与仲裁协议具有最密切联系的法律。同时，若当事人默示的法律选择导致仲裁协议无效，则应当推翻默示选择阶段的推定，适用与仲裁协议具有最密切联系的法律。因此，该案中虽然法官认定当事人对仲裁协议的默示法律选择为主合同的准据法巴西法，但由于适用巴西法可能会使仲裁协议无效，法官最终适用了与仲裁协议具有最密切联系的仲裁地法。②

---

① 参见文稳、陈卫佐：《仲裁协议实质有效性准据法的确定：新方法的视角》，载《青海社会科学》2018年第3期；单晓慧：《国际商事仲裁协议效力准据法的新确定方法》，载《仲裁研究》2020年第2期。

② See Sulamérica Cia. Nacional de Seguros S.A. and Others v. Enesa Engenharia S.A. and Others, [2012] EWCA Civ 638.

在对该案的分析中,有学者将主要精力集中于"三步分析法"的三个层次上,并认为这三个层次所指向的法律已经形成了较为固定的搭配,即"明示的法律选择—默示的法律选择(主合同准据法)—最密切联系原则(仲裁地法)"。笔者认为,在我国将主合同准据法适用于仲裁协议的最大障碍是我国立法明确否认了默示的法律选择。[1]对Sulamérica案的此种解读或许有待商榷。一方面,默示的法律选择不一定指向主合同准据法,相反,在Sulamérica案判决作出后不久的Habas v. VSC案中,法官认为,当事人对仲裁地的选择可以视为对仲裁协议法律适用的默示选择,而原告Habas公司则极力主张主合同准据法与仲裁协议有最密切联系原则,并试图说服法官适用主合同准据法。[2]在更多的案件中,法官甚至不会说明其选择适用主合同准据法或仲裁地法是由于其可以被视为默示的法律选择,抑或与仲裁协议有最密切联系,只能认为,"其或许与默示的法律选择有关,或许与最密切联系原则有关"[3]。另一方面,何种情况下才能认为当事人存在默示的法律选择在英国也多有争议。在Enka v. Chubb案(以下简称"Enka案")中,部分法官认为,该案中当事人并未存在默示的法律选择,仲裁地法的适用是适用最密切联系原则所得出的答案;另一部分法官则认为,即便在主合同的准据法并非当事人明确选择而产生的情况下,主合同的准据法仍然可以视为当事人对仲裁协议默示的法律选择。[4]通过上述现象不难看出,"三步分析法"的第二步是否存在、何种法律会被在第二步以及第三步中适用,很大程度上取决于个案中法官的自由裁量——但这种自由裁量的结果,总会指向使仲裁协议有效的法律。[5]有鉴于此,我国学

---

[1] 参见聂羽欣:《国际商事仲裁协议准据法的确定——英国法和中国法比较考察》,载《商事仲裁与调解》2022年第3期。

[2] See Habas Sinai Ve Tibbi Gazlar Istihsal Endustrisi AS v. VSC Steel Company Ltd., [2013] EWHC 4071.

[3] William Day, Applicable Law and Arbitration Agreements, 80 The Cambridge Law Journal 238, 240(2021).

[4] See Enka Insaat Ve Sanayi AS v. "Insurance Company Chubb" & Ors, [2020] UKSC 38.

[5] See Sabrina Pearson, Sulamérica v. Enesa, The Hidden Pro-validation Approach Adopted by the English Courts with Respect to the Proper Law of the Arbitration Agreement, 29 Arbitration International 115, 124(2014).

者提出,在当事人不具有明确法律选择的情况下,法官实际上就是在依照最密切联系原则,寻找最有利于仲裁协议有效的法律。① 这种观点最近也得到了英国学者的认可,该学者在分析 Enka 案时指出,相对于通过"三步分析法"猜测当事人潜在的法律选择,直接适用最密切联系原则作为缺省原则完成法律适用显然更为恰当。②

从本质上看,法官适用"三步分析法"的过程,实际上就是隐秘地适用有效性原则的过程。法官的任务是在当事人没有进行明示法律选择的情况下,选择最有利于仲裁协议生效的法律,无论是当事人默示的法律选择,抑或是最密切联系原则,实际上都只是法官合理化自身法律选择的依据。法官通过法律适用的分析,选择了能使国际仲裁协议生效的法律。当其为仲裁地的法律时,法官(通过默示的法律选择,抑或最密切联系原则)适用仲裁地的法律;当其为主合同准据法时,法官适用该法律。③ 由是,在"三步分析法"中,英国法院巧妙地将最密切联系原则从法律适用原则转变为了法律解释的工具。④

英国司法实践中,有效性原则与最密切联系原则之间的互动兼顾了法律适用的形式正当性和适用结果的实质可接受性,值得我国参考和借鉴。依据《仲裁法(修订)(征求意见稿)》第 90 条的规定,在当事人既没有约定意思自治,又未明确仲裁地的情况下,法官就进入了第三层次的法律选择中。此时,法官依照规定可以适用法院地法,而在法院地法可能使仲裁协议无效的情况下,法官则应当以有效性原则为导向,适用主合同准据法等最有利于仲裁协议有效的法律。但无论法官在这种情况下最终适用何种法律,都可以将最密切联系原则为解释工具对自身的法律选择进行证成。这种将最密切联系

---

① 参见文稳、陈卫佐:《仲裁协议实质有效性准据法的确定:新方法的视角》,载《青海社会科学》2018 年第 3 期。

② See William Day, Applicable Law and Arbitration Agreements, 80 The Cambridge Law Journal 238, 240(2021).

③ See Gary B. Born, International Commercial Arbitration, Third Edition, Kluwer Law International, 2021, p. 583.

④ 参见文稳、陈卫佐:《仲裁协议实质有效性准据法的确定:新方法的视角》,载《青海社会科学》2018 年第 3 期。

原则纳入仲裁协议法律适用的操作模式兼具必要性与可行性。

三、必要性:作为法律选择理由的最密切联系原则

(一)准据法的选择需要理由

法官对准据法的选择并非随意进行,而是需要说明合乎逻辑的理由和依据,对自身法律选择结果的正当性加以论述。法律选择理由的说明体现了法官更多地依靠理性来作出判断,而不是诉诸非理性的情感因素。[1] 不加说明地进行法律选择是专断而粗暴的,而符合法治化的恰当法律选择则需要遵循一定的方法进行证成。[2] 作为我国国际私法先驱之一的李双元教授曾指出,国际私法需要解决的最重要的两个问题,一个是为什么某一法律能够得到适用;另外一个是如何选择出合适的法律。[3] 事实上,上述第一个问题很大程度上就是对法律选择结果的正当性进行证成的问题。在国际私法的历史中,包括"法则区别说""国际礼让说""既得权说"在内的大多数理论,实际上都致力于解决该问题。毋庸讳言,在我国,由于国际私法理论的高深晦涩和法官对于法律选择问题重视的不足,法官(也包括仲裁员)存在不对法律选择的理由加以说明就径直适用法律(特别是适用法院地法)的做法,甚至"干脆不适用任何法律"[4] 抑或"适用双重法律"[5]。由于上述现象过于普遍,最高人民法院甚至不得不明确要求,法官在撰写涉外民商事纠纷的裁判文书时,应当首先对该案应适用的法律作出分析和判

---

[1] 参见〔英〕尼尔·麦考密克:《法律推理与法律理论》,姜峰译,法律出版社2018年版,第8页。

[2] 参见翁杰:《论涉外民事裁判中法律选择的证立问题》,载《法律科学(西北政法大学学报)》2015年第5期。

[3] 参见李双元:《论国际私法关系中解决法律选择的方法问题》,载《中国法学》1984年第3期。

[4] 宋连斌:《中国国际私法的实践困境及出路》,载中国国际私法学会主编:《中国国际私法与比较法年刊·2002》(第五卷),法律出版社2002年版,第14页。

[5] 宋连斌:《涉外仲裁协议效力认定的裁判方法——以"仲裁地在香港适用英国法"为例》,载中国国际私法学会主办:《中国国际私法学会2010年年会暨涉外民事关系法律适用法研讨会论文集》。

断,并说明理由。绝不能无视法律适用问题而想当然地适用本国法,也不能只得出关于适用法律的结论而不阐述原因。① 诚然,由于某些原因,法官可能事先就已经在心中产生了一个目标法律,譬如,由于司法政策和便利性的原因,法官在内心或许早已经选定了法院地法作为案涉法律关系的准据法②;又譬如,在有效性原则的驱使下,法官会选择有利于仲裁协议有效的法律。这种情况下法官所述理由和所作论证,或许从实质上看是虚伪的、表面的、带有强烈功利主义色彩的,但却仍然是必要的。这种公开的说理和阐述,可以提升法律选择结果的正当性和对于当事人的可接受性③,正如法官对于案件的处理结果未必符合当事人的意愿,但却能够通过裁判文书中详尽的说理使当事人接受和信服④。

(二) 特殊的冲突规范形式强化了说理的重要性

仲裁协议冲突规范的特殊形式强化了法官说理的重要性。如果仲裁协议的冲突规范显名地引入了有效性原则,采取了"满足其一即有效"的形式,那么,法官在进行法律选择时,无须过于在意说理的问题。毕竟在这种"法官被动选择的冲突规范"中,法官所需要做的只是依次根据连结点所指向的准据法,判断仲裁协议的有效性,当有任一准据法能够使仲裁协议有效时,法律选择的过程即宣告结束。换言之,在这种形式的冲突规范中,法官无须考虑对准据法作出具体的选择,自然也就不存在说理的必要。⑤ 然而,在仲裁协议冲突规范的第三层次中,法律只规定法官"可以适用"法院地法,法官当然也可以出于某种原因适用其他法律。由此,该冲突规范实际上就变成了类似于《涉外民事关系法

---

① 参见《最高人民法院审理涉外商事案件适用法律情况的通报》。
② 参见何其生、许威:《浅析我国涉外民事法律适用中"回家去的趋势"》,载《武汉大学学报(哲学社会科学版)》2011年第2期。
③ 参见翁杰:《论涉外民事裁判中法律选择的证立问题》,载《法律科学(西北政法大学学报)》2015年第5期。
④ 参见于晓青:《法官的法理认同及裁判说理》,载《法学》2012年第8期。
⑤ 参见肖永平、丁汉韬:《论〈法律适用法〉中无条件选择性冲突规范的适用》,载《法律科学(西北政法大学学报)》2017年第4期。

律适用法》第41条的"法官主动选择的冲突规范"。在这种冲突规范中,法官并不受具体的成文法约束,可以根据自己对个案的判断选择连结点。因而,为保证法律选择的正当性和说服力,法官就必须将自己进行法律选择的考量过程和价值追求以说理的形式在判决中体现。[①]

有效性原则是否能成为法官的论据和理由,使得相关的法律选择具备正当性?答案是值得商榷的。一方面,我国在《涉外民事关系法律适用法》第25条、第29条中,依据结果选择理论明确地规定法官应当选择有利于保障弱者或被扶养人权益的法律,此时,法官自然可以且应当以有利于保障弱者或被扶养人权益原则进行法律选择的说理论证,《仲裁司法审查规定》第14条也作出了类似的规定。然而,在《仲裁法(修订)(征求意见稿)》第90条中,这种明确的有利于仲裁协议生效原则的规定却付之阙如。同时,虽然《仲裁司法审查规定》第14条针对《涉外民事关系法律适用法》第18条规定中第二层次的法律适用明确规定了有效性原则,但在《仲裁法(修订)(征求意见稿)》第90条将第二层次法律适用的"仲裁机构所在地"连结点删除后,《仲裁司法审查规定》第14条已经不具有实质性的意义。另一方面,《涉外民事关系法律适用法》第25条、第29条和《仲裁司法审查规定》第14条的规定均为法官可以在有限的准据法中(且都与案涉法律关系有实际联系)依照有利于保障弱者权益或仲裁协议生效的原则进行选择,但在《仲裁法(修订)(征求意见稿)》第90条的第三层次法律适用中,法官理论上却可以选择任一国家的法律作为准据法。[②] 如果法官仅仅为了使仲裁协议有效,而选择一个与仲裁协议没有太多关系和牵连的法律来判断其效力,则法律选择将会失去其原本的意义,只需要对所有国际商事仲裁协议的效力一律采用某个最低的标准进行判断即可。[③]

---

① 参见翁杰、李蕊:《论我国涉外民事法律适用中法官自由裁量权的适度空间》,载《时代法学》2021年第4期。

② 与此种情况类似的是阿尔及利亚的立法,《阿尔及利亚民事和行政程序法典》第1040条规定,就仲裁协议的实质内容而言,如果其符合仲裁员(法官)认为适当的法律,即为有效。

③ 事实上,美国的一些判例即采用了所谓"国际最低标准"判断仲裁协议效力。See Gary B. Born, International Commercial Arbitration, Third Edition, Kluwer Law International, 2021, pp. 567-568.

因此,英国理论界普遍认为,有效性原则仅仅是一种"无声的选择"①,其意义更多地表现在对具体的法律进行选择时起到方法论的作用,法官仍然需要采用一定理论解释自己法律选择的正当性。

(三)借助最密切联系原则说理契合《涉外民事关系法律适用法》第2条之规定

相较于有效性原则,最密切联系原则显然能更好地完成说理的任务。最密切联系原则认为,某地法律之所以能够作为某项法律关系的准据法,是因为该地与该项法律关系具有最密切联系,由是,适用该地法律最能展现该项法律关系的特征,能使法律纠纷获得最好的解决。正如学者所言,相较于"法则区别说"或"法律关系本座说",最密切联系原则从"管辖权选择"上升到了"结果选择",为法律选择提供了更为充分和明确的理由。②事实上,借助最密切联系原则对仲裁协议的法律选择进行说理也契合了《涉外民事关系法律适用法》的相关规定。

我国有学者指出,《涉外民事关系法律适用法》第18条仅包括两个层次的法律选择,当无法确定仲裁地和仲裁机构所在地时,就应当根据《涉外民事关系法律适用法》第2条的规定,适用与该涉外民事关系有最密切联系的法律。但与此同时,《仲裁法司法解释》第16条和《最高人民法院关于适用〈中华人民共和国涉外民事关系法律适用法〉若干问题的解释(一)》[以下简称《法律适用法司法解释(一)》]第14条又规定了此种情况下应当(可以)适用法院地法,两者之间或有相互矛盾之处。③事实上,《法律适用法司法解释(一)》第14条将《仲裁法司法解释》第16条"适用法院地"的表述改为"可以适用法院地法"就已经回答了上述问题。也即,在《法律适用法司法解释(一)》第14条中,法院地法只是与仲裁协议具有最密切联系的法律之一,法官

---

① See Sabrina Pearson, Sulamérica v. Enesa, The Hidden Pro-validation Approach Adopted by the English Courts with Respect to the Proper Law of the Arbitration Agreement, 29 Arbitration International 115, 124(2014).

② 参见沈涓:《合同准据法理论的解释》,法律出版社2000年版,第113页。

③ 参见宋常蕊:《从司法实践看国际商事仲裁协议法律适用新发展》,载北京仲裁委员会/北京国际仲裁中心组编:《北京仲裁》(第100辑),中国法制出版社2017年版,第119页。

可以选择适用法院地法,也可以选择其他与仲裁协议有最密切联系的法律。对我国有关文件进行上述考察不难看出,我国立法者也认为应当将最密切联系原则作为仲裁协议第三层次的法律选择原则。一方面,由于最密切联系原则具有被解释的可能,我国立法者为有效性原则的"隐秘"引入留下了空间[①];另一方面,我国立法者又通过最密切联系原则对法官适用有效性原则进行法律选择作出了限制,法官需要在有效性原则指导下,对选择的法律与仲裁协议具有最密切联系进行证成。

四、可行性:最密切联系原则与有效性原则"互动"之可能

(一)有效性原则修补了最密切联系原则之缺陷

如果说最密切联系原则对有效性原则的适当限制使得最密切联系原则具有被引入的必要性,那么有效性原则对最密切联系原则过于宽泛自由裁量权缺陷的修补则使最密切联系原则具有被引入的可能。最密切联系原则在为法官进行法律选择带来更多的灵活性的同时,其赋予法官的过宽泛的自由裁量权的缺陷也广为学术界诟病,这种缺陷的后果即法官的法律选择确定性不足,难以保障当事人的合理预期。世界各国之所以逐渐放弃将最密切联系原则作为仲裁协议的法律适用规则,并代之以仲裁地法这一确定的连结点,也是由于上述原因。就保证仲裁协议的有效性而言,如果任由法官恣意地根据最密切联系原则进行法律选择,则有可能会出现法官认为具有最密切联系的法律不利于仲裁协议生效的情况,难以保障当事人将争端提交仲裁的预期。此时,"隐名"地适用有效性原则作为法官选择适用法律的考量因素,确保法官在自由裁量范围内选择最有利于仲裁协议生效的法律,就可以在很大程度上解决上述担忧。事实上,这种通过确定法官自由裁量的要求和条件从而对法官适用最密切联系原则作出限制的方法已经得到了西方各国实践的普遍认可。譬如,《美国第二次冲突法重述》第6条第2款就列举了法官作出法律选择时应当考量的七

[①] 参见马一飞:《涉外仲裁协议的法律适用——〈涉外民事关系法律适用法〉第18条理解与适用》,载《学术交流》2013年第8期。

项因素,而有效性原则与其中的"对正当期望的保证"和"结果的确定性"等因素即具有异曲同工之妙。

(二)有效性原则指向的准据法具有被解释为最密切联系之可能

将最密切联系原则纳入仲裁协议法律适用的可行性还在于,法官依据有效性原则所选择的准据法,从形式和实质上看,都有被解释为与仲裁协议具有最密切联系的可能性。

从形式上看,我国有关立法并未明确规定只有仲裁地法才有可能与仲裁协议具有最密切联系,仲裁地法只是在通常情况下与仲裁协议具有最密切联系。相反,根据我国理论界和司法实践的观点,包括主合同准据法、法院地法等法律均有被解释为与仲裁协议具有最密切联系原则的可能。[1]

从实质上看,仲裁协议有效的法律解释与仲裁协议有最密切联系并不违背最密切联系原则的制度内涵。追求法律选择结果的恰当性是最密切联系原则最为突出的特点之一,正如学者所言,在最密切联系原则的要求下,法官的法律选择实际上就是一个不断进行比较、优中选优的过程。[2]在某些国家的立法中,最密切联系原则甚至成了法律选择结果适当性的矫正标尺,当确定的法律选择规则可能导致选择适用法律结果有失公正时,法官可以径直另行选择与案涉法律关系有最密切联系的法律。[3]而仲裁协议依据准据法是否有效,又是衡量法律选择结果是否恰当公正的重要维度。合同当事人各方不可能在缔约过程中,意图使仲裁协议这一合同中的重要条款无效。[4]因此,法律选择中应充分地体现这一明确意图,以便使仲裁协议具有效力的解释优先于会使协议无效的其他解释。[5]在国际商会仲裁院的一个稍早裁

---

[1] 参见马一飞:《涉外商事合同准据法对仲裁条款的适用——以仲裁条款独立性为视角》,载《商事仲裁与调解》2021年第1期;朱克鹏:《国际商事仲裁的法律适用》,法律出版社1999年版,第59页。
[2] 参见沈涓:《合同准据法理论的解释》,法律出版社2000年版,第115页。
[3] 参见王胜明:《涉外民事关系法律适用法若干争议问题》,载《法学研究》2012年第2期。
[4] See Enka Insaat Ve Sanayi AS v. Insurance Company Chubb & Ors, [2020] UKSC 38.
[5] See FirstLink Inv. Corp. Ltd. v. GT Payment Pte Ltd., [2014] SGHCR 12.

决中,仲裁员更是一针见血地指出,仲裁协议与维护其存在的法律的关系总比否认其存在的法律的关系更为密切。① 如此,虽然有效性原则难以直接作为法律适用的理由,但可以通过最密切联系原则的结果考量特征成为法律适用的重要参考因素。"隐秘"适用有效性原则并非司法对仲裁的"恩惠",而是对当事人意思自治的尊重②,是最密切联系原则的应有之义。

结语

习近平总书记强调,要努力让人民群众在每一个司法案件中感受到公平正义,而直接影响当事人权利义务关系的司法裁判结果,显然是决定当事人是否能够感受到公平正义的最重要一环。一个能让当事人感受到公平正义的裁判结果,不仅需要有实质上的正当性和可接受性,更需要有对这种正当性和可接受性的裁判说理,并以当事人看得见的方式展现出来。在仲裁协议第三层次的法律适用中,在以有效性原则为法律选择规则的基础上,引入最密切联系原则作为法律选择解释原则,即较好地兼顾了法官法律选择形式上和实质上的正当性和可接受性。一方面,以有效性原则作为法律选择的实质导向原则可以最大程度地保障当事人将争端提交仲裁的预期;另一方面,以最密切联系原则作为法律选择解释方法,不仅契合《涉外民事关系法律适用法》第 2 条的规定,更能恰当地向当事人展示法律选择的过程和依据,提升当事人对法律选择结果的可接受性。上述操作模式对于提升我国仲裁司法审查规范化和精细化水平,促进仲裁事业健康有序发展具有不可忽视的重要意义。

(莫之颖、王鸣杰　审校)

---

① See ICC Case No. 7154, 121 J.D.I. (Clunet) 1059, 1061 (1994).
② 参见宋连斌:《涉外仲裁协议效力认定的裁判方法——以"仲裁地在香港适用英国法"为例》,载中国国际私法学会主办:《中国国际私法学会 2010 年年会暨涉外民事关系法律适用法研讨会论文集》。

第三方资助国际商事仲裁法律问题研究

郑增辉[*]

摘要:近年来,第三方资助在国际商事仲裁领域发展迅猛,其在促进公平正义实现的同时,也由于其本身的逐利性和私密性引发了诸多问题。已经有许多国家和地区开始探索适合本土的第三方资助规制模式,然而,目前我国的法律和仲裁规则都未能对国际商事仲裁领域的第三方资助进行有效规制。本文在参考了国际仲裁机构和各代表国家对于第三方资助规制经验的基础上,结合我国当前国际商事仲裁的实践,提出了适合我国的第三方资助规制模式。

关键词:第三方资助;国际商事仲裁;披露义务;独立性;公正性

引言

国际商事仲裁具有效率高、保密性强等独特优势,是当事人解决国际商事纠纷的重要手段。但国际商事仲裁的费用很高,并非所有当事人都有足够的资金提起仲裁程序,为维护自身的合法权益,有些缺乏资金的当事人便只能寻求他人的帮助。于是,近年来,第三方资助在国际商事仲裁领域应运而生了。作为一种新型的投资方式,第三方资助虽然带有明显的逐利性,但在推动公平正义方面也具有重要意义。由于第三方资金的帮助,一些缺乏资金的当事人可以借助国际商事仲裁来维护自己的合法权益。但是,第三方资助人也给国际商事仲

---

[*] 上海市崇明区人民法院商事审判庭五级法官助理,上海海事大学法律硕士。

裁程序带来了一些新的挑战。

已经有一些国家或地区制定了法律法规来规范这一行为,许多仲裁机构也在修改其仲裁规则,从而促进第三方资助的健康发展。我国已经开始出现了一些专门的第三方资助机构,比如,深圳前海鼎颂法务创新集团有限责任公司。如果内地某一国际商事仲裁案件中出现了第三方资助的情形,那么现有的法律和仲裁规则都不能有效地发挥约束作用。因此,如何有效地规制第三方资助国际商事仲裁是一个亟须解决的重要问题。

一、第三方资助国际商事仲裁的内涵与发展

近年来,第三方资助在国际商事仲裁领域发展迅猛,许多学者已经开始对国际商事仲裁领域的第三方资助进行研究,并取得了丰硕的研究成果,但目前各国学者对第三方资助的相关研究理论尚未达成共识。

(一)第三方资助的内涵

1. 第三方资助的定义

第三方资助具有十分悠久的历史。在古罗马时期,拥有权势和金钱的贵族通过资助诉讼的一方当事人开展诉讼,从而谋求利益。这种方式与今天的第三方资助十分相似。近几年,第三方资助开始蓬勃发展,但是目前学术界对于资助人的主体范围和资助的形式仍然存在很大的争议,因此,对第三方资助尚未形成统一的定义。

笔者认为,国际商事仲裁领域的第三方资助应当是某一国际商事仲裁纠纷之外的第三方主体,通过资助其中一方当事人参与国际商事仲裁程序,在获得积极结果后,从该方当事人所获收益中获得一定比例回报的制度。根据这个定义,国际商事仲裁中第三方资助应当具备三个要素:受资助人、第三方资助人、资助协议。

2. 第三方资助的运行方式

第三方资助的运行方式如图1所示:

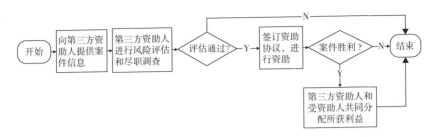

图 1　第三方资助的运行方式

由此可见,第三方资助人的最终目的是营利。如果受资助人在仲裁程序中未能取得积极结果,或者仲裁结果达不到资助人原本的预期,那么资助人很可能会面临巨大的损失,包括但不限于高昂的仲裁费用等。因此,仲裁裁决的结果是影响资助人收益最主要的因素。资助人在与受资助人签订资助协议之前,必然会对案件的具体情况进行全面审查,准确评估可能付出的成本以及可能得到的回报,综合考虑各方面的因素,再决定是否给予资助。

(二)第三方资助的发展历程

1. 第三方资助国际商事仲裁的产生

第三方资助最初起源于诉讼领域"帮助诉讼"与"包揽诉讼"的方式。[①] 随着社会的不断发展,国际经济贸易往来日益频繁,随之而来的是大量矛盾纠纷的出现,而国际商事仲裁则是解决这些矛盾纠纷十分高效便捷的方式。但国际商事仲裁的仲裁费用是十分高昂的,有时候一方当事人难免会存在缺乏资金的情况。于是,国际商事仲裁领域的第三方资助便产生了。

2. 第三方资助国际商事仲裁的发展

在英美法系国家中,澳大利亚最早对仲裁领域第三方资助的合法性予以了确认。后来,威尔士和英格兰的地方法院通过判例确定可以

---

① 参见宋锡祥、吴瑶芬:《国际商事仲裁第三方资助利益冲突的合理规制及其借鉴意义》,载《海峡法学》2018年第2期。

通过第三人资助来进行诉讼与仲裁。2016 年发布的《新加坡国际仲裁中心投资仲裁规则》第一次对第三方资助在该国仲裁领域内的适用作出了明确的规定。新加坡律政部发布的《对民法有关修正的议案》,对禁止助讼和包揽诉讼的规定予以废除。

近年来,我国内地已经开始出现了一些专业的第三方资助机构,然而,我国内地的立法目前对于第三方资助国际商事仲裁尚未有明确的规定,仅有《中国国际经济贸易仲裁委员会国际投资争端仲裁规则(试行)》第 27 条对国际投资仲裁领域中第三方资助的概念、披露义务和仲裁费用的分担方式等作出了规定。随着第三方资助行业的不断发展,仅仅以此对第三方资助进行规制,对于我国国际商事仲裁的实践而言是远远不够的。

二、规制第三方资助国际商事仲裁的必要性

第三方资助有着重要的优势和功能,对仲裁程序的顺利进行和当事人合法权益的保护都有着重要意义。然而,第三方资助的本质是一种投资方式,使其引发了许多问题。因此,对于第三方资助国际商事仲裁进行有效规制是十分必要的。

(一)第三方资助国际商事仲裁的优势及功能

1. 为当事人提供实现公平正义的途径

国际商事仲裁是人们解决国际商事纠纷的重要途径,但是由于费用较高,部分当事人在缺乏足够资金的情况下,即使很可能取得案件的胜利,也会因为没有足够的经济基础而无法申请仲裁。[1] 对于这些缺乏足够资金的当事人而言,第三方资助国际商事仲裁最重要的意义就在于为他们提供了实现公平正义的机会。[2] 有了资助人提供的资金,

---

① 参见石毓晶:《国际商事仲裁中第三方资助法律规制研究》,华东政法大学 2019 年硕士论文,第 18 页。

② 参见张康:《第三方资助国际商事仲裁法律问题研究》,外交学院 2020 年硕士论文,第 8 页。

当事人的资金匮乏问题得到了解决,并获得了启动和维持国际商事仲裁的机会,从而可以通过国际商事仲裁主张自己的合法权利、寻求损害赔偿。①

2. 防止仲裁程序的滥用

许多学者认为,第三方资助使得一些原本很难胜诉的案件进入到仲裁程序中,导致了滥诉现象。笔者对此并不认同。相反,笔者认为,第三方资助在一定程度上可以防止仲裁程序的滥用。一方面,第三方资助人不是慈善家,而是风险投资者,对申请资助的当事人会进行严格的筛选;另一方面,由于第三方资助人往往拥有专业法律人员和风险评估人员,有利于当事人在寻求第三方资助失败后认清第三方资助人拒绝资助的原因,重新审视自身的情况,并选择通过调解或和解等纠纷解决方式来化解纠纷,避免了当事人随意提起仲裁程序。

3. 平衡仲裁双方当事人的地位,促进案件的尽快审理

在一些标的额较大、双方经济实力悬殊的案件中,有的当事人会凭借自身经济实力的优势,利用程序规则来拖延审理,这不仅会加大仲裁庭的工作压力,不利于仲裁案件的尽快审理,而且还会使得另一方当事人的损失不断扩大。而经济实力较弱的一方在获得了第三方资助后,其经济实力会得到一定的提升,双方当事人的地位得到了一定的平衡,另一方当事人不敢再贸然利用程序规则拖延案件的审理。另外,第三方资助人为了尽快获取利益,也会积极主动地推动国际商事仲裁程序的顺利进行。

4. 实现仲裁败诉风险的转移

在某些情况下,当事人会因为无法预估自己胜诉的可能性,不愿意承担败诉风险,从而放弃商事仲裁。有了第三方资助,败诉风险转移给资助人。资助人在承担了败诉风险的同时,也获得了分配胜诉利益的可能。而且资助人往往会与保险公司进行合作,通过商业保险将这一风险进一步分散,从而增强自己防御风险的能力。比如,美国的伯富德资本(Burford Captial)就是通过与保险公司合作,来实现风险

---

① 参见张光磊:《第三方诉讼融资:通往司法救济的商业化路径》,载《中国政法大学学报》2016 年第 3 期。

的分散和转移。

(二)第三方资助在实践中可能存在的问题

1. 利益冲突和信息披露问题

许多资助人会要求受资助人提供大量案件的具体信息,受资助人向资助人披露有关案件的情况是第三方资助存在的前提和基础。但是,受资助人向资助人披露的信息可能会涉及其他仲裁参与者的商业秘密和商业信誉,这些信息原本可能只会有双方当事人和仲裁员知晓,如果向第三方资助人透露,很可能会侵害第三人的合法权益。

同时,信息披露背后所隐含的是各方之间的利益冲突的问题,由于资助协议的达成往往仅需受资助人和第三方资助人达成合意即可,资助关系很难被他们之外的第三人知晓,可能会造成当事人的代理律师与第三方资助人,以及仲裁员与第三方资助人的利益冲突问题,比如,仲裁员或者当事人的代理律师可能曾在第三方资助人的有关公司从事法律顾问,仲裁员兼职的单位可能会与第三方资助人之间存在利益关系等。

2. 保密性问题

实践中,各国的仲裁机构规定仲裁员、仲裁当事人和其他仲裁参与人不得将与仲裁程序有关的信息向与仲裁无关的第三人披露。一般而言,只有在当事人有约定或者存在法定事由的情况下,当事人才可以向案外人披露案件的有关信息。因此,如果没有取得对方当事人的同意,受资助的一方当事人私自向第三方资助人提供案件的具体信息,确实是违反保密义务的。

许多当事人出于自身利益的考虑,都不会同意对方为了寻求第三方资助而将案件信息透露给他人。可若不透露有关案件信息,当事人就很难得到第三方的资助,这就使得想要获得资助的当事人陷入了十分尴尬的境地。因此,如何在保障当事人合法权益的情况下,维护国际商事仲裁案件的保密性是目前亟须解决的重要问题。

3. 仲裁费用的分担问题

仲裁费用是影响第三方资助仲裁发展的重要因素。一方面,高昂的仲裁费用是许多当事人选择寻求第三方资助的主要原因;另一方面,仲裁费用的分担也直接影响当事人是否选择国际商事仲裁。在国际商事仲裁中,主要采用由当事人意思自治、由仲裁庭自由裁量或者由败诉方承担仲裁费用等方式来决定仲裁费用的分担。

除此之外,对于第三方资助仲裁的费用能否向仲裁相对方索赔的问题,许多国家采取了不同的规定。在仲裁费用由败诉方承担的原则下,当受资助人获得胜诉裁决时,其向仲裁庭提出要求对方当事人赔偿其因寻求第三方资助人而支出的费用的请求能否得到支持也是一个值得思考的问题。在当前实践中,尚未对此形成一致意见。

4. 仲裁费用的担保问题

在国际商事仲裁中,为了保证被申请人在案件获得胜利时顺利获得费用补偿,仲裁庭有权要求申请人提供费用担保。在第三方资助的情况下,如果仲裁庭了解到一方当事人存在第三方资助人,而受资助人可能面临败诉裁决时,仲裁庭很可能会据此要求受资助人提供一定的费用担保。

实践中,资助协议通常会对仲裁费用进行事先约定,但是未必会约定担保费用的承担。如果被申请人向仲裁庭申请费用担保,仲裁庭要求受资助人提供费用担保,同时这一担保的金额很大,那么让受资助人承担该担保费用会极大地加重受资助人的费用负担。

5. 仲裁员的公正性和独立性问题

对于仲裁员来说,保持公正性和独立性是最基本的要求。对第三方资助而言,由于是独立于案件之外的第三人提供资助,仲裁员与第三方资助人之间很可能会产生利益冲突,这就可能会对仲裁员的公正性和独立性产生很大影响。

为保证仲裁员在审理案件时可以保持公正性和独立性,许多法律和仲裁规则都对仲裁员提出了要求,比如,《联合国国际贸易法委员会国际商事仲裁示范法》第12条规定仲裁员在出现可能产生影响独立性和公正性的情况时负有向各方当事人说明的义务;第18条规定仲裁员应当对仲裁当事人平等相待。我国《仲裁法》第34条也要求仲裁员有义务做到案件裁决的公正与独立,并对仲裁员应当回避的具体情况作出了说明。之所以仲裁员的公正性与独立性受到各个国家的重视,是因为国际商事仲裁中的仲裁员一般都是兼职的,具备多重身份,所以其公正性更有可能受到各方面的影响,与案件中的当事人或资助人存在利害关系的可能性较高。

三、第三方资助国际商事仲裁的国际规制经验探究

世界各个国家和地区第三方资助的发展情况并不相同,英国、新加坡和中国香港特别行政区(以下简称香港特区)等发展迅速的国家和地区都已经制定了符合当地实践的第三方资助规制模式,探究这些先进的规制经验具有重要意义。

(一)中国香港特区对第三方资助的规制模式

1. 通过修改仲裁条例承认了第三方资助的合法性

2017年6月14日,我国香港特区《2017年仲裁及调解法例(第三者资助)(修订)条例》顺利通过,明确允许第三方资助适用于仲裁程序和调解程序。其中,第10A条对于第三方资助的概念作出了定义和解释,对第三方资助者应符合的标准也作出了明确的规定。2018年11月1日生效的《香港国际仲裁中心机构仲裁规则(2018)》第44条明确规定了第三方资助中信息披露的主体、内容、对象和时间等。2018年12月7日,香港特区律政司发布了《第三方资助仲裁实务守则》,该守则在2019年2月1日开始正式实施。其中,对于资助协议、出资者资本充足要求、利益冲突、保密性、控制权、披露、仲裁费用、资助终止的理由、投诉程序等多个方面都进行了详细的规定,为第三方资助构建了较为完善的规制体系。[①]

2. 对第三方资助作出了详细且全面的规定

香港特区对第三方资助人设置了最低标准,比如,要求第三方资助人拥有至少2000万元港币的可用资本,在至少36个月内,承担根

---

① 参见香港特区《第三方资助仲裁实务守则》第2.3条至第2.18条。

据其所有资助协议的总体出资负债,就资本充足程度承担持续的披露义务等,从而确保受资助人可以得到稳定充足的资金支持。同时,对于资助协议的内容进行了规定,要求该协议内容明确具体且不具有误导性,要求资助人须采取合理措施确保在签订协议之前,受资助人已知晓就该协议寻求独立法律意见的权利。[1]在资助协议中应当包括第三方资助人的名称和其在香港的送达地址,赋予了仲裁庭在利益冲突、披露信息、仲裁费用等方面的自由裁量权,也对受资助人设定了披露第三方资助的义务。

(二)英国对第三方资助的规制模式

1. 以判例的形式确认了第三方资助的合法性

英国有着禁止帮助诉讼的法律传统,其最初认为第三方资助是破坏公共政策的表现,因此在司法实践中,一直否认第三方资助的合法性。后来随着经济社会的发展,这一法律传统受到了冲击,1886年英国枢密院在审理 Ram Coomar Coondoo & Chunder Canto ookerjee 一案时表明,如果第三方资助本身不会影响司法公正,有利于实现公平正义,那么就不应该以违反公共政策作出裁判。2005年英国上诉法院在 Arkin v. Borchard Lines Ltd. and others 一案中表示,第三方资助协议不会破坏公共政策,不会过分地干涉案件审理,第三方资助有利于司法制度的完善和发展。在这个判例中,英国上诉法院对于第三方资助的合法性给予了明确的确认,标志着英国终于彻底承认了第三方资助的合法性。

2. 通过行业自律对第三方资助进行自律监管

英国最大的特点在于其通过行业自律的方式来对第三方资助进行自律监管,这一监管方式十分灵活。为了规制第三方资助人的行为,2011年11月,民事司法理事会发布了《诉讼出资者行为守则》,指定由诉讼资助者协会负责对第三方资助行业进行自律监管。2018年1月,诉讼资助者协会发布了最新版《英国诉讼资助者行为守则》,对协

---

[1] 参见香港特区《第三方资助仲裁实务守则》第2.3条。

会中的第三方资助人进行监管。

行业自律监管的模式虽然可以及时调整以应对第三方资助在实践中遇到的问题,但是也存在着一定的缺陷。由第三方资助人组成的行业组织首先要维护的必然是行业的整体利益,因此,其作出的某些规定可能并不会优先考虑维护受资助人的利益。

(三)新加坡对第三方资助的规制模式

1. 通过修改立法的形式确立了第三方资助的合法地位

2017年1月,新加坡国会通过的《新加坡民法(修正案)法案》正式废除了"禁止助讼与帮讼分利"的原则,确立了第三方资助的合法地位。[①]2017年3月1日,《新加坡民法(第三方资助)条例(2017)》生效,第2条明确规定了第三方资助适用于国际仲裁程序及其他与国际仲裁相关的程序。当前新加坡对第三方资助制度的规定仅仅适用于国际仲裁领域,承认了该领域中第三方资助的合法性,但同时也设置了"不能违反公共政策"作为兜底条款。同时,也对于第三方资助人的资质进行了明确规定,对第三方资助中资助的标准和设立方式也进行了详细的规定。

2. 通过修订《新加坡法律执业法》和《新加坡法律职业(职业行为)规则》规范律师的行为

2015年,《新加坡法律职业法》和《新加坡法律职业(职业行为)规则》,以适应第三方资助对法律从业人员带来的冲击。《法律职业(职业行为)规则》第49A条规定了法律从业人员的披露义务,同时对披露的时间也作出了规定。第49B条则规定法律从业者或法律执业者不得直接或间接持有第三方资助人的任何股份或其他所有权权益,法律从业人员或律师事务所不得从第三方资助人处收取任何佣金、费用或收益分成。

---

① See Indranee Rajah S.C., Civil Law (Amendment) Bill 2016 Second Reading, http://www.nas.gov.sg/archivesonline/data/pdfdoc/20170110002/2R%20Speech%20-%20Civil%20Law%20Amendment%20Bill%202016.pdf, accessed Apr. 18, 2021.

四、第三方资助国际商事仲裁在中国的发展路径

我国的第三方资助发展尚处于起步阶段,虽然国内已经出现了一些专门从事第三方资助的机构,但是目前第三方资助国际商事仲裁的实践十分稀少。我国目前的法律既未对第三方资助作出明确禁止,也没有有效的规制措施。因此,探索出适合我国的第三方资助规制模式是当前学者们的研究重点,笔者以为应从以下方面展开。

(一)修改仲裁规则规制第三方资助的发展

1. 规定强制性的披露义务

第一,增加受资助人和第三方资助人作为披露义务的主体。

一般的仲裁案件中,当事人不会成为披露义务的主体。但由于资助协议仅需资助人和受资助人双方达成合意即可成立,仲裁机构和对方当事人无法知晓第三方资助人的存在。因此,笔者认为必须对受资助人和第三方资助人都设定一定的披露义务,包括披露的对象、时间和内容等。①

目前,我国《中国国际经济贸易仲裁委员会仲裁规则(2015)》第31条仅仅对仲裁员规定了披露义务,而没有对仲裁当事人和第三方资助人设立披露义务。放眼国内外,2014年10月23日,国际律师协会理事会决议通过了《国际律师协会国际仲裁利益冲突指引(2014)》(以下简称《IBA指引》),其中第一部分第7条就详细规定了当事人的告知义务。根据《IBA指引》的规定,受资助人是披露义务的主体。笔者认为,应当要求受资助的一方当事人就第三方资助的有关内容向参与仲裁的所有各方以及仲裁庭作出披露。同时,也应当对第三方资助人设立披露义务,要求第三方资助人向仲裁庭披露其资本充足的情况,使仲裁庭可以确信其有能力对当事人提供足够的资助。要求第三方资助人对于其与仲裁员之间存在的可能影响案件公正审理的直接或间接关系承担披露责任,保证第三方资助人与仲裁员之间不存在利

---

① 参见赵勇、方祖鹏:《国际商事仲裁中第三方资助者与仲裁员的利益冲突与防范》,载《西部学刊》2020年第12期。

益关系。

第二,披露的时间应当尽早。

一般情况下,受资助人和第三方资助人都应当在首次开庭前就履行披露义务,越早进行信息披露,越有利于仲裁程序的顺利进行。但有时候,受资助人是在仲裁程序审理过程中才找到合适的资助人,从而达成了资助协议,此时受资助人或第三方资助人都只能在签署资助协议后向仲裁庭进行信息披露。对于此种情况下的披露时间,香港特区《仲裁条例》规定,如果资助协议是在仲裁展开之后订立的,则应当在订立资助协议后的 15 日内进行披露。笔者认为,国际商事仲裁案件的审理应当以快捷高效为重要原则,设置 15 日的披露时间过长,很容易影响仲裁案件的审理进程,因此,应当适当缩短披露的时间,在签署资助协议后 3 日内向仲裁庭进行信息披露更为合适。

第三,披露的内容应包括第三方资助人的身份信息和资助协议的全部内容。

根据目前国际上对第三方资助有关披露的实践,对披露内容的规定主要包括资助人身份和资助协议的内容。但是对资助协议内容的披露程度尚未形成一致意见,争议的焦点在于披露资助协议的全部内容,还是仅披露与资助有关的条款,或者是仅需要披露资助协议的存在即可。

《中国国际经济贸易仲裁委员会国际投资争端仲裁规则(试行)》第 27 条第 2 款规定了仲裁当事人的披露义务。同时规定仲裁庭有权命令当事人披露有关第三方资助的情况。但是,并没有规定对资助协议的披露程度。

笔者认为,披露的内容应当包括资助人的身份信息和资助协议的全部内容。因为如果不对资助协议全部内容进行披露,那么仲裁庭就无法知晓受资助人和第三方资助人在资助协议中约定了哪些内容。在资助协议的签订过程中,受资助人往往处于相对弱势的地位,对资助协议的全部内容进行披露,一定程度上可以避免资助人利用自己的优势地位过分压迫受资助人的情况,也有利于仲裁庭更加全面地了解案件。披露资助协议的全部内容有利于更好地维护公平正义。对于披露资助协议的全部内容可能侵犯隐私的问题,各地的仲裁规则都对仲裁庭、仲裁员和仲裁当事人设定了保密义务,因此,只要将资助协议的内容放入保密义务的相关规定中,就可以尽可能减少对受资助人和第三方资助人双方资助协议隐私的侵犯。

2. 设定第三方资助人的保密义务

当前我国的仲裁实践中对第三方资助人的保密义务缺乏相应的规定。《中国国际经济贸易仲裁委员会仲裁规则(2015)》第38条第2款只是为双方当事人及其仲裁代理人、仲裁员、证人、翻译、仲裁庭咨询的专家和指定的鉴定人等设定了保密义务。

笔者认为,虽然第三方资助人不是仲裁协议的当事人,仲裁庭在案件审理的过程中可能没有权利对第三方资助人提出要求,但是仲裁机构可以通过仲裁规则来设定第三方资助人的保密义务,规定在存在第三方资助的情形下,第三方资助人不得将所获取的有关仲裁程序的信息进行泄露。如果当事人选择适用了该仲裁规则,那么该仲裁规则就可以对其资助人产生约束力。比如,可以对《中国国际经济贸易仲裁委员会仲裁规则(2015)》第38条第2款进行修改,加入第三方资助人,改为"不公开审理的案件,双方当事人及其仲裁代理人和资助人、仲裁员、证人、翻译、仲裁庭咨询的专家和指定的鉴定人,以及其他有关人员,均不得对外界透露案件实体和程序的有关情况",或者也可以对"其他有关人员"作出解释,将第三方资助人纳入保密义务的责任主体范围内。

3. 合理确定仲裁费用的分担与担保

《中国国际经济贸易仲裁委员会国际投资争端仲裁规则(试行)》第27条第3款规定,仲裁庭可以考虑第三方资助的具体情况后,对仲裁费用作出裁决。但是具体如何裁决,仲裁规则没有作出详细规定。同样,《中国国际经济贸易仲裁委员会仲裁规则(2015)》第52条第2款仅仅确认了败诉方承担仲裁费用的原则,也未就败诉方具体应当承担哪些费用,以及仲裁费用的担保作出明确规定。

因此,应当既要明确当受资助人被要求提供担保时,第三方资助人是否需要承担担保费用,又要明确当受资助人败诉时,第三方资助人所需承担的费用范围,还要明确当受资助人胜诉时,可以向对方当事人索赔的费用范围。[①] 笔者认为,第三方资助人理应帮助受资助人提供担保。因为受资助人往往就是因为资金匮乏而无法独自提起仲裁程序,如果再要求其提供高额的费用担保,这对受资助人而言是十分不利的。

另外,在受资助人败诉时,应当由第三方资助人承担仲裁费用,这也是第三方资助作为一种投资的风险所在。对于受资助人应按资助协议支付给第三方资助人的报酬部分,应当认定为仲裁费用,由败诉方承担。原因在于,受资助人应按资助协议支付给资助人的报酬部分与其聘请律师所支付的律师费具有相似的性质,都是受资助人为维护自己的合法权益而付出的必要支出。如果对方当事人依法按照约定履行自己的义务,那么受资助人就不必花费这些费用来维护自己的合法权益,因此,第三方资助的费用理应由败诉方承担。但是在个案中,应当具体考虑案件的裁决结果、案件的标的金额、付给资助人报酬的金额,以及胜诉方当事人及代理人的实际工作量等情况,公平公正地作出裁决,以免第三方资助人和受资助人恶意夸大支付给第三方资助人的报酬,从而损害对方当事人的合法权益。对此可以赋予仲裁庭一定的自由裁量权。

4. 制定关于第三方资助人的相关标准

纵观其他国家和地区在国际商事仲裁领域的规定,可以发现其都对第三方资助人设定了一定的标准。例如,我国香港特区要求第三方资助人满足一定的最低标准,比如资本充足要求,从而确保受资助人可以得到稳定充足的资金支持。《英国诉讼资助者行为守则》设置了500万英镑作为第三方资助人的最低资本标准,并要求第三方资助人持续向诉讼资助者协会披露其资本充足的情况。新加坡则规定,资助人不能是争议的当事方,且应当具备资助仲裁程序的专项资金,资金的总额不低于500万新加坡元。

笔者认为,当前国际市场上第三方资助人的资质良莠不齐,第三

---

① 参见吴维锭:《商事仲裁第三方资助的规制逻辑:"准当事人"学说探析》,载北京仲裁委员会/北京国际仲裁中心组编:《北京仲裁》(第110辑),中国法制出版社2020年版,第125—127页。

方资助人在仲裁案件审理过程中撤资或破产的现象时有发生。为保障国际商事仲裁各方的合法权益,有必要制定关于第三方资助人的相关标准,比如,对开展第三方资助业务的公司的实缴资本规定最低金额,对于公司内法律专业人员数量作出要求,对公司近5年的经营状况作出要求等。具体标准的设定还需要长期实践的积累以及各界专家的共同研讨。

(二)通过行业组织进行自律监管

1. 加强代理人行业组织的自律监管

目前我国律师协会在第三方资助方面尚未对律师提出明确要求。律师执业行为规范、律师协会行业规则和准则的修订难度较小,可以很好地对第三方资助中出现的新问题在短时间内作出迅速反应,从而达到良好的规制效果。

目前的国际商事仲裁的实践中,确实存在部分第三方资助人为受资助人指定律师,或者律师向其代理的仲裁申请人推荐资助人的情况,因此,律师与第三方资助人之间不可避免地会存在一定的利益关系。笔者认为,可以在当前的《律师执业行为规范》中加入有关第三方资助的内容,要求律师或律师事务所不得违法与第三方资助人及其关联公司产生任何经济上的联系,也不得与第三方资助人及其关联公司的高级管理人员存在利害关系。应当使代理人明确在仲裁案件中其是受资助人的代理人,而不是资助人的代理人,应当对受资助人负责,时刻以受资助人的利益为重,不能为了一己私利损害受资助人的合法权益。

2. 建立专门的资助人行业组织

虽然我国的第三方资助行业发展尚处于起步阶段,成立专门的资助人行业组织的条件尚不成熟,但是也应当逐步尝试成立专门的资助人行业组织。

首先,可以为资助人设立准入门槛,比如,资金规模达到多少金额以上,具备法律专业人员的数量达到多少名以上或者近几年内的经营状况如何等;其次,行业组织要定期对资助人进行管理培训,可以设置一定的培训指标,努力提高资助人的专业素质和职业素养;最后,制定内部的惩戒标准,对于资助人干预当事人的代理律师办理案件、在案件审理过程中恶意撤资、利用自身优势地位压迫受资助人、故意延迟出资影响案件的审理等情况作出相应的惩罚。

(三)修改《仲裁法》,进行法律规制

1. 以第三方资助的大量案件实践为前提

我国《仲裁法》颁布于1994年,至今只经历了两次修改。近年来,随着我国仲裁实践的不断发展,现行《仲裁法》中的一些问题也渐渐显露出来,学术界和实务界都发出了对《仲裁法》进行修改的呼声。

但是笔者认为,从我国当前的仲裁实践来看,由于第三方资助的案件很少,我国司法机关和仲裁机构都缺乏实际经验,尚不具备在《仲裁法》中对第三方资助进行全面规制的条件。若过早地制定详细的法律对于第三方资助仲裁进行监管,则可能会出现法律不符合当前我国实践的情况。在前文所述的仲裁规则、行业组织对第三方资助进行规制后,势必会增加有关第三方资助仲裁的案例。因此,《仲裁法》的修改应当以第三方资助的大量案件实践为前提,只有经过案例的不断积累,再在《仲裁法》中加入第三方资助仲裁的相关内容才是比较合理的。

2. 明确第三方资助的定义和合法性

笔者认为,在《仲裁法》的修改中,不便将第三方资助国际商事仲裁作出单独的区分。第三方资助国际商事仲裁只是国际仲裁的一个组成部分,可以在现行《仲裁法》第四章"仲裁程序"中加入第四节"第三方资助仲裁",对第三方资助进行规定,这样既可以明确国际商事仲裁中第三方资助的合法化,也可以同时包括所有的国内仲裁和国际投资仲裁等其他领域的国际仲裁。

此外,由于第三方资助本身具有一定的局限性,前文所述的各种问题都很难在短时间内通过制定完善的法律来解决。因此,笔者认为,对第三方资助的立法规制虽有必要性,但目前的立法不应过于详细,不宜进行大规模的立法活动,可以仅仅对第三方资助的定义和合法性作出确认,而其他细节的问题则依靠仲裁规则和行业自律组织进行调整。

结论

国际商事仲裁领域的第三方资助在平衡仲裁双方当事人的地位,帮助受资助人实现公平正义的同时,也引发了许多问题,比如:信息披露和利益冲突问题、保密性问题、仲裁费用的分担和担保问题、仲裁员的公正性和独立性问题等。面对这些可能引发的问题,笔者参考了国际仲裁机构和各代表国家及地区对于第三方资助的规制经验,结合我国当前国际商事仲裁的实践,提出了适合我国的第三方资助规制模式。对于我国而言,应该充分发挥仲裁机构的作用,通过修改仲裁规则对第三方资助在国际商事仲裁中的运用进行指引和规制,利用代理人行业自律组织进行充分的自律规制,并逐步成立专门的资助人行业组织。在实践成熟后再对《仲裁法》进行修改,从立法上对第三方资助的定义和合法性进行确认。

(肖鹏　审校)

东北亚仲裁发展观察

李虎、周广俊、乌英格、金瑛、苏晓凌、吴强

摘要：仲裁具有高效、灵活、保密性强等特点，《承认及执行外国仲裁裁决公约》使众多缔约成员仲裁裁决易于跨国承认执行，在国际经贸争议解决中发挥重要作用。东北亚地区的商事活动日益频繁，而东北亚地区国家多元，仲裁制度存在差异，商业贸易往来争议解决呈现多元化、专业化趋势。本文对中国、俄罗斯、蒙古国、韩国、朝鲜、日本六个国家展开研究，介绍各国仲裁机构、仲裁规则、仲裁立法等相关发展成果并进行比较，为东北亚区域仲裁的法律制度研究提供参考。

关键词：国际商事仲裁；国别研究；仲裁规则；东北亚区域

随着全球化进程的加速，东北亚地区的商事活动日益频繁。作为解决经贸争议的重要手段，仲裁以其高效、灵活和保密性强的特点，在东北亚地区得到广泛应用。东北亚区域仲裁制度的发展，在呈现出专业化、多元化趋势的同时，也面临诸多挑战。本文选取了东北亚区域目前仲裁制度已有一定发展基础的国家，从多个维度介绍各国仲裁机构、仲裁规则与仲裁立法等相关发展成果，以期为东北亚区域仲裁法律制度研究提供相应参考。

中国篇 *

中国海事仲裁委员会（以下简称"中国海仲"）于 1959 年在中国

---

* 本篇作者为李虎，中国海事仲裁委员会副主任兼秘书长。

国际贸易促进委员会内设立,是我国内地唯一一家以处理海事海商争议为特色的国家级涉外仲裁机构,对外代表着中国海事仲裁的国际形象。得益于中国持续推进的高水平对外开放,近年来,中国海仲涉外海事仲裁业务快速发展。

一、扬帆四海

2022年,中国海仲共计受理案件190件,其中,涉外海事案件34件,涉港澳海事案件15件,案件涉及25个境外当事人、32个国家和地区。2023年,截至10月31日,中国海仲新受理案件1078件,其中涉外海事案件26件,涉港澳台海事案件23件,案件涉及38个境外当事人、23个国家和地区。

该等案件涉及全球各大洲的国家和地区,主要包括南非、菲律宾、马来西亚、越南、以色列、埃及、巴基斯坦、俄罗斯、意大利、美国、德国、日本、巴西、开曼群岛、英属维尔京群岛、百慕大以及我国港澳台地区等。

上述涉外海事案件整体呈现如下趋势:

(1)争议金额过亿的案件明显增多;

(2)船舶燃油加注、海上工程、光伏设备、船舶股权转让等新类型纠纷出现,同时船舶建造、船舶管理、船舶留置、船舶打捞、船舶抵押、共同海损、船舶物料和备品供应、码头租赁、海上人身损害、海上保险,以及海运欺诈等传统海事海商案件数量稳步增长;

(3)双方当事人均为外国人的国际海事案件,以及当事人约定采用英文程序、适用外国实体法的案件陆续出现;

(4)案件涉及的诸如外国法的查明与适用等法律问题日益复杂。

二、改弦更张

为保障、促进涉外海事仲裁的发展,中国海仲更新仲裁员名册,修订机构仲裁规则并制定临时仲裁规则,不断推动仲裁国际化发展。

中国海仲 2021 年的《仲裁员名册》中共有仲裁员 826 名,其中,我国港澳台地区及外籍仲裁员增至 123 人,来自 36 个国家和地区,为中外当事人在具体案件中选定仲裁员提供了更大的便利。

在仲裁管理方面,《中国海事仲裁委员会仲裁规则(2021)》(以下简称 2021 年《仲裁规则》)在国内实现若干突破。该规则首次作出如下规定:

(1)对电子送达、视频开庭、视频作证、电子签名以及网络安全和隐私及数据保护作出全面规定,认可了信息技术在常规仲裁中的广泛应用;

(2)对仲裁证据规则予以较为系统的规定,便于仲裁庭正确查明案件事实;

(3)区分案件经办人和仲裁庭秘书,厘清机构和仲裁庭之间的职责范围,防范利益冲突,提高仲裁透明度;

(4)明确将向当事船舶船长送达作为仲裁文书送达的方式之一,适应海事仲裁实践的特别需求。

此外,2021 年《仲裁规则》在进一步尊重当事人意思自治的同时,赋予仲裁庭更为自主的权限,强化其审慎裁判义务,推动机构仲裁向"轻管理"过渡。

对仲裁庭组成进行优化规定。当事人可以在机构《仲裁员名册》外选定仲裁员。当事人无法共同指定首席仲裁员的,由双方当事人所选定的两位仲裁员共同指定;在期限内无法指定的,由机构指定。

强化仲裁庭的职责权限和责任担当。规定仲裁庭在组成后应立即组织召开案件管理会议,以决定可能采取的程序措施、审理裁决的路线图和时间表;明确仲裁庭有权要求当事人就案外人对仲裁程序的资助或对仲裁结果所具有的经济利益予以披露;要求仲裁庭在确定开庭审理日期时,应慎重考虑庭前文件交换是否充分以及开庭审理的条件是否具备,切实提高庭审质效。

仲裁费用灵活管理。明确当事人可特别约定选择将机构管理费和仲裁员报酬分开的收费办法,进一步与国际接轨。

三、创新与展望

在我国内地仲裁市场逐步对外开放的时代背景下,2022年,中国海商法协会发布实施《中国海商法协会临时仲裁规则》,供其会员及中外当事人约定选择适用。中国海仲同步配套发布《中国海事仲裁委员会临时仲裁服务规则》。两规则有机衔接,相互配合,共同在内地率先开展临时仲裁服务,进一步促进中国涉外海事仲裁的发展。

2023年6月30日,由中国海仲担任指定机构的内地第一起涉港临时仲裁案件顺利裁决,实现了内地临时仲裁案件零的突破。

随着《区域全面经济伙伴关系协定》(RCEP)的生效实施,亚太经济发展会更加迅速,潜力巨大。海事仲裁在国际航运贸易纠纷解决中的重要作用亦将愈发凸显。中国海仲将一如既往地为中外当事人提供优质高效的仲裁服务,与国内外仲裁机构并肩同行,团结协作,共同为国际仲裁的健康发展作出更大的贡献。

(杨意茹 审校)

俄罗斯篇[*]

俄罗斯具有悠久的仲裁传统,其工商会下设的两家仲裁机构一直在东欧地区享有广泛的影响力,也积累了大量的仲裁专业人才。但在国内和国际双重因素的影响之下,俄罗斯不得不在2015年对仲裁制度进行重大改革,以应对俄罗斯面临的政治、经济和法律方面的挑战。2022年之后,由于西方国家对俄罗斯开始了史无前例的极限制裁,导致其仲裁制度和实践再次面临重大挑战,各方面的不确定性风险急剧增加。充分了解俄罗斯的基本仲裁制度和司法实践,提前预判俄罗斯仲裁可能存在的各种风险,对于从争议解决方式方面降低投资和贸易过程中的风险具有重要的意义。

---

[*] 本篇作者为周广俊,北京市信达律师事务所主任,莫斯科国立大学法律系硕士研究生。

综上可以看出,俄罗斯仲裁制度的改革,以及其仲裁实践所体现出来的特殊性,都是俄罗斯为了维护其国家利益和保护本国企业利益而采取的应对措施。尽管俄罗斯法院体系不支持仲裁,但由于俄罗斯是《纽约公约》的成员国,依然要遵守世界公认的仲裁基本原则,所以在目前俄罗斯遭受全面制裁的世界局势中,同时考虑到俄罗斯法院体系的公正性和不确定性,仲裁依然是解决与俄罗斯相关的商事争议的首选方式。

一、悠久的商事仲裁传统

早在苏联时期,商事仲裁就已经成为解决民事争议的重要方式之一。1932年6月17日,苏联人民委员会和中央执行委员会作出决议,成立全苏商会对外贸易仲裁委员会,这是苏联第一个常设仲裁机构。①此决议相当于全苏商会对外贸易仲裁委员会的条例(章程),虽然只有13条,但由于是当时苏联的最高权力机关作出的,且对仲裁过程中的诸如管辖权、选定和指定仲裁员、保全措施、仲裁收费和仲裁裁决执行等问题均作出了相应规定,在之后的很长一段时间里一直是苏联仲裁立法的纲领性文件。

全苏商会1932年发布的一份资料显示,之所以设立对外贸易仲裁委员会,是由于当时苏联已经得到西方的承认,对外贸易开始增长,并且在和意大利、匈牙利、土耳其等许多国家签订的贸易条约中都规定通过仲裁解决争议。②苏联还和德国、拉脱维亚订立了仲裁条约。但当时普遍适用的临时仲裁,既不能让新生的社会主义苏联感到放心,也不能为苏联外贸企业积累和总结经验。因此,借鉴当时西方国家商会组织下设仲裁机构的组织形式,苏联决定成立自己的常设仲裁机构。

俄罗斯联邦工商会国际商事仲裁院前任主席卡马罗夫曾经说

---

① Постановление Центрального Исполнительного Комитета и Совета народных комиссаров Союза ССР от 17 июня 1932 года (СЗ СССР 1932 г. №48, СТ.281).

② Ежемесячник Всесоюзной торговой палаты 8-9, августа - сентября, 1932.

过,在苏联时期,人们对商事仲裁非常信任和尊重,这一点在对外国仲裁裁决的承认和执行方面更加突出。一直到1992年,针对俄罗斯企业的外国仲裁裁决在俄罗斯都是自动履行的,根本不需要申请强制执行。

仲裁对俄罗斯的司法体系也产生了根本性的影响。在多次的司法体系改革之后,在俄罗斯的国家法院系统中,除一般的普通管辖法院之外,还有一个专门处理经济纠纷案件的仲裁法院系统,但这个仲裁法院并不是仲裁机构,而是国家法院。其按照俄罗斯的诉讼法律程序处理经济纠纷案件,行使的是国家审判权,这就是所谓的仲裁法院不"仲裁"。① 在中俄经贸实践中,俄方当事人提供的合同文本约定的争议解决方式大多数为在俄罗斯仲裁法院诉讼解决,但很多时候中方当事人都是误以为此仲裁法院是仲裁机构而接受了这种争议解决条款,导致纠纷发生后不能申请仲裁,而只能去俄方当事人所在地的仲裁法院诉讼解决。

二、2015年仲裁改革的背景

2013年12月12日,俄罗斯总统普京在发表国情咨文时指出,俄罗斯的经济纠纷解决机制与国际先进经验还有距离,俄罗斯应当认真提高仲裁机构的权威性。为此,普京要求俄罗斯政府和俄罗斯工业家企业家联盟、俄罗斯联邦工商会在最短的时间内从根本上完善仲裁制度,并且向国家杜马提出立法建议。②

在普京提出要求之后,俄罗斯政府各个相关部门迅速行动,基本上是以俄罗斯司法部和俄罗斯联邦工商会为主导,对仲裁法和相关法律进行了大幅度的修改。笔者认为,俄罗斯修改仲裁法有国内和国际两方面的原因。

---

① 参见田晔:《仲裁法院不"仲裁"？俄罗斯司法体制掠影》,载信达立律师事务所网站(http://www.xindalilaw.com/newsitem/278196466),访问日期:2023年9月9日。

② Послание Президента РФ Федеральному Собранию от 12.12.2013, https://www.consultant.ru/document/cons_doc_LAW_155646/.

国内方面,由于2002年《俄罗斯联邦仲裁机构法》对设立仲裁机构没有任何限制,也没有相应机制对仲裁机构进行适当的监督,其结果就是任何一个法人都可以成立仲裁机构,仲裁机构鱼龙混杂,业务水平参差不齐,很多人滥用仲裁机构进行违法犯罪活动。这种情况持续了很多年,使得人民对仲裁的公正性、独立性和仲裁员的裁判水平产生严重的不信任,在司法实践中选择仲裁作为争议解决方式的情况也越来越少。

国际方面,俄罗斯政府在一系列仲裁案件中败诉,被判决承担巨额赔偿,尤其是2014年7月28日,位于海牙的常设仲裁法院裁定俄罗斯政府向尤科斯石油公司前股东支付500亿美元的赔偿。[1]这使得俄罗斯政府强烈意识到,国际商事仲裁是一把危险的"双刃剑",如果控制不好,极有可能给控制俄罗斯经济命脉的大型国有公司造成致命伤害,对俄罗斯政府也十分危险,所以,有必要从法律上进行改革,以便可以控制国际商事仲裁的不确定性。

可以说,俄罗斯商事仲裁改革的本质,就是要将仲裁的权力掌握在俄罗斯政府可以信任的少数人手里。

在这样的大背景之下,新《俄罗斯联邦仲裁法》于2015年12月29日通过[2],并于2016年9月1日实施,成为管理仲裁的基本法律,而1993年7月7日生效的《俄罗斯联邦国际商事仲裁法》继续作为管理国际仲裁的特殊法律。

三、现行俄罗斯仲裁法的主要特点

2015年的仲裁改革奠定了现行俄罗斯仲裁法的基础,一方面加强市场准入,严格仲裁机构的设立审批,限制临时仲裁的适用,另一方面开始允许外国仲裁机构进入俄罗斯市场,明确允许部分公司争议通过

---

[1] 参见崔铮:《仲裁裁决俄政府赔尤科斯三股东500亿美元》,载仲裁网(https://china-arbitration.com/index/news/detail/id/1805.html),访问日期:2023年9月9日。

[2] 参见《俄罗斯联邦仲裁法》,周广俊、王天怡译,载中国国际经济贸易委员会、中国海事仲裁委员会、中国国际商会仲裁研究所编:《仲裁与法律》(第134辑),法律出版社2017年版。

仲裁方式解决。

(一)仲裁机构的设立由登记制改为审批制

《俄罗斯联邦仲裁法》第九章对仲裁机构的设立主体、审批程序、设立单位的法律责任等都作出了详细规定,明确仲裁机构的设立由之前的登记制转变为审批制,不仅审批的条件非常严格,而且是否能够成功批核完全取决于审批机关,没有法律机制可以监督。

常设仲裁机构只能由非营利性组织设立。俄罗斯联邦国家权力机关、俄罗斯联邦主体国家权力机关、地方自治机关、国家机构和地方机构、国有集团、国家公司、政党、宗教组织,以及律师事务所、俄罗斯联邦地区律师协会、俄罗斯联邦律师协会、公证员协会、联邦公证员协会不得设立常设仲裁机构。不过,俄罗斯联邦律师协会和其他公司、基金会,以及5家研究机构作为发起人成立了俄罗斯现代仲裁学院(非营利性组织,2016年8月17日注册成立),然后以俄罗斯现代仲裁学院的名义设立了俄罗斯仲裁中心,也获得了俄罗斯联邦政府的批准。笔者认为,这是俄罗斯政府特意为俄罗斯法律界人士发出的一张仲裁机构牌照。

常设仲裁机构的审批条件包括:第一,常设仲裁机构的仲裁规则、推荐仲裁员名册需要符合《俄罗斯联邦仲裁法》的要求;第二,设立该机构的非营利性组织及其发起人(股东)的信息真实;第三,设立该机构的非营利性组织发起人(股东)的构成、信誉及其活动范围和性质可以保障高水平地开展常设仲裁机构的活动,包括对相应机构的设立和活动提供财务保障,可以保障该机构在俄罗斯联邦进行仲裁推广活动。

外国仲裁机构申请俄罗斯常设仲裁机构的资质,不需要符合上述条件,但需要符合《俄罗斯联邦仲裁法》规定的两个特殊条件:第一,享有广泛认可的国际信誉;第二,如果准备管理俄罗斯国内仲裁案件,必须在俄罗斯设立分支机构。第二个条件是2018年12月27日增加的,之前没有这样的规定。

最初的法律规定,常设仲裁机构的资质由俄罗斯联邦政府审批,2018年12月27日之后改为由俄罗斯联邦司法部审批。

《俄罗斯联邦仲裁法》第 50 条规定了常设仲裁机构的设立单位的责任,只有在存在故意和严重过失的情况下,常设仲裁机构的设立单位才仅仅以赔偿由于常设仲裁机构未履行或者未适当履行其仲裁管理职能或其行使常设仲裁机构规则规定之义务给当事人造成之损失的形式对仲裁当事人承担民事法律责任。对于仲裁员行为(不作为)造成的损失,设立常设仲裁机构的非营利性组织对仲裁当事人不承担民事法律责任。

在这一次的仲裁改革中,俄罗斯针对常设仲裁机构的审批采用了一个非常主观的标准,即设立常设仲裁机构的非营利性组织发起人(股东)的构成、信誉及其活动范围和性质可以保障高水平地开展常设仲裁机构的活动,包括对相应机构的设立和活动提供财务保障方面,可以保障该机构进行旨在在俄罗斯联邦推广仲裁的活动。

这种立法完全不符合俄罗斯立法原则和传统,但也只有这种规定,才能够人为地控制仲裁机构的数量,将不可靠或者不希望的机构排除在外。这一条款在俄罗斯饱受争议和批评,但正是基于这一机制,审批机关可以完全自主决定是否发放仲裁机构牌照。

(二)争议的可仲裁性受到限制

在立法层面,俄罗斯将争议的可仲裁性更多地交给其他联邦法律去解决,而仲裁法只负责规范仲裁程序问题。《俄罗斯联邦仲裁法》第 3 条和第 4 条规定,民事法律关系当事人之间的争议根据当事人协议可以交由仲裁解决,其他联邦法律可以对某些类型的争议是否允许交由仲裁解决作出限制性规定。也就是说,仲裁法只是原则性规定民事法律关系争议可以仲裁,但任何联邦法律都可以规定某些争议不可以仲裁。

在《俄罗斯联邦仲裁法》之外,俄罗斯的其他法律又规定了很多具体事项是不可以通过仲裁解决的。比较常见的是,行政法律关系案件和其他公共法律关系案件、破产争议、大部分公司争议、反垄断争议、知识产权争议,以及基于俄罗斯私有化法律调整之关系而产生的争议。

(三) 限制临时仲裁的适用

临时仲裁在俄罗斯是有历史传统的,以往俄罗斯法律对临时仲裁并没有任何限制或者禁止,但在 2015 年仲裁改革之后,越来越多的单行法律明确将某些特定类型的争议排除在临时仲裁适用范围之外,只能由常设仲裁机构进行仲裁。

2018 年 12 月 27 日,俄罗斯通过第 531 号联邦法律,对《俄罗斯联邦仲裁法》作出第三次修改,其中第 44 条第 20 款明确规定,任何个人和法人,如果没有按照《俄罗斯联邦仲裁法》获得常设仲裁机构的牌照,则禁止履行管理仲裁的职能,如指定仲裁员、决定仲裁员回避和仲裁员权力终止问题,以及其他与进行临时仲裁有关的行为,如收取仲裁费、经常性为仲裁开庭或者仲裁会议提供场地等。同时,也不得发布这方面的广告(包括互联网广告),不得公开提供临时仲裁服务。如果违反前述禁止性规定,仲裁机构或者临时仲裁仲裁庭所作出的裁决将被视为违反《俄罗斯联邦仲裁法》规定的仲裁程序。同时,该法律也对《俄罗斯联邦广告法》作出修订,增加了第 30.2 条,规定如果没有按照《俄罗斯联邦仲裁法》获得常设仲裁机构的牌照,就不得对仲裁活动(包括临时仲裁活动)发布广告,包括在互联网发布广告。

在新《俄罗斯联邦仲裁法》实施之后,很多早已存在的仲裁机构无法获得牌照,就规避法律以临时仲裁的方式提供仲裁服务。上述法律通过之后,这些无牌照机构的"擦边球"就没办法继续了,否则其仲裁裁决将被视为违反法定程序而得不到承认和执行。

临时仲裁在 2015 年仲裁改革之后被"封杀",原因只有一个,就是俄罗斯政府需要将仲裁的权力掌握在"自己人"手里,而在临时仲裁中难以做到这一点。

(四) 大部分公司争议不能通过仲裁解决

在 2015 年仲裁改革之后,公司争议原则上可以通过仲裁解决,但相应的限制也很多。同时,如果其他联邦法律将某些公司争议排除适用仲裁解决,则相关公司争议也不可以通过仲裁解决。在具体的适用时间方面,根据2015年12月29日第409号《关于实施仲裁法的联邦法》第13条第7款之规定,只有在2017年2月1日之后,仲裁协议才可以约定将公司争议交由仲裁解决。在此之前签署的关于公司争议的仲裁协议,均被视为无法执行的仲裁协议。

根据《俄罗斯联邦仲裁程序法典》第33条第2款和第225.1条明确的排除性规定,以下公司争议不可以通过仲裁方式解决:与法人召开股东会有关的争议;公证员对有限责任公司股权交易进行公证活动而产生的争议;由于对国家机构、地方自治机关和被联邦法律授予特定国家权力或者其他公共权力的机关、组织和公职人员的非规范性法律文件、决定和行为(不作为)申请撤销而发生的争议;针对战略行业经营性公司的争议;与法人股东除名有关的争议;公司回购已发行股票引发的争议;等等。

同时,对于某些可以仲裁解决的公司争议,必须交由制定了公司争议专门仲裁规则的仲裁机构解决,没有制定专门规则的仲裁机构是无权受理的。

对于中国企业参与比较多的战略行业公司(能源、矿业),股东之间的大部分争议也是不能仲裁解决的,只能交由俄罗斯的仲裁法院诉讼解决。

(五)当事人可以书面形式作出优先约定

为了体现当事人的意思自治,《俄罗斯联邦仲裁法》在某些事项上授予当事人特殊权利,如果当事人以书面形式作出约定,则当事人的约定享有优先效力,包括:

(1)如果根据仲裁规则,仲裁员的回避申请被仲裁员指定机构驳回,则提出回避申请的一方当事人不得再向有管辖权的法院提出回避申请;

(2)如果仲裁庭作出有管辖权的决定,则各方当事人均不得再向有管辖权的法院提出管辖权异议;

(3)不需要进行开庭审理;

(4)只能从仲裁机构推荐仲裁员名册中选定或者指定仲裁员;

(5) 仲裁裁决是终局的,不可撤销。

四、俄罗斯目前主要的商事仲裁机构

《俄罗斯联邦仲裁法》生效至今,只有 5 家新设仲裁机构获得批准,加上之前被豁免审批的俄罗斯联邦工商会下设的 2 家仲裁机构,俄罗斯境内目前总计只有 7 家常设仲裁机构可以提供仲裁服务,它们是:

1. 俄罗斯联邦工商会国际商事仲裁院(成立于 1932 年,规则备案日期:2020 年 5 月 15 日)

Международный коммерческий арбитражный суд при Торгово-промышленной палате Российской Федерации (МКАС)

网址:http://mkas.tpprf.ru/ru/

2. 俄罗斯联邦工商会海事仲裁委员会(成立于 1930 年,规则备案日期:2017 年 2 月 7 日)

Морская арбитражная комиссия при Торгово-промышленной палате Российской Федерации (МАК)

网址:http://mac.tpprf.ru/ru/

3. 现代仲裁学院俄罗斯仲裁中心(批准日期:2017 年 4 月 27 日,规则备案日期:2019 年 10 月 10 日)

Российский арбитражный центр при автономной некоммерческой организации "Российский Институт современного арбитража" (РАЦ)

网址:https://centerarbitr.ru/

4. 俄罗斯工业家企业家联盟仲裁中心(批准日期:2017 年 4 月 27 日,规则备案日期:2020 年 2 月 7 日)

Арбитражный центр при Общероссийской общественной организации "Российский союз промышленников и предпринимателей" (РСПП)

网址:https://arbitration-rspp.ru/

5. 非营利性组织体育仲裁院下设的国家体育仲裁中心常设仲

机构(批准日期:2019 年 4 月 25 日,规则备案日期:2021 年 2 月 1 日)

Национальный Центр Спортивного Арбитража при автономной некоммерческой организации "Спортивная Арбитражная Палата" (АНО «Спортивная арбитражная палата»)

网址:http://sportarbitrage.ru/

6. 俄罗斯机器制造者联盟全俄企业主行业协会下设的仲裁机构(批准日期:2021 年 5 月 18 日,规则备案日期:2021 年 8 月 13 日)

Арбитражное учреждение при Общероссийском отраслевом объединении работодателей «Союз машиностроителей России» (Арбитражное учреждение при ОООР «СоюзМаш России»)

网址:https://arbitr.soyuzmash.ru/

7. 自治非营利组织国家燃料和能源综合体仲裁发展研究所下设的仲裁中心(批准日期:2021 年 8 月 5 日,规则备案日期:2021 年 8 月 27 日)

Арбитражный центр при Автономной некоммерческой организации «Национальный институт развития арбитража в топливно-энергетическом комплексе» (Арбитражный центр при АНО НИРА ТЭК)

网址:https://www.arbitration-niratec.ru/

同时,作为此次改革的最大受益者,俄罗斯联邦工商会国际商事仲裁院开始在俄罗斯全境开设分支机构,目前已经设立了 22 家仲裁中心,基本上形成了一家独大的局面。[①]

俄罗斯仲裁法没有明确禁止境外仲裁机构进入其仲裁服务市场,境外仲裁机构进入俄罗斯仲裁服务市场目前有两种途径:第一,境外的任何法人和自然人都可以在俄罗斯设立非营利性组织,然后以该组织名义申请设立常设仲裁机构;第二,现有的其他国家或地区的仲裁机构也可以在俄罗斯直接申请常设仲裁机构资质,而不必先在俄罗斯成立非营利性组织,只要该机构享有广泛认可的国际信誉。

目前,已经有 4 家国际仲裁机构获得俄罗斯联邦政府的批准,可

---

① 参见俄罗斯联邦工商会国际商事仲裁院网站(http://mkas.tpprf.ru/ru/),访问日期:2023 年 9 月 9 日。

以在俄罗斯管理仲裁案件：

1. 香港国际仲裁中心（批准日期：2019年4月25日）

Гонконгский международный арбитражный центр (ГМАЦ)

Hong Kong International Arbitration Centre (HKIAC)

网址：https://www.hkiac.org/

2. 维也纳国际仲裁中心（批准日期：2019年7月4日）

Венский международный арбитражный центр

Vienna International Arbitral Centre (VIAC)

网址：https://www.viac.eu/en/

3. 国际商会国际仲裁院（批准日期：2021年5月18日）

Международный арбитражный суд при Международной торговой палате

The ICC International Court of Arbitration

网址：http://court.iccwbo.ru/

4. 新加坡国际商事仲裁中心（批准日期：2021年5月18日）

Сингапурский международный арбитражный центр

Singapore International Arbitration Centre (SIAC)

网址：https://www.siac.org.sg/

但是，由于这4家仲裁机构在俄罗斯均没有开设分支机构，所以还不能管理大部分的俄罗斯国内争议案件，只能管理特定类型的俄罗斯国内争议案件。目前，只有俄罗斯两个特别行政区（设立在加里宁格勒和滨海边疆区）主体之间的争议或者在特别行政区进行活动形成的相关合同所引发的争议，外国仲裁机构才可以管理，而这种类型的案件数量非常有限，导致外国仲裁机构在俄罗斯仲裁服务市场的参与程度有限。

五、俄罗斯商事仲裁实践中需要注意的几个问题

（一）俄罗斯为应对西方制裁设立强制专属管辖制度

2020年6月8日，第171号联邦法律对《俄罗斯联邦仲裁程序法典》

进行修订,对受到制裁的俄罗斯实体(包括俄罗斯公民和外国法人)给予特殊的司法保护。即使前述主体签订了仲裁条款,但如果仲裁是在对俄罗斯实施制裁的国家进行的,则俄罗斯仲裁法院自动获得对受制裁个人和法人所涉争议的专属管辖权,除非国际条约或者当事人协议另有约定。同时设立禁诉令制度,如果仲裁协议的当事人不遵守专属管辖制度,则俄罗斯仲裁法院可以判决该当事人承担惩罚性赔偿金。

这一法律规定使得俄罗斯当事人可以滥用权利,导致仲裁条款的有效性、可执行性以及仲裁裁决在俄罗斯境内的可执行性无法确定。如果仲裁裁决裁定俄罗斯实体承担违约责任,而俄罗斯实体无法履行合同义务是由于其受到制裁,则该仲裁裁决可能被不予承认和执行。

该专属管辖制度对于中国公司同样适用。如果中国公司与俄罗斯公司约定,仲裁在对俄罗斯不友好的地区进行,按照俄罗斯仲裁条款,这一约定无效或者无法执行,故发生争议后只能到俄罗斯仲裁法院诉讼解决,这实际上剥夺了中国当事人根据合同进行仲裁的权利。

在 2022 年 2 月 24 日之后,由于西方主要国家都已经对俄罗斯实施了制裁,导致俄罗斯公司已经无法选择西方国家的仲裁机构,使得我国香港特别行政区(以下简称香港特区)成为俄罗斯公司选择最多的司法管辖区,香港国际仲裁中心成为他们首选的争议解决机构。但是,2023 年 6 月 8 日,圣彼得堡市和列宁格勒州仲裁法院在第 A56-129797/202 号案件中作出了一个令人意外且影响深远的裁决。① 该案法官认定,香港特区的法律体系建立在与英国和其他普通法国家相似的普通法原则基础上,英国和欧洲法官在香港特区司法系统中起着重要作用,并在香港特区高等法院上诉法庭担任法官,所以,香港特区作为一个司法管辖区对俄罗斯是不友好的,进而导致双方当事人约定的在香港国际仲裁中心进行仲裁的条款依据俄罗斯法律是无效的,俄罗斯仲裁法院取得相应案件的专属管辖权。如果该案的裁决最终得到俄罗斯联邦最高法院的支持,将导致约定在香港特区进行仲裁的仲裁条款无效,约定在香港特区进行仲裁将对外国当事人产生极其不利的

---

① 参见周广俊:《俄罗斯法官认定香港属于对俄罗斯不友好的司法管辖区》,载"北京市信达立律师事务所"微信公众号,2023 年 8 月 29 日。

影响。

(二)《中苏交货共同条件》规定的强制仲裁

1990年3月13日,中华人民共和国对外经济贸易部和苏维埃社会主义共和国联盟对外经济联络部在北京签订《由中华人民共和国向苏维埃社会主义共和国联盟和由苏维埃社会主义共和国联盟向中华人民共和国交货共同条件议定书》(1990年7月1日生效),其附件为《由中华人民共和国向苏维埃社会主义共和国联盟和由苏维埃社会主义共和国联盟向中华人民共和国交货共同条件》(以下简称《中苏交货共同条件》)。其序言部分明确规定,中华人民共和国的外贸企业和组织同苏维埃社会主义共和国联盟有权经营外贸业务的企业和组织之间的一切供货,若在他们之间的合同中没有因为货物的特点和(或)交货的特殊性而另有规定,都按照下列交货共同条件执行。[1]

《中苏交货共同条件》第52条规定,与合同有关的一切争执,如果双方通过谈判或信函未能解决,不应由一般法庭管辖,而应通过仲裁解决,办法如下:

(1)如果被诉方是中华人民共和国的外贸企业和组织,则由设在北京的中国国际贸易促进委员会中国国际经济贸易仲裁委员会根据该委员会的规则进行仲裁;

(2)如果被诉方是苏维埃社会主义共和国联盟的企业和组织,则由设在莫斯科的苏联工商会仲裁庭根据该庭的条例进行仲裁。

按照《中苏交货共同条件》第52条的规定,中国和苏联企业之间的供货合同实施强制仲裁,除非双方当事人排除《中苏交货共同条件》的适用,或者另行约定了有效的争议解决条款,否则就是"原告就被告",通过仲裁解决。

但是,在《中苏交货共同条件》签订之后不久苏联即告解体,导致

---

[1] 参见《由中华人民共和国向苏维埃社会主义共和国联盟和由苏维埃社会主义共和国联盟向中华人民共和国交货共同条件议定书(北京,1990年3月13日)》,载中俄法律网(http://www.chinaruslaw.com/CN/CnRuTreaty/JudicatoryCoo/2009128161610_236431.htm),访问日期:2023年9月9日。

在实践中两国仲裁机构和司法机关对该条约是否继续适用出现过不同的处理方式。

中国方面,根据《中苏交货共同条件》第52条的规定,中国国际经济贸易仲裁委员会已经受理了多起俄罗斯公司依据该条约对中国公司提起的仲裁,并且作出了仲裁裁决。

俄罗斯方面,俄罗斯的司法机关曾经对《中苏交货共同条件》的国际条约地位不予认可。依法承继苏联工商会仲裁庭地位的俄罗斯联邦工商会国际商事仲裁院曾公开书面解释,在当事人没有书面协商一致的情况下,该仲裁院无权依据《中苏交货共同条件》第52条对供货合同争议行使管辖权。但是,随着司法实践的不断发展,俄罗斯方面的立场也在发生变化。据笔者所知,在俄罗斯联邦工商会国际商事仲裁院发布的仲裁案例中,已经明确表示可以依据《中苏交货共同条件》第52条受理相应的合同争议。①

笔者认为,在苏联解体之后,俄罗斯宣布对苏联订立的国际条约继续行使权利并承担相应义务,即俄罗斯联邦继承苏联的全部国际条约,使得该条约在俄罗斯和中国之间继续适用。1999年4月28日,中国与俄罗斯进行外交换文,对中国与苏联在1949年至1991年间订立的条约进行了清理,在双方约定终止的条约中没有《中苏交货共同条件》。由于中国实际承认俄罗斯继承苏联的国际条约,且双方至今均未声明终止《中苏交货共同条件》,所以,《中苏交货共同条件》属于有效的国际条约,应该继续在中国和俄罗斯之间适用。如果两国企业在供货合同中没有排除《中苏交货共同条件》的适用,或者没有就争议解决问题另行约定,则应当按照《中苏交货共同条件》办理或执行,其第52条规定的仲裁条款也自动强制适用。

(三)俄罗斯法律下的仲裁裁决终局性

根据《俄罗斯联邦仲裁法》第40条和俄罗斯联邦最高法院的司

---

① РЕШЕНИЕ КОЛЛЕГИИ АРБИТРОВ МКАС ПРИ ТПП РФ ОТ 28.07.2017 ПО ДЕЛУ N M-19/2017, https://apkrfkod.ru/pract/reshenie-kollegii-arbitrov-mkas-pri-tpp-rf-ot-28072017-po-delu-n-m-192017/?.

法解释,如果仲裁协议的当事人书面明确约定仲裁裁决是终局的,则俄罗斯法院不得再进行司法干预,不得再对仲裁裁决进行实质性的改变,包括不予承认或者不予执行。在俄罗斯的司法实践中,当事人书面明确约定仲裁裁决是终局裁决时,当事人针对该仲裁裁决提起的司法审查,法院在程序上通常是不予受理的。

当然,实践中也有例外,如果俄罗斯法院认为仲裁裁决违反俄罗斯公共秩序,也会对仲裁裁决进行司法审查。①

一般来说,在订立仲裁条款时,如果约定的仲裁机构在俄罗斯,俄罗斯当事人会坚持要求加入关于仲裁裁决终局性的表述,如"仲裁裁决是终局的,对双方当事人具有约束力";而当仲裁机构在俄罗斯以外时,俄罗斯当事人会坚持要求删除这一表述。笔者认为,这是有经验的俄罗斯律师试图通过仲裁条款的约束,为俄罗斯当事人在海外保留对仲裁裁决提起司法审查的权利,而让对方当事人在俄罗斯失去这一权利。

(四)俄罗斯法院可能在仲裁司法审查中滥用公共秩序理由

针对公共秩序问题,俄罗斯联邦最高仲裁法院和俄罗斯联邦最高法院都多次以司法解释和指导案例的方式作出解释和定义,当前将公共秩序定义为构成建设俄罗斯联邦经济、政治和法律体系且具有最高强制性、普遍性、特殊社会和公共意义的基础性的法律基础(原则)。②

虽然俄罗斯联邦最高法院给出了认定原则,但在司法实践中,对于何谓基础性的法律原则,俄罗斯各级法院往往根据各自的理解得出不同的解释,通常都是扩大解释,导致仲裁裁决在实践中经常被以违反公共秩序为由而撤销或者不予承认或者不予执行。对俄罗斯各级

---

① Определение Верховного Суда № 305-ЭС23-5624 25 августа 2023 по делу № А40-193861/2022, https://kad.arbitr.ru/Document/Pdf/019d6701-1eb0-4e60-bdcd-e361afb07ee1/2a0a23c5-db3a-488a-9348-8e7221e350ea/A40-193861-2022_20230825_Opredelenie.pdf?isAddStamp=True.

② Постановление Пленума ВС от 10 декабря 2019 г.№ 53 «О выполнении судами РФ функций содействия и контроля в отношении третейского разбирательства, международного коммерческого арбитража», https://www.vsrf.ru/documents/own/28587/.

法院滥用公共秩序理由的裁决,俄罗斯最高法院在实施司法监督时也是从宽掌握,导致公共秩序成为俄罗斯拒绝承认和执行外国仲裁裁决的法宝,可以说无往而不利!

综上可以看出,俄罗斯仲裁制度的改革,以及其仲裁实践所体现出来的特殊性,都是俄罗斯为了维护其国家利益和保护本国企业利益而采取的应对措施。尽管俄罗斯法院体系不支持仲裁,但由于俄罗斯是《纽约公约》的成员国,依然要遵守世界公认的仲裁基本原则,所以在目前俄罗斯遭受全面制裁的世界局势中,同时考虑到俄罗斯法院体系的公正性和不确定性,仲裁依然是解决与俄罗斯相关的商事争议的首选方式。

(杨意茹　审校)

蒙古国篇[*]

一、介绍

从早期的蒙古国开始,游牧民族和牧民之间关于财产的纠纷都是在总督办公室解决的,彼时不称作法院,而是把案件提交给当地一位精明、诚实、受人尊敬的长老,由他来辨明是非。

蒙古国自1929年起奠定了设立仲裁机构的法律基础;1930年,经济理事会下设立仲裁委员会;1940年,成立国家仲裁处;1960年,成立对外贸易仲裁处。

在20世纪30—40年代,仲裁以传统模式发展,并迈出了允许自由谈判和选择仲裁员的第一步。当时,政府辖下的经济理事会发挥了适当的作用。因此,仲裁发展的这一阶段值得特别关注。

在1940—1990年期间,国家仲裁机构解决了政府与工业部门、工会、合作社、生产和服务组织之间因合同而产生的纠纷,这与其他国家

---

[*] 本篇作者为乌英格,蒙古国国际仲裁中心仲裁员。

解决贸易和商业纠纷的专门法院制度类似。在社会主义制度下，承认国家和集体财产，并以统一的政策和计划管理国家的经济和商业活动，国家仲裁机构在部长会议或政府的直接监督下工作是适当的。

1982年，仲裁机构划归最高法院管理，1987年后不久，仲裁院成为部长会议下的国家仲裁处。根据1989年的《蒙古国仲裁机构法》，国家仲裁处曾被划归司法部和仲裁部管辖一段时间，这表明国家仲裁处是专门解决行业和企业之间的纠纷的专门商事法庭。当时还没有独立的仲裁制度。

可以从1960年成立的对外贸易仲裁委员会来了解相对独立的仲裁制度。

2003年的《蒙古国仲裁法》为建立独立、自由的仲裁制度奠定了法律基础，该法详细规定了设立常设仲裁机构、遴选临时仲裁员的条件。

今天，仲裁仍然根据双方的协议解决与蒙古国的贸易、投资和商业活动等经济或非物质价值/财富相关的任何合同产生的争议，具有管理和组织仲裁活动职能的常设仲裁机构已在蒙古国建立，并继续稳定运行。因此，应该说蒙古国政府一贯支持的正确的争议解决方法的政策、法律框架以及仲裁发展的国际趋势对独立的国内仲裁制度的形成产生了积极的影响。

可以说，蒙古国的仲裁组织形成的外部条件直接受到了外国仲裁经验的影响，其中包括俄罗斯的立法理念和法律经验。

根据1924年《苏联仲裁委员会规则》，仲裁委员会负责处理大型工业集团和公司之间的民事纠纷；最高人民经济委员会下设仲裁委员会，处理商业组织之间的纠纷。

苏联于1931年废除这些委员会，成立了仲裁委员会，直至今日，俄罗斯联邦仍然保留着这个处理贸易争端和经济实体相关事务的国家仲裁组织制度。

1940年11月12日，蒙古国部长会议第43次会议解决了蒙古国工业部门之间的财产纠纷，制定了国家仲裁规则14条，国家财产争议解决仲裁办公室批准并执行了解决仲裁案件规则，该规则共四章，47

条,这一规则也成为处理仲裁纠纷的第一部规则。

　　根据这些规则和条例,蒙古国官方部门和工业部门之间发生的财产纠纷,由部长会议下的国家仲裁解决,而部长会议制定了选择国家仲裁的程序。

　　蒙古国于 1962 年加入经济互助委员会。1972 年 5 月,在莫斯科通过了《以仲裁解决经济互助委员会成员国之间由经济和科学技术合作关系引起的民法纠纷公约》(以下简称《莫斯科公约》),该公约由附属于各成员国的外贸仲裁组织执行。

　　1972 年,保加利亚共和国、匈牙利共和国、德意志民主共和国、越南人民共和国、波兰人民共和国、罗马尼亚社会主义共和国和苏维埃社会主义捷克斯洛伐克政府共同签订了《莫斯科公约》。经济互助委员会的成员国同意,政府间产生的争端由该公约解决,公约的原则和想法将根据每个国家的特点加以适用。在该公约缔约国间进行经济、科学和技术合作的过程中,各组织之间因合同和其他民事权利关系所产生的争端通过仲裁解决。1975 年 2 月 26 日,蒙古国商会会长批准了《对外贸易仲裁委员会程序规定》,作为对《莫斯科公约》和当时国际公认的国际法的指导。

　　同时,国内组织和它们之间的合同纠纷由国家仲裁办公室解决。

　　蒙古国部长会议于 1960 年 7 月 2 日批准第 295/194 号决议,批准商会对外贸易仲裁委员会第 3 条,并指示于 1960 年批准该规则。但是直至 1962 年,商会才采用对外贸易仲裁委员会的规则。

　　对外贸易仲裁委员会解决蒙古国的对外贸易协会和其他被授权的组织在履行与对外贸易协会、公司、企业与该国商会签订的协议、合同的过程中发生的重大争议。对外贸易仲裁委员会常常挑选具有经济和法律知识的人来裁决案件。

　　1975 年 2 月 26 日,蒙古国商会领导人会议通过了蒙古国商会对外贸易仲裁委员会处理案件的程序的相关规定。仲裁委员会设主任、副主任各 1 名,仲裁员 15 名,秘书 1 名,并按规定聘用高学历、高素质人员。

　　程序规定,仲裁案件应当根据当事人约定的文件、资料进行审查,根据提交的书面材料进行裁决,对当事人提出请求或者拒绝的理由所引用的情况进行反驳,并按照决策机构确定的方式提供原件或者经核验的副本,以决策机构确定的方式审查证据,建立并实施由仲裁员凭自由心证对证据进行评估的程序。此外,对决策、决策内容、决策通知、决策执行都进行了规范。

仲裁员的决定是终局的,具有约束力。仲裁员自愿作出决定。非自愿的、不服从的决定由法律强制执行。当时还没有法院介入仲裁程序的概念。商会对外贸易仲裁委员会已成立并开展活动,负责审查国际合同关系引起的争议。

为了在法制改革的框架内完善仲裁机构的运作、结构和组织,仲裁从法院分离出来,并整合到一个法律部门,一个新的"司法和仲裁部"成立了。在司法和仲裁部成立之前,蒙古国人民代表大会于1989年6月24日首次批准了《蒙古国仲裁组织法》。

蒙古国的仲裁机构曾多次进行这样的结构性变革。目前的蒙古国国际仲裁中心(Mongolian International Arbitration Centre,MIAC)隶属于蒙古国国际与国家仲裁中心(Mongolian International and National Arbitration Centre,MINAC),自1960年开始运作,是国际公认的蒙古国常设仲裁机构。该仲裁机构在蒙古国的21个省设有分支机构,是亚太仲裁协会的成员,并与20多个国际仲裁机构合作。该仲裁机构由51名本国仲裁员和11名外籍仲裁员(来自中国、俄罗斯、德国、日本、波兰)组成,共计62名法律、经济、金融、矿业等方面的专家。

蒙古国国际仲裁中心不仅通过仲裁处理经济及商业相关协议和交易引起的争议,而且还在蒙古国国内推动和发展仲裁活动,开展培训和研究,提供法律咨询,出版与正在进行的仲裁业务相关的书籍和杂志。

二、现代蒙古国仲裁法与法律规制解决

仲裁的概念在蒙古国并不是新生事物。在苏联体系制度下,蒙古国曾于1960年成立了第一个仲裁法庭,以解决对外贸易争端。然而,商事仲裁直到21世纪初才以一种针对商业的替代性争议解决方法的

现代形式发展起来。

在蒙古国,《蒙古国仲裁组织法》和《蒙古国对外贸易仲裁法》等法律规定了关于仲裁的制度。2003年,蒙古国根据《联合国国际贸易法委员会国际商事仲裁示范法》(以下简称《示范法》)制定的《蒙古国仲裁法》获得通过。

《蒙古国仲裁法》分别于2007年8月3日、2011年2月10日、2012年5月22日进行了修订,但没有体现出实质性的变化。

作为政府改善商业和投资法律基础设施计划的一部分,蒙古国修订了《蒙古国仲裁法》,自2017年2月27日生效。该法也被称为"修订的《蒙古国仲裁法》"。修订的《蒙古国仲裁法》以2006年《示范法》为基础,除少数例外情况外,承认蒙古国为示范法管辖区。此外,修订的《蒙古国仲裁法》还增加了一些附加条款。

随着MIAC案件量的稳步增加,蒙古国首都乌兰巴托的民事上诉法院正在审查大量寻求法院协助和干预仲裁程序的申请。民事上诉法院最近裁判的案件有助于阐明法院对仲裁的一般立场和对修订的《蒙古国仲裁法》某些条款的解释,特别是关于撤销仲裁裁决的理由。

三、修订后的仲裁法

2003年的《蒙古国仲裁法》松散地以最初的1985年《示范法》为基础,没有充分解决仲裁的一些重要问题,从而造成了仲裁程序与法院之间关系的不确定性。因此,修订的《蒙古国仲裁法》参照2006年《示范法》,严格遵循其措辞,以确保表述更加清晰,并确保仲裁的法律框架完整。

下文将讨论修订的《蒙古国仲裁法》的主要变化特点。

(一)国际仲裁与国内仲裁的区别

修订的《蒙古国仲裁法》既适用于国际仲裁,也适用于国内仲裁,并对每一种仲裁程序规定了实质上相似的处理措施。根据《示范法》

的规定,国际仲裁被定义为符合以下条件的仲裁:

(1)仲裁协议订立时,当事人的营业地在不同国家的;

(2)当事人的营业地与仲裁地不同,根据仲裁协议确定的;

(3)商事关系中实质性义务的履行地或者与争议事项有最密切联系地与当事人的营业地不同的;

(4)当事人明确约定仲裁协议的标的物涉及一个及以上国家的。

根据修订的《蒙古国仲裁法》的规定,不属于上述定义范围的仲裁被视为国内仲裁。

虽然这两种仲裁的原则、标准和实质要求相同,但修订的《蒙古国仲裁法》对国际和国内仲裁的程序要求略有不同。例如,就国际仲裁而言,当事人可以在收到仲裁裁决书之日起90天内向法院提出撤销仲裁裁决的申请;而对于国内仲裁,这一时限缩短至30天。

此外,在国际仲裁中,民事上诉法院履行与仲裁有关的大多数法院职能,包括对仲裁员的质疑和撤销仲裁裁决的所有申请。法院的这种专属管辖权旨在促进司法部门在国际仲裁方面的司法知识的发展。

民事上诉法院最近判决的案件有助于阐明法院对仲裁的一般立场和对修订的《蒙古国仲裁法》某些条款的解释,特别是关于撤销仲裁裁决的理由的解释。

(二)可仲裁性

修订的《蒙古国仲裁法》解决的关键问题之一是蒙古国法律下可通过仲裁解决的争议范围。可通过仲裁解决的争议范围经"除非该争议属于法院的专属管辖,否则仲裁协议中提及的任何争议均可仲裁"的规定得到扩大。同时,修订的《蒙古国仲裁法》的颁布还伴随着对若干部门法规进行的修订,其中包括《蒙古国证券市场法》《蒙古国石油法》和《蒙古国特许法》等法律的修正案。这些修正案在各自的法律中明确增加仲裁作为一种可能的争议解决机制,从而限制了根据国内立法必须提交法院专属管辖的案件数量。

以下简要概述根据蒙古国法律和修订的《蒙古国仲裁法》关于消

费者和破产纠纷的具体规定不可仲裁的事项。

1. 属于蒙古国专属管辖的事项

根据《蒙古国民事诉讼法》的规定,下列事项属于蒙古国法院的专属管辖权,因此不可仲裁:

(1) 与蒙古国境内不动产的所有权、占有权和使用权有关的纠纷;

(2) 与根据蒙古国法律设立的法人实体的重组或清算有关的争议,以及由法人实体、其分支机构或代表处作出的决议或决定引起的争议;

(3) 关于蒙古国法院和其他公共行政机关作出的登记有效性的争议;

(4) 与蒙古国行政机关对专利、商标和其他知识产权(IP)权利的注册有效性有关的争议,以及与 IP 权利注册申请有关的争议;

(5) 与蒙古国法院判决执行有关的争议或与执行请求有关的争议。

此外,蒙古国于 1995 年成为《纽约公约》的签署国,并根据《关于互惠和商业保留的声明》批准了该公约。

适用后者是因为根据蒙古国法律,非商业性质的问题,如人的地位和婚姻纠纷,完全属于法院的专属管辖范围。此外,根据《蒙古国劳动法》的规定,法院对涉及工会(集体纠纷)和个别雇员的劳资纠纷具有最终和专属管辖权。

2. 消费者纠纷

修订的《蒙古国仲裁法》明确承认消费者纠纷的可仲裁性,对涉及消费者权益争议的仲裁未作实质性限制。但是,它确实对消费者仲裁协议提出了形式上的要求。为了保护一般条款中包含了仲裁条款的标准合同中的消费者当事人,仲裁协议只有在纠纷发生后由当事人以书面形式订立,并载明仲裁地点的情况下才有效。

3. 破产

修订的《蒙古国仲裁法》对破产问题的可仲裁性采取了较为宽松的态度。如果符合下列所有条件,无论破产问题是否为核心问题,法院均可以将涉及破产问题的所有争议提交仲裁裁定:

(1) 就该争议存在仲裁协议;

(2) 破产程序当事人在破产程序开始前已订立仲裁协议;

(3)管理人或受托人未拒绝包含仲裁协议的合同。

4. 有限的法院介入

修订的《蒙古国仲裁法》广受好评的其中一个关键方面是法院对仲裁程序的干预范围仅限于其明确规定的情形,而这些情形主要是为了支持仲裁的正常运作。根据《示范法》的规定,仲裁当事人和/或仲裁庭可在以下方面寻求法院协助:

(1)临时措施的准予和执行;
(2)选定仲裁员;
(3)对仲裁员的质疑和终止仲裁员的职务;
(4)取证;
(5)对维持管辖权的仲裁裁决提出异议;
(6)撤销仲裁裁决;
(7)裁决的承认和执行。

5. 仲裁员的权力

根据修订的《蒙古国仲裁法》的规定,仲裁庭有权根据国际公认的"Kompetenz-Kompetenz"原则,就案件的管辖权,包括仲裁协议的效力作出裁决。根据2006年对《示范法》所作的修订,仲裁庭拥有使用临时措施和执行初步命令的广泛权力。

在费用成本责任的分摊方面,之前的2003年《蒙古国仲裁法》规定了仲裁庭按比例分摊成本的方法,即当事人根据其在案件上的实际胜诉比例承担费用,而这些费用不包括法律代理费用。相比之下,修订的《蒙古国仲裁法》明确规定除非当事人另有约定,否则代理费将纳入仲裁费用,仲裁费用由仲裁庭自行决定,由仲裁庭决定由当事人支付的仲裁费用的比例和金额。

6. 保密性

修订的《蒙古国仲裁法》明确规定,除非当事人另有约定,当事人、仲裁庭和仲裁机构对仲裁程序中交换的所有仲裁裁决、裁定和资料负有保密义务。这种保密义务有三种例外情况:

(1)根据法律要求须强制披露的;
(2)出于保护或执行权利的需要而披露的;

(3) 在仲裁程序中为撤销或者执行仲裁裁决而披露的。

7. 撤销、拒绝承认和执行裁决的理由

修订的《蒙古国仲裁法》所规定的撤销仲裁裁决并拒绝承认和执行其在蒙古国境内仲裁裁决的理由,严格反映了《示范法》第 34 条和第 36 条所列举的理由。包括:

(1) 由于一方当事人无行为能力而缺乏有效的仲裁协议,或仲裁协议在其所适用的法律下无效,且蒙古国法律未作任何说明;

(2) 违反正当程序,未能将指定仲裁员或仲裁程序的适当通知送达另一方,或该方因其他原因无法陈述其案件;

(3) 超出仲裁庭的权限,即裁决所涉及的争议不在提交仲裁申请的范围内,或该裁决包含了对提交仲裁申请范围之外的事项的决定;

(4) 仲裁庭的组成或仲裁程序不合规,包括仲裁庭的组成或仲裁程序不符合当事人的协议约定,除非该协议与修订的《蒙古国仲裁法》的强制性规定相冲突,或者没有达成该协议;

(5) 关于拒绝承认或执行的裁决,仅该裁决尚未对当事人产生约束力,或已被作出该裁决的国家或该裁决所在国的法院撤销或中止;

(6) 法院认为争议事项根据蒙古国法律不能通过仲裁解决,或裁决与蒙古国公共政策相冲突。

对于国际仲裁而言,民事上诉法院是接受所有撤销裁决申请的指定法院。出于成本和时间效率的考虑,对法院的撤销裁决没有进一步的上诉。

关于承认和执行仲裁裁决,该申请必须向对被申请人或被申请人的资产有管辖权的一审法院提出。

由此可见,修订的《蒙古国仲裁法》完全符合《示范法》的规定。

结语

在联合国国际贸易法委员会的网站上,蒙古国被登记在承认和纳入《示范法》的国家名单中。但是,在内容上还需要对修订的《蒙古国仲裁法》的一些条款和规定进行审查,正确适用与仲裁相关的蒙古国法律术语,并统一标准。

(付慈 审校)

朝鲜篇
——简述《朝鲜涉外经济仲裁法》及对朝鲜仲裁管辖权的思考*

朝鲜民主主义人民共和国(以下简称朝鲜)于1948年9月9日宣告成立。此后很长一段时间内,由于国际环境及其特有的政治经济体系,朝鲜并没有成功地建立起本国的良好经济结构,对外经济关系具有依赖性和局限性。[①]1991年,苏联解体导致朝鲜失去了煤矿、石油和钢铁的供应,朝鲜的经济遭到了重创。随着苏联解体和东欧剧变,朝鲜的贸易也受到了巨大的冲击,在巨大的贸易冲击下,朝鲜并没有成功地进行经济关系的再调整,工业体系几乎全面崩盘。同时,失去工业投入的农业产出也直线下降,致使传统的计划经济体制的运作逐渐困难,朝鲜彻底陷入了困境。因此,朝鲜开始对内进行经济体制改革,对外进行开放,制定了许多吸引外商投资、促进经济贸易发展的政策。自20世纪90年代起,朝鲜相继出台了数十部法律法规,如《朝鲜外国人投资法》《朝鲜合营法》《朝鲜合作法》《朝鲜外国人企业法》《朝鲜外国投资银行法》《朝鲜外国投资企业会计法》《朝鲜外国人投资企业劳动法》《朝鲜外国人投资企业和外国人税法》《朝鲜外国人投资企业破产法》等。

为了更好地吸引外资进入朝鲜,1995年(朝鲜主体84年)2月22日,朝鲜最高人民会议常设会议第52号决定通过了《朝鲜对外经济合同法》,又分别于1999年(朝鲜主体88年)2月26日、2008年(朝鲜主体97年)8月19日,由朝鲜最高人民会议常设委员会政令进行了修正补充。1999年(朝鲜主体88年)7月21日,朝鲜最高人民会

---

* 本篇作者为金瑛,北京盈科(沈阳)律师事务所合伙人。
① 参见全丽阳:《简述朝鲜国际私法及其对本国经济的影响》,载《东北亚经济研究》2018年第3期。

议常设委员会第875号政令通过了《朝鲜涉外经济仲裁法》,又分别于2008年(朝鲜主体97年)7月29日、2014年(朝鲜主体103年)7月23日,由朝鲜最高人民会议常设委员会进行了修正补充。至此,朝鲜建立了一个与世界各国接轨的外商投资纠纷解决机制,即涉外经济仲裁制度,这对于外商投资的保护无疑是至关重要的。本篇将简述《朝鲜涉外经济仲裁法》的主要内容,对比与国际惯例及我国商事仲裁制度的不同之处,并探讨其存在的一些问题及未来可能的修改方向。

一、立法背景

自1992年制定《朝鲜外国人投资法》以来,朝鲜就一直加快制定与外商投资相关的一系列法律的进程,但从吸引外资的成效角度来讲,并没有收到显著的效果。[1]当然,这与朝鲜特有的经济体制密切相关,但其所处的复杂的国际关系与相对闭塞的人文环境使得外国投资者不敢轻易进入,尤其是不完善的外国人投资相关法律体系更无法保障外国投资者的权益,很难获得外国投资者的信赖,导致外国投资者在选择对外投资时,比起陌生又闭塞的朝鲜,更容易选择东南亚等对外国投资者来说更加"值得信赖"的国家。因此,朝鲜必须建立与国际接轨的外商投资纠纷解决体制。而由于朝鲜特殊的经济体制,国内商事纠纷案件并不普遍,采取民事诉讼方式解决外商投资纠纷也并不符合国情,因此仲裁这种国际上被普遍接受的商事纠纷解决机制便成了首选。从制定《朝鲜涉外经济仲裁法》即能够看出,朝鲜已经充分意识到,必须完善外国投资者在朝鲜进行商业活动的纠纷解决机制,才能解决外国投资者对陌生法律环境的顾虑。

---

[1] 参见崔东日、吴东镐:《朝鲜对外商投资的法律保护——以制度考察为中心》,载《延边大学学报(社会科学版)》2013年第2期。

二、主要内容

《朝鲜涉外经济仲裁法》共七章,由65个条文组成,下面将以章为单位分别介绍《朝鲜涉外经济仲裁法》的内容。

(一) 涉外经济仲裁法的基本

《朝鲜涉外经济仲裁法》第一章为涉外经济仲裁法的基本。

其中,该法第3条规定了仲裁委员会、涉外经济仲裁的特点。明确规定涉外经济纠纷中,进行涉外贸易、投资、服务的过程中发生的纠纷由朝鲜国际贸易仲裁委员会审理;海事经济活动过程中发生的纠纷,由朝鲜海事仲裁委员会审理;有关计算机软件的纠纷,由朝鲜计算机软件仲裁委员会审理。涉外经济仲裁不设管辖地区和审级,以仲裁部作出的裁决为最终决定。

该法第4条规定了涉外经济仲裁的管辖范围,明确有两种纠纷可以用涉外经济仲裁程序来解决:第一,有涉外因素且当事人之间有仲裁协议的对外经济活动过程中发生的纠纷;第二,有权的国家机关委托仲裁委员会用涉外经济仲裁程序解决的纠纷。与国际上普遍的商事仲裁不同,朝鲜的国际仲裁还增加了一类案件的管辖权,即有权的国家机关委托仲裁委员会用涉外经济仲裁程序解决的纠纷。这类案件通常情况下并不存在当事双方的仲裁协议,而是纠纷被诉至当地法院以后,由当地法院移交的案件。这种情况下,仲裁委员会行使的管辖权就与国际通行的仲裁管辖权不同,本篇将在下一部分具体论述。

该法第8条对提出管辖异议的权利及其效力作出了规定,即当事人明知正在进行根据仲裁协议可能不符合该法规定的仲裁程序,而未立即或在指定期限内提出异议,仲裁程序继续进行的,视为当事人放弃提出异议的权利。这就意味着,朝鲜的国际仲裁程序区别于国际通行的商事仲裁程序,是存在应诉管辖的,即使不存在仲裁协议,只要被申请人未提出管辖异议,就视为放弃提出异议的权利。

根据该法第10条和第11条的规定,朝鲜保障仲裁部审理案件中的自主性,不得干涉仲裁部审理案件;尊重国际法和国际惯例,并同国际机构、外国开展涉外仲裁的合作和交流。虽然上述两个规定与国际惯例有所不同,但从此处规定能够看出,朝鲜依然在向国际社会表达其愿意开放的姿态以及对国际贸易仲裁国际化的认同。

(二)仲裁协议

《朝鲜涉外经济仲裁法》第二章为仲裁协议。

其中第12条、第13条规定仲裁协议需要以书面形式达成,此部分内容与我国仲裁法规定类似。但与我国仲裁法的规定不同的是,该法规定,虽没有明确的书面仲裁协议,但有其他书面证据能够证明双方以口头或行动等方式达成仲裁协议的,也可认定为达成仲裁协议。

与前述第8条应诉管辖的规定相对应,第14条规定,如当事人之间未达成书面仲裁协议,当事人一方请求仲裁而对方当事人未反对,或未提出抗辩的,也可以认定为达成仲裁协议。

第15条规定,仲裁协议如超出法定仲裁受理范围,或当事人在达成仲裁协议时无行为能力,或仲裁协议是受胁迫达成的,仲裁协议无效。

此外,第16条还规定,在不违反仲裁协议的前提下,当事人可以向仲裁委员会、仲裁部或法院等机关申请财产保全措施。

(三)仲裁部

《朝鲜涉外经济仲裁法》第三章为关于仲裁部,即仲裁庭的规定。根据该法规定,仲裁部的组成人数可以由当事人商定,没有协议时则为1人或3人。

第21条规定了选定仲裁员的程序,由3名仲裁员组成仲裁部,当事人各自选定1名仲裁员后,由被选定的仲裁员共同选定首席仲裁员。如当事人未选定仲裁员,或两名仲裁员未能选定首席仲裁员,则由仲裁委员会指定。由1名仲裁员组成仲裁部的情况下,当事人如未能达成一致意见,则可根据一方当事人的要求,由仲裁委员会指定。这种情况下,当事人不可以对仲裁庭组成人员提出异议。可以说,在由 2 名被选定的仲裁员共同指定首席仲裁员这个规定上，在双方对首席仲裁员无法达成一致意见时，朝鲜要比我国大多数仲裁委员会由仲裁委员会主任指定的惯常做法更加与时俱进。但对独任仲裁员提出异议的权利的限制在相当大的程度上又限制了当事人在选定仲裁员的程序中的意思自治，不得不说是非常矛盾的。

第 25 条到第 27 条则规定了关于仲裁员回避的内容。值得注意的是，提出回避申请的时间贯穿整个仲裁审理程序，自获知回避事由之日起 10 日内提交申请即可。另外，仲裁部在作出不予回避的情况下，申请回避一方还可以向仲裁委员会再次提出回避申请。

第 28 条至第 30 条为仲裁部的权利、对仲裁部审理范围的异议及异议的处理。第 31 条、第 32 条则是关于临时措施的申请和解除。

(四) 仲裁程序

《朝鲜涉外经济仲裁法》第四章为仲裁程序。

第 33 条明确了当事人在该法规定的仲裁程序中享有同等的地位，有充分陈述自己主张的权利。

与国际通行的仲裁程序相似，根据《朝鲜涉外经济仲裁法》第四章的规定，当事人可以对仲裁程序、仲裁场所、仲裁语言、鉴定人及证人的参与等达成协议。仲裁委员会和仲裁部也应按照当事人之间达成的协议进行相关的仲裁程序。但是笔者认为，此处规定的"仲裁场所"并不能当然地理解为"仲裁地"，根据第 35 条第 2 款"没有当事人之间的协议时，仲裁部可以根据当事人的便利及解决案件的整体情况指定仲裁场所"的表述，笔者更倾向于将此处"仲裁场所"的含义理解为"开庭地"。

不得不说，《朝鲜涉外经济仲裁法》赋予仲裁部在仲裁程序中极大的权利。如上文所述，仲裁部不仅有权力决定仲裁协议是否有效，也可以对仲裁员的回避问题作出决定。

在第 37 条中，还规定了在当事人未对仲裁语言达成协议时，由仲裁部决定仲裁语言；只有在仲裁部没有决定时，才以朝鲜语进行仲裁。

另外，第 38 条还规定，仲裁部如果认为当事人变更或补充仲裁请求的内容或者抗辩的内容不合理,可能导致延迟审理案件,可以不予考虑。此外,仲裁部还可以通过与当事人进行协商,决定口头审理或书面审理。此处,笔者认为所谓的"口头审理"和"书面审理"的含义并非字面意思,而是指开庭或不开庭审理。

第 39 条还赋予仲裁部在仲裁申请人与被申请人中的某一方无正当理由而未参加仲裁或未提交证据时,直接依照提交的证据受理案件并予以裁决的权利;反之,如当事人另有协商或仲裁庭认为其有正当理由,也可以不按照上述规定予以裁决。

在调查取证方面,第 42 条还规定,仲裁部可以根据当事人的申请或在认为有必要时,进行调查取证,或委托相关机关进行调查取证。且当事人也可以根据仲裁部的授权,进行委托调查取证。

仲裁的被申请人可以依据第 44 条的规定,在仲裁审理结束之前针对申请人的请求提出与仲裁相关的反请求,但仲裁部如认为反请求可能导致迟延审理,也可以不受理反请求。

(五)裁决

《朝鲜涉外经济仲裁法》第五章为仲裁程序。

第 45 条"裁决的准据法由当事人达成协议决定,当事人未对裁决的准据法达成一致时,仲裁部应适用与纠纷案件有最密切联系并认为最可行的法律。此时,还应当考虑合同条件和国际惯例予以决定或裁决"的规定是 2014 年修改后的《朝鲜涉外经济仲裁法》新增的内容。在此次修改前,《朝鲜涉外经济仲裁法》对审理涉外仲裁案件的准据法并没有明确[①],2008 年修正的《朝鲜对外经济合同法》第 42 条规定,"依照当事人的协议可以向第三国仲裁机关提请解决"[②],这种看似可以对仲裁机构、仲裁地进行约定的内容,与在朝鲜进行涉外仲裁适用的准据法并没有直接关系。通过这次对于准据法条款的增加,尤其是

---

① 参见崔东日、吴东镐:《朝鲜对外商投资的法律保护——以制度考察为中心》,载《延边大学学报(社会科学版)》2013 年第 2 期。

② 《朝鲜对外经济合同法》第 42 条规定:"有关合同的意见分歧以协商的方法求得解决。在以协商的方法未能解决时,依照共和国规定的仲裁秩序加以解决。依照当事人的协议可以向第三国仲裁机关提请解决。"

对国际惯例的适用,也可以看出朝鲜在涉外仲裁领域与国际社会慢慢接轨的期待。

第46条规定了仲裁部的议事方法。仲裁裁决由3名仲裁员组成的仲裁部应按照多数仲裁员的意见作出,如有当事人的协议或仲裁部成员的协议,则由首席仲裁员来确定议事方法。

第47条和第48条则规定了当事人在仲裁进行过程中随时可以和解、调解。和解决定和调解决定与仲裁裁决书具有同等的效力。

第49条至第51条规定了裁决书必须以书面形式作出,且由仲裁员签字。由3名仲裁员组成仲裁部的,需要有多数仲裁员的签字方可作出裁决书。裁决书应当写明裁决所依据的事由和裁决书的作出日期和裁决场所等内容。

除作出仲裁裁决之外,仲裁部可在仲裁申请人申请撤回仲裁申请时、仲裁申请人与被申请人达成仲裁程序终结的协议时、仲裁部认为没有必要继续仲裁程序或者无法继续仲裁程序时,决定终结仲裁程序。但是在仲裁申请人申请撤销仲裁申请,而被申请人不同意撤销时,如仲裁部认为继续仲裁程序并作出最终裁判符合被申请人的合法利益,则仲裁部不应终结仲裁程序。

第53条和第54条还规定了仲裁部可以在仲裁裁决书作出之后对计算错误及书写错误进行更正,或对遗漏的裁决进行补充裁决。另外,还赋予当事人就有疑问的部分向仲裁部申请解释的权利。

(六)裁决的效力及撤销申请

《朝鲜涉外经济仲裁法》第六章是关于仲裁裁决书的效力与撤销仲裁裁决的内容。

本章规定了仲裁裁决自裁决书作出之日起生效。与国际惯例一样,对仲裁裁决存在异议的当事人可以向法院申请撤销仲裁裁决。但是,与我国仲裁法中向仲裁委员会所在地中级人民法院申请撤销仲裁裁决的规定不同,《朝鲜涉外经济仲裁法》并没有具体规定向哪个地方、哪一级别的法院申请撤销仲裁裁决,在实践中可能还存在不明确之处。申请撤销仲裁裁决的期限为自当事人收到仲裁裁决书、更正书、解释书或补充裁决书之日起2个月。与我国仲裁法中一方当事人申请执行仲裁裁决,而另一方当事人申请撤销裁决的,人民法院应当裁定中止执行,待裁定是否撤销仲裁裁决后,根据裁定恢复执行或终结执行的规定不同,《朝鲜涉外经济仲裁法》则规定,法院对仲裁裁决作出予以执行的决定后,当事人不得申请撤销仲裁裁决。在笔者曾经代理的一起案件中,就看到过平壤市法院作出予以执行的判定书。也就是说,朝鲜法院在受理申请执行仲裁裁决的案件时,首先需要审查仲裁裁决书是否符合予以执行的条件,很显然,这与国际惯例并不一样,这在第七章第62条中也再次印证。该条规定,法院或者有关机关自收到申请执行裁决文件之日起30日内审核申请文件,最终以判定或决定的形式予以执行。

与国际惯例不一样的是,《朝鲜涉外经济仲裁法》中申请撤销仲裁裁决的事由也颇具特色。第一,当事人在签订仲裁协议时,根据准据法的规定为无行为能力人的;第二,根据当事人协议的约定或当事人未达成协议时根据朝鲜法律规定,仲裁协议无效的;第三,当事人在选定仲裁员的程序或其他仲裁程序中未得到适当通知,或因不得已的事由无法进行抗辩的;第四,裁决内容不符合或超出仲裁协议范围的;第五,仲裁部的组成或仲裁程序,不符合该法规定的有效仲裁协议的条件的,或达成仲裁协议时不符合该法规定的。由于《朝鲜涉外经济仲裁法》与国际惯例最大的不同是,即使没有当事人之间的仲裁协议,也可以受理涉外仲裁案件,因此申请撤销仲裁裁决的事由也随之变更。而第二项"根据朝鲜法律规定,仲裁协议无效"的规定,对于外国投资者来说,更是因为对朝鲜相关法律规定的不熟悉,很难产生信任感。因此,除仲裁相关法律外,其他朝鲜法律的对外公开也是非常必要的。

(七)裁决的执行

《朝鲜涉外经济仲裁法》第七章不仅规定了对朝鲜本国仲裁裁决的执行程序,还覆盖了对外国仲裁裁决的承认与执行。与我国的做法不同的是,当事人可以直接或通过仲裁委员会向法院或其他有关机关申请执行仲裁裁决。法院或其他机关收到申请后还需要审核,最终以判决、裁定的形式确认予以执行。如可供执行财产在朝鲜国境外,也可以向该国相应的审判机关申请执行裁决书。朝鲜的司法机关也可以根据本国相关法律规定承认和执行外国仲裁部作出的仲裁裁决书,但是在下列情形下可以不予承认和执行外国仲裁裁决:第一,根据准据法的规定,当事人签订仲裁协议时为无行为能力人,或根据当事人指定的法律或仲裁审理国家的法律,仲裁协议无效的;第二,当事人在选定仲裁员的程序或其他仲裁程序中未得到适当通知,或因不得已的事由无法进行抗辩的;第三,裁决内容不符合或超出仲裁协议范围的;第四,仲裁部的组成或仲裁程序不符合仲裁协议或仲裁审理国家相关法律规定的;第五,裁决书未对当事人生效,或仲裁审理国家的审判机关根据该国法律认定撤销或不予执行的;第六,仲裁的纠纷根据仲裁审理国家法律规定,为不可仲裁的纠纷的;第七,执行仲裁裁决会对朝鲜国家主权、安全、社会秩序造成损害的。可以看出,由于《朝鲜涉外经济仲裁法》第4条规定的以涉外仲裁程序解决的纠纷的范围,不仅包括当事人之间存在仲裁协议的涉外经济活动纠纷,还包括有权的国家机关委托仲裁委员会以涉外经济仲裁程序解决的纠纷,因此后续撤销仲裁裁决的规定及不予承认外国仲裁裁决的规定中也作了相应修改。与国际惯例不同,《朝鲜涉外经济仲裁法》没有对"当事人之间没有仲裁协议或事后未达成仲裁协议"的情况作出限制,仅要求对"达成仲裁协议时当事人是否具有民事行为能力"作出审查。

三、对于朝鲜仲裁管辖权的思考

如上文所述,对于外国投资者来说,《朝鲜涉外经济仲裁法》中存在的最大问题即为,朝鲜的仲裁还包含当事人之间不存在仲裁协议,而有权力的国家机关委托仲裁的案件。2015年朝鲜国际贸易仲裁委员会也相应地颁布了新版《仲裁规则》。其中,第3条第6款相应地增加了"仲裁委员会审理并解决有权力的国家机关指定仲裁委员会以涉外经济仲裁程序解决的纠纷"的规定。

与世界上大部分国家关于国际仲裁的通行做法不同,朝鲜的仲裁显然被赋予更多的政府强制性的色彩。从上述法律规定来看,可以理解为朝鲜的贸易仲裁委员会有权管辖两类案件:一类是国际上通常所理解的仲裁管辖案件,即当事人之间协议选择由朝鲜国际仲裁机构管辖的涉外经济纠纷案件;另一类则是有权力的国家机关认为交由仲裁机构审理更为适当而移交给仲裁机构的案件。其中第一类案件与我国,以及其他大部分国家的国际仲裁概念基本一致,无须赘述。但是与国际上通行做法非常不同的第二类案件,其性质到底是仲裁还是判决,非常值得讨论。

仲裁作为当今世界上最为普遍的一种非诉讼争议解决方式,在解决商事纠纷,尤其是国际商事纠纷领域发挥着积极的重要作用。但似乎各国法律规定与仲裁规则都没有给仲裁一个明确的定义。例如,《联合国国际贸易法委员会国际商事仲裁示范法》(以下简称《示范法》)第一章"总则"中,第 2 条"定义及解释规则":"在本法中:(a)'仲裁'是指无论是否由常设仲裁机构进行的任何仲裁……";第二章"仲裁协议"备选案文一第 7 条"仲裁协议的定义和形式":"(1)'仲裁协议'是指当事人同意将他们之间一项确定的契约性或非契约性的法律关系中已经发生或可能发生的一切争议或某些争议交付仲裁的协议。仲裁协议可以采取合同中的仲裁条款形式或单独的协议形式……";第二章"仲裁协议"备选案文二第 7 条"仲裁协议的定义和形式":"'仲裁协议'是指当事人同意将其之间一项确定的契约性或非契约性的法律关系中已经发生或可能发生的一切争议或某些争议交付仲裁的协议"。我国《仲裁法》第 2 条规定:"平等主体的公民、法人和其他组织之间发生的合同纠纷和其他财产权益纠纷,可以仲裁。"对于"仲裁"一词,国际上最普遍接受的一种观点是美国学者加里·B.博恩在《国际仲裁:法律与实践》一书中写到的,"当事人合意将争议提交给由双方选择的,或双方指定的非政府裁决机构,并由其遵循中立的、给予任一方陈述案情机会的审裁程序,作出具有约束力的裁决的程序"。

从上述对仲裁和仲裁协议的定义来看,仲裁具有四个方面的特征:一是当事人的合意;二是仲裁解决纠纷的机构是非政府裁决机构;三是中立的审裁程序;四是具有约束力的裁决。

因此,仲裁管辖权与司法管辖权的不同主要为以下几个方面。

(一)权力来源的不同

仲裁解决纠纷的权力来源于双方或几方当事人的协议选择和指定,而民商事诉讼的司法管辖权来自国家的司法主权,以国家主权为基础。可以说,国际商事仲裁中的仲裁管辖权,不仅不以国家主权为基础,而且还建立在主权国家对其国家主权的自主限制这一基础上。在国际商事纠纷中,仲裁管辖权是当事人之间形成的仲裁协议赋予仲裁庭对纠纷案件进行审理和作出对各方均有约束力的结论的权力,这与国家在拥有司法主权的前提下,一国法院或其他有权司法机关依照国家法律规定行使的司法管辖权,存在本质上的区别。仲裁管辖权和司法管辖权,其权力来源的不同,决定了仲裁和诉讼的性质亦不相同。仲裁管辖权来自各方当事人之间的仲裁协议,这是仲裁存在的前提和依据。如果不存在仲裁协议,或仲裁协议存在瑕疵,仲裁是否拥有管辖权就存在争议。实践中,当事人请求法院确认仲裁协议无效的案件比比皆是。而司法管辖权的来源则是一国司法主权的行使,其管辖权是来自一国法律,甚至是宪法的规定,其权力的来源毋庸置疑。可以说仲裁条款对司法管辖权的协议排斥,本身就来源于国家通过仲裁法相关的特殊法律规定,自主地限制了其司法主权的行为。因此,朝鲜仲裁的两类案件中,只有第一类案件的权力来源是符合仲裁管辖权特征的。而不同于第一类案件,由国家有权机关指定通过仲裁程序解决的第二类纠纷的审理权力,仍然来自国家的公权力,丝毫不受当事人意思自治的影响。

(二)审裁机构的不同

仲裁机构是区别于国家司法机关的非政府裁决机构,这是仲裁区别于诉讼的一个典型特征。涉外民事诉讼是在国家司法审判机关,由国家司法审判人员来完成的。但无论是机构仲裁或是临时仲裁,均是非政府裁决机构,或是非政府工作人员作出的中立性判断。仲裁中,当事人有权选择特定的专业人士作为仲裁员,或选择特定的仲裁机构在他们不能就仲裁员的选定达成一致时来为他们指定仲裁员。当事人在协议选择仲裁机构或约定仲裁员的资质条件等具体要求之前,可以对不同仲裁机构的规则加以对比,就双方可能发生争议的特点和需求进行协商,最终将双方都可以接受的选择落到纸面上。这就使得仲裁员的中立性和专业性更容易被当事人认可,毕竟地域或资格等因素都是经过双方当事人的考虑和协商的。而诉讼中,当事人是不被赋予选择审判人员的权利的。从这一点来看,朝鲜仲裁的两种案件确实都符合这类特征,均是在其涉外仲裁机构,按照涉外仲裁程序来完成的。但在实践中,当事人是否能够不受外力干扰而自由选择仲裁员,仲裁员在审理案件过程中的独立性和中立性如何,都有待确认。

(三)强制性和当事人的意思自治程度的不同

涉外民事诉讼的管辖权是由具有国家强制力的一国司法机关所享有,其管辖权的实现是法定的、强制的。由于诉讼管辖权是以国家权力为基础,从而具有强制性,提起民事诉讼不需以对方当事人的同意作为必要条件。虽然民事诉讼中也允许当事人协议选择管辖法院,但并非所有的案件都可以由当事人协议选择管辖法院,通常只有商事类案件才可以协议选择与案件具有实际联系的法院管辖,且不得违反级别管辖、专属管辖等许多限制。而国际商事仲裁管辖权的行使,则是由非政府民间组织性质的仲裁庭来完成,这样的民间组织不具有任何法律赋予的司法机关强制性权力。因此,在整个行使国际商事仲裁管辖权的过程中,仲裁庭缺乏强制性权力和物质手段来保障国际商事仲裁管辖权的行使。为保证国际商事仲裁程序的顺利进行,仲裁管辖权的行使通常需求助于司法机关的支持与协助。例如在我国,仲裁庭在财产保全、证据保全等方面都需要法院的支持与协助。另外,《示范法》在确认当事人的意思自治原则地位的同时,也明确了当事人的选择应当服从《示范法》的相关强制性规定。但是不可否认,在国际商事仲裁中,当事人的意思自治原则占据举足轻重的地位。从上述分析来看,朝鲜仲裁的第二类案件,在案件被提起的时候,很明显是具有强制性的,因为当事人之间并没有协议选择仲裁来解决纠纷。但是一旦案件被受理,从组成仲裁庭到仲裁裁决书的作出,又均根据仲裁规则来进行,当事人的自主性又重新被保障,而案件受理在本质上而言却毫无自主权,不得不说非常矛盾。

从上述分析综合来看,朝鲜仲裁的第二类案件,即有权力的国家机关(例如朝鲜中央裁判所)指定仲裁机构按照涉外仲裁程序进行审理的案件,其管辖权力的来源是国家法律规定,出自国家的司法主权,而非平等的主体之间根据双方当事人合意,协议选择的结果。案件的受理由国家权力机关来决定,但案件的审理过程却由仲裁机构的仲裁规则来确定;案件在受理阶段具有国家强制性,但审理阶段却又具有当事人的自主性。因此笔者认为,虽然这类案件的法律文书在形式上无疑是仲裁机构作出的仲裁裁决书,但其实质却是仲裁机构接受司法机关的委托,代为行使国际司法审判权的结果。换句话说,其仲裁裁决书并非普遍意义上的"仲裁裁决书",而更具有司法"判决书"的特征。在笔者代理的一起在我国承认与执行朝鲜国际贸易仲裁委员会裁决书的案件中,笔者就曾主张虽然案涉裁决书名为"仲裁裁决书",但无论是从双方没有达成过仲裁协议,或是仲裁申请人曾向朝鲜法院起诉,后朝鲜中央裁判所将案件移送至朝鲜国际贸易仲裁委员会审理的过程来看,其实质上都应该是仲裁委员会接受中央司法机关中央裁判所的委托,代为行使了司法管辖权的结果,因此该案应当确认其性质为民事判决书,适用《中华人民共和国和朝鲜民主主义人民共和国关于民事和刑事司法协助的条约》第 3 条的规定予以承认,最终我国法院也根据该条约作出了裁判。

四、《朝鲜涉外经济仲裁法》存在的一些问题

(一)仲裁的开始阶段

除上文所述朝鲜的仲裁管辖权存在的问题以外,第一类与国际惯例相同的,存在仲裁协议的仲裁案件依然存在签订仲裁协议方面的一

些问题。根据朝鲜的法律体系,尤其是《朝鲜对外经济合同法》第11条的规定,交易金额较大或者具有国家意义的合同订立应当经中央贸易领导机关或者有关机关批准。该法第18条也规定,危害国家安全或给经济利益造成损失的合同,以及欺骗或强迫订立的合同不具备效力。① 因此,外国投资者与朝鲜的企业签订商事合同首先需要面对的难关就是即使双方都同意仲裁协议,如果仲裁协议不能被中央贸易领导机关批准,或以第18条的规定否认其仲裁协议的效力,那么就意味着仲裁根本无法开始。而上述条文中的"具有国家意义""经济利益造成损失"等条文的理解又并不明确。实践中确实也存在一些对外经济合同因违反相关法律规定,而被朝鲜相关机关认定无效的情形,这种可能使自由裁量权被无限放大的做法,无疑是不会给外国投资者带来多少信心的。

(二)法律细节上缺乏公开性,仲裁部被赋予的权力过大

《朝鲜涉外经济仲裁法》虽然规定了涉外经济纠纷由朝鲜国际贸易仲裁委员会、朝鲜海事仲裁委员会、朝鲜计算机软件仲裁委员会审理解决,但这三个组织的具体情况、组成人员、仲裁规则、仲裁员名录等是普通人难以得知的,即使在现今互联网普及的社会,也很难找到相关的信息,甚至朝鲜的其他法律规定也属于外国投资者、外国法律从业人员很难获取的信息。另外,根据上文所述,仲裁部被赋予了相较于国际惯例更大的权力,而仲裁部在审理案件时是否能够保证其独立性、中立性,不受其他行政机关的干涉,这一点对于外国投资者来说并不明确,这也就使得外国投资者对在朝鲜进行涉外仲裁的信任度非常有限且难以短时间内大幅提高。因此,加大相关法律规定及仲裁信息的透明度,尽快与国际社会接轨,对于朝鲜涉外仲裁的发展而言非常紧迫。

---

① 参见《朝鲜对外经济合同法》(2008年修正版)。

(三) 加入《承认及执行外国仲裁裁决公约》的紧迫性

自 1958 年 6 月 10 日,《承认及执行外国仲裁裁决公约》(又称《纽约公约》)签订以来,世界上大部分国家和地区已经陆续加入了该公约。2023 年 1 月 17 日,东帝汶宣布加入《纽约公约》,成为该公约第 172 个缔约方。但是朝鲜目前为止并没有加入《纽约公约》,因此在朝鲜作出的仲裁裁决书无法根据《纽约公约》在境外获得承认与执行,外国仲裁裁决书也无法根据该公约在朝鲜获得承认与执行,而是需要依据朝鲜与其他国家签订的双边条约申请承认与执行。我国与朝鲜于 2003 年签订了《中华人民共和国和朝鲜民主主义人民共和国关于民事和刑事司法协助的条约》,其内容包括相互承认民事判决书,却并未包含相互承认仲裁裁决书。与中国签订的双边条约尚且未能包含承认仲裁裁决,便可以想象朝鲜与其他国家关于相互承认与执行仲裁裁决的情况是何种光景。换句话说,朝鲜目前缺乏与国际社会相互承认仲裁裁决的依据,因此加入《纽约公约》就迫在眉睫。但是又因为其仲裁管辖权的与众不同,使得其加入《纽约公约》必然将面临巨大的困难。即使顺利加入《纽约公约》,后续根据该公约修改相关国内立法也必然会面临不小的挑战。

结语

首先,虽然《朝鲜涉外经济仲裁法》的内容很大程度地借鉴了《示范法》,却同时兼具许多朝鲜特有的规定。该法虽然确立了符合朝鲜国情的纠纷解决机制,却仍然存在不少不符合国际惯例的情况。最典型的例子便是上文所述的即便各方当事人之间不存在仲裁协议,有权力的国家机关也可以将案件委托给仲裁委员会,按照涉外经济仲裁程序审理的案件。这类案件在司法实践中,其案件结果的性质到底是法院判决,还是仲裁裁决,迄今缺乏明确定论,使得案件结束后是否能在朝鲜境外得到承认与执行变得模糊不定。因此,包含这类具有朝鲜特色的特殊规定的《朝鲜涉外经济仲裁法》,与国际接轨还有待进一步细化和完善。

其次,虽然《朝鲜对外经济合同法》等诸多法律达成了保护外商投资的基本内容,如确立了保护外商投资企业合法权益的原则[1],禁止政府对外商投资企业进行国有化[2],允许外商投资企业将收入合法转出[3],保护外商投资企业的商业秘密[4]等,但是仍存在许多政策不能完全落地的情况。另外,在具体争议解决的实践中,仲裁协议是否能够签订需要得到政府有关部门的审批,即使不存在仲裁协议,朝鲜的仲裁委员会很可能也具有管辖权,仲裁规则等具体规定难以被外界知晓,仲裁的公正性与中立性还缺乏可信度等,需要进一步完善外商投资相关的纠纷解决机制。

再次,由于朝鲜是为数不多未加入《纽约公约》的国家之一,其仲裁裁决的效力对于外国投资者来说并不友好,因此,将涉外仲裁作为外商投资的纠纷解决机制就显得尤为单薄。其具有朝鲜特色的规定,使得朝鲜加入《纽约公约》也存在不小的阻力,因此尽快加入《纽约公约》,并根据公约内容修改、完善其本国立法,是朝鲜引进外国外商投资首先需要解决的问题之一。

最后,朝鲜近年来为了吸引外商投资促进国内经济发展,相继出台、修订了许多鼓励和保护外商投资的法律法规,不断地填补和完善其外商投资法律方面的空白,对吸引外商投资和促进本国经济发展具有非常重要的积极意义。但是不得不说,在这一系列的举措中,仍存在许多与国际社会不接轨、具有鲜明朝鲜特色的规定,还有待进一步修正。希望在不久的将来,能够看到一个真正开放化、发展化、与国际社会接轨的现代化朝鲜仲裁法律体系,为外国投资者在朝投资提供更多的保护机制与信心,为朝鲜的经济发展提供更好的法律基础。

(杨意茹　审校)

---

[1] 参见《朝鲜外国人投资法》(2011年修正版)第4条。
[2] 参见《朝鲜外国人投资法》(2011年修正版)第18条。
[3] 参见《朝鲜外国人投资法》(2011年修正版)第20条。
[4] 参见《朝鲜外国人投资法》(2011年修正版)第21条。

韩国篇

——韩国仲裁业概况及其法制建设 *

韩国是东亚三国之一,其经济体量虽无法和中、日匹敌,但在世界范围内也属于重要经济体。此外,近年来中韩之间贸易往来频繁,虽因世界形势变化,政治方面经历多次低谷,但2023年以前,韩国的第一大贸易伙伴连续多年都是中国,同时韩国在中国贸易伙伴序列中也一直位居前五。国际仲裁与跨境贸易伴生,涉韩民商事争议在我国并不鲜见,因此,了解韩国的仲裁业状况及韩国仲裁法制环境对我国学术界及实务界而言都有必要。本篇拟从韩国仲裁产业政策导向及现状、韩国仲裁法制建设两个方面尝试简要描绘韩国仲裁业及仲裁法律的基本样貌。

一、韩国仲裁产业政策导向及现状

(一)仲裁产业化思想的形成和法律出台

仲裁起源于商人之间高效解决争议的需要,第一次世界大战之后,为了经济复苏和促进国际经贸往来,国际商会得以设立,随后有了ICC国际仲裁院以及确保仲裁裁决得到跨国执行的国际公约。韩国仲裁的起源也与本国经济发展需要密切相关。1962年韩国第一个经济开发五年计划实施,交易量迅速增加,争端也随之显著增加。为此,韩国政府与韩国工商业界于1966年设立本国的常设仲裁机构——大韩商事仲裁院,并制定了韩国第一部仲裁法。但是,在相当长的一段时间里,仲裁在韩国并不是解决商事争议经常选择的手段。

21世纪之后,对国际仲裁的认识有了新的变化,即国际仲裁除了是一种有效的争议解决手段,还可以被视为法律服务的一种,案件如能留在本国审理,与之相关的产业均将从中获益。韩国当时对外贸易额以及对外投资稳步增加,韩国企业在外国进行仲裁的案件也同步

---

* 本篇作者为苏晓凌,法学博士,北京德和衡律师事务所律师。

增多，法律服务费用主要由韩国企业一方承担，因此法律服务贸易赤字日渐增加。以减小法律服务贸易赤字、发展仲裁法律服务为目的，2010年以后，业界围绕建设首尔为仲裁地的设想进行了较多的讨论，主要理由是，首尔位于美国、中国、日本等韩国主要贸易国的中间地带，具有地理上的优势，而且韩国法制遵循大陆法传统，可以提供与新加坡、中国香港特别行政区等英美法系法域不同的差别化服务。在这种设想指导下，2013年5月，由大韩律师协会、首尔市政府、大韩商事仲裁院共同出资，在首尔设立了首尔国际仲裁中心（Seoul International Dispute Resolution Center）。首尔国际仲裁中心是为国际仲裁提供国际化高标准服务的设施，并不是管理案件的仲裁机构，但提高了仲裁界对首尔的认知度，建成之后ICC仲裁案件不少在首尔开庭审理，就仲裁产业化而言，可以说取得了一定成果。在此基础上，仲裁产业化的设想从相关业界扩展到政府层面，法务部开始主导对国际仲裁产业化的讨论，到2016年11月，《韩国仲裁产业振兴法》出台，并于2017年6月28日开始施行，促进并发展仲裁产业开始正式成为被提高到法律层面的韩国产业政策。①

(二) 仲裁产业振兴法下相关举措

《韩国仲裁产业振兴法》主要涉及基本计划的制定、产业振兴基础的构建、仲裁专门人才的培养、国际争端案件在韩国审理的引导、财政支援，以及自律性运营的保障等方面。按照《韩国仲裁产业振兴法》的要求，2018年12月，法务部制定了《韩国仲裁产业振兴基本计划》（以下简称《基本计划》）并向社会公开。《基本计划》从仲裁产业基础的强化、竞争力的确保、扩大留在本国审理的国际仲裁案件范围等多个方面对整个产业进行了规划，随后逐步采取了相应的落实措施。

1. 仲裁产业基础的强化

仲裁产业基础的强化涵盖了专门人才的培养和法律制度的整备两个方面。

---

① 《韩国仲裁产业振兴法》出台背景参见：오현석，"중재산업진흥법에 대한 평가 및 국제중재 활성화를 위한 법정책적 제언"《선진상사법률연구》통권 제103호，2023.7.

在人才培养方面,主要的措施是在法学院邀请仲裁专家举办研讨会;选拔法学院学生到外国仲裁机构访问或实习;针对不同行业的企业,按照所属不同行业进行仲裁实务的教育;开设线上课程;等等。大韩商事仲裁院是法务部指定的唯一仲裁教育主管机关,2019 年 5 月 20 日,大韩商事仲裁院内部设立仲裁教育院,开设了 ADR 基本课程、国内仲裁专家课程、娱乐仲裁专家课程等一系列课程。

在法律制度整备方面,《基本计划》提出,随时听取大韩商事仲裁院、大韩仲裁员协会、学术团体、公司律师、企业家以及建设、海运行业从业者的各种法制改善建议和意见。此外,组建仲裁机构、学界以及实务界专家组成的咨询委员会,委托进行相关课题研究、召开学术大会等。

2. 仲裁产业竞争力的确保

在这方面,《基本计划》主要涉及两个方面,一是仲裁硬件设施建设,二是加强仲裁机构的各方面力量。

对于仲裁硬件设施建设,由法务部主导,在 2013 年建成的首尔国际仲裁中心基础上又扩建综合仲裁中心。综合仲裁中心于 2018 年正式开启运营,仲裁办公场所的面积从原来的三四百平方米扩建到 1911 平方米,同时引入线上审理平台。对于硬件设施的运营主体,曾有人提议学习新加坡,另设专门运营设施的法人①,但最终还是交由大韩商事仲裁院运营。

关于强化仲裁机构的力量,法务部一方面计划系统化教育培训从事案件处理的人员,另一方面认为国际投资仲裁作为仲裁新领域可以进一步挖掘,因此组织人力展开对国际投资仲裁的调查分析。

3. 引导国际仲裁案件在韩国审理

《基本计划》曾表示要对如何引导案件以韩国为仲裁地在韩国审理展开研究并为此成立战略委员会,但目前未见相关报告,也未见战略委员会成立的公开消息。

《基本计划》还规划支持大韩商事仲裁院在海外设立代表处,开展宣传及沟通工作,开展"Seoul ADR Festival"等活动,加深公众对首尔

---

① 국제중재실무회,"북합중재센터의 설립 및 운영방안에 관한 연구",법무부 용역보고서,2017 년 6 월,301 면.

为仲裁地的印象等。

(三)《韩国仲裁产业振兴法》及《基本计划》实施的现状

韩国产业振兴计划经济上主要依靠财政拨款,主体上则主要交由韩国唯一的仲裁机构——大韩商事仲裁院来实施。

1. 仲裁机构的组织结构

因为大韩商事仲裁院是唯一的实施主体,因此仲裁产业振兴计划实施以来,大韩商事仲裁院的组织机构有了比较大的变化,新设组织多,职能也相对庞杂,截至目前,大韩商事仲裁院的组织机构具体组成如图1所示。①

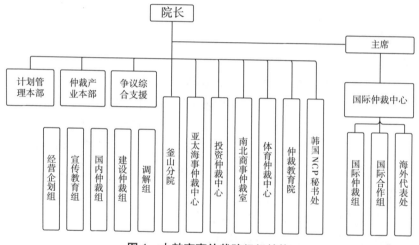

图 1　大韩商事仲裁院组织结构

从以上组织图可见,国际仲裁被单独分离出来,设立国际仲裁中心,有相对独立的人员管理和组织运营,显示出较高的地位。但是与国际案件紧密相关的投资仲裁以及海事仲裁又未纳入国际仲裁中心运营,其职能区分与实际管理存在模糊之处。

2. 对大韩商事仲裁院的财政支援

法务部给予大韩商事仲裁院一定规模的财政支援。2017年总计

---

① 参见大韩商事仲裁院官网(http://www.kcab.or.kr/servlet/kcab_kor/intro/1511),访问日期:2023年11月4日。

给予财政支援 11.51 亿韩元,用于召开海外说明会、宣传以及引导国际仲裁在韩国审理等相关措施的支出。2018 年拨款 24.1 亿韩元用于租用仲裁审理的房屋租金或补助、视频系统建设等。仲裁审理设施启用之后,从 2018 年之后,每年大约获得 25 亿韩元左右的财政支援。① 但是大韩商事仲裁院审理案件所用建筑物是租用的,需要支付租金,财政支援的相当一部分用于租金的支付,分配给国际仲裁所需专门人才的经费保障并不十分充足。

3. 案件受理情况

根据大韩商事仲裁院统计资料,从 2018 年开始到 2022 年,大韩商事仲裁院受理的仲裁、调解案件如表 1 所示。②

表 1 2018—2022 年大韩商事仲裁院受理案件情况

		2018 年		2019 年		2020 年		2021 年		2022 年	
		数量/件	金额/亿韩元	数量/件	金额/亿韩元	数量/件	金额/亿韩元	数量/件	金额/亿韩元	数量/件	金额/亿韩元
仲裁	国内	331	5923	373	8886	336	4146	450	7949	304	4136
	国际	62	1432	70	1159	69	1670	50	511	38	738
调解	国内	881	148	830	354	696	108	484	79	531	51
	国际	80	62	59	330	51	44	28	74	23	133

从受理案件数量看,自 2018 年仲裁产业振兴计划发布起,除 2019 年国际仲裁受理案件数增加外,2020 年以后反而是逐年下降,其中新冠疫情是否是导致这一结果的主要因素,尚且存疑。

4. 海事仲裁

在 2018 年 3 月之前,大韩商事仲裁院没有专门的海事仲裁机构,

---

① 오현석,"중재산업진흥법에 대한 평가 및 국제중재 활성화를 위한 법정책적 제언"《선진상사법률연구》통권 제 103 호, 2023.7.

② 根据大韩商事仲裁院公布统计数据整理。

海事案件按照其是国内案件还是国际案件分别交由国内仲裁组和国际仲裁组处理。在仲裁产业化政策导向下,2018年3月,由大韩商事仲裁院在釜山设立亚太海事仲裁中心,这是韩国国内唯一的海事仲裁机构。2019年8月,《韩国海事仲裁规则》制定并施行。但是海事仲裁传统上绝大多数是在韩国之外进行,因此韩国海事仲裁的量比较小。近年来,韩国学界对引导海事争议在韩国解决的讨论比较热烈,但主要方向集中在专门海事法院的设立方面,仁川、釜山等港口城市正在激烈争取第一个海事法院的选址。本篇限于篇幅,对韩国海事仲裁不再展开说明。

二、仲裁产业化导向下韩国仲裁法制建设

《韩国仲裁产业振兴基本计划》已满五年,尽管从实际效果看,并未达到当初设想的打造首尔为国际仲裁中心地的目标,但法制建设并不落后。《韩国仲裁法》(2016年修订并实施)[①]全方位吸收《联合国国际贸易法委员会国际商事仲裁示范法》(以下简称《示范法》)修订的内容,司法实践中也注意维护仲裁友好型法制环境。同年,韩国国内唯一仲裁机构大韩商事仲裁院[②]修订国际仲裁规则,吸收世界其他主要仲裁机构仲裁规则的精华,同时出版《2016年大韩商事仲裁院国际仲裁规则解释书》,方便当事人及从业者理解和适用。

(一)《韩国仲裁法》

1. 修订背景

《韩国仲裁法》最初制定于1966年,1973年进行过一次局部的修订。1999年,《韩国仲裁法》进行了全面修订,除与司法制度有冲突的部分外,全面采纳了《示范法》的内容和体例。2006年《示范法》修订,韩国学界开始呼吁国内法也作出相应的修订和改善,这是韩国这次

---

① 2020年《韩国仲裁法》又有一次修订,但仅限于第40条一条,内容是为了与产业振兴法案一致,在原来规定的产业通商部之外,又增加法务部作为仲裁机构财政支援的主体。

② 尽管大韩商事仲裁院是韩国唯一仲裁机构,但韩国仲裁法允许临时仲裁,也为临时仲裁提供司法上的协助。

启动仲裁法修订的一个动因。另一个修法动因当然还是仲裁产业化政策的推动,作为仲裁产业振兴计划的一环,必须保持仲裁法制的先进性。

2016年《韩国仲裁法》修订起始于2012年7月,法务部先组成《韩国仲裁法》修订任务小组,之后正式组成《韩国仲裁法》修订委员会,着手对《韩国仲裁法》修订方案进行讨论和设计。从2013年3月到2014年10月底,修订委员会召开了20次会议,最终形成了修订草案。2014年,韩国法务部与韩国大韩商事仲裁院共同主持召开名为"修订仲裁法案的主要争点和各国的修订方向"的研讨会,这次研讨会上公开了修订草案。2015年8月,法务部宣布对《韩国仲裁法》的修订立法预告,向社会各界公开征求意见。2015年10月14日,法务部召开律师、教授等仲裁领域专业人士参加的公听会,就仲裁法修订草案听取意见。2016年5月新修订的《韩国仲裁法》(以下简称新《韩国仲裁法》)公布,同年11月30日开始实施。

2. 基本指导思想

因为这次修订的动因之一是《示范法》的修订,因此韩国《仲裁法》的修订也主要集中在对《示范法》新修订内容的借鉴和模仿方面。微观上,这次《韩国仲裁法》的修订紧跟《示范法》的修订,重点对仲裁协议的签订方式和仲裁庭的临时处分权限等作了相应的修订。宏观指导思想上,韩国业界对是否要继续保持与《示范法》相同的体系进行了讨论。韩国相关业界最终形成的意见相对保守,认为英国、法国等仲裁先进国家在考虑《示范法》的意见和立场的同时并没有全面采用《示范法》的立法,亚洲地区的新加坡和中国香港特别行政区在借鉴《示范法》的同时也都引入了自己独有的制度,但是对于韩国来说,制定"有韩国特色"的独特仲裁法还为时尚早。基于这种判断,这次修订意见是尽可能尊重既有的模仿《示范法》的体系,增加《示范法》没有的规定或者另行作出规定。

3. 主要修订内容

(1)可仲裁事项范围的扩大。

原《韩国仲裁法》将可仲裁的对象表述为"私法上的纠纷",新《韩国仲裁法》仿照德国立法例,将仲裁对象表述为"财产权上的纠纷及当事人可以和解解决的非财产权上的纠纷"（第3条）。按照这个规定，不正当竞争相关纠纷、专利等知识产权纠纷也可以以仲裁方式解决。

（2）仲裁协议书面性要件的放宽。

原《韩国仲裁法》有对仲裁协议书面性要件的规定，并按照《示范法》的方式列举了可以认定为满足书面性要件的几种情况。2006年《示范法》就仲裁协议的书面性要件提供了两种方案供选择：一是保留书面性要件的规定，但同时规定，只要仲裁协议的内容以任何形式被记录下来就满足书面性要件；二是全面废除书面性要件的规定。

这次修订工作中，修订委员会认为，现在大部分国家都还保留书面性要件的要求，且从当事人可预见性考虑，不宜采用全面废除书面性要件这样激进的方案，因此建议保留。新《韩国仲裁法》与《示范法》的第一种方案宗旨一致，只是表述方式有所不同（第8条第3款）。按照现在的方案，不管仲裁协议是以口头还是行为方式作出，只要其内容被记录下来就满足书面性要件的要求，且通过电报、邮件等电子方式作出的意思表示，只要可以被确认，也满足书面性要件的要求。并且当事人交换的申请书和答辩状有仲裁的意思表示，而对方并不表示反对的，也满足书面性要件的要求。

（3）对临时措施作出系统性规定，赋予临时措施可执行性。

2006年《示范法》修改的中心内容是在临时措施方面，因此《韩国仲裁法》的这次修改在这方面也进行了较多的讨论。新《韩国仲裁法》以第18条中的8个条款对临时措施（韩国称为临时性处分）作了较为系统的规定，《示范法》中除初步命令（preliminary order）的规定没有被引入之外，其他有关临时措施的规定几乎被全盘接受，比较重要的修改至少有以下两个方面。

一是仿照《示范法》对"临时措施"进行定义。新《韩国仲裁法》第18条第1款首先肯定了仲裁庭有依据一方当事人的申请采取临时措施的权力，这是对原《韩国仲裁法》有关规定的保留。随后，新《韩国仲裁法》在第2款中对"临时措施"作出定义，规定：临时措施是指仲裁庭以仲裁裁决的方式或者其他方式在仲裁裁决下达之前命令一方当事人履行下列内容的暂定性的处分措施：①到纠纷事案的仲裁裁决下达时为止,保持原状或者恢复原状;②防止对仲裁程序本身有现实或者当前危害或影响的措施,或者禁止可能有上述危险或者影响的行为;③对可能成为仲裁裁决执行对象的财产提供保全措施;④与纠纷解决有关联性或者重要性的证据的保全。对照《示范法》第17条的规定可以发现,《韩国仲裁法》这次修订是对《示范法》的全面接受。

二是赋予临时措施可执行性。在原《韩国仲裁法》中,仲裁庭作出的临时措施是对程序问题的处理,不属于对纠纷实体问题的处理,因此采取的法律形式是"决定"。因为韩国法院执行的对象是"裁决",所以临时措施不属于法院可以执行的对象。针对这个问题,这次修订在第18条之7[1]赋予法院对临时措施的执行权力,并作出了相关详细规定。与赋予临时措施可执行性相应,新《韩国仲裁法》也对拒绝执行的事由[2]作出了规定,其内容基本与《示范法》第17I条一致。

---

[1] 《韩国仲裁法》第18条之7(临时措施的承认和执行)
(1)当事人欲强制执行仲裁庭下达的临时措施的,可以向法院申请强制执行。
(2)该临时措施取消、中止、变更的,申请承认和执行临时措施的当事人或其对方当事人应当及时告知法院。
(3)仲裁庭就临时措施对担保的提供未作出决定或者有可能侵害第三人权利的,接受或执行临时措施申请的法院认为有必要时,可以命令申请承认和执行临时措施的一方当事人提供与之相当的担保。
(4)执行临时措施准用《民事执行法》中保全处分的有关规定。

[2] 《韩国仲裁法》第18条之8(拒绝承认及执行的事由)
(1)只有属于下列任意一项时才可以拒绝承认或执行临时措施。
①临时措施的对方当事人提出异议,法院认定属于下列任何一种情况的。
A.临时性措施的对方当事人对属于下列任何一种情况的事实进行了说明的。
a.属于第36条第(2)款第①项A或者D的事实;
b.临时措施的对方当事人就仲裁员的选定或者仲裁程序没有获得适当通知或者因为其他事由没能进行辩论的事实;
c.临时措施处理的是不属于仲裁协议约定的争议的事实或者临时措施处理的是偏离仲裁协议范围的事项的事实。但,临时措施可以区分为属于仲裁协议对象的部分和不属于仲裁对象部分的,仅可拒绝不属于仲裁对象的部分。
B.就临时措施,不按照法院或者仲裁庭命令提供担保的。
C.临时措施被仲裁庭撤销或者中止的。
②法院依职权认定属于下列任意一种情况的。
A.法院不具有执行临时措施权力的。但法院为执行临时措施,不变更临时措施的实体,且在必要的范围内决定变更临时措施的,不在此限。
B.存在第36条第(2)款第②项A或者B所述事由的。
(2)按照第18条之7接到承认和执行申请的法院在作出决定时不得审理临时措施的实体内容。
(3)法院对第(1)款事由作出的判断仅对临时措施的承认和执行有效。

(4)证据方面强化法院对仲裁的支持并允许仲裁庭对证据直接进行调查。

在证据调查方面,这次修订强化了法院对仲裁的支持。在原《韩国仲裁法》下,仲裁过程中需要对第三人进行证据调查的,仲裁庭可以委托法院进行证据调查,法院进行证据调查后将结果送交仲裁庭。在修订过程中,修订委员会认为,这种委托法院进行证据调查的方法在某些时候比较有效,但是在运用询问证人等证据调查方法时,由仲裁庭直接进行,更有利于仲裁员形成正确的心证,因此应当在现行委托法院调查证据这种方式之外,为仲裁庭直接进行证据调查打开大门。基于这种考虑,新《韩国仲裁法》增加了"法院对证据调查的协助"一条[①],规定"仲裁庭请求法院协助证据调查的,法院可以命令证人或者持有文件的人出席仲裁庭或者将必需的文件提交仲裁庭"。按照这个规定,在需要对证据进行调查时,仲裁庭可以根据情况,或者委托法院进行证据调查,或者请求法院协助,命令证人出席仲裁庭,由仲裁庭对证人进行直接询问。

(5)简化仲裁裁决的承认和执行程序。

原《韩国仲裁法》下,对仲裁裁决,需要按照"宣布允许执行程序",获得法院的执行判决,然后才可以执行,其程序相对比较烦琐。这次修订明确仲裁裁决与确定判决有相同的效力,在执行时无须再获得法院的"执行判决",而是由法院以"决定"形式作出即可,以保证仲裁裁决可以迅速有效地得到执行。

[①] 第28条(法院对证据调查的协助)
  (1)仲裁庭可依职权或者当事人申请,请求法院进行证据调查或者协助进行证据调查。
  (2)仲裁庭请求法院进行证据调查的,应当书面指定调查文书上要记载的事项以及其他证据调查所必需的事项。
  (3)法院依第2款进行证据调查的,仲裁员或者当事人在获得审判长许可后可参与证据调查。
  (4)法院按照第2款进行调查的,在证据调查结束后,应当将询问证人记录的原本、鉴定书原件等证据调查记录原件无迟延地交给仲裁庭。
  (5)仲裁庭申请法院协助进行证据调查的,法院可以命令证人或持有文件者出席仲裁庭或者将必要的文件提交仲裁庭。
  (6)仲裁庭应当向法院缴纳必要的证据调查费用。

(6)确认仲裁庭有权确定仲裁费用的承担和迟延利息的支付。

《示范法》没有规定当事人无约定时仲裁费用如何分担以及迟延利息如何支付,韩国法律中也无相关规定。修订过程中,修订委员会认为,应当在法律中明确仲裁庭有权确定仲裁费用的承担,为仲裁庭作出相关裁决提供法律依据。新《韩国仲裁法》允许仲裁庭在当事人无约定的情况下决定仲裁费用支出的分担①,同时赋予仲裁庭决定迟延利息的权力②。

(7)修改一些不必要的限制性规定,简化仲裁裁决的执行。

这次修订还删除了一些不必要且给实际操作带来麻烦的限制性规定。比如原《韩国仲裁法》规定,仲裁裁决作出后不仅要送达当事人,仲裁裁决的原本还要交法院保管(原《韩国仲裁法》第32条第4款);申请执行仲裁裁决时,仲裁裁决的正本或者经正当认证的副本、仲裁协议的原本或者经正当认证的副本应当提交法院;仲裁裁决或者仲裁协议以外语做成的,应当提交经正当认证的韩语翻译本(原《韩国仲裁法》第37条第2款)。这些规定中的"正本""正当认证"究竟是何含义并不明确,有些也并无必要。比如仲裁裁决的原件由仲裁机构和当事人保管,本无必要交给法院保管。基于便利当事人的考虑,这次修订均作了相应的修改。关于仲裁裁决书的保管,新《韩国仲裁法》规定,仅在当事人申请的情况下,法院才保管仲裁裁决书(新《韩国仲裁法》第32条第4款)。关于仲裁裁决执行的程序,新《韩国仲裁法》规定,当事人申请执行时只要提交"副本"即满足条件,仲裁裁决以外语作出的,仅规定提交韩语翻译本,删除了原规定中翻译件须经"正当认证"的要求(新《韩国仲裁法》第37条)。

4. 对新《韩国仲裁法》的简评

这次《韩国仲裁法》的修订是在打造韩国为国际仲裁中心的战略

---

① 《韩国仲裁法》第34条之2(仲裁费用的负担)
当事人之间若无另行约定,则仲裁庭可以考虑仲裁案件的各种情节,决定仲裁程序中支出费用的分担。
② 《韩国仲裁法》第34条之3(迟延利息)
当事人之间若无另行约定,则仲裁庭在仲裁裁决时,可以考虑仲裁案件的各种情节,命令支付自己认为适当的迟延利息。

规划下进行的,因此主要着眼点就是改善本国仲裁法制,努力打造一个对仲裁有亲和力的法律环境。一方面,韩国认识到自己国家仲裁实践发展的现状,遵从仲裁普遍性的要求,不追求国别特色,老老实实参考《示范法》的模板,因此整体上看,其修订中规中矩,但基本上能够与众多仲裁先进国家以及世界仲裁发展趋势保持一致。另一方面,这次修订注意规范仲裁与法院的关系,强调法院对仲裁的支持和协助,但排除法院的不当干涉,赋予仲裁庭对某些事项作出决定的权限,特别是在临时措施方面,这次修订进行了比较详细的整合,全面接受《示范法》关于临时措施的规定,并对国内程序法作出衔接性的规定,提高了操作便利性。鉴于临时措施在实务中特别是在国际商事仲裁实务中的重要意义,这一修订因为有利于仲裁裁决的最终实现,显然会加强当事人选择仲裁作为纠纷解决手段的信心。此外,简化程序,方便仲裁程序的进行和执行,都有利于当事人,最终也将有利于本国仲裁业的发展。

(二)大韩商事仲裁院 2016 年《国际仲裁规则》

大韩商事仲裁院针对国内案件和国际案件分别制定了仲裁规则。但是大韩商事仲裁院所说的国际案件要比我国所说的涉外案件的范围窄。按照大韩商事仲裁院 2016 年《国际仲裁规则》第 2 条的定义,国际仲裁是指两种情况:一种是当事人至少一方的营业所在国外的;另一种情况是仲裁协议约定的仲裁地不在韩国的。前者,如果当事人有多个营业所,则主营业所在国外的,属于国际仲裁;如果没有营业所,则经常居所在国外的,属于国际仲裁。

1. 历史沿革

2007 年之前,大韩商事仲裁院受理的国际仲裁案件非常少,有些年份甚至只有 0 件,因此不存在国际仲裁规则,无论案件有无涉外因素,一概适用统一的仲裁规则。随着涉外案件的出现,由国际仲裁专家组成的国际仲裁实务会开始着手推进国际仲裁规则的制定。2007 年,大韩商事仲裁院第一个国际仲裁规则出台。但是,2007 年《国际仲裁规则》适用的前提是当事人明确约定适用,否则仍将适用原仲规则,这就导致虽然有国际仲裁规则,但在实务当中却很少得到适用。为了提升韩国国际仲裁竞争力,2011年大韩商事仲裁院再次修订仲裁规则,一方面变更规则名称,明确区分为国内仲裁规则和国际仲裁规则,另一方面修改原来国际仲裁规则中明示约定适用才能适用的规定,改为当事人未明确排除国际仲裁规则适用的,则国际仲裁案件适用国际仲裁规则。① 随着国际仲裁规则适用范围的扩大,适用国际仲裁规则的仲裁案件数开始增多,到2014年已有54件之多。

2012年之后,国际上主要仲裁机构纷纷修订其仲裁规则,韩国也顺应这一国际趋势,开始着手对2011年《国际仲裁规则》作进一步修订。2015年,新的《国际仲裁规则(修正案)》提交韩国大法院并获得承认,2016年6月1日之后受理的案件适用新的《国际仲裁规则》(以下简称2016年《国际仲裁规则》)。

2. 2016年《国际仲裁规则》主要变化

2016年《国际仲裁规则》的变化主要涉及以下几个方面②:

(1)通知及书面材料提交的电子化。

为了程序进行的方便、快捷,2016年《国际仲裁规则》第2条允许当事人以电子邮件、传真等可以留下记录的电子方式提交证据及其他书面材料,也允许仲裁院及秘书处以同样的方式发送通知,但是为了避免发送失败或错误的责任,电子送达的地址应当是当事人指定或同意的地址。但是当事人申请仲裁时,不能采用电子方式提交申请书,而是需要向秘书处提交书面材料及相应的副本(第8条)。

(2)仲裁员公正性、独立性主动陈述义务。

2016年《国际仲裁规则》之前,仲裁员接受指定时,只有在认为自己可能具有影响公正性或独立性的因素时才需要向秘书处告知。2016年《国际仲裁规则》第10条规定,仲裁员接受指定时,要在仲裁院制式的公正性、独立性陈述书上署名,实际上对仲裁员附加了陈述、

---

① 以上修订过程参见:김대훈,차경자:"대한상사중재원 중재규칙의 최근개정내용에 관한 고찰",〈중재연구〉제22권 제3호,2021.3.

② 主要修订内容参见:윤병철,이병우:"대한상사중재권 국제중재규칙개정에 관하여",〈중재〉344호,2015 가을겨울;大韩商事仲裁院:〈2016년국제중재규칙해석서〉.

告知义务,从而提高仲裁员对这一问题的认识。

(3)仲裁员的确定。

2016年《国际仲裁规则》将确定仲裁员的最终权力赋予秘书处,按照其第13条的规定,当事人指定仲裁员或者边裁确定首席仲裁员时,在秘书处确认该指定时才发生效力。之前的规则规定仲裁员一旦被指定即发生效力,当事人对仲裁员的独立性或公正性提出异议时,仲裁庭的组成逻辑上便不够合理。这一规定的目的是仲裁机构的秘书处可以就仲裁员回避事由进行讨论并作出决定。

(4)当事人的追加。

争议存在多方当事人时,如果能够在一个仲裁程序中予以解决,无疑是高效的。2016年《国际仲裁规则》对追加当事人作出了规定。按照第21条的规定,当事人及被追加当事人均同意被追加当事人参加仲裁的,或者被追加当事人与仲裁当事人之间有同一个仲裁协议,被追加当事人书面同意参加仲裁程序时,仲裁庭可以根据当事人的申请追加当事人。同时,即使追加当事人也不影响仲裁庭的构成。

这个规定实际上还意味着,判断是否追加当事人的权限在仲裁庭。追加当事人不变更仲裁庭构成的规定则是为了不影响仲裁庭审理案件的进程,防止造成程序过分迟延。

(5)多份合同的合并审理。

2016年《国际仲裁规则》增加了多份合同合并仲裁的规定。按照第22条的规定,秘书处初步判断合同中有适用国际仲裁规则的仲裁协议,多个请求是基于同一个交易或者持续发生的交易产生的,允许基于多份合同发生的仲裁请求只提交一个申请书。

(6)紧急仲裁员作出的紧急处分。

2016年《国际仲裁规则》新增紧急仲裁员制度(附则3),当事人可以在仲裁程序正式开始前,即提交仲裁申请的同时,或者提交申请后但仲裁庭尚未组庭时,向秘书处提交书面申请,请求紧急仲裁员作出临时性保全措施。紧急仲裁员为1名,秘书处在收到申请书后2个工作日内指定。当事人在收到指定紧急仲裁员通知书之日或者得知紧急仲裁员有回避事由之日的翌日起的2个工作日内可以提出回避申请,秘书处对是否回避作出决定。紧急仲裁员可以以开庭、电话会议等方式,或者仅依据当事人提交的书面材料,作出临时性保全措施。紧急仲裁员应当在被指定之日起15日之内就是否作出临时性保全措施作出决定。仲裁庭组庭后,紧急仲裁员作出的临时性保全措施继续有效,视为仲裁庭作出的。紧急仲裁员或者仲裁庭可以变更、中止或者取消临时性保全措施。临时性保全措施作出之日起3个月之内没能组庭,或者当事人撤回仲裁申请、未预缴仲裁费用、仲裁庭无权限的,随着仲裁程序的终结,临时性保全措施失效。仲裁庭组庭当时,紧急仲裁员自动失权,除非当事人另行约定,否则紧急仲裁员不能成为该争议的仲裁员。

以上仅为主要变动或新增条文,除此之外,2016年《国际仲裁规则》还有细节上的修改。例如,仲裁申请的合并方面,明确赋予当事人提交意见陈述的机会(第23条);对仲裁申请的撤回增加规定,明确答辩书提交之后当事人才撤回仲裁申请的,为了保护被申请人利益,只有取得被申请人同意,仲裁申请才能撤回(第34条);仲裁简易程序适用案件标的额从2亿韩元增加到5亿韩元(第43条);等等。

据悉,近年大韩商事仲裁院正在着手对2016年《国际仲裁规则》作进一步修订,2022年8月已正式成立规则修订委员会,修订方案于2023年11月召开公听会公开听取意见。[①]

结语

《韩国仲裁产业振兴基本计划》实施已逾5年,从实际业绩看,并未达到最初设想的目标。从硬件上看,开庭审理案件的场所面积缩小。从实际收案数看,大韩商事仲裁院3年新冠疫情期间国际仲裁受理案件数呈下降趋势。但是从法律环境的改善而言,《韩国仲裁法》的修订实现了法制的改善,近年法院的相关案例、判例也大都贯彻了当前先进的仲裁理念,体现了打造仲裁友好型国家的宗旨和精神。

---

① 参见韩国经济网(https://www.hankyung.com/article/202311080881i),访问日期:2023年11月9日。

目前韩国并未放弃仲裁产业化的方向。相关业界认为,仲裁产业化计划实施结果不佳的原因至少包括政府财政支援不够,导致高水平人员无法招募,仲裁机构内部运行机制设置不合理等。针对这些问题,业界也提出了不少建言和方案。比如提出应该由独立法人运营仲裁审理硬件设施,保持法律稳定性和确定性,充分利用韩国地理上的优势,依托韩国大陆法传统创造与英美法不同的差别化法律服务等。①法务部也于2022年下半年委托法学院教授等对如何促进仲裁产业化进行比较法的研究,主要对标新加坡仲裁业的优势,提出自己的改善方案等。②然而是否能够像预想的一样实现韩国产业政策导向的目的,显然还需要实践的检验。

（陈末末　审校）

日本篇
——关于日本司法机关对仲裁裁决的司法审查及判例运用的考察*

引言

随着贸易自由主义和贸易多边主义的不断发展,跨国投资贸易和经济合作日益频繁,各国之间已经形成了相互融合、密不可分、彼此依存的态势。国际经济交流体量的增大,也使得跨国商事纠纷频发。如何建立公平公正、快速高效并能够以国家司法强制力为后盾保障执行的纠纷解决机制,日益为国际商事主体所关注、重视。

以国家司法强制力为后盾保障执行的跨国纠纷解决机制主要有司法判决和作为民间纠纷解决机制的国际仲裁两种方式。在采取司

---

① 参见https://www.ajunews.com/view/20230319102825939,访问日期：2023年11月9日。
② 参见韩国政策研究管理系统网站(https://www.prism.go.kr/homepage/entire/researchDetail.do?researchId=1270000-202200083&menuNo=I0000002),访问日期：2023年11月9日。
* 本篇作者为吴强,北京德和衡（上海）律师事务所高级联席合伙人。

法判决作为纠纷解决方法时,对于双方当事人均为该国国内居民的案件,其财产也基本在该国内,在该国内对其财产采取强制执行措施没有障碍。但跨国纠纷的对方当事人及其财产处于外国时,该国内司法管辖权及判决效力无法及于域外,该国内判决在外国的强制执行有赖于两国之间签订的相互承认和执行外国判决的司法互助协定或相互承认和执行司法判决的互惠原则。

具体到中日之间,中日两国未签订相互承认和执行外国判决的司法互助协定,也未形成相互承认和执行司法判决的互惠原则。中国方面最早且较为典型的拒绝承认执行日本判决的为大连市中级人民法院作出的"五味晃事件"裁定,其依据为最高人民法院于1995年6月26日对辽宁省高级人民法院作出的复函。[①]最高人民法院确定的对日本判决不予承认和执行的原则一直沿用至今,目前尚未出现过与此相反的裁定。在此之后,日本方面同样认为,由于中日之间未签订两国间司法互助协定,且从上述大连市中级人民法院及最高人民法院的复函来看,日本判决在中国无法得到承认和执行,中日之间缺乏《日本民事诉讼法》第118条规定的"相互保证"要件,中国法院作出的判决在日本亦应不予承认和执行。2003年4月9日,大阪高等法院作出判决,首先作出了"由于中国人民法院作出的判决缺少'相互保证'要件,对其在日本的效力不予承认"的判决。之后,针对原告中国人根据南京市的法院作出的判令日本作者及出版社对侵害南京大屠杀目击证人名誉一事予以民事赔偿的判决,请求东京地方法院予以强制执行的申请,2015年3月20日,东京地方法院沿袭前述2003年4月9日大阪高等法院的判决,同样以中日之间不存在相互保证为由驳回了原告的强制执行请求。之后,东京高等法院作出维持东京地方法院的判决,驳回上诉的裁定。2016年4月20

[①] 参见《最高人民法院关于我国人民法院应否承认和执行日本国法院具有债权债务内容裁判的复函》,最高人民法院在该复函中明确:"关于日本国民五味晃向大连市中级人民法院申请承认和执行日本国横滨地方法院小田原分院具有债权债务内容的判决和熊本地方法院玉名分院所作债权扣押命令及债权转让命令,我国人民法院应否承认和执行问题,经研究认为,我国与日本国之间没有缔结或者参加相互承认和执行法院判决、裁定的国际条约,亦未建立相应的互惠关系。根据《中华人民共和国民事诉讼法》第二百六十八条的规定,我国人民法院对该日本国法院裁判应不予承认和执行。"(〔1995〕民他字第17号)

日，日本最高法院亦作出维持东京地方法院和东京高等法院判决的裁定，从而日本在最高法院层面确立了对中国法院判决不予承认和执行的原则。①

一方面，鉴于很多国家之间均不存在承认和执行司法判决的司法互助协定或未形成相互承认和执行司法判决的互惠关系，除非在被告所在国提起诉讼，否则原告所在国司法机关作出的商事判决均存在无法取得被告所在国司法机关承认和执行的障碍。于是，跨国交易合同较少将司法管辖作为解决纠纷的手段。另一方面，很多国家均为《承认及执行外国仲裁裁决公约》（以下简称1958年《纽约公约》）缔约国。该公约第1条规定："仲裁裁决，因自然人或法人间之争议而产生且在声请承认及执行地所在国以外之国家领土内作成者，其承认及执行适用本公约。本公约对于仲裁裁决经声请承认及执行地所在国认为非内国裁决者，亦适用之。"该公约第3条规定："各缔约国应承认仲裁裁决具有拘束力，并依援引裁决地之程序规则及下列各条所载条件执行之。承认或执行适用本公约之仲裁裁决时，不得较承认或执行内国仲裁裁决附加过苛之条件或征收过多之费用。"根据1958年《纽约公约》的上述规定，加入该公约的缔约国均有义务承认和执行其他缔约国仲裁机构作出的仲裁裁决，从而为某一缔约国仲裁机构作出的仲裁裁决在其他缔约国以司法强制力予以执行提供了保证，使得国际商事当事人通过仲裁解决国际商事纠纷成为较为常见的方式。

中日两国均为1958年《纽约公约》缔约国（日本于1961年批准，中国于1987年批准），依照该公约，中日两国均已存在相互承认和执行对方国仲裁机构作出的仲裁裁决的死法判决或裁定。本篇试图通过对仲裁裁决的日本司法审查制度以及实际判例运用进行考察，探讨日本司法机关对于仲裁裁决进行司法审查的裁量标准，从而为我国企业在与日本的经济交往中如何更好地将仲裁作为纠纷解决手段提供参考和借鉴。

---

① 村上幸隆「日中間における判決の承認・執行の現状と仲裁利用の際の留意点」（日中経協ジャーナル277号31頁、2017年2月）。

一、日本司法机关对仲裁裁决进行司法审查的制度概要

(一)国内仲裁裁决与外国仲裁裁决的区分

《日本仲裁法》于2004年8月颁布,2005年3月1日起施行。在该仲裁法颁布前,对于国内仲裁裁决的承认和执行主要适用原《日本民事诉讼法》第801条、第802条的规定。1961年日本加入1958年《纽约公约》之后,对于外国仲裁机构作出的仲裁裁决的承认和执行,根据《日本宪法》第98条第2款确立的尊重及优先适用国际条约原则,日本法院在司法审查中优先适用1958年《纽约公约》的有关规定,同时准用原《日本民事诉讼法》第801条、第802条的规定。在司法判例的运用中,一般以1958年《纽约公约》第4条为积极要件[1],以1958年《纽约公约》第5条为消极要件进行审查[2],即以满足第4条的积极

---

[1] 1958年《纽约公约》第4条:
一、声请承认及执行之一造,为取得前条所称之承认及执行,应于声请时提具:
(甲)原裁决之正本或其正式副本;
(乙)第二条所称协定之原本或其正式副本。
二、倘前述裁决或协定所用文字非为援引裁决地所在国之正式文字,声请承认及执行裁决之一造应备具各该文件之此项文字译本。译本应由公设或宣誓之翻译员或外交或领事人员认证之。

[2] 1958年《纽约公约》第5条:
一、裁决唯有于受裁决援用之一造向声请承认及执行地之主管机关提具证据证明有下列情形之一时,始得依该造之请求,拒予承认及执行:
(甲)第二条所称协定之当事人依对其适用之法律有某种无行为能力情形者,或该项协定依当事人作为协定准据之法律属无效,或未指明以何法律为准时,依裁决地所在国法律系属无效者;
(乙)受裁决援用之一造未接获关于指派仲裁员或仲裁程序之适当通知,或因他故,致未能申辩者;
(丙)裁决所处理之争议非为交付仲裁之标的或不在其条款之列,或裁决载有关于交付仲裁范围以外事项之决定者,但交付仲裁事项之决定可与未交付仲裁之事项划分时,裁决中关于交付仲裁事项之决定部得予承认及执行;
(丁)仲裁机关之组成或仲裁程序与各造间之协议不符,或无协议而与仲裁地所在国法律不符者;
(戊)裁决对各造尚无拘束力,或业经裁决地所在国或裁决所依据法律之国家之主管机关撤销或停止执行者。
二、倘声请承认及执行地所在国之主管机关认定有下列情形之一,亦得拒不承认及执行仲裁裁决:
(甲)依该国法律,争议事项不能以仲裁解决者;
(乙)承认或执行裁决有违该国公共政策者。

要件且无第 5 条拒绝承认和执行的消极要件为前提,对外国仲裁裁决予以承认和执行。① 在《日本仲裁法》颁布施行前,按照以上司法审查原则,日本法院对于中国仲裁机构(主要为中国国际经济贸易仲裁委员会)作出的多起仲裁裁决均作出了承认和执行的判决和裁定。②

1958 年《纽约公约》第 7 条第 1 款规定:"本公约之规定不影响缔约国间所订关于承认及执行仲裁裁决之多边或双边协定之效力,亦不剥夺任何利害关系人可依援引裁决地所在国之法律或条约所认许之方式,在其许可范围内,援用仲裁裁决之任何权利。"中国与日本之间于 1974 年签订了《日本国与中华人民共和国之间关于贸易的协定》(以下简称《日中贸易协定》,签订同年生效),其中第 8 条就日本国法人或自然人与中国贸易机构之间签订的商事合同或与此相关的纠纷解决进行了规定,该条第 4 款规定:"两缔约国就仲裁裁决应当按照被请求执行国家法律所规定的条件,相关机关负有执行的义务。"从上述 1958 年《纽约公约》第 7 条第 1 款及《日中贸易协定》第 8 条第 4 款的规定可看出,在两国间签订了关于商事仲裁的双边协定时,双边协定的规定应优先于 1958 年《纽约公约》适用,1958 年《纽约公约》与《日中贸易协定》的关系可理解为一般法与特殊法的关系,从而不应影响两国间协定的适用。该观点在日本法院作出的关于承认和执行中国仲裁机构作出的裁决的判决中得以确立③,且获得学说上的支持④。由此,依照《日中贸易协定》第 8 条第 4 款的规定,对于向日本司法机关申请承认和执行中国仲裁机构作出的仲裁裁决而言,可解释为日本司法机关负有按照日本国内法所规定的条件予以执行的义务。对此,日本学界也认为,对于承认外国仲裁机构作出的仲裁裁决,可直接援

---

① 小岛武司·高桑昭编『注釈と論点 仲裁法』(青林書院、2007 年)245—246 頁。

② 代表性的判例有:冈山地裁平成五年七月十四日判决、东京地裁平成五年七月二〇日判决、东京地裁平成六年一月二七日判决、东京地裁平成七年六月十九日判决、横滨地裁平成十一年八月二五日判决、东京地裁平成一三年六月二〇日判决、大阪地裁平成二三年三月二五日决定等。介绍相关判决的文献请参考:吉野正三郎·斎藤明美「中国の仲裁判断の日本における承認と執行 – 最近の裁判例を中心に – 」判例タイムズ 861 号 24 頁以下。

③ 横浜地裁平成十一年八月二五日判决,判例タイムズ 1053 号 269 頁。

④ 小岛武司·高桑昭编『注釈と論点 仲裁法』(青林書院、2007 年)267 頁。

引《日本仲裁法》第45条关于撤销事由的规定,且该第45条第1款中规定的撤销事由与1958年《纽约公约》第5条规定的不予承认的消极事由在本质上亦无差异。① 《日本仲裁法》颁布施行后,其第3条第3款规定,第八章的规定(即仲裁裁决的承认及执行决定)适用仲裁地为日本国内及仲裁地为日本国外的情形;其第45条第1款亦规定,仲裁裁决(无论仲裁地是否为日本国内,以下章节亦同)与确定判决具有同一效力,但基于该仲裁裁决的民事执行,应当按照此条规定作出执行决定。该两条规定明确了日本国内仲裁裁决与外国仲裁裁决承认和执行手续的同一性,外国仲裁机构作出的仲裁裁决的承认与执行的法律依据直接指向《日本仲裁法》的相关规定。

鉴于上述分析,除《日本仲裁法》明确不适用外国仲裁裁决的规定外,对于日本国内仲裁裁决及外国仲裁裁决均可适用《日本仲裁法》相关承认与执行的相关规定,且通过下述对《日本仲裁法》相关仲裁裁决承认和执行规定的考察,可得出《日本仲裁法》所规定的仲裁裁决的承认与执行要件与1958年《纽约公约》第4条规定的积极要件及第5条规定的消极要件并无本质区别,故对于区分日本国内裁决与外国仲裁裁决的承认与执行方面的差异已无实际意义。下文将以《日本仲裁法》的规定为中心考察日本司法机关对仲裁裁决的司法审查制度。

(二)日本司法机关对仲裁裁决进行司法审查的制度概要

根据《日本仲裁法》的相关规定,对于仲裁裁决的司法审查主要为仲裁裁决的撤销、仲裁裁决的承认、仲裁裁决的执行三个方面。

1. 仲裁裁决的撤销

《日本仲裁法》第七章是关于撤销仲裁裁决的规定。其第44条第1款首先规定了仲裁裁决的撤销须依仲裁当事人申请而提起,同时规定了可撤销仲裁裁决的具体事由。该条第1款规定,当事人在有下述事由时可向法院申请撤销仲裁裁决:

---

① 高杉直「日本における外国判決および外国仲裁判断の承認・執行」(法政論集2018年276号416頁)。

第一,仲裁协议因当事人的行为能力不具有效力的;

第二,仲裁协议根据当事人达成一致的应适用仲裁协议的指定法令(没有指定时为日本法令),因当事人限制行为能力以外的事由不具有效力的;

第三,申请人在仲裁员选任程序及仲裁程序中没有接到根据日本法令(关于法令无关公共秩序规定的事项当事人之间有协议的,为该协议)所必需的通知的;

第四,申请人在仲裁程序中无法防御的;

第五,仲裁裁决中包含超出仲裁协议或仲裁程序中申请范围的裁决内容的;

第六,仲裁庭的组成或仲裁程序违反日本法令(关于法令无关公共秩序规定的事项当事人之间有协议的,为该协议)的;

第七,仲裁程序中的申请,根据日本法令,是关于不能作为仲裁协议对象的纠纷的;

第八,仲裁裁决的内容违反日本公序良俗的。

该条还规定了当事人提出撤销仲裁裁决的期限(第44条第2款,即在仲裁裁决副本送达通知日起经过3个月或依照第46条规定执行决定确定时不得提出);规定了即时上诉制度(第44条第4款及第8款);规定了适用一般民事诉讼的口头辩论和当事人双方到庭审理质证期日制度(第44条第5款)以及当事人举证责任制度和职权主义(第44条第6款,即对于第1款第1项至第6项所列举事由,仅限于当事人证明存在该事由的情形,法院方可撤销仲裁裁决,而对于第1款第7项至第8项所列举事由,法院可依据职权而撤销)等。

另外,需要注意的是,仲裁裁决的撤销并不适用外国仲裁机构作出的仲裁裁决,而仅针对以日本国内为仲裁地所作出的仲裁,包括外国仲裁机构以日本国内为仲裁地所作出的仲裁裁决。其主要考虑是,对于外国仲裁机构作出的仲裁裁决的撤销进行司法审查属于该仲裁地司法机关的司法管辖权,而日本法院的司法管辖权无法及于域外,阻止该仲裁裁决在域外的法律效力。日本法院对外国仲裁机构作出的裁决不予承认和执行,就足以阻止该外国仲裁裁决在日本国内发生法律效力。因而对于外国仲裁裁决的撤销,日本法律既不能也无须对此作出规定。因此,《日本仲裁法》第3条第1款规定仲裁裁决的撤销适用于仲裁地为日本国内的情形,第45条第2款第7项规定的对仲裁裁决不予执行的事由中,也明确了仲裁裁决被其所属国司法机关撤销时,应作出拒绝执行的决定。依照上述规定,在日本国内对外国仲裁地仲裁机构作出的仲裁裁决提起撤销手续,将被日本法院驳回。可见,对于国际仲裁裁决的撤销属于该仲裁地所在国司法机关的专属管辖成为被国际普遍认可的规则。①

2. 仲裁裁决的承认与执行

《日本仲裁法》第八章是关于承认与执行仲裁裁决的规定。其中第45条规定了对仲裁裁决的承认手续。根据第45条第1款的规定,除非存在该条第2款明确规定的拒绝承认事由,否则自其在仲裁地确定发生效力时,与确定判决具有同一效力,即在日本国内自动认可其效力。该条规定与《日本民事诉讼法》第118条同样采用了自动承认主义,而无须由当事人提起承认仲裁裁决的申请程序,便可请求法院作出执行决定的申请。虽然《日本民事诉讼法》第118条及1958年《纽约公约》第1条第3款采取了相互主义原则,但《日本仲裁法》第八章并未采取相互主义原则将国内仲裁地与外国仲裁地作出的仲裁裁决予以区分。因此,依照《日本仲裁法》第八章的规定,即使是未加入1958年《纽约公约》的国家或地区作出的仲裁裁决,亦得以在日本被承认和执行(如中国台湾地区作出的仲裁裁决)。②

《日本仲裁法》第45条第2款规定了该条第1款仲裁裁决与确定判决自动具有同一效力的除外事由(即拒绝承认事由),将第45条第2款规定的承认除外事由与第44条第1款规定的撤销事由相对照,可看出仲裁裁决的不予承认事由与撤销事由基本一致。即第45条第2款第1项至第6项分别与第44条第1款第1项至第6项相同,第45条第2款第8项、第9项分别与第44条第1款第7项、第8项相同(就

---

① 小島武司·高桑昭编『注釈と論点 仲裁法』(青林書院、2007年)252—253頁。
② 高杉直「日本における外国判決および外国仲裁判断の承認·執行」(法政論集2018年276号417頁)。

该两条款之第2项、第3项及第6项的规定,因日本司法机关无须对依照外国法律对外国仲裁地作出的仲裁裁决进行撤销审查,语句上第44条用语为"日本之法令",第45条用语为"仲裁地所属国之法令",该区别仅为上下文语境措辞之差异,在实质上并无不同)。两条款的唯一不同点在于,第45条第2款第7项规定了"根据仲裁地所属国法律(仲裁程序适用法律为仲裁地所属国以外的国家之法律时,为该国法律)仲裁裁决尚未确定的,或者仲裁裁决被其所在国司法机关撤销的,或者其效力停止的"。因为如上所述,外国仲裁地作出的仲裁裁决其本身不成为日本司法机关进行审查的撤销对象,关于其效力的司法管辖权属于仲裁地所在国司法机关,需要在对外国仲裁裁决的承认条款中追加第45条第2款第7项规定的情形,即在该仲裁裁决已被仲裁地所属国司法机关撤销或者不具有法律效力时,当然也不可能再得到日本司法机关的承认和执行。

《日本仲裁法》第45条第3款规定了针对第1款第5项仲裁裁决中包含超出仲裁协议或仲裁程序中申请范围的裁决内容时的处理方法,即从该仲裁裁决中可区分出有关同项规定事项部分的,将该部分与该仲裁裁决的其他部分分别视为各自独立的仲裁裁决,适用该款规定;对于未超出仲裁协议或仲裁程序中申请范围的裁决内容,予以限定后进行承认和执行。这与第44条第7款针对第1款第5项仲裁裁决中包含超出仲裁协议或仲裁程序中申请范围的裁决内容时,就超出部分可进行区分的,仅就仲裁裁决的该超出部分予以撤销的趣旨亦是完全相同的。

《日本仲裁法》第46条规定了仲裁裁决的执行决定手续。第46条第1款规定,根据仲裁裁决欲进行民事执行的当事人以被申请人为债务人可向法院提出请求执行决定的申请。该条第8款规定了拒绝执行的条件,即法院对于第1款的请求执行决定的申请,认为有前条第2款各项所列举事由之一的(即第45条第2款规定的承认除外事由,该款第1项至第7项所列举之事由,仅限于被申请人证明存在该事由),可驳回该请求执行决定的申请。该条款中对于拒绝执行决定的事由要件直接援引了关于仲裁裁决承认除外的第45条第2款规定的事由要件,而如上所述,第45条第2款规定的拒绝承认仲裁裁决的事由要件也与第44条第1款规定的撤销仲裁裁决的事由要件基本一致。由此,拒绝执行决定的事由要件与拒绝承认以及撤销仲裁裁决申请的事由要件具有实质上的同一性。

该条还规定了执行中止程序(第46条第3款),即向法院提出请求撤销或停止仲裁裁决效力的申请且法院认为必要时,可中止第1款规定的执行申请程序,但法院可责令该中止申请人向他方当事人提供担保;规定了对于请求执行决定申请的管辖法院及管辖移送(第46条第4款、第5款),即执行案件由第5款各项规定的法院及根据请求目的或对债务人可进行扣押财产所在地有管辖权的法院专属管辖,该管辖法院在认为必要时可根据申请或依照职权,将该案件全部或部分向其他法院移送;规定了对于管辖决定的即时抗告制度(第46条第6款)及对执行决定的即时抗告制度(第46条第10款,准用第44条第8款之规定);规定了执行程序中适用一般民事诉讼的口头辩论和当事人双方到庭审理质证期日制度(第46条第10款,准用第44条第5款之规定);规定了仲裁裁决中包含超出仲裁协议和仲裁程序中申请范围的裁决内容时,且超出部分与未超出部分可进行区分时,对于未超出仲裁协议和仲裁程序中申请范围的裁决内容可予以限定后进行执行(第46条第9款,准用第45条第3款之规定)。

3. 对仲裁裁决撤销、不予承认与执行事由的归类

如上所述,拒绝执行决定的事由要件与拒绝承认以及撤销仲裁裁决申请的事由要件具有实质上的同一性,可以《日本仲裁法》第45条第2款列举的仲裁裁决承认除外事由规定为基础,对仲裁裁决撤销、不予承认与执行事由进行大致的归类。

《日本仲裁法》第45条第2款共列举了9项对仲裁裁决不予承认的事由,可大致作出如下归类:

第一,关于仲裁协议的有效性事由(第1项、第2项)及仲裁裁决包含超出仲裁协议或仲裁申请范围裁决内容的事由(第5项)。仲裁协议非为有效时,当然成为拒绝承认的事由。因为作为民间纠纷解决机制的仲裁制度本身,是以当事人之间的仲裁协议为基础,基于当事

人就争议事项的解决达成合意的意思自治原则方可启动仲裁程序。作为判断仲裁协议有效性的准据法，依据当事人指定的法律（无指定时则为仲裁地所在国法律），但关于当事人行为能力的准据法，依照国际司法的基本原则，当事人为自然人时原则上为其本国法，为法人时则为设立地法律。对于第5项规定的仲裁裁决包含超出仲裁协议或仲裁申请范围裁决内容的事由，因就超出部分事项作出裁决缺失当事人合意这一启动仲裁的前提条件，对该超出部分事项作出裁决相当于没有达成仲裁协议，故亦成为不予承认和执行仲裁裁决的事由。

第二，关于仲裁程序适正性事由（第3项、第4项、第6项）。作为民间纠纷解决机制的仲裁制度虽然将纠纷解决手段让渡给当事人意思自治，但也必须保障仲裁程序适当、公正地进行，即仲裁程序的适正性。仲裁程序中如存在未对当事人进行适当的通知、当事人在仲裁程序中无法进行防御抗辩或仲裁庭的组成及仲裁程序本身违法等仲裁程序方面的重大瑕疵，则当然成为拒绝承认仲裁裁决的事由。

第三，关于仲裁裁决非为有效的事由（第7项）。即，根据仲裁地所属国法律，仲裁裁决尚未确定的，或者仲裁裁决被其所在国司法机关撤销的，在日本当然也不具有效力，成为拒绝承认仲裁裁决的事由。

第四，关于依照日本法律不能成为仲裁协议适格对象的纠纷事由及违反日本公序良俗的事由（第8项、第9项）。即，依照日本法律，某些纠纷事项（如艺术价值的优劣、专利权的有效性等）并非仲裁协议的适格对象，对该等事项作出的仲裁裁决，应拒绝承认和执行。违反日本公序良俗是指仲裁裁决与日本基本法律秩序不相容。仲裁裁决被法院认定为违反日本公序良俗的，成为拒绝承认和执行仲裁裁决的事由，如仲裁程序中作伪证，或者仲裁员有收受贿赂行为，严重影响仲裁裁决公正性，可因违反公序良俗而拒绝承认和执行。[①] 关于仲裁适格及违反公序良俗的拒绝承认和执行事由，即使当事人未进行主张和举证，法院仍可依照职权进行调查。

---

① 唐津恵一「仲裁判断が手続の公序に反するとして取り消された事例」ジュリスト1447号109頁。

二、日本司法机关对仲裁裁决进行司法审查的判例运用

以下介绍两起日本司法机关对仲裁裁决进行司法审查的判例,通过对上面归类的司法机关对撤销、拒绝承认和执行仲裁裁决相关事由的裁量标准进行考察,以探讨日本司法机关对于拒绝承认和执行仲裁裁决相关事由的裁量标准在司法实践中是如何把握和运用的。

(一)东京地方裁判所 2010 年 7 月 28 日决定(X 株式会社与 American International Underwriters, Ltd., 申请撤销仲裁裁决案件)[①]

1. 案件概要

仲裁案外人中国台湾地区半导体制造商 A 公司在 1998 年采购 X 株式会社制造销售的半导体制造装置用于半导体工厂的运营。因 X 株式会社制造销售的半导体制造装置存在缺陷,A 公司工厂遭遇火灾并全损。A 公司向三家保险公司进行火灾险理赔,并从再保险的 Y 公司获取了保险金。Y 公司向 A 公司支付保险金后取得对 X 株式会社的代位求偿权。之后 Y 公司基于与 X 株式会社达成的仲裁协议,以日本为仲裁地向美国仲裁协会提起仲裁,请求 X 株式会社赔偿损失。仲裁机构于 2009 年 7 月 14 日作出仲裁裁决,主要以以下理由部分支持了 Y 公司的仲裁请求:①X 株式会社违反了设备警示义务;②警示义务的违反与本次火灾具有相当程度的因果关系。

X 株式会社不服仲裁裁决,向东京地方法院提起撤销仲裁裁决。其撤销理由为:①申请人 Y 公司在本案仲裁程序中并未主张违反警示义务,仲裁裁决却以此为由认定了 X 株式会社的责任,属于基于 X 株式会社无法防御抗辩的事由而作出该裁决;②该案以中国台湾地区相关规定为准据法几乎无法认可申请人 Y 公司的主张,而仲裁裁决却认定了警示义务的存在及本警示义务的违反与损害具有相当程度的因果关系,且责令作出巨额赔偿,该裁决内容违反日本公序良俗;③该案仲裁裁决的仲裁程序违反当事人之间的仲裁协议。

---

① 東京地決平成 21 年 7 月 28 日判例タイムズ 1304 号 292 頁。

2. 法院决定要旨

驳回 X 株式会社提起的撤销仲裁裁决申请。主要理由如下：

第一，针对 X 株式会社的第①点撤销理由，法院认为：《日本仲裁法》第 44 条第 1 款第 4 项规定的趣旨，应当将其解释为仅限于实施了使当事人无法到场质证、依据当事人完全无法认知的资料作出裁决等对于当事人几乎没有给予防御机会的严重违反程序保障的情形，法院方可撤销仲裁裁决。该案仲裁程序中 Y 公司已主张了 X 株式会社警示义务的违反及与损害结果的因果关系，因而，仅以当事人未将其认识为重要争点的情况，不能将其认定为符合该项撤销事由。

第二，针对 X 株式会社的第②点撤销理由，法院认为：从《日本仲裁法》第 4 条关于仲裁程序仅限于仲裁法规定法院可行使其职权的规定看，仲裁裁决应当得到最大限度的尊重，《日本仲裁法》第 44 条第 1 款第 8 项规定的趣旨，不应当将其解释为只是在仲裁庭进行事实认定或法律判断被认为不合理时法院即可撤销仲裁裁决，而应当将其解释为仅限于在认为仲裁裁决实现的法律结果违反日本公序良俗的情形下，法院方可撤销仲裁裁决。X 株式会社认为仲裁裁决认定违反警示义务及其与损害结果的因果关系从而作出巨额赔偿的裁决违反了日本的公序良俗，这仅仅是主张本案仲裁庭在事实认定和法律判断上存在不合理，而无法找到作出巨额赔偿金额以外的特殊事由。因而，不能将其认定为本案仲裁裁决所实现的法律结果违反了日本的公序良俗。

第三，针对 X 株式会社的第③点撤销理由，法院认为：该主张系 X 株式会社在收到仲裁裁决的 3 个月后重新追加提出的，在申请撤销仲裁裁决后，只要超出了《日本仲裁法》第 44 条第 2 款所规定的期限，再重新主张追加同条第 1 款第 1 项至第 6 项的事由，违反了同条第 2 款的规定而不能被认可。因为该种行为将产生阻止仲裁裁决早期确定的结果。

3. 考察

该案中法院对于申请人提出的撤销仲裁事由是否符合《日本仲裁法》第 44 条第 1 款第 4 项规定的当事人在仲裁程序中无法防御、第 44 条第 1 款第 8 项规定的违反日本公序良俗，以及第 44 条第 2 款规定的撤销期限期满后重新追加新的撤销事由是否符合该款规定等作出了决定。对该案申请撤销仲裁裁决的决定中,法院将第 44 条第 1 款第 4 项规定的在仲裁程序中无法防御事由限定在严重违反程序保障且该违反与影响仲裁裁决的结果具有盖然性;将第 44 条第 1 款第 8 项规定的违反日本公序良俗事由限定在仲裁裁决实现的结果违反日本公序良俗,而非仲裁事实的认定或法律判断存在不合理;将第 44 条第 1 款第 1 项至第 6 项的事由的追加提出期限同样限定为该条第 2 款规定的收到仲裁裁决之日起 3 个月内。法院对于以上三点作出的裁量判断,在之前尚无先例,法院提示了对上述问题的判断标准,在司法实践中具有参考和启示意义。①

(二) 东京地方裁判所 2012 年 6 月 13 日决定 (X 株式会社与美国法人 Y 申请撤销仲裁裁决案件)②

1. 案件概要

日本法人 X 株式会社系运用美国法人 Y 拥有的利用高炉渣泽生产玻璃的专利技术(日本专利)在日本运营进行产品制造销售的合资企业。因 X 株式会社在 2006 年之后未向 Y 支付技术服务费并要求重新审定技术服务费,就该事宜未能与 Y 达成一致。于是 X 株式会社向 Y 通知合同无效或解除,Y 于 2009 年 12 月 16 日以 X 株式会社为被申请人向一般社团法人日本商事仲裁协会提起仲裁,仲裁庭作出了支持 Y 请求 X 株式会社支付技术服务费的仲裁裁决。

X 株式会社不服仲裁裁决,向东京地方法院主张撤销仲裁裁决。其撤销理由为:在该案仲裁程序中,尽管未认可技术服务费为合资企业的利益分配,但仲裁庭却将其作为没有争议的事实并作出仲裁裁决,如仲裁庭就技术服务费的性质进行确切的事实认定则将得出完全不同的结论。因而,仲裁裁决不当地侵害了 X 株式会社的防御利益,妨碍了保障 X 株式会社的适正手续和保障 X 株式会社接受审理的权利,违反了《日本仲裁法》第 44 条第 1 款第 8 项手续上的公序良俗,

---

① 東京地決平成 21 年 7 月 28 日判例タイムズ 1304 号 293 頁。
② 高橋一章「仲裁廷における仲裁判断が仲裁法 44 条 1 項 8 号に反すると判断された事例」(東京地決平成 23 年 6 月 13 日)、ジュリスト 1456 号 152 頁。

根据第44条第1款第8项应当予以撤销。

2. 法院决定要旨

认可X株式会社提起的撤销仲裁裁决申请。主要理由如下：

首先，从关于仲裁程序的仲裁法规定及其趣旨来看，仲裁程序违反程序上的公序时，根据该程序作出的仲裁裁决的内容无法承担与手续公序相一致的程序，因而违反了基本法律秩序，不能承认其作为具有国家强制力保障的纠纷解决效力。其次，按照日本法律，专利权消灭后限制该技术的使用或对该技术的实施课以支付实施许可费的义务，属于不公正交易，很可能构成反垄断法规定的违法行为，既然反垄断法上的违法行为同样违反公序良俗而极有可能无效，那么技术服务费的性质认定相当于影响仲裁裁决主文的重要事项。该案仲裁裁决将当事人之间有争议的影响仲裁裁决主文的重要事项——技术服务费的性质作为无争议的事实而不再作出判断，违反了手续上的公序，应解释为相当于第44条第1款第8项规定的撤销事由。

3. 考察

该案仲裁裁决将有争议的事实作为无争议事实予以认定的情形与上一案件当事人未主张违反警示义务而仲裁庭认定对方当事人责任的情形大致相似，均属于仲裁庭对于案件具体事实的认定，而对于两件仲裁裁决是否属于第44条第1款第8项规定的违反日本公序撤销事由的裁量判断，该决定却作出了撤销仲裁裁决这一与前案截然不同的决定。该决定作为日本法院作出的撤销仲裁裁决申请的首例决定而广受关注，并在日本学界引起很大反响。反对该决定理由和要旨的学者不在少数。反对该决定的主要理由为：作为第44条第1款第8项规定的事由，应当解释为仅仅限定在仲裁裁决的内容违反公序予以适用，对于程序违反以同款第3项、第4项及第6项的规定已完全可以对应，将有争议的事实作为无争议事实予以认定的仲裁裁决作为程序问题适用该项规定令人质疑，只有在将其定性为内容判断时方有可能适用该项规定。而法院将其作为程序问题适用第44条的相关撤销事由时，只有在仲裁庭完全无视一方当事人主张、一方当事人采取欺诈、伪证或贿赂仲裁员等重大程度的手续保障违反时方可适用。本来仲裁裁决对于事实认定或法律适用即便存在错误,也不应成为撤销裁决的事由。因此,即使仲裁庭未将技术服务费的性质作为争点予以判断而作出仲裁裁决,仲裁裁决书中有不完备之处,而以手续上的公序违反为由将该裁决予以撤销,不得不使人深感疑惑。①

结语

通过以上关于日本司法机关对仲裁裁决的司法审查的制度概要及判例运用的考察可看出,《日本仲裁法》颁布施行后,日本司法机关对于仲裁裁决的承认与执行不再区分国内仲裁裁决和外国仲裁裁决,两者均可适用《日本仲裁法》第45条及第46条的规定,而拒绝承认和执行的事由也与第44条规定的撤销事由实质上一致。

虽然日本司法机关对于作出撤销仲裁裁决的决定存在较为罕见的先例,经检索目前尚未发现公开出版物刊载有其他撤销仲裁裁决的法院决定,亦未发现撤销外国仲裁裁决的案例。总体上,日本司法机关对仲裁裁决进行司法审查时,对作出撤销仲裁裁决的裁量标准掌握严格,以防止动摇将仲裁裁决作为国际纠纷解决的基本机制,防止损害当事人通过意思自治将仲裁作为终局解决纠纷手段的可信赖性。这与我国对于外国仲裁裁决的拒绝承认和执行采取更为严格的审查程序以维护国际仲裁裁决的信赖性的趣旨相同。②目前,我国企业与日本经济交流和合作日益频繁,商事纠纷不断多发,鉴于法院管辖司法判决在域外执行效力的障碍,作为国际商事主体的当事人将更经常地约定仲裁作为纠纷解决手段,可期待国际仲裁在纠纷解决机制中发挥更大作用。

(张傲霜　审校)

---

① 唐津恵一「仲裁判断が手続の公序に反するとして取り消された事例」ジュリスト1447号110頁。

② 《最高人民法院关于人民法院处理与涉外仲裁及外国仲裁事项有关问题的通知(2008年修订)》规定,拒绝承认和执行外国仲裁裁决须由高级人民法院报最高人民法院回复后方可作出。

试论以集团公司名义订立仲裁协议的效力扩张

曾玉洁*

摘要:随着经济全球化的不断深化,国际经济交往主体的组织形式日益多样,仲裁案件的争议主体已不再局限于合同双方当事人。在国际商事仲裁的实践中,仲裁协议的效力出现了有条件地向第三人扩张的现象。在一起涉外海事仲裁案件中,申请人依据以集团公司名义订立的仲裁协议提出仲裁申请,被申请人以申请人不是仲裁协议签字方为由提出管辖权异议,双方当事人就仲裁机构的管辖权问题发生了争议。本文拟以该案件为出发点,重点选取代理理论、公司集团理论和公平合理期待原则,结合国内外司法实践案例,分析在我国现行法律制度框架下,以集团公司名义订立仲裁协议效力扩张于集团内部未签字成员的理论适用,并在此基础上提出完善我国仲裁协议效力扩张法律制度的建议。

关键词:集团公司;仲裁协议;效力扩张

一、基本案情

S集团公司与注册在美国的C公司签订《货物运输代理合同》,合同前言部分约定,S集团公司代表附件3列明子/分公司与C公司就美国各港口的货运代理事宜签订本合同。同时,双方约定本合同项下

---

* 大连海事大学法学硕士,广东律坊律师事务所专职律师。

产生的纠纷应提交中国海事仲裁委员会。

H公司是S集团公司在华南地区从事货运代理业务的子公司。2019年,T公司与H公司签订《海运(货运出口代理)合同》,委托H公司办理货运出口相关业务。合同约定非因T公司原因造成货物被盗窃,或货物所有权被不当转移,由H公司承担全部赔偿责任。随后,H公司依据S集团公司与C公司之间的《货物运输代理合同》,委托C公司办理涉案货物在美国港口的货运代理事宜。

案涉货物到达目的港后,因美国海关通知查验被转移至指定查验堆场,并在等待查验期间被盗。H公司向T公司作出赔偿后,依据S集团公司与C公司之间《货物运输代理合同》中的仲裁协议,提出仲裁申请向C公司追偿。在仲裁庭首次开庭前,C公司提出管辖权异议,认为其与H公司之间不存在仲裁协议,H公司就该案无权提起仲裁。

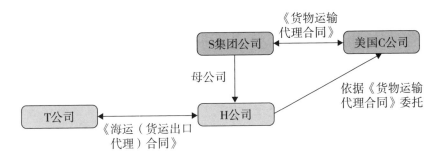

图1 案件简图

二、问题的提出

所谓仲裁协议效力扩张,是指符合有效要件的仲裁协议,在某些特定的情形下,因仲裁协议非签字人基于某种行为实质上享有合同权利且履行合同义务而推定其具有仲裁的意思表示,而使其受仲裁协议约束的情形。[①] 2000年,联合国国际贸易法委员会仲裁工作组第

---

① 参见张贤达:《国际商事仲裁协议效力扩张法律问题研究》,大连海事大学2018年博士学位论文,第18—19页。

三十二届会议审议了仲裁实践中的若干典型例子。该会议报告认为，当出现以下情形时，可将仲裁协议效力扩张至合同签署方之外的第三方：①仲裁庭或法庭对仲裁协议形式要件作扩张解释；②提单转让；③利他合同；④代理；⑤合同转让；⑥代位清偿；⑦法人的合并或分立；⑧关联方或关联交易；⑨公司集团理论。①上述报告虽不具有国际法效力，但反映了仲裁协议效力扩张的重要趋势。在此后的研究过程中，仲裁协议效力扩张理论被分为两大类：一是民法理论，主要包括衡平禁止反言原则、公平合理期待原则、诚实信用原则、代理理论、受益第三人原则；二是公司法理论，主要包括揭开公司面纱原则和公司集团理论。

对比国际商事仲裁的理论与实践，我国现行法律规范中对仲裁协议效力扩张的规定尚处于相对缺失的状态。我国《仲裁法》未规定仲裁协议效力扩张。相关司法解释中规定了仲裁协议效力扩张的四种适用情形，包括：当事人订立仲裁协议后合并、分立；因当事人死亡而发生继承；债权债务全部或者部分转让②；非涉外的保险人代位求偿③。随着经济全球化进程的迅速推进和现代企业的组织形式、经营模式的巨大变革，涌现出一系列新型组织形式，如集团公司、供应链伙伴等。其中，企业集团化管理的出现为传统仲裁法律制度带来了新的挑战。集团公司与合同相对方签订的合同中包含仲裁协议，同一集团的其他成员作为该仲裁协议的非签字方是否受该仲裁协议的约束成为解决现代商业纠纷的前提问题。本文将选取与集团公司仲裁协议效力扩张关系最密切的代理理论、公司集团理论和公平合理期待原则，结合国内外相关司法实践案例逐一进行分析。

---

① 参见联合国国际贸易法委员会仲裁工作组第三十二届会议文件《解决商业争端所涉某些问题可能的统一规则：调解、临时保护措施、仲裁协议的书面形式秘书长的报告》（文件编号：A.CN.9/WG.II/WP.108/Add.1）。

② 参见《最高人民法院关于适用〈中华人民共和国仲裁法〉若干问题的解释》（2008年调整）第8条、第9条。

③ 参见《全国法院民商事审判工作会议纪要》第98条。

三、以集团公司名义订立仲裁协议效力扩张的理论适用分析

(一)基于代理理论的仲裁协议效力扩张分析

仲裁协议效力扩张适用于非签字方的一种情况是,该非签字方一直就是仲裁协议的实质当事人。这种情况主要存在于委托代理关系中。一般说来,代理关系的实质是由代理人缔结、履行合同,法律后果由被代理人承担,而且代理人在行为时是基于为被代理人利益。因此,代理人在以代理身份签署仲裁协议时,代理人与相对人的意图均是使被代理人受仲裁协议的约束。因此,有必要首先从代理理论入手,分析以集团公司名义订立仲裁协议对集团内部未签字成员的效力扩张。

1. 显名代理情形下的仲裁协议效力扩张

我国《民法典》第162条规定:"代理人在代理权限内,以被代理人名义实施的民事法律行为,对被代理人发生效力。"从该规定可知,显名代理的构成包括四个要件:一是存在可代理的行为;二是代理人须为意思表示,这里的意思表示既包括向他人发出意思表示的积极代理,也包括受理他人意思表示的消极代理;三是代理人在代理权限内行为,即代理行为不应超出授权的范围,否则构成无权代理;四是代理人以被代理人名义行为,该要件体现了我国代理理论的显名原则,即代理人在实施民事法律行为时,应向相对人亮明自己的身份。据此,在显名代理情形下,集团公司订立仲裁协议的实质当事人是合同中明示的集团内部成员公司,即使该成员公司未在仲裁协议上签字,也应受到该仲裁协议的约束。

2. 隐名代理情形下的仲裁协议效力扩张

与显名代理相对应,我国参照《国际货物销售代理公约》引入了隐名代理理论。我国《民法典》第925条规定:"受托人以自己的名义,在委托人的授权范围内与第三人订立的合同,第三人在订立合同时知道受托人与委托人之间的代理关系的,该合同直接约束委托人和第三人;但是,有确切证据证明该合同只约束受托人和第三人的除外。"从代理归属效果看,本条与第162条的代理归属效果相同,唯一区别在

于是以代理人名义还是以被代理人名义。①

根据合同相对性原则,委托人与受托人之间的委托合同对第三人没有约束力,而受托人以自己名义与第三人签订的合同,一般也仅在受托人与第三人之间产生约束力。但根据本条规定,受托人以自己名义与第三人签订合同,在符合下列条件的情况下直接约束委托人和第三人。

(1)在委托人的授权范围内。

受托人实施的法律行为必须在委托人授权范围内。如果受托人没有获得授权或者超越授权范围,则不符合本条的构成要件。需要注意的是,这里的授权范围,并非合同层面的委托范围或者受托范围,而是代理层面的代理权限范围。②

(2)第三人在订立合同时知道代理关系。

受托人与第三人签订的合同要约束委托人和第三人,核心要素是第三人知道受托人背后的代理关系。在实践中,对第三人"知道"的程度和范围存在较大争议。有观点认为,应当对"知道"作如下限定性的解释:首先,除知道存在代理关系外,还应当知道具体的被代理人,以区别于行纪;其次,应当知道委托授权的内容和期限,确保受托人没有超出委托授权范围。③也有观点认为,本条所表述的是知道代理关系,这意味着第三人要知道代理事实,至于具体的被代理人,则无须构成第三人必须知道的内容;另外,由于本条将代理人在授权范围内与第三人订立合同作为其适用的构成要件之一,故在解释上可以认为第三人知道的内容不包括授权的内容和权限。④

上述两种观点中,笔者倾向于第二种观点。虽然委托与代理关系密切,但是两者之间存在明显区别,委托只涉及委托人与受托人之间

---

① 参见最高人民法院民法典贯彻实施工作领导小组编著:《中国民法典适用大全(合同卷)》,人民法院出版社2022年版,第1253页。
② 参见最高人民法院民法典贯彻实施工作领导小组编著:《中国民法典适用大全(合同卷)》,人民法院出版社2022年版,第1255页。
③ 参见王利明:《合同法研究(第3卷)》(第2版),中国人民大学出版社2015年版,第717—718页。
④ 参见朱虎:《代理公开的例外类型和效果》,载《法学研究》2019年第4期。

的法律关系,不涉及第三人;代理则涉及代理人、被代理人及第三人三方法律关系。本条中的"在委托人的授权范围内与第三人订立的合同"要件是约束受托人的,不应作为第三人"知道"的要件构成。如果要求第三人必须知道代理的具体内容和权限,对第三人而言未免过于苛刻,实践中也难以实现。

(3)没有确切证据证明该合同只约束受托人和第三人。

该条件为消极要件,如果有证据证明该合同只约束受托人和第三人,则此时该合同不能直接约束委托人和第三人。"有确切证据证明"的情形通常可包括:第一,合同中明确约定该合同仅约束受托人和第三人;第二,合同中虽然没有明确约定,但依据合同相关条款和相关事实,可以确定受托人和第三人仅希望在双方之间产生法律拘束力;第三,合同中明确约定"由受托人先行承担责任"或类似描述。

3.间接代理情形下的仲裁协议效力扩张

我国《民法典》第926条是关于间接代理的规定。需要指出的是,间接代理并非真正的代理,不会产生代理的三方关系。但在特殊情况下,间接代理可以发生直接代理的部分效力。[①] 对于间接代理情形下的仲裁协议效力扩张,我国司法实践中持否定态度。在申请人北方万邦物流有限公司申请撤销(2012)海仲京裁字第001号仲裁裁决一案中,各级人民法院的审查意见如下:

天津海事法院在其审查意见中指出:"在合同签订时,万邦公司并不知道卓域公司与金源公司之间存在代理关系,即万邦公司在签订仲裁协议时是与卓域公司达成了合意,而不是其他主体,金源公司并未参与仲裁条款的签订,亦与万邦公司无其他形式的仲裁协议。卓域公司在仲裁协议签订后,向万邦公司披露其有委托人,主张其委托人与万邦公司之间亦可依据仲裁协议进行仲裁,这种主张使万邦公司面临了在其签订仲裁协议时亦不能明确仲裁主体的局面,违背了仲裁的自愿原则。因此,应认定万邦公司与金源公司之间不具有仲裁

---

① 参见最高人民法院民法典贯彻实施工作领导小组主编:《中华人民共和国民法典合同编理解与适用(四)》,人民法院出版社2020年版,第2504—2505页。

协议。"①

天津市高级人民法院对该案的审查意见为:"万邦公司在订立代理合同之初并不知道金源公司为实际委托人,当卓域公司向金源公司披露万邦公司后,金源公司援引《中华人民共和国合同法》第四百零三条之规定介入代理合同并将争议提交仲裁的行为,仅能说明金源公司单方同意采取仲裁方式解决争议。其后,万邦公司向海事仲裁委提出管辖权异议的行为,系其就拒绝通过仲裁方式解决与金源公司争议所作出的明确意思表示。据此,我院认为万邦公司与金源公司之间未就采用仲裁方式解决纠纷达成合意。"②

最高人民法院在该案的请示复函中,同意了天津海事法院和天津市高级人民法院的审查意见,最终撤销了中国海事仲裁委员会(2012)海仲京裁字第001号仲裁裁决。由此可见,我国司法实践中,对于在订立仲裁协议时未披露委托人的隐名代理,不能基于委托人的介入权而使受托人与第三人之间的仲裁协议效力扩张至委托人。

(二)基于公司集团理论的仲裁协议效力扩张分析

"公司集团理论"的概念可以概括为:若公司集团中的某一成员与第三人签订了包含仲裁条款的合同,集团中其他成员虽未签署合同,但实质性参与了该合同的谈判、订立、履行或终止,则这些公司就在事实上形成了同一经济实体,该成员公司与第三人之间的合同,包括仲裁协议对于该同一经济实体内的任何成员公司均具有约束力,包括未签字的成员公司。③该理论最早出现在国际商会仲裁院的经典案例Dow Chemical v. Isover Saint Gobain(以下简称"Dow Chemical案")

---

① 《最高人民法院关于申请人北方万邦物流有限公司申请撤销(2012)海仲京裁字第001号仲裁裁决一案的请示的复函》[(2013)民四他字第5号]。
② 《最高人民法院关于申请人北方万邦物流有限公司申请撤销(2012)海仲京裁字第001号仲裁裁决一案的请示的复函》[(2013)民四他字第5号]。
③ See Stavros L. Brekoulakis, Third Parties in International Commercial Arbitration, Oxford University Press, 2010, pp. 154-164.

的仲裁裁决中。[1]在之后的仲裁实践中,国际商会仲裁院根据具体案情就公司集团理论的要件作出了进一步的分析和论证。例如,在国际商会仲裁院第5130号案例中,仲裁庭认为,集团内的所有公司都隶属于该集团,且均参与到一个复杂的国际贸易法律关系中,且这一集团的利益超越了其中各个公司的利益,因此应当视公司集团为一个经济实体,集团内的所有公司均应受仲裁协议的约束;在国际商会仲裁院第6519号案例中,仲裁庭认为,非签字方如果能够证明其已通过明示或默示的方式接受仲裁协议的约束,或者其积极参与合同签订前的磋商阶段,或者其已被直接牵连到包含有仲裁协议的合同中,那么该非签字方就当受仲裁协议的约束;在国际商会仲裁院第7604号和第7610号案例中,仲裁庭认为,仲裁协议的效力扩张需要证明仲裁程序中所涉及的所有当事人对非签字方加入包含仲裁条款的合同,成为合同当事人的共同意愿,或者能够推定在非签字方明确知道合同的情况下,仍然同意受该合同的约束。

总结 Dow Chemical 案及后续有关公司集团理论的经典案例,可归纳适用公司集团理论将以集团公司名义订立的仲裁协议效力扩张至集团内部未签字成员公司的要件如下:

1. 公司集团构成同一经济实体

仲裁庭在考虑适用公司集团理论时,首先会考察仲裁协议的签字方与非签字方数个公司之间的公司结构,这就要求签字方与非签字方成员之间建立起"紧密的集团结构"和"密切的组织与经济联系",即构成"同一经济实体"。[2]

"紧密的集团结构"和"密切的组织与经济联系"通常体现在两个方面:

第一,各个公司之间存在关联关系,如母子公司、联营企业、合营企业等。例如,某一集团公司的母公司占据控制地位,其下属子公司

---

[1] See Dow Chemical v. Isover Saint Gobain, ICC Case No.4131 of September 23,1982, 9 Y.B. Commercial Arbitration,1984, pp. 131-137.

[2] See Stavros L. Brekoulakis, Third Parties in International Commercial Arbitration, Oxford University Press, 2010, p. 154.

等成员需要根据母公司的指示负责执行,该母子公司通常会被认定为构成紧密的集团。

第二,各个公司之间对于资金、人力资源、商标等的共享。如在 Dow Chemical 案中,仲裁庭运用公司集团理论将仲裁协议效力扩张至非签字母公司的一项重要理由是,美国母公司拥有签字子公司所使用商标的所有权,且子公司并非无偿使用该商标,即签字子公司与非签字母公司共享了同一商标的使用权。①

2. 非签字方实质性参与了包含仲裁协议的合同

一方面,仲裁协议的签字方与非签字方满足同一经济实体的适用条件后,判断仲裁协议效力是否向非签字方扩张的另一个重要判断因素是,非签字方是否实际参与了包含仲裁协议的合同。非签字方的实质性参与被认为是仲裁协议效力扩张的要件之一,其主要原因是其后果通常是导致第三人有合理理由认为多个公司的身份产生了混同。②并且,实质性参与能够从另一个角度证明同一经济实体的存在。另一方面,实质性参与能够表明非签字成员已默示接受仲裁协议的约束。③在仲裁实务中,非签字方是否积极地参与了包含仲裁协议的合同的磋商、缔结、履行、终止的一个或多个阶段,是判断实质性参与的主要因素。仲裁庭往往结合案件中涉及的相关情况进行综合判断。在国际商会仲裁院第 6519 号仲裁案的裁决中,仲裁庭表明,如果能够通过有效或暗示的方式证明非签字方参与了合同,或者能够证明他们在合同的磋商阶段扮演重要的角色,或者他们直接地被牵连到包含仲裁条款的主合同中,那么,仲裁协议的主体就可以扩张至非签字方。

3. 各方当事人受仲裁协议约束的意愿

当事人的合意是仲裁程序存在的前提,也是仲裁机构取得案件管

---

① See Stavros L. Brekoulakis, Third Parties in International Commercial Arbitration, Oxford University Press, 2010, p. 155.

② 参见池漫郊:《论仲裁条款在关联公司中效力范围之界定——基于"公司集体理论"及"刺破公司面纱理论"的比较研究》,载北京仲裁委员会编:《北京仲裁》(第 66 辑),中国法制出版社 2008 年版,第 80 页。

③ 参见任媛媛:《国际商事仲裁中的"公司集团理论"研究》,载北京仲裁委员会编:《北京仲裁》(第 70 辑),中国法制出版社 2009 年版,第 47 页。

辖权的基础。因此,合意是适用公司集团理论所必须考虑的关键因素。只有证明当事人之间就非签字方作为仲裁协议当事人达成合意,才可能扩张仲裁协议效力,无论这种同意是当事人的明示还是默示。① 在实践中,法院和仲裁庭的惯常做法是,依据非签字方成员实质性参与合同的事实行为推定当事人默示的共同意思是同意仲裁协议。② 此外,若集团内部非签字公司积极地参与到合同的签订、履行以及终止过程中,这也可视为是以默示同意的方式对主合同中仲裁条款的约束表示同意。③ 但也有学者对这一观点表示反对,认为非签字方成员实质性参与合同的行为本身不足以导致仲裁协议效力向非签字方成员的必然延伸。④

笔者认为,考察各方当事人是否具有受仲裁协议约束的意愿,仲裁庭应站在独立第三方的立场,根据具体案情和各方当事人的行为进行判断。根据合同的具体约定,合同相对方在签订合同时存在与集团公司整体开展业务的意图,该合同涉及集团公司内部各方面的整体运营,则通常可以认定合同相对方与集团整体订立合同的意愿,集团公司未签字方实际参与合同的行为,可以推定其有受合同中仲裁协议约束的意愿。

(三)基于公平合理期待原则的仲裁协议效力扩张分析

公平合理期待原则是由预期利益制度发展而来的。其定义为:合同双方的预期利益是双方在签订合同时所期待的合同承诺发生的交易和可能带来的重要经济利益;而在一方没有按照约定适当履行合同义务时,对其行为的控诉、对自己利益损失的计算是以公平作为价值规范作出的。⑤ 在特定情况下,法院或仲裁庭考虑当事人的期待及该期

---

① See Bernard Hanotiau, Complex Arbitrations- Multiparty, Multicontract, Multi-issue and Class Actions, Kluwer Law International, 50(2005).

② See Stavros L. Brekoulakis, Third Parties in International Commercial Arbitration, Oxford University Press, 2010, p. 154.

③ See Stepham Wilske, Laurence Shore and Jan-Michael Ahrens, "the Group of Companies Doctrine"-Where Is It Heading? American Review of International Arbitration 17, 76(2006).

④ 参见任媛媛:《国际商事仲裁中的"公司集团理论"研究》,载北京仲裁委员会编:《北京仲裁》(第70辑),中国法制出版社2009年版,第51页。

⑤ 参见张利宾:《美国合同法:判例、规则和价值规范》,法律出版社2007年版,第3页。

待的公平合理性,结合案件争议具体情形,考虑仲裁协议的效力扩张范围,决定是否令非合同当事人参与仲裁。

按照文义解释,运用公平合理期待原则判断仲裁协议效力扩张应重点考虑两方面的标准:一是公平,即平衡兼顾各方当事人的利益;二是合理,即各方当事人期待仲裁的本意不因仲裁协议扩张而改变。随着公平合理期待原则在现代合同法制度中得到广泛的肯定,该原则已成为国际商事仲裁协议效力扩张至非签字方的重要理论原则,得到了包括我国在内的许多国家的司法实践认可。

山西省大同华建水务有限公司与北京朗新明环保科技有限公司执行案①是研究我国仲裁协议效力扩张问题的一个典型案例。该案涉及仲裁协议两次效力扩张。第一次为因公司合并导致权利义务主体变更情形下的扩张,在朗新明公司与华建实业公司、孔志强签订股权转让合同后,华建实业公司与华建房地产公司吸收合并,合并后的华建房地产公司合法承继了华建实业公司在上述两份合同中的权利和义务。第二次为合同权利义务转让情形下的效力扩张,华建房地产公司将其对朗新明公司的债权债务全部转让给华建水务公司,由华建水务公司享有合同权利、履行合同义务。

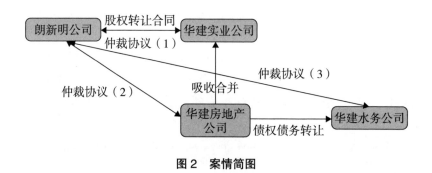

图 2　案情简图

北京市第一中级人民法院在该案裁定书中指出:无论是华建实业公司还是吸收合并华建实业公司的华建房地产公司,均没有与朗新明

---

① 参见北京市第一中级人民法院(2020)京 01 执异 70 号执行裁定书。

公司就仲裁协议在发生公司吸收合并、股权转让等情形下是否适用、有效等问题作出约定，亦没有当事人在受让债权债务时对仲裁条款明确表示反对，也不存在当事人之间订立了单独仲裁协议的情形，在发生公司吸收合并、债权转让的情形下，朗新明公司以盖章的形式对上述内容予以确认，并未提出对关于股权转让的补充合同中约定的委托经营收益条款不再履行的主张。①

对于朗新明公司来说，其作为合同当事人签署包含仲裁协议的合同，即表明了选择仲裁的意愿。在原合同相对方华建实业公司被华建房地产公司吸收合并，及此后华建房地产公司向华建水务公司转让合同的过程中，各方当事人均未就合同中的仲裁条款提出反对意见，也未作出其他约定。在发生纠纷后，当事人选择以仲裁方式解决纠纷，足以说明各方均有以仲裁方式解决纠纷的意愿。法院基于公平合理期待原则下各方利益的考量，将仲裁协议的效力扩张至华建水务公司，以仲裁的方式解决朗新明公司与华建水务公司之间的纠纷，并未违反各方的意愿，亦不损害各方的利益，体现了对当事人仲裁合意的尊重和维护。②

(四)以集团公司名义订立仲裁协议效力扩张理论在我国的适用

我国《民法典》第10条规定："处理民事纠纷，应当依照法律；法律没有规定的，可以适用习惯，但是不得违背公序良俗。"本条中所规定的民法法源包括法律以及不违背公序良俗的习惯。法源是法律适用过程中裁判依据的来源，是裁判所要依循的权威依据③，也是人民法院、仲裁机构在处理民事纠纷时据以作出裁判的规则。根据本条的规定，笔者认为，在我国现行法律框架下，以集团公司名义订立仲裁协议效力扩张理论应按照如下规则适用：第一，应优先适用代理理论；第二，公司集团理论在现阶段暂不宜适用；第三，以公平合理期待原则为

---

① 参见北京市第一中级人民法院(2020)京01执异70号执行裁定书。
② 参见栗俊海、徐梓程：《仲裁协议的效力扩张》，载《人民司法》2021年第23期。
③ 参见雷磊：《习惯法作为法源？——以〈民法总则〉第10条为出发点》，载《环球法律评论》2019年第4期。

补充。

1. 优先适用代理理论

我国是成文法国家,法律是排在第一位的法源,处理民事纠纷首先应当适用法律。作为一项独立的法律制度,我国《民法典》中设专章对代理作出了明确的规定,包括代理的适用范围、类型、效力等。因此,在涉及以集团公司名义订立仲裁协议效力扩张的具体争议中,人民法院、仲裁机构应首先按照法律的相关规定,依据代理的具体情形和条件,判断仲裁协议效力是否向集团内部未签字成员扩张。

结合前文对代理理论的分析,笔者认为,在集团公司以自己名义订立仲裁协议的情况下,仲裁协议的效力可依据显名代理、隐名代理的相关法律规定扩张适用于集团内部未签字成员,适用要件应包括三个方面:第一,集团公司应在订立仲裁协议前取得相应集团成员公司的授权;第二,集团公司应在订立合同时,或在合同中加入关于集团公司与集团内部成员公司之间存在代理关系的条款,表明代理关系的存在,在仲裁协议订立后委托人行使介入权不发生效力扩张;第三,集团公司没有明确表示仲裁协议仅约束其与合同相对方。在满足以上要件的情况下,以集团公司名义订立的仲裁协议效力可扩张适用于集团内部未签字成员公司。

2. 公司集团理论在现阶段暂不宜适用

关于公司集团理论的适用,有学者提出可将其视作商人习惯法、国际商会仲裁先例。[1]但笔者认为该观点失之偏颇。我国是成文法国家,判例在我国不是有效的法源,而通常作为民法法源的"习惯",应该是国家认可的民事习惯。[2]《最高人民法院关于适用〈中华人民共和国民法典〉总则编若干问题的解释》第2条第1款对我国《民法典》中的"习惯"作出了解释,该条规定:"在一定地域、行业范围内长期为一般人从事民事活动时普遍遵守的民间习俗、惯常做法等,可以认定为民

---

[1] 参见任媛媛:《国际商事仲裁中的"公司集团理论"研究》,载北京仲裁委员会编:《北京仲裁》(第70辑),中国法制出版社2009年版,第47页。

[2] 参见最高人民法院民法典贯彻实施工作领导小组主编:《中华人民共和国民法典总则编理解与适用(上)》,人民法院出版社2020年版。

法典第十条规定的习惯。"

作为一种解释仲裁协议效力向非签字方扩张的新理论,公司集团理论顺应了目前鼓励和支持仲裁的趋势,但该理论目前仅在少数机构和国家尝试适用,国际上明确承认该理论的国家寥寥无几,其适用结果也引起了较广泛的争论。例如,瑞士对公司集团理论持谨慎态度,瑞士法院就明确表示"瑞士法并不在意公司集体的概念,(瑞士法)仍旧坚持公司与其股东相互独立、母子公司之间相互独立"[①]。又如英国一直对公司集团理论持质疑并拒绝的态度。在 Peterson Farms 一案中,英国法院明确表示"英国法下没有公司集团理论这一概念"[②]。可见,公司集团理论在国际商事领域并未达到"长期"和"普遍遵守"的标准。此外,我国作为传统的成文法国家,目前未在任何形式的法律规范中明确接受公司集团理论,我国司法实践中也尚未出现援引该理论作出仲裁协议效力扩张的相关案例。因此,该理论暂不宜作为对以集团公司名义订立仲裁协议的效力扩张的认定依据。如跨国集团公司需采取以集团公司名义签署合同,由集团整体参与的模式开展业务,应尽量在合同中约定选择国际商会仲裁或选择以法国等承认公司集团理论的国家为仲裁地或以其法律作为仲裁协议的准据法。

3. 以公平合理期待原则为补充

从公平合理期待原则的具体内容看,该原则实际上是我国公平、自愿、诚信三项民法基本原则的结合。其中,公平原则要求民事主体在从事民事活动时,要兼顾他人利益和社会公共利益,不能有失公允;自愿原则是指,民事主体在民事活动中有权按照自己的意思设立、变更、终止民事法律关系,并自觉承担由此带来的法律后果;诚信原则要求所有民事主体在从事任何民事活动时,秉持诚实、善意,信守自己的承诺。

上述三项基本原则体现了《民法典》所维护的社会基本价值,对

---

① Bernard Hanotiau, Problems Raised by Complex Arbitration Involving Multiple Contracts- Parties- Issues: An Analysis 18 J. Int'l Arb:261, 281-282(2001).

② John Leadley & Liz Williams, Peterson Farms, There is no Group of Companies Doctrine in English Law, International Arbitration Law Review, 112(2004).

规范民事主体的行为、培养社会成员的价值理念具有重要作用。民法基本原则因具有高度抽象性和概括性,有利于克服成文法的局限性,授予法官自由裁量权,通过运用民法基本原则实现法的续造和漏洞填补。但另一方面,民法基本原则具有较大的"弹性",在司法实践中适用基本原则应遵循"具体规则穷尽"原则:第一,法律有具体规定时,应优先适用该具体规定,不能直接适用民法基本原则;第二,在没有法律具体规定时,如能以类推适用类似法律规定的,也不得适用民法基本原则;第三,只在以类推适用等漏洞补充方法仍不能解决时,才能适用民法基本原则。由此可见,民法基本原则只能处于具体法律规定的补充地位,这就决定了在具体案件中,只有在现行法律没有规定,或者依据现行法律规定处理,会造成当事人之间实质上的不公平或使社会利益遭受损害的情况下,司法机关才可以适用民法基本原则。因此,在处理以集团公司名义订立的仲裁协议效力扩张争议时,在没有法律具体规定的情况下,法院、仲裁机构可以公平合理期待原则为补充,结合具体案情作出判断。

四、我国以集团公司订立仲裁协议效力扩张的法律制度完善

《纽约公约》确立了仲裁协议的书面形式要件。该公约第2条第1款规定:"各国应当承认当事人将可仲裁纠纷提交仲裁的书面仲裁协议。"同时,公约对其缔约国提出要求:书面仲裁协议是仲裁裁决被各国承认及执行的必备条件之一。我国于1987年正式加入《纽约公约》,并根据《纽约公约》的要求对仲裁协议的形式和内容作出了规定。我国《仲裁法》第16条规定:"仲裁协议包括合同中订立的仲裁条款和以其他书面方式在纠纷发生前或者纠纷发生后达成的请求仲裁的协议。仲裁协议应当具有下列内容:(一)请求仲裁的意思表示;(二)仲裁事项;(三)选定的仲裁委员会。"从该规定可以看出,我国对仲裁协议采取了严格的效力认定规则。在形式要件方面要求具备严格的"书面方式",在内容方面要求具备"选定的仲裁委员会"。对仲裁协议严

格的效力认定规则,导致在仲裁实践中出现了许多仲裁协议被认定为无效的情形,客观上限制了我国仲裁协议效力扩张理论和实践的发展。

随着我国"一带一路"倡议和自贸区战略的不断深化,国际商事纠纷的类型复杂化、主体多元化等新特点也不断凸显,完善多元化争议解决机制,特别是我国的仲裁制度,成为我国法治工作的重点。改变仲裁协议严格的效力认定规则,为仲裁协议效力扩张提供更多法律制度空间,应作为我国仲裁法律制度改革的第一步。

(一) 以立法形式承认默示仲裁协议

在全球性经济贸易往来日益密切的背景下,为了适应经济社会发展的需要,2006 年《联合国国际贸易法委员会国际商事仲裁示范法》(以下简称《示范法》)放宽了对仲裁协议书面形式的要求,不但建议放弃仲裁协议书面形式的强行规则,还规定:"在申诉书和答辩书的交换中当事一方声称有协议而当事他方不否认即为书面协议。"①《示范法》实际上是通过确认当事人不否认的行为而确定具有仲裁的合意,表明了对默示仲裁协议的认可。

所谓默示仲裁协议是指当事人一方对于另一方用书信或者其他书面形式向其表示仲裁的意思,在没有明确给予答复的情况下构成的该方对于此仲裁意思的默示接受。② 尽管其在形式上与书面仲裁协议不同,但其实质仍是当事人间同意以仲裁方式解决争议的意思表示。随着仲裁实践的发展,许多国家和地区的法律都认可默示仲裁协议。如《韩国仲裁法》第 8 条将当事人予以答辩之行为认为是对仲裁协议的认可;又如我国台湾地区"仲裁法"第 22 条规定,只要当事人参与仲裁且未提出异议即默认仲裁协议之存在;再如我国澳门特别行政区《自愿仲裁法》规定,仲裁一方当事人认为存在仲裁协议,另一方当事人未否认,且参加仲裁程序陈述,则视为双方当事人达成了书面仲裁

---

① 参见《联合国国际贸易法委员会国际商事仲裁示范法》第 7 条第 2 款。
② 参见张建华:《仲裁新论》,中国法制出版社 2002 年版,第 105 页。

协议。

为顺应仲裁实践的发展,我国司法部于2021年7月发布了《仲裁法(修订)(征求意见稿)》。与现行《仲裁法》相比,《仲裁法(修订)(征求意见稿)》对仲裁协议的规定作了重大的修改。《仲裁法(修订)(征求意见稿)》第21条规定:"仲裁协议包括合同中订立的仲裁条款和以其他书面方式在纠纷发生前或者纠纷发生后达成的具有请求仲裁的意思表示的协议。一方当事人在仲裁中主张有仲裁协议,其他当事人不予否认的,视为当事人之间存在仲裁协议。"这一修改扩大了仲裁协议的书面形式,简化了仲裁协议的实质要件,是我国仲裁制度尊重当事人意思自治的进步表现。但上述修改仅采取"不予否认"这一消极标准认定当事人的意思表示,具有较大的模糊性,在仲裁实践中可能导致不公平的现象,最终有违尊重当事人意思自治的初衷。

仲裁协议的本质是当事人之间就争议解决方式达成的合同,笔者认为,在规定默示仲裁协议时,可借鉴《民法典》合同编中关于当事人以其实际行动订立合同的相关规定,增加结合当事人的积极行为如实际参与合同、主动参与仲裁程序等综合判定各方当事人之间仲裁协议的成立。如默示仲裁协议在我国仲裁法律制度中得到确认和完善,以集团公司名义订立的仲裁协议效力扩张将具备法律依据,在合同相对人不反对集团内部未签字成员依据集团公司订立的仲裁协议参与仲裁程序,或集团内部未签字成员实际参与仲裁程序即可视为合同相对人与集团内部未签字成员之间也存在仲裁协议,进而实现仲裁协议的效力扩张。

(二)采用"原则+列举"模式规范仲裁协议扩张

我国《仲裁法》第19条第1款规定:"仲裁协议独立存在,合同的变更、解除、终止或者无效,不影响仲裁协议的效力。"该规定是国际商事仲裁协议效力扩张的关键条款。对该规定中的"合同变更"采用不同理解,仲裁协议的效力可能产生截然不同的结果。如将"合同变更"狭义地理解为合同内容的变更,则通常不影响仲裁协议的效力;如采取广义理解,"合同变更"还可包括合同主体变更。笔者认为,从体系解释的角度，《仲裁法》第 19 条中的"合同变更"应采取广义理解。否则，我国《仲裁法》司法解释关于合并、分立、继承和债权债务转让时，仲裁协议效力扩张至合同外第三人的规定将失去存在的空间。即便"合同变更"包括合同主体的变更，我国现行仲裁相关法律仍无法触及以集团公司名义订立仲裁协议效力是否可向集团内部未签字成员扩张的问题。因此，有必要通过法律制度的完善，对仲裁协议效力扩张的适用标准和适用情形作出更明确的规定。

目前，各国对仲裁协议效力扩张的法律制度构建模式主要包括两种：一种是原则性规定，即只对仲裁协议效力扩张的适用要件作原则性规定，将具体认定标准交给法官；另一种是列举式规定，即对仲裁协议效力扩张的具体情形一一进行列举。从现行立法看，我国目前采取的是第二种模式。鉴于以集团公司名义订立仲裁协议效力扩张问题通常涉及多重主体，且具体案件情况较复杂，笔者倾向于采取"原则＋列举"模式对以集团公司名义订立仲裁协议效力扩张问题作出规定。

采取"原则＋列举"模式首先需要确定仲裁协议效力扩张的"原则"部分。通过本文第三部分的分析，笔者认为，将以集团公司名义订立的仲裁协议效力扩张至集团内部未签字成员的适用原则应为：非签字方虽未在仲裁协议上签字，但已经实质性地加入仲裁协议之中，并明示或默示接受仲裁协议的约束。对于"列举"部分，虽然我国司法解释已规定了几种仲裁协议效力扩张的情形，但随着经济社会的迅速发展，一些已经具备仲裁协议效力扩张条件的情形仍未包含在内。因此，为进一步完善我国仲裁制度，应适当增加以下三类仲裁协议效力扩张的类型：第一，以集团公司名义订立仲裁协议时，集团内部未签字方实际参与合同并愿意接受仲裁协议约束的，仲裁协议效力应扩张适用于该未签字方；第二，母子公司之间存在混同时仲裁协议效力应予以扩张；第三，基于代理关系等情况的仲裁协议效力扩张。仲裁协议效力扩张相对于双方仲裁协议而言属于特殊情况，必须在满足特定条件的情况下才能适用。因此，采用"原则＋列举"模式对仲裁协议效力扩张的条件作出规定，更能保证该特殊规则的准确适用，以利仲裁庭查清案件事实，辨明当事人之间的权利义务和责任，最终达到仲裁程序定分止争的目的。

结论

随着社会经济的不断发展,仲裁作为一种高效便捷的争议解决手段,在化解国际商事纠纷中所起的作用日益显著。与西方发达国家相比,仲裁协议效力扩张在我国仲裁理论和实践中较少涉及。本文从笔者经办的仲裁案件出发,通过分析与集团公司仲裁协议效力扩张关系最密切的代理理论、公司集团理论和公平合理期待原则,得出在我国现行法律框架下,以集团公司名义订立仲裁协议效力扩张理论适用规则应为优先适用代理理论,公司集团理论在现阶段暂不宜适用,并以公平合理期待原则为补充的结论。在此基础上,为进一步完善我国以集团公司名义订立仲裁协议效力扩张的法律制度,提出了应以立法形式承认默示仲裁协议,并采用"原则 + 列举"模式规范仲裁协议效力扩张的建议。

(付慈　审校)

商事仲裁中逾期提交证据涉及的若干法律问题研究

陈 晶[*]

摘要：证据制度是商事仲裁的重要内容。证据提交期限，是仲裁证据制度的核心要素之一，在特定情况下，逾期提交证据的效力如何，对案件结果会起到扭转乾坤的作用。不同的仲裁机构，对于逾期提交证据的程序、后果等规定不尽相同，仲裁庭（仲裁员）对于逾期提交证据也常常采取从宽兼从柔的态度。实践中，当事人无法如期提交证据、滥用证据提交期限、故意逾期提交证据等情形，影响了仲裁的程序正义以及案件独立公正审理，并存在（国内）仲裁裁决可能因此被撤销的风险。因此，对于仲裁庭、当事人而言，熟悉并严格依照仲裁机构仲裁规则处理逾期提交证据问题，显得尤为重要。当一方当事人出现违反仲裁规则并逾期提交证据的情形，另一方当事人（特别是代理律师）应当根据仲裁规则，积极采取合法的应对措施，以最大限度维护自身合法权益。逾期提交证据的行为，与证据持有人故意隐瞒证据及仲裁裁决的撤销存在关联性。建议我国仲裁机构适时引入"强行披露证据"制度，赋予仲裁庭行使"强制披露令"的权力，并配套相应的廉洁制度，对仲裁庭随意采信逾期提交证据的行为予以约束，规范逾期提交证据的程序和法律后果，以保证仲裁的独立公正。

关键词：商事仲裁；逾期提交证据；违反仲裁规则；撤销裁决；强行证据披露

---

[*] 中国人民公安大学法学院副教授。

一、研究逾期提交证据具有重要意义

(一)证据制度无论在民事诉讼还是商事仲裁中,都占有重要地位,是商事争议解决的核心

在商事仲裁中,证据的收集、整理、提交和出示,在整个仲裁活动中起着关键作用,是仲裁庭独立公正审理案件的重要环节,也是当事人和代理律师赢得仲裁的关键,同时,也是仲裁庭形成自由心证的重要环节,其重要性不言而喻。目前在我国立法层面上,仅仅原则性地规定了证据规则,例如《仲裁法》第43条规定:"当事人应当对自己的主张提供证据。仲裁庭认为有必要收集的证据,可以自行收集。"国内各个商事仲裁机构也没有统一的证据规则,各个仲裁机构的仲裁规则中有关具体证据规则的规定也不尽相同,有的只是根据《仲裁法》作出了原则性规定,有的作出较为详细的规定。在证据规则中,关于逾期提交证据的规定,不同的仲裁机构规定的内容大同小异,但是还是有差别,这就要求对当事人所选定的仲裁机构的仲裁规则熟悉、了解、掌握并加以准确应用,以公平合理实现仲裁目的。

(二)研究逾期提交证据具有重要理论和实践价值

证据提交期限,是仲裁证据制度的核心要素之一。一般而言,双方当事人都会在仲裁庭征求双方同意后的规定期限内完成证据的提交。但是,在特定情况下,当事人无法在仲裁庭规定以及双方当事人同意的期限内提交证据时,就涉及证据逾期提交的法律问题。逾期提交证据,是仲裁证据规则中一个特殊的例外情形,常常并不容易引起相关方面的重视,以逾期提交证据作为题目,同时结合仲裁实践进行深入研究的并不多见。逾期提交的证据,对案件结果起到扭转乾坤作用的情形,实践中也会遇到。由于不同仲裁机构的仲裁规则,关于逾期提交证据规定不尽相同,仲裁庭(仲裁员)对于逾期提交证据也常常采取从宽兼从柔的态度,仲裁当事人也存在滥用逾期提交证据相关规则的情形。因此,仲裁员和当事人,特别是代理律师,应当对不同的仲

裁机构以及相关的规定做到胸有成竹,才能够得心应手地运用。对逾期提交证据进行专门的研究和剖析,并依法采取积极应对举措,无论是对于当事人、仲裁机构、仲裁员,还是代理律师,都具有重要的理论意义和实践价值。同时,对于维护仲裁制度的独立公正以及维护当事人的合法权益,都将起到至关重要的作用。

对逾期提交证据了解并运用,对于仲裁各个参与方都具有重要价值。特别是对于当事人以及代理律师而言,如果当事人认为逾期提交证据隐含着暗箱操作、人为设计圈套等严重影响公正审理裁决的情形,则应当采取相应的法律措施,避免出现举证不能、对逾期提交证据应对失误等;同时,也涉及如何应对逾期提交的证据被仲裁庭接受的情形,如何依照仲裁规则提交附条件的质证意见,如何明确反对书面质证以及要求开庭质证,如何在质证意见中明确提出保留日后要以隐瞒证据或违反仲裁规则为由提出撤销之诉,等等。再者,要避免仲裁庭通过"当事人自行核对证据原件"等灵活的仲裁程序取代对"逾期提交证据应开庭质证"的法定程序[①],遇到这种情形时要旗帜鲜明地提出异议,明确提出以下具体意见:开庭出示证据并进行质证与核对证据原件是根本不同、不能相互替换的,在仲裁庭主持下的开庭质证为法定程序,仲裁庭故意缺席并随意变更质证程序,是严重违反仲裁程序的行为。这样的积极稳妥作为,为仲裁当事人在日后依法撤销仲裁裁决奠定扎实的基础。

对于仲裁庭而言,熟知并严格依据仲裁规则进行裁决,审慎处理逾期提交的证据,也具有重要意义。仲裁庭应严格遵守规则,对案情、案卷、证据做到通盘把握,心中有数;对于证据提交的期限进行充分及时的说明,并记录在案;在特定情况下,可以根据仲裁规则的规定,就逾期提交证据申请作出是否同意延期的书面决定;严守法律和廉政底线。避免由于程序违反仲裁规则规定而导致裁决被撤销或不予执行

[①] 根据《仲裁法》和不同仲裁机构仲裁规则的一般性规定,庭审后提交的证据,在仲裁庭释明以及当事人明确表示同意的情况下,可以采取书面形式质证;否则,则应根据《仲裁法》第45条关于"证据应当在开庭时出示"的一般性强制规定,进行开庭出示并质证。

的情况发生。①

二、"逾期提交证据"与"违反仲裁规则"的关系

关于仲裁的证据制度,由于《仲裁法》仅仅作了原则性的规定,因此,各个仲裁机构的仲裁规则,就成为仲裁庭、当事人(包括代理律师)需严格遵守的仲裁行为规范。如果违反仲裁规则的规定,则存在证据不被仲裁庭接受而导致的仲裁失利或者裁决被撤销等风险。下面就国内几个重要的仲裁机构的相关规定分别进行论述。

(一)国内几个仲裁机构的有关规定

1. 北京仲裁委员会

北京仲裁委员会(以下简称"北仲")《仲裁规则》规定:仲裁庭有权要求当事人在一定期限内提交证据材料,当事人应当在要求的期限内提交;逾期提交的,仲裁庭有权拒绝接受。当事人另有约定或者仲裁庭认为有必要接受的除外。当事人未能在规定的期限内提交证据,或者虽提交证据但不能证明其主张的,负有举证责任的当事人承担因此产生的不利后果。②

根据北仲《仲裁规则》的规定,可能产生一个困境,即:在一方当事人逾期提交证据,同时仲裁庭认为有必要接受的情况下,仲裁规则关于逾期提交证据应承担不利后果的规定就成了一纸空文。同时,仲裁规则完全授权仲裁庭,对于逾期提交证据是否有必要接受作出决定,但是对于作出决定的时间、程序、条件等,并未作出明确的规定。这样的话,对于案件的公平审理,以及如何确保当事人享有同等的逾期举证的权利,似乎出现了比较矛盾的规定,在实践操作中,可能会出现争议。同时,北仲的规定,是否与《仲裁法》有关证据必须开庭出示

---

① 根据《最高人民法院关于适用〈中华人民共和国仲裁法〉若干问题的解释》第20条的规定,《仲裁法》第58条规定的"违反法定程序",是指违反仲裁法规定的仲裁程序和当事人选择的仲裁规则可能影响案件正确裁决的情形。因此,如果仲裁庭违反仲裁规则并可能影响公正裁决,则可能面临被撤裁的风险。

② 参见《北京仲裁委员会/北京国际仲裁中心仲裁规则(2015)》第32条。

的强制性规定相悖,是否存在限制或者剥夺当事人开庭质证的权利,值得进一步探讨。

2. 中国国际经济贸易仲裁委员会

中国国际经济贸易仲裁委员会(以下简称"贸仲")仲裁规则规定:仲裁庭可以规定当事人提交证据的期限。当事人应在规定的期限内提交证据。逾期提交的,仲裁庭可以不予接受。当事人在举证期限内提交证据材料确有困难的,可以在期限届满前申请延长举证期限。是否延长,由仲裁庭决定。当事人未能在规定的期限内提交证据,或虽提交证据但不足以证明其主张的,负有举证责任的当事人承担因此产生的后果。①

中国海事仲裁委员会(以下简称"中国海仲")仲裁规则作出了和贸仲仲裁规则比较一致的规定。

3. 上海国际经济贸易仲裁委员会

上海国际经济贸易仲裁委员会(以下简称"上仲"),与贸仲的规定基本一致。当事人应当对其申请、答辩和反请求所依据的事实提供证据加以证明。仲裁庭可以规定当事人提交证据的期限。当事人应在规定的期限内提交。逾期提交的,仲裁庭可以不予接受。当事人在举证期限内提交证据材料确有困难的,可在期限届满前申请延长举证期限。是否延长,由仲裁庭决定。②

4. 深圳国际仲裁院

深圳国际仲裁院(以下简称"深仲")规定,仲裁庭可以决定举证期限,当事人应当在该期限内提交证据。逾期提交的,仲裁庭有权拒绝接受。当事人对自己的主张承担举证责任。仲裁庭有权决定当事人的举证责任。③

上述仲裁规则,对于逾期提交证据仲裁庭是否有权接受,仅北仲规定了在两种情形下仲裁庭可以接受,其他的机构都没有明确规定是

---

① 参见《中国国际经济贸易仲裁委员会仲裁规则(2015)》第 41 条举证规定。
② 参见《上海国际经济贸易仲裁委员会(上海国际仲裁中心)仲裁规则(2015)》第 37 条举证规定。
③ 参见《深圳国际仲裁院仲裁规则(2016)》第 39 条举证规定。

否有权接受,只是规定仲裁庭有权拒绝接受。这样的话,在实践中,就会产生一个疑问,如果仲裁规则没有规定仲裁庭可以接受逾期提交证据,那么,仲裁庭在证据提交期限届满后,决定接受一方当事人的证据,是否属于违反仲裁规则?如果不属于违反仲裁规则的情形,那么,规定举证期限的意义何在?

(二)贸仲的仲裁规则,对于逾期提交证据的接受与拒绝,作了较为详细的规定,实践中的操作性较强

针对逾期提交证据,贸仲仲裁规则[①]考虑得比较全面,既考虑到当事人的合法权利,也赋予了仲裁庭相应的权力。同时,为了将仲裁庭和当事人两方的权利义务平衡,作出了相应的程序性规定。首先,明确规定了举证期限,以及当事人在举证期限内提交证据的强制性义务。其次,同时也规定了无法如期提交证据的救济程序,即在规定期限内提交证据确有困难需要提前提出申请,并经过仲裁庭决定同意。规则仅赋予仲裁庭不接受逾期提交证据的权力,但是,规则并没有赋予仲裁庭可以任意接受逾期提交证据的权力。最后,对于逾期提交证据仲裁庭是否有权接受,规则采取了保守的态度,明确规定了限制性条件,并规定了详细操作程序:第一,必须以书面形式提出申请;第二,必须在举证期限届满前提出;第三,是否延长举证期限,由仲裁庭作出决定。同时,仲裁规则也明确规定了未能在规定期限内提交证据的法律后果,即"负有举证责任的当事人承担因此产生的后果"。

根据仲裁规则规定,逾期提交证据,如果没有严格依照仲裁规则规定的程序和条件寻求救济,则应当承担举证不能的法律后果。简言之,仲裁规则仅仅赋予仲裁庭对于逾期提交证据不予接受的权力,但是,仲裁规则并没有赋予仲裁庭在举证期限届满后可以随意接受证据的权力。笔者认为,仲裁庭在面对逾期提交证据且没有按仲裁规则规定提前提出申请时,应当严格依照该规定,不应接受为妥。

[①] 《贸仲仲裁规则》第41条规定,仲裁庭可以规定当事人提交证据的期限。当事人应在规定的期限内提交证据。逾期提交的,仲裁庭可以不予接受。当事人在举证期限内提交证据材料确有困难的,可以在期限届满前申请延长举证期限。是否延长,由仲裁庭决定。

但是，当事人一定要根据所选择仲裁机构的仲裁规则，因地制宜，依照选定的仲裁规则进行证据的提交，以保证在仲裁程序中的主动与合法。

（三）在实践中，逾期提交证据违反仲裁规则的常见情形及法律后果

以贸仲的仲裁规则为例，对于当事人或者代理律师而言，常见的违反仲裁规则的情形包括：

第一，没有在举证期限内提出逾期提交证据的申请。仲裁庭一般会在征求双方当事人同意的基础上，规定一个合理的证据提交期限，该期限一般在开庭之后，由办案秘书整理并打印出来一份"庭审要点"，由双方当事人各签一份，作为约束双方当事人的证据提交期限。第二，虽然在仲裁庭规定的举证期限内提出了逾期提交证据申请，但是阐明的理由不够充分全面。一般而言，如果希望延期举证，应当将逾期提交的证据的名称、依法取证难以在举证期限内完成、该证据对于案件具有重大影响等理由阐述清楚，争取获得仲裁庭的认可和支持。第三，没有对仲裁庭接受逾期提交证据提出异议。在仲裁实践中，也会遇到这样的情况，即仲裁庭在没有明确释明的情况下，接受一方当事人逾期提交证据，而对于另一方当事人的逾期提交证据拒绝接受，违反了仲裁规则中"仲裁员不代表任何一方当事人，应独立于各方当事人，平等地对待各方当事人"①，"在任何情形下，仲裁庭均应公平和公正地行事，给予双方当事人陈述与辩论的合理机会"②等规定，另一方当事人对仲裁庭违反仲裁规则的做法，没有及时以书面形式提出异议。第四，没有及时要求或请求仲裁庭要求对方当事人出示证据。如果当事人无法如期提交的证据，为另一方当事人所有，却故意隐瞒、拒绝出示、提供，正确的做法是，当事人应当当庭明确提出，或者以书面形式提出，或者请仲裁庭要求对方将故意隐瞒的证据出示提交。这样强制披露证据的要求是非常必要的，但是，许多当事人却由于种种

---

① 参见《贸仲仲裁规则》第24条仲裁员的义务的规定。
② 参见《贸仲仲裁规则》第35条审理方式的规定。

原因而怠于提出。

对于当事人或代理律师而言,如果出现上述情形,往往会由于处理不当导致丧失提供证据机会、失去日后提出撤销裁决的有利条件等法律后果。

对于仲裁庭而言,为了保证仲裁程序公正透明,避免出现程序瑕疵,避免出现裁决被撤销的潜在风险,以下事项需要引起注意。第一,没有释明。仲裁庭是保证庭审程序正义的主要力量,而仲裁是基于当事人对仲裁制度和仲裁机构的充分信任而产生的,因此,仲裁庭在审理案件过程中,应当充分尊重当事人的意见,做到充分释明,具体到逾期提交证据而言,就是要在征求双方当事人明示同意基础上,明确规定举证期间,并阐明逾期提交证据的不利法律后果,以避免事后引发当事人不满。第二,没有平等对待双方当事人。如果仲裁庭确实认为当事人逾期提交证据的请求合理而同意延期提交证据的话,仲裁庭应当给予另一方当事人同样待遇,无论另一方当事人是否需要,除非当事人明确表示拒绝。第三,没有作出是否接受逾期提交证据的决定而随意接受逾期提交的证据。依照贸仲仲裁规则,如果仲裁庭认为举证期限确需延长,一般而言,需要根据当事人提出的申请作出相应的决定,并通过仲裁机构及时充分释明给双方当事人,而非不经释明、不经决定而随意接受逾期提交证据。

仲裁庭如果在举证期限方面存在违反仲裁规则的情形,有可能因为违反仲裁规则的法定理由,而导致被人民法院撒销裁决的风险,同时,对于机构的美誉度也是一种伤害。

针对逾期提交证据需要把握以下几个要点:

无论是代理律师,还是当事人,在提交仲裁机构时,对于逾期提交证据的规定要学习并掌握,以便于维护自身程序权利,避免出现举证逾期并承担相应不利法律后果的情形。第一,仲裁规则的精准了解和把握。第二,了解掌握逾期提交程序和条件。不同的仲裁机构,规定不同,法律后果也不尽相同。第三,严格依照规则规定的条件、程序和时间行使申请的权利。第四,对于仲裁庭是否同意延长的决定,要有充分预案和应对措施。对于逾期提交证据,应注意:其一,尽可能针对仲裁请求、答辩或者反请求,提前将证据的取证工作做完整、全面、扎实、充分。其二,对案情研判做到细致、全面、自洽,避免出现延期举证的情形。其三,如果根据案情的发展,出现了对案件的公正审理具有重大影响的新证据,当事人应当在严格依照仲裁庭规定的期限内,阐明理由和必要性,依法向仲裁庭提出延期举证申请。其四,如果出现一方延期举证申请被仲裁庭拒绝,另一方当事人逾期提交证据却被接受的情形,一方当事人要据理力争,以仲裁庭应当给予双方当事人平等仲裁权利为由,要求仲裁庭对于双方当事人逾期提交证据给予平等待遇。其五,如果仲裁庭拒绝一方当事人的逾期举证申请,而接受另一方当事人逾期提交的证据,也没有提前向当事人予以充分、明确的释明,则一方当事人可以在裁决书作出后,根据《仲裁法》第58条"仲裁庭的组成或者仲裁的程序违反法定程序的"为由,请求法院对仲裁裁决予以撤销。其六,关于仲裁庭在庭审后出具的"庭审要点",如果不同意仲裁庭提出的证据提交期限,不同意对于庭后提交证据进行书面审理的话,则可以保留自己的权利,在"庭审要点"上明确表达自己的异议。

三、逾期提交证据与证据持有人故意隐瞒证据(及撤销裁决之间)的关联性

这是一个实践中常遇到的问题,本文前面部分已有提及,此处作为一个问题单独论述,希望当事人高度重视,深刻理解并加以应用,为日后撤销裁决打下坚实的基础。我国法律明确规定,对方当事人隐瞒了足以影响公正裁决的证据的[①],可以作为撤销仲裁裁决的法定理由。实践中常常碰到的难题是,取证方希望取得的证据,往往被另一方当事人所持有,而证据持有人又拒绝出示或披露所掌握的证据,这样的话,对于取证方而言,往往难以获取。但是,这并不意味着取证方只有消极等待,相反,取证方应当根据法律和仲裁规则的规定,制定积极的仲裁策

---

① 《仲裁法》第58条第1款第(五)项的规定。

略,并采取全面稳妥的应对措施,维护自身的仲裁权利,并为日后以证据持有人故意隐瞒证据为由申请撤销裁决打下基础,创造条件。

当事人逾期提交的证据,一般是对方当事人持有。我国由于缺乏强制披露制度,所以,一般情况下,证据持有人不会将不利于自己的证据披露或提供给仲裁庭。对于取证方而言,由于缺乏强制力的救济手段,往往难以在仲裁庭规定的举证期间取得关键证据。根据我国仲裁法和司法解释的规定,对于撤销裁决以及对于仲裁裁决不予执行的制度设计,既是对故意隐瞒证据行为的惩罚性规定,也是对取证方的一种事后救济手段,仲裁当事人应当充分理解并将该项规定作为维护自身权益的重要手段。

取证方在无法提交证据的情况下,要重点把握"逾期提交证据""故意隐瞒"①"撤销裁决"②三个法律制度的规定,并周密地进行相应的专业安排。对于故意隐瞒证据的行为,负有提交证据义务的一方当事人,在仲裁庭规定期限内如无法及时取得证据,应当根据仲裁规则规定,及时向仲裁庭提交"延期举证申请书",在申请书中应明确以下事项:明确对方当事人故意隐瞒证据的行为、明确故意隐瞒证据的名称以及该证据对案件公正审理的关键作用、明确要求对方当事人出示或者提交证据的意思表示、明确对方当事人拒绝出示或者提交证据的行为。上述每一个环节,都应提供相应证据佐证并形成证据闭环。其目的在于:取证方虽然无法在规定期限内取得证据,但是要明确提出逾期提交证据的申请;如果仲裁庭拒绝当事人申请,且存在影响公正裁决的情形,则上述每个环节的安排,可以作为日后申请法院撤销仲裁裁决的法定理由。当然,申请撤销需要考虑的因素是多方面的,具有严格的限制条件,其中关键的一条,就是要有充分的证据证明,是否对当事人的权利有实质性影响,是否可能对于案件的公正正确裁决产生重大影响。而上述环节的各种安排,也应围绕这一点展开。

---

① 《仲裁法》第58条第1款(五)项规定,当事人提出证据证明对方当事人隐瞒了足以影响公正裁决的证据的,可以向仲裁委员会所在地的中级人民法院申请撤销裁决。
② 《仲裁法》第58条第2款规定,人民法院经组成合议庭审查核实裁决有前款规定情形之一的,应当裁定撤销。

四、对于仲裁庭擅自接受一方当事人逾期提交的证据,对方当事人如何正确应对?

在仲裁实践中,这种情况虽不常见,但是一旦发生,对于当事人仲裁权利的影响巨大。鉴于此,本文将这个问题予以专门讨论,以期对当事人有所借鉴和参考。

第一,借鉴我国法院的司法实践,法院考虑当事人的主观方面以及证据与事实的关联程度而决定是否接受和采纳。根据我国在民事诉讼中的法律规定和司法实践,关于逾期举证的法律效力并非一概而论,常常会根据当事人主观上是否故意或者重大过失而采取不同态度。在司法实践中,如果一方当事人以对方当事人逾期提交证据为由而不予质证,人民法院能否采信该份证据? 最高人民法院没有采取一刀切的简单做法,而是采取了区别对待的方式。① 根据该规定,人民法院应当根据当事人逾期提供证据的主观过错程度区别对待:对于当事人因故意或者重大过失逾期举证提供的证据,人民法院可以根据其同案件基本事实是否有关联,决定是否采纳;反之,对于当事人非因故意或者重大过失逾期举证提供的证据,人民法院应当采纳。

第二,司法实践对于仲裁的借鉴意义。在民事诉讼中,针对当事人逾期提供的案件证据,另一方当事人不应简单以逾期提交为由拒绝或者放弃质证。在仲裁中,如果遇到一方当事人逾期提交证据时,另一方当事人应当分析,对方是否存在违反仲裁规则的情形,该证据是否应当进行开庭质证,该逾期提交的证据与案件基本事实是否有关,逾期提供的证据对于案件的基本事实是否有证明价值,并作出正确判断。切记不要简单以对方逾期提交证据为由,拒绝质证,而应当在阐明上述情形的前提下,积极应对,并进行质证,以避免承担不利的法律后果。

第三,对于仲裁而言,如果一方当事人遇到仲裁庭接受证据持有

---

① 《最高人民法院关于适用〈中华人民共和国民事诉讼法〉的解释》第 102 条第 1 款、第 2 款规定:"当事人因故意或者重大过失逾期提供的证据,人民法院不予采纳。但该证据与案件基本事实有关的,人民法院应当采纳,并依照民事诉讼法第六十五条、第一百一十八条第一款的规定予以训诫、罚款。当事人非因故意或者重大过失逾期提供的证据,人民法院应当采纳,并对当事人予以训诫。"

方逾期提交证据的情形,比较稳妥的应对策略是,在仲裁庭规定的质证期限内作出积极质证的反应。但是,该质证意见应明确表明是附条件的质证,并明确提出异议。质证所附条件主要包括:明确己方的反对意见,明确表示仲裁庭接受逾期提交证据违背仲裁规则;明确要求对于逾期提交的证据,进行开庭出示、质证;明确提出在日后的救济途径中,己方将会依据法律规定,申请撤销仲裁裁决。这样,对于保护当事人自身权益,促进仲裁庭公平公正独立仲裁,迫使对方当事人回归依法仲裁轨道等,将会起到积极的作用。

五、关于逾期提交证据的立法建议

鉴于立法的复杂性和难度,建议仲裁机构借鉴其他国际仲裁机构的经验,引入强制披露证据的规定。同时,强化仲裁庭权力的行使应严格遵守相关法律规定,并建议仲裁庭在行使强制披露令权力的同时,签署廉洁承诺书,以维护仲裁员和仲裁制度的公信力。

(一)国际仲裁机构的有关规定

1. 香港国际仲裁中心(HKIAC)的有关规定

关于仲裁证据制度,香港国际仲裁中心没有区分举证期限是否逾期,对仲裁庭是否有权拒绝或者接受作出了明确规定,值得内地仲裁机构参考和借鉴。主要内容有如下几个方面:第一,关于证据提交的期限为"在仲裁过程中"。第二,关于证据提交方式,包括两种形式,即当事人提交,或者仲裁庭要求当事人提交。第三,关于提交时间点为"随时"。第四,关于仲裁庭是否接受证据,仲裁规则明确赋予仲裁庭有权"接受或拒绝接受任何文件、附件或其他证据"[①]。

2. 瑞典斯德哥尔摩商会(SCC)仲裁院的有关规定

SCC 仲裁院作出了类似的证据披露规定,只是强调了需"应一方

[①] 《2018 香港国际仲裁中心机构仲裁规则》第 22.3 款规定:"在仲裁过程中,仲裁庭可随时允许或要求当事人提交仲裁庭认为与案件相关并对案件结果有重要影响的文件、附件或其他证据。仲裁庭有权接受或拒绝接受任何文件、附件或其他证据。"

当事人的要求,仲裁庭可以指令当事人一方提供可能与案件结果有关的任何文件或其他证据"。①

3. 美国仲裁协会(AAA)有关规定

AAA 也有和 SCC 仲裁院、HKIAC 相似的规定,但是更强调仲裁庭的权力和认知判断,即"仲裁庭在仲裁程序过程中,可随时要求当事人提交仲裁庭认为必要的或适当的其他文件、证物或证据"。② AAA 同时规定,当法律授权仲裁员传唤证人或者索取文件时,仲裁员可以自行或根据任何一方当事人的要求这样做。③

4. 伦敦国际仲裁院(LCIA)有关规定

LCIA 仲裁规则规定,仲裁庭有权力指令任何当事人向仲裁庭和其他当事人提供任何仲裁庭认为有关的并在其占有、保管或权力范围之内的文件和任何类别文件以供查阅,并提供副本。④

(二)关于如何完善逾期提交证据的建议

第一,建议增加强行证据披露制度。但是鉴于立法修改的难度大、程序难,建议可以在通过对仲裁规则的修改,在遵守法律规定前提下,在仲裁法框架内,借鉴新加坡、美国、伦敦、斯德哥尔摩国家和地区等经验,结合我国国情,赋予仲裁庭强行证据披露的权力。这样可以在现有法律框架内,大大降低对隐藏证据的获取难度,提高仲裁效率,促进仲裁公平,提升当事人对仲裁制度的信心。

第二,建议在仲裁规则中明确规定,仲裁庭非经规则规定的条件和程序,无权随意接受逾期提交的证据。

第三,建议在仲裁规则中明确规定,如果仲裁庭认为必要,且理由充分,需要经过双方当事人同意,可以接受逾期提交的证据,但是,需要对双方给予同等待遇,即双方当事人都同时享有平等的逾期提交证据的机会。可以参考《中国国际经济贸易仲裁委员会证据指引》的有

---

① 参见《斯德歌尔摩商会仲裁院仲裁规则》第 26 条第 1 款规定。
② 参见《美国仲裁协会国际仲裁规则》第 19 条第 3 款规定。
③ 参见《美国仲裁协会商事仲裁规则》第 35 条规定。
④ 参见《伦敦国际仲裁院仲裁规则》第 22 条关于仲裁庭的附加权力的规定。

关规定。①

第四,建议在仲裁规则中明确规定,如果仅仅接受一方当事人逾期提交的证据,而拒绝另一方的同样要求,视为严重违反仲裁规则的行为;同时,配套仲裁员个人以及仲裁机构廉洁制度的建设,明确相关仲裁员的行为规范及其责任。

第五,关于逾期提交证据的规定,如果授权仲裁庭权力,应建立在仲裁员独立公正基础上。基于我国目前仲裁界的现状,枉法仲裁、"朋友案""跑风漏气"等现象时有发生,为了维护仲裁的声誉,形象,维护当事人合法权益,保证案件审理和裁决尽可能公平合理,对于逾期提交证据,倾向于参考贸仲的规定,并结合强行证据披露以及相关的仲裁员廉政保证制度,共同努力促进中国的仲裁生态系统不断发展成熟。

(耿迪　审校)

---

① 《中国国际经济贸易仲裁委员会证据指引》第二章"举证、取证与证据交换"之第5条"举证期限"第(二)款规定:"当事人在举证期限内提交证据确有困难的,可在期限届满前书面阐明理由,向仲裁庭申请延长举证期限。仲裁庭应根据当事人申请延期理由的充分程度,决定是否准予延期。允许一方延期举证的,仲裁庭亦应同时考虑适当延长另一方的举证期限。"

CHINA REVIEW OF MARITIME AND COMMERCIAL ARBITRATION (VOL. 2)

Regional Coordination and Practical Development of International Arbitration

Studies About Issues Related to the ADR Mechanism on Civil and Commercial Disputes in the Guangdong-Hongkong-Macao Greater Bay Area

Written by Li Hu[*]   Translated by Li Taoxi[**]

Abstract: The ADR mechanism for the civil and commercial disputes is a vital project for the deep integration development of the Greater Bay Area. Due to the different jurisdictions of Guangdong, Hongkong and Macao, the regional legal conflicts do exist objectively. It is acknowledged that profound research and reasonable management on relevant issues are required in constructing and optimizing the ADR mechanism for the civil and commercial disputes in the Area. These issues fall into 2 main categories of non-litigation and litigation, which may be divided into 7 questions. Questions concerning non-litigation are connection of arbitration and mediation rules of the three regions, qualification and ethical conduct of arbitrators and mediators, recognition and enforcement of arbitration award and settlement agreement, and access to the professional legal service providers; ques-

---

[*] Vice Chairman & Secretary General of China Maritime Arbitration Commission (CMAC). The author would like to acknowledge his thanks to Ms. Qi Ji, the Director of the Case Administration Division of CMAC Arbitration Court and Ms. Mo Zhiying, the Case Manager of the Coordination and Supervision Division of CMAC Secretariat for their assistance, support and extensive comments on the drafts.

[**] Undergraduate student, the School of International Relations, Renmin University of China (RUC), majoring in international political economy, and minoring in law from the RUC Law School.

tions concerning litigation include construction of connection mechanism and platform of litigation, arbitration and mediation, transformation and cross-border enforcement of commercial settlement agreement, arbitration award and court decision in the Greater Bay Area, and the construction of information platform. Since the construction of the ADR mechanism for the civil and commercial disputes in the Area is a systematic project, there are two basic principles which need to be paid more attention on. The first is to possess international perspective and the second is to confirm and adopt the norm of "seat of dispute resolution".

Keywords: The ADR Mechanism for the Civil and Commercial Disputes in the Greater Bay Area; Litigation; Arbitration; Mediation

In September 2021, the Central Committee of the Communist Party of China and the State Council printed and released *the Comprehensively Deepening the Reform and Opening-up Plan of Qianhai Shenzhen-Hong Kong Modern Service Industry Cooperation Zone (the Qianhai Shenzhen-Hong Kong Plan)* and *the Overall Plan for the Construction of Hengqin Guangdong-Macao Deep Cooperation Zone (the Hengqin Guangdong-Macao Plan)*. The Qianhai Shenzhen-Hong Kong Plan states to construct high quality passage of key position for opening-up to the outside world, promote the opening-up of legal affairs, and establish the international legal service center and international commercial dispute resolution center in the Qianhai Cooperation Zone, exploring the connection of cross border legal rules under different legal systems and building the regional platform for resolving international commercial disputes where litigation, mediation and arbitration separate from but also connect with each other. *The Hengqin Guangdong-Macao Plan* requires to enhance legal safeguard, promote judicial communication and cooperation between Guangdong and Macao, establish and perfect the ADR mechanism for commercial dispute including international commercial trial, arbitration and mediation. In June 2022, the State Council printed and released *Over-*

all Plan for Deepening Comprehensive Cooperation among Guangdong, Hong Kong, and Macao towards the World in Nansha, Guangzhou (the Nansha Guangdong-Hongkong-Macao Plan), stating to create rule connection and mechanism connection highland, build the first-class business environment, perfect ADR mechanism, and build the one-stop platform for civil and commercial dispute resolution so as to promote the information exchange and mechanism connection of the ADR approaches such as litigation, arbitration and mediation. The above-mentioned three plans have clarified the requirements for the construction of the ADR mechanism for the civil and commercial disputes in the Greater Bay Area.

As an approach of high-end modern legal service, the ADR mechanism for the civil and commercial disputes is a vital project included in the joint cooperation of Guangdong, Hongkong and Macao with the Greater Bay Area and imposes significant impact on the deep integration development of the Greater Bay Area. Due to the different legal systems implemented by Guangdong, Hongkong and Macao, the regional legal conflicts do exist objectively. Therefore, it is acknowledged that profound research and reasonable management on relevant issues are required in the promoting process of constructing and optimizing the ADR mechanism for the civil and commercial disputes in the Greater Bay Area. Referred to the relative requirements of the three plans above, these issues fall into two main categories of non-litigation and litigation, which may be divided into 7 questions. Questions concerning non-litigation are connection of arbitration and mediation rules of the three regions, qualification and ethical conduct of arbitrators and mediators, recognition and enforcement of arbitration award and settlement agreement, and access to the professional legal service providers. Questions concerning litigation include construction of connection mechanism and platform of litigation, arbitration and mediation, transformation and cross-border enforcement of commercial settlement agreement, arbitration award and court decision in the Greater Bay Area, and the construction of information platform.

China Maritime Arbitration Commission (CMAC) set up its Hong Kong Arbitration Center in 2014 and its Greater Bay Area Arbitration Center (South China Sub-Commission) in Guangzhou in 2023 to provide nearby arbitration service; signed cooperation agreement with Guangzhou Maritime Court in 2017, developing the working mechanism for entrusted mediation; in 2021, signed MOU with eBRAM International Online Dispute Resolution Centre Limited and WTC Macao Arbitration Center to deepen mutual cooperation and communication, and participate actively in the construction of the ADR mechanism for the civil and commercial disputes in the Greater Bay Area. By doing so, CMAC has accumulated certain amount of successful experience and made a number of achievements accordingly.

I. Non-litigation

1.1 Connection of Arbitration and Mediation Rules

1.1.1 Arbitration Rules

As a rule, international arbitration is under the regulation of the law (*lex arbitri*). If the parties reach an agreement on the seat of arbitration, the parties' agreement prevails; in the absent of the parties' agreement, the arbitral tribunal shall decide the seat of arbitration, which is usually the location of the arbitration institution. The formulation of the institutional arbitration rules in the three regions cannot violate the mandatory provision of arbitration laws in each region. Therefore, it is rather apparent that the different provisions of the arbitration laws in the three regions can result in the divergence of arbitration rules and practice, and thus create problems in the connection between arbitration rules. These problems are mainly reflected in the following aspects:

First, who is to decide the jurisdiction of arbitral cases?

In the Chinese Mainland, according to the arbitration law, the jurisdiction of cases shall be decided by arbitration institution. While under

Hong Kong and Macao arbitration law, it is the arbitral tribunal that decides its jurisdiction over the cases in accordance with *the Competence to Competence Theory* adopted in international arbitration.

Second, who is to decide the challenge to arbitrators?

In the Chinese mainland, according to the arbitration law, arbitration institution (the chairperson of arbitration commission) shall decide the challenge to arbitrators. Whereas, in Hong Kong and Macao, the decision may by reference to the law be made by the arbitral tribunal, and the competent court possesses the final say.

Third, who is to decide the preservation and interim measure in arbitration?

According to the law of the Chinese Mainland, preservation shall be decided by the competent court. In Hong Kong, the preservation and interim measure against the party to the arbitration shall be decided by the arbitral tribunal but those against directly the third party shall be decided by the court. In Macao, the court decides the preservation while the arbitral tribunal decides the interim measure.

Fourth, who is to decide important procedural matters such as the seat of arbitration and language?

The majority of the arbitration rules in the Chinese Mainland stipulates that it is up to the arbitration institutions' decision, while under arbitration rules of Hong Kong and Macao, the decision shall be made by the arbitral tribunal.

Fifth, can a case manager of institution serve as a secretary of arbitral tribunal?

According to the usual practice of international arbitration, arbitration institution by its self does not resolve disputes but provides managing service for dispute resolution such as arbitration and etc. As the judge of the case, arbitral tribunal is responsible for the procedure and merit of the case, meanwhile hear the case and render award. Institution may appoint its staff member as case manager to manage the case on behalf of it, who is not allowed to serve as the secretary of arbitral tribunal. The arbitral tribunal may appoint arbitration professionals as its secretary who provides the tribunal with professional assistance, and whose task shall be decided by the tribunal. In the Chinese Mainland, the case manager of the institution actually also assumes secretary after the formation of arbitral tribunal. Yet in Hong Kong, the member staff of the institution can be appointed as secretary by the tribunal, but cannot be appointed as case manager for the same arbitration.

Sixth, can an arbitrator serve as a mediator in the arbitration proceedings?

In Chinese Mainland, Hong Kong and Macao, arbitrator may by law serve as mediator during the arbitration to mediate case (combination of arbitration with mediation), but there are different requirements for substantive and confidential details of the case acquired from mediation after mediation fails and arbitration resumes[①].

There are 3 ways to tackle the problems brought about by the distinctions among arbitration rules of the 3 regions. Firstly, by taking the chance of revising *Chinese Arbitration Law*, the top-level design can be enhanced, to comprehensively solve the problems such as decision on ar-

---

① According to Section 33 of Hong Kong Arbitration Ordinance, if "confidential information is obtained by an arbitrator from a party during the mediation proceedings conducted by the arbitrator as a mediator", "and, those mediation proceedings terminate without reaching a settlement acceptable to the parties, the arbitrator must, before resuming the arbitral proceedings, disclose to all other parties as much of that information as the arbitrator considers is material to the arbitral proceedings". According to Article 55 para 4 of Macao Arbitration Law, if the settlement agreement cannot be reached with the termination of mediation proceedings, the arbitrator must disclose to all other parties the information which is material to the arbitral proceedings. Article 51 of Arbitration Law of People's Republic of China has made regulations for mediation during arbitration, but does not clarify how to deal with the parties' important data and information acquired by the arbitrators during mediation proceedings. Usually, in practice, the issue is under the regulation of the institutional arbitration rules. Article 56 para 9 of CMAC Arbitration Rules 2021 stipulates that, "where conciliation is not successful, neither of the parties may invoke any view, proposition, statement, acceptance or opposition as proposal or proposition expressed by either party or by the arbitral tribunal in the conciliatory process to use as grounds for any claim, defense or counterclaim in the subsequent arbitral proceedings, judicial proceedings, or any other proceedings."

bitration jurisdiction, interim measures and challenge to arbitrators. Secondly, the arbitration institutions of Chinese Mainland are encouraged to revise their arbitration rules so as to improve connections and link up with the international practice. The CMAC Arbitration Rules 2021 stipulated that the decision on arbitration jurisdiction shall be made by CMAC, but if necessary, CMAC could delegate such power to the arbitral tribunal, which has made CMAC arbitration not only accord with the provisions of *Chinese Arbitration Law*, but also keep pace with the international common practice nowadays. The CMAC Arbitration Rules 2021 further clarify that significant procedural matters such as the language and seat of arbitration and etc may be decided by the arbitral tribunal. The tribunal can appoint CMAC staff member as its secretary, provided that the appointed staff is not the case manager of the same arbitration. Thirdly, it is necessary to enhance and promote the workable practice of "combination of arbitration with mediation" originated from Chinese Mainland so that the understanding can be improved, differences can be reserved while advantage can be exerted fully with seeking for the common ground.

1.1.2 Mediation Rules

Compared to arbitration, mediation is more flexible and convenient. In mediation, mediator does not enjoy the power to award the disputes, but to manage intercession and interposition, assist both parties to unscramble the dispute, clarify responsibilities, understand each other and promote both parties to reach a consensus, sign the settlement agreement and perform it in the due course. Within the Greater Bay Area, the Chinese Mainland and Macao belong in general to Civil Law system, but Hong Kong complies with Common Law jurisdiction. The corresponding English term for the Chinese phrase "调解" under the Civil Law tradition is "conciliation", in which conciliator is more active and positive, and may put forward to the proposals for the parties' reference. The corresponding English word for the Chinese phrase "调解" under the Common Law tradition is "mediation", in which mediators mainly encourage and promote parties to reach an a settlement agreement.

Hong Kong has formulated its *Mediation Ordinance*, but there is no specialized commercial conciliation legislation in the Chinese Mainland and Macao. The mediation institutions of 3 regions may make their mediation rules, provided that the rules do not violate the mandatory provisions of relevant laws of the region where the institution is located. Despite the different roles of mediation institutions and mediators in the 3 regions, the mediation is ultimately aiming to push parties to reach a settlement agreement. Therefore, there is no substantial barrier to the connection among the mediation rules of the 3 regions. Mediation institutions in the Greater Bay Area can improve coordination, enhance the application of mediation and enrich the practice of mediation.

1.2 Qualification and Ethical Conduct of Arbitrators and Mediators

1.2.1 Arbitrators

Internationally, relevant international conventions and national arbitration laws both impose substantive requirements on the qualification of arbitrators, which is independence and impartiality. There is little requirement of other form aside from that. For instance, The Swedish arbitration act provides definitely that an arbitrator shall be independent and impartial. Various worldwide famous arbitration institutions including International Arbitration Court of International Chamber of Commerce (ICC), Arbitration Institute of Stockholm Chamber of Commerce (SCC) and London Court of International Arbitration (LCIA) do not formulate their panels of arbitrators, and some other arbitration institutions such as Singapore International Arbitration Center (SIAC) and etc. do possess their panels, but the majority of which are recommendatory to the parties. On the other hand, numerous international maritime and commercial disputes have been submitted to *ad hoc* arbitration where the institutional management is not necessary in principle. Potential professionals acquire certification by attending arbitrator training program hosted by the independent associations with high credibility like Charted Institute of Arbitrators (CIArb) and etc, and thus raise the opportunity of being appointed as arbitrators by the parties or the arbitration institutions in specific cases. Professional associations such as International Bar Association (IBA) have also formulated their model ethical rules of arbitrators so that the parties of the arbitration choose to apply or the tribunal decides to apply in the arbitration.

The arbitration market in Hong Kong is generally speaking well made. Professionals usually acquire accredited certification by the training course and the membership provided by the independent associations such as CIArb East Asia Branch and etc. Along with their professional experience, they may apply for the listed arbitrator of arbitration institutions, or be appointed by parties to serve as arbitrator in *ad hoc* arbitration. Hong Kong International Arbitration Center (HKIAC) also provides with arbitration training program, but does not have a strict requirement of accredited certification over candidate arbitrators. Obviously, the corresponding training certificate has a significant impact on the access to HKIAC's panel of arbitrators. The HKIAC's panel is of the nature of recommendation, for the reference of the parties when appointing their arbitrators in arbitration. The Center has also formulated its *Code Ethical Conduct*.[①] In Macao, traditionally, civil and commercial disputes are mostly resolved through court litigation, and the development of commercial arbitration is relatively lag behind. Before its return, there were special provisions for arbitration in the civil procedure law of Macao. After return, Macao has made its *Arbitration Law* in May of 2020 to promote and regulate the arbitration in Macao. The Macao Arbitration Association has been

---

① *HKIAC's Code of Ethical Conduct* is for arbitrators of the arbitrations administered by HKIAC, who will also be bound by other codes of practice or conduct imposed upon them by virtue of membership of primary professional organizations. See www.hkiac.org/arbitration/arbitrators/code-of-ethical-conduct, accessed July 24, 2022.

established in 2014, providing the services related to arbitration such as seminars and training. In Chinese Mainland, aside from substantive requirement of "independence and impartiality", *the Chinese Arbitration Law* has provided the statutory requirements known as "three eight-years professional working experience and two senior titles" (三八两高) for the candidate arbitrators. All arbitration institutions select their candidate arbitrators in accordance with the statutory grounds and the institutions' additional requirements, formulate the code of ethical conduct, and manage the training for their listed arbitrators. The majority of the arbitration institutions is implementing the system where the parties are only allowed to appoint arbitrators from on the institutions' panel of arbitrators.[①] The China Arbitration Association is still in the process of organization, consequently, there is at present no third-party independent institution with good reputation for arbitration training and certification. In practice, the rules for candidate arbitrator selection and the codes of ethical conduct implemented by different arbitration institutions are also different.

By comparation, it is apparent that there are vast differences with regard to qualification and ethical conduct of arbitrators in three regions of Guangdong, Hong Kong and Macao. Given that arbitration market of the Chinese Mainland has been continuously opened and that *ad hoc* arbitration is gradually accepted[②], it is significant that Chinese Mainland

---

① *The CMAC Arbitration Rules 2021* has in the first time definitely provided the panel is recommendatory. According to Art. 30 of the CMAC Rules, "CMAC maintains a Panel of Arbitrators which uniformly applies to CMAC and Shanghai Headquarters/sub-commissions/arbitration centers. Parties may nominate arbitrators from the Panel of Arbitrators provided by CMAC, or from outside CMAC's Panel of Arbitrators. Unless otherwise decided by CMAC, the Sole Arbitrator or Presiding Arbitrator shall be nominated or appointed from CMAC's Panel of Arbitrators." "Nomination of arbitrators from outside CMAC's Panel of Arbitrators should comply with the law of the seat of arbitration."

② Internationally, the model *ad hoc* arbitration rules are in most of cases made by the institutions such as the maritime arbitrators associations. On 18 March 2022, the China Maritime Law Association (CMLA) firstly in Chinese Mainland released its *Ad Hoc Arbitration Rules*, and CMAC in the meantime released its *Rules as Appointing Authority in Ad Hoc Arbitration* to provide together the *ad hoc* arbitration service in Chinese Mainland.

accelerates to set up *China Arbitration Association*, and formulates the uniform professional regulations for the training, certification and ethical conduct of arbitrators. Guangdong, Hong Kong and Macao can enhance cooperation, jointly assessing and evaluating third party training and certificating institutions with high credibility which provide with arbitrators training and certification service in the Greater Bay Area so as to improve qualification and ethical conduct of arbitrators and promote the credibility of arbitration in the Area.

1.2.2 Mediators

The situation related to the qualification and ethical conduct of mediators in the three regions is similar to that of the arbitrators mentioned above. In this regard, Hong Kong has already had the independent institution for training and certification of mediators. In Chinese Mainland, there is no unified rules for the qualification and ethical conduct of mediators or third-party institution to provide certification service so far, and as a result, some commercial mediation institutions (e.g. The Mediation Center of China Council for the Promotion of International Trade) has formulated their own rules in practice. Similarly, Guangdong, Hong Kong and Macao can strengthen cooperation to appoint the co-recognized independent institutions for training and certification of mediators in the Area, and thus promote the positive development of the mediation in the region.

1.3 Issues Concerning the Recognition and Enforcement of Arbitration Award and Settlement Agreement

1.3.1 Arbitration Award

The relevant mechanism about the mutual recognition and enforcement of arbitration awards among Guangdong, Hong Kong and Macao is already relatively perfect. In the first place, China acceded to *the United Nations Convention on the Recognition and Enforcement of Foreign Arbitral Awards (the New York Convention)* in 1986, and the Convention has come into force in China since 1987. The member states of the Convention have reached 170 by now. All arbitration awards made in China (including Hong Kong and Macao) can be recognized and enforced in other member states of the Convention. In the second place, the China Supreme People's Court signed with Hong Kong *the Arrangement of Mutual Recognition and Enforcement of Arbitral Award between Hong Kong SAR and Chinese Mainland* in 1999, and signed with Macao the same arrangement in 2007. In 2013, Hong Kong and Macao signed the arrangement with each other. The relevant content of the 3 arrangements, especially the grounds for refusing recognition and enforcement of the arbitral awards is the same as that of *the New York Convention*. As a result, the recognition and enforcement of arbitral awards with each other among the 3 regions are conducted rather smoothly. The judicial authorities of the 3 regions may improve coordination related to the application of the arrangements, further unify the standards of judication and promote the quality and efficiency of recognition and enforcement of arbitral awards of the regions.

1.3.2 Settlement Agreement

There is no mechanical arrangement concerning the mutual recognition and enforcement of settlement agreement between the Chinese mainland and Hong Kong and Macao.

Mediation is a process where the mediators encourage and assist both parties to address their disputes and reach a settlement agreement. Settlement agreement is a new contract between both parties that mainly requires both sides to fulfill automaticallg. Since settlement agreement is not legally enforceable, unless explicitly stipulated, settlement agreement cannot be directly enforced by courts like court decision or arbitral award. In 2019, *the United Nations Convention on Recognition and Enforcement of Settlement Agreement Resulting from International Mediation (the Singapore Convention on Mediation)* has made express regulations about this. According to *the Singapore Convention on Mediation*, international settlement agreements reached through international commercial mediation can be recognized and enforced in the member states of the Convention. This has successfully addressed the problem of enforcement of settlement agreements resulting from international commercial mediation.

China has ratified *the Singapore Convention on Mediation* in 2019. After the Convention came into effect, the international commercial settlement agreement reached through mediation conducted by the mediation institutions in China (including Hong Kong and Macao) could be recognized and enforced in other member states of the Convention, unless the settlement agreement was involved with one of the statutory grounds for refusing recognition and enforcement under the Convention. As for the 3 regions of Guangdong, Hong Kong and Macao, on the one hand, it is appropriate to strengthen cooperation and improve coordination, perfect the environment of rule of law in Area, and speed up the construction of credit system in order to effectively enhance the rate of automatic performance of settlement agreements resulting from mediation. On the other hand, it can be taken into consideration that, at the appropriate time, by reference to *the Singapore Convention on Mediation*, the judicial authorities in the Chinese mainland sign with Hong Kong and Macao the relevant arrangements on mutual recognition and enforcement of settlement agreements so as to technically address such issue in the Area.

1.4 Issues Concerning the Access to the Professional Legal Service Providers

First of all, as an alternative dispute resolution aside from court litigation, both arbitration and mediation obey the "principle of parties' autonomy". The parties by themselves decide and choose arbitration or mediation through arbitration agreement or mediation agreement concluded by them. In international arbitration, the choice of the seat of arbitration is more important compared to that of arbitration institutions. The arbitration is under the regulation of the national laws of the seat of arbitration, which determine the competent court to assist and supervise the arbitration as well as the nationality of the arbitration award (the arbitral award is deemed to be made at the seat of arbitration), and thus decide the legal basis of the enforcement of arbitral award (the law of the seat of arbitration or regional arrangement or international convention). Unless otherwise agreed by the parties, the arbitral tribunals usually decide to adopt the law of the seat of arbitration as the law applicable to the substance of the disputes in accordance with the conflict rules of the international private law. The 3 regions may advance the cooperation, enhance the international credibility of ADR in the Area and attract more domestic and foreign parties to choose the Greater Bay Area as the destination of dispute resolution.

Secondly, as for the mutual access to the professional legal service providers of the 3 regions, Hong Kong and Macao both maintain an open policy. CMAC has already founded its Hong Kong Arbitration Center in 2014, which like Hong Kong International Arbitration Center is a company limited by guarantee (non-profit institution) registered in accordance with the Hong Kong Law. According to *Macao Regulation on Setting up and Operation of Arbitration Institutions 2019*, the arbitration institutions in the Chinese Mainland may set up their branch offices in Macao. So far, there is no unified regulation about the matter that foreign arbitration institutions or arbitration institutions from Hong Kong and Macao set up their branch offices in the Chinese Mainland. In practice, Shanghai and Beijing Municipal People's Governments have made the policies to support the arbitration institutions of Hong Kong, Macao and foreign countries set up their branch offices in Shanghai and Beijing. *The Qianhai Shenzhen-Hong Kong Plan* has expressly provided that, "the ADR service providers such as well-known arbitration institutions outside the Chinese Mainland may set up their branch offices in Qianhai Cooperation Zone which shall be registered at the Guangdong Provincial Department of Justice and put on record at the Ministry of Justice, to deal with the arbitral business with regard to civil and commercial disputes arising from the foreign-related commercial, maritime and investment affairs." As one of the regions in the Area, Guangdong province may also actively consider to adopt the similar policies. The revised draft Chinese Arbitration Law has responded to the matter that the arbitration institutions from Hong Kong, Macao and foreign countries may set up their branch offices in the Chinese Mainland which shall be registered at the Provincial Department of Justice and put on record at the Ministry of Justice. In reality, in addition to arbitration administered by Chinese mainland arbitration institutions, it is an ideal decision for the Chinese Arbitration Law to also uniformly regulate all the other arbitration taking place in the Chinese Mainland (arbitration administered by Hong Kong and Macao institutions, foreign institutions as well as international institutions).

II. Litigation

2.1 Issues Concerning the Construction of Connection Mechanism and Platform of Litigation, Arbitration and Mediation

From the perspective of court litigation, with regard to the ADR connection mechanism in the Greater Bay Area, it is believed that the China Supreme People's Court's practice of constructing "one-stop" ADR mechanism and platform may be by reference taken into consideration.

By way of setting up the international commercial courts, the Supreme People's Court has formulated the rules to create the "one-stop" ADR mechanism and platform where the specific arbitration institutions and mediation institutions in both the Mainland and Hong Kong SAR have been invited to participate so that litigation, arbitration and mediation are reasonably connected and the ADR service may be provided. For the relevant international commercial disputes, if the parties are willing to resolve them through arbitration or mediation, the court may propose the parties to choose arbitration institutions or mediation institutions on the platform for arbitration or mediation. On the other hand, the court will provide direct support for such arbitrations and mediations, by confirming the validity of arbitration agreement, deciding the application for preservation of property and evidence, performing judicial review, judicially confirming the settlement agreement resulting from mediation and etc.

Given that different judicial systems and jurisdictions of the 3 regions in the Area, the 3 regions may jointly build up the "one-stop" civil and commercial dispute resolution mechanism and platform of the Greater Bay Area and formulate the operational rules, under which the courts and arbitration institutions and mediation institutions from the 3 regions should be clarified through consultation; the courts of the 3 regions on the platform may direct the parties within or outside the Area to resolve their disputes through litigation, arbitration and mediation, and offer subject to the different seats for dispute resolution more convenient support for the resolution of disputes according to the respective law provisions and mutual arrangements① of the 3 regions (arrangements about mutual recognition and enforcement of arbitral award, assistance of interim measures as well as recognition and enforcement of civil and commercial judgements).

2.2 Issues Concerning Transformation and Cross-border Enforcement of Commercial Settlement Agreement, Arbitral Award and Court Decision in the Area

The settlement agreement resulting from mediation is not enforceable in law so far, and cannot be directly enforced by the court. In the

---

① As stated above, the arrangements about arbitration among the Mainland and Hong Kong and Macao have been well done. On 29 January 2024, the arrangement on mutual recognition and enforcement of civil and commercial judgements by the courts of the Mainland and Hong Kong ASR has come into force officially. If the arrangement on mutual recognition and enforcement of the settlement agreement resulting from commercial mediation can be signed and come into effect in the coming years among the Mainland, Hong Kong and Macao, the relevant arrangements over litigation, arbitration and mediation among the Mainland, Hong Kong and Macao is going to be more perfect, which will substantially promote the development of the ADR mechanism for the civil and commercial disputes in the Greater Bay Area.

Mainland, the settlement agreement may be enforced by the 3 means of being transformed into other legal instruments. Firstly, Parties may initiate an arbitration according to the arbitration clause contained in the settlement agreement to the chosen arbitration institution, which may form a sole arbitrator tribunal to hear the case in a summary procedure and make in accordance with the settlement agreement the consent award① that can be enforced by law. Secondly, the settlement agreement may be submitted by the parties to the competent court for judicial confirmation and transformed into the court decision to be enforced by law. Lastly, the settlement agreement may be submitted to the notary office for notarization and transformed into the notarial document to be legally enforced by the court. Under the present legal framework of Hong Kong and Macao, it is not forbidden to transform the settlement agreement resulting from the independent mediation into the arbitral award by the means of arbitration.

As discussed above, the mechanisms of mutual recognition and enforcement of arbitral awards among the Mainland, Hong Kong and Macao are thoroughly integrated and working well. From the perspective of ADR mechanism in the Greater Bay Area, it is advisable to encourage the parties to transform their settlement agreements into arbitral awards, which can be recognized and enforced in the Mainland, Hong Kong and Macao under the arrangements for mutual enforcement of arbitral awards. Aside from that, such arbitral awards could also be recognized and enforced abroad according to *the New York Convention*. The parties may

---

① The Article 56 Para 10 of CMAC Arbitration Rules 2021 reads: "Where the parties have reached a settlement agreement 44 CMAC Arbitration Rules by themselves through negotiation or conciliation before the commencement of an arbitration, either party may, based on an arbitration agreement concluded between them that provides for arbitration by CMAC and the settlement agreement, request CMAC to constitute an arbitral tribunal to render an arbitral award in accordance with the terms of the settlement agreement. Unless otherwise agreed by the parties, the Chairman of CMAC shall appoint a Sole Arbitrator to constitute such an arbitral tribunal, which shall examine the case through procedures it considers appropriate and render an award. The specific procedures and time period for rendering the award shall not be subject to the provisions of other articles of these Rules".

also have their settlement agreements be transformed into the court's decision that can be enforced in the Mainland and Hong Kong according to the arrangement for mutual enforcement of civil and commercial judgements between the Mainland and Hong Kong. However, at present there is no arrangement to back mutual enforcement of civil and commercial judgements between the Mainland and Macao. The enforcement of civil and commercial judgements of the Mainland, Hong Kong and Macao abroad still needs to be conducted on the basis of international judicial assistance. Taking these factors into consideration, under the current circumstance where the Mainland, Hong Kong and Macao have not made the arrangement for mutual recognition and enforcement of the settlement agreements from mediation, it is the most ideal and practical choice to transform the settlement agreements into the arbitral awards.

2.3 Issues concerning the Construction of Information Platform

Guangdong, Hong Kong and Macao may jointly construct the Greater Bay Area information platform of civil and commercial dispute resolution as a carrier of the civil and commercial dispute resolution mechanism of the Greater Bay Area, to promote the litigation and ADR services of the 3 regions for the choice of the parties within or outside the Area. Additionally, the platform may also provide the relevant legal database and newsletter of the 3 regions, thoroughly assisting the merging development of the Greater Bay Area.

In the process of constructing and improving the civil and commercial dispute resolution mechanism of the Greater Bay Area, there are two basic principles which need to be paid more attention on. The first principle is to possess international perspective and formulate the mechanism from the regional and even international level, being in line with the international rules and practice. The second is to confirm and adopt the norm of "seat of dispute resolution". No matter the parties within or outside the Area choose which institution and what kind of dispute resolution to resolve their disputes, the dispute resolution shall be regulated under the respective laws of the Mainland, Hong Kong or Macao as the seat of dispute resolution chosen by the parties.

The construction of the civil and commercial dispute resolution mechanism of the Greater Bay Area is a systematic project, which requires thorough implementation of the above three Plans for building up the Greater Bay Area, reaching common consensus, strengthening mutual cooperation, and systematically promoting with continuous effort.

An Analysis of Frontier Issues in the Amendment of Arbitration Law

Cui Qiang[*]

Abstract: The current "Arbitration Law", enacted in 1995, deviates significantly from international practice. Against the backdrop of widespread recognition in academia and practice that revision is needed, the Ministry of Justice released the "Arbitration Law (Amendment) (Draft for Comments)" in 2021. In this paper, we conduct research on the important issues in this revision and put forward suggestions for improvement and perfection on the basis of analyzing the highlights of relevant system reform. The following viewpoints are put forward in this paper: The ad hoc arbitration system in China is facing objective bottlenecks that need to be overcome and the role of pilot programs in FTZs and the leading effect of institutional arbitration still need to be fully utilized accordingly; the amendment concerning competence-competence requires further deliberation due to potential conflicts with the court's the prior review mechanism; the application of emergency arbitrator procedures and interim measures need to address challenges related to the effectiveness of enforcement; the judicial review mechanism of arbitration needs to be improved in terms of improving the system of setting aside arbitral awards and abolishing the system of non-enforcement of arbitral awards.

Keywords: amendment of Arbitration Law; ad hoc arbitration; com-

---

[*] Bachelor of Law of Peking University; LLM of University of Pennsylvania Law School; Partner of Commerce & Finance Law Offices; Arbitrator of China Maritime Arbitration Commission and China International Economic and Trade Arbitration Commission.

petence-competence; emergency arbitrator; interim measure; arbitration judicial review

As a socialized dispute resolution mechanism, the arbitration system has undeniable value in serving commercial relations. China's commercial arbitration system can be traced back to the early days of the founding of the PRC, and since the reform and opening up, in order to meet the actual needs of global economic integration and national governance modernization, the arbitration system has also begun to innovate while paying attention to the international experience and local conditions. The current Arbitration Law of the People's Republic of China (hereinafter referred to as the "Arbitration Law") came into effect on September 1, 1995, ending the situation in which various types of arbitration were subject to an administrative management system and arbitral institutions were mostly attached to administrative authorities[1], and elevating the arbitration system to the status and level of the basic law of the country. However, although this version of the Arbitration Law was formulated with reference to the UNCITRAL Model Law on International Commercial Arbitration (hereinafter referred to as the "Model Law")[2], there were still significant differences from the proposed provisions of the Model Law, which to a large extent reflected the transitional nature of the transition period.

---

[1] Article 2 of the Regulations of the People's Republic of China on Economic Contract Arbitration promulgated by the State Council in 1983: The economic contract arbitration authority is the economic contract arbitration committee established by the State Administration for Industry and Commerce and local administrations for industry and commerce at various levels.

[2] For example, Article 19(1) of the Arbitration Law stipulates that the arbitration agreement exists independently, and the modification, rescission, termination or invalidity of the contract shall not affect the validity of the arbitration agreement, which refers to a certain extent to Article 16(1) of the Model Law. Article 16(1) of the Model Law states: The arbitral tribunal may rule on its own jurisdiction, including any objections with respect to the existence or validity of the arbitration agreement. For that purpose, an arbitration clause which forms part of a contract shall be treated as an agreement independent of the other terms of the contract. A decision by the arbitral tribunal that the contract is null and void shall not entail ipso Jure the invalidity of the arbitration clause.

Therefore, the academic community began to pay attention to the issue of amending the Law shortly after its implementation. The Standing Committee of the National People's Congress (NPC) subsequently amended the Arbitration Law twice in 2009 and 2017[1], but the main purpose of these two amendments was to solve the problem of misplaced provisions caused by the amendment of the Civil Procedure Law of the People's Republic of China (hereinafter referred to as "Civil Procedure Law") and to adapt to the reform of the unified qualification exam for legal professions, without involving substantive changes to the provisions.

With the passage of time, discussions in the practical and academic circles about the lag in legislation of the Arbitration Law and the urgent need for revision have gradually formed a considerable amount of voice. In response, the Standing Committee of the Thirteenth NPC published the legislative plan on September 7, 2018, listing the revision of Arbitration Law as one of the 47 second-category legislative projects, that is, "draft laws that need to be worked on urgently and submitted for consideration when conditions are ripe".[2] On July 30, 2021, the Ministry of Justice released the "Arbitration Law (Amendment) (Draft for Comments)"[3], making a drastic revision to the Arbitration Law after 26 years. The Draft for Comments takes into account the gap between the existing Arbitration Law and international practice in a more comprehensive manner, and makes a number of fundamental changes and attempts, which promptly

---

[1] After the implementation of the current Arbitration Law, it was amended twice by the Decision of the Standing Committee of the National People's Congress on Amending Some Laws (issued on August 27, 2009; implemented on August 27, 2009) and the Decision of the Standing Committee of the National People's Congress on Amending Eight Laws, including the Law of the People's Republic of China on Judges (issued on September 1, 2017; implemented on January 1, 2018).

[2] See Legislative Planning of the Standing Committee of the 13th National People's Congress, accessed June 2, 2023, https://www.gov.cn/xinwen/2018-09/08/content_5320252.htm.

[3] See Notice of the Ministry of Justice on the "Arbitration Law of the People's Republic of China (Amendment) (Draft for Comments)" for Public comments, https://www.moj.gov.cn/pub/sfbgw/lfyjzj/lflfyjzj/202107/t20210730_432967.html., accessed December 25, 2024.

led to a lively and extensive discussion in the arbitration practice and academic community after its publication. With regard to the many cutting-edge issues involved in this revision, this paper focuses on the topics of ad hoc arbitration, competence-competence, emergency arbitrator procedures and interim measures, and reform of judicial review mechanism for arbitration from the author's experience.

I. There are Objective Bottlenecks in the Ad Hoc Arbitration System to be Broken Through

1.1 From Systematic Denial to Limited Acceptance of Ad Hoc Arbitration System under Current Law

In the law and practice of international commercial arbitration, the concept of arbitration includes institutional arbitration and ad hoc arbitration (or non-institutional arbitration). Institutional arbitration, as the name implies, refers to arbitration in which the arbitration proceedings are administered by a specialized permanent arbitral institution in accordance with its own promulgated arbitration rules; ad hoc arbitration, by contrast, refers to arbitration in which the parties conduct their arbitration proceedings pursuant to the arbitration agreement without an arbitral institution to administer or supervise the proceedings.[1] While ad hoc arbitration may be a more unfamiliar concept and form to our practitioners, from an international perspective, ad hoc arbitration dates back even to the ancient Greek period[2] and in fact forms the traditional DNA and institutional core of the international arbitration system[3]. Institutional arbitration, on the other

---

[1] Yang Liangyi, *International Commercial Arbitration*, China University of Political Science and Law Press, 1997, p. 136.

[2] Henry T. King, Jr. & Marc A., "LeForestier: Arbitration in Ancient Greece," 49 *SEP Disp. Resol. J.* 38(1994).

[3] Li Jianzhong, "China's Attempts at Ad Hoc Arbitration: Institutional Dilemmas and Realistic Paths - A Perspective from China's Pilot Free Trade Zone," *Research on Rule of Law* 2(2020).

hand, is widely considered to be a product of the modernization of the arbitration system, with most of the world's major arbitral institutions having been established only between the late 18th and late 20th centuries[①].

China's current Arbitration Law systematically denies the institution of ad hoc arbitration in a relatively implicit manner. Specifically, the current Arbitration Law stipulates that there shall be a clear arbitration agreement between the parties in order to apply for arbitration, and that a valid arbitration agreement shall have the following four basic elements: in a written form, with the intention to request arbitration, with clear items for arbitration, and with a selected arbitration committee.[②] In particular, where an arbitration agreement has not specified or has not specified clearly items for arbitration or the choice of an arbitration commission, the parties may conclude a supplementary agreement; but if a supplementary agreement cannot be reached, the arbitration agreement shall be void.[③] According to the above provisions, as an arbitration not administered by a permanent arbitration institution, ad hoc arbitration does not satisfy the requirement for an arbitration agreement to be effective, which is "with a selected arbitration committee", and its validity is in principle

---

① In accordance with incomplete statistics, the main arbitration institutions in the world were established as follows: the London Court of International Arbitration (LCIA) was established in 1892; the International Chamber of Commerce Arbitration Institute (ICC) was established in 1923; the American Arbitration Association (AAA) was established in 1926; The Arbitration Institute of the Stockholm Chamber of Commerce (SCC) was established in 1949; the China International Economic and Trade Arbitration Commission (CIETAC) was established in 1956; the Hong Kong International Arbitration Center (HKIAC) was established in 1985; and the Singapore International Arbitration Center (SIAC) was established in 1990.

② Article 16 of the Arbitration Law: An arbitration agreement shall include arbitral clauses stipulated in the contract and other written agreements which request arbitration to be made prior to or following the occurrence of a dispute. An arbitration agreement shall include the following: (1) the expression of an application for arbitration; (2) items for arbitration; (3) the chosen arbitration commission.

③ Article 18 of the Arbitration Law: Where an arbitration agreement has not specified or has not specified clearly items for arbitration or the choice of an arbitration commission, the parties concerned may conclude a supplementary agreement. If a supplementary agreement cannot be reached, the arbitration agreement shall be void.

not recognized by the current Arbitration Law. In this regard, the Legal Work Committee of the NPC has explained that historically there was only institutional arbitration but no ad hoc arbitration, and there was a lack of experience in supporting effective ad hoc arbitration.①

On December 30, 2016, the Supreme People's Court issued Opinions of the Supreme People's Court on Providing Judicial Guarantee for the Development of Free Trade Zones (hereinafter referred to as "The Opinions on FTZ Pilot Program"), which made a significant breakthrough in the recognition of the validity of ad hoc arbitration agreements. Article 9(3) of the Opinions adopts a tolerant and supportive attitude towards arbitration agreements without expressly agreed arbitral institutions, although it is only applicable to enterprises registered in the Pilot Free Trade Zones and meeting the "three specific restrictions".② Shortly thereafter, the "Hengqin Pilot Free Trade Zone Interim Arbitration Rules" (hereinafter referred to as "Hengqin Rules") were issued in March 2017 jointly by the Administrative Committee of the Hengqin New Area of the Guangdong Pilot FTZ and the Zhuhai Arbitration Commission. In September of the same year, the China Internet Arbitration Alliance also issued the CIAA Rules for Bridging Ad Hoc Arbitration and Institutional Arbitration. The aforementioned initiatives represent a limited attempt to introduce ad hoc arbitration in China in specific regions and areas, and are considered by academics and practitioners as an opportunity to promote the revision of the current Arbitration Law.

As a continuation of the aforementioned attempt, the Draft for Com-

---

① Jiang Wei, Xiao Jianguo, *Arbitration Law*, People's University of China Press, 2016, p. 22.

② Article 9(3) of The Opinions on FTZ Pilot Program: If enterprises registered in FTZs agree with each other to arbitrate the relevant disputes by specific personnel at a specific location in Chinese Mainland according to specific arbitration rules, such arbitration agreements may be deemed valid. If a people's court believes that the arbitration agreement is invalid, it shall report to the court at a higher level for review. If the superior court agrees with the reporting court, it shall submit its review opinions to the Supreme People's Court and make a ruling after receiving the reply from the Supreme People's Court.

ments issued by the Ministry of Justice in July 2021 for the first time loosens the principled position of the current Arbitration Law, which refuses to recognize the validity of ad hoc arbitration agreements from the legislative level, by proposing to incorporate the ad hoc arbitration system into the legal system of arbitration and defining the relevant specific rules.

On the one hand, the Draft for Comments changes the requirements for the validity of an arbitration agreement under Article 16 of the current Arbitration Law, as reflected in Article 21 of the Draft for Comments, that is, a valid arbitration agreement only needs to satisfy the requirements of "in a written form" and "with the intention to request arbitration", and does not need to have "clear items for arbitration" and "a selected arbitration committee".① In other words, the Draft for Comments no longer requires a selected arbitration committee, thus providing room for the application of ad hoc arbitration and following the trend of respecting the principle of party autonomy in the field of international commercial arbitration.

On the other hand, the scope of ad hoc arbitration is limited to "foreign-related commercial disputes" in the context of China's specific national conditions, domestic arbitration still adopts the form of institutional arbitration, and the parties do not have the right to agree on ad hoc arbitration. The Draft for Comments introduces the concept of "ad hoc arbitral tribunal" in Chapter 7 "Special Provisions on Foreign-Related Arbitration", and clarifies the conditions for the application of the provisions on foreign-related arbitration through Articles 91 to 93, which stipulate the core procedures of ad hoc arbitration such as formation and the recusal of the tribunal.

---

① Article 21 of the Draft for Comments: An arbitration agreement includes arbitration clauses entered into in a contract and an agreement in other written form with the intention to request arbitration before or after a dispute arises. If one party claims in arbitration that there is an arbitration agreement, but the other parties do not deny it, it shall be deemed that there is an arbitration agreement between the parties.

1.2 Objective Obstacles and Future Prospects of the Implementation of Ad Hoc Arbitration in China

1.2.1 Objective Obstacles

Under the background of the increasingly prominent competitive international dispute resolution pattern, the introduction of the ad hoc arbitration system fully reflects the importance attached to the principle of party autonomy in China's arbitration legislation, and it is also a response to the actual needs faced by the internationalization of China's commercial arbitration. However, it cannot be ignored that the introduction of the ad hoc arbitration system in China at this stage still faces the following objective obstacles:

First, the procedural advantages of the ad hoc arbitration system do not fully match the current development of arbitration in China, and there may be consequences of acclimatization.

It is generally accepted that in international arbitration practice, the value of institutional arbitration lies in predictability, while the value of ad hoc arbitration lies in flexibility, and the preference for different values determines the form of arbitration chosen by the parties.① However, the realization of the flexibility goal of the ad hoc arbitration system depends on a well-designed ad hoc arbitration agreement, experienced arbitrators and good cooperation among parties, lawyers and arbitrators. Without the skills, experience, and sense of cooperation in arbitration, the flexibility sought by the parties will be distorted into an arbitrariness that will detract from the original goal of arbitration and lead to an unpredictable outcome.

In China's institutional arbitration practice, arbitral institutions are permanently responsible for appointing arbitrators, determining and collecting arbitration fees, processing requests for recusal of arbitrators,

---

① Namrata Shah and Niyati Gandhi, "Arbitration: One Size Does Not Fit All: Necessity of Developing Institutional Arbitration in Developing Countries," 6 *Journal of International Commercial Law and Technology* Vol. 6, No. 4 (2011).

designating the venue of hearings, keeping and serving documents on the parties, convening expert hearings, and promoting arbitration proceedings, etc. The arbitrators do not address or take responsibility for the above procedural issues; moreover, the parties and their attorneys hardly have any direct face-to-face communication on procedural matters.

With the introduction of ad hoc arbitration, the ad hoc tribunal will be responsible for handling all procedural issues on the basis of respect for party autonomy, which places a high demand on the ability of the parties to understand the procedural rules and cooperate to advance the arrangements. While the parties to an ad hoc arbitration will also jointly select the procedural rules to be followed, this may not always withstand the test of various contingencies. Once the arbitral tribunal fails to deal with the process of negotiating with the parties, organizing and promoting the management of the arbitration procedure, it will not only cause the delay of the arbitration procedure, increase the cost of the arbitration, but may even lead to the revocation of the arbitral award, and the legislation does not provide further solutions to the problems that may arise. In contrast, arbitral institutions can conduct clear, unambiguous and predictable management of the arbitration process, at least to ensure that the advancement and cost of the arbitration are controllable.

Second, ad hoc arbitration lacks effective external supervision. In the absence of an arbitral institution, the system of filing ad hoc arbitral awards as provided for in Article 93 of the Draft for Comments may play a limited role in judicial review.

Under the institutional arbitration system, the arbitral institution serves as a heteronomous mechanism to effectively regulate the professional ethics and discipline of the arbitrators, whereas such a monitoring mechanism does not exist for ad hoc arbitration tribunals formed by the parties themselves. It can even be argued that whether the rights and obligations of the parties can be properly protected depends entirely on the arbitrator's own professional and legal qualities. There is no fixed list of arbitrators for ad hoc arbitration, in theory, anyone can form an arbitral tribunal and sign the arbitral award. Therefore, it cannot be ruled out that criminals use false arbitration to evade foreign exchange regulatory policies and other risks. Independent arbitrators who work full-time as arbitrators are very common in international arbitration, but the vast majority of arbitrators in China are part-time rather than full-time arbitrators, that is, there is no independent professional arbitrator group in China. The quality and credibility of arbitration ultimately depend on the professionalism and ethics of the arbitrators. In the context of the current lack of self-discipline mechanism for arbitrators in China, it is doubtful whether the ad hoc arbitral tribunal can reasonably play the role of "referee" entrusted to it by legislation.

Another advantage of the institutional arbitration system is the supervision of the arbitral award by the arbitral institution, namely the award review system. This system originated from the 1975 edition of ICC Rules of Conciliation and Arbitration, which requires the arbitral tribunal to submit the draft award to the Court of Arbitration for review before signing the award, so as to ensure that the award covers all the issues that the arbitral tribunal needs to respond to.[1] Current Arbitration Law does not explicitly provide for a review system of arbitral awards, but CIETAC was the first to provide in its 1995 Arbitration Rules that draft awards shall be submitted to the Arbitration Commission for review.[2] Subsequently, most of the arbitral institutions in China have followed this practice and made express provisions in their Arbitration Rules. Although

---

[1] Article 21 of ICC Rules of Conciliation and Arbitration (1975): Before signing an award, whether partial or definitive, the arbitrator shall submit it in draft form to the Court. The Court may lay down modifications as to the form of the award and, without affecting the arbitrator's liberty of decision, may also draw his attention to points of substance. No award shall be signed until it has been approved by the Court as to its form.

[2] Article 56(2) of the CIETAC Arbitration Rules (1995): The arbitrator shall submit the draft award to the Arbitration Committee before signing the award. Without prejudice to the arbitrator's independent award, the Arbitration Committee may bring to the arbitrator's attention the question of the form of the award.

there is no such provision in the Arbitration Rules of the Beijing Arbitration Commission, BAC actually has a process of reviewing and approving drafts when handling cases. Although the reviewer does not substantively modify the arbitrator's opinions, such supervision can put pressure on the arbitrator and increase the parties' trust in the arbitration process. Ad hoc arbitration lacks a corresponding review mechanism, and in the absence of an independent group of arbitrators and a competitive arbitrator market in China, the reputation monitoring mechanism cannot play its role, and the quality of ad hoc arbitration awards will be difficult to guarantee.

Article 93(3) of the Draft for Comments stipulates: "The arbitral tribunal shall serve the award to the parties, and submit the service record and the original copy of the award to the intermediate people's court at the place of arbitration for filing within 30 days from the date of service." To some extent, the purpose of this provision is to solve the above-mentioned problem of the lack of a review mechanism for the ad hoc arbitration system, but Draft for Comments lacks an effective explanation of the relationship between the filing system and the effectiveness or enforcement of the awards, which may add burden to arbitral tribunals and courts on the contrary.

First, the core value of ad hoc arbitration lies in the respect and protection of party autonomy, which is a principle universally applied in contracts and deeds. The results of a commercial arbitration award are to be voluntarily performed by the disputing parties, rather than having to be enforced through the courts. If the parties recognize the arbitration result and voluntarily perform the award, it is possible that the award will have been performed the day after it is served; and in the case of applying to the court for enforcement of the award, it is not necessary to file an arbitral award with a Chinese court for a foreign-related award that needs to be enforced overseas. The parties who need to recognize and enforce the award in China will naturally disclose the relevant award to the Chinese court, and the court will review the ad hoc arbitration award and make a ruling in accordance with the review standards. Therefore, the mandatory filing requirement is to some extent a reversal of the legislative intent of the ad hoc arbitration system to respect the principle of autonomy. In practice, there are risks of conflicting with the confidentiality of arbitration, arousing concerns of the parties and affecting the application of the system itself.

Second, under the perspective of comparative law, neither The Convention on the Recognition and Enforcement of Foreign Arbitral Awards (hereinafter referred to as "New York Convention") nor the Model Law imposes a requirement for ad hoc arbitral awards to be filed in courts, and the filing provision of Article 93 of the Draft for Comments lacks a reasonable object of reference.

Third, after years of arbitration practice, the parties have a path dependence on institutional arbitration and a low acceptance of ad hoc arbitration.

As a contracting party to the New York Convention, China's recognition and enforcement of arbitral awards made in the territory of another contracting state are not only for institutional arbitral awards, but also for ad hoc arbitral awards, in accordance with the relevant provisions of the New York Convention. Therefore, one of the biggest criticisms of current practice of not recognizing ad hoc arbitral awards made within Chinese Mainland is that it results in de facto "super-national treatment" - for foreigners.[1] However, such an understanding is inaccurate, because such "super-national treatment" is not related to the nationality of the parties involved, but is attached to the nationality of the arbitral awards, and an overseas ad hoc arbitral award obtained by one party with Chinese nationality can also be recognized and enforced in China. The reason why overseas ad hoc arbitral awards can obtain the same treatment as

---

[1] Liu Jingdong, Liu Yan, "Research on Related Issues of Ad hoc Arbitration System and Judicial Review," in Li Hu, *China Review of Maritime and Commercial Arbitration*, Peking University Press, 2022, p.28.

institutional arbitral awards in China is fundamentally due to the recognition of the quality of overseas ad hoc arbitral awards. Therefore, whether the ad hoc arbitration system can be implemented in China depends on whether the ad hoc arbitration in China can make awards which are not inferior to the quality of institutional arbitration, rather than pursuing the so-called "equality" regardless of reality.

Moreover, according to our observation and practice in the field of arbitration over the years, although overseas ad hoc arbitration awards can be recognized and enforced in China, Chinese enterprises involved in international commercial activities in most cases intend to select institutional arbitration, that is, the Chinese parties show strong preferences for institutional arbitration. For a foreseeable period, ad hoc arbitration will not be fully culturally accepted by Chinese parties, and the subjective confidence and objective environment for arbitration practitioners to promote ad hoc arbitration in China will be lacking.

1.2.2 Future Prospects

Since the promulgation of the current Arbitration Law and the acquiescence of the absence of the ad hoc arbitration system, there have been endless discussions in the academic circles about whether to introduce the ad hoc arbitration system. The vast majority of scholars are supportive, but there are differences in the timing of the introduction. This paper argues that the introduction of an ad hoc arbitration system is necessary to improve the commercial dispute resolution mechanism and to promote the convergence of commercial arbitration in China with international commercial arbitration, especially in special areas such as maritime and aviation. However, in view of the aforementioned objective obstacles, the pace of introduction shall not be too rapid. For some time to come, we shall continue to promote ad hoc arbitration in specific areas and regions, and encourage arbitral institutions to actively participate in the assistance of ad hoc arbitration, so that institutional arbitration can drive ad hoc arbitration. In this regard, this paper also attempts to make the following recommendations, with a view to the eventual steady implementation of the ad hoc arbitration system in China.

First, the scope of application of the ad hoc arbitration system in the FTZs shall be clarified, and the judicial review authority of the ad hoc arbitration in the FTZs shall be uniformly configured.

The Opinions on FTZ Pilot Program allow a limited selection of ad hoc arbitration among enterprises registered in the FTZs. The so-called Free Trade Zone is a multi-functional special economic zone established by law in China with the goal of trade liberalization, and also a pilot zone for the rule of law. Since the establishment of the Shanghai FTZ was approved by the State Council in August 2013, China has established FTZs in several provinces and cities. However, it shall be noted that different FTZs do not have the same level of development and have different jurisdictional models, which has led to the complexity and differences in the implementation of the ad hoc arbitration system in each FTZ.[①] In addition, The Opinions on FTZ Pilot Program set out the "three specific prerequisites" for the application of ad hoc arbitration, but the relevant expressions are too vague to determine their specific connotations, and such uncertainty is bound to block some potential users of ad hoc arbitration. In view of this, it is suggested that the Supreme People's Court shall issue further opinions on the implementation of ad hoc arbitration in FTZs, clarify the scope of application of the ad hoc arbitration system, and make a unified configuration of the judicial review authority of ad hoc arbitration. For example, it may be stipulated that the First Circuit Court of the Supreme People's Court assumes the judicial review responsibility for the ad hoc arbitration in Guangdong, Hainan and other FTZs.

Second, while effectively utilizing the leading role of institutional arbitration for ad hoc arbitration, there is a need to draw the boundaries of

---

① See Liu Ying & Zhang Weijia,"Establishment of Ad hoc Arbitration System in China,"10 *J. WTO & CHINA* 68 (2020).

the participation of arbitral institutions in ad hoc arbitration.

On the one hand, in the international practice of ad hoc arbitration, even if the parties choose ad hoc arbitration, they do not exclude the administrative services provided by the arbitral institutions. In order to promote the ad hoc arbitration system in China at this stage, it is obvious that we also need to draw nutrients from institutional arbitration. Specifically, arbitral institutions can assist in providing applicable procedural rules and necessary procedural services, as well as supervising arbitrators and guaranteeing the enforcement of ad hoc arbitration decisions and awards, which will significantly reduce the uncertainty faced by parties agreeing to ad hoc arbitration and help inexperienced parties and arbitrators to advance the arbitration process in a sustained and effective manner. Moreover, arbitral institutions are the subject that has the closest relationship with arbitrators at this stage, and that is most competent for the guidance and training of arbitrators in ad hoc arbitration.

On the other hand, China has developed a heterogeneous market for institutional arbitration, and arbitral institutions in each FTZ are interested in seizing the emerging ad hoc arbitration market. The Hengqin Rules issued by the Zhuhai Court of International Arbitration clearly has this intention. However, the practice of having arbitral institutions establish ad hoc arbitration rules would largely confuse the boundaries between institutional and arbitration ad hoc arbitration, and there are few international precedents.[①] In order to curb the situation where various arbitral institutions operate independently and compete to formulate ad hoc arbitration rules, and reduce the regional color of ad hoc arbitration rules, it is suggested that a national association formulate ad hoc arbitration rules that can be universally applicable to each FTZ. The recent model of "Ad hoc

---

[①] In accordance with the 2021 International Arbitration Survey Report released by Queen Mary University of London and White & Case LLP, the most popular ad hoc arbitration rules are the United Nations International Trade Commission Arbitration Rules, which are formulated by the United Nations Commission on International Trade Law.

Arbitration Rules" issued by China Maritime Law Association and "Ad hoc Arbitration Service Rules" issued by China Maritime Arbitration Commission can be used for reference.

II. The Details of the Revision of Competence-Competence Need to be Discussed

2.1 Jurisdiction Division Principle of "the Parties Make their own Choice in Litigation and Arbitration, with Courts Take Precedence" is Proposed to be Broken

Under the current legal framework, the division of jurisdiction regarding the confirmation of the validity of an arbitration agreement is mainly stipulated in the Arbitration Law, Interpretation of the Supreme People's Court on Certain Issues relating to Application of the Arbitration Law of the People's Republic of China, and Response of the Supreme People's Court on Several Issues Concerning the Validation of Arbitration Agreements. Based on these relevant provisions, if one party applies to the arbitral institution to confirm the validity of the arbitration agreement, while the other applies to the court, in principle, the court would make a decision, unless the arbitral institution has already made a formal decision; after the arbitral institution has made a decision on the validity of the arbitration agreement, the court could re-determine the validity of the arbitration agreement in cases where the parties apply for revocation of the arbitration award or non-enforcement of the arbitration award, that is, the court holds the final decision on the validity of the arbitration agreement. Although the current law gives the parties the right to choose their own jurisdiction, it is objectively easy to lead to procedural conflicts and a waste of judicial resources.

In particular, if the arbitration proceedings involve multiple respondents, there may even be cases where multiple respondents take turns to initiate arbitration agreement validation proceedings in order to interfere with the normal progress of the arbitration proceedings. Taking a case of confirming the validity of an arbitration agreement heard by the Foshan Intermediate People's Court of Guangzhou City as an example, a company filed an arbitration application for a financial loan contract dispute with the Foshan Arbitration Commission. The application for confirmation of the invalidity of the arbitration agreement resulted in the suspension of the arbitration procedure several times. In desperation, the company had no choice but to file an application for confirmation of the validity of the arbitration agreement against all the arbitration respondents.① Similarly, in a recent shareholder agreement dispute undertaken by the author, the respondent also repeatedly filed lawsuits to confirm the validity of the arbitration agreement to delay the arbitration proceedings.②

Different from the current legal framework, the Draft for Comments has a new competence-competence clause.③ Specifically, when the parties have objections to the validity of the arbitration agreement or the juris-

---

① See Civil Ruling (2021) YUE06MINTE113, the Foshan Intermediate People's Court, Guangdong Province.

② See Civil Ruling (2022) JING04MINTE207, the Beijing Fourth Intermediate People's Court; (2022) JING04MINTE261, the Beijing Fourth Intermediate People's Court; (2022) JING04MINTE486, the Beijing Fourth Intermediate People's Court; (2022) JING74MINTE59, Beijing Financial Court.

③ Article 28 of the Draft for Comments: If a party has any objection to the existence of an arbitration agreement, the issue of validity or equivalent effect, or the jurisdiction of the arbitration case, the party shall raise the objection within the time limit for pleadings stipulated in the arbitration rules, and the arbitral tribunal shall make a decision on the objection. Before the constitution of the arbitral tribunal, the arbitral institution may decide whether to continue the arbitral procedure based on prima facie evidence. Where a party directly raises an objection to the people's court without the procedure prescribed in the preceding paragraph, the people's court shall not accept it. If a party has any objection to the validity of the arbitration agreement or the decision on jurisdiction, the party shall, within ten days of receiving the decision, submit it to the intermediate people's court at the place of arbitration for review. If a party is dissatisfied with the ruling that the arbitration agreement is invalid or that the arbitration case has no jurisdiction, the party may apply to the people's court at the next higher level for reconsideration within ten days from the date of delivery of the ruling. The people's court shall make a ruling within one month of accepting the application for reconsideration. The review by the people's court does not affect the conduct of the arbitration procedure.

diction of the arbitration, they no longer have the option to file a complaint with the court or the arbitral tribunal, but can only file an objection application with the arbitral tribunal. If the arbitral tribunal has not been established at this time, the arbitral institution shall first decide whether to proceed with the arbitral procedure based on prima facie evidence. In addition, without the review of the arbitral tribunal, the parties have no right to directly raise objections to the court. Only after the arbitral tribunal makes a decision can they have the right to appeal to the court, and the review by the court will no longer affect the continuation of the arbitration procedure.

With regard to the above-mentioned reform of introduction of the competence-competence clause, the legislative intention is to simplify the judicial review procedure for the effectiveness of the arbitration agreement, and avoid malicious delay by one party causing damage to the other party's rights, so as to better utilize the advantages of the independent and efficient arbitration system, and at the same time, to adapt to the proposed ad hoc arbitration system.

2.2 Potential Conflicts Between Competence–Competence and the Court's Prior Review Mechanism

While the introduction of competence-competence in the Draft for Comments follows the trend of respecting the independence of arbitration in international commercial arbitration, the fact that competence-competence becomes a precursor to court hearings may cause new procedural delays and is not conducive to achieving the goal of efficiency in arbitration.

Specifically, Article 28(3)&(4) of the Draft for Comments stipulate that the court still retains the pre-supervisory function of the jurisdiction decision made by the arbitral tribunal. If the parties have objections to the jurisdiction decision, they do not need to wait until the award is rendered to challenge the validity of the arbitration agreement by applying for revocation of the arbitral award and non-enforcement of the arbitral award, but can directly request the court to conduct judicial review of the jurisdiction decision.

Article 28(5) of the Draft for Comments provides that the court's review will not affect the arbitration proceedings. However, in practice, the arbitral tribunal may choose to refuse to proceed with the arbitration and wait for the court to finally confirm the validity of the jurisdictional decision in order to avoid the embarrassing situation of being determined by the court to have no jurisdiction after it has proceeded with the proceedings or even rendered an award. In addition, if the arbitral tribunal makes an award and the court later overturns the tribunal's determination of the validity of the arbitration agreement, not only will the costs incurred by the parties and the tribunal in hearing the case be wasted, but whether the arbitral award is automatically invalid or subject to a separate application for setting aside will also become a problem to be solved. If the arbitral award is not automatically invalid, then in order to suspend the enforcement of the arbitral award, the parties will need to file a separate application to the court to set aside the arbitral award and also apply for judicial review of the jurisdictional decision, which is actually an overlap of judicial remedies.

It can be seen that, as a pre-judicial review procedure, competence-competence will not alleviate the problem of procedural delay, on the contrary, it may bring about repeated objections by the parties, repeated review by the court, and even inconsistent conclusions of the previous and subsequent review procedures. In such cases, Judicial efficiency and authority will be greatly degraded.

Generally speaking, jurisdictions that have established the principle of competence-competence usually adopt the ex post facto review approach[1], that is, instead of conducting prior judicial review in the arbitra-

---

[1] William W. Park, "Determining Arbitral Jurisdiction: Allocation of Tasks between Courts and Arbitrators," 8 *Am. Rev. Int'l Arb.* 133 (1997).

tion proceedings, the issue of the validity of the arbitration agreement will be re-examined in the subsequent proceedings to challenge the arbitral award initiated by the parties.

In summary, the legislative intention of this round of amendments to the Arbitration Law to establish the competence-competence is worthy of approval, but the details of the specific system need to be further explored. In particular, it is necessary to focus on and resolve the potential conflicts between competence-competence and judicial review system for the validity of arbitration agreements.

III. Unresolved Issue of Effectiveness of the Enforcement of Decisions on Interim Measures

3.1 Attempts to Introduce Emergency Arbitrator Procedure and its Institutional Difficulties in China

In arbitration proceedings, if one party deliberately takes steps to evade its obligations, such as squandering assets, disposing of disputed objects, or destroying evidence that is crucial to the outcome of the case, the other party may suffer irreparable damage. As a method of dispute resolution, the effectiveness of arbitration will depend on whether the arbitral tribunal has the jurisdiction for interim measures to protect the legitimate interests of the parties in a timely manner. However, given that the most critical point at which interim measures are sought is often the beginning of the dispute, and that the selection of arbitrators and the composition of the arbitral tribunal may take weeks or even months, in order to prevent such inherent limitations from compromising the effectiveness of the relief provided by arbitration, many arbitral institutions have provided for an emergency arbitrator procedure in the arbitration rules to fill this gap.

The emergency arbitrator procedure can be traced back to the Rules for a Pre-Arbitral Referee procedure issued by the ICC International Court of Arbitration in 1990. Since the pre-arbitral referee procedure is optional and the parties are free to choose whether or not to apply it, the rule is seldom applied in practice.[1] In 2006, the International Center for Dispute Resolution (ICDR), the international branch of the American Arbitration Association, first introduced the term "emergency arbitrator" into its arbitration rules, and most of the world's major arbitral institutions have since adopted a similar approach.

As stated in the ICC Arbitration and ADR Commission Report on Emergency Arbitrator Proceedings published in 2019, "Although the procedures and conditions for obtaining emergency interim relief may vary somewhat between different rules, many institutions seem to have determined that EA proceedings fill a perceived void and satisfy a demand from users".[2] Through decades of application, the institutional advantages of the emergency arbitrator procedure are mainly in the following areas:

First, it has many advantages that arbitration procedures usually have, including confidentiality, neutrality, high efficiency, independence, professionalism, and respect for autonomy of the will. In addition, urgency/efficiency is the most prominent feature of the emergency arbitrator procedure, which is reflected in multiple stages, such as the appointment of the emergency arbitrators, the advancement of the proceedings, and the time period for the emergency arbitrator to make the decision. Second, the criteria for the emergency arbitrator to decide whether to provide interim relief are more flexible and security is not mandatory. Third, it can avoid the burden of seeking protective relief from the courts and potential tendencies for local protection. Fourth, The recognition and enforcement of the emergency arbitrators' decisions are not restricted by the law of the jurisdiction where the place of arbitration is, and the procedure can eliminate the difficulty for parties to obtain interim relief in multiple different

---

[1] ICC Arbitration and ADR Commission Report on Emergency Arbitrator Proceedings, accessed June 6, 2023, https://iccwbo.org/news-publications/arbitration-adr-rules-and-tools/emergency-arbitrator-proceedings-icc-arbitration-and-adr-commission-report/.

[2] Id.

jurisdictions.

Although the emergency arbitrator procedure is still blank in China's current legislation, considering that the lack of the procedure cannot adapt to the trend of international arbitration development, and it is difficult to meet the legitimate needs of arbitration parties seeking effective relief, mainstream domestic arbitral institutions have been currently incorporated the emergency arbitrator procedure into their arbitration rules, such as Article 21 of SHIAC China (Shanghai) Pilot Free Trade Zone Arbitration Rules (2015), Article 23 and Article 77 of the CIETAC Rules (2015), Article 63 of the Beijing Arbitration Commission Arbitration Rules (2022), etc.

On the other hand, although the emergency arbitrator procedure has been widely used in China's arbitration practice, there are still many problems in practice, the most notable of which is the enforcement of decisions on interim measures issued by emergency arbitrators.

Specifically, according to Article 84, Article 103 and Article 104 of the current Civil Procedure Law and Article 28 and Article 46 of the Arbitration Law, the legislator has chosen to adopt a "single-track" legislative and operational model in which the courts have exclusive authority to issue interim relief. In other words, the law only authorizes courts to issue preservation measures, but not emergency arbitrators to issue interim measures. Decisions on interim measures issued by emergency arbitrators have no legal basis, therefore, at this stage, it is difficult to apply to the court for enforcement of interim measures made by the arbitral tribunal or the emergency arbitrator, and the effectiveness of the systems relies mainly on the active performance of the parties. In a case represented by the author where the emergency arbitrator procedure was applied, the bank confirmed in a written form that it would execute the order prohibiting payment under the letter of guarantee in question issued by the arbitration committee, thus avoiding the risk of non-implementation of the decision on interim measures.

In practice, parties may indeed be willing to perform on their own initiative, but this is largely due to fear of the discretion of the arbitral tribunal, specifically, the fear that failure to cooperate without justified reasons may be presumed unfavorably, which in turn will affect the outcome of the substantive trial. In addition, the parties may be concerned that the arbitral tribunal may make adverse adjustments in the allocation of arbitration costs due to their refusal to implement the interim measures or breach of the arbitration agreement. However, as noted above, the emergency arbitrator procedure only works after the arbitration is initiated and before the arbitral tribunal is composited, and unless otherwise agreed by the parties, emergency arbitrators are generally not allowed to participate in the subsequent composition of the tribunal. Therefore, the above-mentioned "soft constraints" on the voluntary performance of the parties have limited practical effect, and it is currently uncertain whether the arbitral tribunal can make a presumption unfavorable to one party just because of the non-cooperative attitude of the party to the interim measure decision, at least for now there is no clear institutional support. In addition, if the benefits of violating the decision on interim measure far outweigh the costs, a party may still choose to ignore the decision and the potentially adverse arbitration outcome.[1]

Article 49(2) of the Draft for Comments formally introduces the emergency arbitrator procedure, the common practice in international commercial arbitration, thus giving legitimacy to this procedure at the legal level.[2]

It shall be noted that this clause only generally stipulates the right of

---

[1] Mika Savola, "Access to Arbitral Justice: Time Aspects of Access to Arbitral Justice: Interim Measures and Emergency Arbitrator Proceedings," 23 *Croat. Arbit. Yearb.* 73 (2016).

[2] Article 49(2) of the Draft for Comments: Before the formation of the arbitral tribunal, if the parties need to appoint an emergency arbitrator to take interim measures, they may apply to the arbitration institution for the appointment of an emergency arbitrator in accordance with the arbitration rules. The authority of the emergency arbitrator is reserved until the constitution of the arbitral tribunal.

the parties to apply for the initiation of emergency arbitrator procedure, but it does not touch on the enforcement of the emergency arbitrator's interim measure decisions. However, whether the enforcement effect of the interim measure decisions issued by emergency arbitrators can be obtained determines whether the emergency arbitrator procedure can exert its value. At present, there are still some basic problems that need to be improved urgently. For example, the position of the emergency arbitrator is not clear, and this issue is related to whether the emergency arbitrator's decision is enforceable. Given that an arbitrator can be defined as an individual selected by the parties to a dispute to hear the arguments of the parties and make a binding decision accordingly,[1] and that an emergency arbitrator's decision on interim measures does resolve the parties' dispute and is binding on all parties to the arbitration, it is suggested that legislation shall clarify that emergency arbitrators also belong to the category of arbitrators, so as to give their decisions legality and enforceability at the legal level, which has been clarified arbitration rules/legislation in some countries and regions, such as The CAAI Arbitration (2017) and the Singapore International Arbitration (Amendment) Act (2012).

3.2 Preliminary Exploration on the Discretion and Effectiveness of Interim Measures in the Amendment of the Arbitration Law

3.2.1 The Necessity to Redistribute the Discretion of Interim Measures

Interim measures are immediate and temporary protection measures of rights or property provided for a party until the arbitral tribunal makes a decision on the merits.[2] The interim measures issued by emergency arbitrators have been initially introduced. With reference to the arbitra-

---

[1] See Black's Law Dictionary, 2nd Ed., accessed June 8, 2023, https://thelawdictionary.org/arbitrator/.

[2] See Marianne Roth, "Interim Measures," 3 *Yearbook on International Arbitration* 141(2013).

tion rules and corresponding practices of major domestic and overseas arbitral institutions, interim measures may also be issued by the arbitral tribunal after the composition of the tribunal. Although interim measures are known by slightly different names[1] in accordance with the laws of different countries in different jurisdictions, they all have the same or similar functions. For example, article 17(2) of the Model Law lists four functions of interim measures, namely, "maintaining or restoring the status quo pending determination of the dispute"; "taking action that would prevent, or refrain from taking action"; "providing a means of preserving assets" or "preserving evidence".[2]

In China's previous legislation, the discretion and enforcement authority of interim measures rests with the courts, and the arbitral tribunal can only play the role of a "second hand" in transmitting the application materials.[3] The Draft for Comments makes a great breakthrough in this regard by setting up a section on interim measures in Chapter IV "Arbitration Procedures", which provides detailed provisions on the procedures for deciding on and enforcing interim measures by the arbitral tribunal.

Specifically, the Draft for Comments breaks away from the model that the court has exclusive authority adopted by the current law and

---

[1] In accordance with the Model Law and the United Nations International Trade Commission Arbitration Rules, interim relief measures are called Interim Measures and Preliminary Orders; in accordance with the Singapore International Arbitration Center Arbitration Rules, interim relief measures are called Interim reliefs; in accordance with the HKIAC Arbitration Rules, they are called interim measures of protection.

[2] Article 17(2) of the Model Law: An interim measure is any temporary measure, whether in the form of an award or in another form, by which, at any time prior to the issuance of the award by which the dispute is finally decided, the arbitral tribunal orders a party to: (a) Maintain or restore the status quo pending determination of the dispute; (b) Take action that would prevent, or refrain from taking action that is likely to cause, current or imminent harm or prejudice to the arbitral process itself; (c) Provide a means of preserving assets out of which a subsequent award may be satisfied; or (d) Preserve evidence that may be relevant and material to the resolution of the dispute.

[3] Liu Xiaohong, *Special Research on International Commercial Arbitration*, Law Press, 2009, p. 343.

adopts a model in which the discretion of the court and the arbitral tribunal coexist, giving the arbitral tribunal the discretion to issue including measures of property preservation, evidence preservation, conduct preservation, and other necessary short-term measures. Parties may request interim measures from the relevant court or arbitral tribunal according to their needs after initiating arbitration.① In terms of the legislative model for the discretion of interim measures, in addition to the "free choice model" adopted in the Draft for Comments, there is also the "court subsidiarity approach" adopted in England. In this approach, parties seek to obtain interim measures through the arbitral tribunal and look only to the courts as a last resort.② From a worldwide perspective, there is a market for each of the two legislative models, with the "free choice model" probably prevailing. In the course of the revision of the Model Law, there was also a debate as to whether to continue to adopt the model in which the discretion of the court and the arbitral tribunal coexist, but ultimately the Working Group retained the original model for the purpose of preserving the dual accessibility of interim measures.③

On the whole, the necessity for the law to authorize the arbitral tribunal to decide on interim measures can be summarized in the following

---

① Article 43 of the Draft for Comments: Before or during the arbitration procedure, the parties may request the people's court or the arbitral tribunal to take temporary and emergency measures related to the subject matter of dispute in order to ensure the progress of the arbitration procedure, ascertain the disputed facts or enforce the award. Interim measures include property preservation, evidence preservation, conduct preservation and other short-term measures deemed necessary by the arbitral tribunal.

Article 46(2) of the Draft for Comments: Where the parties apply for preservation measures after initiating arbitration, they may directly submit the application to the people's court of the place where the preserved property is located, where the evidence is located, where the act is performed, where the respondent is located or where the arbitration is located; they may also apply to the arbitral tribunal.

② William Wang, "International Arbitration: The Need for Uniform Interim Measures of Relief," *28 Brooklyn J. Int'l L.* 1059.

③ See Report of the Working Group on Arbitration on the work of its 32nd session (Vienna, 20-31 March 2000), accessed June 10, 2023, https://digitallibrary.un.org/record/ 413924.

aspects:

First, the rights of the parties to choose the procedure shall be respected and guaranteed. The law allows the parties to choose arbitration to resolve disputes and the arbitral tribunal to exercise jurisdiction, which means that the law recognizes the court's waiver of jurisdiction over some specific disputes based on the parties' rights to choose procedures. On this basis, it is a continuation of the legislative trend of respecting the autonomy of the parties to assign the discretion of interim measures and substantive disputes to the arbitral tribunal.

Second, it is conducive to saving judicial resources and improving the efficiency of dispute resolution. Thanks to the comprehensive authority to review substantive disputes, the arbitral tribunal can more accurately assess the possibility of a party winning an action in an actual dispute, and the impact of the preservation measures on the arbitration proceeding and the parties. In addition, the tribunal is able to more acutely identify the parties' requests for abusive preservation measures and the tactical intent behind the requests. The mechanism for the arbitral tribunal to decide on interim measures is more effective in avoiding unnecessary delays and high costs than resorting to the courts.

Third, the authority of discretion is not equivalent to the authority of execution, which will not affect the judicial supervision and necessary judicial review conducted by the courts in the enforcement stage. Specifically, the role of conducting judicial review of the courts in arbitration can be exercised by distinguishing the authority of discretion and enforcement of interim measures in arbitration, and allocating part of the discretion to arbitral tribunals while reserving the authority of enforcement in the courts. However, the review of the arbitral tribunal's decision on interim measures conducted by the courts shall be limited to the procedures, and not involve substantive issues.

Fourth, the disadvantages of the arbitral tribunal exercising its discretion can be resolved through institutional design. There are two notable obstacles to the exercise of the arbitral tribunal's discretion of interim measures: one is the making and release of interim measures before the composition of arbitral tribunal; the other is the enforcement of the arbitral tribunal's decision on interim measures. However, these drawbacks can be solved through reasonable institutional design, such as the introduction of emergency arbitrator procedures and the improvement of the interface mechanism between the authority of discretion of the arbitral tribunals and the authority of enforcement of the courts.

Fifth, it is in line with the practical trend of international commercial arbitration. As the adjudication power of arbitration in solving international economic and trade issues is gradually strengthened, the concept of arbitration independence has been widely recognized, and the arbitral tribunal's discretion of interim measures has also been more and more widely accepted, which is reflected in the Model Law and the arbitration rules of many mainstream international arbitration institutions. In accordance with a survey compiled by scholars, many countries with developed international commercial transactions, such as the United Kingdom, Sweden, Germany, the United States, Singapore and Japan, have also granted legitimacy to arbitral tribunals to issue decisions on interim measures.[①]

3.2.2 Enforceability of Interim Measure Decisions

One of the main disadvantages of decisions on interim measures issued by emergency arbitrators/arbitral tribunals compared to those ordered by courts is their lack of enforceability. The enforcement of decisions on interim measures can be broadly divided into the following three dimensions: first, the enforcement of domestic interim measures orders issued in the territory; second, the enforcement of domestic interim measures orders issued outside the territory; and third, the implementation of overseas interim measures in the territory.

[①] Zhang Shengcui, "A study on the restructuring of the system of arbitration preservation measures in China," *Journal of Shanghai University of Finance and Economics* Vol. 2, 106(2016).

First, in this proposed amendment to the Arbitration Law, parties may apply to a court with competent jurisdiction for enforcement of an interim measure decision ordered by an arbitral tribunal, which preliminarily solves the problem of enforcement of interim measure decisions in the territory.① Of course, the Draft for Comments has not yet clarified the details of the court's review criteria, enforcement procedures and other institutional details. Whether and how the relevant mechanisms can be implemented remains to be further observed.

Second, in the context of Draft for Comments, the parties also have the rights to apply to an extraterritorial court to enforce the interim measure decisions, and the main enforcement mechanisms outside the territory are based on the New York Convention, the PRC has participated in, and the domestic law of the place of enforcement, etc. Specifically, Article 3 of the New York Convention, requires that "each Contracting State shall recognize arbitral awards as binding and enforce them", but does not itself describe what is meant by an enforceable award in a way that expressly includes or excludes decisions on interim measures, which makes it difficult for supporters and opponents of the enforceability of interim measures under the Convention to convince each other. By observing how the courts of various countries deal with such issues, the ambiguity of the New York Convention does leave room for interpretation to determine the implementation of interim measures based on the Convention, but it fails to directly promote the widespread realization of such implementation based on the Convention.

In *Resort Condominiums International Inc. v. Ray Bolwell and Resort Condominiums, Pty. Ltd.*, the Supreme Court of Queensland, Australia ruled

---

① Article 47(2) of the Draft for Comments: Where a party applies to the arbitral tribunal for preservation measures, the arbitral tribunal shall make a decision in a timely manner and require the party to provide a guarantee. After the preservation decision is submitted to the people's court with jurisdiction by the parties or the arbitration institution, the people's court shall implement it in a timely manner in accordance with relevant laws and regulations.

that the interim arbitration order and award was not a "foreign award" within the meaning of the New York Convention and so it could not be enforced under that. The case involved a dispute between the American claimant and the Australian respondent, and the arbitrator issued an interim award requiring the respondent to perform the agreement during the arbitration. However, the court held that the interim award, which could be set aside, stayed or modified in subsequent arbitration proceedings, did not have the legal effect of "finality" and therefore did not satisfy the New York Convention's requirement for an arbitral award to be "binding".

Some countries and regions have taken a positive approach to extend the court's enforcement of interim measure decisions issued by arbitral tribunals, which falls into two main categories: one is to expand the definition of "arbitral award" in the New York Convention to include decisions on interim measures made by arbitral tribunals, including Singapore International Arbitration Act① and Dutch Arbitration Act②, etc. the other is to directly promulgate in legislation that allows courts to implement interim measures decided by arbitral tribunals, such as the Hong Kong Arbitration Ordinance③ and the German Code of Civil Procedure.④

---

① Section 27(1) of the Singapore International Arbitration Act states:"Arbitral award"has the meaning given by the Convention, but also includes an order or a direction made or given by an arbitral tribunal in the course of an arbitration in respect of any of the matters set out in section 12(1)(c) to (j).

② Article 1043b(4) of Dutch Arbitration Act: Unless the arbitral tribunal determines otherwise, a decision by the arbitral tribunal, upon request for an interim measure, is considered to be an arbitral award, to which the provisions of Section Three to Five inclusive of this Title shall be applicable.

③ Section 45(2) of the Hong Kong Arbitration Ordinance: On the application of any party, the Court may, in relation to any arbitral proceedings which have been or are to be commenced in or outside Hong Kong, grant an interim measure.

④ Section 1041(2) of the German Code of Civil Procedure: Upon a party having filed a corresponding petition, the court may permit the enforcement of a measure pursuant to subsection (1), unless a corresponding measure of temporary relief has already been petitioned with a court. It may issue a differently worded order if this is required for the enforcement of the measure.

Finally, the Draft for Comments is unclear as to the domestic enforcement of decisions on interim measures taken outside the territory. Considering that the scale of international economic and trade activities continues to expand, and the ability to resolve disputes has increasingly become an important aspect of countries participating in international competition, it is recommended that separate provisions be made on the recognition and enforcement of decisions on extraterritorial interim measures, and that, on the basis of allowing courts to recognize and enforce decisions on extraterritorial interim measures in principle, the exceptions to such recognition and enforcement, such as conflicts with the public policies of the State, shall be made clear.

IV. The Judicial Review Mechanism for Arbitration Needs to be Improved

The judicial review mechanism for arbitration is a mechanism for courts to review and supervise arbitration activities in accordance with the law. Judicial review of arbitration in China is mainly oriented to the two dimensions of the arbitration agreement and the arbitration award. Under the background that the current revision of the Arbitration Law intends to introduce the competence-competence of the arbitral tribunal, the prior review mechanism for the validity of the arbitration agreement is actually unnecessary. The prior review of arbitral awards is mainly reflected in Article 58 of the Arbitration Law and the system for the parties to apply for cancellation and non-enforcement of arbitral awards stipulated in Article 63 of the Arbitration Law. In recent years, this mechanism has gradually shown itself to be inconsistent with the development trend of commercial arbitration in recent years. In view of this, the Draft for Comments also echoes the reform program on the judicial review mechanism after arbitral awards are made, which is specifically divided into two aspects: firstly, to improve the system for cancellation of arbitral awards; secondly, to abolish the system for non-enforcement of arbitral awards. This paper will introduce and analyze the highlights of the reform of these two parts, and put forward corresponding recommendations for legislative improvement.

4.1 Improvement of the System for Cancellation of Arbitral Awards

4.1.1 Suggestions on Setting Aside Arbitral Awards on Procedural Grounds only

In Chinese Mainland, the legal grounds for the parties to apply for the setting aside of an arbitral award are mainly stipulated in Article 58 of the current Arbitration Law[①]. This provision adopts a legislative structure similar to that of Article 5 of the New York Convention, enumerating the grounds on which the court may review an arbitral award and drawing on the provisions of Article 5, such as "the award has not yet become binding on the parties", "the composition of the arbitral authority or the arbitral procedure was not in accordance with the agreement of the parties" and "the award deals with a difference not contemplated by or not falling within the terms of the submission to arbitration". However, in

---

[①] Article 58 of the Arbitration Law: Where the parties concerned can provide evidence disproving the arbitration award in any of the following circumstances, they may request a cancellation of the arbitration award by an intermediate People's Court at the place where the arbitration commission is located:

(1) there was no arbitration agreement;

(2) items for arbitration were not within the scope of the arbitration agreement or were those upon which the arbitration commission had no right to arbitrate;

(3) the establishment of the arbitration tribunal or arbitration procedures are in contravention of legal proceedings;

(4) the evidence upon which the arbitration award is made was counterfeit;

(5) the other party has concealed evidence to the degree that fairness has been affected;

(6) arbitrators have accepted bribes, resorted to deception for personal gain or perverted the course of justice by the award.

Where the People's Court has formed a collegiate bench and has examined and verified that the award was made under one of the aforesaid situations, it shall order the cancellation of the award.

Where the People's Court decides that it shall make a ruling to the effect that there has been a violation of the public interest, it shall order the cancellation of the award.

addition, Article 58 of the current Arbitration Law also includes two substantive review matters, namely (4) "counterfeit evidence" and (5) "concealed evidence". In past judicial practices, there were serious misuses and abuses of these two grounds for setting aside the award, and some rulings even intervened in the determination of arbitration facts based on these two grounds and set aside the arbitral award accordingly.

For example, there is a ruling that it was unlawful for an arbitral tribunal to award the validity of a contract on the grounds that the contract was formally incomplete and there was no other evidence to prove the authenticity of the contract.① However, the arbitral tribunal has the authority to decide on the probative effect of the evidence, and defective evidence may not always be forged and does not necessarily constitute a ground for cancellation of the award. For another example, there is a ruling that the claimant has concealed evidence to the degree that fairness has been affected on the grounds that the amount of the claim submitted by the claimant has not deducted the amount already paid.② In the reasoning part of the ruling, the court mentioned that the arbitration respondent "shall not bear the adverse consequences caused by the unfairness of the arbitration award due to failure to disclose that the 30,000 yuan has been returned". However, this approach actually amounts to a redistribution of the burden of proof beyond the arbitral tribunal, which violates the original intention of the judicial review mechanism for arbitration. It is undeniable that the realization of substantive justice in arbitration results is the intrinsic value pursued by the judicial review mechanism, but it shall not be at the expense of breaking through the parties' agreements on substantive jurisdiction.

Article 77 of the Draft for Comments integrates and revises the above two grounds for substantive review by expanding the ground for "counter-

---

① See Civil Ruling (2017) LU14MINTE12, the Dezhou Intermediate People's Court, Shandong Province.

② See Civil Ruling (2016) LU05MINTE21, the Dongying Intermediate People's Court, Shandong Province.

feit evidence" to "obtaining an award by fraud", and deleting the ground for "concealed evidence".① The current round of revisions to the Arbitration Law, by narrowing the statutory grounds for setting aside an award, obviously helps limit the court's involvement in substantive issues of arbitration, but still involves both procedural and substantive aspects. It is recommended that the two substantive grounds of review, "counterfeit evidence" and "concealed evidence", be completely deleted.

Firstly, the principle of limited judicial review shall be respected and followed. Since the rights of the parties to present and cross-examine evidence have been adequately protected in the arbitration proceedings, it is not necessary for the court to conduct substantive review of the case as such.

In China's civil and commercial litigation and arbitration system, the principle of "whoever makes the claim shall present evidence" is adopted, and any party is not obliged to take the initiative to prove facts that are unfavorable to itself. Even if the relevant evidence is in the possession of the other party, the party may also request the presentation of evidence during the trial process (including applying for investigation and evidence collection, and evidence preservation measures, etc.), instead of claiming that the other party conceals evidence after the case is over. Moreover, both parties shall have completed their claims or defenses to the authenticity of the evidence during the hearing, rather than claiming cancellation of the award after the end of the arbitration hearing on the ground that the

---

① Article 77 of the Draft for Comments: If the parties submits evidence to prove that the award falls under any of the following circumstances, they may apply to the intermediate people's court at the place of arbitration to cancel the award: (1) There is no arbitration agreement or the arbitration agreement is invalid; (2) The subject matter of the award falls outside the scope of the arbitration agreement or exceeds the scope of arbitration stipulated in this Law; (3) The respondent has not been notified of the appointment of an arbitrator or the conduct of the arbitration procedure, or has failed to make a statement for reasons not attributable to the respondent; (4) The composition of the arbitral tribunal or the procedure of the arbitration violates the statutory procedures or the agreement of the parties, so as to seriously damage the rights of the parties; (5) The award is obtained due to fraudulent acts such as malicious collusion and falsification of evidence; (6) When arbitrating the case, the arbitrators demands and accepts bribes, engaged in malpractice for personal gain, and perverted the law to make an award.

counterparty presented "the evidence upon which the arbitration award is made was counterfeit".

In addition, the exclusion of substantive review by the court is also consistent with the "principle of estoppel". Although the "principle of estoppel" is not expressly stipulated in the Chinese laws, the universality of the jurisprudence in judicial practice has not been affected. If a party recognizes the authenticity of the evidence in the arbitration proceedings but later proposes to set aside the arbitral award on the grounds that the evidence is counterfeit, the court shall not support the claim in violation of the principle of estoppel.①

Secondly, internationally accepted legislation does not stipulate that the parties may apply for review of the substantive content of the arbitral award.② For example, article 34 of the Model Law explicitly provides that the court's review of the setting aside of an arbitral award is limited to a procedural review. The High People's Court of Beijing Municipality has also clearly stipulated in Article 1 of the Main Points of Judicial Review of Domestic Commercial Arbitral Awards that "the court shall not use the substantive errors of the arbitral award as the reason for setting aside, and shall not review the arbitral award with respect to its substantive contents such as the allocation of the burden of proof, the authentication of the evidence, and the determination of the facts". It is suggested that the current round of revision of the Arbitration Law can incorporate this viewpoint by separating the sense of judicial review of arbitration from the awareness of substantive adjudication of the cases, limiting the courts' review to the scope of procedural matters and no longer including any substantive disputes.③

---

① See Civil Ruling (2018) JING04MINTE326, the Beijing Fourth Intermediate People's Court.

② Kong Deyue, "An Empirical Study on the Setting Aside or Non-Enforcement of Arbitral Awards," *Commercial Arbitration and Mediation* Vol. 2(2021).

③ Shen Wei, "Normative Analysis of China's Arbitration Judicial Review System--Emergence, Evolution, Mechanisms and Defects," *Law Forum* Vol. 1(2019).

4.1.2 Suggestions on Granting the Parties the Right of Filing a Reconsideration or an Appeal

Under current Chinese laws, the parties have no right of appeal against the decision to set aside an arbitral award nor can they apply for a retrial, which means they have no right of procedural remedies. In order to standardize the application of judicial review throughout the country, the Supreme People's Court issued the Provisions of the Supreme People's Court on Issues Concerning the Reporting of Cases Involving Judicial Review of Arbitration for Examination and Approval (hereinafter referred to as the "Reporting Provisions"), as a means of supervising the judicial review of arbitral awards by people's courts at lower levels. In accordance with the Reporting Provisions, where a people's court at lower level proposes to revoke an arbitral award issued by a domestic arbitration institution, it shall report the case to the people's court at higher level under this jurisdiction for examination and approval; among them, foreign-related cases or cases involving Hong Kong, Macao or Taiwan Region, and cases in which the grounds for setting aside the award are violation of public interest must be reported to the Supreme People's Court step by step.

While this provision undoubtedly contributes to the standardization of the criteria for judicial review, promotes the development of the arbitration industry and safeguards the legitimate rights and interests of the parties, it fails to properly take into account the requirements for the efficiency of judicial review. Specifically, Article 60 of the current Arbitration Law stipulates that the time limit for applying for cancellation of an arbitral award is two months, and the reporting system has resulted in many cases taking as long as four to six months to process.① Moreover, the people's courts at higher levels respond to reported cases in the form

---

① See "Discerning Concepts and Sorting Out Rules to Enhance the Quality and Efficiency of Review Work - Research Report of the High People's Court of Shaanxi Province on the Review of Arbitration Judicial Review Reporting Cases," in People's Court Daily, 22nd October 2020, p. 8.

of a reply letter, and the parties are absent from the reporting system. This authoritative review mode overemphasizes the leading role of the courts and ignores the role of the parties in the disputes.

The Draft for Comments has taken note of the above-mentioned problems, and stipulates in Article 81 that the parties have the right to file a reconsideration of the ruling to cancel the arbitral award.[①] This provision helps to enhance the transparency of judicial review of arbitration and the participation of the parties, reflecting the efforts made by the legislation to achieve a balance between the protection of the rights of the parties and the efficiency of judicial review.

Furthermore, there are opposing parties in the procedure for applying for cancellation of the arbitral award, and the trial matters involve significant procedural interests or even substantive interests of the parties, which is obviously of a contentious nature. The basic requirements for litigation are neutrality of the judge, personal experience of the judge, transparency of the procedure and equality of the parties. The existing reporting system adopts a written review mode, and the parties have no access to the judge and express their own views and opinions. In contrast, the current amendments to the Arbitration Law intends to grant the parties the right to reconsideration, which is more in line with the modern judicial concept of "people-oriented" and can maximize the respect and protection of the legitimate rights and interests of the parties.

After the introduction of the parties' reconsideration rights, the reporting system will no longer be necessary. However, the hierarchical setting of the Reporting Provisions has its own special public policy considerations, and in order to be compatible with such a hierarchical setting, the level of jurisdiction of cases involving cancellation can be adjusted

---

[①] Article 81 of the Draft for Comments: If the parties are dissatisfied with the ruling to cancel the award, they may apply to the people's court at the next higher level for reconsideration within ten days of receiving the ruling. The people's court shall make a ruling within one month of accepting the application for reconsideration.

accordingly. In addition, in accordance with the current Reporting Provisions, special cases shall be reported to the high people's court and the Supreme People's Court step by step, forming the de facto "cases closed after the second instance" effect, which is inconsistent with two-tier trial system stipulated in Civil Procedure Law. In view of this, it is recommended that the intermediate people's courts shall be responsible for the first instance in general cancellation cases, and the high people's courts shall be responsible for the second instance. For foreign-related cases or cases involving Hong Kong, Macao or Taiwan Region, and cases in which the grounds for setting aside the award are a violation of public interest, it is suggested the high people's court be responsible for the first instance and the Supreme People's Court for the final instance, with reference to the spirit of the Reporting Provisions.

4.1.3 Suggestions for Increasing Application Costs

In accordance with the relevant provisions of the "Rules on the Payment of Litigation Fees", only RMB 400 is required for each application for setting aside an arbitral award.[1] As a result, many parties will apply for the setting aside of the award without justifiable reasons, delaying the fulfillment of the award at a very low cost. If we also take into account the two to three months that can be delayed by applying for non-enforcement of arbitral awards (some courts charge filing fees with reference to the standard for applying for cancellation cases)[2], the losing party in the arbitration can delay the performance of the arbitral award for nearly half a year at a very low cost, which is not conducive to the maintenance of

---

[1] Article 14 of the Rules on the Payment of Litigation Fees: application fees shall be paid in accordance with the following standards respectively: ... (v) RMB 400 for each application to set aside an arbitral award or to recognize the validity of an arbitration agreement.

[2] Article 12 of Provisions on Several Issues Concerning the Handling of Cases of Enforcement of Arbitral Awards by the People's Courts: The people's court shall complete the examination and make a ruling within two months from the date of filing the case for non-enforcement of the arbitral award; if there are special circumstances that require an extension, it may be extended for one month with the approval of the president of the court.

the arbitration's high efficiency and convenience. In view of this, it is necessary to increase the application fees for an application to set aside an arbitral award so that the losing party can prudently exercise its right to seek judicial review of the arbitral award.

4.2 Abolition of the System of Non-enforcement of Arbitral Awards

In accordance with the current law, the parties can request both the setting aside and the non-enforcement of the arbitral award based on the same grounds[①], that is, China adopts a dual review model for arbitral awards. In the previous years of development, the legislation has also tried to clarify the relationship between the two judicial review systems of setting aside and non-enforcement of arbitral awards, and achieved some

---

① Article 244 of the Civil Procedure Law: With respect to an arbitral award of an arbitration organization established pursuant to the law, where one party does not perform, the counterparty may apply to a People's Court which has jurisdiction for enforcement. The People's Court accepting the application shall carry out enforcement. Where the respondent presents evidence to prove that the arbitral award falls under any of the following circumstances, upon examination and verification by the collegiate bench formed by the People's Court, a ruling on non-enforcement shall be made:

(1) The parties concerned have not included an arbitration clause in the contract or have not entered into a written arbitration agreement subsequently;

(2) The arbitration matter does not fall under the scope of the arbitration agreement or the arbitration organization has no right to carry out arbitration;

(3) The composition of the arbitral tribunal or the arbitration procedures is/are in violation of statutory procedures;

(4) The evidence on which the arbitral award is based is forged;

(5) The counterparty has concealed evidence which has an impact on making a fair arbitral award from the arbitration organization; or

(6) The arbitrators have committed bribery or favoritism or perverted the law in making the arbitral award when carrying out arbitration of the case.

Where the People's Court rules that enforcement of the arbitral award is against the public interest, a ruling of non-enforcement shall be made.

A ruling document shall be served on both parties to the arbitration and the arbitration organization.

Where non-enforcement of an arbitral award is ruled by a People's Court, the parties concerned may apply for arbitration again based on the written arbitration agreement between both parties or file a lawsuit with a People's Court.

results①, but failed to solve the problem fundamentally. This paper argues that the dual review model is unnecessary and has many drawbacks.

First, the two systems have the same legal effect, and the repeated use has resulted in a waste of judicial resources. In accordance with article 244(5) of Civil Procedure Law, non-enforcement is sufficient to deprive an arbitral award of its enforceability and res judicata effect, which is equivalent to setting aside the arbitral award in terms of legal effect. Such dual review has led, to some extent, to confusion about jurisdiction and execution authority.

Secondly, the combined use of the two systems will further cause procedural delays and impair the efficiency and expeditiousness of the arbitration system. In accordance with Article 59 of the Arbitration Law, the statutory period for applying for the setting aside of an arbitral award is 6 months from the date of receipt of the award②, which is in itself longer than the time limit for applying for the setting aside of an arbitral award that prevails in extra-territorial jurisdictions (usually 3 months)③. In ad-

---

① Article 26 of Interpretation of the Supreme People's Court on Certain Issues relating to Application of the Arbitration Law of the People's Republic of China in 2006 stipulates that The people's court shall not support a party that pleads for a suspension of enforcement of the arbitration award in the enforcement proceedings by quoting the same reasons used in the same party's rejected application for overturning an arbitration award;

Article 20 of Provisions of the Supreme People's Court on Several Issues Concerning the Handling of Cases of Enforcement of Arbitration Awards by People's Courts in 2018, on the basis of affirming the aforementioned judicial interpretation, perfects the linking mechanism between cancellation and non-enforcement, and clarifies that the review of cancellation of arbitral awards shall take precedence between the two.

② Article 59 of the Arbitration Law: An application by a party for the cancellation of an arbitration award shall be made within six (6) months of its receipt of the application award document.

Article 479 of Interpretation of the Supreme People's Court on the Application of the Civil Procedure Law of the People's Republic of China: Where a party requests a court not to enforce an arbitral award or notarized instrument of a creditor's rights, such request shall be submitted to the court conducting the enforcement before the enforcement is terminated.

③ Article 34(3) of the Model Law: An application for setting aside may not be made after three months have elapsed from the date on which the party making that application had received the award or, if a request had been made under Article 33, from the date on which that request had been disposed of by the arbitral tribunal.

dition, the parties also have the right to apply for non-enforcement of the arbitral award at any time after the commencement of the enforcement proceeding and before the end of the enforcement proceeding, resulting in the validity of the arbitral award remaining in a state of uncertainty until the end of the enforcement. The rapidity of arbitration determines that the arbitration judicial review procedure must be rapid and efficient.[1] At this stage, the overlapping use of the two arbitration judicial review systems is not conducive to the development of the arbitration industry.

Thirdly, the system of non-enforcement of arbitral awards may involve local protectionism. According to Article 2(3) of the Provisions on Several Issues Concerning the Handling of Cases of Enforcement of Arbitral Awards by the People's Courts and Article 58(1) of the Arbitration Law[2], the non-enforcement of arbitral awards is under the jurisdiction of the enforcement court (the court of the place where the person subject to execution/ the property to be enforced is located), which is prone to breed local protectionism. On the other hand, the setting aside of arbitral awards is under the jurisdiction of the court where the arbitration institution is located, which is more conducive to safeguarding the rights of the parties.

In view of this, article 82 of the Draft for Comments proposes to abolish the system of non-enforcement of arbitral awards, and at the same time stipulates that the court has the right to take the initiative to review whether

---

[1] Jiang Xia, *Essentials of Arbitration Judicial Review Procedures*, Xiangtan University Press, 2009, p. 48.

[2] Article 2(3) of Provisions of the Supreme People's Court on Several Issues Concerning the Handling of Cases of Enforcement of Arbitration Awards by People's Courts: If the person subject to enforcement or any non-party applies for not enforcing the arbitration award, the intermediate people's court responsible for enforcement shall file a separate case for investigation. If the enforcement case has been designated to the basic people's court for jurisdiction, the basic people's court shall, within three days after receiving the application for non-enforcement, transfer the case to the original enforcement court for separate filing.

Article 58(1) of the Arbitration Law: Where the parties concerned can provide evidence disproving the arbitration award in any of the following circumstances, they may request a cancellation of the arbitration award by an intermediate People's Court at the place where the arbitration commission is located: ...

the arbitral award is in the public interest.[1] This innovation deserves to be recognized and is also in line with international practice. Although arbitration has a certain quasi-judicial nature, it is still a civil means of dispute resolution, and can only be enforced after being recognized by the authority and endowed with the power of enforcement.[2] The supervisory role played by the court in the enforcement procedure of arbitral awards has been changed from a ruling of non-enforcement upon application to a proactive review and confirmation, while strictly limiting the scope of the review to whether the arbitral award is contrary to the public interest. This approach is conducive to resolving disputes under the current dual review mechanism on the premise of maintaining the court's review role in arbitration.

Conclusion

As a response of the Ministry of Justice to the call of the practical and academic circles on the revision of the Arbitration Law, the Draft for Comments, on the one hand, conforms to the development trend of the international commercial arbitration system, and on the other hand, is a tailor-made initiative based on China's national conditions. Although there are still some ambiguities in the current draft, it is believed that these issues will be gradually resolved in the future evolution and changes. And we also expect the new Arbitration Law to play a greater role and add new vitality in the arena of commercial arbitration in the future.

---

[1] Article 82 of the Draft for Comments: The parties shall perform the award. If a party fails to perform, the other party may apply to an intermediate people's court with jurisdiction for enforcement. If the people's court determines, upon examination, that the enforcement of the award is not contrary to the public interest, it shall rule to confirm the enforcement; otherwise, it shall rule not to confirm the enforcement. The ruling shall be served on the parties and the arbitral institution. Where the award is ruled by the people's court not to be confirmed for enforcement, the parties may apply for arbitration in respect of the dispute in accordance with a renewed arbitration agreement, or they may sue in the people's court.

[2] Zhang Weiping, "Reflection and Adjustment of the Structure of the Existing Judicial Supervision System of Arbitration Enforcement--Another Discussion on the System of Non-Enforcement of Arbitral Awards," *Modern Law* Vol. 1(2020).

The Analysis of the Value Option for Judicial Review for Arbitration

Zhang Silu[*]

Abstract: The value option of judicial review for validity of an arbitration agreement is to respect the consensus of parties toward arbitration, converting from the value option to regulate the consensus of parties toward arbitration. Nevertheless, the value option for judicial review for arbitral awards is to ensure the fairness of the arbitral awards. Nevertheless, the value option for judicial review for arbitral awards is to ensure the fairness of the arbitral awards. Only for the issue which under the control of the parties, the value option for judicial review of arbitral awards is to ensure the fairness of the arbitral awards. Only for the issue which under the control of the parties, the value option for judicial review of arbitral awards is to respect the consensus of parties toward arbitration procedures. The above-mentioned value option reflects the attitude, which is support and supervision, of the courts towards the arbitration. Nonetheless, this is only part of the promotion of international competitiveness for Chinese arbitration, and it is not a matter for the courts. Nonetheless, this is only part of the promotion of international competitiveness for Chinese arbitration, and it is also

---

[*] Lecturer, School of International Law, Northwest University of Political Science and Law, Doctor of Law, Postdoctoral Fellow, Fifth Batch of Young Scholars for Practical Exercise of the Supreme People's Court. Major research : international private law, international commercial arbitration, international carriage of goods.

a part of the effective cohesion and coordination of judicial and arbitration in the diversified dispute resolution mechanism. The effective cohesion and coordination of judicial and arbitration in the diversified dispute settlement mechanism depends more on the top-level design of the arbitration mechanism. The effective cohesion and coordination of judicial and arbitration in the diversified dispute settlement mechanism depends more on the top-level design of the arbitration law to realise the simultaneous advancement of the value option upheld by the court in the judicial review of arbitration, the standardized design of the arbitration law, and the standardized design of the arbitration law. The effective cohesion and coordination of judicial and arbitration in the diversified dispute settlement mechanism depends more on the top-level design of the arbitration law to realize the simultaneous advancement of the value option upheld by the court in the judicial review of arbitration, the standardized operation of the arbitration institution itself and the optimization of the judicial review procedure.

Keywords: validity of an arbitration agreement; judicial review of arbitral awards; diversified dispute resolution mechanism; value option

I. Formulation of the Question

According to Article 1 of the *Provisions of the Supreme People's Court on Several Issues concerning Deciding Cases of Arbitration-Related Judicial Review* (hereinafter referred to as the "Provisions on Arbitration-Related Judicial Review")[①], judicial review of arbitration

---

① Article 1 of the Provisions on Arbitration-Related Judicial Review: "For the purpose of these Provisions," arbitration-related judicial review case "means any of the following cases: (1) A case of an application for recognition of the effect of an arbitration agreement. (2) A case of an application for enforcement of an arbitral award made by a Chinese mainland-based arbitral institution. (3) A case of an application for revocation of an arbitral award made by a Chinese mainland-based arbitral institution. (4) A case of an application for recognition and enforcement of an arbitral award made in the Hong Kong Special Administrative Region, the Macao Special Administrative Region, or Taiwan region. (5) A case of an application for recognition and enforcement of a foreign arbitral award. (6) Other arbitration-related judicial review cases."

mainly contains two aspects, firstly, reviewing the validity of the arbitration agreement; and secondly, reviewing whether there are any statutory grounds for the arbitral award to be set aside or not to be recognised and enforced. Judicial review of arbitration is of great significance to both arbitration and justice.

On the one hand, after judicial review, the validity of the arbitration agreement has been confirmed by the court, thus laying a sound foundation for the arbitral tribunal to carry out the subsequent arbitration procedures. At the same time, after judicial review, the effectiveness of the arbitral award has been recognised by the court, and then can be implemented through the court enforcement procedures to realize the results of the arbitral award. This provides a strong protection for the parties to safeguard their own rights and interests through arbitration .

On the other hand, arbitrations faciliated by valid arbitration agreements can divert a large number of commercial cases from the courts, alleviating the pressure arising out of huge caseloads. At the same time, through the judicial review of arbitration, the court corrects the arbitration award that harms the legitimate rights and interests of the arbitration parties, and can promote the benign development of arbitration, which is an important manifestation of judicial support and supervision of arbitration.

Accordingly, the effective connection and coordination between justice and arbitration in the diversified dispute resolution mechanism depends on a perfect judicial review system of arbitration. Regarding the judicial review system of arbitration, China's scholars have adopted various approaches in their researches. Some put forward proposals to improve the system of arbitral award annulment from the perspective of comparative law.[1] Some, based empirical research, examine the applica-

---

[1] Zhang Shengcui: "On the Improvement of the Arbitral Award Setting Aside System in China", in Journal of Shanghai University of Finance and Economics, No. 1, 2012.

tion of the specific grounds for annulment of arbitral awards[①] or analyse China's current judicial review system of arbitration and put forward the corresponding recommendations for improvement.[②] There is a lack of examination of the value choices adopted by judges in determining whether an arbitration agreement is valid, whether an arbitral award should be set aside, or whether it should be denied recognition and enforcement.

In interpreting the existing judicial review provisions or dealing with issues not covered by the existing judicial review provisions, judges need to be supported by a choice of values to provide them with a yardstick for making their final judgement concerning what is right and what is wrong. Therefore, in the process of judicial review of arbitration, when judges review the validity of an arbitration agreement or the validity of an arbitral award, do they have the same value orientation ? if not, what is the value orientation followed by each of them in reviewing the validity of an arbitration agreement and reviewing an arbitration agreement. Whether the aforementioned value orientation can effectively enhance the international competitiveness of China's arbitration system, and whether it can effectively realise judicial support and supervision of arbitration so as to promote the effective articulation and co-ordination between justice and arbitration in the diversified dispute resolution mechanism is the issue examined in this paper.

II. Value Options for Judicial Review of the Validity of Arbitration Agreements

According to Paragraph 2 of Article 27 of the *Interpretation of the*

---

① Zhang Jiechao, "On the Changes in the Concept of Judicial Review of Arbitration - Based on the Decision of the N Municipal Intermediate Court in Applying for the Annulment of a Domestic Arbitral Award", in Contemporary Jurisprudence, No. 4, 2015.

② Jiang Jianxin and Chen Liwei, "Investigation and Thoughts on Judicial Review of Arbitral Awards - An Empirical Analysis of the Review of Non-enforcement and Application for Annulment of Arbitration", in Law Application, No. 10, 2013.

Supreme People's Court on Several Issues Concerning the Application of the Arbitration Law of the People's Republic of China (hereinafter referred to as the Judicial Interpretation of the Arbitration Law), the court, rather than the arbitration institution, makes the final decision on the validity of the arbitration agreement; whereas according to Paragraph 1 of the same article, once the parties do not raise objections to the arbitration agreement during arbitration proceedings, even if the arbitration agreement does not exist between the parties, the arbitration procedure cannot be considered unlawful. The spirit embodied in this provision is that whether or not there exists a mutual constent to arbitration between the parties is the primary issue in reviewing the validity of the arbitration agreement, and the aforementioned constent is not only embodied in the arbitration agreement, but also in the act of applying for or participating in the arbitration proceedings. Therefore, the value choice of the court in the judicial review of the arbitration agreement should be to respect the parties' mutual constent to arbitration; and the judicial review of the validity of the arbitration agreement is fundamentally a judicial determination and regulation of the parties' consent to arbitration .

Accordingly, the core issue of the value choice of judicial review of the validity of the arbitration agreement is to what extent the respect for the parties' arbitration consent is subject to the limitations of judicial determination and regulation of arbitration consent. According to Article 90 of the 2021 Proceedings of the National Court Work Symposium on Maritime Trial in Foreign Commercial Matters (hereinafter referred to as the Proceedings), the judicial review of the arbitration agreement includes the review of the issues of whether the arbitration agreement has been established, has entered into force, has become invalid, and whether it binds the particular parties. Among these issues, whether the arbitration agreement binds the third party, the determination of the validity of the clause of arbitration before litigation, and the determination of the uniqueness of the arbitration institution are the three most obvious conflicts between the respect for the parties' arbitration agreement and the judicial determination and regulation of the arbitration agreement. Therefore, this paper intends to examine the core issues of the value choice of judicial review of the validity of the arbitration agreement, starting from the three issues mentioned above.

2.1 Whether the Arbitration Agreement Binds Third Parties

The arbitration agreement ultimately embodies the parties' constent to submit the dispute in question to arbitration. ①From the perspective of contractual relativity, an arbitration agreement cannot bind a third party without the express consent by such party. Therefore, the core issue of whether an arbitration agreement can bind a third party lies in the circumstances under which the law can presume that a third party agrees to be bound by an arbitration agreement made between others and also in the reasonable basis for such a presumption. ②Articles 8 and 9 of the Judicial Interpretation of the Arbitration Law stipulate whether a third party is bound by an arbitration agreement concluded between others in the case of a change in the subject matter of the contract and the assignment of claims. In judicial practice, there are still disputes as to whether the insurer is bound by the arbitration agreement between the insured and the third party, and whether the creditor exercising its right of subrogation is bound by the arbitration agreement between the debtor and the sub-debtor.

2.1.1 Whether the Insurer is Bound by an Arbitration Agreement Between the Insured and a Third Party

As to whether the insurer is bound by the arbitration agreement reached between the insured and the third party, Article 98 of the 2019 Proceedings of the National Court Civil and Commercial Trial Work Con-

---

① Zhao Xiowen, International Commercial Arbitration Law (3rd ed.), People's University of China Press, 2012 edition, p. 55.

② Song Lianbin and Luo Xingyu, "The Effect of an Arbitration Agreement on an Insurance Subrogor", in International Law Journal, No. 1, 2021, pp. 84-85.

ference clearly stipulates that "the arbitration agreement reached between the insured and the third party before the occurrence of the insurance accident shall be binding on the insurer." At the same time, this article excludes from the foregoing provisions whether the insurer is bound by the arbitration agreement reached between the insured and the third party in foreign-related civil and commercial cases. On this issue, the consistent opinion of the Supreme People's Court, as reflected in its replies, is that the insurer is not bound by the arbitration agreement in the aforesaid contract unless there is evidence to the contrary that the insurer knew of and agreed to accept the arbitration agreement. For example, the [2005] Min Si Ta Zi No. 29 Reply Letter clearly states: "Since the insurer is not a party to the negotiation of the arbitration clause, the arbitration clause is not an expression of the insurer's intention, and the arbitration clause of the bill of lading does not bind the insurer unless the insurer explicitly expresses its acceptance of the arbitration clause."[①]

In foreign-related cases, the insurer is not bound by the arbitration agreement reached between the insured and the third party. The fundamental reason is that, in maritime cases, especially in liner shipping, the Chinese insurer is often confronted with London arbitration as provided in the bill of lading after it makes the compensation In that case, the Chinese supreme people's court does not recognize a legally binding arbitration agreement on the Chinese insurer so as to safeguard the interests of the country's insurance industry Strictly speaking, this is a reflection of the policy of the law, rather than a theoretically self-evident conclusion. More accurately, in such circumstances, the value orientation of our

---

① Reply of the Supreme People's Court to the Request for Instruction on the Effectiveness of the Arbitration Clause in the Case of Dispute over Cargo Damage in the Contract for the Carriage of Goods by Sea between the People's Republic of China Property and Casualty Insurance Co. Ltd., Shenzhen Branch v. Guangzhou Ocean Shipping Company, (2005) Min Si He Zi 29, 9 October 2005, (2005) Civil IV. Reply to the Supreme People's Court on Whether the Insurer is Bound by the Arbitration Agreement between the Insured and the Third Party in Foreign-related Civil and Commercial Cases, op. cit., pp. 83-84.

courts is more in favour of regulating arbitration consents. And theoretically speaking, to judge whether the insurer, in exercising its subrogation right, is bound by the arbitration agreement reached between the insured and the third party, it is necessary to clarify the relationship between the arbitration agreement and the rights and obligations of the main contract, in order to make clear whether the arbitration agreement should be automatically assigned when the rights and obligations of the main contract are assigned.

Although the arbitration agreement exists independently of the main contract, it should be considered as a procedural obligation attached to the rights and obligations in the main contract. In essence, the arbitration agreement effectively restricts the parties' right of action and obliges them to resolve their disputes through the arbitration proceedings. At the same time, arbitration is based on the consent of the parties. From this perspective, while modern arbitration law no longer insists on the personal nature of arbitration, the relativity of the parties' choice to arbitrate with specific parties in respect of specific disputes should still be respected.[①] In other words, the arbitration agreement is not only a procedural obligation attached to the rights and obligations of the main contract, but also a procedural obligation with relativity. Based on the above analysis, the core issue of whether the insurer is bound by the arbitration agreement between the insured and the third party when exercising its subrogation right is whether it is reasonable for the insurer to be bound by the arbitration agreement, which is a procedural obligation of a relative nature attached to the main contract. In order to clarify this issue, the insurer's subrogation rights can be compared to the assignment of claims.

Article 9 of the Judicial Interpretation of the Arbitration Law provides that the arbitration agreement is automatically assigned upon the

---

① Yao Yu, "The Value Balancing Approach of Arbitration Agreements Accompanying Assignment of Claims - A Re-examination of Debtor Protection", in Journal of China University of Political Science and Law, No. 3, 2022, pp. 285-286.

assignment of a claim, unless the parties have agreed otherwise, or the assignee expressly objected to it at the time of the assignment of the claim or it was unaware of the existence of a separate arbitration agreement. Due to the existence of the proviso, article 9 does not actually recognise that the arbitration agreement, which is a relative procedural obligation attached to the main contract, is necessarily assigned with the main claim upon assignment of the claim. The reason for this is the breach of the identity of the claim by the cession of the claim. The assignment of a claim actually violates the identity of the claim, but the legislation favours the property right attribute of the claim and therefore allows the claim to circulate freely as a form of property. Thus, the assignee is not so much assigning a claim between the assignor and the assignee as it is assigning an independent claim that is consistent with the payment of the aforementioned claim.[①] Consequently, the procedural obligations attached to the original claim between the assignor and the debtor are necessarily not transferred with the assignment of the main claim. Therefore, the basic theory behind article 9 of the Judicial Interpretation of the Arbitration Law is correct, but the problem with this article is that it ignores the fact that the arbitration agreement also has a relative nature. When a claim transfer established by agreement occurs, the debtor has no right to object to the transfer, and as long as it receives notice from the creditor, the transfer of the claim is effective against the debtor. However, this is for substantive rights, while arbitration agreements are not in essence negotiable property rights, but rather consensual agreements between the parties regarding dispute resolution procedures. Therefore, the Supreme People's Court Interpretation on the Application of the Civil Procedure Law of the People's Republic of China which entered into force in 2015 and was revised in 2022 has been consistent in its provisions on the selection

---

[①] Zhuang Jiayuan, "Commentary on Article 79 (Assignment of Claims) of the Contract Law", in Jurist, No. 3, 2017, pp. 1-2.

of competent courts. It provides that the agreement on jurisdiction over a contract shall be applicable to the transferee of the contract upon contract transfer, except where the transferee has no knowledge of the agreement on jurisdiction upon contract transfer, or where jurisdiction is otherwise agreed under the transfer agreement and the original counterparty to the contract has given consent thereto. This priviso is a more appropriate way to regulate. In other words, the transferee and the debtor need to be given the right to negate the binding effect of the arbitration agreement at the time of the transfer of the claim.

The subrogation right of the insurer is generally understood by scholars in China as a kind of statutory transfer of claims.[①] If we follow the above analysis, the insurer and the third party should certainly have the right to object to the binding effect of the arbitration agreement. However, the subrogation right of the insurer and the intentional assignment of claims are very different legal mechanisms for different purposes, leading to the difference in whether the arbitration agreement is automatically assigned or not. The insurer's subrogation right derives from the insurance law's principle of compensateing damages, and its main value is to enable the insured to obtain a quick settlement of the claim and to prevent the insured from obtaining compensation in excess of the actual loss.[②] Thus, subrogation of the insurer focuses on the compensation of damages, whereas claims transfer established by agreement focuses on the circulation of property. After the insurer pays the insured, it acquires the statutory right to claim compensation from third parties. According to the insurance law, which provides for "subrogation of the insured's right to claim compensation from third parties within the limits of the compensation amount", the insurer is actually claiming compensation from third parties in a legal relationship between the insured and the third party,

---

[①] Wen Shiyang and Wu Yiwen, "On the Jurisprudential Basis of Insurance Subrogation Right and Its Scope of Application", in Tsinghua Law, 2010, No. 4, p. 32

[②] Op. cit. p. 28.

which has resulted in an actual loss. Thus, the insurer's subrogation right is more akin to a compulsory general transfer of a debt. In such cases, both the insurer and the third party are of course bound by the arbitration agreement between the insured and the third party.

2.1.2 Whether a Creditor Exercising its Right of Subrogation is Bound by an Arbitration agreement Between the Debtor and the Sub-debtor

Subrogation of creditors is the right of a creditor to exercise in its own name the rights belonging to the debtor in order to preserve its claim.[①] Although the creditor's right of subrogation also bears the title of subrogation, it is fundamentally different from the insurer's right of subrogation. The latter is a statutory cession of a claim, whereas the former is an external effect of a claim. Therefore, the creditor's subrogation right is the creditor's subordinate right to the debtor's claim, a kind of "preservation" right of the claim under the law, rather than the cession of the claim from the debtor.[②] Therefore, the Civil Code of the People's Republic of China (hereinafter referred to as the "Civil Code") stipulates the creditor's subrogation right in the part of contract preservation. Understanding the creditor's right of subrogation from this perspective, the creditor's exercise of the right of subrogation is of course not subject to the arbitration agreement between the debtor and the sub-debtor, but should be exercised in accordance with the subrogation system provided for by law.

At issue is the wording of article 535 of the Civil Code, which states that a request "may be made to the People's Court". Since a request can be made to the court, it can of course also be made to the arbitration institution. However, judging from the judicial practice, taking the most typical case in which the actual constructor is subrogated to the subcontractor

---

① Han Shiyuan, General Introduction to Contract Law (4th ed.), Law Press 2018, p. 433.
② Gao Yinli: "Study on Several Issues of Subrogation Rights of Actual Constructors", in Commercial Arbitration and Mediation, No. 2, 2021, p. 103.

or the illegal subcontractor to claim compensation from the contractor as an example, the courts in China do not support that the actual constructor is bound by the arbitration agreement between the subcontractor or the illegal subcontractor and the contractor. For example, in the case of (2020) Supreme Court Civil Final No. 479,① the Supreme People's Court pointed out that "this case is a litigation caused by the creditor, Yicheng Company, to the extent that the debtor, Dongtai Company, was negligent in exercising its matured claim on the sub-debtor, Xiangdian Company, which caused damages to Yicheng Company, and the litigation was caused by Yicheng Company's action of subrogating to exercise the claim of Dongtai Company against Xiangdian Company in its own name, and it is not a litigation arising from the assignment of the claim." On this basis, the Supreme People's Court held that: "Although Xiangdian Company claimed that the contract signed between Xiangdian Company and Dongtai Company had expressly agreed on an arbitration clause, and that the case should be heard by Xiangtan Arbitration Commission, but since Yicheng Company was neither a party to the contract involved in the arbitration clause nor an assignee of the rights and obligations of the contract involved in the arbitration clause, and that the agreement to submit dipsutes to arbitration is in conflict with special territorial jurisdiction provided for the creditor subrogation litigation stipulated in article 14 of *The supreme people's court on the application of the contract law of the People's Republic of China on a number of issues of the interpretation (a)*. In that sense, the original ruling that the Yicheng company is not subject to the arbitration clause is in accordance with the law.

As can be seen from the Supreme People's Court's findings in this case, firstly, the Supreme People's Court understood that the possibility of petitioning the People's Court was a provision on the creditor's

---

① Civil Judgement of the Second Instance on the Dispute over Subrogation Rights of Creditors of Yicheng New Material Technology (Shanghai) Co., Ltd. and Xiangdian Wind Energy Co., Ltd. (2020) Supreme Court Civil Final No. 479.

rights, not on the manner in which the creditor could exercise its rights; and secondly, the creditor's exercise of its right of subrogation was not a step into the legal relationship between the debtor and the sub-debtor, or a cession by the sub-debtor of its claim. Therefore, the exercise of the creditor's right of subrogation is not the same as the subrogation of an insurer or the assignment of a claim, and requires the preservation of its claim in accordance with the statutory mode of exercising the creditor's right of subrogation - litigation.

Accordingly, when analysing whether the arbitration agreement can bind the third party, the starting point is that the arbitration agreement is a procedural obligation attached to the main contract and is relative in nature. From this point of view, when judging whether the arbitration agreement binds the third party, the basic value choice of our courts is to respect the arbitration agreement of the parties as well as the third party's right to choose arbitration. And when the third party fully enters into the legal relationship between others, unless there are legal policy reasons, the third party shall be bound by the arbitration agreement between others.

2.2 Determination of the Validity of an Arbitration–and–litigation Clause

A typical arbitration-and-litigation clause is that the parties agree to continue to litigate after they have submitted the dipsute to arbitration and obtained a result. Unlike an arbitration-or-litigation clause, an arbitration-and-suit clause often includes clear expressions indicating "arbitration first and litigation after". For instance, the parties may agree to continute if the arbitration was unsuccessful or that the outcome of the arbitration was unsatisfactory. The core of the dispute over arbitration-and-litigation clauses is whether such clauses should be categorised as arbitration-or-litigation clauses and thus be denied validity under article 7 of the Judicial Interpretation of the Arbitration Law.

In the case of (2013) Civil Second Final Word No. 81,[①] the parties agreed on an arbitration clause that reads: "The way to resolve contractual disputes is as follows: if a dispute arises out of the contract, the two parties to the contract will resolve it through consultation; if the consultation fails, the dispute may be submitted to the arbitration committee in the place of the signing of the agreement, and if any of the parties disputes the result of the arbitration, it may be filed with the court in the place of the signing of the contract." With regard to this clause, the Supreme People's Court held that "although the parties in this case agreed that either party could propose arbitration to the Arbitration Commission at the place where the agreement was signed, they at the same time agreed that if any one of the parties objected to the result of the arbitration, it could file a lawsuit with the court at the place where the contract was signed. Such an agreement is inconsistent with the provisions of Article 9(1) of the Arbitration Law of the People's Republic of China regarding 'The arbitration award shall be final', and violates the basic principle that arbitration excludes the jurisdiction of the court." Obviously, the attitude of the Supreme People's Court was clear, and the clause of award before litigation should be regarded as a special type of arbitration-or-litigation clause that was invalid.

However, Article 94 of the Minutes clearly stipulates that "Where the parties have agreed in the arbitration agreement to 'arbitrate first and litigate later' after the dispute has arisen, it does not belong to the invalid circumstances of the arbitration agreement as stipulated in Article 7 of the Judicial Interpretation of the Arbitration Law." Obviously, the Supreme People's Court's attitude towards the arbitration-and-litigation clause has changed fundamentally, turning to recognition instead of denial of the validity of such clause. The value proposition supporting this change

---

① Appeal of Jurisdictional Objections to the Sale and Purchase Contract Dispute between Inner Mongolia Jixiang Coal Co., Ltd. and Tianjin Metallurgical Group Trading Co., Ltd., (2013) Civil Second Final No. 81.

in attitude is to respect the parties' arbitration agreement. According to article 9, paragraph 1 of the Arbitration Law on the arbitral award issued by the parties shall not be the same dispute to the people's court, the "arbitration before litigation" on the litigation agreement is invalid, but does not affect the validity of the arbitration agreement. Such argumentation is based on Article 156 of the Civil Code, which distinguishes between the pre-arbitration part and the post-litigation part while finding that the post-litigation part violates the provisions of the law. On this basis, the validity of the pre-arbitration part is further judged separately.

Such argumentation requires further answers to two potential questions, one of which is whether, if the arbitration part of an arbitration-and-litigation clause is invalid, the litigation part can be a valid choice of court agreement. Since there is an option to respect the parties' agreement to choose arbitration, under the premise that such agreement is invalid and the clause itself provides for a competent court, whether the litigation part can constitute a valid choice of court agreement; and if it can, as a corollary, whether any arbitration-or -litigation clause, as long as the arbitration part is invalid, can be regarded as a valid choice of court clause is an issue that needs to be clarified by the Supreme People's Court. Secondly, the litigation part of the arbitration-and-litigation clause is invalid because the agreement violates the principle of finality of the award; if the parties did not agree on the litigation after arbitration, but agreed on other matters, whether it is also possible to apply the "partially valid, partially invalid" test to determine the validity of the arbitration part of the clause. In other words, the court will need to determine on a case-by-case basis whether the portion of the arbitration agreement that follows the parties' agreement to arbitrate violates a mandatory provision of the arbitration law. Such a provision must constitute a valid mandatory provision in order to negate the validity of the post-arbitration part of the clause. This argumentation necessarily leads to a discussion of which provisions of the arbitration law are mandatory provisions of validity, which is clearly a question without a foregone conclusion. It is debatable whether the initial support for arbitration consensualism, which has led to an arbitrary standard of judicial review of arbitration, is necessary and justified.

2.3 Determination of Uniqueness of an Arbitral Institution

The current Chinese arbitration law does not allow ad hoc arbitration. Although the Opinions of the Supreme People's Court on Providing Judicial Guarantees for the Construction of Pilot Free Trade Zones has made an exceptional policy for ad hoc arbitration conducted in Pilot Free Trade Zones, allowing ad hoc arbitration in compliance with the "three-specifications" principle[①], there have been no such cases in judicial practice. In terms of legislative trends, Article 25 of the Arbitration Law of the People's Republic of China (Revised) (Draft for Opinion) (hereinafter referred to as the Draft for Opinion of the Arbitration Law), which was published for public consultation by the Ministry of Justice in 2021, on the validity of the arbitration agreement, has explicitly canceled the requirement for the arbitration agreement to agree on a sole arbitration institution. The second and third paragraphs of Article 35 of the Exposure

---

① Opinions of the Supreme People's Court on Providing Judicial Guarantees for the Construction of Pilot Free Trade Zones (Fa Fa [2016] No. 34), Article 9, Paragraph 3: "Where enterprises registered in a Pilot Free Trade Zone have agreed with each other to arbitrate the dispute in question at a specific place in the Mainland, in accordance with specific arbitration rules, and by a specific person, such an arbitration agreement may be deemed valid. Where the people's court considers the arbitration agreement to be invalid, it shall report it to a higher court for review. If the higher court agrees with the opinion of the lower court, it shall report its review opinion to the Supreme People's Court and make a ruling after the Supreme People's Court has replied." It should be noted that the opinions on judicial safeguards issued by the Supreme People's Court for FTZs since then no longer refer to procedures that require a response from the Supreme People's Court, such as Article 19 of the Opinions of the Supreme People's Court on the People's Courts' Provision of Judicial Services and Safeguards for the Construction of Beijing's Comprehensive Demonstration Zone for the Expansion and Opening Up of the National Service Sector and the Pilot Free Trade Zone of China (Beijing) (Fafa [2021] No. 11), which reads: "... Supporting the agreement between enterprises registered in the Pilot Free Trade Zone to arbitrate relevant disputes at a specific place, under specific arbitration rules, and by specific persons. ..."

Draft of the Arbitration Law, on the other hand, make additional provisions for arbitration agreements that do not expressly agree on a sole arbitration institution, stipulating how to deal with cases where the agreement on the arbitration institution is unclear and where there is no agreement on the arbitration institution.

Judging from the general trend, the trend of the future revision of the Arbitration Law should be to incorporate ad hoc arbitration. As a result of this trend, the value orientation of the Chinese courts in recent years in determining the uniqueness of an arbitration institution has tended to respect the arbitration agreement of the parties, and to presume, as far as possible, the sole arbitration institution, taking into account the facts of the case and the agreement of the arbitration agreement. Article 93 of the Minutes, in response to Article 3 of the Judicial Interpretation of the Arbitration Law, further clarifies that "the arbitration agreement shall be determined in accordance with the principle of favouring the validity of the arbitration agreement", which is the best illustration of the aforementioned value choice. For example, in the case of (2019) Supreme Law Zhi Civil Final No. 338,① the Supreme People's Court held that the arbitration clause in the contract was "arbitration at the Beijing Municipal Arbitration Commission", and there are three arbitration commissions in Beijing, namely the Beijing Arbitration Commission, the China International Economic and Trade Arbitration Commission, and the China Maritime Arbitration Commission. The literal meaning of the arbitration clause is closest to the "Beijing Arbitration Commission" among the three existing arbitration institutions in Beijing, with the difference lying in only one word. Considering that the parties are not legal or dispute resolution professionals, the court shall not impose too demanding requirements upon them when reviewing the validity of the parties' agreement on the arbitra-

---

① Appeal of Computer Software Development Contract Dispute between Hushang.com (Shanghai) Network Technology Co. and Beijing Mihua Times Technology Co. Ltd, (2019) Supreme Court Zhi Minzhen Final No. 338.

tion institution. Therefore, the arbitration clause should be considered to have agreeed on the sole arbitration institution. In terms of wording, the arbitration clause in this case does not include clear expressions concerning the agreed arbitration institution. Therefore, the Supreme People's Court in this case actually presumed the parties' intention when they concluded the arbitration agreement, and the presumption was based on the value of making the arbitration agreement as effective as possible rather than regulating an inaccurate arbitration agreement.

The essence of the parties' application to the court for confirmation of the validity of the arbitration agreement was that the parties disputed the validity of the arbitration agreement, or more accurately, that one party believed that the validity of arbitration agreement is defective while the other party disagreed. [1]Therefore, in the judicial review procedure of the validity of the arbitration agreement, the court could not ask the parties about the true meaning of the arbitration agreement. Thus, in determining the validity of the arbitration agreement, the court is, strictly speaking, presuming the intention of the parties. As in the case cited above, the conclusion of the Supreme People's Court was in effect that the parties, in concluding the arbitration agreement, should have expressed the intention of choosing the Beijing Arbitration Commission.

According to the above methodology, when the court determines whether the parties have agreed upon the sole arbitration institution in their arbitraiton agreement, the conclusion cannot be based on the facts that occur after the signing of the arbitration agreement. Instead, the court should judge whether the agreement between the parties, at the time of conclusion of the arbitration agreement, pointed to the sole arbitration institution. However, in the case of (2019)Supreme Court Civil Final No.

---

[1] Xie Shisong, ed., Commercial Arbitration Law (2nd ed.), Higher Education Press 2022, pp. 331-332.

1500,[1] the Supreme People's Court held that the parties entered into the arbitration clause with the intention of choosing to resolve the dispute by arbitration and chose the Arbitration Committee established at the place where the project was located. When CLP Hong Kong and Shipping Company filed a lawsuit at the Fujian Higher People's Court in February 2019, there had been an arbitration institution named Cross-Strait Arbitration Centre established at the place where the project was located in accordance with the Chinese Arbitration Law. The uncertainty of the arbitration clause has been eliminated and the arbitration clause should be found valid. Obviously, the court determined the validity of the arbitration agreement retrospectively on the basis of facts occurring after the conclusion of the arbitration agreement. This approach is flawed, and could only be endorsed for its full respect of the parties' arbitration agreement.

In addition to article 3 of the Judicial Interpretation of the Arbitration Law, article 6 of the Judicial Interpretation also stipulates on how to determine whether the parties have agreed upon the sole arbitration institution in their arbitraiton agreement. In accordance with the value orientation of respecting the parties' mutual consent to arbitration, the judicial practice has gradually relaxed the criteria for interpreting Article VI. For example, in (2019) Shaan 01 Min Special No. 351,[2] the parties agreed in the contract that they should submit the dispute to "the Arbitration Commission established at the place where the project is located". The location of the project in question was in the Yangling Demonstration Zone in Shaanxi Province, but there was no arbitration committee in the Yangling Demonstration Zone. The Intermediate People's Court of Xi'an held that since Yangling Demonstration Zone was one of the areas under the direct ad-

---

[1] Civil Ruling of the Second Instance on the Construction Contract Dispute between CECC Harbour and Navigation Construction Company Limited and Pingtan Comprehensive Experimental Zone Land Reserve Centre, (2019) Supreme Court Civil Final No. 1500.

[2] Xi'an Fangzhou Construction Labour Service Co Ltd and Jiangsu Nantong Sanjian Group Co Ltd Application for Confirmation of the Validity of Arbitration Agreement Special Procedural Civil Ruling, Xi'an Intermediate People's Court, (2019) Shaan 01 Mint No. 351

ministration of Shaanxi Province, and there were a number of arbitration committees within Shaanxi Province. The arbitration committee at the location of the project agreed upon by the parties could not correspond to a specific arbitration committee. According to Article 6 of the Judicial Interpretation of the Arbitration Law, the arbitration agreement in question was invalid. As the judgement in this case was made in 2020, according to Article 3 of the Relevant Provisions of the Supreme People's Court on the Reporting and Verification of Arbitration Judicial Review Cases (hereinafter referred to as the "Reporting and Verification Provisions") which had not yet been amended at that time,[①] since the case denied the validity of the arbitration agreement and the parties' domiciles were in different provinces, it was necessary to report such case to the Supreme People's Court for verification. Therefore, the determination of the case actually reflected the Supreme People's Court's opinions behind its review. Apparently, the Supreme People's Court has adopted an extended interpretation for the concept of "a certain place" as stipulated in Article 6 of the Judicial Interpretation of the Arbitration Law. With regard to "a certain place" in this article, it should not be limited to a specific place, but rather to judge from the perspective of administrative jurisdictions whether there is a sole arbitration institution in the upper administrative jurisdiction of a

---

① Article 3 of the Relevant Provisions of the Supreme People's Court on Issues Concerning the Reporting and Verification of Arbitration Judicial Review Cases (Legal Interpretation [2017] No. 21): "In the non-foreign-related Hong Kong, Macao and Taiwan arbitration judicial review cases as stipulated in Article 2, Paragraph 2 of these Provisions, the Higher People's Court intends to agree with the Intermediate People's Courts or the Specialised People's Courts, after examination, to find that the arbitration agreement is invalid, and that the arbitration agreement will not be enforced or set aside in China The Higher People's Court shall report to the Supreme People's Court for review and approval under the following circumstances, and only after the Supreme People's Court has reviewed and approved the case shall it make a ruling in accordance with the Supreme People's Court's review and approval opinion: (a) the domicile of the parties to the arbitration case for judicial review extends across the provincial-level administrative regions; (b) the arbitral awards of arbitral institutions in the Mainland of China shall be refused to be enforced or set aside on the basis that they are contrary to the social and public interests." It should be noted that Article 3(1) was deleted after the 2021 amendment to the Reporting and Verification Provisions.

certain place; if there is, the arbitration agreement can likewise be deemed valid.

For example, in (2019) Shaan 01 Min Te 37,[①] the arbitration agreement provides that disputes will be "submitted to the arbitration committee established at the place where the party files the lawsuit is located". This clause clearly involves not only the determination of whether it constitutes an arbitration-or-litigation clause, but also the determination of whether there exists a sole arbitraiton institution as the place where the party files the lawsuit is located remains uncertain. The Xi'an Intermediate People's Court, after reviewing the case, held that since the domiciles of the parties to the contract were located in Xi'an City of Shaanxi Province, and Shiyan City of Hubei Province, respectively, and as there was only one arbitration institution in each of these two places, the arbitration institution was one and only when either party to the contract applied for arbitration. Therefore, according to Article 6 of the Judicial Interpretation of the Arbitration Law, the Arbitration Commission at the location of the applicant for arbitration shall be regarded as the agreed arbitration institution. If strictly in accordance with Article 6 and Article 7 of the Judicial Interpretation of the Arbitration Law, this case is one in which the validity of the arbitration agreement should be denied, not only because both litigation and arbitration appear in the arbitration agreement; and more so because the location, which is the party where the party files the lawsuit is located, is uncertain. As the case was decided in 2019, it was required to be reported to the Supreme People's Court under the Reporting and Verification Provisions, which had not yet been amended at that time. Therefore, the final decision over this case was actually also the review opinion of the Supreme People's Court. From the final conclusion, the Supreme People's Court adopted an extended interpretation for the concept of

---

[①] Li Zhenqing and Huachanda Intelligent Equipment Group Corporation Application for Confirmation of the Effectiveness of the Arbitration Agreement Special Procedural Civil Ruling, Xi'an Intermediate People's Court, (2019) Shaan 01 Min Special No. 37.

"a certain place" under Article 6 of the Judicial Interpretation of the Arbitration Law, i.e., that "a certain place" is a certain place for a specific party, not a certain place for all parties to the arbitration agreement. And since the conclusion of the case did not involve Article 7 of the Judicial Interpretation of the Arbitration Law, it can be inferred that, as judged by the Supreme People's Court in (2019) Supreme Law Zhi Min Jun 338, laxity in the wording of an arbitration agreement will not materially affect the validity of the arbitration agreement unless the extent of such laxity clearly indicates that the parties are attempting to resolve the dispute through both litigation and arbitration, which in turn constitutes an arbitration-or-litigation clause.

Accordingly, under the premise that the pace of incorporating ad hoc arbitration in our legislation is getting faster and faster, our courts are less and less inclined to deny the validity of the arbitration agreement on the basis that the arbitration institution agreed upon by the parties is not one and only, unless the courts, having taken all the facts and the arbitration clause into consideration, cannot find the specific arbitration institution the parties intend to agree upon. This is obviously an important manifestation of respect for the parties' arbitration agreement. However, this respect does not come without a price, and the inevitable consequence is that the courts need more exhaustive fact-finding. In the past, the judicial review of arbitration agreement obviously did not include the courts investigation over the arbitration institutions, either over those in the respective administrative regions or those located in different parties' domiciles. With an extended interpretation of the "a certain place", such fact-finding is inevitable. Of course, if the future arbitration law adopts ad hoc arbitration, the court of course does not need to conduct the above fact-finding. But in the present, whether too much tolerance of the parties' free agreement upon arbitration institution, which increases the burden of the investigation by the courts, is necessary is still a question to be answered. Whether the courts' findings concerning the content of the arbitration agreement based upon so much in-depth fact-finding can be considered to be the expressions of true intentions of the parties is open to disputes.

In summary, without considering the appropriateness of the path adopted by the court in reviewing the validity of the arbitration-and-litigation clause as well as in determining the uniqueness of the arbitration institution, the viewpoint of this article is that, Since the General Office of the CPC Central Committee and the General Office of the State Council jointly issue the "Opinions on Improving the Arbitration System and Enhancing the Credibility of Arbitration" on 31 December 2018, for the purpose of fully carrying out the important instruction "Putting the Alternative Dispute Resolution Mechanism to the Front" made by President Xi Jinping at the Central Political and Legal Work Conference, the orientation of the court for judicial review of the effectiveness of the arbitration agreement is obviously to shift from heavy regulation of the parties' arbitration consensual to the maximum support of the parties' arbitration consensual, and many of the arbitration agreements that have been found to be invalid in the past judicial practice, such as the arbitraiton-and-litigation arbitration agreement, have been supported by the judiciary instead.

III. Value Options for Judicial Review of Arbitral Awards

According to Article 17 of the Judicial Interpretation of the Arbitration Law, the procedure for judicial review of arbitral awards, which is more similar to the trial supervision procedure, is to review arbitral awards that have entered into force based upon very limited legal grounds. Theoretically, the grounds for setting aside or not recognising and enforcing an arbitral award are generally categorised into grounds against the jurisdiction of the arbitral tribunal, including the non-existence of an arbitration agreement, arbitrability and overruling; procedural grounds of review, i.e., violation of the statutory or agreed arbitration procedures; and substantive grounds of review. ①Since arbitrability is a purely legislative choice, and has nothing to do with the choice of value in judicial review; while the problem of overruling is fundamentally that the arbitral tribunal has ruled on the substantive legal relationship over which it has no jurisdiction, this paper examines the choice of value in determining the over-award in the part of substantive causes of review. Accordingly, this paper discusses the value choice of the court in the judicial review of arbitral awards, starting from the procedural and substantive grounds of review respectively.

3.1 Value Choices of Review on Procedural Grounds

After an arbitral award has been rendered, there are two main situations in which a party may challenge an arbitral award on the basis of a violation of statutory or agreed arbitration procedures: first, where the arbitration procedure itself was flawed and the arbitral tribunal failed to deal effectively with the flaw during the arbitration proceedings; and, second, where the party is dissatisfied with the outcome of the arbitration and seeks to negate the validity of the arbitral award on the basis of a violation of the statutory or agreed procedures. The first situation involves the right of the parties to object; the second situation centres on the question of how to find a violation of the statutory or agreed-upon arbitration procedure to the extent that it may affect the fair determination of the case.

3.1.1 Parties' Right to Object

Respecting the parties' consent to arbitration, in addition to respecting the parties' consent to choose arbitration, has the additional implication that the parties may make a special agreement on the arbitration procedure according to their needs. Such special agreement can be reflected not only in the arbitration agreement, but also through the waiver of the

---

① Nigel Blackaby et al. *Redfern and Hunter on International Arbitration*, Oxford University Press, 2015, p. 581.

right to challenge. That is to say, even if the arbitration procedure violates the arbitration rules or the special agreement of the parties on the arbitration procedure, as long as the parties waive the objection, they actually change the arbitration rules or the special agreement on the arbitration procedure by their deeds. Therefore, in the judicial review procedure of the arbitral award, if the party then raises a defence on the procedural defects that have been waived, it will certainly violate the principle of honesty and good faith.

Paragraph 3 of Article 14 of the *Provisions of the Supreme People's Court on Several Issues Concerning the Handling of Cases on the Enforcement of Arbitral Awards by the People's Courts* (hereinafter referred to as the "Enforcement Provisions") provides for the waiver of the right to object to the arbitration proceedings at the level of judicial interpretation. The article stipulates three conditions that must be met simultaneously for the waiver of the right to object to the arbitration proceedings: (1) a party knew or ought to have known of the defects in the arbitration proceedings upon special prompting; (2) that party participated in the arbitration proceedings or continued with the arbitration proceedings; and (3) that party did not raise any objections. The foregoing conditions may also be used in judicial review of the setting aside of an arbitral award to determine whether a party has exercised its right to waive its objection to the arbitral proceedings.

In arbitration practice, in most cases, the arbitral tribunal will, at the first hearing, ask the parties whether they have objections to the arbitration proceedings that have already taken place. It can be seen that the provisions of the Enforcement Provisions on the waiver of the right to object to the arbitration proceedings are based on arbitration practice and do not impose excessive requirements on the manner in which the parties may object. If the parties indicate that they have no objection under the aforementioned circumstances, then in the subsequent judicial review procedure, the court usually does not support the parties' argument for setting aside or not recognising and enforcing the arbitral award in respect of the defects of the arbitration procedure; if the parties indicate that they have objections, then the arbitral tribunal must resolve the defects of the arbitration procedure raised by the parties, or the court is bound to set aside or not to recognise and enforce the arbitral award on the basis of the violation of the statutory or agreed arbitration procedure. Arbitral awards. It goes without saying that when it comes to the parties' right to object, the court's value choice as to whether to set aside or not to recognise and enforce an arbitral award is to respect the parties' arbitration agreement.

Two points need to be added. One is that the waiver of the right to challenge is provided for in the arbitration rules formulated by several major arbitration institutions in China. For example, Article 69 of the Arbitration Rules of the Shenzhen International Arbitration Institute (SIAC) as amended in 2022, Article 13 of the Arbitration Rules of the Guangzhou Arbitration Commission (GAC) in 2021, Article 10 of the Arbitration Rules of the China Maritime Arbitration Commission (CMAC) as amended in 2021, Article 10 of the Arbitration Rules of the China International Economic and Trade Arbitration Commission (CIETAC) in 2015. The contents of these rules are basically the same, setting out three requirements that must be satisfied concurrently with respect to the waiver of the right to object: (1) a party knew or ought reasonably to have known of the defects in the arbitral proceedings; (2) the party still participated in the arbitral proceedings or continued with the arbitral proceedings; and (3) the party failed to object in a timely manner and in writing. In terms of the manner in which the challenge is to be made, the requirements of the former arbitration rules are higher than those of article 14, paragraph 3, of the Enforcement Provisions, but the former arbitration rules do not provide for the requirement of a special reminder to the parties.

Secondly, there is another dimension to the waiver of the right to challenge at the stage of judicial review. From the perspective of the parties, this involves whether the parties can make a special agreement or special waiver of the subject matter of judicial review;[①] From the perspective of the court, this involves whether the parties must raise all the objections in one go in the procedure for setting aside the arbitral award, or else lose the right to raise objections in the procedure for enforcing the arbitral award. Unfortunately, Article 26 of the Judicial Interpretation of the Arbitration Law only stipulates that a party cannot raise the same subject matter in both the setting-aside and enforcement proceedings, and does not deal with the waiver of the right to object at the stage of judicial review of the arbitration. As there are no clear legislative provisions and no judicial practice involving the right to waive objections at the judicial review stage of arbitration, this article will not further discuss the right to waive objections at the judicial review stage.

3.1.2. Determinations that May Affect the Fairness of the Case

According to Article 20 of the Judicial Interpretation of the Arbitration Law, violation of statutory or agreed procedures may lead to the setting aside of an arbitral award only to the extent that it may affect the correct decision of the case. In contrast, article 14, paragraph 1, of the Enforcement Provisions and article 101 of the Minutes of the Meeting, regarding the violation of statutory or agreed procedures, use the wording that it may affect the fair decision of the case. From this change in wording, it is easy to see that the concept of judicial review of the violation of statutory or agreed procedures has changed from ensuring the correctness of arbitral awards to safeguarding the impartiality of arbitral awards. Although an incorrect arbitral award must be unjust, an arbitral award that violates procedural justice is an unjust arbitral award even if it is substantively correct. Clearly, the change in wording is an advancement in the concept of judicial review.

The finding of a causal link between a violation of statutory or

---

[①] For more details on this issue, see: Li Hongjian, "The Dilemma of Judicial Review of Arbitration and Its Response", in Law Application, No. 8, 2021, pp. 49-50.

agreed procedures and an unfair arbitral award is necessarily implied from the use of the phrase "may affect" in article 20 of the Judicial Interpretation of the Arbitration Law, article 14, paragraph 1, of the Enforcement Provisions and article 101 of the Minutes. If the causal link is direct, such as when an arbitral award is made without proper notice to a party, the requirement of probable effect is clearly satisfied. Whether an indirect causal link may also fulfil the likely effect requirement is therefore a question to be examined. For example, in the case of (2021) Shaan 01 Min Special 170,① the arbitral tribunal made its determination of the cost of the labour cost adjustment amount in question based mainly on the calculation method it consulted with the costing professional body and taking into account the relevant quotas. According to Article 31 of the Arbitration Rules of the Xi'an Arbitration Commission, "the arbitration tribunal shall organise the parties to conduct cross-examination of evidence collected by the arbitration tribunal", the Xi'an Intermediate People's Court held that: "the arbitration tribunal, without organising the parties to conduct cross-examination of the calculation method, took the calculation method as the main basis for its decision, and the arbitration tribunal's decision was not based on any evidence collected by the arbitration tribunal. The Xi'an Intermediate People's Court held that "the arbitral tribunal, without organising any cross-examination between the parties on the cost calculation method, took the calculation method as the main basis for deciding the case, which was obviously a violation of the arbitration procedure", and accordingly set aside the arbitral award. The core judgement of the case was that it was the process of determining the evidence in the case that was procedurally flawed, while it was the arbitral award based on the evidence in the case that was set aside, and the court clearly used an indirect causal link to determine the impact of the procedural flaws on

---

① Xi'an University of Electronic Science and Technology and Xianyang First Construction Engineering Co., Ltd. Application for Special Procedural Civil Ruling on Annulment of Arbitral Award, Xi'an Intermediate People's Court, (2021) Shaan 01 Min Special No. 170.

the outcome of the arbitral award.

The phrase "may affect" does not in itself completely exclude an indirect causal link, but its scope is entirely at the discretion of the court. Thus, the core element in determining a breach of statutory or agreed arbitration procedures is actually the impartiality of the decision. It is clear that the court's value proposition in this judgement process is to achieve justice between the parties. Therefore, using the fairness of the award as the standard of review means in practice that the court can judge the arbitral award to a certain extent in terms of its substantive nature. If the arbitral award does not fairly determine the dispute between the parties, the court needs to further judge whether the procedural defects raised by the parties in setting aside or refusing to recognise and enforce the arbitral award can establish a causal link with the outcome of the arbitration. If the answer is in the affirmative, the arbitral award in question will be set aside or not recognised and enforced as a result of a violation of the statutory or agreed arbitration procedure.

In summary, when judicially reviewing procedural grounds, the court's value choice is to strike a balance between respecting the parties' consent to arbitration and ensuring the impartiality of the arbitral award. As the parties have the final say on the arbitration procedure, the court first needs to judge whether the parties have waived the right to object by exercising the arbitration procedure, which essentially changes the rules of the arbitration procedure; if not, to ensure the fairness of the arbitral award becomes the value choice of the court when making whether to find that the arbitral award is in violation of the statutory or agreed arbitration procedure. Under this value choice, once the court establishes a causal link between procedural defects and an unfair arbitral award through factual findings, it will make an affirmative judgement that the arbitral award has violated the procedural grounds for judicial review.

3.2 Review of the Value Option of the Matter of Fact

The substantive grounds for review of domestic arbitral awards under China's current arbitration law and its judicial interpretations include overruling, falsification or concealment of evidence, damaging the legitimate rights and interests of third parties, and contravening the public interests of society. At the theoretical level, over-award and falsification or concealment of evidence reflect the court's value orientation of ensuring the impartiality of arbitral awards. Overruling is to solve the problem of the arbitral tribunal's determination of a legal relationship that it does not have the authority to rule on, and falsification or concealment of evidence is to solve the problem of the incorrect facts on which the legal relationship ruled on by the arbitral award is based. These determinations were made in order to ensure that the arbitral award's determination of the legal relationship between the parties was fair.

The grounds for review of damage to the legitimate rights and interests of a third party and violation of the public interest of society are intended to address the issue of arbitral awards that have damaged the legitimate rights and interests of a specific third party or an unspecified third party, respectively. On the face of it, this is not a reflection of the value orientation of ensuring the impartiality of arbitral awards. However, if the arbitral award is understood as a contract between the parties, the damage to the legitimate rights and interests of third parties and against the public interest of the review of the subject matter is actually to solve the negative externalities of the contract. And once this negative externality is solved, it is also reversed to achieve justice between the parties. Therefore, just as there are two meanings of respecting the consent of the parties to arbitration, to ensure the impartiality of the arbitral award also has two sides. The positive side is that the arbitral award adjudicates disputes between the parties fairly; the negative side is that it overcomes the negative externalities of an unjust arbitral award. These two sides are reflected in different substantive grounds of review.

To argue judicially whether the value orientation of the court in reviewing substantive grounds is to ensure the impartiality of the arbitral award, it is necessary to examine a substantive ground of review not provided for in the Arbitration Law and its Judicial Interpretation - new evidence. Due to the nature of arbitration being final, if new evidence capable of overturning the arbitral award emerges after the arbitral award has been made, unless the parties agree to re-arbitrate, neither the arbitral tribunal, the arbitral institution, nor the court has proper grounds to overturn the arbitral award that has already come into effect. This is actually an extreme case of respecting the parties' consent to arbitration, i.e., the parties, having chosen arbitration as a means of dispute resolution, have to bear the possible drawbacks of a single award. Therefore, in cases of new types of evidence, courts are actually faced with a sharp conflict between respecting the parties' arbitration consent and ensuring the impartiality of arbitral awards. How the court deals with this conflict can effectively illustrate the value orientation of the court when reviewing substantive matters; it can also effectively illustrate what value orientation the court prioritises in the judicial review of arbitral awards. In (2020) Liao 02 Enforcement Dispute No. 267, the arbitral award in question recognised the loss proved by the applicant through two pieces of evidence, but the respondent obtained new evidence to prove that the applicant's loss did not exist during the enforcement proceedings. The case was ultimately rejected on the grounds of concealment of evidence, but it did not strictly comply with the requirements of Article 16(1)(c) of the Arbitration Enforcement Provisions, which states that "the opposing party shall be required to produce, or the arbitral tribunal shall be requested to order the submission of, the evidence". The Court's final finding was that the evidence provided by the respondent was sufficient to prove that there was a possibility that the claimant had concealed evidence during the arbitration process, and that the concealed evidence had clearly led to an unfair arbitral award. It is not difficult to see that this path of argumentation is consistent with the path of argumentation for finding that a violation of a statutory or agreed arbitral award may affect a fair award. Although the case cannot be considered as a typical situation of substantive grounds for judicial review by the courts in China, it is sufficient to show that the courts, when confronted with unjust arbitral awards, will, through the method of interpretation, try as much as possible to encompass the facts of the case into the statutory grounds for judicial review, and thus set aside or refrain from recognising and enforcing the unjust arbitral awards.

Accordingly, this paper argues that in reviewing arbitral awards, courts are more concerned with the fairness of arbitral awards and respect the parties' consent to arbitrate only to an appropriate extent, i.e., on matters that the parties can decide on their own. The reason for this is that the fundamental purpose of judicial review of arbitral awards is to rectify the lack of an ex post facto monitoring mechanism in the arbitration system itself and the consequent unfairness of the arbitration results that may result. Therefore, judicial review of arbitral awards is a limited review, and the courts will not intervene in arbitral awards as long as the arbitral awards are able to adjudicate disputes between the parties in a fair manner.①

IV. Practical Utility of the Value Choice of Judicial Review of Arbitration for the Effective Articulation and Coordination of Diversified Dispute Resolution Mechanisms

The value choice of our courts in judicially reviewing the validity of an arbitration agreement is to respect the consent of the parties in choosing arbitration, while the value choice in judicially reviewing an arbitral award is to ensure the fairness of the arbitral award. On this basis, this

---

① Hossein Abedian, *Judicial Review of Arbitral Awards in International Arbitration-A Case for an Efficient System of Judicial Review.* Journal of International Arbitration, 2011, Volume 28 Issue 6, p. 555.

Part attempts to answer the following two questions raised in Part I:

First, whether the above value orientation can effectively enhance the international competitiveness of China's arbitration system. Since the 18th National Congress of the Party, China's arbitration cause has been advancing by leaps and bounds. In 2018, the number of cases received by arbitration institutions nationwide and the subject matter of such cases were equivalent to the sum of the 15 years prior to the implementation of the Arbitration Law.[①] From the point of view of the court, respecting the parties' arbitration consent can effectively divert commercial cases and add more fuel to China's arbitration cause, which is already developing at a high speed. From the perspective of the arbitration institution, a large number of cases into the arbitration process, it is inevitable to standardise the operation of the arbitration process as the fundamental basis. Otherwise, once there are quality problems of arbitral awards, the court from the point of view of ensuring the impartiality of arbitral awards will inevitably need to revoke or not recognise and enforce these defective arbitral awards. This is not only a waste of arbitration resources, but also reduces the confidence of the parties to choose arbitration. Obviously, the value choice upheld by our courts in the judicial review of arbitration is only one aspect of China's arbitration career to enhance international competitiveness, and it is more important for arbitration institutions themselves to enhance the credibility of arbitration through standardised development.

Secondly, whether this value orientation can effectively realise judicial support and supervision of arbitration, thereby promoting the effective interface and coordination between justice and arbitration in the diversified dispute resolution mechanism. It is indisputable that the value choice of our courts in judicially reviewing the validity of the arbitration agreement - respecting the consent of the parties to choose arbitration - is the

---

[①] The Fourth Civil Trial Division of the Supreme People's Court, edited by the Supreme People's Court, Annual Report of the Supreme People's Court on Judicial Review of Commercial Arbitration (2019), People's Court Press 2021, p. 17.

most important support for the cause of arbitration, and the court humbly explains its own jurisdiction to support the parties to resolve their disputes through arbitration, which is a self-governing means of dispute resolution; because the arbitral award cannot justly Decide the dispute between the parties, and deny the effectiveness of arbitral awards, on the surface is a deterrent to arbitration, but in fact it can not only warn the arbitration personnel to be cautious in the use of power, to protect the healthy development of the arbitration industry, but also conducive to safeguarding the legitimacy and credibility of arbitral awards. [1]Therefore, the value choice of our courts in the judicial review of arbitration can effectively realise the judicial support and supervision of arbitration.

Promoting the effective interface and coordination between justice and arbitration in a diversified dispute resolution mechanism is a three-part project, one of which is the value choice upheld by the courts in the judicial review of arbitration. Respect the parties' arbitration agreement, promote more commercial cases through arbitration; correct the legitimate rights and interests of the parties to the arbitral award, maintain fairness between the parties and eliminate the negative externalities of such arbitral awards. The second is the standardised operation of arbitration institutions themselves. Improving the quality of arbitral awards enhances the competitiveness of arbitration as a means of dispute resolution. The third is the procedural optimisation of the judicial review system. [2]Increase the transparency, party participation and procedural efficiency of the judicial review process. From the perspective of effective articulation and coordination of diversified dispute resolution mechanisms, the above three points must be synchronised and jointly promoted. Therefore, a more

---

[1] Zhu Ke, "Trying to Discuss the Basic Principles of Judicial Review of International Commercial Arbitration", in Henan Social Science, No. 11, 2016, p. 54.

[2] Regarding the procedural optimisation of the current judicial review system of arbitration, please refer to: Shen Wei, "Normative Analysis of China's Judicial Review System of Arbitration - Origin, Evolution, Mechanisms and Defects", in LLF, No. 1, 2019, pp. 124-125.

fundamental way to effectively connect and coordinate the judicial and arbitration aspects of the diversified dispute resolution mechanism is to implement the concept of diversified dispute resolution, amend the current arbitration law, and promote the above trinity of projects in an integrated manner. Relying solely on the value choices made by the courts in the judicial review process of arbitration will not solve the procedural problems that exist in the current judicial review process itself, nor will it solve the problem of irregularities in the operation of arbitration institutions.

Conclusion

Value choices in judicial review of arbitration are of great significance in interpreting existing legislative provisions and dealing with borderline cases. In order to give full play to the role of arbitration in the diversified dispute mechanism, the value choices adopted by the people's courts in reviewing arbitration agreements have shifted from regulating the arbitration agreement to making the arbitration agreement as effective as possible. The Minutes reflect a significant shift in the value choices made by the courts in judging the validity of arbitration agreements. In the review of arbitral awards, the court to a certain extent involved in the review of the substantive results of the arbitral award, in order to ensure the fairness of the arbitral award, which seems to deviate from the judicial review of arbitration only procedural review of the general principle. However, at a time when China's arbitration institutions are springing up and flourishing, in order to enhance the credibility of arbitration, this deviation is appropriate to a certain extent.

The Choice of Law of the Arbitration Agreement: New Approach Towards the Application of the Closest Connection Principle

Zhang Wenkai[*]

Abstract: Under the current legislative framework of Chinese Mainland, the validation principle has been applied in a silent way as the third step of the choice of law rules to determine the law applicable to the arbitration agreements. The English courts' adoption of the closest connection principle in the determination the choice of law governing the arbitration agreements is worth being learning from. From the perspective of necessity, the special form of the conflict rules concerning arbitration agreements has added to the importance of reasoning, while reasoning cannot be conducted with a "silent" validation principle.Incorporating of the closest connection principle as a choice-of-law rule also meet the pro-arbitration approach under the Law of the People's Republic of China on Choice of Law for Foreign-related Civil Relationships. From the perspective of feasibility, the article suggests the hidden pro-validation approach would be a preferable way to determine the closest connecting factors and thus to manage the uncertainty resulting from the largely unfettered discretion afforded to the arbitrators in applying the closest connection principle.

---

[*] Master's Candidate, School of Law, Sun Yat-sen University, Research Direction: Litigation Law and Arbitration Law.

The article concludes that incorporation of the closest connection principle into the hidden pro-validation approach will give effect to parties' agreements to arbitrate, therefore ensure the applicable law to meet the requirements of legitimacy and acceptability with respect to the formal and substantive validity of the arbitration agreement.

Keywords: arbitration agreement; choice of law; the closest connection principle; the validation principle

Deciding the law governing an arbitration agreement in foreign related arbitrations is crucial among all choice-of-law issues in international commercial disputes, as it determines the validity of an arbitration agreement, the realization of the parties' consent for arbitration, jurisdiction of arbitral tribunal, recognition and enforcement of an arbitral award. Influenced by legislation and judicial practice of western countries, an increasing number of Chinese legal theorists have advocated that Chinese laws should include as many close connections as possible for the choice-of-law conflict rules governing arbitration agreement, and Chinese courts should adopt the pro-validation approach (hereinafter the validation principle) for the determination of the proper law of arbitration agreement.[①] These proposals have been partially adopted in Article 14 of the Provisions of the Supreme People's Court on Several Issues Concerning Deciding Cases of Arbitration-Related Judicial Review. Whilst the Revised Draft of the PRC Arbitration Law (hereinafter the Revised Draft of the PRC Arbitration Law) for public consultation issued on 30 July 2021 by the PRC

[①] Song Lianbin and Huang Jin, "Arbitration Law of the People's Republic of China (Comments on the Draft Revision)," 4 *Law Review* (2003); Wen Jian and Chen Weizuo, "The Determination of the Law Applicable to the Substantive Validity of Arbitration Agreements: Perspectives on a New Approach," 3 *Qinghai Social Science* (2018); Shan Xiaohui, "A New Approach to Determining the Law Applicable to the Validity of International Commercial Arbitration Agreements," 2 *Arbitration Study* (2020); Chen Zhi, "The Applicability of the Law of the Main Contract to the Arbitration Clause - From the Perspective of the Validation Principle," 2 *Arbitration Study* (2019).

Ministry of Justice stipulates some of the widely accepted practices and proposed some welcome changes in areas including the validity of the arbitration agreement (Article 90), it fails to mandate the application of the validation principle. Some critics have suggested that the Revised Draft of the PRC Arbitration Law should reiterate the validation principle to protect the reasonable and fair expectations of the parties, thus arbitration institutions in Chinese Mainland may enjoy growing influence worldwide.① According to Article 90 of the Revised Draft of the PRC Arbitration Law, there are essentially three stages to find the law governing the validity of the arbitration agreement:(1) the law agreed by parties to apply to the arbitration agreement;(2) the law of the seat; (3) the PRC law. Article 90 of the Revised Draft of the PRC Arbitration Law adopts the general principle under Article 18 of the Law of the People's Republic of China on Choice of Law for Foreign-related Civil Relationships (hereinafter PRC Law on Choice of Law) and expressly stipulates the concept "seat of arbitration" rather than "the location of the arbitration institution", yet it becomes less likely to follow the Swiss legislation mode or that of the Articles 22 and 32 of the PRC Law on Choice of Law by expressly stipulating the validation principle. In that case, the validation principle may only possibly be silently adopted by courts as a possible ground but at stage three for choice of law where no contractual choice governs.② In light of this, the article analyzes the judicial practice of the English courts that also have applied the validity principle in a "silent" way and suggests that the close connection principle may provide grounds and analysis of the support for judicial decisions making. In the greater detail below, the article analyzes the two modes of application of the validation principle,

---

① Nie Yuxin, "The Determination of the Law Applicable to International Commercial Arbitration Agreements: Comparison between English and Chinese Laws," 3 *Commercial Arbitration and Mediation* 75 (2022).

② Ma Yifei, "Laws Applicable to Foreign-Related Arbitration Agreements-Understanding and Application of Article 18 of the Law of the People's Republic of China on the Law Applicable to Foreign-Related Civil Relations," 8 *Academic Exchange* 77 (2013).

and examines the necessity and feasibility of incorporating the close connection principle into choice-of-law rules for arbitration agreements.

I. The Closest Connection Principle as a Source of Choice of Law for Foreign-related Arbitration Agreements

The closest connection principle is one of the most widely-used existing approaches to determine the law that governs the international commercial contracts where the parties have not chosen the applicable law. An arbitration agreement in nature is a form of private law regardless its contractual aspect, jurisdictional aspect, or *sui generis* nature.[1] Neither Chinese private international law nor that of other jurisdictions excludes the arbitration clause or agreement from international commercial contracts by limiting its scope to the substantive rights and obligations of parties to contracts.[2] Therefore the closest connection principle plays a vital role in finding the proper law governing the arbitration agreement.[3] "There is no ground to prevent a judicial authority from following the closest connection principle while determining the law applicable to an arbitration agreement".[4] Legislations and judicial practices of jurisdictions worldwide show that courts often equally treat the arbitration agreements and general commercial contracts and take "party autonomy - the closest connection principle" approach to determine the law governing such agreements.[5] For instance, Article 218 of the Restatement (Second) of Conflict of Laws establishes

---

[1] Wang Lan, "General Theories and Legislation Interpretation of the Law Applicable to Arbitration Agreement," 5 *Gansu Theory Research* 158 (2013).

[2] Zhu Kepeng, *Applicable Laws in International Commercial Arbitration*, Law Press China, 1999, p.59.

[3] Li Shuangyuan, *New Approach on the Practice of International Economic and Trade Law*, Hunan University Press, 1996, p.401.

[4] Zhu Kepeng, *Applicable Laws in International Commercial Arbitration*, Law Press China, 1999, p.59.

[5] Huang Jin and Chen Weizuo, "Applicable laws in International Commercial Arbitration," 4 *Law Review* 15 (1993).

the conflict-of-law rules of general contracts shall also apply to arbitration agreements, providing that in the absence of a choice of law by the parties, the validity and scope of the arbitration agreement will be governed by the law with which the arbitration agreement was most closely connected.

Nevertheless, the closest connection principle has been criticized for its uncertainty and unpredictability resulting from the largely unfettered discretion afforded to the judges. With a view of promoting greater uniformity and effective application of the choice-of-law rules, a number of national laws and international treaties have gradually departed from the closest connection principle to the seat of arbitration – the law and jurisdiction in which the arbitration agreement is likely to have its closest and most real connection.[1] Article V (1)(a) of the Convention on the Recognition and Enforcement of Foreign Arbitral Awards (hereinafter the New York Convention) sets forth limited and exhaustive grounds on which recognition and enforcement of an arbitral award may be refused by a competent authority in the Contracting State where recognition and enforcement is sought. It enables the courts of a Contracting State to refuse recognition and enforcement in two situations: first, if "the parties to the arbitration agreement ... were, under the law applicable to them, under some incapacity" and, second, if the "arbitration agreement is not valid under the law to which the parties have subjected it or, failing any indication thereon, under the law of the country where the award was made." Commentaries and judicial practices have suggested that Article V(1)(a) sought to lay down a principle that, in absence of a choice of law in the arbitration agreement, the law of the chosen arbitral seat would govern the arbitration agreement.[2] Under current Chinese legal frame-

---

[1] Ma Yifei, "Laws Applicable to Foreign-Related Arbitration Agreements - From the Perspective of the Independence of Arbitration Clauses," 1 *Commercial Arbitration and Mediation* 145(2021).

[2] Gary B. Born, *International Commercial Arbitration* (Third Edition), Kluwer Law International, 2021, p529.

work, law of the seat – one of the factors having closest connection with the arbitration agreement - has been adopted as a general choice-of-law principle in the Interpretation of the Supreme People's Court concerning Some Issues on Application of the Arbitration law of the People's Republic of China (hereinafter the Judicial Interpretation on PRC Arbitration Law), the PRC Law on Choice of Law, Interpretations of the Supreme People's Court on Several Issues Concerning Application of the Law of the People's Republic of China on Choice of Law for Foreign-Related Civil Relationships (hereinafter the Judicial Interpretation on Choice of Law) and the Revised Draft of the PRC Arbitration Law. It is noted that law of the place of the arbitration institution is also taken as a traditional approach in some of the above laws and judicial interpretations since the current PRC Arbitration Law only provides for institutional arbitration. [1]

In recent years, the validation principle has been gradually developed and broadly adopted by the legislations and judicial practices of western countries. Both Swiss Arbitration Law and Spanish Arbitration Act seek to preserve the validity of the arbitration agreement and apply a "most favorable criteria" approach, as long as the applicable law complies with any connecting factor closely related to the arbitration agreement, similar to that of Articles 22 and 32 of PRC Law on Choice of Law.[2] Likewise, several noted theoretical studies in China have suggested the validation principle shall be expressly established as part of the choice-of-law rules of the arbitration agreement, where the place has the closest connection with the dispute has been frequently identified as a connecting factor. For instance, in Recommendations for the Revised PRC Arbitra-

---

[1] Wu Yuyang, "Study on Law of the Location of the Arbitration Institution as the Law Applicable to the Arbitration Agreement," 4 *Beijing Arbitration Quarterly* 154(2020).

[2] Such conflicting norms, also known as "the passive approach on choice of law", reflect the purpose of legislation to maintain the legal validity to the maximum extent. Xiao Yongping and Ding Hantao, "The Unconditional Application of Conflict of Laws in the Law of the People's Republic of China on the Law Applicable to Foreign-Related Civil Relations," 4 *Science of Law (Journal of Northwest University of Politics and Law)* 177(2017).

tion Law drafted by Wuhan University Institute of International Law, general validation principle, along with the law most closely connected with the arbitration agreement, law of the seat, law applicable to the contract, are identified as presumptive choice-of-law approaches under the validation principle.① Furthermore, Professor Wen Jian, Professor Chen Weizuo and Professor Shan Xiaohui have also suggested the law most closely connected with the arbitration agreement should be included as a choice-of-law approach, together with law of the seat, law of the place of the arbitration institution and law of the forum.② However, Article 90 of the Revised Draft of the PRC Arbitration Law 2021 maintains the basic framework of the Article 16 of the Interpretation on PRC Arbitration Law 2006, reflecting that China's legislative trends towards the application of the validation principle remains unchanged.

Evolution of the closest connection principle as a choice of law rule for the foreign-related arbitration agreements has experienced a boom-to-bust circle. Upon the express adoption of validation principle, the closest connection principle has been taken as part of the choice-of-law rules yet with less attention among various connecting factors. On the contrary, under current Chinese legal framework where the hidden pro-validation approach is followed, in what way the closest connection principle could play a more important role in the conflict of laws in China? In addition to explore the legal significance of the closest connection principle, it is necessary to examine the historical threads of hidden pro-validation approach followed by the English courts with respect to the proper law of the arbitration agreement.

---

① Song Lianbin and Huang Jin, "Arbitration Law of the People's Republic of China (Comments on the Draft Revision)," 4 *Law Review* 97(2003).

② Wen Jian and Chen Weizuo, "The Determination of the Law Applicable to the Substantive Validity of Arbitration Agreements: Perspectives on a New Approach," 3 *Qinghai Social Science* 139(2018); Shan Xiaohui, "A New Approach to Determining the Law Applicable to the Validity of International Commercial Arbitration Agreements," 2 *Arbitration Study* 27(2020).

II. Noval Framework for Application of the Closest Connection Principle Under the Hidden Pro-validation Approach

The validation principle, as it applies to arbitration, can be illustrated in Hamlyn & Co v. Talisker Distillery and Others dating back to 1890s. The cases of Sulamérica CIA Nacional de Seguros SA and others v. Enesa Engenharia SA and others ("Sulamérica") in the English Court of Appeal have provided a welcome guidance on which law governs the arbitration agreement. In order to determine which law should apply to the arbitration agreement, the Lord Justices of Appeal (Moore-Bick LJ giving the leading judgment) laid down a three-stage enquiry, namely (i) whether there is an express choice, (ii) whether any choice can be implied, and (iii) which system of law has the closest and most real connection. The three stages should be embarked on separately but nonetheless in that order. Applying the three-stage enquiry to the facts, it was decided that the parties' express choice of Brazilian law as the governing law of the substantive contract was not sufficient evidence of an implied choice of Brazilian law applied to the arbitration agreement. Moreover, the application of Brazilian law would have had the effect of undermining the validity of the arbitration agreement. Given that London was the seat of the arbitration, it was held that the governing law of the arbitration agreement was English law.①

Some Chinese commentators have argued that each of the three-stage tests refers to a certain law, namely "express law-implied law (law of the main contract)-law has the closest connection (law of the seat)". As the implicit choice of law is expressly denied by the PRC Arbitration Law, it becomes one of the biggest challenges for law of the main contract

---

① Sulamérica Cia. Nacional de Seguros S.A. and Others v. Enesa Engenharia S.A. and Others, [2012] EWCA Civ 638

applied to the arbitration agreement.[1] However, above analysis of the Sulamérica is debatable. For one, implied choice of law does not necessarily direct towards law the main contract law. In Habas Sinai Ve Tibbi Gazlar Istihsal Endustrisi v. VSC Steel Co Ltd, Habas (the claimant) challenged the award on the ground the arbitral tribunal erred in finding that there was a binding arbitration agreement. As the Turkish law had the closest and most real connection with the dispute, it was the law governing the substantive contract. Therefore, Turkish law should be the law applicable to the arbitration agreement. The court considered the decision of Sulamérica and concluded that, given that lack of an express choice of substantive law, law of the seat, namely the English law, should be deemed as an implied choice of law applicable to the arbitration agreement.[2] In more precedents, judges did not take the clear cut tests as mentioned above. Instead, the law of the main contract or the law of the seat is held to be the law gonverning the arbitration agreement merely because it is associated with "the implied law that indicates the choice and intention of the parties or the law that most closely connected with the disputes shall be applied".[3] For another, English jurisprudence has been divided into different approaches to identification of "an implied choice". In the recent judgement in Enka Insaat Ve Sanayi A.S. v. OOO Insurance Company Chubb [2020] UKSC 38 ("Enka"), when deciding on the gverning law of the arbitration agreement, the Court of Appeal applied the English common law rules for resolving conflicts of law and established at the second stage of the enquiry that there is an implied choice for the seat, and this would be the general rule, subject only to any particular features

---

[1] Nie Yuxin, "Determination of the Law Applicable to International Commercial Arbitration Agreements: Comparison Between the English and Chinese Laws," 3 *Commercial Arbitration and Mediation* 72(2022).

[2] Habas Sinai Ve Tibbi Gazlar Istihsal Endustrisi AS v. VSC Steel Company Ltd, [2013] EWHC 4071.

[3] William Day, "Applicable Law and Arbitration Agreements," 80(2) *The Cambridge Law Journal* 238-240(July 2021).

of the case demonstrating powerful reasons to the contrary. However, the members of the Supreme Court were not unanimous in the route they took to arrive at their decision, notably on the important issue of the position of English law on the governing law of agreements to arbitrate. Essentially, two possible approaches have emerged when it comes to determining the law applicable to arbitration agreements, absent an express choice of governing law for the contract:(i) The first involves determining the law that governs the main contract, and presuming that this is also the law that governs the arbitration agreement;(ii) The second involves the presumption that the parties' choice of a seat of arbitration reflects their choice of governing law for the arbitration agreement more generally.[①] From the above majority-minority divide in Enka, whether the implied choice or a default positive rule of law will be taken largely depends on the court in exercising its discretion on a case-by-case basis. The English Courts relied on the principle of contractual interpretation that the contract should be interpreted so that it is valid rather than ineffective.[②] As some Chinese scholars suggested, if there is no choice of the parties (expressly or implied) of the law applicable to the arbitration agreement, the court actually takes the approach of finding the law most conducive to the validity of the arbitration agreement in accordance with the principle of the closest connection.[③] This view is also reflected in a paper by an English scholar William Day, which presents an analysis of Enka. He agrees with the default application of the closest connection as a defeat principle to select the governing law, which would be more appropriate than the strict appli-

---

[①] Enka Insaat Ve Sanayi AS v. OOO "Insurance Company Chubb" & Ors, [2020] UKSC 38.

[②] Sabrina Pearson, "Sulamérica v. Enesa: The Hidden Pro-validation Approach Adopted by the English Courts with Respect to the Proper Law of the Arbitration Agreement," 29 *Arbitration International* 115, 124(2014).

[③] Wen Jian and Chen Weizuo, "The Determination of the Law Applicable to the Substantive Validity of Arbitration Agreements: Perspectives on a New Approach," 3 *Qinghai Social Science* 135-136(2018).

cation of the three-stage enquiry.①

In essence, behind the three-stage enquiry lies a consistent hidden pro-validation approach followed by the English courts. The court applies the validation principle for purpose, that is, to choose the law most conducive to the validity of the arbitration agreement where no law is chosen by the parties. Whether the law potentially applied is deemed as the implied choice of the parties or determined under the closest connection principle, the courts' decision is rationalized upon the pro-validation approach. "In other words, the court tends to apply laws under which the arbitration agreement is valid. The validation principle provides that, if the arbitration agreement is valid under law of the seat, law of the seat will be upheld; same in the case of law of the substantive contract."② In the three-stage enquiry, the English Courts have developed the closest connection principle from a conflict-of-law doctrine to a judicial interpretation instrument in the process of finding the correct law applicable to the arbitration agreement.③

The English Courts took a broad approach to the application of the validation principle and the closest connection principle, to questions about the scope of the arbitration agreement as well as disputes about its substantive validity. Such approach sets a good reference for China's lawmaking. According to Article 90 of the Draft Revision of the PRC Arbitration Law, in the absence of a specified choice of law or a seat of arbitration, the court will jump directly to the third stage, that is, applying law of the forum. In the event the arbitration agreement is invalid under law of the forum, courts should follow the validation principle and de-

---

① William Day, "Applicable Law and Arbitration Agreements," 80(2) *The Cambridge Law Journal* 238,240(July 2021).

② Gary B. Born, International Commercial Arbitration (Third Edition), Kluwer Law International, 2021, p583.

③ Wen Jian and Chen Weizuo, "The Determination of the Law Applicable to the Substantive Validity of Arbitration Agreements: Perspectives on a New Approach," 3 *Qinghai Social Science* 135-136(2018).

termine applicable laws under which the arbitration agreement is valid, including law of the main contract. No matter which law is finally applied to the arbitration agreement, the closest connection principle is a judicial interpretation instrument in the choice-of-law context. It is both necessary and feasible to incorporate the closest connection principle into the choice of law analysis.

III. Necessity: the Closest Connection Principle as Basis for Choice of Laws

3.1 Rationale Behind Choice of Laws

Judicial decisions on governing law on the arbitration agreement shall not be rendered arbitrary. Rather, reasonable grounds are required for sound legal decision-making. Effective legal reasoning on choice of laws highlights the reasons for decisions are justified rather than irrational.[①] When a judge makes a decision without reasonable grounds or adequate considerations of the circumstances, it is said to be arbitrary and capricious. Instead, rule-based legal reasoning must meet the criteria and forms of justification.[②] According to Professor Li Shuangyuan, one of the leading private international law scholars in Chinese Mainland, there are two key issues in private international law: one is why specific laws could be applied, and the other is how to determine the proper law.[③] Essentially, the first issue above is, to a large extent, a question of the applicability of the chosen law. In the evolution of private international law, various approaches such as "the doctrine of statutes", "the doctrine of interna-

---

[①] Neil MacCormick, translated by Jiang Feng, *Legal Reasoning and Legal Theory*, Law Press China, 2018, p.8.

[②] Weng Jie, "Justifiability of Choice of Law in Foreign-Related Civil Adjudications and Arbitrations," 5 *Science of Law (Journal of Northwest University of Politics and Law)* 187 (2015).

[③] Li Shuangyuan, "Choice of Law Methods in Private International Law," 3 *China Legal Science* 161-162 (1984).

tional comity" and "the doctrine of vested rights" have been developed to solve this problem. Due to the complexity of private international law and less attention the Chinese Courts paid to the choice-of-law rules, some Chinese judges (including arbitrators) might determine the applicable law (especially the law of the forum) of an arbitration agreement without providing sufficient legal reasons, even "fail to determine any applicable law" ① or "determine more than one applicable law" ②. Considering the far-reaching effect of the above manifest disregard challenge, the Chinese Supreme Court has elaborated significantly that a reasoned judicial decision on foreign-related civil and commercial disputes must include the applicable law and the court's analysis of how the law was selected and applied. The court should neither directly apply the law of the forum, nor determine the applicable law without sufficient legal reasoning behind the decision.③ Subject to the judicial policy and convenience, some courts may tend to find, for instance, the law of the forum, as the governing law of an arbitration agreement;④ Other courts, though, driven by the pro-validity approach, may be inclined to apply a body of law in favor of the validity of the arbitration agreement. Under these circumstances, it is significant to provide sufficient basis in the court's decision, even if the approach followed is criticized hypocritical, superficial or utilitarian. A well-reasoned decision is important because it can enhance the legitimacy

---

① Song Lianbin, "The Practical Dilemma and solutions of Private International Law in China", in China Society of Private International Law, *Chinese Yearbook of Private International Law and Comparative Law 2002 (vol. 5)*, Law Press China, 2002, p.14.

② Song Lianbin, " Methods for Determining the Validity of Foreign-related Arbitration Agreements - Taking 'Arbitration in Hong Kong with English Law to Apply' as an Example," 11 *Political Science and Law* 8(2010).

③ Circular of the Supreme People's Court on the Application of Laws in Foreign-related Commercial Trials [Fa (2003) 121].

④ He Qisheng and Xu Wei, "Analysis of the 'Homeward Trend' in the Choice of Law for Foreign-related Civil Relationships in China," 2 *Wuhan University Journal (Philosophy & Social Science)* (2011).

and acceptability of the rulings of the court.① Regardless of the unfavorable decisions, the parties are more willing to accept a well-reasoned decision based on a formal, deliberative written opinion issued by the court.②

3.2 Distinct Form of Conflict-of-law Rules Highlights the Importance of Legal Reasoning

The differences between conflict of laws, in so far as it is concerned with the choice of the applicable law governing the arbitration agreement, address the importance of legal reasoning. In the event that the validation principle becomes a established conflict-of-law principle, namely "the law presumes that the interpretation that upholds the validity of the arbitration agreement will prevail", legal justification for judicial decisions based on reasoning is less of a concern. In this "passive mode of choice of law", the court only needs to consider whether the applicable law determined by the connecting factors gives effect to the arbitration agreement. The law applicable to the validity of the arbitration agreement will be determined. In other words, under the pro-validation approach, it is of less necessity to determine which laws to apply in a particular situation, or to interpret the process of finding the law.③ Nevertheless, the third stage of the choice-of-law test stipulates the court "may" apply law of the forum, meaning the court may also apply laws other than law of the forum. Thus, the choice-of-law test has become "an active choice by the court" similar to Article 41 of the PRC Law on the Choice of Law. Under this approach, courts are not bound by specific statutory laws in decision making to the choice

---

① Weng Jie, "Justifiability of Choice of Law in Foreign-Related Civil Adjudications and arbitrations," 5 *Science of Law (Journal of Northwest University of Politics and Law)* 186 (2015).

② Yu Xiaoqing, "The Judicial Decision Towards Legal Justification and Legal Reasoning," 8 Law Science 81(2012).

③ Xiao Yongping and Ding Hantao, "The Unconditional Application of Conflict of Laws in the Law of the People's Republic of China on the Law Applicable to Foreign-Related Civil Relations," 4 *Science of Law (Journal of Northwest University of Politics and Law)* 176-177(2017).

of law but establish the presumptive connecting factors based on the circumstances. To ensure legitimacy and persuasion, a reasoned judgement should reflect the judicial values and analysis of the determination through adequate reasoning.[①]

Is validation principle an effective ground enhancing justification of choice of law? The answer is debatable, though. On one hand, Articles 25 and 29 of the PRC Law on Choice of Law expressly stipulate that courts should choose laws conducive to protecting the rights and interests of the vulnerable groups, therefore the judge should follow such approach in the judicial decision making. Similar provisions could be found in Article 14 of the Provisions on Judicial Review of Arbitration. However, this type of explicit pro-arbitration provision is absent in Article 90 of the Draft Revision of the PRC Arbitration Law. In addition, Article 14 of the Provisions on Judicial Review of Arbitration explicitly stipulates the validation principle, in compliance with the second step of the choice-of-law test under Article 18 of the PRC Law on Choice of Law, which refers to law of the location of the arbitration institution or law of the seat. However, the location of the arbitration institution is no longer a connecting factor under Article 90 of the Draft Revision of the PRC Arbitration Law. In this sense, Article 14 of the Provisions on Judicial Review of Arbitration will have no substantial meaning. On the other hand, according to Articles 25 and 29 of the PRC Law on Choice of Law, together with Article 14 of the Provisions on Judicial Review of Arbitration, courts may determine applicable laws in a limited scope (that have real connections with the legal relations) upon the principle of protecting the rights and interests of the vulnerable groups or the validation principle. However, at the third stage of the choice-of-law test under Article 90 of the Draft Revision of the PRC Arbitration Law, courts may choose any national law as the govern-

---

[①] Weng Jie and Li Rui, "Space of Choice and Judicial Discretion in the Law of the Application of Law for Foreign-related Civil Relations of the People's Republic of China", 4 *Presentday Law Science* 34 (2021).

ing law.① Assume that courts determine an applicable law under which the arbitration agreement is valid yet it has little connection with the case, the choice of laws will lose its foundation, thus mere minimum criteria are required in regard with the validity of the international arbitration agreements.② In this regard, the English legal theorists generally consider that the validation principle is merely a "silent approach".③ It plays a methodological role to guide the choice of laws, yet additional principles are required to interpret the legitimacy of judicial decision-making.

3.3 The Reasoning Based upon Closest Connection Principle Meets the Requirement of the Article 2 of the PRC Law on Choice of Law

Compared with the validation principle, the closest connection principle plays a more effective role in legal reasoning. The closest connection principle means the application of the law of a country or a region which is most closely connected with the foreign element. In this regard, the closest connection principle plays an important role in the conflict of law as the court must balance various factors and find out the factors most closely related to the case to determine the applicable law. Some studies have noted that compared with the "theory of statutes" "seat of legal relationship theory", closest connection principle has been established as "choice of result" instead of "choice of jurisdiction", for the purpose of improving the justification of the choice of law.④ Moreover, closest

---

① A similar approach is found in Algerian law, pursuant to Article 1040 of the Algerian Code of Civil and Administrative Procedure, as to substance, an arbitration agreement is valid if it complies with the law that the arbitrator (judge) regards appropriate.

② "International minimum standard" has been adopted in several cases in United States for determining the validity of an arbitration agreement. Gary B. Born, *International Commercial Arbitration (Third Edition)*, Kluwer Law International, 2021, p567-568.

③ Sabrina Pearson, Sulamérica v. Enesa: The Hidden Pro-validation Approach Adopted by the English Courts with Respect to the Proper Law of the Arbitration Agreement,29 Arbitration International 115, 124(2014).

④ Shen Juan, *Interpretation of the Theory of the Laws Applicable to Contracts*, Law Press China, 2000, p.113.

connection principle as part of the choice-of-law test for the arbitration agreement is also complied with the relevant provisions of the PRC Law on Choice of Law.

Some Chinese scholars have noted that Article 18 of the PRC Law on Choice of Law includes a two-step choice of law test: (i) the chosen laws by the parties, (ii) if no law has been chosen, the laws at the locality of the arbitral authority or of the arbitration seat. In the event that the locality of the arbitral authority or the arbitration seat cannot be determined, according to Article 2 of the PRC Law on Choice of Law, the laws which have the closest relation with the foreign-related civil relationship shall apply. Nevertheless, the provisions are contradictory between Article 16 of the Interpretation on Application of the PRC Arbitration Law (2018) and Article 14 of the Interpretation of the PRC Law on Choice of Law I (2021).① Indeed, "law of the forum shall apply" stipulated in Article 16 of the Interpretation on Application of the PRC Arbitration Law (2018) has been revised as "law of the forum may apply" in Article 14 of the Interpretation on the PRC Law on Choice of Law I (2021). That is to say, under Article 14 of the Interpretation of the the PRC Law on Choice of Law I (2021), law of the forum is one of the laws that have closest connections with the arbitration agreement, therefore courts may choose other laws with which the arbitration agreement is closely connected. From the above analysis, we could deduce that the initiative of Chinese lawmakers is to adopt the closest connection principle at the third step of the choice of-law test. For one, the closest connection principle may bring room for the application of the hidden pro-validation approach.② For another, the closest connection principle also set restrictions on the application of

---

① Song Changrui, "New Developments in the Laws Applicable to International Commercial Arbitration Agreements: From the Perspective of Judicial Practice," 2 *Beijing Arbitration Quarterly* 119 (2017).

② Ma Yifei, "Laws Applicable to Foreign-Related Arbitration Agreements-Understanding and Application of Article 18 of the Law of the People's Republic of China on the Law Applicable to Foreign-Related Civil Relations," 8 *Academic Exchange* 77 (2013).

validation principle, namely courts should prove the applicable law determined by the validation principle has the closest connection to the arbitration agreement.

IV. Feasibility: Bridging the Validation Principle with the Closest Connection Principle

4.1 A proper Application of the Validation Principle as a Remedy for Limitations of the Closest Connection Principle

Neither the closest connection principle nor the validation principle has proven fully satisfactory. The closest connection principle as an established test could remedy the logical limits of the validation principle; the validation principle could regulate the broad judicial discretion under the closest connection principle. The closest connection principle brings more flexibility in making choices, but it also has been widely criticized for its excessive discretionary power. The closest connection principle is found to have many problems in the implementation process, such as uncertain judicial decisions and unpredictable result. To remedy these insufficiencies, courts in various jurisdictions have gradually abandoned the closest connection principle as a general choice-of-law rule governing the arbitration agreement. Instead, seat of arbitration has been taken into account as a connecting factor determining the *lex arbitri*. As far as the validity of the arbitration agreement is concerned, if courts are allowed to freely choose the law based on the closest connection principle, it is possible that the arbitration agreement with which the law has the closest connection would be invalid, thus it is difficult to guarantee the parties' expectation in arbitration. Accordingly, in the validity of the arbitration agreement, the above problems can be solved, if the court, within its discretion, choose the law under which the arbitration agreement is valid. In western countries, widely recognized mechanism of judicial discretion has been designed to guide the application of the closest connection principle.

For example, Article 6 (2) of Restatement (Second) of Conflict of Laws of the U.S lists seven factors that courts should rely on when determining the choice of law, and identifying factors such as "guarantee of legitimate expectations" and "certainty of results" are similar to the validation principle.

4.2 The Law Referred by the Validation Principle May Have the Closest Connection with the Arbitration Agreement

The feasibility of incorporating the closest connection principle into the choice-of-laws lies on that the law that would validate the arbitration agreement may have the closest connection with the arbitration agreement both in form and essence.

In formal way, law of the seat is not the only law that has the closest connection with the arbitration agreement under the Chinese legal framework; rather, law of the seat is adopted as a general but merely one of the potentially applicable choices of law governing the arbitration agreement. According to the jurisprudence and judicial practice in China, courts may also apply laws - such as the law governing the main contract or law of the forum –which may be interpreted to be the one having the closest connection with the arbitration agreement.①

In essence, it is not against the main purpose of the closest connection principle where the law condusive to the validity of the arbitration agreement is interpreted as the one having the closest connection with the arbitration agreement A distinctive function of the closest connection principle is to examine whether the law of the arbitration agreement is proper. As some scholars noted, under the closest connection principle, finding the potentially applicable choices of law is actually a process of

---

① Ma Yifei, "Laws Applicable to Foreign-Related Arbitration Agreements - From the Perspective of the Independence of Arbitration Clauses," 1 *Commercial Arbitration and Mediation* 145(2021); Zhu Kepeng, *Applicable Laws in International Commercial Arbitration*, Law Press China, 1999, p.59.

continuous comparison and selection of the best..① In some jurisdictions, the closest connection principle has been employed as a test for justification of the choice of law. When the presumptive choice-of-law rules may cause an unjustified judicial decision, courts can directly choose the law that has the closest connection with the legal relationship involved.② Moreover, whether the arbitration agreement is valid under the applicable law is also an important dimension to measure the appropriateness and fairness of the choice of law. "It is unlikely that the parties to the contract intended to invalidate the arbitration agreement/clause during the contracting process." ③Therefore, "parties' true intention should be fully reflected in the choice of laws, that is, courts must always prioritize the pro-arbitration approach over other approaches that would invalidate the arbitration agreement." ④ In an earlier ICC arbitral award, the arbitrator noted that "an arbitration agreement always has closer connections with the law that upholds its validity than that undermines it." ⑤ Although it is difficult to directly apply the validation principle as a basic rule of choice of law, it may serve as an important reference for choice of law through the established closest connection principle. The adoption of the hidden pro-validation approach is not a judicial favor for arbitration, but a respect for the autonomy of the parties,⑥ which is also the rightful meaning of the closest connection principle.

---

① Shen Juan, Interpretation of the Theory of the Laws Applicable to Contracts, Law Press China, 2000, p. 115.
② Wang Shengming, "Several Issues Concerning the Law of the Application of Law for Foreign-related Civil Relations of the People's Republic of China," 2 *Chinese Journal of Law* 189 (2012).
③ Enka Insaat Ve Sanayi AS v. OOO "Insurance Company Chubb" & Ors, [2020] UKSC 38.
④ FirstLink Inv. Corp. Ltd v. GT Payment Pte Ltd, [2014] SGHCR 12.
⑤ ICC Case No. 7154, 121 J.D.I. (Clunet) 1059, 1061 (1994).
⑥ Song Lianbin, " Methods for Determining the Validity of Foreign-related Arbitration Agreements - Taking 'Arbitration in Hong Kong with English Law to Apply' as an Example," 11 *Political Science and Law* 5(2010).

Conclusion

Chinese President Xi Jinping stressed that we must work hard to ensure that the people feel fairness and justice prevail in each and every judicial case. Whether the parties can see in a judicial case that justice is served is mostly attributable to the judicial decisions of parties' rights and obligations reached by a court. Likewise, an arbitral award - just as final and binding as a court judgement - is critically important to an arbitration. Well-reasoned arbitral awards are a safeguard against arbitrary adjudication and ensure the proper delivery of justice, but also increase public trust in the judicial system. Good reasoning also facilitates acceptance of the judgment by the parties and by the general public. At stage three of the choice-of-law rules, introduction of the closest connection principle as a rule of interpretation based on the validation principle will keep the balance between the formal and substantive legitimacy and acceptability of the courts' choice of law. On one hand, the validation principle as the substance of choice of law-oriented principle can maximize the protection of the parties to submit the dispute to arbitration expectations;

on the other hand, the closest connection principle as a rule of interpretation of choice of law is not only in line with the provisions of Article 2 of the Law on the Application of Laws, but also more appropriately to the parties to the process of choice of law and the basis for the enhancement of the parties to the results of the choice of law acceptability. The above operation mode is of great significance in enhancing the standardization and refinement of China's judicial review of arbitration and promoting the healthy and orderly development of arbitration.

Study on the Legal Issues of the Third Party Funding for International Commercial Arbitration

Abstract: In recent years, the third-party financing has developed rapidly in the field of international commercial arbitration. While promoting the realization of fairness and justice, it has caused many problems due to its profit-driven and private nature. In recent years, many countries and regions have begun to explore the regulation mode of third-party financing suitable for their own countries, but China's laws and arbitration rules have not carried out good regulation of third-party financing in the field of international commercial arbitration now. This paper draws on the experience of international arbitration institutions and representative countries on the regulation of third-party financing, combined with the current practice of international commercial arbitration in China, and puts forward the regulation model of third-party financing suitable for our country.

Keywords: third-party financing; international commercial arbitration; disclosure obligation; impartiality; independence

Introduction

International commercial arbitration has unique advantages such as high efficiency and strong confidentiality, and has become an important means for parties to resolve international commercial disputes. However, the cost of international commercial arbitration is high, and not all parties have sufficient funds to initiate arbitration proceedings. In order to protect their legitimate rights and interests, some parties lacking funds can only seek help from others. Therefore, in recent years, third-party funding has emerged in the field of international commercial arbitration. As a new type of investment method, third-party funding, although clearly profit oriented, is also of great significance for promoting fairness and justice. Due to the assistance of third-party funds, some parties lacking funds can use international commercial arbitration to safeguard their legitimate rights and interests. However, third-party sponsors have also brought some new challenges to international commercial arbitration procedures.

In recent years, some countries or regions have formulated laws and regulations to regulate this behavior, and many arbitration institutions are also modifying their arbitration rules to promote the healthy development of third-party funding. In recent years, there have been some specialized third-party funding institutions in China, such as Shenzhen Qianhai DS Legal Capital Co., Ltd. If there is a situation of third-party funding in an international commercial arbitration case in Chinese Mainland, the current laws and arbitration rules cannot effectively play a binding role. Therefore, how to effectively regulate third-party funding for international commercial arbitration is an important issue that urgently needs to be studied.

I. The Connotation and Development of Third Party Funding for International Commercial Arbitration[①]

In recent years, third-party funding has developed rapidly in the field of international commercial arbitration. Many scholars have begun

---

① Zheng Zenghui, male, born in February 1996, Assistant Judge of the Commercial Trial Division of Chongming District People's Court, Shanghai, with a Master's degree in Law (non legal) from Shanghai Maritime University

to study third-party funding in the field of international commercial arbitration, producing rich research results. However, scholars from various countries have not yet reached a consensus on the relevant research theories of third-party funding.

1.1 The Connotation of Third Party Funding

1.1.1 Definition of Third-party Funding

Third party funding has a very long history. In ancient Rome, nobles with power and money sought benefits by sponsoring one party to a lawsuit. This approach is very similar to today's third-party funding. In recent years, third-party funding has begun to flourish, but there is still significant controversy in the academic community regarding the scope of the sponsor and the form of funding. Therefore, a unified definition of third-party funding has not yet been formed.

The author believes that third-party funding in the field of international commercial arbitration should be a third-party entity outside of a certain international commercial arbitration dispute. By funding one of the parties to participate in international commercial arbitration proceedings, a system can obtain a certain proportion of returns from the profits obtained by that party after the case is successful. According to this definition, third-party funding in international commercial arbitration should have the following three elements: the recipient, third-party sponsor, and funding agreement.

1.1.2 The Operation Mode of the Third-party Funding System

The operation methods of third-party funding are mostly shown in the following figure:

From this, it can be seen that the ultimate goal of third-party sponsors is to make profits. If the sponsored party fails to win in the arbitration proceedings or the arbitration result does not meet the sponsor's original expectations, then the sponsor is likely to face significant losses, including but not limited to high arbitration costs. Therefore, the outcome of the arbitration award is the most important factor affecting the benefits of the sponsor. Before signing a funding agreement with the recipient, the sponsor will inevitably conduct a comprehensive review of the specific situation of the case, accurately evaluate the various costs that may be incurred and the potential returns on benefits, comprehensively consider various factors, and then decide whether to grant funding.

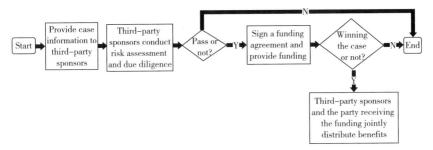

Figure 1   Flow Chart of Third Party Funding

1.2 Development History of Third Party Funding

1.2.1 The emergence of Third-party Funding for International Commercial Arbitration

The third-party funding system originated from the methods of "assisting litigation" and "contracting litigation" in the field of litigation.[①] With the continuous development of society, international economic and trade exchanges are becoming increasingly frequent, leading to the emergence of a large number of contradictions and disputes. International commercial arbitration is a highly efficient and convenient way to solve these contradictions and disputes. However, the arbitration costs of international commercial arbitration are very high, and sometimes one party

---

[①] Song Xixiang, Wu Yaofen: *Reasonable Regulation of Third Party Funding for Conflict of Interest in International Commercial Arbitration and Its Significance for Reference*, the 6th issue the Cross-straits Legal Science, p74(2018).

may inevitably lack funds. Thus, third-party funding in the field of international commercial arbitration emerged.

1.2.2 The Development of Third Party Funding for International Commercial Arbitration

Among countries under the Anglo American legal system, Australia was the earliest to confirm the legality of third-party funding in the field of arbitration. Later, local courts in Wales and England determined through precedents that litigation and arbitration could be conducted through third-party funding. The Singapore International Arbitration Center issued the "Investment Arbitration Rules" in 2016, which for the first time made clear provisions on the application of third-party funding in the field of arbitration in the country. The bill on amendments to the Civil Law issued by the country's legal department will abolish the prohibition of assisting in litigation and soliciting litigation.

In recent years, some professional third-party funding institutions have emerged in Chinese Mainland, such as Shenzhen Qianhai DS Legal Capital Co., Ltd. However, there is currently no clear definition of third party funding for international commercial arbitration in Chinese Mainland's legislation. Only Article 27 of the China International Economic and Trade Arbitration Commission International Investment Arbitration Rules provides provisions on the concept of third party funding, disclosure obligations, and the sharing of arbitration fees in the field of international investment arbitration.[1] With the continuous development of the third party funding industry, regulating third party funding alone is far from enough for the practice of international commercial arbitration in China.

---

[1] Article 27 of *the China International Economic and Trade Arbitration Commission International Investment Arbitration Rules*.

II. Necessity of Regulating Third Party Funding for International Commercial Arbitration

Third party funding has important advantages and functions, and is of great significance for the smooth progress of arbitration proceedings and the protection of the legitimate rights and interests of the parties. However, the essence of third-party funding is an investment method, which has caused many problems. Therefore, it is necessary to effectively regulate third-party funding for international commercial arbitration.

2.1 Advantages and Functions of Third Party Funding for International Commercial Arbitration

2.1.1 Provide Avenues for Parties to Achieve Fairness and Justice

International commercial arbitration is an important way for people to solve international commercial disputes. However, due to its high cost, some parties may not be able to apply for arbitration even if they lack sufficient funds and may win the case due to insufficient economic foundation.[1] For these parties who lack sufficient funds, the most important significance of third-party funding for international commercial arbitration lies in providing them with opportunities to achieve fairness and justice.[2] With the funding provided by the sponsor, the problem of financial scarcity for the parties has been resolved, and they have been given the opportunity to initiate and maintain international commercial arbitration, allowing them to assert their legitimate rights and seek compensation for damages through international commercial arbitration.[3]

---

[1] Shi Yujing: *Research on the Legal Regulation of Third Party Assistance in International Commercial Arbitration*, Master's Thesis of East China University of Political Science and Law, June 2019, p. 18.

[2] Zhang Kang: *Research on Legal Issues of Third Party Funding for International Commercial Arbitration*, Master's Thesis of the School of Foreign Affairs, June 2020, p. 8.

[3] Zhang Guanglei: *Third Party Litigation Financing: A Commercial Path to Judicial Remedies*, Journal of CUPL, 2016, Issue 3, p. 26.

2.1.2 Preventing the Abuse of Arbitration Procedures

Many scholars believe that third-party funding has led to some previously difficult to win cases being brought into arbitration proceedings, leading to excessive litigation. The author does not agree with this. On the contrary, the author believes that third-party funding can to some extent prevent the abuse of arbitration procedures. On the one hand, third-party funders are not philanthropists, but venture capitalists. They will strictly screen the parties applying for funding and select the cases they believe have a higher probability of winning for funding. On the other hand, due to the fact that third-party sponsors often have professional legal personnel and risk assessment personnel, in some cases where the probability of winning is not very high, the parties involved may recognize the reasons why the third-party sponsor did not provide funding to them, re-examine their current situation, and consider giving up arbitration and choosing dispute resolution methods such as mediation or settlement to resolve the dispute, This avoids the parties from arbitrarily initiating arbitration proceedings.

2.1.3 Balancing the Status of Both Parties Involved in Arbitration and Promoting the Speedy trial of Cases

In some cases where the subject matter has significant value and the economic strength of both parties is significantly different, some parties may use procedural rules to delay the trial based on their own economic strength. This not only increases the working pressure of the arbitration tribunal and is not conducive to the prompt trial of the arbitration case, but also causes the losses of the other party to continue to expand. After receiving third-party funding, the party with weak economic strength will have a certain improvement in its economic strength, and the positions of both parties will be balanced. The other party will no longer dare to rashly use procedural rules to delay the trial of the case. In addition, third-party sponsors will actively promote the smooth progress of international commercial arbitration procedures in order to obtain benefits as soon as possible.

2.1.4 Transfer of Risk of Arbitration Failure

In some cases, the parties may abandon commercial arbitration due to their inability to predict their likelihood of winning the case and unwillingness to bear the risk of losing the case. With the existence of third-party funding, the risk of losing a lawsuit is transferred from the recipient to the sponsor. The sponsor not only bears the risk of losing the lawsuit, but also has the possibility of distributing the benefits of winning the lawsuit. Moreover, sponsors often collaborate with insurance companies to further diversify this risk through commercial insurance, thereby enhancing their ability to defend against risks. For example, Burford Capital in the United States achieves risk diversification and transfer through cooperation with insurance companies.

2.2 Possible Problems with Third Party Funding in Practice

2.2.1 Conflict of Interest and Information Disclosure Issues

Many sponsors require the recipient to provide a large amount of specific information about the case, and disclosing the information about the case to the recipient is a prerequisite and foundation for the existence of third-party funding. However, the information disclosed by the sponsored party to the sponsor may involve the trade secrets and commercial reputation of other arbitration participants, which may have only been known to both parties and arbitrators. If disclosed to a third-party sponsor, it is likely to infringe on the legitimate rights and interests of the other party.

At the same time, the underlying issue behind information disclosure is the conflict of interest between all parties. As the conclusion of funding agreements often only requires the consent of the recipient and third-party sponsors, their funding relationship is difficult for third parties outside of them to know, which can lead to conflicts of interest between the parties' lawyers and third-party sponsors, as well as between arbitrators and third-party sponsors, For example, the arbitrator or the lawyer representing the party may have worked as a legal advisor in the relevant company of the third-party sponsor, and the unit where the arbitrator works part-time may have an interest relationship with the third-party sponsor.

2.2.2 Confidentiality Issues

In practice, arbitration institutions in various countries stipulate that arbitrators, arbitration parties, and other arbitration participants shall not disclose information related to the arbitration procedure to third parties unrelated to the arbitration. Generally speaking, only when the parties have agreed or there are legal reasons, can the parties disclose relevant information about the case to outsiders. Therefore, it is indeed a breach of confidentiality obligation for the sponsored party to provide specific information about the case to a third-party sponsor without obtaining the consent of the other party.

However, many parties, out of their own interests, do not agree to the other party disclosing case information to others in order to seek third-party funding. If relevant case information is not disclosed, it will be difficult for the parties to obtain third-party funding, which puts them in a very awkward situation when they want to obtain funding. Therefore, how to maintain the confidentiality of international commercial arbitration cases while safeguarding the legitimate rights and interests of the parties is an important issue that urgently needs to be addressed.

2.2.3 The Issue of Sharing Arbitration Costs

Arbitration fees are an important factor affecting the development of third-party funded arbitration. On the one hand, the high arbitration costs are the main reason why many parties choose to seek third-party funding; On the other hand, the sharing of arbitration costs will directly affect the parties' choice whether to conduct international commercial arbitration. In the practice of international commercial arbitration, the allocation of arbitration costs is mainly determined by the autonomy of the parties, the discretion of the arbitration tribunal, or the assumption of arbitration costs by the losing party.

In addition, many countries have adopted different regulations in practice regarding the issue of whether third-party funded arbitration costs can be claimed from the arbitration counterpart. Under the principle that the arbitration costs are borne by the losing party, it is also worth considering whether the request made by the aided party to the arbitration tribunal to compensate the other party for the expenses incurred in seeking third-party assistance can be supported when the aided party obtains a successful award. There is no consensus on this in current practice.

2.2.4 The Issue of Guarantee for Arbitration Fees

In international commercial arbitration, in order to ensure that the respondent can smoothly obtain cost compensation in the event of a successful case, the arbitration tribunal has the right to require the applicant to provide cost guarantees. In the case of third-party funding, if the arbitral tribunal becomes aware of the existence of a third-party sponsor by one party, and the sponsored party may face a losing award, the arbitral tribunal is likely to demand that the sponsored party provide a certain amount of cost guarantee based on this.

In practice, funding agreements usually stipulate arbitration fees in advance, but may not necessarily stipulate the responsibility for guarantee fees. If the respondent applies for a fee guarantee to the arbitration tribunal, and the arbitration tribunal requires the sponsored party to provide a fee guarantee, and the amount of this guarantee is large, then making the sponsored party bear the guarantee cost will greatly increase the burden of the sponsored party's expenses.

2.2.5 The Issue of Impartiality and Independence of Arbitrators

For arbitrators, maintaining fairness and independence is the most basic requirement. For third-party funding, as it is provided by a third party independent of the case, there may be conflicts of interest between the arbitrator and the third-party sponsor, which may have a significant impact on the arbitrator's independence and impartiality.

In order to ensure the impartiality and independence of arbitrators in the trial of cases, many laws and arbitration rules have put forward many requirements for arbitrators. For example, Article 12 of *the United Nations Model Law on International Commercial Arbitration* stipulates that arbitrators shall disclose any circumstances likely to give rise to justifiable doubts as to his impartiality or independence, and Article 18 stipulates that the parties shall be treated with equality and each party shall be given a full opportunity of presenting his case.① Article 34 of China's Arbitration Law also requires arbitrators to have the obligation to ensure the fairness and independence of the case award, and specifies the specific circumstances in which arbitrators should avoid.② The reason why the independence and impartiality of arbitrators are valued by various countries is because in international commercial arbitration, arbitrators are generally part-time and therefore have multiple identities to participate in the award. Therefore, their impartiality is more likely to be affected by various factors, and there is a higher possibility of having an interest relationship with the parties or sponsors in the case.

III. Exploration of International Regulation Experience of Third Party Funding for International Commercial Arbitration

The development of third-party funding in various countries and regions around the world is not the same. Rapidly developing countries and regions such as Hong Kong, the United Kingdom, and Singapore have already developed third-party funding regulatory models that comply with local practices. Exploring these advanced regulatory experiences is of

---

① Article 12 & Article 18, *United Nations Model Law on International Commercial Arbitration*, https://uncitral.un.org/sites/uncitral.un.org/files/media-documents/uncitral/en/19-09955_e_ebook.pdf

② Article 34, *Arbitration Law of the People's Republic of China*, https://cicc.court.gov.cn/html/1/218/62/83/444.html

great significance for China.

3.1 Regulatory Model for Third Party Assistance in Hong Kong, China

3.1.1 Recognition of the Legality of Third-party Funding Through Amendment of Arbitration Regulations

On June 14, 2017, *Arbitration and Mediation Legislation (Third Party Funding) (Amendment) Ordinance 2017 (Commencement)* was successfully passed in Hongkong, explicitly allowing third-party assistance to apply to arbitration and mediation proceedings. The concept of third-party funding has been defined and explained, and the standards that third-party funders should meet have been clearly defined.① The 2018 Administered *Hong Kong International Arbitration Center (HKIAC) Arbitration Rules*, which came into effect on November 1, 2018, clearly stipulate the subject, content, object, and time of information disclosure in third-party funding.② On December 7, 2018, the Hong Kong Department of Justice issued a notice on *the Code of Practice for Third Party Funded Arbitration*, which was officially implemented on February 1, 2019. Among them, detailed provisions have been made on various aspects such as funding agreements, capital adequacy requirements for investors, conflicts of interest, confidentiality, control rights, disclosure, arbitration fees, reasons for termination of funding, complaint procedures, etc., establishing a relatively complete regulatory system for third-party funding.③

3.1.2 Detailed and Comprehensive Regulations Have Been Made for

---

① *Arbitration and Mediation Legislation (Third Party Funding) (Amendment) Ordinance 2017 (Commencement)*, https://www.legco.gov.hk/yr18-19/english/subleg/sub18_260.htm

② *2018 Administered Arbitration Rules* (HKIAC), https://www.hkiac.org/arbitration/rules-practice-notes/hkiac-administered-2018

③ Article 2.3 - 2.18, *Code of Practice for Third Party Funded Arbitration*, https://gia.info.gov.hk/general/201812/07/P2018120700601_299064_1_1544169372716.pdf#:~:text=Code%20of%20Practice%20for%20Third%20Party%20Funding%20of,third%20party%20funding%20of%20arbitration%20in%20Hong%20Kong.

Third-party Funding

Hong Kong has set certain minimum standards for third-party sponsors, such as requiring them to have at least HKD 20 million in available capital, bear all overall investment liabilities under all their funding agreements for a period of at least 36 months, and assume continuous disclosure responsibility for capital adequacy, in order to ensure that recipients can receive stable and sufficient financial support. At the same time, provisions have been made for the content of the funding agreement, requiring it to be clear, specific and not misleading, and requiring the sponsor to take reasonable measures to ensure that the recipient is aware of the right to seek independent legal opinion on the agreement before signing it.[①] The funding agreement should include the name of the third-party sponsor and their delivery address in Hong Kong, giving the arbitral tribunal discretion in conflicts of interest, disclosure of information, arbitration fees, and other aspects. It also imposes an obligation on the recipient to disclose third-party funding.

3.2 UK's Regulatory Model for Third Party Funding

3.2.1 Confirmed the Legality of Third-party Funding in the Form of Precedents

The UK has a legal tradition of prohibiting assistance in litigation. Initially, it believed that third-party funding was a manifestation of undermining public policy, so it has been denied the legality of third-party funding in judicial practice. Later, with the development of the economy and society, this legal tradition suffered a certain impact. In 1886, the British Privy Council stated in the Ram Coomar Coondoo & Chunder Canto ookerjee case that if third-party funding itself does not affect judi-

---

① Article 2.3, *Code of Practice for Third Party Funded Arbitration*, https://gia.info.gov.hk/general/201812/07/P2018120700601_299064_1_1544169372716.pdf#:~:text=Code%20of%20Practice%20for%20Third%20Party%20Funding%20of,third%20party%20funding%20of%20arbitration%20in%20Hong%20Kong.

cial fairness and is conducive to achieving fairness and justice, then decisions should not be made based on violating public policies. In the Arkin v Borchard Lines Ltd and others case in 2005, the British Court of Appeal stated that third-party funding agreements will not undermine public policy, as long as the sponsor does not excessively interfere with the trial of the case, third-party funding is conducive to the improvement and development of the judicial system. In this case, the UK Court of Appeal gave clear confirmation of the legality of third-party funding, marking the UK's complete recognition of the legality of third-party funding.

3.2.2 Self Regulation of Third-party Funding

The biggest feature of the UK is its self-regulation of third-party funding, which is very flexible. In order to regulate the behavior of third-party funders, in November 2011, the Civil Justice Council issued *the Code of Conduct for Litigation Funders*, which designated the Litigation Funders Association to be responsible for self-regulation of the third-party funding industry. In January 2018, the Litigation Funders Association released the latest version of *the Code of Conduct for Litigation Funders*, which regulates third-party sponsors within the association.

Although the model of industry self-regulation can be adjusted in a timely manner to address the problems encountered by third-party funding in practice, there are also certain shortcomings. Industry organizations composed of third-party funders must first safeguard the overall interests of the industry, so certain regulations they make may not prioritize safeguarding the interests of the beneficiaries.

3.3 Singapore's Regulatory Model for Third Party Funding

3.3.1 Established the Legal Status of Third-party Funding Through Legislative Amendments

In January 2017, the Singapore National Assembly passed the Civil Code (Amendment) Act, which officially abolished the principle of "prohibiting litigation and sharing benefits" and established the legal status of third-party funding.① On March 1, 2017, the Singapore Civil Code (Third Party Funding) Regulations 2017 came into effect, which clearly stipulated that third-party funding applies to international arbitration proceedings and other procedures related to international arbitration.② The current regulations on third-party funding system in Singapore only apply to the field of international arbitration, recognizing the legality of third-party funding in this field, but also setting a "cannot violate public policy" as a cover clause. At the same time, clear regulations have been made on the qualification requirements of third-party sponsors, and detailed provisions have been made on the standards and establishment methods of funding in third-party funding.

3.3.2 Standardize the Behavior of Lawyers by Revising the Law on Legal Practice and the Legal Professional Rules

In 2015, Singapore revised the Legal Profession Act and the Legal Profession (Professional Conduct) Rules to adapt to the impact of third-party funding on legal professionals. Article 49A of the Legal Professional (Professional Conduct) Rules stipulates the disclosure obligations of legal practitioners, and also specifies the timing of disclosure.③ Article 49B stipulates that legal practitioners or practitioners shall not directly or indirectly hold any shares or other ownership interests of third-party sponsors, and legal practitioners or law firms shall not receive any commission, fee or profit sharing from third-party sponsors.④

---

① See Indranee Rajah S.C., *CIVIL LAW (AMENDMENT) BILL 2016 SECOND READING*, at http://www.nas.gov.sg/archivesonline/data/pdfdoc/20170110002/2R%20Speech%20-%20Civil%20Law%20Amendment%20Bill%202016.pdf, Apr. 18, 2021.

② Article 2 of the Singapore's Civil Law (Third-Party Funding) Regulations 2017, https://sso.agc.gov.sg/SL-Supp/S68-2017/Published/20170224?DocDate=20170224

③ The article 49A of Singapore's Legal Profession (Professional Conduct) Rules 2015, https://sso.agc.gov.sg/SL/LPA1966-S706-2015

④ The article 49B of Singapore's Legal Profession (Professional Conduct) Rules 2015, https://sso.agc.gov.sg/SL/LPA1966-S706-2015

IV. Development Path of Third Party Funded International Commercial Arbitration in China

The development of third-party funding in China is still in its infancy. Although there have been some specialized institutions engaged in third-party funding in China, the practice of third-party funding for international commercial arbitration is currently very rare. The current laws in China do not explicitly prohibit third-party funding, nor do they have effective regulatory measures. Therefore, how to explore a suitable regulatory model for third-party funding in China is the focus of current research by scholars.

4.1 Revision of Arbitration Rules to Regulate the Development of Third Party Funding

4.1.1 Establish Mandatory Disclosure Obligations

(1) Add beneficiaries and third-party sponsors as subjects of disclosure obligations.

In general arbitration cases, the parties generally do not become the subject of disclosure obligations. However, due to the fact that the funding agreement can only be established by mutual agreement between the sponsor and the recipient, the arbitration institution and the other party cannot be aware of the existence of a third-party sponsor. Therefore, the author believes that it is necessary to establish certain disclosure obligations for both the recipient and third-party sponsors, including the object, time, and content of disclosure.[①]

At present, Article 31 of the Arbitration Rules (2015 Edition) of China International Trade Arbitration Commission only stipulates disclosure obligations for arbitrators, without establishing disclosure obligations for

---

① Zhao Yong, Fang Zupeng: *Conflict of Interest and Prevention between Third Party Funders and Arbitrators in International Commercial Arbitration*, Journal of Western, 12th issue, 2020, pp. 88-90.

arbitration parties and third-party sponsors. Looking internationally, on October 23, 2014, the Council of the International Bar Association (IBA) passed *the IBA Guidelines for Conflicts of Interest in International Arbitration 2014* (hereinafter referred to as the "IBA Guidelines"), in which Part 1, Article 7, specifies the obligation of parties to disclose in detail.[①] According to the IBA Guidelines, the recipient is the subject of the disclosure obligation. The author believes that the party receiving funding should be required to disclose the relevant content of third-party funding to all parties participating in the arbitration and the arbitration tribunal. At the same time, disclosure obligations should also be established for third-party sponsors, requiring them to disclose their sufficient capital to the arbitral tribunal, so that the arbitral tribunal can be confident that they have the ability to provide sufficient support to the parties. Require third-party sponsors to assume disclosure responsibility for any direct or indirect relationship between them and the arbitrator that may affect the fair trial of the case, ensuring that there is no interest relationship between the third-party sponsor and the arbitrator.

(2) The disclosure time should be as early as possible.

In general, both the recipient and third-party sponsors should fulfill their disclosure obligations before the first hearing, and the earlier the information disclosure is, the more conducive it is to the smooth progress of the arbitration proceedings. But sometimes, the sponsored party only finds a suitable sponsor during the arbitration proceedings and reaches a funding agreement. At this time, the sponsored party or third-party sponsor can only disclose information to the arbitration tribunal after signing the funding agreement. For the disclosure time in such cases, the Hong Kong Arbitration Ordinance stipulates that if the funding agreement is entered into after the commencement of arbitration, it should be disclosed

---

[①] Article 7, Section 1, *IBA Guidelines on Conflicts of Interest in International Arbitration*, 2014

within 15 days after the conclusion of the funding agreement. The author believes that the trial of international commercial arbitration cases should be based on the important principle of speed and efficiency. Setting a 15 day disclosure time that is too late can easily affect the trial process of arbitration cases. Therefore, it is more appropriate to shorten the disclosure time and disclose information to the arbitral tribunal within 3 days after signing the funding agreement.

(3) The disclosed content should include the identity information of the third-party sponsor and the entire content of the funding agreement.

According to current international practices regarding disclosure of third-party funding, the regulations on disclosure content mainly include the identity of the sponsor and the content of the funding agreement. However, there is no consensus on the level of disclosure of the content of the funding agreement, and the focus of the dispute is whether to disclose the entire content of the funding agreement, only disclose the terms related to the funding, or only disclose the existence of the funding agreement.

Article 27 (2) of the International Investment Dispute Arbitration China International Economic and Trade Arbitration Commission International Investment Arbitration Rules(For Trial Implementation) stipulates the disclosure obligation of the arbitration parties.[①] At the same time, it is stipulated that the arbitration tribunal has the power to order the parties to disclose information about third-party funding. However, there is no regulation on the level of disclosure of funding agreements.

The author believes that the disclosed content should include the identity information of the sponsor and the entire content of the funding agreement. Because if the entire content of the funding agreement is not disclosed, the arbitral tribunal will not be able to know what content is agreed upon in the funding agreement between the recipient and the third-party

---

① Article 27, *China International Economic and Trade Arbitration Commission International Investment Arbitration Rules(For Trial Implementation)*, http://www.cietac.org/index.php?m=Page&a=index&id=390&l=en

sponsor. During the signing process of the funding agreement, the recipient is often in a relatively disadvantaged position. Disclosure of the entire content of the funding agreement can to some extent avoid the situation where the recipient is excessively oppressed by the sponsor using their advantageous position, and also facilitate the arbitration tribunal to have a more comprehensive understanding of the case. Disclosure of the entire content of the funding agreement is conducive to better maintaining fairness and justice. Regarding the issue of potential privacy infringement by disclosing the entire content of the funding agreement, arbitration rules in various regions have set confidentiality obligations on the arbitration tribunal, arbitrators, and arbitration parties. Therefore, as long as the content of the funding agreement is included in the relevant provisions of confidentiality obligations, it can minimize the infringement of privacy on both the recipient and third-party sponsors of the funding agreement.

4.1.2 Establish Confidentiality Obligations for Third-party Sponsors

The current arbitration practice in China lacks corresponding provisions on the confidentiality obligation of third-party sponsors. Article 38 (2) of *China International Economic and Trade Arbitration Commission (CIETAC) Arbitration Rules(2015)* only sets confidentiality obligations for both parties and their arbitration agents, arbitrators, witnesses, translators, experts consulted by the arbitration tribunal, and designated appraisers.[①]

The author believes that although the third-party sponsor is not a party to the arbitration agreement and the arbitration tribunal may not have the right to demand from the third-party sponsor during the case hearing process, the arbitration institution can set the confidentiality obligation of the third-party sponsor through arbitration rules, stipulating that in the case of third-party sponsored arbitration, the third-party sponsor shall not disclose the information related to the arbitration procedure obtained. If

---

① Article 38, *China International Economic and Trade Arbitration Commission (CIETAC) Arbitration Rules(2015)*, http://www.cietac.org/index.php?m=Page&a=index-&id=106&l=en

the parties choose to apply the arbitration rules, then the arbitration rules can be binding on their sponsors. For example, Article 38 (2) of *China International Economic and Trade Arbitration Commission (CIETAC) Arbitration Rules(2015)* can be modified to include third-party sponsors, For cases that are not publicly heard, both parties, their arbitration agents and sponsors, arbitrators, witnesses, translators, experts consulted by the arbitration tribunal, designated appraisers, and other relevant personnel shall not disclose relevant information about the entity and procedures of the case to the outside world. Alternatively, explanations may be given to "other relevant personnel" to include third-party sponsors within the scope of confidentiality obligations.

4.1.3 Reasonably Determining the Allocation and Guarantee of Arbitration Costs

Article 27 (3) of China International Economic and Trade Arbitration Commission International Investment Arbitration Rules(For Trial Implementation) stipulates that the arbitration tribunal may make an award on arbitration fees after considering the specific circumstances of third-party funding.[①] However, the arbitration rules do not provide detailed provisions on how to award. Similarly, Article 52 (2) of the Arbitration Rules (2015 Edition) of the China International Trade Arbitration Commission only confirms the principle that the losing party shall bear the arbitration costs, and does not make clear provisions on the specific fees that the losing party should bear and the guarantee of arbitration costs.[②]

Therefore, it should be clear whether third-party sponsors need to bear the guarantee costs when the sponsored party is required to provide guarantees; Also, it is necessary to clarify the scope of expenses that

---

[①] Article 27, *China International Economic and Trade Arbitration Commission International Investment Arbitration Rules(For Trial Implementation)*, http://www.cietac.org/index.php?m=Page&a=index&id=390&l=en

[②] Article 52, *China International Economic and Trade Arbitration Commission (CIETAC) Arbitration Rules(2015)*, http://www.cietac.org/index.php?m=Page&a=index&id=106&l=en

third-party sponsors need to bear when the recipient loses the lawsuit; It is also necessary to clarify the scope of expenses that can be claimed from the other party when the aided party wins the lawsuit.① The author believes that third-party sponsors should assist the recipient in providing guarantees. Because the sponsored party is often unable to initiate arbitration proceedings alone due to a lack of funds, requiring them to provide high cost guarantees is very detrimental to the sponsored party.

In addition, when the aided party loses the lawsuit, the arbitration fees should be borne by the third-party aided party, which is also the risk of third-party funding as an investment. The portion of the remuneration that the recipient should pay to the third-party sponsor in accordance with the funding agreement shall be recognized as arbitration fees and borne by the losing party. The reason is that the portion of the remuneration that the recipient should pay to the sponsor in accordance with the funding agreement is similar in nature to the legal fees paid by the lawyer they hire, both of which are necessary expenses paid by the recipient to safeguard their legitimate rights and interests. If the other party fulfills its obligations in accordance with the agreement in accordance with the law, the recipient of the assistance does not need to spend these expenses to protect their legitimate rights and interests. Therefore, the expenses of third-party assistance should be borne by the losing party. However, in individual cases, specific considerations should be taken into account such as the ruling result of the case, the amount of the case's subject matter, the amount of compensation paid to the sponsor, and the actual workload of the winning party and the agent. A fair and impartial ruling should be made to avoid malicious exaggeration of the compensation paid to the third-party sponsor by the third-party sponsor and the recipient, thereby damaging the legitimate rights and interests of the other party. The arbi-

---

① Wu Weiding: *Regulatory Logic of Third Party Funding in Commercial Arbitration: An Analysis of the Theory of" Quasi parties*, Beijing Arbitration Quarterly, 2019, Issue 4, pp. 125-127.

tration tribunal can be granted a certain degree of discretion in this regard.

4.1.4 Develop Relevant Standards for Third-party Sponsors

Looking at the regulations in the field of international commercial arbitration in other countries and regions, it can be found that many countries have set certain standards for third-party sponsors. For example, Hong Kong requires third-party investors to meet certain minimum standards, such as capital adequacy requirements, to ensure that recipients can receive stable and sufficient financial support; The UK Code of Conduct for Litigation Funders sets a minimum capital standard of £5 million GBP for third-party sponsors and requires them to continuously disclose their capital adequacy to the Litigation Funders Association; Singapore stipulates that the sponsor cannot be a party to the dispute and should have special funds to support arbitration proceedings, with a total amount of no less than 5 million SGD.

The author believes that the qualifications of third-party funders in the current international market are uneven, and there are frequent occurrences of third-party funders withdrawing or going bankrupt during arbitration cases. In order to protect the legitimate rights and interests of all parties involved in international commercial arbitration, it is necessary to establish relevant standards for third-party sponsors, such as setting a minimum amount of paid in capital for companies engaged in third-party funding business, setting requirements for the number of legal professionals within the company, and setting requirements for the company's operating status in the past 5 years. The setting of specific standards still requires long-term practical accumulation and joint discussions among experts from all walks of life.

4.2 Self Regulation Through Industry Organizations

4.2.1 Strengthen Self-discipline and Supervision of Agency Industry Organizations

At present, the China Lawyers Association has not yet made clear requirements for lawyers in terms of third-party funding. The revision of the Code of Conduct for Lawyers' Practice and the industry rules and guidelines of the Bar Association is relatively difficult, and can quickly respond to emerging issues in third-party funding in a short period of time, thus achieving good regulatory effects.

In the current practice of international commercial arbitration, there are indeed cases where some third-party sponsors appoint lawyers for the beneficiaries or recommend sponsors to the arbitration applicants they represent. Therefore, there is inevitably a certain interest relationship between lawyers and third-party sponsors. The author believes that a section on third-party funding can be added to the current Code of Conduct for Lawyers, requiring lawyers or law firms not to illegally establish any economic connections with third-party sponsors and their affiliated companies, nor to have any interests with senior management personnel of third-party sponsors and their affiliated companies. The agent should be made clear in the arbitration case that they are the agent of the aided person, not the agent of the aided person, and should be responsible to the aided person, always putting the interests of the aided person first, and not damaging the legitimate rights and interests of the aided person for personal gain.

4.2.2 Establish Specialized Industry Organizations for Sponsors

Although the development of third-party funding industry in China is only in its infancy and does not yet meet the conditions to establish specialized industry organizations for sponsors, efforts should also be made to gradually establish specialized industry organizations for sponsors.

Firstly, the industry organization of the sponsor can establish entry thresholds for the sponsor, such as the amount of funds reached or above, the number of legal professionals or above, or the operating status in recent years; Secondly, industry organizations should regularly provide management training to sponsors, setting certain training indicators and striving to improve their professional and professional qualities; Finally, the industry organization of sponsors can establish internal disciplinary standards and impose corresponding penalties for cases where sponsors interfere with the lawyer representing the parties involved in handling the case, maliciously withdraw funds during the trial process, use their own advantageous position to oppress the beneficiaries, and intentionally delay the trial of cases affected by capital contributions.

4.3 Revise the Arbitration Law to regulate Third-party Funding

4.3.1 Based on the Practice of a Large Number of Cases Funded by Third Parties

The Arbitration Law of the People's Republic of China (referred to as the "Arbitration Law") was promulgated in 1994 and has been rarely revised since its promulgation. In recent years, with the continuous development of arbitration practice in China, some issues in the current Arbitration Law have gradually emerged, and both academic and practical circles have issued calls for amendments to the Arbitration Law.

However, the author believes that based on the current arbitration practice in China, due to the limited number of cases related to third-party funding, the judicial and arbitration institutions in China lack practical experience and do not yet have the conditions for comprehensive regulation of third-party funding in the Arbitration Law. If detailed laws are formulated too early to regulate third-party funded arbitration, there may be situations where the law is not in line with the current practical situation in China. After the arbitration rules and industry organizations mentioned earlier regulate third-party funding, there will inevitably be more cases of third-party funded arbitration. The revision of the Arbitration Law should be based on the practice of a large number of cases funded by third parties. Only after the continuous accumulation and maturity of cases, can the relevant content of third-party funded arbitration be added to the Arbitration Law.

4.3.2 Clarify the Definition and Legality of Third-party Funding

The author believes that in the revision of the Arbitration Law, it is inconvenient to make a separate distinction between third-party funding for international commercial arbitration. Third party funding for international commercial arbitration is only a component of international arbitration. Section 4 "Third party funded arbitration" can be added to Chapter 4 "Arbitration Procedure" of the current Arbitration Law to regulate third-party funding. This can not only clarify the legalization of third-party funding in international commercial arbitration, but also include all domestic arbitration and international investment arbitration in other fields.

In addition, due to the limitations of third-party funding itself, the various problems it faces as mentioned earlier are difficult to solve in a short period of time through the development of sound laws. Therefore, the author believes that although it is necessary to legislate and regulate third-party funding, the current legislation should not be too detailed and should not be subject to large-scale legislative activities. It is possible to only confirm the definition and legality of third-party funding, while other detailed issues rely on arbitration rules and industry self-discipline organizations for adjustment.

Conclusion

Third party funding in the field of international commercial arbitration not only balances the status of both parties involved in arbitration and helps recipients achieve fairness and justice, but also raises many issues, such as information disclosure and conflict of interest issues, confidentiality issues, arbitration cost sharing and guarantee issues, and the fairness and independence of arbitrators. In the face of these potential issues, the author has drawn on the regulatory experience of international arbitration institutions and representative countries and regions regarding third-party funding, combined with the current practice of international commercial arbitration in China, and proposed a suitable regulatory model for third-party funding in China. For our country, we should fully leverage the role of arbitration institutions, guide and regulate the application of third-party funding in international commercial arbitration by modifying arbitration rules, utilize agent industry self-regulation organizations for sufficient self-regulation, and gradually establish specialized funder industry organizations. After sufficient practice, the Arbitration Law will be revised to confirm the definition and legality of third-party funding in legislation.

Observations on the Developments of Arbitration in Northeast Asia

Abstract: Arbitration is characteristic of its high efficiency, flexibility, and confidentiality. The Convention on the Recognition and Enforcement of Foreign Arbitral Awards supported by numerous contracting states of make it easy for arbitral awards to be recognized and enforced across borders, playing an important role in the resolution of international economic and trade disputes. The commercial activities in Northeast Asia are becoming increasingly frequent, and the countries in Northeast Asia are diverse, with differentiated arbitration systems. The resolution of commercial trade disputes is showing a trend towards diversification and specialization. This chapter conducts research on six countries including China, Russia, Mongolia, the Republic of Korea, Democratic People's Republic of Korea, and Japan, introducing and comparing the relevant achievements of arbitration institutions, arbitration rules, arbitration legislation, etc. in each country, providing reference for the developments of arbitration legal system in Northeast Asia region.

Keywords: international commercial arbitration; country-specific research; arbitration rules; Northeast Asia region

With the acceleration of globalization, commercial activities in Northeast Asia are becoming increasingly frequent. Arbitration, as an important means of resolving economic and trade disputes, is widely used in Northeast Asia due to its high efficiency, flexibility, and strong confidentiality. The development of the arbitration system in Northeast Asia is showing a trend of specialization and diversification, but it also faces many challenges. This article collects short essays concerning several Northeast Asia countries where arbitration has been developed over years and introduces progress in arbitration institutions, arbitration rules, and arbitration legislation from multiple dimensions, in order to provide corresponding references for the research of arbitration legal systems in Northeast Asia.

China[*]

In 1959, the China Maritime Arbitration Commission (CMAC) was established as part of the China Council for the Promotion of International Trade (CCPIT), becoming Chinese Mainland's only state-level foreign-related arbitration institution specialising in resolving maritime disputes.

To the world, the CMAC now represents China's standard for foreign-related maritime arbitration, which, due to years of high-level opening-up, is sailing in rapid currents.

I. Worldwide Routes

In 2022, the CMAC handled a total of 190 cases, including 34 foreign-related and 15 concerning Hong Kong or Macau maritime issues, involving 25 overseas parties from 32 countries and regions.

In 2023, as of 31 October, the CMAC handled 1078 new cases, including 26 foreign-related and 23 concerning maritime issues in Hong Kong, Macau and Taiwan, involving 38 overseas parties from 23 countries and regions.

These cases involved a considerable number of countries and regions across all continents including South Africa, the Philippines, Malaysia,

---

[*] The author is Dr. Li Hu, Vice Chairman & Secretary General of China Maritime Arbitration Commission (CMAC).

Vietnam, Israel, Egypt, Pakistan, Russia, Italy, the US, Germany, Japan, Brazil, the Cayman Islands, the BVI and Bermuda, as well as Hong Kong, Macau and Taiwan.

Overall, these foreign-related maritime cases exhibit the following trends:

Significant increase in the number of cases, with more than RMB100 million (USD14 million) in dispute;

Emergence of new types of disputes – involving bunker fueling, offshore engineering, photovoltaic equipment and transfer of ship equity – as the number of traditional maritime cases dealing with the construction, management, retention, salvage and mortgages of ships was generally average, with a steady increase in issues involving supply of materials and spare parts, wharf leasing, personal injury at sea, marine insurance, and shipping fraud;

Emergence of international maritime cases where both sides are foreign parties; English is mutually designated as the language of proceedings; and foreign substantive law is applied as the governing law; and

Increasing complexity of legal issues involved in cases, such as the identification and application of foreign laws.

II. Setting the Sails

To promote continual development and internationalisation of foreign-related maritime arbitration, the CMAC regularly updates its panel of arbitrators and revises its arbitration rules, and has established rules for ad hoc arbitration.

A total of 826 arbitrators constitute the CMAC's 2021 panel, with the number of overseas arbitrators (including those from Hong Kong, Macau and Taiwan) increasing to 123, hailing from 36 countries and regions. This greatly facilitates the selection of arbitrators for Chinese and foreign parties alike.

In arbitration management, the CMAC's 2021 arbitration rules recorded several breakthroughs. For the first time, the rules:

Provided comprehensive regulations on electronic service of notice, video hearing, video testimony and e-signature, as well as cybersecurity and privacy and data protection, recognising the wide application of information technology in conventional arbitration;

Provided systematic rules for arbitration evidence to facilitate the arbitral tribunal ascertaining case facts;

Distinguished between the case manager and secretary of the arbitral tribunal, and clarified the scope of duties between the institution and the tribunal, preventing conflicts of interests while also improving arbitration transparency; and

Clarified service to the captain of the ship involved in the case as a valid form of service of process, adapting to the special needs of maritime arbitration.

In addition, while further emphasising the importance of party autonomy, the 2021 rules granted more autonomous powers to the tribunal, strengthening its duty of care and transitioning the institution to a "light management" system.

Optimal composition of the tribunal. Parties may elect arbitrators outside of the CMAC's own panel. Where parties cannot agree on a presiding arbitrator, two arbitrators, respectively selected by the parties, may do so jointly. Only when a presiding arbitrator cannot be elected within the specified period will it fall to the institution to make an appointment.

Strengthened competence and responsibility. According to the 2021 rules, the tribunal is required to convene a case management meeting immediately after its constitution to determine the possible procedures, as well as the roadmap and timetable of the hearing. The tribunal has the right to require the parties to disclose any third-party funding or financial interests in the outcome of the arbitral award.

Furthermore, the tribunal is required to carefully consider the adequacy of pre-trial exchange of documents and fulfilment of conditions when setting a date for a hearing, in order to maximise efficiency.

Flexible fee management. Special agreements are permitted for parties to separate institution fees and arbitrator fees, which further aligns with international practice.

III. Innovation and Outlook

Echoing the continual opening-up and worldwide exposure of China's domestic arbitration market, the CMAC launched its Ad Hoc Arbitration Rules, making ad hoc arbitration available for its members, as well as Chinese and foreign parties.

Together with the concurrently released CMAC Ad Hoc Arbitration Service Rules, they serve as a pioneer for ad hoc arbitration in Chinese Mainland, further promoting the development of foreign-related maritime arbitration.

On 30 June 2023, the first ad hoc arbitration case in Chinese Mainland, with the CMAC designated as arbitration institution in charge, reached a successful conclusion with the issuance of an award.

With implementation of the Regional Comprehensive Economic Partnership, there is great anticipation of economic growth and potential within the Asia-Pacific. In tandem, maritime arbitration in resolving international shipping trade disputes becomes increasingly important.

The CMAC will work alongside fellow institutions both within and outside China to contribute to the healthy development of international arbitration.

Russia[*]

Russia has a long tradition of arbitration, the two arbitration institutions under the Chamber of Commerce and Industry of the Russian Federation (hereinafter referred to as RF ICC) have enjoyed wide influence in

---

[*] The author is Zhou Guangjun, Director of Beijing Xindali Law Firm, Master of Law of Lomonosov Moscow State University.

Eastern Europe and accumulated a large number of arbitration professionals. However, Russia had to undertake a grand reform of its arbitration system in 2015 to address the challenge in political, economic and legal areas from both domestic and international situations. Due to the unprecedented and extreme sanctions against Russia from the Western world since the Russia-Ukraine crisis in 2022, the Russian arbitration system and practice have faced great challenges again and the risk of uncertainty in all aspects has increased dramatically. As a result, it is of great significance to fully understand the basic arbitration system and judicial practice in Russia to evaluate various potential risks that may exist in Russian arbitration and to reduce the risks in the process of investment and trade in terms of dispute resolution.

From the above, it can be seen that the reform of the Russian arbitration system, as well as the special characteristics of its arbitration practice, are the countermeasures taken by Russia in order to safeguard its national interests and protect the interests of domestic companies. Although the Russian court does not support arbitration, Russia is a member of the Convention on the Recognition and Enforcement of Foreign Arbitral Awards, so it still has to comply with the basic arbitration principles recognized around the world. Therefore, considering the current situation where Russia is subjected to comprehensive sanctions around the world and the impartiality and uncertainty of the Russian court system, arbitration is still the preferred way of resolving commercial disputes related to Russia.

I. A Long Tradition of Commercial Arbitration

As early as the Soviet Union period, commercial arbitration had already become one of the most important ways of settling civil disputes. The Councils of People's Commissars and the Central Executive Committee of the Soviet Union made a resolution on 17 June 1932 to set up the All-Union Chamber of Commerce the Foreign Trade Arbitration

Commission, which is the first permanent arbitral institution in the Soviet Union[1]. This resolution had an equal effect on the Rules (Regulations) of the Foreign Trade Arbitration Commission at the All-Union Chamber of Commerce. Although it only contains 13 articles, it was made by the highest state organ of power of the Soviet Union and regulated issues in the arbitration process such as the jurisdiction, nomination and appointment of arbitrators, preservation and interim measures, arbitration fees and the enforcement of arbitration awards. Since then, the resolution had been the programmatic document of arbitration legislation in the Soviet Union for a long time.

According to the information published by the All-Union Chamber of Commerce in 1932, the reason for establishing the Foreign Trade Arbitration Commission was that foreign trade had been grown as the Soviet Union had already admitted by the Western world and had chosen the arbitration as the means of dispute resolution in the trade treaties with many countries such as Italy, Hungary, Turkey, etc[2]. Also, the Soviet Union had signed arbitration treaties with Germany and Latvia. However, ad hoc arbitration, which was generally applied at that time, could neither reassure the nascent socialist Soviet Union nor accumulate and learn from the experience for Soviet foreign trade companies. As a result, the Soviet Union decided to set up its own permanent arbitral institution referring to the organization form of arbitration institutions under the Western world's chamber of commerce.

The former president of the International Commercial Arbitration Court at the Chamber of Commerce and Industry of the Russian Federation (hereinafter referred to as ICAC at the RF CCI) K. Komarov once said that there was a great deal of trust and respect for commercial arbitration, which was even more pronounced in the recognition and en-

---

① Постановление Центрального Исполнительного Комитета и Совета народных комиссаров Союза ССР от 17 июня 1932 года (СЗ СССР 1932 г. №48, СТ.281).

② Ежемесячник Всесоюзной торговой палаты 8-9, августа - сентября, 1932.

forcement of foreign arbitral awards during the Soviet period. Until 1992, foreign arbitral awards against Russian companies were automatically honoured in Russia, with no need to apply for enforcement at all.

Arbitration also has a fundamental impact on the Russian judicial system. After several judicial system reforms, apart from the ordinary courts of general jurisdiction, there is a system of arbitration courts for special cases of economic disputes in the Russian court system, but the arbitration court is a state court instead of an arbitration constitution. The arbitration court deals with economic disputes according to Russian litigation law procedures, which exercises the state's judicial power, so it is known as an arbitration court not "arbitrate"①. In the economic and trade practice between China and Russia, dispute resolution settlement provided in contract by the Russian parties is usually that the disputes shall be submitted to an arbitration court in Russia. In the mistaken understanding that the arbitration court is an arbitration institution, Chinese parties agree on such dispute settlement clauses, which results in the situation that the disputes were not able to be applied for arbitration and had to be resolved by litigation in the arbitration court seated in the location of the Russian parties.

II. Background of the 2015 Arbitration Reform

On 12 December 2013, Russian President Vladimir Putin addressed in the Remarks that Russia's economic dispute resolution system still had a long way from the international advanced experience and that Russia should seriously improve the authority of arbitration institutions. Therefore Putin expected the Russian government, the Russian Union of Industrialists and Entrepreneurs and the RF ICC to fundamentally improve the

---

① Tian Ye, "Arbitration Courts Don't Arbitrate? A Glimpse of the Russian Judicial System," http://www.xindalilaw.com/newsitem/278196466 (Last visited Sep. 9, 2023).

arbitration system as soon as possible, and submitted the legislative proposals to the State Duma①.

Since Putin's request, the relevant departments of the Russian government acted swiftly. Led by the Ministry of Justice of Russia and the RF ICC mainly, Russia has made substantial changes to the arbitration law and related regulations. In the author's view, there are both domestic and international reasons for Russia to amend its arbitration law:

On the domestic aspect, the Arbitration Procedural Code of the Russian Federation adopted in 2002 did not provide any restrictions on the creation of arbitration institutions, and there was no proper corresponding supervision mechanism for arbitration institutions, resulting that any legal person could set up an arbitration institution, the levels of performance of cohabitation of arbitration institutions vary and the arbitration institutions were abused to carry out illegal and criminal activities. The situation has persisted for many years, causing serious distrust of the impartiality, independence and judicial level of arbitration, and the choice of arbitration as a means of dispute resolution in judicial practice has become less and less common.

On the international aspect, the Russian government has lost a series of arbitration cases and has been judged to be liable for huge amounts of compensation, especially on 18 July 2014, the Russian government was adjudicated to pay \$50 billion compensation to the former shareholders of Yukos by the Permanent Court of International Arbitration②. From this award, the Russian government has become strongly aware that international commercial arbitration is a dangerous "two-edged sword", which may cause a fatal impact on large state-owned companies that control the

---

① Послание Президента РФ Федеральному Собранию от 12.12.2013, https://www.consultant.ru/document/cons_doc_LAW_155646/ (Last visited Sep.9, 2023).

② Cui Zheng, "Arbitration Award of Russian Government paying three Yukos shareholders 50 billion dollars", https://china-arbitration.com/index/news/detail/id/1805.html (Last visited Sep.9, 2023).

lifeblood of the Russian economy if not properly controlled, and it is also very dangerous to the Russian government. Therefore it is necessary to carry out legal reforms in order to control the uncertainty of international commercial arbitration.

It can be said that the essence of the Russian reform in commercial arbitration is to put the power of arbitration in the hands of a few people who can be trusted by the Russian government.

Against the above backdrop, Federal Law No. 382-FZ "On Arbitration in the Russian Federation" (hereinafter referred to as the New Arbitration Law) amended on 29 December 2015 and came into force on 1 September 2016[①], has become the basic law of arbitration, while the Federal Law on International Commercial Arbitration adopted on 7 July 1993, continues to be the special law of international arbitration.

III. Features of the Arbitration Law of Russian

The reform of arbitration law in 2015 laid the foundation of the Russian arbitration law. On the one hand, Russia strengthens market access, strictly approves the creation of permanent arbitration institutions and restricts the application of ad hoc arbitration by the reform. On the other hand, it begins to allow foreign arbitration institutions to enter the Russian market and explicitly allows some corporate disputes to be resolved by arbitration.

3.1 Creation of Arbitration Institutions from Registration to Permission

Chapter 9 of the New Arbitration Law contains detailed provisions on the main entities of the creation of an arbitration institution, the per-

---

① Zhou Guangjun, Wang Tianyi, Huo Xiaoqian, "Federal Law On Arbitration in the Russian Federation(translated version) " Arbitration and Law No.134(Law Press China) (2017).

mission procedure, and the legal liability of the creating organization, etc., making it clear that the creation of an arbitration institution has changed from the previous registration system to the approval system, where not only are the conditions for authorizing an organization to function as an arbitration institution stringent but also whether the approval success depends entirely on the authorities without regulatory mechanism.

Permanent arbitral institutions may only be created by non-profit organizations. Permanent arbitral institutions may not be established by the federal state authorities, state authorities of the constituent entities of the Russian Federation, local self-government authorities, state and municipal institutions, state corporations, state companies, political parties and religious organizations, as well as bar associations, bar chambers of the constituent entities of the Russian Federation and the Federal Bar Chamber of the Russian Federation, notary chambers and the Federal Notary chamber. However, the Federal Bar Chamber of the Russian Federation and other companies and foundations, together with five research institutes, as the initiators established the Russian Institute of Modern Arbitration (a non-profit organization, incorporated on 17 August 2016), and then created the Russian Arbitration Center at the Russian Institute of Modern Arbitration in the name of Russian Institute of Modern Arbitration which was conferred by an act of the authorized federal executive body. The author believes that the authorization to the arbitral institution was specifically issued for the Russian legal profession by the Russian government.

The requirements for creating a permanent arbitral institution include: 1) compliance with the rules of the permanent arbitral institution submitted in accordance with the requirements of this Federal Law and availability with the permanent arbitral institution of a recommended list of arbitrators meeting the requirements of this Federal Law; 2) authenticity of the information on the non-profit organization by which a permanent arbitral institution is created and on its founders (participants), and the reputation of the non-profit organization by which a permanent arbitral institution is created, the scale and nature of its activities subject to the structure of its founders (participants), shall ensure a high level of organization of the functioning of the permanent arbitral institution, including as regards the financial support of creation and functions of the respective institution, and the said organization's carrying out activities aimed at the development of arbitration in the Russian Federation.

A foreign arbitration institution granted the right to function as a permanent arbitral institution does not need to meet the above requirements, but needs to meet two special requirements according to the New Arbitration Law: firstly, the foreign arbitral institution is widely recognized with an international reputation; And secondly, if the foreign arbitral institution intends to administer arbitration of domestic disputes in Russia, it shall presence in the territory of the Russian Federation of a separate division of the foreign arbitral institution or the organization. The second requirement was added via the amendment on 27 December 2018, while there was no such requirement previously.

Permanent arbitral institution used to be approved by the government of the Russian Federation, but after 27 December 2018, it was changed to be approved by the Council for the Development of Arbitration of the Russian Federation.

Article 50 of the New Arbitration Law provides the liability for non-profit organizations under which the permanent arbitral institution was created. The non-profit organization, under which the permanent arbitral institution was created, shall bear civil-law liability to the parties to arbitration only in the form of compensation of damages caused to them as a result of failure to perform or improper performance by the permanent arbitral institution of its functions for the administration of arbitration or related to its performance of its obligations provided by the rules of the permanent arbitral institution, in case of intent or gross negligence. The non-profit organization, under which the permanent arbitral institution was created, shall bear no civil-law liability to the parties to arbitration for the damages caused by the actions (omissions) of an arbitrator.

In this arbitral reform, Russia has adopted a very subjective approval criterion for the creation of a permanent arbitration institution, that the reputation of the non-profit organization by which a permanent arbitral institution is created, the scale and nature of its activities subject to the structure of its founders (participants), shall ensure a high level of organization of the functioning of the permanent arbitral institution, including as regards the financial support of creation and functions of the respective institution, and the said organization's carrying out activities aimed at the development of arbitration in the Russian Federation.

It is completely incompatible with the principles and traditions of Russian legislation, but it is the only provision that makes it possible to artificially control the number of arbitration institutions and exclude unreliable or unwanted institutions. The provision has great controversy and criticism in Russia, but because of this judicial mechanism, it allows the authorized executive body to decide with complete autonomy whether or not to confer the creation of an arbitral institution.

3.2 Restrictions on the Jurisdiction of Arbitration

In Russia, while the Arbitration Law only regulates the arbitration procedure, the jurisdiction of arbitration is provided by other federal laws. According to paragraph 3 and 4 of Article 1 of the New Arbitration Law, arbitration may be instituted with the Parties' agreement to hear disputes between parties to civil law relations, and the other Federal Law may set forth restrictions on referring certain categories of disputes to arbitration. In other words, the New Arbitration Law only provides in principle that disputes in civil law relations can be arbitrated, but the federal law may provide that certain categories of disputes can not be arbitrated.

Aside from the New Arbitration Law, other federal laws provide for many specific categories of disputes not to be heard arbitration, for example administrative disputes and other public legal relation disputes, insolvency disputes, most corporate disputes, antitrust disputes, intellectual property right disputes, and the disputes based on the legal adjustment of privatization in Russia.

3.3 Restrictions on the Application of Ad Hoc Arbitration

Ad hoc arbitration has a historical tradition in Russia, and in the past, there were no restrictions or prohibitions on ad hoc arbitration under Russian law. However, since the 2015 arbitration reform, a growing number of specific laws and regulations explicitly exclude ad hoc arbitration in certain types of disputes, which can only be conducted by a permanent arbitration institution.

On 27 December 2018, Russia adopted Federal Law No. 531-FZ, introducing the third amendment to the New Arbitration Law, in which paragraph 20 of Article 44 provides that the entities that have not obtained the right to function as permanent arbitral institutions may not fulfil separate functions for the administration of arbitration, including the functions for the appointment of arbitrators, resolution of challenges and termination of the mandate of arbitrators, as well as other actions related to conducting arbitral proceedings in an ad hoc arbitration, such as receipt of arbitration fees and charges, regular allocation of premises for oral hearings, etc. Also, the entities may not promote, including on the information and telecommunications network, the "Internet", and/or publicly offer to perform functions for the conduct of arbitration, including functions for the conduct of arbitration by an ad hoc arbitral tribunal. In case of violations of the above prohibitions, the award of an arbitral tribunal, including an ad hoc arbitral tribunal, shall be deemed rendered in violation of the arbitration procedure set forth in this Federal Law. Moreover, amendments to the Federal Law "On Advertising" of 13.03.2006 N 38-FZ came into force and added Article 30.2, which provides that if a permanent arbitration institution has not been authorized by the New Arbitration Law, advertising of arbitration activities (including ad hoc arbitration activities), including advertising on the Internet, is not permitted.

With the New Arbitration Law coming into force, many long-standing arbitration institutions can not be adopted by the authorities, so they tend to circumvent the law by offering ad hoc arbitration services. After the said laws and regulations come into force, there is no way for these unlicensed institutions to get around the ban, as the arbitral awards will not be recognized and enforced because of violating the statutory procedure.

There is only one reason for restricting ad hoc arbitration since the reform of arbitration in 2015 that Russian government needs to keep the power of arbitration in its own hands, which is difficult to do in ad hoc arbitration.

3.4 Most Corporate Disputes Cannot be Arbitrated

After the arbitration reform in 2015, corporate disputes can in principle be arbitrated, but there are many restrictions. At the same time, when other federal laws and regulations exclude certain corporate disputes from the application of arbitral settlement, certain corporate disputes are not arbitral. With regard to the specific time of application, according to paragraph 7 in Article of Federal Law of 29 December 2015 No. 409-FZ, corporate disputes may not be referred to arbitration before 1 February 2017. So the arbitration agreements in respect of corporate disputes made before that date will be deemed non-effective.

According to paragraph 2 in Article 33 and Article 225.1 of the Arbitration Procedural Code of the Russian Federation No. 95-FZ, the following corporate disputes may not be arbitrated: disputes relating to the convening a meeting of the shareholders by companies; disputes of activities of a notary with regard to the notarization of a limited liability company share transaction; disputes arising from applications for annulment of non-normative legal documents, decisions and acts (Inaction) by a state body, a local self-government body, other bodies specially authorized by the federal laws or public officials; disputes with strategic companies;

disputes arising from the expulsion of a shareholder from a company; disputes of the repurchase of stocks, etc.

Meanwhile, for corporate disputes that can be arbitrated, certain corporate disputes must be applied to the arbitration institution that has formulated special arbitration rules for corporate disputes, and the arbitration institutions that do not have specialized rules are not authorized to accept such disputes.

Disputes between shareholders of strategic companies, where Chinese companies are more involved, can not be arbitrated and can only be applied to the arbitration court of the Russian Federation.

3.5 Parties May Make a Prior Agreement in Writing

In order to embody the parties' autonomy, the New Arbitration Law grants special rights to the parties in certain matters, and the agreement of the parties has a preferential effect if the parties make in writing, including:

If, under the arbitration rules, an arbitrator's application for disqualification is rejected by the arbitrator's appointing authority, the party making the disqualification may not make a further application for disqualification to a court of competent jurisdiction;

If the arbitral tribunal makes a jurisdictional decision, none of the parties may further challenge jurisdiction in a court with competent jurisdiction;

No hearings are required;

Arbitrators may only be selected or appointed from the recommended list of arbitrators of the arbitral institution;

The arbitral award is final and irrevocable.

IV. Current Main Commercial Arbitration Institutions in Russia

Since the New Arbitration Law has come into force, only 5 new permanent arbitral institutions have been licensed. Together with two permanent arbitral institutions of the RF CCI, which were previously exempted from approval, there are currently only seven permanent arbitral institutions in Russia that can provide arbitration services, namely:

International Commercial Arbitration Court at the Chamber of Commerce and Industry of the Russian Federation (Established in 1932, rules registered on 15 May, 2020)

Международный коммерческий арбитражный суд при Торгово-промышленной палате Российской Федерации (МКАС)

Website: http://mkas.tpprf.ru/ru/

Maritime Arbitration Commission at the Chamber of Commerce and Industry of the Russian Federation (Established in 1930, rules registered on7 February, 2017)

Морская арбитражная комиссия при Торгово-промышленной палате Российской Федерации (МАК)

Website: http://mac.tpprf.ru/ru/

Russian Arbitration Center at the Russian Institute of Modern Arbitration (licensed on 27 April, 2017, rules registered on 10 October, 2019)

Российский арбитражный центр при автономной некоммерческой организации "Российский Институт современного арбитража" (РАЦ)

Website: https://centerarbitr.ru/

Russian Arbitration Centre at Russian Union of Industrialists and Entrepreneurs(licensed on 27 April, 2017, rules registered on 7 February, 2020)

Арбитражный центр при Общероссийской общественной организации "Российский союз промышленников и предпринимателей" (РСПП)

Website: https://arbitration-rspp.ru/

Russian Sports Arbitration Center at All-Russian Union of Public Associations "Russian Olympic Committee" (Licensed on 25 April, 2019, rules registered on 1 February, 2021)

Национальный Центр Спортивного Арбитража при автономной некоммерческой организации "Спортивная Арбитражная Палата" (АНО «Спортивная арбитражная палата»)

Website: http://sportarbitrage.ru/

Russian Arbitration Center at the All-Russian Industrial Association of Employers "Union of Russian Machine Builders" (Licensed on 18 March, 2021, rules registered on 13 August, 2021)

Арбитражное учреждение при Общероссийском отраслевом объединении работодателей «Союз машиностроителей России» (Арбитражное учреждение при ООOР «СоюзМаш России»)

Website: https://arbitr.soyuzmash.ru/

Russian Arbitration Center at the autonomous non-profit organization the "National Institute for the Development of Arbitration in the Fuel and Energy Complex" (Licensed on 5 August, 2021, rules registered on 27 August, 2021)

At the same time, as the biggest beneficiary of this reform, the ICAC at the RF CCI started to open branches all over Russia and has now set up 22 arbitration centers, essentially creating a dominant situation[①]. The New Arbitration Law does not explicitly prohibit foreign arbitral institutions from entering its arbitration services market, and there are currently two ways to enter: first, any legal and natural person abroad can set up a non-profit organization in Russia and then apply for the creation of a permanent arbitral institution in the name of the organization; second, existing arbitral institutions from other countries can also apply for the qualification of permanent arbitral institution in Russia directly without the need of setting up a non-profit organization, as long as the institution enjoys a widely recognized international reputation.

Currently, four international arbitration institutions have received

---

① http://mkas.tpprf.ru/ru/otdeleniya/ (Last visited Sep.9, 2023).

approval from the authorized federal executive body of the Russian Federation to accept arbitration cases in Russia:

Hong Kong International Arbitration Centre (HKIAC) (Approved on 25 April, 2019)

Гонконгский международный арбитражный центр (ГМАЦ)

Website: https://www.hkiac.org/

Vienna International Arbitral Centre (VIAC) (Approved on 4 July, 2019)

Венский международный арбитражный центр

Website: https://www.viac.eu/en/

The ICC International Court of Arbitration (Approved on 18 May, 2021)

Международный арбитражный суд при Международной торговой палате (ICC)

Website: http://court.iccwbo.ru/

Singapore International Arbitration Centre (SIAC) (Approved on 18 May, 2021)

Сингапурский международный арбитражный центр

Website: https://www.siac.org.sg/

However, since none of the four arbitral institutions has a branch in Russia, they are not yet able to accept most of the Russian domestic disputes but only specific types. Currently, only disputes between parties in two Russian Special Administrative Regions (established in Kaliningrad and Primorsky Krai) and disputes based on contracts related to activities carried out in the Special Administrative Regions can be applied to the foreign arbitral institutions, and the number of such types of cases is few, resulting in the limited participation of foreign arbitral institutions in the market of arbitration services in Russia.

V. Issues to be Noticed in the Practice of Commercial Arbitration in Russia

5.1 Mandatory Exclusive Jurisdiction System Established in Russia in Response to the Western World's Sanctions

However, since none of the four arbitral institutions has a branch in Russia, they are not yet able to accept most of the Russian domestic disputes but only specific types. Currently, only disputes between On 8 June 2020, the Arbitration Procedural Code of the Russian Federation is amended by Federal Law of the Russian Federation No. 171-FZ, which gives special protection to the Russian entities being sanctioned (including Russian citizens and foreign legal persons). Even if an arbitration clause has been signed by the aforementioned entities, if the arbitration takes place in a country that has imposed sanctions on Russia, the Russian arbitration court automatically acquires exclusive jurisdiction over disputes of individuals and legal persons being sanctioned, unless there is an international treaty or parties has made agreements otherwise. At the same time, a system of injunctions has been established that a Russian arbitration court may award punitive damages against a party if the party fails to comply with the exclusive jurisdiction.

This legal system makes it possible for Russian parties to abuse their rights, resulting in the uncertainty of the validity and enforceability of arbitration clauses and the foreign enforceability of arbitral awards.

If a Russian party is awarded to be liable for breach of contract, while the Russian party's failure to perform the contract obligations is due to the imposition of sanctions, the arbitral award may not be recognized and enforced.

The exclusive jurisdiction system also applies to Chinese companies. If Chinese companies agree with Russian entities on the seat of arbitration in a Russia-unfriendly country, where the arbitration clause is invalid or unenforceable according to the Russian arbitration laws, the disputes should apply to the arbitration court, resulting in the deprivation of the Chinese party's right to arbitration under the agreement.

After 24 February 2022, as major Western countries had imposed sanctions on Russia, Russian companies are no longer able to choose arbitration institutions in Western countries, making Hong Kong Special Administrative Region (hereinafter referred to as Hong Kong) the most favorable seat of arbitration for Russian companies, and therefore Hong Kong International Arbitration Centre is the first chosen institution. However, the arbitration court of St. Petersburg of the Leningrad Region made a surprising and far-reaching judgement in Case No. 56-129797/2022 on 8 June 2023[①]. The judge found that due to the legal system in Hong Kong is based on common law principles similar to the United Kingdom and other common law countries, and English and European judges play an important role in Hong Kong's judicial system and sit as judges on the Court of Appeal of the High Court of Hong Kong, Hong Kong is unfriendly to Russia as the seat of arbitration, which results that the arbitration agreement of choosing the Hong Kong International Arbitration Centre as the arbitration institution by the parties is invalid, thus the arbitration court has the exclusive jurisdiction. If the decision of this case is ultimately upheld by the Supreme Court of the Russian Federation, it will lead to the invalidation of the arbitration clause where parties agree to arbitrate in Hong Kong, which will have an extremely unfavourable impact on foreign parties who agree on Hong Kong as the seat of arbitration.

5.2 Compulsory Arbitration under the Sino-Soviet Common Conditions of Delivery

On 13 March 1990, the Ministry of Trade of the Central People's Government of the People's Republic of China and International Depart-

---

① Zhou Guangjun, "Russian Judge Finds Hong Kong to be an Unfriendly Jurisdiction to Russia".

ment of the Communist Party of the Union of Soviet Socialist Republics signed the Protocol on the Common Conditions of Delivery of Goods from the People's Republic of China to the Union of Soviet Socialist Republics and of Goods from the Union of Soviet Socialist Republics to the People's Republic of China (entered into force on 1 July 1990) in Beijing, with the annexes thereto as Common Conditions for the Delivery of Goods Between the Soviet Union and the People's Republic of China (hereinafter referred to as the Sino-Soviet Common Conditions of Delivery). The preamble expressly provides that all deliveries between foreign trade enterprises and organizations of the People's Republic of China and enterprises and organizations of the Union of Soviet Socialist Republics entitled to carry on foreign trade operations shall be made in accordance with the following common conditions of delivery, insofar as they are not otherwise stipulated in the contract between them by reason of the special characteristics of the goods and/or special features of delivery①.

Article 52 of the Sino-Soviet Common Conditions of Delivery provides that all disputes relating to the contract or to the contract if the parties fail to settle by negotiation or correspondence, shall not be subject to the jurisdiction of the general courts but shall be settled by arbitration as follows:

If the respondent is a foreign trade enterprise or organization of the People's Republic of China, the arbitration shall be conducted by the China International Economic and Trade Arbitration Commission (hereinafter referred to as CIETAC) at the China Council for the Promotion of International Trade in Beijing in accordance with the rules of the commission;

If the respondent is an enterprise or organization of the Soviet Union, the arbitration shall be conducted by the arbitration tribunal at the Cham-

---

① Protocol on the Common Conditions of Delivery of Goods from the People's Republic of China to the Union of Soviet Socialist Republics and of Goods from the Union of Soviet Socialist Republics to the People's Republic of China, http://www.chinaruslaw.com/CN/CnRuTreaty/JudicatoryCoo/2009128161610_236431.html(Last visited Sep.9, 2023).

ber of Commerce and Industry of the Soviet Union in Moscow, in accordance with the regulations of the Tribunal.

In accordance with Article 52 above, supply agreements between Chinese and Soviet enterprises are subject to arbitration mandatorily. Unless the parties have excluded the application of the Sino-Soviet Common Conditions of Delivery or have otherwise agreed on a valid dispute settlement clause, the dispute shall be resolved by arbitration under the general territorial jurisdiction.

However, shortly after the signing of the Sino-Soviet Common Conditions of Delivery, the Soviet Union collapsed, leading to different practices between the arbitration institutions and judicial authorities of the two countries as to whether the treaty continued to apply.

As for China, in accordance with Article 52 of the Sino-Soviet Common Conditions of Delivery, CIETAC had accepted a number of arbitrations initiated by Russian companies against Chinese companies on the basis of the Treaty and had issued arbitral awards.

As for Russia, judicial authorities had once refused to recognize the Sino-Soviet Common Conditions of Delivery as an international treaty. ICAC at the RF CCI, which is the successor to the Foreign Trade Arbitration Commission, has once publicly explained in writing that the arbitration commission was not authorized to exercise jurisdiction over disputes in supply agreements on the basis of Article 52 of the Sino-Soviet Common Conditions of Delivery without a writing agreement by the parties. However, with the continuous development of judicial practice, Russia is changing its attitude towards the treaty. As far as the author knows, ICAC at the RF CCI has clearly indicated in the arbitration cases issued that the corresponding disputes of the supply agreements can be accepted according to Article 52 of the Sino-Soviet Common Conditions of Delivery[①].

---

① РЕШЕНИЕ КОЛЛЕГИИ АРБИТРОВ МКАС ПРИ ТПП РФ ОТ 28.07.2017 ПО ДЕЛУ N M-19/2017, https://apkrfkod.ru/pract/reshenie-kollegii-arbitrov-mkas-pri-tpp-rf-ot-28072017-po-delu-n-m-192017/? (Last visited Sep.9, 2023).

In the author's opinion, as Russia has declared that it would exercise the rights and assume the obligations continuously with respect to the international treaties concluded by the Soviet Union, i.e., the Russian Federation would succeed to all the international treaties of the Soviet Union, the treaty of the Sino-Soviet Common Conditions of Delivery remains effective. On 28 April 1999, China and Russia relisted the current effective treaties signed between China and the Soviet Union from 1949 to 1991 via the diplomatic exchanged notes between China and Russia, where the Sino-Soviet Common Conditions of Delivery was not among the treaties agreed to terminate. Since China has recognized the Russian succession to the international treaties of the Soviet Union practically and neither of the countries has made a declaration of the termination of the Sino-Soviet Common Conditions of Delivery so far, the the Sino-Soviet Common Conditions of Delivery is valid and should be applied between China and Russia continually. If the enterprises of the two countries have not excluded the application of the Sino-Soviet Common Conditions of Delivery in the supply agreements or have not otherwise made the agreement on the settlement of disputes, the agreements should follow the treaty, in which the Article 52 thereof should be applied automatically and mandatorily.

5.3 Finality of Arbitral Awards Under the Russian Laws

According to Article 40 of the New Arbitration Law and the judicial interpretations of the Supreme Court of the Russian Federation, if the parties directly agree to provide that the arbitral award shall be final for the parties in writing, the final arbitral award can neither be judicial interfered nor be subject to annulment by the Russian court, including not being recognized or enforced by the court. In Russian judicial practice, the court usually rejects the application of the parties of any judicial review when the parties make the agreement in writing that the arbitral award is final. Of course, there are exceptions in practice that the court may make a judicial review of an arbitral award if it is considered to violate the Russian public order[①].

Generally, when making an arbitration clause, if the parties agree to arbitrate in Russia, the Russian party will insist on adding a statement about the finality of the arbitral award, such as "the arbitral award shall be final and binding for the parties"; if the parties agree to arbitrate outside Russia, the Russian party will insist deleting the express above. In the author's view, this is an attempt by experienced Russian lawyers to preserve the right of the Russian party in foreign countries through the arbitration clause to apply for the judicial review to the arbitral award, while depriving the right to apply for the judicial review of foreign party in Russia.

5.4 Possible Abuse of the Public Order Exception by Russian Courts in the Judicial Review of Arbitral Awards

The Supreme Arbitration Court of the Russian Federation and the Supreme Court of the Russian Federation have repeatedly interpreted and defined the public order exception by means of judicial interpretations and guiding cases, currently defining the meaning of public order as the fundamental legal basis (principle) that constitutes the economic, political and legal system of the Russian Federation and has the characteristic of the highest obligatory, university and special meaning for social and public[②].

Although the Supreme Court of the Russian Federation gives the determination of the principles of public order, Russian courts at all levels tend to make their own interpretations on the fundamental legal basis,

---

① Определение Верховного Суда № 305-ЭС23-5624 25 августа 2023 по делу № A40-193861/2022, https://kad.arbitr.ru/Document/Pdf/019d6701-1eb0-4e60-bdcd-e361af-b07ee1/2a0a23c5-db3a-488a-9348-8e7221e350ea/A40-193861-2022_20230825_Opredelenie.pdf?isAddStamp=True (Last visited Sep.9, 2023).

② Постановление Пленума ВС от 10 декабря 2019 г. № 53 «О выполнении судами РФ функций содействия и контроля в отношении третейского разбирательства, международного коммерческого арбитража», https://www.vsrf.ru/documents/own/28587/ (Last visited Sep.9, 2023).

which are often over expansive and different from each other, resulting in the arbitral awards being frequently being annulled, not being recognized or not being enforced because of the violation of public order in practice. The judicial supervision of the Russian Supreme Court is also lenient to the abuse of public order by all levels of the Russian courts, therefore public order exception has become the invariably favourable reason for Russia to refuse the recognition and Enforcement of Foreign Arbitral Awards.

In conclusion, it can be seen that the reform of the Russian arbitration system, as well as the particularities of its arbitration practice, are the countermeasures taken by Russia to protect the interests of the nation and the native enterprises. Despite the fact that the Russian judicial system does not support arbitration, Russia has signed the Convention on the Recognition and Enforcement of Foreign Arbitral Awards, so it still has to comply with the basic principles of arbitration universally acknowledged. Therefore, based on the global situation where Russia is subjected to comprehensive sanctions, as the judgments made by the Russian court are considered to be unfair and uncertain, arbitration is still the preferred way of resolving commercial disputes related to Russia.

Mongolia[*]

Introduction

From early times in Mongolia, disputes between nomadic and herder peoples regarding the property were settled in the governor's office, not called the court at that time, by submitting the case to a local shrewd, honest, well-respected elder who taught him the right and the wrong.

---

[*] The author is Ukhbaatar UYANGAA, Arbitrator of the Mongolian International Arbitration Center, Chairwoman of the Board of Legal Development & Reform Institute of Mongolia, Ph.D candidate of the Renmin University of China.

In Mongolia, since 1929, the legal framework for arbitration was established, in 1930 an organization was founded, namely the Arbitration Commission under the Economic Council, the State Arbitration Department, and the Foreign Trade Arbitration established respectively in 1940 and 1960.

In the 1930-1940, arbitration was developed in a truly classical sense, and the first step was taken to allow the freedom to negotiate and choose arbitrators. At this time, the Economic Council under the Government had an appropriate role. For this reason, this stage of the development of arbitration deserves a special consideration.

During the period of 1940s-1990s, the state arbitration organization settled disputes arising from contracts between government and industry departments, unions, cooperatives, production, and service organizations, which is similar to the specialized court system that resolves trade and commercial disputes in other countries. Under the socialist system, which recognized state and cooperative property and managed the economic and business activities of the country with a unified policy and plan, it was appropriate for the state arbitration organization to work under the direct supervision of the Council of Ministers or the Government.

In 1982, the arbitration institution was transferred to the management of the Supreme Court, and soon after 1987, the arbitration court became the State Arbitration Department under the Council of Ministers. According to the 1989 Law on Arbitration Institutions, it was assigned to the Ministry of Justice and Arbitration for a short period of time, which showed that the State Arbitration Department was a type of trade and commercial court that exclusively resolved disputes between industries and enterprises. At that time, there was no independent system of arbitration.

A relatively independent arbitration system can be understood as the Foreign Trade Arbitration Commission established in 1960.

The 2003 Arbitration Law formed the legal basis for the establishment of an independent and free arbitration system. The law regulates in detail the conditions for establishing a permanent arbitration organization and selecting an *ad hoc* arbitrator.

Today, arbitration still resolves disputes arising from any contract related to economic or non-material values, wealth, such as trade, investment, and business activities of Mongolia, based on the agreement of the parties. Permanent arbitration institutions with the function of providing management and organization of arbitration activities have been established in our country and continue to operate stably. Thus, it should be said that the consistent policies of the Government of Mongolia to support the correct method of dispute resolution, the legal framework, and international trends in the development of arbitration have a positive impact on the formation of an independent, private arbitration system.

It can be considered that the external conditions for the formation of the arbitration organization were directly influenced by the arbitration experience of foreign countries, including the legislative concept and legal experience of Russia.

The 1924 Rules of the Arbitration Commission of the USSR, according to which the arbitration commission handled civil disputes between large industries and offices, and the Arbitration Commission was established under the Supreme Council of People's Economy to handle disputes between business organizations.

The Soviet Union abolished these commissions in 1931 and established the Arbitration Board. The system of the State Arbitration Organization, which deals with trade disputes and economic entities, is still preserved in the Russian Federation.

At the 43rd meeting of the Council of Ministers of the Mongolian People's Republic on November 12, 1940, property disputes between the industrial departments of the Mongolian People's Republic were resolved, and the state arbitration rules, with 14 articles, as well as between the official industrial departments The State Arbitration Office for Settlement of Property Disputes approved and enforced the rules on the settlement of arbitration cases with chapters and 47 articles, which became the first rule for handling arbitration disputes.

According to these rules and regulations, property disputes arising between official and industrial departments in the country were decided by the State Arbitration under the Council of Ministers. The Council of Ministers had established a procedure for choosing state arbitration.

Mongolia joined the Council for Mutual Economic Assistance in 1962. In May 1972 Moscow adopted the Convention on the Settlement by Arbitration of Civil Law Disputes Resulting from Relations of Economic and Scientific-Technical Cooperation between the member countries of the Economic Mutual Assistance Council by the Foreign Trade Arbitration Organization attached to the Chambers of Commerce of the member countries.

This 1972 Moscow Convention was established by the government of the Republic of Bulgaria, the Republic of Hungary, the German Democratic Republic, the People's Republic of Vietnam, the People's Republic of Poland, the Socialist Republic of Romania, and the Soviet Socialist Czechoslovakia. For the countries that are members of the Auxiliary Council for Economic Relations, it was agreed that disputes arising between governments would be resolved by this convention, and that the principles and ideals of the convention would be applied in accordance with the characteristics of each country. In the course of economic, scientific and technical cooperation of the participating countries in this convention, disputes arising from contracts and other civil rights relations between the organizations are settled by arbitration. As a guide to this convention and internationally accepted international legal acts at that time, the Presidents of the Chamber of Commerce of the Republic of Mongolia approved the Regulations on Proceedings by the Foreign Trade Arbitration Commission on February 26, 1975 to follow the rules.

At the same time, domestic organizations and contractual disputes between them were resolved by the state arbitration office.

The Council of Ministers of the Mongolian People's Republic approved Resolution No. 295/194 dated July 2, 1960, in clause 3 of the Foreign Trade Arbitration Commission under the Chamber of Commerce, and instructed to approve the rules in 1960, But the Chamber of Commerce did not adopt the rules of the Foreign Trade Arbitration Commission until 1962.

The Foreign Trade Arbitration Commission resolves material disputes between the foreign trade associations of the Mongolian People's Republic and other authorized organizations during the execution of agreements/contracts concluded with foreign trade associations, firms and companies, and the Chamber of Commerce of the country used to wor к. The arbitration commission used to select people with economic and legal knowledge to decide the cases.

At the meeting of the leaders of the Chamber of Commerce of the Mongolian People's Republic on February 26, 1975, the procedure for handling cases by the Foreign Trade Arbitration Commission under the Chamber of Commerce was approved. The arbitration commission had a chairman and a deputy chairman, 15 arbitrators and a secretary, and employed highly educated and qualified people according to the regulations.

The procedure stipulated that the arbitration case should be reviewed on the basis of documents and materials, which the parties agree on, the case should be settled based on the submitted written materials, file counterclaims, provided evidence, refuted the circumstances cited by the parties as the basis for their claims or refusal, and the evidence. The process of providing the original or its certified copies, examining the evidence in a manner determined by the decision-making body, and evaluating the evidence by the arbitrators with their own internal confidence has been established and implemented.

In addition, decision-making, its content, notification of decision, and implementation of decision-making are regulated.

The decision of the arbitrator shall be final and binding. The applicants will voluntarily carry out the decision. Enforcement of non-voluntary, non-compliant decisions will be carried out by law.

At that time, there was no concept of court involvement in arbitration proceedings.

The Arbitration Commission under the Chamber of Commerce was established and implemented its activities with the responsibility of reviewing disputes arising from international contractual relations.

In order to improve the operation, structure, and organization of the arbitration within the framework of the legal reform, the arbitration was separated from the court and integrated into a legal department, and a new "Ministry of Justice and Arbitration" was established.

Thus, before the establishment of the Ministry of Justice and Arbitration, the People's Assembly of the People's Republic of Mongolia approved the Law on Arbitration Organization of the Republic of Mongolia for the first time on June 24, 1989.

Mongolia's arbitration organization has repeatedly made such structural changes, It can be considered that the current Mongolian International Arbitration Center (MIAC) under the MNICC has been operating since 1960, and is an internationally recognized permanent arbitration in Mongolia. The arbitration has branches in 21 provinces of Mongolia, is a member of the Asia-Pacific Arbitration Association, and cooperates with more than 20 international arbitral institutions. The arbitration consists of 51 national and 11 foreign (Russia, China, Germany, Japan, Hong Kong, Poland), a total of 62, specialists in law, economics, finance, and mining.

MIAC not only handles disputes arising from contracts and deals of economic and business related agreements through arbitration, but also promotes and develops arbitration activities in Mongolia, conducts training and research, represents domestically and abroad, provides legal advice, and publishes books and magazines relevant to arbitration operation which is underway.

I. Modern Mongolian Arbitration Law and Legal Regulation Settlement

The concept of arbitration is not new in Mongolia. The country established its first arbitration court in 1960, under the former Soviet regime, to resolve foreign trade disputes. However, commercial arbitration has developed in its modern guise as an alternative dispute resolution method for businesses only since the 2000s.

In Mongolia, there were laws such as the Laws on the Arbitration Organization and the Laws on Foreign Trade Arbitration of the People's Republic of Mongolia that regulated relations related to arbitration. In 2003, the Arbitration Law, which was developed in accordance with the Model Law on International Commercial Arbitration (hereinafter referred to as the "Model Law") of the International Trade Law Commission of the United Nations, was approved.

The Arbitration Law was amended on August 3, 2007, February 10, 2011, and May 22, 2012, but no fundamental change is reflected.

As part of the government's plan to improve the legal infrastructure for business and investment, Mongolia revised its Arbitration Law with effect from 27 February 2017, which is known as the Revised Arbitration Law or the 2017 Law. The 2017 Law is based on the 2006 version of the UNCITRAL Model Law, with few exceptions, resulting in the recognition of Mongolia as a Model Law jurisdiction. The 2017 Law also enacts a number of additional provisions.

Along with the steady increase in MIAC's caseload, the Court of Civil Appeals in the Mongolian capital of Ulaanbaatar is reviewing a sizeable number of applications seeking court's assistance and intervention in arbitral proceedings. Recent cases decided by the Court of Civil Appeals help to shed light on the court's general stance on arbitration and the interpretation of certain provisions of the Revised Arbitration Law, in particular with regard to the grounds for setting aside arbitral awards.

"*The Revised Arbitration Law is based on the 2006 version of the UNCITRAL Model Law, with few exceptions, resulting in the recognition of Mongolia as a Model Law jurisdiction... [It] was therefore aimed at adopting the Model Law by strictly following its wording to ensure greater clarity and secure a legal framework for arbitration.*"

II. The Revised Arbitration Law

Although Mongolia's previous Arbitration Law of 2003 was said to be loosely based on the original Model Law of 1985, it did not adequately address a number of important aspects of arbitration, thus creating uncertainties as to the relationship between the arbitral process and the courts. The 2017 Law was therefore aimed at adopting the 2006 Model Law by strictly following its wording to ensure greater clarity and securing a legal framework for arbitration.

Key features of the changes made by the Revised Arbitration Law are discussed below.

2.1 The Distinctions Between International and Domestic Arbitration

The 2017 Law applies to both international and domestic arbitration and provides for substantially similar treatment of each process. In line with the Model Law, international arbitration is defined as an arbitration in which:

(1) The parties to an arbitration agreement have, at the time of concluding that agreement, their places of business in different countries;

(2) The place of business of the parties is different from the seat of the arbitration, if determined in, or pursuant to, the arbitration agreement;

(3) The place where a substantial part of the obligations of the commercial relationship is to be performed or the place with which the subject-matter of the dispute is most closely connected is different from the

place of business of the parties; or

(4) The parties have expressly agreed that the subject-matter of the arbitration agreement relates to more than one country.

An arbitration that does not fall within the ambit of the above definition is regarded as a domestic arbitration under the 2017 Law.

Although the principles, standards and substantive requirements for both types of arbitration remain the same, the Revised Arbitration Law sets out slightly different procedural requirements for international and domestic arbitration. For example, in respect of international arbitration, a party may submit its application to set aside an arbitral award to the court within 90 days of the date on the award was received, whereas this time limit is shortened to 30 days for domestic arbitration.

Further, in international arbitration, the Court of Civil Appeals performs most court functions relating to arbitration, including all applications to challenge arbitrators and set aside arbitral awards. This exclusive jurisdiction of the Court is intended to facilitate the development of judicial expertise in international arbitration within the judiciary.

"The recent cases decided by the Court of Civil Appeals help to shed light on the Court's general stance on arbitration and the interpretation of certain provisions of the Revised Arbitration Law, in particular with regard to the grounds for setting aside arbitral awards."

2.2 Arbitrability

One of the key issues addressed by the Revised Arbitration Law is the scope of arbitrability of disputes under Mongolian law. The scope of disputes that can be settled by arbitration is expanded by a stipulation that "any dispute that is referred in an arbitration agreement is arbitrable unless such dispute falls within the exclusive jurisdiction of the court". At the same time, the enactment of the 2017 Law was accompanied by amendments to a number of sectoral statutes, including, among others, the Securities Market Law, the Petroleum Law and the Concession Law.

These amendments expressly added arbitration as a possible dispute resolution mechanism in the respective laws, thus limiting the number of matters that must be exclusively referred to the court under domestic legislation.

A brief summary of the matters that are not arbitrable under Mongolian law and specific provisions of the 2017 Law with regard to consumer and bankruptcy disputes is set out below.

2.2.1 Matters Falling Within the Exclusive Jurisdiction of Mongolian Courts

Pursuant to the Civil Procedure Code of Mongolia, the following matters fall within the exclusive jurisdiction of Mongolian courts and are therefore non-arbitrable:

> Disputes relating to the ownership, possession and use of immovable property located in the territory of Mongolia;
>
> Disputes relating to the reorganization or liquidation of a legal entity established under Mongolian law and disputes arising out of resolutions and decisions made by the legal entity, its branches and representative offices;
>
> Disputes relating to the validity of registration by Mongolian courts and other public administrative offices;
>
> Disputes relating to the validity of registration of patents, trademarks and other intellectual property (IP) rights by a Mongolian administrative office and disputes relating to the application of registration of IP rights;
>
> Disputes relating to the enforcement of court judgments in Mongolia or disputes relating to requests for enforcement.

Further, Mongolia became a signatory to the New York Convention in 1995 and ratified it subject to declarations regarding the reciprocity and commercial reservations. The latter was applied because, pursuant to Mongolian law, issues of a non-commercial nature, such as the status of persons and matrimonial disputes, fall exclusively within the jurisdiction of the courts. In addition, the courts have final and exclusive jurisdiction over labour disputes involving both trade unions (collective disputes) and individual employees under the Labour Law of Mongolia.

2.2.2 Consumer Disputes

The Revised Arbitration Law expressly acknowledges the arbitrability of consumer disputes and imposes no substantive restrictions concerning the arbitration of disputes involving consumer rights. It does, however, set out formal requirements for consumer arbitration agreements. In order to protect consumer parties to arbitration clauses contained in standard general terms of contract, an arbitration agreement is only effective if it is made in writing by the parties after the dispute has arisen and the place of arbitration is specified in such an agreement.

"One of the key issues addressed by the Revised Arbitration Law is the scope of arbitrability of disputes under Mongolian law. The scope of disputes that can be settled by arbitration is expanded by a stipulation that any dispute that is referred in an arbitration agreement is arbitrable unless such dispute falls within the exclusive jurisdiction of the court."

2.2.3 Bankruptcy

The Revised Arbitration Law takes a liberal approach with regard to the arbitrability of bankruptcy issues. If all of the following conditions are satisfied, the court may refer any and all disputes involving bankruptcy issues, whether or not a bankruptcy issue is a core issue, for determination by arbitration:

> there is an arbitration agreement in respect of the dispute;
> the party subject to the bankruptcy proceedings entered into the arbitration agreement before those proceedings commenced; and
> the administrator or trustee did not reject the contract containing the arbitration agreement.

2.2.4 Limited Court Involvement

One of the key aspects of the Revised Arbitration Law commended by the arbitration community and users is that the scope of intervention by the court in the arbitral process is limited to those circumstances expressly provided for by the 2017 Law, these having been designed mainly to support the proper functioning of arbitration. Consistent with the Model Law, parties to an arbitration and/or an arbitral tribunal may seek court assistance in respect of:

(1) the grant and enforcement of interim measures;

(2) the appointment of arbitrators;

(3) challenges to arbitrators and termination of their mandates;

(4) the taking of evidence;

(5) challenges to tribunal decisions upholding jurisdiction;

(6) the setting aside of arbitral awards; and

(7) the recognition and enforcement of awards.

2.2.5 Powers of Arbitrators

Under the Revised Arbitration Law, the arbitral tribunal is empowered to rule on its own jurisdiction, including as to the validity of the arbitration agreement, in line with the internationally accepted principle of Kompetenz-Kompetenz. Further, tribunals are vested with broad power to grant interim measures and preliminary orders, in line with the amendments made to the Model Law in 2006.

With regard to the allocation of liability for costs, the previous Arbitration Law of 2003 imposed a proportional method for cost allocation by tribunals, i.e, that parties bore costs in line with their actual success on the merits, and that such costs did not include fees for legal representation. By contrast, the Revised Arbitration Law expressly includes legal costs in the costs of arbitration and provides that, unless otherwise agreed by the parties, the costs of arbitration are at the discretion of the tribunal, which may decide in what proportion and in what amount costs should be paid by the parties.

2.2.6 Confidentiality

The Revised Arbitration Law expressly imposes an obligation of confidentiality on parties, arbitral tribunals and arbitral institutions in respect of all arbitral awards, orders and information exchanged during arbitral proceedings, unless the parties agree otherwise. There are three exceptions to this confidentiality obligation:

(1) mandatory disclosure pursuant to a legal requirement;

(2) disclosure necessary to protect or enforce a right; and

(3) disclosure in the course of proceedings to set aside or enforce an arbitral award.

2.2.7 Grounds for Setting Aside and Refusing Recognition and Enforcement of Awards

The grounds for setting aside an arbitral award and refusing its recognition and enforcement in the territory of Mongolia set forth in the Revised Arbitration Law strictly mirror those enumerated in Art 34 and 36 respectively of the Model Law. They include:

(1) Lack of a valid arbitration agreement due to a party's incapacity or the arbitration agreement not being valid under its applicable law, failing any indication thereon, under Mongolian law;

(2) Violation of due process by way of failure to give proper notice of the appointment of an arbitrator or of the arbitral proceedings to a party or that party otherwise having been unable to present its case;

(3) Excess of the arbitral tribunal's authority, i.e, that the award deals with a dispute not contemplated by or not falling within the terms of the submission to arbitration, or contains decisions on matters beyond the scope of the submission to arbitration;

(4) Irregularities in the composition of the arbitral tribunal or the arbitral procedure, including that the composition of the tribunal or the arbitral procedure was not in accordance with the agreement of the parties, unless such an agreement was in conflict with a mandatory provision of the 2017 Law or, failing such agreement, was not in accordance with it;

(5) With regard to the refusal of recognition or enforcement, only that the award has not yet become binding on the parties or has been set aside or suspended by a court of the country in which, or under the law of

which, that award was made; or

(6) The court finds that the subject-matter of the dispute is not capable of settlement by arbitration under Mongolian law or the award is in conflict with the public policy of Mongolia.

For international arbitration, the Court of Civil Appeals is the designated court to receive all applications to set aside awards. As a matter of cost- and time-efficiency, there is no further appeal from set aside decisions of the court.

With regard to the recognition and enforcement of an arbitral award, the application must be filed with the Court of First Instance having jurisdiction over the respondent or the respondent's assets.

"One of the key aspects of the Revised Arbitration Law commended by the arbitration community and users is that the scope of intervention by the court in the arbitral process is limited to those circumstances expressly provided for in the Law which are designed mainly to support the proper functioning of arbitration."

It can be concluded that the newly approved Revised Arbitration Law of Mongolia is fully in line with the Model Law.

Conclusion

On the website of the International Law Commission of the United Nations, Mongolia is registered in the list of countries that have recognized and internalized the Model Law. However, there is still a need to review some articles and provisions of the Revised Arbitration Law in terms of content, to correctly assign Mongolian legal terms related to arbitration, and to get used to using one line.

Democratic People's Republic of Korea

A Brief Introduction to the DPRK Laws on Foreign Economic Arbitration and Reflections on the Arbitral Jurisdiction in the DPRK[*]

The Democratic People's Republic of Korea (hereinafter referred to as DPRK) was proclaimed on September 9, 1948, and for a long period of time thereafter, due to the international environment with its peculiar political and economic system, it did not succeed in establishing a good economic structure in the country, and its foreign economic relations were depended and limitted[①]. In 1991, the DPRK's economy was hit hard as the collapse of the Soviet Union led to the loss of supplies of coal, oil and steel. With the collapse of the Soviet Union and the Drastic Changes in Eastern Europe, the DPRK's trade also suffered a huge impact. Under the huge trade shock, the DPRK did not succeed in re-adjusting its economic relations and its industrial system almost completely collapsed. At the same time, agricultural output plummeted because of the loss of industrial inputs, which made the operation of the traditional planned economic system progressively more difficult and fall into complete disarray. As a result, the DPRK began to reform its economic system internally and open up to the outside world, while starting to formulate a number of policies to attract foreign investment and promote economic and trade development. Since the 1990s, the DPRK has successively introduced several laws and regulations, such as the DPRK Foreign Investment Law, Contractual Joint Venture Law, Equity Joint Venture Law, Foreign Enterprise Law, Foreign-Invested Banks Law, Accounting Law for Foreign-Invested Businesses, Labor Law for Foreign-Invested Enterprises, Taxation Law

---

  * The author is Jin Ying, Partner of Beijing Yingke Law Firm Shenyang Office.
  ① Quan Liyang, "Preliminary Study on Private International Law of DPRK and Its Impact on Its Own Economy", 3 Northeast Asia Economic Research, 112-120(2018).

for Foreign-Invested Enterprises and Foreign Individuals and Bankruptcy Law for Foreign-Invested Enterprises.

In order to better attract foreign investment into the DPRK, the Foreign Economic Contract Law of the DPRK was adopted on February 22, 1995 (Juche 84), as Decision No. 52 of the Standing Committee of the Supreme People's Assembly, amended and supplemented on February 26, 1999 (Juche 88), and August 19, 2008 (Juche 97). Besides, Foreign Economic Arbitration Law of the Democratic People's Republic of Korea (hereinafter referred as "Foreign Economic Arbitration Law") was adopted on July 21, 1999 (Juche 88), as Directive No. 875 of the Presidium of the Supreme People's Assembly, then respectively amended and supplemented on July 29, 2008 (Juche 97), and amended and supplemented on July 23, 2014 (Juche 103). By now, the DPRK has established a dispute settlement mechanism for foreign investment in line with that of the world, i.e., the foreign-related economic arbitration system, which is undoubtedly crucial for foreign investment protection. This article will briefly describe the main contents of the Foreign Economic Arbitration Law of the DPRK, and compare to the international practices and China's commercial arbitration system to discuss some existing problems and possible directions for future amendment.

I. Legislation Background

Since the enactment of the Foreign Investment Law in 1992, the DPRK has been speeding up the process of enacting a series of laws related to foreign investment, but it has not achieved significant results in terms of the effectiveness of attracting foreign investment[1]. It's certain that due to the unique economic system of DPRK, the complex interna-

---

[1] Cui Dongri, Wu Donghao, "Legal Protection of Foreign Investments in DPRK——Centered on relevant systems", 46 Journal of Yanbian University(Social Science), 35-41(2013).

tional relations and relatively closed cultural conditions make foreign investors hesitate, as the imperfect foreign investment legal system is unable to protect the rights and interests of foreign investors, it is difficult to gain the trust, which leads to the fact that foreign investors, comparing to the unfamiliar and closed DPRK, prefer those trustworthy countries such as Southeast Asia countries. Therefore, the DPRK must develop a dispute resolution system for foreign investment that is in line with international standards. Due to the special economic system of the DPRK, domestic commercial disputes are not common, while initiating civil litigation to resolve disputes over foreign investment is not in line with the national conditions. Therefore, arbitration, which is the most internationally accepted commercial dispute resolution mechanism, becomes the preferred choice. The enactment of the Foreign Economic Arbitration Law shows that the DPRK is fully aware of the need to improve the dispute settlement mechanism for foreign investors' commercial activities to address their concerns about the unfamiliar legal environment.

II. Main Contents

The Foreign Economic Arbitration Law consists of seven chapters and sixty-five articles. The contents will be introduced in the following chapters.

2.1 Basics of the Foreign Economic Arbitration Law

Chapter I is the basis of the Foreign Economic Arbitration Law.

Article 3 thereof stipulates the arbitration committees and characteristics of foreign-related economic arbitration. It clearly stipulates that, among the foreign-related disputes, disputes arising from foreign-related trade, investment and services shall be heard by the DPRK International Trade Arbitration Commission; disputes arising in the course of maritime economic activities shall be heard by the DPRK Maritime Arbitration

Commission (hereinafter referred to as "DMAC"); and disputes relating to computer software shall be heard by the DPRK Computer Software Arbitration Commission (hereinafter referred to as "DCSAC"). Foreign-related economic arbitration has neither jurisdiction nor forum level jurisdiction, and the final decision shall be made by an award issued by the Arbitration Department.

Article 4 stipulates the jurisdiction of foreign-related economic arbitration and makes it clear that there are two types of disputes that can be resolved by foreign-related economic arbitration: 1. disputes arising in the course of foreign economic activities with foreign-related elements and an arbitration agreement between the parties; and 2. disputes entrusted to the arbitration committee by a state authority to be resolved by foreign-related economic arbitration procedures. Unlike the common international commercial arbitration, the DPRK international arbitration accepts one more type of case, i.e., disputes entrusted to the arbitration committee by the state authority to be resolved by foreign economic arbitration proceedings. This type of case usually does not involve an arbitration agreement between the parties but is transferred by a local court since the dispute reaches the local court. In such cases, the jurisdiction exercised by the arbitration committee is different from the internationally accepted arbitration jurisdiction, as will be discussed in the next section.

Article 8 provides for the right to raise jurisdictional objections and its effects. That is, if a party is aware that arbitration proceedings are being conducted under the arbitration agreement that may not be in accordance with the law, and the party fails to raise an objection immediately or within the designated period of time, the arbitration proceedings continue, which is deemed that the party has waived the right to raise an objection. This suggests that international arbitration proceedings in the DPRK are distinguished from internationally accepted commercial arbitration proceedings by the existence of *forum prorogatum*, i.e. even if the arbitration agreement is absent, the right to object is deemed to have been waived as long as the respondent fails to object to the jurisdiction.

In accordance with Article 10 and 11, the DPRK guarantees the independence of the Arbitration Department in the hearing of cases and the authority shall not interfere with the Arbitration Department hearing the cases. It respects international law and practice and develops cooperation and exchanges with international institutions and foreign countries in foreign-related arbitration. Although the above articles are different from international practices, it can still be seen that the DPRK is expressing its willingness to open up to the international community and its recognition of the internationalization of international trade arbitration.

2.2 Arbitration Agreement

Chapter II of the Foreign Economic Arbitration Law deals with the arbitration agreement.

Article 12 and 13 state that the arbitration agreement shall be in writing, which is similar to provisions of China Arbitration Law. However, unlike China's arbitration rules, the law provides that it can be recognized as an arbitration agreement as the written evidence proves that the parties orally or by action reach an agreement on arbitration without a clear written arbitration agreement.

Corresponding to the aforementioned *forum prorogatum* in Article 8, Article 14 provides that, in the absence of a written arbitration agreement between the parties, an arbitration agreement may be deemed to have been reached if one of the parties requests arbitration and the other party does not object to it or raise a defence.

Article 15 provides that an arbitration agreement is null and void if it exceeds the statutory range of arbitration, or if the parties are incompetent to act or coerced into reaching the arbitration agreement.

In addition, Article 16 provides that the parties may apply property preservation measures to an arbitration committee, arbitration department, court, or authorities subject to the arbitration agreement.

2.3 Arbitration Departments

Chapter III of the Foreign Economic Arbitration Law is devoted to the arbitration departments, i.e. the arbitral tribunal. According to the Law, the number of arbitrators in the arbitration department may be decided by the parties, or in cases where there is no agreement by the parties, the number of arbitrators shall be one person or three people.

Article 21 provides the procedure for the selection of arbitrators. In cases where the arbitration department is sought to be composed of three arbitrators, the parties shall each select one arbitrator, then the two selected arbitrators shall select a head arbitrator and, in cases where the parties have not selected arbitrators or the two selected arbitrators have not been able to select a head arbitrator, the arbitration committee shall select them. In cases where the arbitration department is sought to be composed of one arbitrator, if the parties cannot agree on the selection of an arbitrator during the period determined, the arbitration department shall select an arbitrator according to the requirements of one party. In this situation, the parties may not raise an opinion about a decision made by the arbitration committee. It can be said that the provision that two selected arbitrators jointly appoint the head arbitrator is more prior than China, which generally provides that the head arbitrators shall be appointed by the director of the arbitration committee when the parties fail to reach an agreement. However, the considerable restriction on challenging the sole arbitrator limits the autonomy of the parties in the process of selecting, which is extremely contradictory. Article 25 to 27 provide the exclusion process for arbitrators. It is worth noting that the time for filing an application for disqualification lasts throughout the entire arbitration proceeding, within 10 days from the date of noticing the reasons for disqualification. In addition, if the arbitration department decides not to disqualify the arbitrator, the party applying for disqualification may submit another application for disqualification to the arbitration committee again.

Article 28 to 30 deal with the rights of the arbitration department, lodgement of opinion related to the arbitration department and the handling of such opinion. Article 31 and 32 deal with the application and lifting of temporary measures.

2.4 Arbitration Process

Chapter IV of the Foreign Economic Arbitration Law deals with the arbitration process.

Article 33 clarifies that the parties enjoy equal status in the handling of dispute cases and may sufficiently state their alleged facts.

Similar to the internationally prevailing arbitration procedures, according to this chapter of the Foreign Economic Arbitration Law, the parties may agree on the arbitration process, the place of arbitration, arbitration language, the participation of expert witnesses, and so on. The arbitration committee and the arbitration department shall also conduct the relevant arbitration procedures in accordance with the agreement reached between the parties. However, the author believes that the "place of arbitration" herein shall not be interpreted as the "seat of arbitration". According to the description of the second paragraph of Article 35 that "In cases where there is no agreement between the parties, the arbitration department shall determine the place of arbitration by taking into consideration the convenience to the parties and the general situation relating to resolving a case", the author tends to understand the meaning of the "place of arbitration" as the "place of hearing".

It must be said that the DPRK Foreign Economic Arbitration Law grants the arbitration department a great deal of power in arbitration proceedings. As mentioned above, the arbitration department not only has the right to decide whether the arbitration agreement is valid or not but also can decide on the exclusion of arbitrators.

According to Article 37, it is also provided that the arbitration department shall decide the arbitration language in the absence of an agreement between the parties, and only where there is no decision of the arbitration department, shall it be Korean.

In addition, Article 38 provides that the arbitration department accepts that the amendment or supplementation of the content of a claim or content of a defence of a party is unreasonable and would delay the resolution of a case, it may not give approval for it. Besides, the arbitration department can decide whether it will hold an arbitration hearing orally or on papers when it comes to an agreement with the parties. In this context, the author believes that the meaning of "hearing orally or on the papers" is not literal, but rather hearings with or without a hearing.

Article 39 also gives the arbitration department the right to accept a case and make a decision directly on the basis of the evidence submitted when one of the parties fails to participate in the arbitration hearing or submit evidence without a lawful reason; on the contrary, where there is a different agreement between the parties or the arbitration department accepts that there is a lawful reason, the foregoing provision shall not be applied.

Regarding the investigation and collection of evidence, Article 42 stipulates that the arbitration department may, upon application of a party or as necessary, conduct an evidentiary investigation or request an evidentiary investigation from a court or the authorities concerned. The party may also request an evidentiary investigation after receiving the approval of the arbitration department.

A defendant may apply for a counterclaim arbitration for an arbitral case it has received according to Article 44, while the arbitration committee may choose not to accept the counterclaim arbitration if the counterclaim arbitration would delay the handling of the arbitral case.

2.5 Arbitral Award

Chapter V of the Foreign Economic Arbitration Law deals with arbitration procedures.

The rule of Article 45 that "the governing law of the arbitral award shall be determined by agreement between the parties. If there is no agreement between the parties related to the governing law of the arbitral award, the arbitration department must apply the law it accepts to be most closely related to the dispute case and capable of being applied" is a new addition to the Foreign Economic Arbitration Law, which was amended in 2014. Prior to this amendment, the applicable law of hearing foreign-related arbitration cases was not clear in the Foreign Economic Arbitration Law[1], only referring to Article 42 of the Foreign Economic Contract Law on the relative content agreeing the seat and committee of arbitration that "according to the agreement of the parties, they may also be raised to resolve before an arbitral institution of a third country"[2], which is not directly related to the applicable law for foreign arbitration in the DPRK. The addition of the provisions on the applicable law, especially the application of international practice, also shows that the DPRK is looking forward to converging with the international community slowly in the field of foreign-related arbitration.

Article 46 provides for the method for the arbitration department. Decision-making for an arbitration department composed of three arbitrators shall be made by majority decision or, in cases where there is an agreement between the parties or agreement between the members of the arbitration department, the head arbitrator shall make the final decision.

Article 47 and 48 provide for reconciliation and conciliation by the parties at any time and at any stage of the handling of the arbitral case. The decision to reconcile or conciliate has the same effect as the arbitral award.

---

[1] Cui Dongri, Wu Donghao, "Legal Protection of Foreign Investments in DPRK——Centered on relevant systems", 46 Journal of Yanbian University(Social Science), 35-41(2013).

[2] Foreign Economic Contract Law of the Democratic People's Republic of Korea (2008), Article 42 "Differences in opinion related to contracts shall be resolved by method of agreement. In cases where they cannot be resolved by method of agreement, they shall be resolved according to an arbitration process determined by the Democratic People's Republic of Korea. According to the agreement of the parties, they may also be raised with an arbitral organ of a third country to be resolved."

Article 49 to 51 provide that the award must be in writing and signed by the arbitrators. An arbitral award document from an arbitration department composed of three arbitrators requires the signature of a majority of the arbitrators before it is made. The award shall state things such as the reasons that are the basis of the arbitral award, the drafting date of the arbitral award document, and the place of arbitration.

Besides making an arbitral award, the arbitration department may decide to conclude the arbitration when the plaintiff withdraws the suggestion of arbitration; when the plaintiff and defendant have agreed to conclude the arbitration; or when the arbitration department accepts that continuing the arbitration is unnecessary or impossible. However, despite the plaintiff withdrawing the suggestion of arbitration, the defendant does not consent and has a proper interest in finally resolving the dispute, the arbitration department accepts that it must not conclude handling the arbitral case.

Article 53 and 54 also provide the possibility for the arbitration department to correct calculation or wording defects in the arbitral award document or to make a supplementary arbitral award for a claim that is made but the issue is not included in the arbitral award document. In addition, the parties are given the right to apply to the arbitration department for an interpretation of the part of the award that is in doubt.

2.6 Legal Effect of Arbitral Awards and Cancellation

Chapter Ⅳ of the Foreign Economic Arbitration Law deals with the legal effect of arbitral awards and the cancellation of an arbitral award. This chapter stipulates that an arbitral award takes effect from the date on which the award is made. In accordance with international practice, a party with an opinion on an arbitral award may raise an opinion that it should be cancelled.

However, unlike the China Arbitration Law which provides that an application for cancelling the arbitral award shall be made to the Intermediate People's Court where the arbitration commission is situated, the Foreign Economic Arbitration Law does not specify the place or the hierarchy of the court for cancellation, which leads to be ambiguities in practice. The validity period for an application to cancel an arbitral award shall be 2 months from the day the parties received the arbitral award document or its corrected version, interpreted version, or supplemental arbitral award document. Unlike the China Arbitration Law that when one party applies for the enforcement of an arbitral award and the other party applies for cancellation, the court shall decide to suspend the enforcement, and after deciding whether or not to set aside the arbitral award, resume the enforcement or termination in accordance with the decision, the Foreign Economic Arbitration Law stipulates that the party may not apply for canceling the arbitral award since the court has made a decision on the arbitral award to be enforced. In a case for which the author once represented, the decision by the Pyongyang Municipal Court to enforce the award has been seen. In other words, when the court of the DPRK receives an application for the enforcement of an arbitral award, it first examines whether the arbitral award meets the conditions for enforcement, which is obviously not the same as the international practice, as evidenced again in Article 62 of Chapter Ⅶ, stating that the court or authorities concerned must review the application document and execute the arbitral award with a finding or a decision within 30 days of the day the application for the execution of arbitral award is received.

Different from international practice, the reasons for raising the cancellation of an arbitral award in the Foreign Economic Arbitration Law of the DPRK are also quite distinctive. Specifically, they are as follows: i. A party was an incompetent person to act according to the governing law at the time of the arbitration agreement; ii. The arbitration agreement has no legal effect under the law designated by the parties or, in cases where the parties did not designate the law, according to the law of the DPRK; iii. A party did not receive appropriate notification about the selection of the arbitrator or the arbitration process or that they could not protest for unavoidable reasons; iv. The arbitral award took as its subject a dispute that is not the arbitration agreement, or that it exceeded the scope of the arbitration agreement; v. In cases where the composition of the arbitration department or the arbitration process contravenes the agreement of parties complying with this law, or in cases where there is no agreement between the parties, it is a violation of this law. Since the biggest difference between the Foreign Economic Arbitration Law of the DPRK and international practice is that a foreign-related arbitration can be accepted even if there is no arbitration agreement between the parties, the grounds for raising the cancellation of an arbitral award have also changed. The second paragraph of Article 57, that "The arbitration agreement has no legal effect under the law" is difficult for foreign investors to trust due to their lack of familiarity with DPRK's laws and regulations. Therefore, it is necessary to disclose the laws of the DPRK in addition to the arbitration-related laws.

2.7 Execution of Awards

Chapter Ⅶ of the Foreign Economic Arbitration Law not only provides the procedures for the execution of the arbitral award in the DPRK but also covers the approval and execution of arbitral awards made by arbitration institutions of other countries. Unlike China's practice, the parties may apply to the court or the authorities for enforcement of the arbitral award either directly or through the arbitration committee. Upon receipt of the application, the court or the authorities also needs to review the application document and executes the arbitral award with a finding or a decision. If the property to be executed according to the arbitral award is beyond the territory of the DPRK, the application may be made to a court of the given country for the execution of the arbitral award. Judicial authorities of the DPRK may also approve and implement arbitral awards made by foreign arbitration departments in accordance with the regulations of the DPRK but may reject the approval and implementation of foreign arbitral awards if: i. The party was a person incompetent to act at the time of the arbitration agreement according to the governing law, or the fact that an arbitration agreement does not have legal effect under the law designated by the parties or, in cases where the parties did not designate a law, the arbitration agreement does not have legal effect under the law of the country that conducted the arbitration hearing; ii. The party did not receive appropriate notification for the selection of an arbitrator or the arbitration process or could not protest for unavoidable reasons; iii. The arbitral award took as its subject a dispute that is not the arbitration agreement, or that it exceeded the scope of the arbitration agreement; iv. In cases where the composition of the arbitration department or the arbitration process did not comply with the agreement of the parties, or in cases where there is no agreement between the parties, did not comply with the laws and regulations of the country that conducted the arbitration hearing; v. The arbitral award does not yet imposes effect upon the parties or that the arbitral award has been cancelled or its execution has been suspended by a court according to a law of the country that made the arbitral award; vi. The given dispute cannot is unabitratable according to the law of the country that made the arbitral award; vii. The execution of the arbitral award would cause hindrance to the sovereignty, safety, or social order of the DPRK. It can be seen that since in Article 4 of disputes resolved using foreign economic arbitration, the Foreign Economic Arbitration Law stipulates that not only the disputes having occurred in foreign economic activity processes where there is an arbitration agreement between the parties together with a foreign factor but also the disputes where an authorized state institution has authorized the arbitration committee to resolve the dispute through foreign economic arbitration process, the provisions on the cancellation and rejection of arbitral awards have been amended accordingly. Unlike international practice, the Foreign Economic Arbitration Law does not restrict the fact that "there is no arbitration agreement or no arbitration agreement reached afterwards between the parties", but only requires an examination of whether "the parties had the capacity for civil conduct at the time of reaching the arbitration agreement".

III. Reflections on the DPRK Jurisdiction of Arbitration

As mentioned above, the biggest problem for foreign investors of the Foreign Economic Arbitration Law is that the arbitration in the DPRK also covers cases where there is no arbitration agreement between the parties while the arbitration is entrusted by the authorized State institution. The DPRK International Trade Arbitration Committee (DITAC) promulgated a new version of its Arbitration Rules in 2015, in which Article 3.6 was added to read as follows "The arbitration committee hears and resolves disputes that have been entrusted to the arbitration committee by authorized state institution to resolve the dispute through foreign economic arbitration process".

Unlike the common practice of international arbitration in most countries of the world, the arbitration in the DPRK has obviously been given more governmental-coercive influence. From the above articles, it can be understood that DITAC is authorized to have jurisdiction over two types of cases. One is the common arbitration jurisdiction understood internationally, i.e., the cases where there is an arbitration agreement between the parties that disputes shall be submitted to DITAC together with a foreign economic factor; The other is the cases that have been transferred to the arbitration committee by the authorized state institution considering it more appropriate to be heard by the arbitration committee. The first type of case is basically in line with the concept of international arbitration in China and most other countries, so there is no need to go into detail. However, the nature of the second type of case, which is very different from the prevailing international practice, is open to discuss whether it is an arbitration or a judgment.

As one of the most common forms of alternative dispute resolution in the world today, arbitration plays a positive and important role in the settlement of commercial disputes, especially in the field of international commercial disputes. However, it seems that the legal provisions and arbitration rules of various countries have not given a clear definition of arbitration. For example, Article 2 of Definitions and Rules of Interpretation in Chapter I "General Provision" of UNCITRAL Model Law on International Commercial Arbitration (hereinafter referred to as "UNCITRAL Model Law") provides that "arbitration" means any arbitration whether or not administered by a permanent arbitral institution; Article 7 of definition and form of the arbitration agreement in chapter II "Arbitration Agreement" option I provides that (1) "Arbitration Agreement" is an agreement by the parties to submit to arbitration all or certain disputes which have arisen or which may arise between them in respect of a defined legal relationship, whether contractual or not. An arbitration agreement may be in the form of an arbitration clause in a contract or in the form of a separate agreement; Article 7 of the definition of arbitration agreement in chapter II "Arbitration Agreement" option II provides that an "Arbitration Agreement" is an agreement by the parties to submit to arbitration all or certain disputes which have arisen or which may arise between them in respect of a defined legal relationship, whether contractual or not. Besides, Article 2 of the China Arbitration Law provides that contractual disputes and other disputes arising from property rights and interests between citizens, legal persons and other organizations of equal status in law may be submitted for arbitration. One of the most internationally accepted views of the term "arbitration" is from the book International Arbitration: Law and Practice by Gary B. Born that arbitration is a process in which parties to a dispute agree to submit to a non-governmental adjudicatory body chosen by, or appointed by, the parties, which will render a binding decision following a neutral adjudicatory process that allows either party to present the facts of the case.

According to the above definitions of arbitration and arbitration agreement, arbitration has 4 aspects of characteristics: 1) the agreement of the parties; 2) a non-government adjudicative body for the settlement of disputes; 3) a neutral adjudicative process; and 4) a binding award.

Therefore arbitral jurisdiction differs from judicial jurisdiction in the following ways:

3.1 Source of Rights

The right of arbitration to settle disputes originates from the choice and designation of the agreement from the two or several parties, while the jurisdiction of civil and commercial litigation comes from the judicial sovereignty of the state and is based on state sovereignty. It can be said that the arbitration jurisdiction in international commercial arbitration is not only not based on state sovereignty, but on the basis of the sovereign state's autonomous limitation of its state sovereignty. In international commercial disputes, arbitration jurisdiction is formed by the arbitration agreement between the parties that gives the arbitral tribunal the right to hear the dispute case and make binding conclusions, which is essentially different from the jurisdiction of courts or other competent judicial authorities in accordance with the provisions of the law and regulations by the state under the premise of the state in possession of judicial sovereignty. Arbitration jurisdiction and judicial jurisdiction come from different sources of power, which determines the nature of arbitration and litigation are not the same. Arbitration jurisdiction originates from the arbitration agreement between the parties, which is the premise and basis for the existence of arbitration. If there is no arbitration agreement, or when the arbitration agreement is defective, there is a controversy whether the arbitration has jurisdiction. In practice, cases abound in which the parties request the court to confirm the invalidity of the arbitration agreement. The source of jurisdiction is the exercise of a state's judicial sovereignty, and the jurisdiction originates from the laws and regulations of a state, possibly including the constitution, so the source of the right is unquestionable. It can be said that the agreed exclusion of jurisdiction by the arbitration clause comes from the special arbitration provisions via the related law and regulation of the state. Therefore, in the two types of cases in DPRK's arbitration, only the first type of case has a source of authority that is consistent with the jurisdictional character of arbitration. But unlike the first type of case, the right to hear the second type of dispute, which is transferred by the authorized state institution to be heard under the arbitration procedure, is still derived from the authority, which is unaffected by the parties' autonomy in no way.

3.2 Adjudicative Bodies

Distinguished from the state judicial authorities, the arbitration institution is a non-governmental adjudicating organization, which is a typical feature of arbitration distinguished from litigation. Foreign-related civil litigation is made by the judges of the state judicial authorities. However, both institutional arbitration and *ad hoc* arbitration are non-government tribunals where the neutral judgement is made by non-government adjudicators. In arbitration, the parties have the right to choose particular professionals to act as arbitrators or to choose a particular arbitral institution to appoint arbitrators for them when they can not reach an agreement on arbitrators. The parties can compare the rules of different arbitration institutions and negotiate on the characteristics and needs of the possible disputes before making the agreement on specific requirements such as the choice of an arbitration institution and the qualifications of arbitrators, and ultimately make an agreement accepted by both parties in writing. Based on the above, parties are more likely to accept the neutrality and professionalof the arbitrators, as factors such as the seat of the arbitration and the qualifications required are considered and negotiated between the parties. On the contrary, the parties are not given the right to choose their trial judge. From this point of view, two types of cases arbitrated in the DPRK do conform to the characteristics above, which were completed at its foreign-related arbitration institutions and in accordance with the foreign-related arbitration procedures. However, it remains uncertain whether the parties were able to choose arbitrators autonomously without external interference and whether the arbitrators were independent and neutral in hearing the cases in practice.

3.3 Enforceability and Party's Autonomy

Jurisdiction of foreign-related civil litigation is enjoyed by the state's judicial branch with national binding power, and its realization is statutory and mandatory. As the jurisdiction of the lawsuit is based on national sovereignty and thus is mandatory, it is unnecessary for the other party to consent. Although civil litigation may allow the parties to agree to choose the court with jurisdiction, the parties can not be allowed to choose the court in all cases. Usually, only in commercial cases may parties choose the court with practical connection to hear the cases by the agreement, not violating the hierarchy jurisdiction and the territorial jurisdiction. On the contrary, the exertion of the jurisdiction of international commercial arbitration is carried out by the arbitral tribunals of non-governmental civil institutions, which do not have the mandatory power conferred by law similar to judicial authorities. Therefore, in the whole process of exercising international commercial arbitration jurisdiction, the arbitral tribunal lacks the compulsory power and material means to guarantee the exercise of international commercial arbitration jurisdiction. In order to ensure the progress of international commercial arbitration proceeding smoothly, the exercise of the arbitration jurisdiction usually requires the support and assistance of judicial authorities. For example, in China, the arbitral tribunal needs the support and assistance of the court in property preservation and evidence preservation. In addition, the UNCITRAL Model Law not only confirms the status of the principle of party autonomy but also makes clear that the choice of the parties should be subject to the relevant mandatory provisions of the UNCITRAL Model

Law. However, it is still undeniable that the principle of party autonomy occupies a pivotal position in international commercial arbitration. From the above, it is clear that the second type of DPRK arbitration is mandatory when the case is initiated, as there is no agreement between the parties to choose arbitration to resolve the dispute. However, once the case is accepted, from the formation of the arbitral tribunal to the issuance of the arbitral award, the parties' autonomy is guaranteed again, while the nature of the case acceptance has no autonomy, which is very contradictory. From the above analyses, the second type of arbitration case in the DPRK is mandatory when it is proceeding as the parties do not reach an agreement of arbitration. But once the case is accepted, the autonomy of the parties is guaranteed again as the process through the constitution of the arbitral tribunal to the arbitral award proceeds according to the arbitration rules, where the autonomy of the parties is guaranteed again while the acceptance of the case is a lack of autonomy basically, making the provision inconsistent.

Generally speaking, the jurisdiction of the second type of arbitration cases in the DPRK, i.e., the cases that are heard by the arbitration institution appointed by the state authority through the foreign-related arbitration procedure, where the source of jurisdiction is the provisions of the state law, which comes from the judicial sovereignty of the state, instead of the agreement of the equal parties. The acceptance of the case is decided by the authority but the procedure of the case is in accordance with the arbitration rules of the arbitration institution. The acceptance of the case presents the mandatory of the state while the hearing of the case presents the autonomy of the parties. Therefore, the author considers that although the form of the legal document of this type of case is the arbitration award made by the arbitral institution, the legal document is the result of the arbitral institution exercising international judicial jurisdiction on behalf of the judicial authorities with authorization. In other words, this type of arbitral award is not the same as the arbitral award in general practice, as it has the characteristics of judicial judgment. In real case represented by the author in China of the recognition and enforcement of the award of the DITAC, the court agrees with the view that the legal documents made by the arbitral institution shall be recognized as the judgement and applies the Article 3 of Ratifying the Treaty on Civil and Criminal Judicial Assistance between the People's Republic of China and the Democratic People's Republic of Korea, as the Central Court of the DPRK transferred the case to the DITAC while the parties had not been reached an agreement of arbitration or submitted to the court of DPRK, leading the fact that the DITAC exercises the power of the judicial jurisdiction on behalf the authorized state institution, and eventually, the court made a decision in accordance with the Treaty.

IV. Problems of the Foreign Economic Arbitration Law of the DPRK

4.1 Inception of Arbitration

In addition to the problems with the DPRK's arbitration jurisdiction described above, the first type of arbitration cases similar to the international practice where an arbitration agreement exists still remains the problems in signing the arbitration agreement. Under the DPRK's legal system, particularly Article 11 of the Foreign Economic Contract Law of the DPRK, the entry into a contract with a large trading sum or with significance to the State, shall receive the approval of the central trade guidance institution or the given institution. Similarly, Article 18 of the Foreign Economic Contract Law of the DPRK provides that contracts that hinder the safety of the country or cause damage to its economic interests, or contracts concluded through deception or coercion, may not have legal effect[1]. Therefore, even if the parties reach an arbitration agreement,

---

[1] Foreign Economic Contract Law of the Democratic People's Republic of Korea (2008).

the arbitration could not be started if the arbitration agreement was not approved by the central trade guidance institution or have no legal effect according to Article 18 of the Foreign Economic Contract Law. Moreover, the meaning of "significance to the State" and "cause damage to its economic interests" remain uncertain. There is no doubt that foreign investors lack confidence because of the discretionary power amplified without restriction while some foreign economic contracts have been invalidated by the relevant authorities of the DPRK due to violation of relevant laws in practice.

4.2 Non-publicity of the Details of Laws and Excessive Powers of the Arbitration Departments

Although the Foreign Economic Arbitration Law stipulates that foreign-related economic disputes are heard by the DITAC, the DMAC and the DCSAC, the specifics of these three organizations, such as their constituents, arbitration rules, personnel and panel of arbitrators are difficult for ordinary people to know. It is also difficult to find relevant information on the Internet while nowadays the Internet is widespread. Even the other regulations of the DPRK are difficult for foreign investors and foreign legal practitioners to obtain. In addition, according to the above, the arbitration departments have been given more power than international practice, and it remains uncertain to foreign investors whether the arbitration departments can ensure independence and neutrality in hearing cases without interference from other authorities, which limits the trust of the DPRK's international arbitration system from foreign investors and discourages the trust increasing in a short period of time. Therefore, it is particularly urgent for the DPRK to increase the transparency of relevant legal provisions and arbitration information, and to connect with the international community as soon as possible.

4.3 Urgency of the accession to the Convention on the Recognition and Enforcement of Foreign Arbitral Awards

Since the signing of the Convention on the Recognition and Enforcement of Foreign Arbitral Awards (hereinafter referred to as the "New York Convention") on June 10, 1958, most of the countries and regions in the world have acceded to the convention successively. On January 17, 2013(2023?), the Democratic Republic of Timor-Leste announced its accession to the New York Convention as the 172nd Contracting Party to the convention. However, as the DPRK has not acceded to the New York Convention so far, neither the arbitral awards made in the DPRK cannot be recognized and enforced outside the DPRK under the New York Convention, nor the foreign arbitral awards can be recognized and enforced in the DPRK under the convention, which needs the bilateral treaties signed between the DPRK and other countries to recognize and enforce instead. The treaty between China and the DPRK on Civil and Criminal Judicial Assistance signed in 2003 is, regulating the the mutual recognition of civil and criminal judgments but does not include the mutual recognition of arbitral awards. Even if the bilateral treaty with China fails to include the recognition of arbitral awards, it can be imagined that the situation of mutual recognition and enforcement of arbitral awards between the DPRK and other countries is pessimistic. In other words, the DPRK currently lacks the legal basis for mutual recognition of arbitral awards with the international community, leading to the need to accede to the New York Convention imminently. However, it is bound to face great difficulties in acceding to the New York Convention because of the unique arbitration jurisdiction. Furthermore, even if the DPRK accedes to the New York Convention successfully, the subsequent revision of domestic legislation in accordance with the New York Convention will certainly face considerable challenges.

Conclusion

Firstly, although the Foreign Economic Arbitration Law of the DPRK is largely referred to the UNCITRAL Model Law, it contains various special provisions peculiar to the DPRK. The Foreign Economic Arbitration Law establishes a dispute resolution mechanism that is in line with the DPRK's national conditions, but there are still a number of provisions that are not in line with international practices. The most typical example is the second type of case mentioned above, in which a powerful state authorities can appoint cases without an arbitration agreement between the parties to the arbitration committee in accordance with foreign arbitration procedures. There is a lack of clarity on whether the nature of the legal documents of the cases is a court judgement or an arbitral award in practice, making it ambiguous whether the case can be recognized and enforced outside the DPRK. Therefore, with such special provisions, the Foreign Economic Arbitration Law of the DPRK is yet to be further refined and improved in line with international standards.

Secondly, although the DPRK has reached the basic content of protecting foreign investment, such as establishing the principle of protecting the rights and interests of foreign investment enterprises[①], prohibiting the state nationalizing the property of foreign investment enterprises[②], allowing the foreign investment enterprises to remit the profits and other income outside of the territory of the country without restriction[③], and guaranteeing of secrecy over business administration of the foreign investment enterprises[④], etc. through the Foreign Economic Contract Law and relative laws and regulations, the legislation can not fully put into practice.

In addition, the dispute settlement mechanism related to foreign

---

① Article 4, Foreign Investor Law of the Democratic People's Republic of Korea (2011).
② Article 18, Foreign Investor Law of the Democratic People's Republic of Korea (2011).
③ Article 20, Foreign Investor Law of the Democratic People's Republic of Korea (2011).
④ Article 21, Foreign Investor Law of the Democratic People's Republic of Korea (2011).

investment needs to be further improved via the practice, answering the concerns such as whether an arbitration agreement needs to be approved by the relevant government departments, whether the arbitration commission of the DPRK has the jurisdiction if there is no arbitration agreement, it is difficult for outsiders to know the specific rules like the arbitration rules of the arbitration commission, and the independence and neutrality of the arbitration is still lack of credibility, etc.

Moreover, as the DPRK is one of the few countries that has not acceded to the New York Convention, the effectiveness of its arbitration awards is uncertain to foreign investors, so it lacks reliability for foreign investment to use arbitration as a dispute resolution mechanism. Also, because of the special provisions in the DPRK, there is considerable resistance to the DPRK to accede to the New York Convention. Therefore, it is one of the priority issues for DPRK in order to introduce foreign investment that the DPRK accedes to the New York Convention as soon as possible and to amend and improve its domestic legislation in accordance with the New York Convention.

Finally, in order to attract foreign investment and promote domestic economic development, the DPRK has successively introduced and amended many laws and regulations to encourage and protect foreign investment in recent years, and constantly filled and improved the gaps in its foreign investment laws, which is of great significance in attracting foreign investment and promoting domestic economic development. However, it must be said that there are still many provisions in this series of initiatives that are not in line with the international community and remain distinctive characteristics of the DPRK, which are yet to be further amended. It is hoped that a modern arbitration legal system of the DPRK that is truly open, developed and in line with the international community, will provide foreign investors with more protection mechanisms and confidence in investing in the DPRK, and provides a better legal basis for the economic development of the DPRK in the near future.

Republic of Korea

Overview of Republic of the Arbitration Industry and its Legal System Development[*]

Republic of Korea, as one of the three countries in East Asia, is an important economy in the world, although its economic volume cannot match that of China and Japan. In addition, despite the political relationship between China and Republic of Korea goes ups and downs due to the changing world, trade between the two countries has been frequent in recent years. Before 2023, China has been the largest trading partner of Republic of Korea for many years, and Republic of Korea has also been among the top five trading partners of China. International arbitration and cross-border trade are closely related, and civil and commercial disputes involving Republic of Korea are not uncommon in China, therefore, it is necessary for both academics and practitioners in China to study the industrial policy and legal environment of arbitration in Republic of Korea. This article attempts to briefly depict the basic appearance of arbitration industry and arbitration law from the aspects: industrial policy orientation and current status, and legal system of arbitration in Republic of Korea.

I. Industrial Policy Orientation and Current Status of the Arbitration of Republic of Korea

1.1 Formation of the Idea of Arbitration Industrialization and Enactment of Laws

Arbitration originated from the need for efficient dispute resolution among merchants. After World War I, in order to promote economic recovery and international trade, the International Chamber of Commerce (ICC) was established, followed by the ICC International Court of Arbitration and the

---

[*] The author is Su Xiaoling, Doctor of Laws, Attorney of Beijing DHH Law Firm.

international convention that ensure arbitral awards are enforceable across borders. The origins of arbitration in Republic of Korea are also closely related to the needs of the country's economic development; in 1962, when the first five-year economic development plan was implemented in Republic of Korea, the transaction volume increased rapidly, and commercial disputes also increased significantly. For this reason, the government together with the business community of Republic of Korea established the national permanent arbitration institution, the Korean Commercial Arbitration Board (KCAB) in 1966 and enactment of the first arbitration law of Republic of Korea. However, for quite some time, arbitration was not a frequently chosen means of resolving commercial disputes in Republic of Korea.

In the wake of the 21st century, a new understanding of international arbitration has emerged, that is, in addition to being an effective means of dispute resolution, international arbitration can be viewed as a type of legal service, from which industries would benefit if the case stays in their home country. Along with the steadily increasing volume of foreign trade and investment in Republic of Korea at that time, the number of arbitration cases of domestic companies arbitrated in foreign countries has also increased, and the cost of legal services is mainly borne by them, resulting in a growing trade deficit in legal services. With the aim of reducing the trade deficit and developing arbitration legal services, a lot of discussions around the idea of building Seoul as an arbitration seat have been held since 2010. The main reasons for this are that Seoul is geographically located in the middle of the major trading partners of Republic of Korea such as the U.S., China, and Japan, and that the legal system of of Republic of Korea is of the civil law tradition, and that Seoul may be able to provide differentiated services from those provided by the common law jurisdictions such as Singapore and Hong Kong SAR. Based this orietantion, the Seoul International Dispute Resolution Center (SIDRC) was established in May 2013 in Seoul with joint funding from the Korean Bar Association, the Seoul Metropolitan Government, and the KCAB. The

SIDRC operates a facility that provides internationalized and high-standard services for international arbitration. Although it is not an arbitration institution that administers cases, it has raised awareness of Seoul among the arbitration community, and a number of ICC arbitration cases have been heard in Seoul since its completion, which could be said to achieve certain results with regard to the industrialization of arbitration. On this basis, the idea of industrialization of arbitration was extended to the government level, and the Ministry of Justice began to lead the discussion on it. In 2017, the Arbitration Industry Promotion Act was enacted and came into force on June 28, 2017, which marked the formalization of the promotion and development of the arbitration industry on a legal level[①].

1.2 Measures under the Arbitration Industry Promotion Act

The Arbitration Industry Promotion Act (hereinafter referred to as the "Promotion Act") mainly deals with the establishment of master plan, creating foundation to promote arbitration industry, cultivation of arbitration specialists, the guidance of international dispute cases to be heard in Republic of Korea, financial support, and the guarantee for autonomic operation. In accordance with the requirements of the Promotion Act, the Ministry of Justice formulated and released the Basic Plan for the Promotion of the Arbitration Industry (hereinafter referred to as the "Basic Plan") in December 2018. The Basic Plan maps out the arbitration industry as a whole in a number of aspects, including strengthening the foundation of the arbitration industry, ensuring competitiveness, and expanding international arbitration cases hearing in Republic of Korea, followed by gradual implementation measures.

1.2.1 Strengthening the Foundation of the Arbitration Industry

The strengthening of the foundation of the arbitration industry cov-

---

[①] Background of the Arbitration Industry Promotion Act: 오현석, "중재산업진흥법에 대한 평가 및 국제중재 활성화를 위한 법정책적 제언",〈 선진상사법률연구〉 통권 제 103 호, July 2013.

ers both the training of specialized personnel and the improvement of the legal system.

With regard to the cultivation of arbitration specialists, the main measures are inviting arbitration experts to attend law school's seminars; selecting law school students for visits or internships at foreign arbitration institutions; educating employees of companies in different industries on different arbitration practices; and offering online courses, etc. The KCAB is the sole competent authority for arbitration education designated by the Ministry of Justice, and the Arbitration Education Institute was established within the KCAB on May 20, 2019, to offer a series of courses, such as the ADR Basic Course, the Domestic Arbitration Specialist Course, and the International Arbitration Specialist Course.

With regard to the improvement of the legal system, the Basic Plan proposes to listen to various suggestions and opinions on the improvement of the legal system from the KCAB, the Korean Association of Arbitrators, academics, corporate lawyers, entrepreneurs, and practitioners in the construction and maritime industries at any time. In addition, the Basic Plan proposes the formation of an advisory committee composed of experts from arbitration institutions, academia and the practical community, commissioning research on relevant topics, holding academic conferences, and so on.

1.2.2 Ensuring Competitiveness

The ensuring competitiveness also covers two aspects, one is the construction of arbitration facilities, and the other is strengthening of arbitration institutions in all aspects.

For the construction of arbitration facilities, the Ministry of Law has taken the lead in expanding the Integrated Arbitration Center on the Seoul International Arbitration Center completed in 2013. The Integrated Arbitration Center officially operated in 2018, and the area of the arbitration office was expanded from about 300 to 400 square meters to 1,911 square meters, and introduced a platform for online hearings. As for the main body to operate the hardware facility, there was a proposal[①] to set up a separate corporation specializing in the operation of the facility, similar to Singapore, but in the end, it was handed over to the KCAB.

With regard to the strengthening of arbitration institutions, the Ministry of Justice plans to provide systematically training to the personnel handling cases on the one hand, and on the other hand, organize research on international investment arbitration, a new field which is believed to be worth of further exploring.

1.2.3 Expanding International Arbitration Cases Hearing in Republic of Korea

The Basic Plan states that a study will be conducted on how to induce cases to be heard and arbitrated in Republic of Korea, and that a strategy committee will be established for this purpose, but there has been no report on this, nor has there been any public announcement of the establishment of the strategy committee.

The Basic Plan also designs to support the establishment of representative offices of the KCAB overseas, promote advocacy and communications and organize events such as the Seoul ADR Festival to enhance the public's perception of Seoul as the seat of arbitration.

1.3 Current Status of Implementation of the Promotion Act and the Basic Plan

The implementation of the Promotion Act relies mainly on financial allocations, and the main body is the KCAB, the only arbitration institution in Republic of Korea.

1.3.1 The Structure of the KCAB

Due to the KCAB is the sole implementing body, the organization of the KCAB has changed considerably since the implementation of the

---

[①] 국제중재실무회, "북합중재센터의 설립 및 운영방안에 관한 연구", 법무부 용역보고서, June 2017, Page 301.

Promotion Act for the Arbitration Industry, with a large number of newly established organizations and a relatively large number of functions, and as of today, the specific composition of the KCAB's organization can be shown in the chart below①.

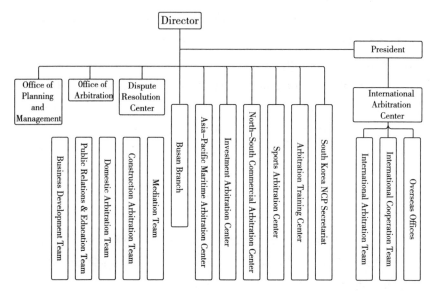

Figure 1 Organizational structure of the Korean Commercial Arbitration Institute

As can be seen from the above organizational chart, international arbitration has been separated and an International Arbitration Center has been established, with relatively independent personnel management and operation, showing a higher status. However, investment arbitration and maritime arbitration, which are closely related to international cases, are not included in the the International Arbitration Center, and there are ambiguities in the division of functions and actual management.

1.3.2 Financial Support for the KCAB

The Ministry of Justice grants financial support to the KCAB on a cer-

---

① See the official website of the Korean Commercial Arbitration Board: http://www.kcab.or.kr/servlet/kcab_kor/intro/1511, accessed Nov. 4, 2023.

tain scale. In 2017, a total of 1,151 hundred million won was provided for expenses related to overseas presentation, publicity, and measures to guide international arbitration cases to be heard in Republic of Korea, etc. In 2018, 2,410 hundred million won was allocated for the rental of arbitration hearings, construction of video systems, etc. After the opening of the arbitration hearing facilities, financial support of approximately 2,500 hundred million won will be given annually from 2018 onwards[①]. However, as the arbitration hearings of the KCAB are rented and require rent payments, a significant portion of the financial support is used for the rent, and the allocation of funds of specialists for international arbitration is not sufficiently secured.

1.3.3 Case Receipt[②]

According to the statistics of the KCAB, the receipt of arbitration and mediation cases of the KCAB from 2018 to 2022 can be expressed in the chart below:

Table 1　Cases Accepted by the Korean Commercial Arbitration Court from 2018 to 2022

		2018		2019		2020		2021		2022	
		Amount/Cases	Sum/Hundred million won	Amount/Cases	Sum/Hundred million won	Amount/Cases	Sum/Hundred million won	Amount/Cases	Sum/Hundred million won	Amount/Cases	Sum/Hundred million won
Arbitration	Domestic	331	5923	373	8886	336	4146	450	7949	304	4136
	International	62	1432	70	1159	69	1670	50	511	38	738
Mediation	Domestic	881	148	830	354	696	108	484	79	531	51
	International	80	62	59	330	51	44	28	74	23	133

---

① 오현석,"중재산업진흥법에 대한 평가 및 국제중재 활성화를 위한 법정책적 제언",〈 선진상사법률연구〉통권 제 103 호 , June 2023.

② Based on statistics published by the KCAB.

In terms of the number of cases received, since the release of the Promotion Act in 2018, the number of international arbitration cases has declined yearly from 2020, except for an increase in 2019, where it is doubtful whether the COVID-19 is the main factor contributing to this outcome.

1.3.4 Maritime Arbitration

Prior to March 2018, there was no maritime arbitration institution within the KCAB, and maritime cases were referred to the Domestic Arbitration Team or the International Arbitration Team depending on whether they were domestic or international cases. Guided by the policy of industrialization of arbitration, the Asia-Pacific Maritime Arbitration Center was established in Busan by the KCAB in March 2018, which is the only maritime arbitration institution in Republic of Korea. In August 2019 the Maritime Arbitration Rules were formulated and put into effect. However, most maritime arbitration has traditionally been conducted outside of Republic of Korea, and the volume of maritime arbitration in Republic of Korea is relatively small. In recent years, there has been a hot discussion about promoting maritime disputes to be resolved in Republic of Korea among academics, but the main direction has focused on the establishment of maritime courts, with port cities such as Incheon and Busan fiercely fighting for the location of the first maritime court. Given space constraints, the information of maritime arbitration of Republic of Korea will not be further developed.

II. Legal System Construction of Arbitration of Republic of Korea Under the Orientation of Arbitration Industrialization

It has been five years since the introduction of the Basic Plan, and although the goal of making Seoul the center of international arbitration as envisioned at the beginning have not been achieved, the legal system construction is not lagging behind. The Arbitration Act was amended and implemented in 2016[1], incorporating all aspects of the revised UNCITRAL Arbitration Model Law, and attention was paid to maintaining an arbitration-friendly legal environment in judicial practice. In the same year, the KCAB, the only domestic arbitration institution in Republic of Korea[2], revised its international arbitration rules, absorbing the essence of the arbitration rules of other major arbitration institutions in the world, and published the 2016 *KCAB International Arbitration Rules Commentary* for the convenience of the parties and practitioners in understanding and applying the rules.

2.1 The Arbitration Act

2.1.1 Background of Amendment of the Arbitration Act

The Arbitration Act, which was originally enacted in 1966 and partially revised in 1973, was comprehensively revised in 1999, adopting the contents and style of the UNCITRAL Model Law on Arbitration, except for those that conflict with the judicial system. When the UNCITRAL Arbitration Model Law (hereinafter referred to as the "Arbitration Model Law") was revised in 2006, academics began to call for corresponding revisions and improvements in domestic law, which was one of the reasons for Republic of Korea to initiate the revision of the Arbitration Act. Another reason for the revision is the policy of industrialization of arbitration, which is part of the Basic Plan, and the need to maintain the advancement of legal system of arbitration.

The revision of the Arbitration Act (2016) began in July 2012, when

---

[1] The Arbitration Act was amended once again in 2020, but only to Article 40, which was to add the Ministry of Justice as the main body of financial support for arbitration institutions, in addition to the Ministry of Industry, Trade and Commerce, which was originally provided for, in order to be consistent with the Promotion Act.

[2] Although the KCAB is the sole arbitration institution in Republic of Korea, the Arbitration Act permits ad hoc arbitration and also provides judicial assistance for ad hoc arbitration.

the Ministry of Justice formed the Task Force for the Revision of the Arbitration Act and then formally constituted the Committee for the Revision of the Arbitration Act, starting to discuss and design a proposal for the revision of the Arbitration Act. From March 2013 to the end of October 2014, the Revision Committee held 20 meetings, resulting in a draft revision, and in 2014, the Ministry of Justice and the KCAB co-hosted a seminar titled "Major Controversies in the Revision of the Arbitration Act and the Revisions of Other Countries," at which the draft revision was accessible to the public. In August 2015, the Ministry of Justice announced that it would conduct a legislative preview of the revision of the Arbitration Act and solicit opinions from public. On October 14, 2015, the Ministry of Justice convened a public hearing for lawyers, professors, and other arbitration professionals to receive opinions on the draft revision of the Arbitration Act. The Arbitration Law was published in May 2016 and came into force on November 30 of the same year (hereinafter referred to as the "2016 Arbitration Act").

2.1.2 Basic Idea of the 2016 Arbitration Act

Since one of the motivations for this revision is the amendment of the Arbitration Model Law, the revision of the Arbitration Act also focuses on borrowing and imitating the Arbitration Model Law. At the micro level, the 2016 Arbitration Act follows the revision of the Arbitration Model Law and focuses on the manner of the arbitration agreement and the arbitral tribunal's authority to issue interim sanctions. At the macro level, the industry practitioners discussed whether to maintain the same system as the Arbitration Model Law. In the end, they formed a relatively conservative opinion, considering that advanced countries in arbitration, such as the UK and France, do not fully adopt the system and legislation of the Arbitration Model Law while taking into account the opinions and positions of the Arbitration Model Law, and that Singapore and Hong Kong in the Asian region have introduced unique systems while borrowing some contents from the Arbitration Model Law. However, it is still too early for Republic of Korea to enact a unique arbitration law "with national characteristics". Based on the above mentioned, the basic idea of this revision is to respect the established system modeled on the Arbitration Model Law as much as possible, and to add new provisions that are not found in the Arbitration Model Law.

2.1.3 Main Revisions

(1) Expansion of the scope of arbitrable matters.

While the old Arbitration Act expressed the arbitrable objects as "disputes in private law", the 2016 Arbitration Act, modeled on the German legislation, expresses the arbitrable objects as "disputes over property rights and disputes over non-property rights that can be resolved by the parties through conciliation" (Article 3). According to this provision, disputes related to unfair competition, patents and other intellectual property disputes can also be resolved by arbitration.

(2) Relaxation of the requirement of written arbitration agreement.

The old Arbitration Act had provisions on the written arbitration agreement and enumerated, in the manner of the Arbitration Model Law, the circumstances in which the element of writing could be found to be satisfied. The 2006 Arbitration Model Law provided two options to choose, firstly, to retain the requirement of the element of writing, but at the same time to provide that the element of writing was satisfied insofar as the content of the arbitration agreement was recorded in any form; and secondly, to abolish the requirement of the element of writing altogether.

During the revision of Arbitration Act, the Revision Committee recommended the written elements to be retained, considering that the requirement of written elements is still retained in most countries and that it would be inappropriate to adopt such a radical option as the total abolition of written elements in view of the predictability of the parties. The Arbitration Act 2016 shares the purpose of the first option of the Arbitration Model Law, but is formulated differently (article 8, paragraph 3). According to the current proposal, the requirement of the element of writing is fulfilled as long as the content of the arbitration agreement is recorded, regardless of whether the agreement is made orally or by conduct, and as long as the expression of intent made by electronic means such as telegrams, telecommunication, mail, etc., can be confirmed. Moreover, if the content of statement of claim and statement of defense exchanged by the parties have the intention of arbitration, and the other party does not object to it, the requirement of written elements is also satisfied.

(3) Regulation of Interim Measures and Their Enforceability.

The 2006 revision of the Arbitration Model Law centered on interim measures, so the revision of the Arbitration Act has been discussed a lot in this regard as well. The 2016 Arbitration Act provides for interim measures (known as provisional sanctions in Republic of Korea) in a systematic manner with eight articles in Article 18. It has adopted these provisions on interim measures regulated in the Arbitration Model Law except for the provision on preliminary order, and has at least two important modifications.

The one is, the definition of "interim measure" is modeled on the Arbitration Model Law. Firstly, Paragraph 1 of Article 18 of the 2016 Arbitration Act affirms the power of the arbitral tribunal to take interim measures on the application of one party, which is a reservation from the old Arbitration Act. Subsequently, the 2016 Arbitration Act defines "interim measure" in Paragraph 2, "An interim measure is any temporary measure, by which, at any time prior to the issuance of the award by which the dispute is finally decided, the arbitral tribunal orders a party to perform any of the following subparagraphs: (1) maintain or restore the status quo pending determination of the dispute; (2) take action that would prevent current or imminent harm or prejudice to the arbitral proceeding itself, or prohibiting action that may cause such harm or prejudice; (3) Provide a means of preserving assets subject to the execution of an arbitral award; (4), Preserve evidence that may be relevant and material to the resolution of the dispute." After a comparison of the provisions of Article 17 of the Arbitration Model Law, we can see that 2016 Arbitration Act is a full acceptance of the Arbitration Model Law.

The other one is, interim measures are given enforceability. Under the old Arbitration Act, interim measures issued by an arbitral tribunal are dealing with a procedural matter, and not a substantive matter of disputes, and therefore the legal form is a "decision". Since the object of enforcement by courts is "judgment", interim measures are not subject to enforcement by the courts. To address this issue, the amendment empowers courts to enforce interim measures in Article 18-7[①] and provides detailed provisions in this regard. Corresponding to the granting of enforceability to interim measures, the 2016 Arbitration Act also provides for the grounds for refusal of enforcement[②], the content of which is basically the

---

① Article 18-7 Recognition and Enforcement of Interim Measures
(1) The party who intends to seek compulsory execution on the basis of the interim measure may file a petition with a court to seek a decision that authorizes the execution.
(2) The party who is seeking or has obtained recognition or enforcement of an interim measure shall promptly inform the court of any termination, suspension or modification of that interim measure.
(3) The court where recognition or enforcement of an interim measure is sought may, if it considers it necessary, order the requesting party to provide appropriate security if the arbitral tribunal has yet to make such an order with respect to the interim measure or where such a decision is necessary to protect the rights of third parties.
(4) The provisions concerning preservative measures in the *Civil Execution Act* shall apply mutatis mutandis to the execution of interim measures.
② Article 18-8 Grounds for Refusing Recognition or Enforcement
(1) Recognition or enforcement of an interim measure may be refused only if it falls under one of the following subparagraphs:
A. At the request of the party against whom the interim measure is invoked if the court is satisfied that:
(a) The other party to the interim measure proves any of the following facts:
(i) A fact under Article 36 (2) 1 (a) or (d);
(ii) The fact that the other party to the interim measure was not able to present his or her case because the party was not given proper notice of the appointment of an arbitrator or of the arbitral proceeding or due to any other cause or event;
(iii) The fact that the dispute subject to the interim measure is not eligible for an arbitration agreement or that the interim measure is beyond the scope of the arbitration agreement. Provided that the recognition or execution of the interim measure only for the part not eligible for an arbitration agreement may be denied, if the part eligible for the arbitration agreement is separable from the part ineligible for the arbitration agreement; (Turn to the next page)

same as that of Article 17 I of the Arbitration Model Law.

(4) Strengthening Court's Assistance for Arbitration with Respect to Evidence and Allowing Taking the Evidence Directly by the Arbitral Tribunal.

In terms of taking evidence, this amendment strengthens the court's assistance for arbitration. Under the old Arbitration Act, if taking evidence from a third party in an arbitration is needed, the arbitral tribunal could entrust the court to conduct the investigation, and the results from the court would be sent to the arbitral tribunal. The Revision Committee held the view that entrusting the courts to take evidence was more effective at certain occasions, but that, when applying methods of questioning of witnesses or other investigation of evidence, it would be more conducive to the formation of inner conviction by the arbitrators if the they were carried out directly by the arbitral tribunal, and that therefore there should be a gateway for the arbitral tribunal to take evidence directly, in addition to the current method. Based on this consideration, the 2016 Arbitration Act adds an article on "Court Assistance in Taking Evidence"①, which

---

(Follow the previous page)

(b) Where an asset has not been provided as security for the interim measure according to an order issued by the court or the arbitral tribunal;

(c) Where the interim measure has been terminated or suspended by the arbitral tribunal.

B. Where the court, ex officio, finds that either of the following grounds exists:

(a) Where the court has no authority to execute the interim measure: Provided, That the foregoing shall not apply where the court makes a decision to alter the interim measure to the necessary extent, without altering the substance of the interim measure, in order to execute the interim measure;

(b) Where any of the grounds set forth in Article 36 (2) 2 (a) or (b) exists.

(2) No court shall examine the substance of an interim measure when it makes a decision on a petition filed to seek the recognition or execution of the interim measure under Article 18-7.

(3) The judgment of a court based on any of the grounds referred to in paragraph (1) shall be valid only for the decision on the recognition and execution of the relevant interim measure.

① Article 28 Court Assistance in Taking Evidence

(1) The arbitral tribunal may, ex officio or upon the request of a party, request a court to take evidence or request for the court's assistance in taking evidence.

(2) When an arbitral tribunal requests a court to take evidence, the arbitral tribunal may specify, in writing, the matters to be recorded in the evidence examination (Turn to the next page)

provides that "when the arbitral tribunal requests a court to cooperate in taking evidence, the court may order such persons as a witness or document holder to appear before the arbitral tribunal or order them to submit necessary documents to the arbitral tribunal." According to this provision, when there is a need to take evidence, the arbitral tribunal may, depending on the circumstances, either entrust the court to do so or request the court's assistance in ordering the witnesses to attend the hearing examined them directly by the arbitral tribunal.

(5) Simplification of Procedures for Recognition and Enforcement of Arbitral Awards.

Under the old Arbitration Act, the enforcement of an arbitral award required the obtaining of an enforcement judgment from the court in accordance with a "procedure for declaring the permission of enforcement", which was a relatively complex procedure. This amendment clarifies that an arbitral award has the same legal effect as a judgment, and that it is no longer necessary to obtain an "enforcement judgment" from the court but rather a "decision" from the court, in order to ensure that arbitral awards can be enforced promptly and effectively.

(6) Confirmation of the competence of the arbitral tribunal to determine the bearing of the arbitration costs and the payment of interest for delay.

The Arbitration Model Law does not provide for the allocation of the arbitration costs or the payment of interest on delay in the absence of

---

(Follow the previous page) reports and other particulars required in the evidence-taking.

(3) When a court takes evidence according to paragraph (2), the arbitrator or parties may participate in taking evidence with the permission of the presiding judge.

(4) In the case of paragraph 2, the court shall, without delay after taking evidence, send to the arbitral tribunal the records on taking evidence such as a certified copy of reports on the examination of witnesses or a certified copy of reports on the examination of evidence.

(5) When the arbitral tribunal requests a court to cooperate in taking evidence, the court may order such persons as a witness or document holder to appear before the arbitral tribunal or order them to submit necessary documents to the arbitral tribunal.

(6) The arbitral tribunal shall pay expenses incurred in taking evidence to the court.

agreement by the parties, nor does the law of Republic of Korea. During the revision, the Revision Committee supported to empower the arbitral tribunal to determine the burden of arbitration costs in the law, providing a legal basis for the arbitral tribunal to make the relevant award. The 2016 Arbitration Act allows the arbitral tribunal to determine the sharing of the arbitration costs in the absence of agreement by the parties[①], and also gives the arbitral tribunal the power to determine interest for delay[②].

(7) Revision of unnecessary restrictive provisions to simplify the enforcement of arbitral awards.

The amendment also removes a number of restrictive provisions that were unnecessary and troublesome in practice. For example, the old Arbitration Act stipulated that not only the arbitral award should be served on the parties after it was made, but also the original copy of the award shall be sent to and deposited with the competent court (Article 32, Paragraph 4 of the old Arbitration Act); When applying for the enforcement of an arbitral award, the duly authenticated original award and the original arbitration agreement or a duly certified copy thereof shall submit to the court; if the award or arbitration agreement is made in a foreign language, a duly certified translation into the Korean language shall be accompanied (Article 37, Paragraph 2 of the old Arbitration Act). The meaning of "original", "copy" and "duly authenticated or certified" in these provisions is not clear, and some requirements are not necessary. For example, the original of an arbitral award is kept by the arbitral institution and the parties, and there is no need for it to be kept by the court. In the consideration of fa-

---

① Article 34-2 Allocation of Arbitration Costs
Unless otherwise agreed by the parties, the arbitral tribunal may determine the allocation of costs of arbitration incurred in the arbitral proceedings, considering all circumstances of the relevant arbitration case.

② Article 34-3 Past Due Interest
Unless otherwise agreed by the parties, the arbitral tribunal may order either party to pay past due interest, if it finds it appropriate in making an arbitral award, considering all circumstances of the relevant arbitration case.

cilitating the parties, the amendments have been made accordingly. The 2016 Arbitration Act provides that an arbitral award shall be deposit by the court only if the parties so request (Article 32, Paragraph 4 of the 2016 Arbitration Act). With respect to the procedure for the enforcement of arbitral awards, the 2016 Arbitration Act provides that the parties only need to submit a "copy" of the arbitral award when applying for enforcement to the court; and where the arbitral award is made in a foreign language, only the Korean translation is required to be submitted, and the requirement for the translation to be "duly certified" under the original provision has been deleted (Article 37 of the 2016 Arbitration Act).

2.1.4 Brief Comments on the 2016 Arbitration Act

The revision of the Arbitration Act was carried out under the strategic plan to establish Republic of Korea as an international arbitration center, and therefore, the main focus was to improve the domestic arbitration legal system and strive to create a legal friendly environment to arbitration. On the one hand, the amendment recognizes the current situation in Republic of Korea of the development of arbitration practice, complies with the universal requirement arbitration, does not pursue country-specific characteristics, and accepts the template of the Arbitration Model Law, so the amendment on the whole is moderate but basically consistent with the development trend of the many advanced countries in arbitration as well as the world trend of arbitration. On the other hand, the revision draws attention to regulating the relationship between arbitration and courts, emphasizes the support and assistance of courts to arbitration, and meantime excludes the undue interference of courts, and grants the arbitral tribunal the authority to make decisions on certain matters. Especially in the aspect of interim measures, the revision carries out a comprehensive consolidation, fully accepts the provisions of the Model Law on interim measures, and articulates on domestic procedural law, which improves the operation and convenience for arbitration. Because of the significance of interim measures in practice, especially in international commercial arbitration, this amendment, as it facilitates the realization of arbitral awards, will obviously strengthen the confidence of parties in choosing arbitration as a means of dispute resolution. In addition the more simplified procedures which facilitates the conduct and enforcement of arbitral proceedings will benefit the parties and ultimately the development of arbitration in Republic of Korea.

2.2 The 2016 KCAB International Arbitration Rules (hereinafter referred to as the "2016 Rules")

KCAB arbitration has separate arbitration rules for domestic and international cases. However, the scope of international cases referred to by the KCAB is narrower than the scope of foreign-related cases in China. As defined in Article 2 of the 2016 Rules, "international arbitration" refers to two types of cases: those in which at least one of the parties has its place of business abroad, and those in which the seat of arbitration agreed upon in the arbitration agreement is outside Republic of Korea. In the former type, where the parties have multiple places of business, the arbitration is international if the principal place of business is abroad, and where there is no place of business, the arbitration is international if the parties have their habitual residence abroad.

2.2.1 Background of Development

Prior to 2007, the KCAB received very few international arbitration cases, and in some year the number was zero, so there were no international arbitration rules, and the KCAB Arbitration Rules were applied for all cases regardless of whether it is foreign related. With the emergence of foreign-related cases, the International Arbitration Practice Association, which is composed of international arbitration experts, started to promote the development of international arbitration rules, and the first international arbitration rules of the KCAB were introduced in 2007. However, in 2007, the application of the international arbitration rules was subject to the explicit agreement of the parties to apply them, otherwise the Arbitration Rules would still apply, which resulted in the fact that international arbitration rules were seldom applied in practice. In order to enhance the competitiveness of international arbitration of Republic of Korea, the KCAB revised its arbitration rules again in 2011 with two big changes. The one is changing the name of the rules to distinguish between domestic and international arbitration rules clearly; the other is amending the original provision that the international arbitration rules are only applicable if they are expressly agreed upon by the parties, to the international arbitration rules are applicable to the international arbitration case unless otherwise the parties expressly exclude the rules to apply.① And with the expansion of the scope of application of the International Arbitration Rules, the number of arbitration cases applied by the International Arbitration Rules have been increasing, with as many as 54 cases by 2014.

After 2012, major international arbitration institutions revised their arbitration rules, and Republic of Korea started to revise the 2011 Arbitration Rules in line with the trend. The 2015 amendments to the International Arbitration Rules were submitted to and recognized by the Supreme Court of Republic of Korea, and the New International Arbitration Rules (the 2016 Rules) are applicable to cases received after June 1, 2016.

2.2.2 Main Changes to the 2016 Rules

The main developments to the 2016 Rules relate to the following aspects②:

(1) Electronic submission of notices and other materials.

For a more facilitate and expedite proceedings, Article 2 of the 2016 Rules allows the parties to submit evidence and other written materials by electronic means which are recordable such as e-mail, fax, etc., and also allows the Court of Arbitration and the Secretariat to send notices in the

---

① For the revision process, see: 김대훈, 차경자: "대한상사중재원 중재규칙의 최근 개정내용에 관한 고찰", < 중재연구 >Vol.22, No. 3, March 2021.

② For the revision, see: 윤병철, 이병우 : "대한상사중재권 국제중재규칙개정에 관하여", < 중재 > No. 344 호, Fall Winter 2015; The KCAB: <2016 International Arbitration Rules>.

same way, but in order to avoid sending failures or errors, the address for electronic service shall be the address designated or agreed by the parties. However, when a party applies for arbitration, it cannot submit its Statement of Claim by electronic means, but is required to submit written materials and corresponding copies to the Secretariat (Article 8).

(2) Obligation of arbitrators to make statements voluntarily of the impartiality and independence.

Prior to the 2016 Rules was carried out, an arbitrator was only required to inform the Secretariat when accepting an appointment if he or she believed that he or she might have facts affecting impartiality or independence. However, Article 10 of the 2016 Rules provides that when accepting an appointment, an arbitrator shall sign his or her name to the Statement of Impartiality and Independence made by the KCAB, which in effect imposes a statement and informing obligation on the arbitrator, thereby raising the arbitrators' awareness of this issue.

(3) Determination of arbitrators.

The 2016 Rules vest the final authority for the determination of arbitrators in the Secretariat and, under article 13 of the 2016 Rules, the appointment of an arbitrator by the parties or the determination of the presiding arbitrator by two side arbitrators does not take effect until the Secretariat confirms the appointment. The previous regulation of the constitution of the arbitral tribunal provided that the appointment of an arbitrator took effect once the arbitrator had been appointed, which did not justify in the logic when the parties challenged the independence or impartiality of the arbitrator. The revision of this provision is to allow the Secretariat of the arbitral institution to discuss and decide on the challenge of an arbitrator.

(4) Joinder of additional parties.

When there are multiple parties to a dispute, it is more efficient if the dispute can be resolved in a single arbitration proceeding. The 2016 Rules provide for the joinder of additional parties. According to Article 21 of the Rules, the arbitral tribunal may allow third parties to be joined in the arbitration proceedings by application of a party, provided that (a) all parties and the additional party have all agreed in writing to the joinder of the additional party to the arbitration proceedings; or (b) the additional party is a party to the same arbitration agreement with the parties and the additional party has agreed in writing to the joinder in the arbitration proceedings. Besides, this shall not affect the constitution of the arbitral tribunal.

This provision also implies that the arbitral tribunal has the competence to determine whether to add a party or not. The provision that the addition of parties does not affect the composition of the arbitral tribunal is to prevent undue delay in the proceedings.

(5) Single arbitration under multiple contracts.

The 2016 Rules added provisions for consolidation of arbitration under multiple contracts. Pursuant to Article 22 of the Rules, the Secretariat may allow submission of claims arising out of multiple contracts within a single Request, provided that the Secretariat is prima facie satisfied that all of the contracts provide for arbitration under the Rules, the arbitration agreements' compatibility is recognized, and the claims arise out of the same transaction or series of transactions. The Secretariat shall appoint a sole emergency arbitrator.

(6) Emergency measures by emergency arbitrator.

According to the Appendix 3 of the 2016 Rules, a party seeking conservatory and interim measures may, concurrent with or following the submission of the Request but before constitution of the arbitral tribunal, apply in writing to the Secretariat for conservatory and interim measures by an emergency arbitrator. The Secretariat shall appoint a sole emergency arbitrator within two business days from its receipt of the application for Emergency Measures. Any party may challenge an emergency arbitrator to the Secretariat within two business days from the date on which the party receives the Notice of Appointment or the date on which the party becomes aware of the emergency arbitrator having grounds to challenge, and the Secretariat shall make a decision on the challenge. The emergency arbitrator may hold a hearing or proceed by a telephone conference and/or written submissions in lieu of a formal hearing to make emergency measures, and he or she the decision within 15 days from his or her appointment. The Emergency Measures shall be deemed to be conservatory and interim measures granted by the Arbitral Tribunal when it is constituted. The Emergency Measures shall remain in effect until the Arbitral Tribunal modifies, suspends or terminates such Emergency Measures. And the Emergency Measures shall no longer be effective, if: the Arbitral Tribunal is not constituted within 3 months of the decision granting the Emergency Measures; or the arbitration proceeding is terminated because the continuation of the arbitration proceedings has become unnecessary or impossible for any reason, such as withdrawal of the Request for Arbitration or failure to pay the Advance on Costs. The power of the emergency arbitrator shall be terminated upon constitution of the Arbitral Tribunal, and the emergency arbitrator may not act as the arbitrator in the same dispute, unless otherwise agreed by the parties.

The above are only the major changes or additions, and the 2016 Rules also amended in details. For example, in respect of consolidation of arbitration claims, the parties are expressly given the opportunity to submit statements of opinion (Article 23); provisions of withdrawal of arbitration claims are added to make it clear that if a party withdraws an arbitration claim after the statement of defense has been submitted, the arbitration claim can only be withdrawn with the consent of the respondent in order to protect the respondent's interests (Article 34); and the subject matter of the cases subject to the simplified procedures for arbitration has been increased from 200 million won to 500 million won (Article 43) and so on.

It is reported that in recent years, the KCAB has been working on further revisions to the 2016 Rules, and the Rule Revision Committee has been formally established in August 2022, and the revision program will be held in November 2023 for public hearings[①].

---

① https://www.hankyung.com/article/202311080881i, accessed Nov. 9, 2023.

Conclusion

It's almost five years after the implementation of the Basic Plan, and the goals initially envisaged has not reached from the results. In terms of hardware, the space of hearing rooms reduced in size; in aspect of the caseload, the number of international arbitration cases during the three-year epidemic has been on a downward trend. However, when talking about the improvement of the legal environment, the amendment of the Arbitration Act has realized the improvement of the legal system, and most of the relevant court cases and jurisprudence in recent years have been compliance with the advanced concept of arbitration, reflecting the purpose and spirit of creating an arbitration-friendly country.

Republic of Korea has not stop industrializing arbitration. The industry has attributed at least some of the reasons for the poor results of the industrialization program to the lack of financial support from the government, which has prevented the recruitment of high-quality personnel, and to the unreasonable set-up internal operating mechanisms of arbitration institutions. In response, the industry has put forward a number of suggestions and proposals. For example, it has been proposed that an independent corporation should operate the arbitration hearing facilities to maintain legal stability and certainty, and that of Republic of Korea should take full advantage of its geographic location to create differentiated legal services based on its civil law tradition, as opposed to common law[1]. The Ministry of Justice has also commissioned professors from law school and other experts to conduct a comparative law study on how to promote the industrialization of arbitration in the second half of 2022, with a focus on benchmarking the strengths of Singapore's arbitration industry and proposing improvement plans[2]. However, whether the purpose can be

---

[1] https://www.ajunews.com/view/20230319102825939, accessed Nov. 9, 2023.

[2] https://www.prism.go.kr/homepage/entire/researchDetail.do?researchId=1270000-202200083&menuNo=I0000002, accessed Nov. 9, 2023.

realized as expected in the policy of industrialization needs to be tested in practice.

Japan

The Examination of the Judicial Review of Arbitral Awards and the Application of Precedents by Japanese Judicial Authorities[*]

Introduction

With the continuous development of trade liberalism and trade multilateralism, cross-border investment, trade and economic cooperation have become increasingly frequent, and countries have formed a trend of mutual integration, inseparable and interdependence. The increasing volume of international economic exchanges has also led to frequent transnational commercial disputes. How to establish a dispute settlement mechanism that is fair, just, fast and efficient, and can be backed by the national judicial force to ensure the implementation is increasingly concerned and valued by international commercial subjects.

The transnational dispute resolution mechanism with the support of national judicial force to ensure execution mainly includes two methods, which are the judicial judgment and the international arbitration, for a civil dispute resolution. When judicial judgment is adopted as the method of dispute resolution, if both parties are residents in the country and their property is basically in the country, there is no obstacle to taking enforcement measures against their property in the country. However, when the

---

[*] The author is Wu Qiang, Senior Co Partner of Beijing DHH (Shanghai) Law Firm. Translated by Zhang Aoshuang.

other party of a transnational dispute and its property are in a foreign country, the jurisdiction and the effect of the judgment in the country cannot extend beyond the region. The enforcement of the domestic judgment in a foreign country depends on the mutual recognition and enforcement of foreign judgments signed between the two countries, or whether the principle of mutual recognition and enforcement of judicial judgments has been formed.

Specifically, China and Japan have not signed an agreement on mutual recognition and enforcement of foreign judgments, nor have they formed the principle of mutual recognition and enforcement of judicial judgments. The earliest and relatively typical refusal of China to recognize the enforcement of Japanese judgments was the Wu Weihuang case ruling made by the Dalian Intermediate People's Court, based on the reply of the Supreme People's Court to the Liaoning Higher People's Court on June 26, 1995.① The principle of non-recognition and non-enforcement of Japanese judgments established by the Supreme People's Court has been applied to this day, and no ruling to the contrary has ever been made. After that, the Japanese side also held that since Japan and China had not signed the agreement on mutual judicial assistance between the two countries, and, from the above-mentioned reply letters from the Dalian Intermediate People's Court and the Supreme People's Court showing that

---

① See the Reply Letter of the Supreme People's Court on Whether Chinese People's Courts should recognize and enforce the judgments of Japanese courts with creditor's rights and Debts, in which the Supreme People's Court clarified: "With regard to the application of Japanese national Wu Weihuang to the Dalian Intermediate People's Court for recognition and enforcement of the judgment of the Odawara Branch of the Yokohama District Court of Japan with creditor's rights and debts and the order of creditor's rights seizure and creditor's rights transfer made by the Tamina Branch of the Kumamoto District Court, whether the Chinese people's Court should recognize and enforce the issue, after research, China and Japan have not concluded or participated in international treaties on mutual recognition and enforcement of court judgments and rulings, nor have they established corresponding reciprocal relations. In accordance with Article 268 of the Civil Procedure Law of the People's Republic of China, the Chinese people's Court shall not recognize or enforce the judgment of the Japanese court." (1995) Minta No. 17).

Japanese judgments could not be recognized and enforced in China, Japan and China lacked the "mutual guarantee" required by Article 118 of the Japanese Civil Procedure Law, judgments made by Chinese courts should also not be recognized and enforced in Japan. On April 9, 2003, the Osaka High Court issued a judgment, first ruling that, "Due to the absence of the" mutual guarantee "requirement, the validity of the judgment made by the Chinese people's Court shall not be recognized in Japan". Subsequently, in response to the plaintiff's request for compulsory enforcement by the Tokyo District Court based on the judgment made by the Nanjing People's Court, which ordered Japanese authors and publishers to provide civil compensation for the infringement of the reputation of witnesses to the Nanjing Massacre, the Tokyo District Court followed the previous judgment of the Osaka High Court on April 9, 2003, and rejected the plaintiff's request for compulsory enforcement on the grounds that there was no mutual guarantee between Japan and Japan. Afterwards, the Tokyo High Court made a ruling to uphold the judgment of the Tokyo District Court and dismiss the appeal. On April 20, 2016, the Supreme Court of Japan also upheld the judgments of the Tokyo District Court and the Tokyo High Court, thus establishing the principle of non-recognition and enforcement of Chinese court judgments at the level of the Supreme Court of Japan.[①]

In view of the fact that there is no mutual judicial assistance agreement for the recognition and enforcement of judicial decisions or no reciprocal relationship for the mutual recognition and enforcement of judicial decisions between many countries, unless a lawsuit is filed in the country where the defendant is located, the commercial judgments made by the judicial authorities of the country where the plaintiff is located have obstacles that cannot be recognized and enforced by the judicial authorities of the country where the defendant is located. As a result, jurisdiction

---

① 村上幸隆「日中間における判決の承認・執行の現状と仲裁利用の際の留意点」(日中経協ジャーナル 277, page 31, February 2017).

is rarely used as a means of dispute resolution in cross-border transaction contracts. On the other hand, many States are parties to the New York Convention on the Recognition and Enforcement of Foreign Arbitral Awards (hereinafter referred to as the "1958 New York Convention"). Article 1 of the Convention provides that this Convention shall apply to the recognition and enforcement of an arbitral award arising out of a dispute between natural or legal persons and made in the territory of a State other than the State in which recognition and enforcement are claimed. This Convention shall also apply to arbitral awards which the State in which the claim is made for recognition and enforcement considers to be non-domestic. Article 3 of the Convention provides that each State Party shall recognize the arbitral award as binding and enforce it in accordance with the rules of procedure of the place where the award is invoked and with the conditions set out in the following articles. The recognition or enforcement of an arbitral award in the application of this Convention shall not be subject to unduly onerous conditions or impose excessive fees compared with the recognition or enforcement of an arbitral award of a State. In accordance with the above provisions of the 1958 New York Convention, States Parties to the Convention are obliged to recognize and enforce arbitral awards made by the arbitral institutions of other States Parties, thus providing a guarantee that arbitral awards made by the arbitral institutions of one State Party can be enforced by judicial force in other States Parties, so it has become a more common way for international commercial parties to resolve international commercial disputes through arbitration.

Both China and Japan are parties to the 1958 New York Convention (ratified by Japan in 1961 and by China in 1987), in accordance with which judicial judgments or orders for mutual recognition and enforcement of arbitral awards made by the other country's arbitration institutions already exist in China and Japan. This paper attempts to investigate the judicial review system of arbitral awards in Japan and the application of actual precedents, and explore the judicial standards for judicial review of arbitral awards in Japan, so as to provide references for Chinese enterprises to better use arbitration as a means of dispute resolution in their economic exchanges with Japan.

I. Summary of the Judicial Review System of Arbitral Awards by Japanese Judicial Organs

1.1 The Distinction Between Domestic and Foreign Arbitral Awards

The Arbitration Law of Japan was promulgated in August 2004 and came into force on March 1, 2005. Before the promulgation of the Arbitration Law, the recognition and enforcement of domestic arbitral awards were mainly governed by Articles 801 and 802 of the old Civil Procedure Law. After Japan acceded to and ratified the 1958 New York Convention in 1961, with respect to the recognition and enforcement of arbitral awards made by foreign arbitration institutions, the Japanese courts gave priority to the relevant provisions of the 1958 New York Convention in judicial review in accordance with the principle of respect for and priority application of international treaties established in Article 98, paragraph 2, of the Japanese Constitution. At the same time, the provisions of Articles 801 and 802 of the old Civil Procedure Law are allowed to apply. In the application of judicial precedents, Article 4 of the 1958 New York Convention is generally regarded as a positive element[1] and Article 5 of the

---

[1] Article 4 of the 1958 New York Convention reads as follows:
(1) obtain the recognition and enforcement mentioned in the preceding article, the party applying for recognition and enforcement shall, at the time of the application, supply:
(a) duly authenticated original award or a duly certified copy thereof;
(b) riginal agreement referred to in article II or a duly certified copy thereof.
(2) If the said award or agreement is not made in an official language of the country in which the award is relied upon, the party applying for recognition and enforcement of the award shall produce a translation of these documents into such language. The translation shall be certified by an official or sworn translator or by a diplomatic or consular agent.

1958 New York Convention as a negative element in the review,[1] that is, when the positive element of Article 4 is satisfied and there is no negative element of Article 5 that refuses to recognize and enforce, the foreign arbitral awards are recognized and enforced.[2] Before the promulgation and implementation of the Japanese Arbitration Law, in accordance with the above principles of judicial review, Japanese courts had recognized and enforced a number of arbitral awards made by Chinese arbitration institutions (mainly the China International Economic and Trade Arbitration

---

[1] Article 5 of the 1958 New York Convention reads as follows:

(1) Recognition and enforcement of the award may be refused, at the request of the party against whom it is invoked, only if that party furnishes to the competent authority where the recognition and enforcement is sought, proof that:

(a) The parties to the agreement referred to in article II were, under the law applicable to them, under some incapacity, or the said agreement is not valid under the law to which the parties have subjected it or, failing any indication thereon, under the law of the country where the award was made; or

(b) The party against whom the award is invoked was not given proper notice of the appointment of the arbitrator or of the arbitration proceedings or was otherwise unable to present his case; or

(c) The award deals with a difference not contemplated by or not falling within the terms of the submission to arbitration, or it contains decisions on matters beyond the scope of the submission to arbitration, provided that, if the decisions on matters submitted to arbitration can be separated from those not so submitted, that part of the award which contains decisions on matters submitted to arbitration may be recognized and enforced; or

(d) The composition of the arbitral authority or the arbitral procedure was not in accordance with the agreement of the parties, or, failing such agreement, was not in accordance with the law of the country where the arbitration took place; or

(e) The award has not yet become binding on the parties, or has been set aside or suspended by a competent authority of the country in which, or under the law of which, that award was made.

(2) Recognition and enforcement of an arbitral award may also be refused if the competent authority in the country where recognition and enforcement is sought finds that:

(a) The subject matter of the difference is not capable of settlement by arbitration under the law of that country; or

(b) The recognition or enforcement of the award would be contrary to the public policy of that country.

[2] 小島武司・高桑昭編『注釈と論点 仲裁法』(青林書院、2007 年)245-246 頁

Commission).①

Article 7, paragraph 1, of the 1958 New York Convention provides that nothing in this Convention shall affect the validity of multilateral or bilateral agreements between Contracting States concerning the recognition and enforcement of arbitral awards, nor shall it deprive any interested party of any right to invoke arbitral awards in a manner permitted by the law or treaty of the State in which the award is invoked, to the extent permitted by it. In 1974, Japan and China signed the Agreement on Trade between Japan and the People's Republic of China (hereinafter referred to as the "Japan-China Trade Agreement", which entered into force in the same year), Article 8 of which provides for the settlement of commercial contracts or disputes arising therefrom concluded between Japanese legal or natural persons and Chinese foreign trade institutions. Paragraph 4 of the article provides: "The two Contracting States shall, in respect of the arbitral award, comply with the terms and conditions stipulated in the laws of the State in which the application is sought, and the relevant authorities shall have the obligation to enforce it." It can be seen from the above provisions of Article 7 (1) of the 1958 New York Convention and Article 8 (4) of the Japan-China Trade Agreement that when a bilateral agreement on commercial arbitration is concluded between the two countries, the provisions of the bilateral agreement shall prevail over the 1958 New York Convention. The relationship between the 1958 New York Convention and the Japan-China trade Agreement can be understood as the relationship between general law and special law. And thus shall not affect the application of the agreement between the two countries. This view has been established in the judgments of Japanese courts recognizing and en-

---

① Representative cases include:岡山地裁平成五年七月十四日判決、東京地裁平成五年七月二〇日判決、東京地裁平成六年一月二七日判決、東京地裁平成七年六月十九日判決、横浜地裁平成十一年八月二五日判決、東京地裁平成一三年六月二〇日判決、大阪地裁平成二三年三月二五日決定等。介绍相关判决的文献请参考:吉野正三郎・斎藤明美「中国の仲裁判断の日本における承認と執行—最近の裁判例を中心に—」判例タイムズ861号24頁以下.

forcing the awards made by Chinese arbitral institutions[①]. Thus, in accordance with Article 8, paragraph 4, of the Japan-China Trade Agreement, for the application to the Japanese judicial authorities for recognition and enforcement of the arbitral award made by the Chinese arbitration institution, it can be interpreted as that the Japanese judicial authorities have the obligation to enforce the award in accordance with the conditions stipulated in the domestic law of Japan. In this regard, the Japanese academic community also believes that for the recognition of an arbitration award made by a foreign arbitration structure, the provisions of Article 45 of the Arbitration Law on the grounds for revocation can be directly invoked, and the grounds for revocation stipulated in the first paragraph of Article 45 are essentially not different from the negative grounds for non-recognition stipulated in Article 5 of the New York Convention of 1958.[②] After the promulgation and implementation of the Japanese Arbitration Law, the Article 3 (3), the rules in Chapter 8 (that is, the recognition and enforcement decision of the arbitration award) that apply for arbitration seated domestically or abroad, and Article 45 (1) of the Arbitration Law stipulates that the arbitration award (whether the place of arbitration is in Japan or not, the following sections are the same) has the same effect as the definitive award. However, in the case of civil enforcement based on the arbitral award, the enforcement decision shall be made in accordance with the next article of Article 45. These two provisions make it clear that the procedures of recognition and enforcement for domestic arbitral awards in Japan and foreign arbitration award are identical, and the legal basis for recognition and enforcement of arbitral awards made by foreign arbitral institutions can be the relevant provisions of the Arbitration Law of Japan directly.

---

① 横浜地裁平成十一年八月二五日判決, 判例タイムズ 1053 号 269 頁 .], and has received theoretical support [小島武司・高桑昭編「注釈と論点 仲裁法」(青林書院、2007年)267頁.

② 高杉直「日本における外国判決および外国仲裁判断の承認・執行」(法政論集 2018 年 276 号 416 頁).

In view of the above, except to the foreign arbitral awards that the Japanese Arbitration Law expressly does not apply to, the relevant provisions of the Japanese Arbitration Law on recognition and enforcement of arbitral awards in Japan and foreign arbitral awards are applicable to both domestic and foreign arbitral awards in Japan, and through the following review of the provisions on recognition and enforcement of arbitral awards in Japan Law, it can be concluded that there is no essential difference between the requirements for recognition and enforcement of arbitral awards stipulated in the Japanese Arbitration Law and the positive requirements stipulated in Article 4 and the negative requirements stipulated in Article 5 of the 1958 New York Convention. Therefore, it is of no practical significance to distinguish the differences between the recognition and enforcement of arbitral awards made in Japan and foreign counties. Therefore, the following paragraph is an examination to the judicial review system of arbitral awards in Japan by judicial organs, focusing on the provisions of the Japanese Arbitration Law.

1.2 Summary of the Judicial Review System of Arbitral Awards by Japanese Judicial Organs

According to the relevant provisions of the Arbitration Law of Japan, judicial review of arbitral awards mainly includes three aspects: the cancellation of arbitral awards, the recognition of arbitral awards, and the enforcement of arbitral awards.

1.2.1 Cancellation of Arbitral Awards

Chapter 7 of the Japanese Arbitration Law provides for the cancellation of arbitral awards. Paragraph 1 of Article 44 of the Arbitration Law first stipulates that the cancellation of an arbitral award shall be initiated upon the application of the parties to the arbitration and then stipulates the specific reasons for the cancellation of an arbitral award. That is, the first paragraph of this article provides that a party may apply to the court for revoking an arbitral award if:

(a) An arbitration agreement is invalid due to the capacity of the parties;

(b) The arbitration agreement is invalid for reasons other than the limitation of the parties' capacity, in accordance with the law appointing the arbitration agreement to which the parties have agreed (in the absence of such stipulation, it shall be Japanese law);

(c) The applicant has not received the necessary notice during the arbitrator selection procedure and the arbitration procedure according to the Japanese law (if there is an agreement between the parties on matters not covered by the public order provisions of the law, the agreement shall apply);

(d) where the applicant is unable to defend itself in the arbitration proceedings;

(e) The arbitral award contains contents of the award on matters beyond the scope of application in the arbitration agreement or arbitration proceedings;

(f) The composition of the arbitral tribunal or the arbitration procedure violates Japanese laws and regulations (if there is an agreement between the parties on matters not related to public order in the laws, the agreement shall apply);

(g) The application in the arbitral proceedings is about a dispute that cannot be the subject of an arbitration agreement according to Japanese law;

(h) The contents of the arbitral award are contrary to the public order and good customs of Japan.

This article also provides for the time limit for the parties to file a request for cancellation of the arbitral award (paragraph 2 of Article 44, that is, three months after the date of the notice of service of the copy of the arbitral award or when the decision is made in accordance with Article 46), an immediate appeal system (Article 44, paragraphs 4 and 8), the system of oral debate and cross-examination period for both parties to appear in court in general civil proceedings (Article 44, paragraph 5), as well as the system of burden of proof and the doctrine of authority (Article 44, paragraph 6, that is, for the reasons listed in paragraphs 1 to 6 of paragraph 1, the court can only cancel an arbitral award if the parties prove the existence of the reasons. And for the reasons listed in paragraphs 7 to 8 of the first paragraph, the court may revoke it according to the exercise of its powers).

In addition, it should be noted that the cancellation of arbitral awards does not apply to arbitral awards made by foreign arbitration institutions. It only applies to arbitral awards seated in Japan, including arbitral awards made by foreign arbitration institutions in Japan. The main consideration is that judicial review of the cancellation of an arbitral award made by a foreign arbitral institution belongs to the jurisdiction of the judicial organ of the arbitration place, and the jurisdiction of the Japanese courts cannot extend beyond the region, preventing the legal effect of the arbitral award outside the region. If a Japanese court does not recognize and enforce an award made by a foreign arbitral institution, it is sufficient to prevent the foreign arbitral award from taking legal effect in Japan. Therefore, Japanese law can not and do not need to regulate the cancellation of foreign arbitral awards. Therefore, Article 3, paragraph 1, of the Arbitration Law stipulates that Chapter VII (cancellation of an arbitral award) shall apply to situations where the place of arbitration is in Japan. Among the reasons for non-enforcement of an arbitral award provided for in Article 45, paragraph 2, paragraph 7, it also clarifies the decision of refusing to enforce an arbitral award when it is revoked by the judicial authority of the country to which the arbitral award belongs. In accordance with the above provisions, the application for the cancellation of an arbitration award made by a foreign arbitral institution in Japan will be rejected by the Japanese court. It can be seen that the cancellation of an international arbitral award is under the exclusive jurisdiction of the judicial organ of the country where the arbitration is seated, which has become a universally recognized rule internationally.[①]

1.2.2 Recognition and Enforcement of Arbitral Awards

Chapter VIII of the Japanese Arbitration Law provides for the recognition and enforcement of arbitral awards. Article 45 of the Law stipulates the procedures for recognition of arbitral awards. According to paragraph 1 of Article 45, unless there exists any cause for refusal of recognition specified in paragraph 2 of that article, it shall have the same effect as the final award when it becomes effective at the place of arbitration, that is, it shall be automatically recognized as effective within Japan. The doctrine of automatic recognition is also adopted in Article 118 of the Civil Procedure Law. Without the need for the parties to file an application for recognition of the arbitral award, they may request the court to make an application for enforcement of the decision. Although Article 118 of the Civil Procedure Law and Article 1, paragraph 3, of the 1958 New York Convention adopt the principle of mutualism, Chapter VIII of the Japanese Arbitration Law does not adopt the principle of mutualism, distinguishing the arbitral awards seated in Japan from the arbitral awards seated in foreign countries. Therefore, in accordance with the provisions of Chapter VIII of the Arbitration Law, even arbitral awards made by countries or regions that have not acceded to the 1958 New York Convention can be recognized and enforced in Japan (such as arbitral awards made in Taiwan).[②]

Paragraph 2 of Article 45 provides for the reasons for the exclusion of the arbitral award automatically having the same effect as the definitive award (i.e. the reasons for refusal of recognition). By comparing the reasons for the exclusion of recognition provided for in Article 45 (2) with the reasons for revocation provided for in Article 44 (1), it can be seen that the reasons for non-recognition of the arbitral award and the reasons for cancellation are basically the same. That is, items 1 to 6 of the second

---

① 小島武司・高桑昭編『注釈と論点 仲裁法』(青林書院、2007 年)252-253 頁.
② 高杉直「日本における外国判決および外国仲裁判断の承認・執行」(法政論集 2018 年 276 号 417 頁).

paragraph of Article 45 are the same as items 1 to 6 of the first paragraph of Article 44, and items 8 and 9 of the second paragraph of Article 45 are the same as items 7 and 8 of the first paragraph of Article 44 respectively (for the provisions of items 2, 3 and 6 of the two articles, since the Japanese judicial organs do not need to revoke the review of arbitral awards made in accordance with foreign laws on foreign places of arbitration, the wording of Article 44 "the law of Japan", and the wording of Article 45 "the law of the country where the arbitration is located" is different only in the context of the wording, and there is no difference in substance). The only difference between the two articles is the Article 45, paragraph 2, paragraph 7, that provides for "where the arbitral award has not been determined according to the law of the country where the arbitration place is located (the law of a country other than the country where the arbitration place is located is the law of that country), or the arbitral award has been revoked by the judicial authority of the country where the arbitral award is located, or its effect has ceased". As mentioned above, an arbitral award made at a foreign arbitration place is not itself subject to review by the judicial authorities of Japan, and the jurisdiction for its effect belongs to the judicial authorities of the country where the arbitration place is located, so it is necessary to add the provisions of Article 45, paragraph 2, paragraph 7, to the recognition of foreign arbitral awards. That is, if the arbitral award has already been cancelled by the judicial organ of the country where the arbitration place is located or has no legal effect, it can no longer be recognized and enforced by the judicial organ of Japan.

Paragraph 3 of Article 45 provides for the handling of the arbitration award contained in paragraph 1 (5) which exceeds the scope of application in the arbitration agreement and arbitration proceedings, that is, if part of the same provision can be distinguished from the arbitration award, this part and other parts of the arbitration award shall be regarded as separate arbitral awards and the provisions of this paragraph shall apply. The contents of the award that do not exceed the scope of application in the arbitration agreement and arbitration proceedings shall be recognized and enforced after being limited. This is exactly the same as the principle of paragraph 7 of Article 44 focuing on the paragraph 1(5), that when an award including exceeded the scope of application in the arbitration agreement and arbitration proceedings, which can be distinguished, the exceeded part can be cancelled only.

Article 46 of the Arbitration Law provides for the procedures for the execution of an arbitral award. Paragraph 1 of Article 46 provides that a party wishing to carry out civil enforcement on the basis of an arbitral award and the respondent being the debtor may file an application with the court for enforcement of the decision. Paragraph 8 of this article stipulates the conditions for refusal of enforcement, that is, if the court considers that an application for enforcement of a decision made in paragraph 1 has one of the reasons listed in paragraph 2 of the preceding article (that is, the reasons excluded from recognition provided for in paragraph 2 of Article 45, the reasons listed in paragraphs 1 to 7 of this paragraph are limited to proof by the respondent of the existence of such reasons), the application for enforcement of a decision may be rejected. The conditions of refusal to enforce the decision in this article directly invoke the conditions of the second paragraph of Article 45 on the exclusion of recognition of arbitral awards, and as mentioned above, the conditions of the refusal of recognition of arbitral awards in the second paragraph of Article 45 are basically the same as the conditions of the cancellation of arbitral awards in the first paragraph of Article 44. Therefore, the elements of the refusal to enforce the decision are essentially identical with the elements of the refusal to recognize and revoke the arbitral award.

This article also provides for the procedure of suspension of enforcement (Article 46, paragraph 3), that is, when an application for cancellation or suspension of the effect of an arbitral award is made to the court and the court deems it necessary, the application for enforcement provided for in paragraph 1 May be suspended, but the court may order the applicant for suspension to provide security to the other party; It provides for the jurisdiction of the application for an enforcement decision and the transfer of jurisdiction (Article 46, paragraphs 4 and 5), that is, the enforcement decision has the exclusive jurisdiction of the court provided in Article 5 and of the court having jurisdiction over the place where the debtor's property may be seized according to the purpose of the request, and the court where the jurisdiction of may, if deemed necessary, acting on the application or ex parte, transfer the whole or part of the case to another court; It provides for an immediate system of protest against jurisdictional decisions (article 46, paragraph 6) and an immediate system of protest against enforcement decisions (article 46, paragraph 10, with the use of Article 44, paragraph 8); It provides for the application of oral debate in general civil proceedings and the cross-examination period system for both parties to appear in court (Article 46, paragraph 10, may use the provisions of Article 44, paragraph 5); It provides that when the arbitral award contains the content of the award beyond the scope of application in the arbitration agreement and arbitration proceedings and the exceeded part can be distinguished from the non-exceeded part, the content of the award that does not exceed the scope of application in the arbitration agreement and arbitration proceedings can be limited before execution (Article 46, paragraph 9, shall be applicable to the provisions of Article 45, paragraph 3).

1.2.3 Classification of the Reasons for Cancellation, Non-recognition and Non-enforcement of Arbitral Awards

As mentioned above, the elements of refusal to enforce a decision are essentially identical with those of refusal to recognize or revoke an arbitral award, and the elements of refusal to recognize or revoke an arbitral award can be roughly classified on the basis of the provisions of the exceptions for recognition of an arbitral award listed in paragraph 2 of Article 45.

In the second paragraph of Article 45 of the Arbitration Law, a total of nine reasons for refusing to recognize an arbitral award are listed, which can be roughly classified as follows:

First, the reasons for the validity of the arbitration agreement (Items 1 and 2) and the reasons for the arbitration award to contain contents beyond the scope of the arbitration agreement or arbitration application (Items 5). If the arbitration agreement is not valid, it shall, of course, be a cause for refusal of recognition. This is because the arbitration system itself, as a mechanism for civil dispute settlement, is based on the arbitration agreement between the parties and the principle of autonomy of the parties' will to resolve the matter in dispute. The applicable law to judge the validity of an arbitration agreement shall be the law designated by the parties (in the absence of such a designation, it shall be the law of the country where the arbitration place is located). However, the applicable law concerning the capacity of the parties shall, in accordance with the basic principles of international justice, be the domestic law when the parties are natural persons and the law of the place of establishment when they are legal persons in principle . As for items 5 the arbitral award which contains matters beyond the scope of the arbitration agreement or the application for arbitration, the award on the matters beyond the scope of the arbitration agreement is equivalent to the absence of an arbitration agreement and the reason for not recognizing and enforcing the arbitral award is that the award on the matters beyond the scope of the arbitration agreement lacks the consent of the parties to initiate arbitration.

Second, the reasons for the integrity of arbitration proceedings (Items 3, 4 and 6). Although the arbitration system, as a civil dispute settlement mechanism, cedes the means of dispute resolution to the autonomy of the parties, it must also ensure the proper and fair conduct of the arbitration procedure, that is, the integrity of the arbitration procedure. If there are major defects in the arbitration procedure, such as the failure to give proper notice to the parties, the inability of the parties to defend themselves in the arbitration procedure, or the illegality of the composition of the arbitral tribunal and the arbitration procedure itself, it will certainly be the grounds for refusing to recognize the arbitral award.

Third, the reasons why an arbitral award is not valid (Item 7). That is, if the arbitral award has not been determined according to the laws of the country where the arbitration place is located, or if the arbitral award has been revoked by the judicial authority of the country where the arbitration place is located, it will certainly have no effect in Japan and become a cause for refusal of recognition of the arbitral award.

Fourth, the causes of disputes that are not eligible for arbitration agreement under Japanese law and the causes that violate Japanese public order and good customs (Items 8 and 9). That is, certain disputes (such as the merits of artistic value, the validity of patent rights) are not eligible subjects of arbitration agreement under Japanese law, and arbitration awards made on these matters are refused to be recognized and enforced. Violation of Japanese public order and good customs means that the arbitral award is incompatible with the basic legal order of Japan. If an arbitral award is found by the court to be in violation of Japanese public order and good customs, it shall be grounds for refusing to recognize and enforce the arbitral award. For example, if perjury is committed in the arbitration proceedings, or the arbitrator has accepted bribes, and the fairness of the arbitral award is seriously affected, it may be refused to recognize and enforce as a violation of public order and good customs.[①] With regard to the grounds for refusal to recognize or enforce an arbitration award that violates public order and good customs, even if the parties have not made a claim and provided evidence, the court may still investigate in accordance with its functions and powers.

---

① 唐津恵一「仲裁判断が手続的公序に反するとして取り消された事例」ジュリスト 1447 号 109 頁.

II. The Application of Judicial Review in the Judicial Precedents of Arbitral Awards by Japanese Judicial Organs

The following are two cases of judicial review of arbitral awards by Japanese judicial organs. By examining the above categories of judicial organs' discretion standards for revoking, refusing to recognize and enforcing arbitral awards, we will explore how discretion standards for refusing to recognize and enforce arbitral awards are held and applied in judicial practice by Japanese judicial organs.

2.1 Tokyo District Court Decision of July 28, 2010 (X Co., Ltd. vs. American International Underwriters, Ltd., Application for Revocation of Arbitral Award)[①]

2.1.1 Summary of the Case

In 1998, Company A, a semiconductor manufacturer in Taiwan, purchased a semiconductor manufacturing device manufactured and sold by Company X for the operation of a semiconductor factory. Due to the defect of the semiconductor manufacturing equipment manufactured and sold by Company X, the factory of Company A suffered a fire and was completely damaged. Company A made fire claims with three insurance companies and received insurance money from Company Y, a reinsurer. Company Y paid Company A and obtained a subrogation against Company X. Then Company Y, based on the arbitration agreement reached with Company X, filed an arbitration to the American Arbitration Association seated in Japan and requested Company X to compensate for the loss. The arbitration institution made an arbitration award on July 14, 2009, partially supporting the arbitration claim of Company Y on the grounds that (1) Company X violated the equipment warning obligation, and (2) the violation of the warning obligation had a considerable degree of causal

---

① 東京地決平成 21 年 7 月 28 日判例タイムズ 1304 号 292 頁.

relationship with the fire.

X Company refused to accept the arbitration award and filed a petition with the Tokyo District Court to revoke the arbitration award. The reasons for rescission are as follows: (1) Company Y did not claim breach of the duty of warning in the arbitration proceedings of the case, but the arbitration award found Company X's responsibility on this ground, so the award was made on the basis of reasons that Company X could not defend; (2) Taking Taiwan Law as the applicable law, the claim of applicant Y Company can hardly be recognized, but the arbitration award found that the existence of the warning obligation and the violation of the warning obligation and the damage have a considerable degree of causal relationship, and ordered a huge amount of compensation. The content of the award violates the public order and good customs of Japan; And (3) the arbitration procedure of the arbitration award in this case violates the arbitration agreement between the parties.

2.1.2 The Gist of the Court's Decision

The application filed by X Company to set aside the arbitration award is rejected. The main reasons are as follows:

First, in view of X Company's point (1), the court held that: The interest set forth in paragraph 1 (4) of Article 44 of the Arbitration Law shall be interpreted as limiting the cancellation of an arbitration award to cases of serious violation of procedural safeguards, such as making it impossible for the parties to be present to cross-examine the proceedings, making an award based on information that the parties are completely unaware of, and giving the parties little opportunity to defend themselves. In the arbitration procedure of this case, Company Y has asserted the violation of Company X's warning obligation and the causal relationship with the result of damage. Therefore, only the circumstances that the parties did not recognize it as an important issue cannot be regarded as meeting the grounds for revocation.

Secondly, in view of X Company's second reason for revocation, the court held that: In view of Article 4 of the Arbitration Law, which provides that arbitration proceedings are limited to the Arbitration Law and that the court may exercise its powers, the arbitral award shall be respected to the maximum extent, and the purpose of paragraph 1 (8) of Article 44 of the Arbitration Law shall not be interpreted as meaning that the court may revoke an arbitral award only when the finding of fact or legal judgment made by the arbitral tribunal is deemed unreasonable. Instead, it should be interpreted to mean that the court may revoke an arbitral award only when it considers that the legal result achieved by the arbitral award is contrary to the public order and good customs of Japan. Company X believes that the award of a huge amount of compensation for the violation of the duty of warning and the causal relationship between the award and the result of damage violates the public order and good customs of Japan. This is only a claim that the arbitral tribunal in this case made unreasonable facts and legal judgments, and could not find special reasons other than a huge amount of compensation. Therefore, it cannot be regarded as a violation of the public order and good customs of Japan for the legal result achieved by the arbitral award.

Third, regarding X Company's reason for cancellation (3), the court held that: This claim is made by X Company three months after the receipt of the arbitration award. After the application for the cancellation of the arbitration award, as long as the time limit stipulated in paragraph 2 of Article 44 of the Arbitration Law is exceeded, the new claim for the addition of items 1 to 6 of paragraph 1 of the same article violates the provisions of paragraph 2 of the same article and cannot be recognized. This is because such an act will have the result of preventing the early determination of the arbitral award.

2.1.3 Investigation

In this case, the court made a decision on whether the grounds for cancellation of arbitration proposed by the applicant conform to the provisions of Article 44, paragraph 1, item 4 of the Arbitration Law that the parties could not defend themselves in the arbitration proceedings, Article 44, paragraph 1, item 8 stipulated that the violation of Japanese public order and good customs , and to the provisions of Article 44, paragraph 2 stipulated that whether the addition of new grounds for cancellation after the expiration of the period for cancellation. In its decision on the application for cancellation of the arbitral award in this case, the court limited the indefensible causes provided for in paragraph 1 (4) of Article 44 to a serious breach of procedural safeguards and the probability that such breach would affect the outcome of the arbitral award; The violation of Japanese public order and good customs stipulated in paragraph 1 (8) of Article 44 is limited to the violation of Japanese public order and good customs as a result of the arbitral award, rather than the unreasonableness of the determination of arbitral facts or legal judgment; The time limit for refiling the causes in item 1 to 6 of paragraph 1 of Article 44 shall also be limited to three months from the date of receipt of the arbitration award as provided in item 2 of that article. The court's judgment on the above three points has no precedent before, and the court has indicated the judgment standards on the above issues, which has reference and enlightenment significance in judicial practice.①

2.2 Tokyo District Court Decision of June 13, 2012 (X Co., Ltd. vs. Y US Legal Entity, Request for revocation of arbitration award event)②

2.2.1 Summary of the Case

X Corporation, a Japanese corporation, operates a joint venture to manufacture and sell products in Japan using the patented technology (Japanese patent) of glass production from blast furnace slag owned by Y Corporation, an American corporation. As X has not paid Y the technical

---

① 東京地決平成 21 年 7 月 28 日判例タイムズ 1304 号 293 頁.
② 高橋一章「仲裁廷における仲裁判断が仲裁法 44 条 1 項 8 号に反すると判断された事例」(東京地決平成 23 年 6 月 13 日)、ジュリスト 1456 号 152 頁.

service fee since 2006 and has requested a reappraisal of the technical service fee, it cannot reach an agreement with Y on this matter. Therefore, X notified Y that the contract was invalid or terminated, and Y filed an arbitration to the Japan Commercial Arbitration Association with X as the respondent on December 16, 2009, and the arbitral tribunal made an arbitration award supporting Y's request for X to pay the technical service fee.

X is not satisfied with the arbitration award and files a petition with the Tokyo District Court to revoke the arbitration award. The reason for the cancellation is that, although the technical service fee was not recognized as the distribution of benefits of the joint venture in the arbitration procedure of this case, the arbitral tribunal regarded it as an undisputed fact finding and made an arbitration award. If the arbitral tribunal had made an exact fact finding of the nature of the technical service fee, it would have reached a completely different conclusion. Therefore, the arbitral award unduly infringes X's defense interests, hinders the protection of X's proper procedures and the protection of X's right to accept the hearing, and violates the public order and good customs in the procedures of Article 44, Paragraph 1(8), of the Arbitration Law. It should be revoked according to Article 44, paragraph 1(8).

2.2.2 The Gist of the Court's Decision

The court acknowledge X Company's application for setting aside the arbitration award. The main reasons are as follows:

First of all, from the perspective of the provisions of the Arbitration Law on arbitration procedures and its interest, when the arbitration procedure violates the public order of the procedure in Japan, the content of the arbitration award made according to the procedure cannot bear the procedure consistent with the public order of the procedure, so it violates the basic legal order in Japan and cannot be recognized as the effect of dispute settlement with the guarantee of state compulsory force. Secondly, according to the Japanese law, the obligation to restrict the use of the technology or pay the implementation license fee for the implementation of the technology after the expiration of the patent right is an unfair transaction, which is likely to be an illegal act under the anti-monopoly law. Since the illegal act under the anti-monopoly law also violates the public order and good customs and is likely to be invalid, the determination of the nature of the technology service fee is equivalent to an important matter affecting the main text of the arbitration award. The arbitration award in this case regards the nature of the technical service fee, which is an important matter affecting the main text of the arbitration award in dispute between the parties, as an undisputed fact and no longer makes a judgment, which violates the public order of the formalities in our country and should be interpreted as equivalent to the cancellation of Article 44, paragraph 1(8).

2.2.3 Investigation

The circumstances in which the arbitration award in this case affirms the disputed facts as undisputed facts are roughly similar to those in the previous case in which the parties did not claim breach of the duty of warning and the arbitral tribunal determined the liability of the other party, both of which belong to the arbitral tribunal's determination of the specific facts of the case. However, as to whether the two arbitral awards belong to the discretionary judgment of Article 44, paragraph 1(8) of the revocation against the Japanese public order, the decision made a completely different decision from the revocation of the arbitration award in the previous case. This decision, as the first decision made by a Japanese court to revoke an arbitral award, has attracted wide attention and caused great repercussions in the Japanese academic community. There are not a few scholars who oppose the reasons and thrust of the decision. The main reasons for opposing the decision are as follows: As a matter of Article 44, paragraph 1(8), should be interpreted as limited to the content of the arbitral award is contrary to public order, which is fully compatible with the procedural violation of the provisions of paragraphs 3, 4 and 6 of the same paragraph, and the application of this provision as a procedural matter to an arbitral award where a disputed fact is recognized as an undisputed fact is questionable. It is possible to apply this provision only if it is defined as a content judgment. And when the court applies the relevant grounds for rescinding Article 44 as a matter of procedure, it can only be applied when the arbitral tribunal completely disregards the claims of a party and a party commits a breach of procedural safeguards to a significant degree, such as fraud, perjury or bribery of the arbitrator. Even if there are errors in the determination of facts or the application of law in the original arbitral award, it should not be a cause for rescission of the award. Therefore, even if the arbitral tribunal did not determine the nature of the technical service fee as an issue and made the award, and there are inadequacies in the arbitral award, the cancellation of the award on the ground of a breach of public order in formalities is deeply questionable.[①]

Conclusion

It can be seen from the above investigation on the outline of the judicial review system of arbitral awards by Japanese judicial organs and the application of cases, that after the promulgation and implementation of the Arbitration Law of Japan, the recognition and enforcement of arbitral awards by Japanese judicial organs will no longer distinguish between domestic arbitral awards and foreign arbitral awards, and the provisions of Articles 45 and 46 of the Arbitration Law of Japan shall apply to both. And the reasons for refusing to recognize and enforce arbitral awards are essentially the same as the reasons for revocation stipulated in Article 44.

Although there are relatively rare precedents for the Japanese judicial organs to make a decision to revoke an arbitral award, so far any other court decision to revoke an arbitral award in public publications has

---

① 唐津恵一「仲裁判断が手続的公序に反するとして取り消された事例」ジュリスト 1447 号 110 頁.

not been found, nor has any case of revoking a foreign arbitral award via a search. On the whole, the Japanese judicial authorities have strictly adopted the criteria for judicial review of arbitral awards to revoke arbitral awards, so as to avoid undermining the basic mechanism for international dispute settlement of arbitral awards and undermining the trustworthiness of the parties to use arbitration as a final means of dispute settlement through autonomy of will. This is the same as China's interest in maintaining the trustworthiness of international arbitral awards by adopting stricter review procedures for the refusal to recognize and enforce foreign arbitral awards.[①] At present, the economic exchanges and cooperation between Chinese and Japanese enterprises are becoming more frequent, and commercial disputes are becoming more frequent. In view of the obstacles to the extraterritorial enforcement of judicial judgments under the jurisdiction of courts, the parties who are the subject of international commercial matters will more often agree on arbitration as a means of dispute resolution, and it is expected that international arbitration will play a greater role in the dispute resolution mechanism.

---

① According to the Notice of the Supreme People's Court of the People's Republic of China on the Handling of Issues Related to Foreign Arbitration and Foreign Arbitration Matters by People's Courts (Revised in 2008), refusal to recognize and enforce foreign arbitration must be submitted by the High People's Court to the Supreme People's Court for a reply since it can be made.

Study on the Expansion of the Validity of Arbitration Agreements Concluded in the Name of a Group Company

Zeng Yujie[*]

Abstract: With the deepening of economic globalization and the increasingly diverse organizational forms of international economic exchanges, the subject of disputes in arbitration cases is no longer limited to the parties to the contract. In the practice of international commercial arbitration, the validity of the arbitration agreement has been conditionally expanded to a third party. In a foreign-related maritime arbitration case, the claimant filed an application for arbitration on the basis of an arbitration agreement concluded in the name of a group company, and the respondent raised a jurisdictional objection on the ground that the claimant was not a signatory to the arbitration agreement, and a dispute arose between the parties over the jurisdiction of the arbitration institution. Taking this case as the starting point, this paper intends to focus on the agency theory, the company group theory and the principle of fair and reasonable expectations, combine domestic and foreign judicial practice cases, analyze the theoretical application of the extension of the validity of arbitration agreements in the name of group companies to unsigned members within the framework of China's current legal system, and put

[*] L.L.M, Dalian Maritime University, Practice lawyer of Guangdong Lvfang Law Firm.

forward suggestions for improving the legal system for expanding the validity of arbitration agreements in China on this basis.

Keywords: Group Company; Arbitration Agreement; Validity Expansion

I. Basic Facts

Group S entered into a Cargo Shipping Agency Contract (hereinafter referred to as "Contract") with Company C, a company registered in the United States (U.S.), and it is agreed in the preamble of the Contract that the Contract is concluded by Group S, on behalf of its subsidiaries/branches listed in Annex3, with Company C for the purpose of freight forwarding to various ports in the U.S. Simultaneously, the parties agreed that disputes arising from this contract should be submitted to the China Maritime Arbitration Commission (CMAC).

Company H is a subsidiary of Group S engaging in shipping and forwarding agency business in Southern China. In 2019, Company T signed a contract, namely Shipping (Export Agency) Contract with Company H entrusting Company H to handle cargo-export related business. It is agreed in the aforementioned contract that Company H shall bear the full liability where the goods are stolen or the ownership hereof is inappropriately transferred without due reasons of the Company T. Subsequently, Company H entrusted Company C with the cargo shipping and forwarding issues in the U.S. ports on the basis of the Contract between Group S and Company C.

After the goods in question arrived at POD, they were transferred to the designated inspection yard due to the inspection notification by the U.S. Customs, the cargo, however was stolen while waiting for inspection. Given the arbitration agreement incorporated in the Contract, Company H, upon making compensation to Company T, filed an application for arbitration to claim damages from Company C. Prior to the first hearing of the arbitral tribunal, Company C demurred to the jurisdiction arguing that there was no arbitration agreement between them, therefore, Company H had no right over initiating the arbitration.

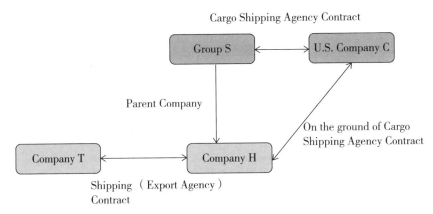

Figure 1　Sketch Map of the Subject Case

II. Problems Raised

The so-called expansion of the validity of the arbitration agreement refers to the valid arbitration agreement under the situation where, the arbitration agreement is presumed to be binding upon the signatory, who is also presumed to have the intention of arbitration, rather than rights and obligations being deferred from *de facto* behaviors of the signatory's[①]. In 2000, the UNCITRAL Working Group on Arbitration, at its 32nd Session, considered a number of typical examples in arbitration practice. The Session Report considered that the validity of an arbitration agreement could be extended to third parties besides the signatories to the contract in the following circumstances where: 1. due to the expansive interpretation by an arbitral tribunal or court of the formal elements of the arbitration

---

① Zhang Xianda, "Research on Legal Issues of Expansion of International Commercial Arbitration Agreements," 2018 Doctoral Degree Dissertation, Dalian Maritime University, pp. 18-19.

agreement; 2. Transfer of a bill of lading; 3. Third-party beneficiary contract; 4. Agency; 5. Contract assignment; 6. Debts discharged on behalf; 7. Mergers or separation of a legal person; 8. Related parties or connected transactions; 9. Theory of the group company①. Although the above report has no legal binding force under the international legal framework, it reflects an important trend in the expansion of arbitration agreement. In the course of research since then, the theories of the expansion of arbitration agreement have been divided into two main categories: first, civil law theories, which mainly include the principle of equitable estoppel, the principle of fair and reasonable expectation, the principle of good faith, the theory of agency, and the principle of third-party-beneficiary; And second, corporate law theories, which mainly include the principle of piercing the corporate veil and the theory of group company.

Compared to the theory and practices of international commercial arbitration, there relatively, remains a loophole in the current legal norms on the expansion of the validity of the arbitration agreement in China. Under Arbitration Law of the People's Republic of China (hereinafter referred to as "China Arbitration Law"), there is no stipulation that provides the expansion of the validity of the arbitration agreement. The relevant judicial interpretation of the arbitration agreement provides for the expansion of the validity in the following applicable circumstances, i.e., party merges or separates after committing to an arbitration agreement; Inheritance after death of the party; Assignment, in whole or in part, of claims and debts②; Subrogation of non-foreign-related insurer③. With the rapid advancement of eco-

---

① See Report of the Secretary-General on Possible Uniform Rules for the Settlement of Certain Questions relating to Commercial Disputes: Conciliation, Interim Measures of Protection, Written Forms of Arbitration Agreements, Document No. A.CN.9/WG. II/WP.108/Add.1. at 32nd Session of UNCITRAL Arbitration Working Group.

② See Art 8&9, Interpretation of the Supreme People's Court on Certain Issues Concerning the Application of the Arbitration Law of the People's Republic of China.

③ See Art 98, Minutes of the National Courts' Civil and Commercial Trial Work Conference.

nomic globalization and the great changes in the organizational forms and business models of modern enterprises, a series of new organizational forms emerged, such as group companies and supply chain partners. Among them, the emergence of enterprise group management has brought new challenges to the traditional arbitration legal system. The contract signed between the group company and the contractual counter-party includes an arbitration agreement, and whether other members under the same group company, the non-signatory of the arbitration agreement, shall be bound by the arbitration agreement has become a prerequisite for the resolution of modern commercial disputes. This article will focus on the agency theory, the group company theory and the doctrine of fair and reasonable expectation, which are most closely related to the expansion of the validity of the arbitration agreement of group company, and analyze the relevant domestic and international judicial practice cases.

III. Analysis of the Application of Theory to the Expansion of the Validity of Arbitration Agreements Concluded in the Name of a Group Company

3.1 Expansion of the Validity of Arbitration Agreements Based on Theory of Agency

The expansion of the validity of the arbitration agreement applies to a non-signatory if such non-signatory has always been the substantive party to the arbitration agreement. It usually emerges in the context of principal-agent relationship. Generally speaking, the essence of the agency relationship is that the agent concludes and performs the contract upon the interests of the principal's, and the legal consequences are subsequently borne by the principal. Therefore, when an arbitration agreement is concluded by an agent, the intention of both agent and the counter-party is to bind the principal to the agreement hereof. Hence, it is necessary to proceed with the theory of agency to analyze the validity of expansion of an arbitration agreement concluded in the name of a group of companies on the non-signatory members of the group.

3.1.1 Expansion of the Validity of the Arbitration Agreement in the Context of a Disclosed Principal

It is provided in Article 162 of the Civil Code of the People's Republic of China (hereinafter referred to as "Civil Code of China") that, "A juridical act performed by an agent in the name of the principal within the power conferred on the agent shall be binding on the principal." It thus could be presumed that there are four elements composing the disclosed agency, which are, firstly, the act to be represented; Secondly, the agent's expression of intent which includes not only the positive agency action of showing expression of intent to other people but also the negative agency action of accepting others' expression of intent; Thirdly, the acts within the delegated authority, i.e., the agent's acts should not be beyond the delegated authority, or else it constitutes unauthorized agency; Fourthly, the agent acts in the name of the principal, it reflects the principle of theory of agency, that is, when the agent performs civil legal acts, the relationship of agency should be revealed to relative persons. Accordingly, under the context of disclosed agency, the substantive party to the arbitration agreement concluded by the group company is the member within the group company expressly stated in the contract, even if the member company has not signed the arbitration agreement *pro ce*, it shall be bound by the arbitration agreement by all means.

3.1.2 Expansion of the Validity of the Arbitration Agreement in the Case of Undisclosed Agency

In contrast to disclosed agency, China has introduced the theory of undisclosed agency with reference to the Convention on Agency in the International Sale of Goods. According to Article 925 of Civil Code of China, "Where an agent, acting within the scope of authority granted by the principal, concludes a contract with a third person in his own name, if the third person is aware of the agency relationship between the agent and the principal, the said contract shall directly bind the principal and the third person, unless there is definite evidence establishing that the said contract binds only the agent and the third person." In terms of the effect of attribution of agency, this article has the same effect of attribution of agency as Article 162, the only difference being whether it is in the name of the agent or in the name of the principal①.

According to the privity of contract, an entrustment contract between a trustor and a trustee is not binding on third party, where a contract concluded in the own name of a trustee with a third party is generally binding merely between themselves. Under this article, however, a contract concluded by the trustee in its own name with a third party shall directly bind the trustor and the third party if the following requirements are satisfied.

(1) Within the scope of the principal's authorization.

The legal act performed by the trustee must be within the scope of the trustor's authorization. If the trustee is not authorized or the agency action exceeds the scope of authorization, the constituent elements of this article are not met yet. It is noteworthy that the scope of authorization mentioned here is not the entrustment or fiduciary at the contractual level, but the scope of authority at the agency level②.

(2) Understanding of the agency relationship by the third party at the time of the conclusion of the contract.

The contract signed between the trustee and the third party shall be hereto binding upon them, of which core element is the third party has an understanding of the agency relationship underneath. In practice, there is a considerable controversy over the extent and sphere of "understanding" of the third party. It has been argued that "understanding" should be interpreted as follows: First, besides understanding the existence of an

---

① Leading Group of the Supreme People's Court for the Implementation of the Civil Code, *A Complete Guide to the Application of the Civil Code of China – Vol. 5*, People's Court Press (2022), p. 1253.

② Ibid, p. 1255.

agency relationship, it is also necessary to know the principal in the case to distinguish it from the relationship of brokerage; Second, the content and duration of the entrustment should be aware of to ensure that the trustee does not act beyond the scope of the authorization①. It is also held that what is expressed in this article is that understanding of the agency relationship, which means the fact of agency should be known by the third party, while it is unnecessary to have an understanding of the principal which is not constituted as the contents third party-must-know. In addition, since this article regards the conclusion of a contract between the agent and a third party within the scope of the authorization as one of the constituent elements of its application, it therefore can be interpreted that the content known to the third party does not include the content and authority of the authorization②.

Of the above two perspectives, the author tends to agree with the second view. Although the relationship between the entrustment and the agent is tight, there is a clear difference between them, and the entrustment only involves the legal relationship between the settlor and the trustee rather than the third party. Agency, on the contrary involves the tripartite legal relationship between the agent, the principal and the third party. The "contract concluded with a third party within the scope of the principal's authorization" in this article is binding on the trustee and should not be constituted as an element of the third party's "knowledge". It is too harsh for the third party to require the third party to know the specific content and authority of the agency, which is also difficult to achieve in practice.

(3) There is no conclusive evidence indicating that the contract binds only the trustee and the third party.

---

① Wang Liming, "Research on Contract Law (Vol. 3)," China Renmin University Press (2015), pp. 717-718

② Zhu Hu, "Types and Effects of Exceptions to the Disclosure of the Agency," *Legal Research, Vol. 4*, (2019).

This is a negative element, should there be conclusive evidence proving that the contract binds only the trustee and the third party, the contract would directly bind the principal and the third party in no way. The course of "conclusive evidence" generally includes: first, the contract expressly agrees that the contract binds only the trustee and the third party; Second, even though there are no expressed terms in the contract, it could be inferred from the relevant terms of the contract and relevant facts that the legal binding force is expected only between the said two parties; Third, the contract explicitly stipulates "the trustee shall initially bear the responsibility" or the similar terms and conditions, and it should be known by the third party.

3.1.3 The Validity of the Expansion of the Arbitration Agreement Under the Situation of Indirect Agency

Indirect agency is provided under the Article 926 of Civil Code of China. It should be pointed out that indirect agency is not real agency and do not engender a tripartite relationship of agency. Nevertheless, in special cases, indirect agency possesses partial effect of direct agency[①]. Regarding the expansion of the validity of arbitration agreements under the course of indirect agency, China's judicial practice shows a negative attitude. In the case of applying of annulling the arbitral award of the (2012) Haizhong Jing Arbitration Award No. 001, the review opinions of the people's courts at all levels are as follows:

In the opinion of Tianjin Maritime Court, it is pointed out: "At the time of signing the contract, the agency relationship between Zhuoyu Company and Jinyuan Company was not aware of by Wanbang Company, that is, Wanbang Company reached an agreement with Zhuoyu Company rather than other entities when the arbitration agreement was signed, while Jinyuan Company did not involve in the signing, and there was no

---

① Leading Group of the Supreme People's Court for the Implementation of the Civil Code, *"A Complete Guide to the Application of the Civil Code of China – Vol4,"* People's Court Press (2020), pp. 2504-2505.

other form of arbitration agreement with Wanbang Company. Wanbang Company was confronted with unclarified subject of arbitration when Zhuoyu Company disclosed its principal to Wanbang Company stating that the arbitration could also be initiated between its principal and Wanbang Company after the arbitration agreement was concluded, which overall breach the principle of voluntariness. Hence, it shall be ruled that, there was no arbitration agreement between Wanbang Company and Jinyuan Company①.

Tianjin Higher People's Court's review on the case was "Wanbang did not know that Jinyuan Company was the actual principal at the beginning of signing the agency contract, the act of Jinyuan Company cited Article 403 of the Contract Law of the People's Republic of China intervening in the agency contract and referring the dispute to arbitration could only indicate that Jinyuan Company unilaterally agreed to resolve the dispute by arbitration. Then, the act of Wanbang Company filed a jurisdictional objection with China Maritime Arbitration Commission was a clear indication of its refusal towards resolving the dispute with Jinyuan Company through arbitration. Accordingly, the Court held that there was no consensus between Wanbang Company and Jinyuan Company on resolving the dispute by arbitration."②

The Supreme People's Court agreed with the review opinions of the Tianjin Maritime Court and Tianjin Higher People's Court in its reply of the case, and eventually annuled the (2012) Haizhong Jing Arbitration Award No. 001. As a consequence, it can be concluded that in China's judicial practice, for the cases of undisclosed agency where the principal is not disclosed when concluding the arbitration agreement, the validity of the arbitration agreement between the trustee and the third party cannot be ex-

---

① Reply from the Supreme People's Court to the Report of (2013) Min Si Ta Zi No. 5 on the Annulment of the (2012) Haizhong Jing Arbitration Award No. 001 by the Applicant Beifang Wanbang Logistics Co., Ltd.

② Ibid.

panded to the principal on the basis of exercising the right of intervention.

3.2 Analysis of the Expansion of the Validity of Arbitration Agreements Based on the Theory of Group Company

The concept of "theory of group company" can be summarized as: when a member of a group company enters into a contract with a third party containing an arbitration clause, even if the other members of the group company have not signed the contract but participated substantially in the negotiation, formation, performance or termination of the contract, those companies, as a consequence, are *de facto* forming the same economic entity, and the contract, including arbitration agreements, between the very member of the group company and the third party, is binding on any member company in that same economic entity, including those unsigned companies[1]. This theory first came into public in the arbitral award of Dow Chemical vs Isover Saint Gobain, a classic case before the International Chamber of Commerce (hereinafter referred to as the "ICC") Court of Arbitration[2]. In subsequent arbitration practice, the ICC Court of Arbitration made further analysis and demonstration on the elements of the theory of group company according to the specific facts of the cases. For instance, in ICC Court of Arbitration Case No. 5130, the arbitral tribunal held that all companies in a group company were affiliated to the group company and were involved in a complex international trade legal relationship, and the interests of the group company outweighed that of every individual company therein, therefore, the group company should be treated as an economic entity and all companies in the group company should be bound by the arbitration agreement. In ICC Court of Arbitration Case No. 6519, the arbitral tribunal held, providing that a non-signatory

---

[1] Stavros L. Brekoulakis, "Third Parties in International Commercial Arbitration," Oxford University Press (2010), pp. 154-164.

[2] See Dow Chemical v. Isover Saint Gobain, ICC Case No.4131 of September 23, 1982, 9Y.B. Commercial Arbitration (1984), pp. 131-137.

can prove that it has accepted the arbitration agreement, expressly or implicitly, or that it has actively participated in the negotiation phase prior to the conclusion of the contract, or that it has been directly implicated in a contract containing an arbitration agreement, then it should be bound by an arbitration agreement. In ICC Court of Arbitration Case No. 7604 and No. 7610, the arbitral tribunal held that the common will for non-signatories becoming the parties to the contract of all parties involved in the arbitral proceedings, or the non-signatory had clear knowledge of the contract and consented to be bound by the contract were required to be justified in order to satisfy the validity of the expansion of the arbitration agreement.

Emphasizing Dow Chemical case and subsequent classic cases on the theory of group company, it can be summarized that the requirements for the application of the theory of group company to extend the validity of an arbitration agreement concluded in the name of a company among the group company to unsigned member companies within the group are as follows:

3.2.1 The Group Company Constitutes an Economic Entity

In considering the application of the theory of group company, the arbitral tribunal will primarily examine the corporation structure between several companies of the signatory and non-signatory parties to the arbitration agreement, which requires the establishment of a "tight group structure" and "tight organizational and economic ties" between the signatory and the non-signatory members, namely an "economic entity"①. "Tight group structure" and "close organizational and economic ties" usually embody two aspects:

First, there are relationships between the companies, such as parent and subsidiary companies, associated enterprises, joint ventures, etc. For example, if the parent company of a group company stands on a prominent position, and its subsidiaries and other members are responsible for execution according to the instructions of the parent company, the parent

---

① Stavros L. Brekoulakis n13, 154.

subsidiary is usually identified as forming a tight group company.

Second, the sharing of capital, human resources, trademarks, etc. between companies. For example, in Dow Chemical case, one of the key reasons why the tribunal applied the theory of group company to extend the validity of the arbitration agreement to the non-signatory parent company was that the U.S. parent company had the ownership of the trademark used by the signatory subsidiary with no costs, i.e., the signatory subsidiary company and the non-signatory parent company shared the right to use the same trademark[1].

3.2.2 Non-signatory Party Substantially Participates in the Contract Containing the Arbitration Agreement

Upon the satisfaction of the prerequisite that the signatory and non-signatory party are an economic entity, another important factor in determining whether the validity of the arbitration agreement expands to the non-signatory party is whether the non-signatory party has substantially participated in the contract containing the arbitration agreement. Given the consequence of which usually leads to the identity confusion of several companies by the third party, substantial participation of non-signatories is considered to be one of the predominant elements of the expansion of the validity of the arbitration agreement[2]. Moreover, substantial participation is supportable to the existence of the same economic entity to another degree. On the other hand, substantial participation can demonstrate that non-signatory members have implicitly accepted to be bound by the arbitration agreement[3]. In practice, whether a non-signatory party

---

[1] Stavros L. Brekoulakis n13, 155.

[2] Chi Manjiao, "The Definition of the Scope of Effectiveness of Arbitration Clauses in Affiliated Companies - A Comparative Study Based on the 'Theory of Group Company' and the 'Theory of Piercing the Corporate Veil' ," *Beijing Arbitration Vol. 3* (2008), p. 80.

[3] Ren Yuanyuan, "Study on the 'Theory of Group Company' in International Commercial Arbitration," *Beijing Arbitration Vol. 9* (2009), p. 47.

Bernard Hanotiau, "Complex Arbitrations - Multiparty, Multicontract, Multi-issue and Class Actions," *Kluwer Law International* (2005), p. 50.

has actively participated in one or more phases of the negotiation, conclusion, performance, or termination of a contract including an arbitration agreement is the main factor in determining substantial participation. Arbitral tribunal often holds a comprehensive judgement taking into account the relevant circumstances involved in the case. In Arbitration Award No. 6519 of the ICC Court of Arbitration, the arbitral tribunal indicated that the subject matter of the arbitration agreement may be expanded to non-signatories if it can be proved, either effectively or implicitly, that the non-signatory participated in the contract, or if it can be proved that non-signatory played an important role in the negotiation phase of the contract, or if non-signatory were directly implicated in the main contract where an arbitration clause was incorporated.

3.2.3. Willingness of the Parties to be Bound by the Arbitration Agreement

Consensus of the parties is a prerequisite for the initiation of arbitration proceedings, which is also the ground for the arbitral institution to exercise jurisdiction over the case. Consensus is therefore a key factor must be taken into account when applying the theory of group company. The validity of an arbitration agreement may be expanded only if it is proved that there was consensus between the parties on whether to have non-signatory party as a party to the arbitration agreement, regardless of whether such consent was expressed or implied by the parties[①]. In practice, court and arbitral tribunal have routinely relied on the factual acts of non-signatory party materially participating in the contract to presume that the contractual parties implicitly and jointly intended to agree to the arbitration agreement[②]. In addition, if the non-signatory party within the group company is actively involved in the signing, performance and termination of the contract, this may also be deemed as an implied consent

---

① Bernard Hanotiau, "Complex Arbitrations - Multiparty, Multicontract, Multi-issue and Class Actions," *Kluwer Law International* (2005), p. 50.

② Stavros L. Brekoulakis n 15.

to be bound by the arbitration clause in the main contract[①]. Some scholars, nonetheless, have expressed opposition to this view, arguing that the substantial participation of non-signatory party in a contract is insufficient to result in the necessary extension of the validity of the arbitration agreement to non-signatory party[②].

In the author's view, to examine whether the parties are willing to be bound by the arbitration agreement, the arbitral tribunal ought to stand in the position of an independent third party and make judgement on the basis of the specific facts of the case and the factual acts of the parties. According to the specific agreement of the contract, as the contractual party intends to conduct business with the group company as an economic entity when the contract, and the contract involves the overall operation of the group company in all aspects within the group company, then it can usually be treated as the contractual counter-party's willingness to enter into the contract with the group as an entity, and the substantial participation of the non-signatory party of the group company of the captioned contract can, presumably, be regarded as the willingness to be bound by the arbitration agreement in the contract.

3.3 Analysis of the Expansion of the Validity of Arbitration Agreement Based on the Doctrine of Fair and Reasonable Expectation

The doctrine of "fair and reasonable expectation" is rooted from the regime of "anticipatory benefit". It is defined as: the anticipatory benefit of both parties to the contract is the important economic benefit brought by the business promised when signing the contract; When either party did not properly perform its contractual obligations in accordance with the agreement, the complaint on its misconduct as well as the calculation of own loss of interest of the counter-party shall be made with respect to the fairness as

---

① Stepham Wilske, Laurence Shore and Jan-Michael Ahrens, "'The Group of Companies Doctrine' - Where Is It Heading?" *Review of International Arbitration* 17 (2006), p. 76.

② Chi Manjiao n17, 51.

the value of norms[①]. Under certain particular circumstances, the court or arbitral tribunal considers the expectation of the parties and the fairness and reasonableness of that expectation, takes into account the specific circumstance of the dispute in each case and combines the range of the expansion of the validity of the arbitration agreement, so as to determine whether to hold non contractual party to be involved in arbitration.

According to the textual interpretation, there are two criteria that should be focused on determining the application of the doctrine of fair and reasonable expectation towards the expansion of the validity of the arbitration agreement: first, fairness, i.e., balancing the interests of all parties involved; Second, reasonableness, i.e., the expectation of arbitration shall not be changed with the expansion of the arbitration agreement. Widely affirmed in the modern contract law system, the doctrine of fair and reasonable expectations has become an important theoretical principle of the expansion of the international commercial arbitration agreement to non-signatory parties, and has been recognized by the judicial practice of many countries, including China.

Shanxi Province Datong Huajian Water Co., Ltd. vs Beijing Langxinming Environmental Protection Science and Technology Co., Ltd[②] is a typical case to study the issue of expansion of the validity of arbitration agreement in China, in which two expansions of the arbitration agreement were involved. The first was the expansion of the change of subject of rights and obligations due to the mergers of companies, after Beijing Langxinming Environmental Protection Science and Technology Co., Ltd (hereinafter referred to as "Lang Xinming Co.,Ltd") signed the equity transfer contract with Huajian Industrial Company, Kong Zhiqiang, Huajian Real Estate Company merged with Huajian Industrial Company, Huajian Real Estate Company legally inherited the rights and obligations

---

① Zhang Libin, "U.S. Contract Law: Jurisprudence, Rules, and Norms of Value," Beijing: Law Press (2007 Edition), p. 3.

② See (2020) Jing 01 Enforcement No. 70 Civil Ruling.

of Huajian Industrial Company in the above two contracts after mergers. The second was the expansion of the transfer of contractual rights and obligations, in which all creditor's rights and debts against Lang Xinming Co., Ltd were assigned to Huajian Water Company from Huajian Real Estate Company, Huajian Water Company enjoyed the contractual rights and fulfilled the contractual obligations.

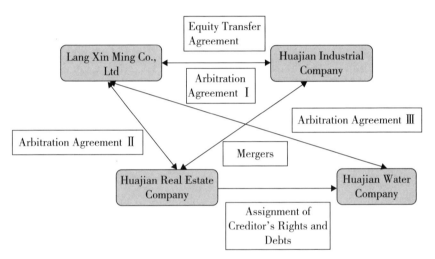

Figure 2 Sketch Map of the Facts of the Case

Beijing First Intermediate People's Court held in its ruling, that: "Neither Huajian Industrial Company nor Huajian Real Estate Company which merged Huajian Industrial Company, had reached any agreement with Langxinming Co., Ltd on the applicability and validity of the arbitration agreement on mergers or transfer of equity, and no party explicitly objected to the arbitration clause when it accepted the creditor's rights and debts or concluded an independent arbitration agreement. In the course of mergers of the company and assignment of creditor's rights, Langxinming Co., Ltd confirmed the aforesaid fact in the form of sealing and raised no claim about termination of entrusted operation income clause agreed in the supplementary contract regarding the transfer of the equity."①

For Langxinmin Co., Ltd, it showed its willingness of selecting arbitration by signing a contract as a contractual party including an arbitration agreement. In this case, Huajian Industrial Company, the original contractual counter-party was merged by Huajian Real Estate Company, and the contract was assigned from Huajian Real Estate Company to Huajian Water Company, the parties herein neither objected against the arbitration clause in the contract nor reached any other agreement. As the dispute arose, all parties involved chose to resolve the dispute by arbitration, which indicated the intentions of all parties to resolve the dispute by arbitration. Based on the interests of the parties under the doctrine of fair and reasonable expectation, the court expanded the validity of the arbitration agreement to Huajian Water Company. Settling the dispute between LangXinming Co., Ltd and Huajian Water Company by arbitration is not against the willingness of the parties and harming the interests of the parties but embodies the respect towards consensus of arbitration of all parties②.

3.4 The Application of the Expansion of the Validity of Arbitration Agreements Concluded in the Name of a Group Company in China

Article 10 of Civil Code of China stipulates: "Civil disputes shall be resolved in accordance with the law; Or if the law is silent, customs may apply, but not contrary to public order and good morals." The sources of civil law provided for in this article include laws and customs that are not contrary to public order and morals. The sources of law are the source of the basis for adjudication in the process of applying law, and it is the au-

---

① See (2020) Jing 01 Enforcement No. 70 Civil Ruling.
② Li Junhai, Xu Zicheng, "Expansion of the Validity of Arbitration Agreements," *People's Justice (Cases), Vol. 23* (2021), p. 106.

thoritative reason for how judgments should be made[①]. It is also the rule on which the courts and arbitration institutions relied making judgments when handling civil disputes. In line with this article, the author argues that under the current legal framework of China, the theory of expanding the validity of arbitration agreements concluded in the name of a group company should be applied regarding the following rules: first, the theory of agency should be applied in priority; Second, the theory of group company shall not be applied at current stage; Third, it is complemented by the doctrine of fair and reasonable expectations.

3.4.1 Theory of Agency Applied in Priority

China is a statutory law country, what ranks first as the sources of law and shall be applied dealing with civil disputes is the law. As an independent legal system, Civil Code of China has set up a specific chapter of clear provisions on agency, including the scope, type, validity, etc. Hence, in the specific dispute involving the validity of expansion of the arbitration agreement concluded in the name of group company, court and the arbitration institution should firstly justify whether the validity of the arbitration agreement is expanded to the non-signatory members of the group company in accordance with the relevant provisions of the law basing on the specific circumstances and conditions of agency.

Together with the previous analysis of theory of agency, the author believes that, when a group company enters into an arbitration agreement in its own name, the arbitration agreement is applicable to the non-signatory members within the group company on the basis of the expansion of validity according to relevant provisions of the law on disclosed agency and undisclosed agency, the elements of application should be around three aspects: first, the group company should obtain authorization of the corresponding company prior to concluding the arbitration agreement;

---

① Li Junhai, Xu Zicheng, "Expansion of the Validity of Arbitration Agreements," *People's Justice (Cases), Vol. 23* (2021), p. 106.

Second, the group company should, at the time of the conclusion of the contract, or incorporate a clause on the agency relationship between the group company and its group member, indicating that the agency relationship exists and there will be no expansion of the principal's proforma right to interfere; Third, there is no explicit expression of group company that the arbitration agreement binds only contractual parties. Where the above conditions are satisfied, the validity of the arbitration agreement concluded in the name of a group company is expansive to the non-signatory members of the group company.

3.4.2 The Theory of Group Company is Inapplicable at Current Period

Per the application of the theory of group company, some scholars have proposed that it can be regarded as the customary law of merchants or the arbitration precedent of ICC[①]. On the contrary, the author thinks the above opinion is not appropriate. China is a statutory law country, where precedent is not an eligible source of law, and by "custom" which is usually deemed as a source of civil law of China should be the state-recognized civil customs[②]. Paragraph 1, Article 2 of the Interpretation of the Supreme People's Court on Several Issues Concerning the Application of the General Provisions of the Civil Code of the People's Republic of China provides an explanation of the "custom" in Civil Code of China. The article states "Folk customs, usual practices, etc., which have long been generally observed by the general public in engaging in civil activities within a certain geographical area or industry shall be recognized as the customs stipulated under Article 10 of the Civil Code of China."

As a new theory to explain the expansion of the validity of arbitration agreements to non-signatories, the theory of group company follows

---

[①] Chi Manjiao n17.

[②] Leading Group of the Supreme People's Court for the Implementation of the Civil Code, "Understanding and Application of the General Provisions of the Civil Code of the People's Republic of China Vol. I.".

the current trend of encouraging and supporting arbitration. But the theory has only been attempted to be applied in a few institutions and countries, and few countries in the world have explicitly recognized the theory, and the results of its application have triggered a wider argument. Switzerland, for example, has taken a prudent attitude towards the theory. The Swiss court stated that "Swiss law would not focus much on the concept of group entity, rather, [it] still insists on the independence of the company from its shareholders, and the independence of the parent company and the subsidiary." ① Further, UK has shown persistent skepticism to the theory of group company. In Peterson Farm case, the UK court explicitly elaborated that "There is no such concept of the theory of group company under English law." ② As can be seen above, the theory of group company has not met the criteria of "long standing" and "commonly applied" in the field of international commerce.

Additionally, as a traditional statutory law country, China has not accepted the theory of group company in any form of legal norms, and there is no case in China's judicial practice invoking the theory of group company to expand the validity of arbitration agreement. Thus, the theory is not suitable, at the time being, as the ground for the expansion of the validity of the arbitration agreement concluded in the name of group companies. If a multinational company needs to sign the contract merely in its own name with the business conducted by its various branches, it shall endeavor to reach the consensus of the contract in choosing the ICC for arbitration, or selecting a country that recognizes the theory of group company, such as France, as the place of arbitration, or to use its law as the applicable law of the arbitration agreement.

---

① Bernard Hanotiau, "Problems Raised by Complex Arbitration Involving Multiple Contracts- Parties- Issues: An Analysis," *18 J. Int'l Arb. 261* (2001), pp. 281-282.

② John Leadley, Liz Williams and Peterson Farms, "There is no Group of Companies Doctrine in English Law," *International Arbitration Law Review* (2004), p.112.

3.4.3 Complemented by the Doctrine of Fair and Reasonable Expectations

Given the specific content of the doctrine of fair and reasonable expectations, it is a combination of the three basic civil law principles in China, i.e., fairness, voluntarism and good faith. Among them, the principle of fairness requires the parties to civil legal relations to take the interests of others and public interest into consideration when engaging in civil activities in a fair way; The principle of voluntarism refers to, that parties to civil legal relations are entitled to create, modify, or terminate civil legal relations according to their own wills in civil activities, and consciously bear the legal consequences; The principle of good faith requires that the parties to civil legal relations shall conduct civil activities by adhering to honest and fulfilling their promises.

The above three basic principles embody the basic social values and norms maintained by the Civil Code of China and play an important role in regulating the conducts of parties to civil legal relations and cultivate the values of social members. The basic principles of civil law are highly abstract and general in nature, which is conducive to overcoming the limitations of the statutory law and empower judges with discretionary to renew and fill the loopholes of the law through the application of the basic principles of civil law. On the other hand however, there is much greater "flexibility" of the civil law principle, in judicial practice, the application of the basic principles should follow the rule of "specific rules exhausted": firstly, when there is a specific provision of law, the specific provisions should be given priority, rather than directly applied basic principles of civil law; Secondly, in the absence of specific provisions of the law, if identical legal provisions can be identified and applied by analogy, the basic principles of civil law shall not be applied; Thirdly, the basic principles of civil law shall be applied only when the loopholes cannot be solved by analogy and other supplementary methods. It can be concluded that the basic principles of civil law can only be in the position of supplementing to specific legal provision, saying in specific cases, the judicial authority cannot apply the basic principles of civil law unless there are no designated provisions in the laws applied, or the legal provisions applied will result in substantial unfairness between the parties, or it will cause damages to public interests. Therefore, when dealing with disputes over the expansion of the validity of an arbitration agreement concluded in the name of a group company, the court and arbitration institution may complement the principle of fair and reasonable expectations and make a judgement in light of the specific circumstances of the case if the specific provision of law is in absence.

IV. Improvement of the Legal System for the Expansion of the Validity of Arbitration Agreements Concluded by Group Company in China

New York Convention confirms the proforma written element of arbitration agreement. Paragraph 1, Article 2 of the Convention provides "Each contracting state shall recognize an agreement in writing under which the parties undertake to submit to arbitration⋯" At the same time, the Convention requires that the written arbitration agreement is one of the necessary conditions for the recognition and enforcement of arbitral awards by all countries. China formally acceded to New York Convention in 1987, and in accordance with the requirements of New York Convention on the formality and content of the arbitration agreement. Article 16 of China Arbitration Law provides: "An arbitration agreement shall include the arbitration clauses stipulated in the contract and any other written agreement for arbitration concluded before or after a dispute occurs. An arbitration agreement shall contain the expression of request for arbitration, arbitration items and the arbitration commission chosen. It can be seen from this provision that China has adopted strict rules for determining the validity of arbitration agreements. In terms of requirements of formality, it is required to have a strict "written form", and in terms of content, it is required to have a "selected arbitration commission". In practice, the strict rules for determining the validity of arbitration agreements have led to many cases in which arbitration agreements are found to be invalid, which objectively restricts the development of the development of theory and practice of the expansion of the validity of arbitration agreements in China.

With the in-depth progress of China's "Belt and Road" and free trade zone strategies, new characteristics such as the complexity of the types of international commercial disputes and the diversification of subjects have also become prominent.The improvement of diversified dispute resolution mechanisms, especially China's arbitration system, has become the focus of China's rule of law. Switching from the strict rules for determining the validity of arbitration agreements and providing more flexibility for the legal system on the expansion of the validity of arbitration agreements should be the first step towards the reform of China's arbitration legal system.

4.1 Legislative Recognition of Implied Arbitration Agreement

In order to meet the needs of economic and social development, the UNCITRAL Model Law on International Commercial Arbitration 2006 (hereinafter referred to as the "Model Law") eases the requirements for the written form of arbitration agreement, not only proposes to waive the mandatory rule for written form of arbitration agreements, but also provides that: "…an arbitration agreement is in writing if it is contained in an exchange of statements of claim and defense in which the existence of an agreement is alleged by one party and not denied by the other."[①] In fact, the Model Law proves its recognition of implied arbitration agree-

---

[①] See paragraph 2, Article 7, UNCITRAL Model Law on International Commercial Arbitration 2006.

ment by confirming the non-deniable conduct of the parties indicating that the consensus of arbitration is reached.

The so-called implied arbitration agreement refers to one party's implied acceptance of the counter-party's intention, in writing or other written form, to arbitrate in the absence of an express reply from that party[1]. Although it is distinguished from a written arbitration agreement in form, the essence of which is still an expression of the parties' intention to agree to resolve the dispute by arbitration. Along with the development of arbitration practice, the laws of many countries and regions recognize implied arbitration agreements. For example, Article 8 of the Arbitration Law of the Republic of Korea regards the parties' conduct of defending as an endorsement of the arbitration agreement; Article 22 of the Arbitration Law of Taiwan Region stipulates that as long as the parties participate in the arbitration and raise no objection, the implied arbitration agreement is accepted then; Voluntary Arbitration Law of Macao stipulates that if one party to the arbitration believes that an arbitration agreement exists, the counter-party, instead of denying it, participates in the arbitration procedure, it would be taken as that the parties have reached a written arbitration agreement.

In response to the development of arbitration practice, the Ministry of Justice of the People's Republic of China (MOJ) issued the Arbitration Law of the People's Republic of China (Amendments) (Draft for Comments) (hereinafter referred to as the "Arbitration Law Amendments Draft") in July 2021. Compared with the currently effective Arbitration Law, Arbitration Law Amendments Draft makes significant changes to the provisions of arbitration agreement. Article 21 of the Arbitration Law Amendments Draft provides "An arbitration agreement includes an arbitration clause entered into in a contract and an agreement reached in other written form before or after the occurrence of a dispute with an expression

---

[1] Zhang Jianhua, "New Theory of Arbitration", China Legal Press (2002), p.105.

of intent to arbitrate. Where one party asserts the existence of an arbitration agreement in the arbitration and the other party does not deny it, then it shall be deemed that an arbitration agreement exists between the parties." This amendment expands the written form of the arbitration agreement and simplifies the substantive elements of the arbitration agreement, which is a progressive manifestation of China's arbitration system's respect towards the parties' autonomy. However, the above-mentioned amendment only adopts the negative criterion of "do not deny" to determine the parties' expression of will, a relatively ambiguous approach that may lead to unfairness in arbitration practice, and ultimately violates the original intention of respecting the parties' autonomy.

The core of arbitration agreement is a dispute-resolving agreement concluded by parties, the author believes that when providing for implied arbitration agreements, the relevant provisions of the Contract Chapter of the Civil Code of China on parties entering into contracts with their actual actions shall be referred to, and the establishment of an arbitration agreement between the parties can be comprehensively determined by combining the parties' positive conducts, such as actual participation in the contract and active participation in arbitration proceedings. If the implied arbitration agreement is confirmed and improved under China's arbitration legal system, the expansion of the validity of the arbitration agreement concluded in the name of the group company will be grounded with a legal basis, and so long as the contractual counter-party does not object to the participation of non-signatory member within the group company in the arbitration procedure in accordance with the arbitration agreement concluded by the group company, or the actual participation of the non-signatory member in the arbitration procedure within the group company, it can be regarded as the existence of an arbitration agreement between the contractual counter-party and the non-signatory member within the group company, thereby the expansion of the validity of the arbitration agreement is achieved.

4.2 Adopt "Principle + Enumeration" Model to Regulate the Expansion of Arbitration Agreement

Paragraph 1, Article 19 of China Arbitration Law stipulates: "An arbitration agreement shall exist independently. Any changes to, rescission, termination or invalidity of the contract shall not affect the validity of the arbitration agreement." This provision is a key to the expansion of the validity of international commercial arbitration agreements. Various interpretations of "changes to contract" in this provision may result in very different consequences for the validity of the arbitration agreement. If "changes to contract" is narrowly defined as changes to the contents of the contract, it will normally not affect the validity of the arbitration agreement; If it is taken broadly, "changes to contract" may also include changes of the parties of the contract. In author's opinion, from the perspective of systematic interpretation, the terminology "changes to contract" in Article 19 of China Arbitration Law should be interpreted in a broad sense. Otherwise for the judicial interpretations of the China Arbitration Law, provisions concerning the expansion of the validity of the arbitration agreement to third parties to the contract under the circumstances of mergers, division, inheritance and assignment of claims and debts will be consistent with the law. Even if "changes to contract" include the change of parties of the contract, China's current arbitration-related laws still cannot address the issue whether the validity of an arbitration agreement concluded in the name of a group company can be extended to non-signatory members within the group company. Therefore, it is necessary to make clearer provisions on the applicable criteria and circumstances for the expansion of the validity of arbitration agreements through the improvement of the legal system.

At present, there are two main ways to construct the legal system for the expansion of the validity of arbitration agreement in different jurisdictions, one is the principled stipulation, which means the applicable requirements for the expansion of the validity of the arbitration agreements are stipulated in principle, while the specific determination criteria are at the discretion of the judge; The other is an enumerative provision, that is, the specific circumstances in which the validity of the arbitration agreement is expanded shall be enumerated. China, in tune with the current legislation system, currently adopts the second model. In view of the fact that the issue of expanding the validity of arbitration agreements concluded in the name of a group company generally involves multiple parties, and cases are more complicated, the author prefers to adopt the "principle + enumeration" model to regulate the expansion of the validity of arbitration agreement concluded in the name of a group company.

The "principle" that governs the expansion of the validity of the arbitration agreement shall be decided in advance if the "principle + enumeration" model is applied. Based on the analysis in Part III of this article, the author suggests that the applicable principle for extending the validity of an arbitration agreement concluded in the name of a group company to non-signatory members within the group should be as follows: regardless the non-signatory party has not signed the arbitration agreement, it has substantially joined the arbitration agreement and expressly or implicitly accepts to be bound by the arbitration agreement. For "enumeration" part, although China's judicial interpretations have provided for several situations to which the validity of arbitration agreements is expanded, it is still lagging behind the rapid development of the economy and society, and many unnamed circumstances are excluded. Therefore, in order to further improve China's arbitration system, the following three types of arbitration agreement expansion should be appropriately added. First, when an arbitration agreement is concluded in the name of a group company, if the non-signatory party within the group company actually participates in the contract and is willing to accept the arbitration agreement, the validity of the arbitration agreement should be expanded to it; Second, when there is confusion between a parent company and its subsidiary, the validity of arbitration agreement should be expanded; Third, the validity of arbitration agreement based on agency relationships and other circumstances should be expanded. The extension of the validity of the arbitration agreement is a special case in relation to the arbitration agreement between the parties, it should only be applied once certain conditions are satisfied. Therefore, the adoption of the "principle + enumeration" model to stipulate the conditions for the expansion of the validity of the arbitration agreement can better ensure the accurate application of the special rules, so as to facilitate the arbitral tribunal to ascertain the facts of the case, identify the rights, obligations and responsibilities between the parties, and ultimately achieve the purpose of resolving disputes in arbitration.

Conclusion

With the continuous development of social economy, arbitration plays an increasingly significant role as an efficient and convenient means of dispute resolution in resolving international commercial disputes. Compared with Western countries, the theory and practice of the expansion of the validity of arbitration agreement in China is barely addressed. From the arbitration cases handled by the author, this paper analyzes the theory of agency, the theory of company group and the doctrine of fair and reasonable expectation, which are most closely related to the expansion of the validity of the arbitration agreement of a group company, and concludes that under the current legal framework of China, the theory of agency should be applied in prior in the expansion of the validity of arbitration agreements concluded in the name of a group company, and complemented by the doctrine of fair and reasonable expectation, whereas the theory of group company should not be applied at this stage. On that basis, in order to further improve the legal system of expanding the validity of arbitration agreement entered into by group companies in China, it is proposed that implied arbitration agreement should be recognized in the form of legislation, and the "principle + enumeration" model should be adopted to regulate the expansion of arbitration agreement.

Studies on the Production of Evidence After the Expiry of the Time Period in Commercial Arbitration

Chen Jing[*]

Abstract: The evidence system is an important element of commercial arbitration. The specified time period for producing evidence is one of the core elements of the evidence system in arbitration, and in certain circumstances, the effectiveness of evidence produced after the expiry of the time period sometimes even has a reversing impact upon the outcome of the case. Different arbitral institutions have different provisions on the procedures and consequences of evidence produced after the expiry of the time period, and arbitral tribunals (arbitrators) often accept evidence produced after the expiry of specified time period. In practice, conducts including the parties' failure to produce evidence within the specified time period, the abuse of time period for producing evidence and production of evidence after the expiry of the time period on purpose will affect the procedural justice of arbitration as well as the case examination that is supposed to be fair and independent, possibly leading to the setting aside of (domestic) arbitral awards under the current Chinese arbtration law. Therefore, it is particularly important for the arbitral tribunal and the parties to be familiar with and strictly follow the arbitration rules of the arbitration institution in handling the evidence produced after the expiry

---

[*] Associate Professor, School of Law, People's Public Security University of China.

of the time period.When a party violates the arbitration rules and produces evidence after the expiry of the time period, the other party (especially the attorney) should actively take lawful countermeasures in accordance with the arbitration rules in order to maximize the protection of its legitimate rights and interests. The production of evidence after the expiry of the time period sometimes parallels with the deliberate concealment of evidence by the holder of the evidence, increasing the risk of the arbitral award's being setting aside. It is suggested that China's arbitration institutions should introduce the system of "compulsory disclosure of evidence" at an appropriate time, give the arbitral tribunal the power to exercise the "compulsory disclosure order", support the corresponding integrity system to restrain the arbitral tribunal from arbitrarily admitting evidence produced after the expiry of the time period, and standardize the procedure handling the prodution of evidence after the expiry of the time period and ensure the consistency of relevant legal consequences of producing so as to ensure the independence and impartiality of arbitration.

Keywords: commercial arbitration; evidence produced after the expiry of the time period; violation of arbitration rules; setting aside arbitration award; compulsory disclosure of evidence

I. Significance of Studies on Production of Evidence After the Expiry of the Time Period

1.1 The Evidence System as the Core of Commercial Arbitration

In commercial arbitration, the collection, organization, submission and presentation of evidence is crucial for the arbitral tribunal's independent and impartial examination of the case and discretionary evaluation of evidence and also the key for the parties and their attorneys to win the arbitration. Under the current legal framwork of Chinese Mainland, the rules of evidence are only stipulated in principle. For example, article 43 of the Arbitration Law of the People's Republic of China(the Arbitration Law) stipulates that "Parties shall provide the evidence in support of their own arguments.The arbitral tribunal may, as it considers necessary, collect evidences on its own." China's domestic commercial arbitration institutions also do not have uniform rules of evidence, and the provisions of the arbitration rules of each arbitration institution relating to specific rules of evidence are not the same, with some only making provisions in principle under the Arbitration Law and some making more detailed provisions. Regarding rules on the evidence produced after the expiry of the time period, different arbitration institutions do have much in common with slight differences, demanding parties to be familiar with, understand, comprehend and accurately apply the arbitration rules of the agreed arbitration institution in order to realize the goals of arbitration in a fair and reasonable way.

1.2. The Important Theoretical and Practical Value of Studying on Production of Evidence after the Expiry of the Time Period

The expiry of the time period for producing evidence is one of the core elements of the arbitration evidence system. Generally speaking, both parties will complete the production of evidence within the time period specified by the arbitral tribunal after upon the agreement of both parties.However, in certain circumstances, when the parties are unable to produce evidence within the time period specified by the arbitral tribunal and also agreed by the parties, it will be a legal issue.Production of evidence after the expiry of the time period is a special exception in the rules of evidence in arbitration, which often does not easily attract the attention of the relevant parties.There are not many in-depth studies in this respect. Evidence produced after the expiry of the time period sometimes leads to a complete outcome of the case. As different arbitration institutions have different arbitration rules on the producing evidence after the expiry of the time period, the arbitral tribunal (arbitrator) often adopts a lenient attitude towards it, and the parties also abuse the relevant rules on producing evidence after the expiry of the time period. Therefore, arbitrators and parties, especially attorneys, should be fully aware of the relevant provisions of the different arbitration institutions in order to be able to use them. It is of great theoretical significance and practical value for parties, arbitration institutions, arbitrators and attorneys to conduct special research and analysis on producing evidence after the expiry of the time period and take active measures according to law.At the same time, it will play a vital role in maintaining the independence and justice of the arbitration system and safeguarding the legitimate rights and interests of the parties.

Production of evidence produced after the expiry of the time period is a legal issue worthing understanding and will be of great value to all parties involved in arbitration.In particular, for the parties and their attorneys, if the parties think that the evidence produced after the expiry of the time period implies underhanded operations, artificially designed traps and other circumstances that seriously affect the fairness of arbitration award, they should take the appropriate legal measures to avoid failing to produce the evidence and failing to respond to the evidence produced after the expiry of the time period, and so on;at the same time, it also involves how to deal with the situation where evidence produced after the expiry of the time period is accepted by the arbitral tribunal, how to submit conditional cross-examination comments in accordance with the arbitration rules, how to expressly object to the written cross-examination as well as the request for the oral hearing of the cross-examination, and how to explicitly state in the cross-examination comments that the right to applying for setting aside the arbitration award on the grounds of concealment of evidence or violation of the arbitration rules is preserved in future, and so on. Moreover, it is necessary to avoid the arbitral tribunal replacing the legal procedure of "evidence produced after the expiry of the time period shall be cross-examined in oral hearing"① with "parties' own verification of the original evidence" and other flexible arbitration procedures, clearly raise objections and make clear the following specific opinions: The production and cross-examination of evidence in oral hearing is fundamentally different from the verification of the original evidence and cannot be replaced with each other. Cross-examination in oral hearing under the auspices of the arbitral tribunal is a legal procedure. The arbitral tribunal's intentional absence and arbitrary alteration of the cross-examination procedure is a serious violation of the arbitration procedure. Such positive and prudent action lays a solid foundation for the parties to the arbitration to set aside the arbitral award in accordance with the law in the future.

It is also of great significance for the arbitral tribunal to make an award in strict accordance with the arbitration rules and prudently deal with the evidence produced after the expiry of the time period. The arbitral tribunal shall strictly abide by the arbitration rules, have a thorough grasp of the facts, case files and evidence, fully and promptly explain the time period for the production of evidence and record it, make a written decision on whether or not to agree to the extension of an application for the evidence produced after the expiry of the time period in accordance with the arbitration rules under certain circumstances, strictly abide by the law and the bottom line of integrity to avoid situations in which an award is set aside or not enforced due to a violation of the arbitration rules.②

---

① According to the general provisions of the Arbitration Law and the arbitration rules of different arbitration institutions, the evidence produced after oral hearing may be cross-examined in writing if the arbitration tribunal has clarified and the parties have explicitly expressed their consent. Otherwise, it shall be produced and cross-examined in oral hearing in accordance with the general mandatory provisions of Article 45 of the Arbitration Law on "evidence shall be presented during the hearings"

② In accordance with Article 20 of the Interpretation of the Supreme People's Court on Several Issues concerning the Application of the Arbitration Law of the People's Republic of China, the term "violation of legal procedure" as provided for in Article 58 of the Arbitration Law refers to the circumstances in which the violation of the arbitration procedure prescribed by the Arbitration Law and the arbitration rules chosen by the parties may affect the correct award of the case. Therefore, if the arbitral tribunal violates the arbitration rules and affects the impartiality of the award, there is a risk that the arbitral award may be set aside.

II. The Relationship Between "Producing Evidence After the Expiry of the Time Period" and " Violation of Arbitration Rules"

As for the evidence system of arbitration, since the Arbitration Law only makes provisions in principle, the arbitration rules of various arbitration institutions become the norms of arbitration conduct that the arbitral tribunal and the parties (including the attorneys) must strictly abide by. If the arbitration rules are violated, there is a risk that the evidence will not be accepted by the arbitral tribunal, resulting in the loss of arbitration, or the award will be revoked. Analysezs of of the relevant provisions of several important domestic arbitration institutions are as follows:

2.1 Relevant Provisions of Several Domestic Arbitration Institutions

According to the Arbitration Rules of Beijing Arbitration Commission(BAC)①, the arbitral tribunal has the right to require the parties to produce evidence within a certain time limit, and the parties shall do so within the specified time period; If the evidence was produced after the expiry of the time period, the arbitral tribunal has the right to refuse to admit it unless otherwise agreed by the parties or deemed necessary by the arbitral tribunal. If a party fails to produce evidence within the specified time period, or if the evidence is produced but cannot prove its claims, the party with the burden of proof shall bear the adverse consequences arising therefrom.

Under the BAC Arbitration Rules,a dilemma may arise where a party produces evidence after the expiry of the time period and the arbitral tribunal deems it necessary to admit it. In that case, the provisions of

---

① Article 32 (2) and (3) of Beijing Arbitration Commission/Beijing International Arbitration Center Arbitration Rules (2015).

the arbitration rules regarding the adverse consequences of the evidence produced after the expiry of the time period will become nonsense. At the same time, the arbitration rules fully authorize the arbitral tribunal to make a decision on whether it is necessary to admit the evidence produced after the expiry of the time period. However, there are no clear provisions on the time, procedure and conditions for making such a decision.In this case, it seems that there are contradictory provisions on the fair hearing and how to ensure that the parties enjoy the equal rights to produce evidence after the expiry of the time period, which may accordingly lead to disputes in practice.At the same time, whether the provisions of BAC Arbitration Rules are inconsistent with the mandatory provisions of the Arbitration Law that evidence must be produced in oral hearing, and whether there is any restriction or deprivation of the parties' right to cross-examine evidence in oral hearing, should be worth further discussion.

The Arbitration Rules of the China International Economic and Trade Arbitration Commission (CIETAC) [1] stipulate that the arbitral tribunal may specify the expiry of the time period for the parties to produce evidence. The parties shall produce evidence within the specified time period. The arbitration tribunal may refuse to accept the evidence produced the expiry of the time period.If it is really difficult for the party to produce the evidence within specified time period, it may apply for an extension before the expiry. The arbitration tribunal shall decide whether to extend it. If a party fails to produce the evidence within the specified time period, or if evidence is produced but insufficient to prove his claims, the party with the burden of proof shall bear the consequences arising therefrom.

The Arbitration Rules of China Maritime Arbitration Commission (CMAC) have include provisions consistent with the Arbitration Rules of CIETAC.

Shanghai International Economic and Trade Arbitration Commission

---

[1] Article 41 (2) and (3) of the Arbitration Rules of CIETAC (2015).

(SHIAC)[①] has made rules on production of evidence basically consistent with the provisions of CIETAC. The parties shall produce evidence to prove the facts on which their application, defence or counterclaim is based. The arbitral tribunal may specify the expiry of the time period for the parties to produce evidence. The parties shall produce within the specified time period. The arbitration tribunal may refuse to admit the evidence after the expiry of the time period. If it is really difficult for the party to produce the evidence within the time period, the party may apply for an extension for producing evidence before the expiry period. The arbitration tribunal shall decide whether to extend it.

Arbitraiton Rules of Shenzhen Court of International Arbitration(SCIA)[②] stipulate that the arbitral tribunal may specify the expiry of the time period for producing evidence, and the parties shall produce evidence within the time period. The arbitration tribunal shall have the power to refuse to admit the evidence if the parties fail to produce within the time period. The parties bear the burden of proof for their claims. The arbitral tribunal shall have the power to determine the burden of proof of the parties. As for the issue of whether the arbitral tribunal has the power to admit evidence produced after the expiry of the time period, only BAC has stipulated that the arbitral tribunal can accept it under two circumstances, while other institutions have not made clear whether the arbitral tribunal has the power to accept it, but only the arbitral tribunal has the power to refuse to accept it. In practice, a question arises. If the arbitration rules do not stipulate that the arbitral tribunal has the power to admit the evidence produced after the expiry of the time period, is it a violation of the arbitration rules if the arbitral tribunal decides to admit the evidence after the specified time period of one party? If it is not a violation of arbitration rules, what is the point of specifying the expiry of the time period for pro-

---

① Article 37 (1) and (2) of SHIAC Arbitration Rules (2015).
② Article 39 (1) and (2) of SCIA Arbitration Rules (2016).

ducing evidence?

2.2 The More Detailed and Operational Provisions on the Admission and Refusal of Evidence Produced after the Specified Time Period in Arbitration Rules of CIETAC

Regarding the evidence produced after the specified time period, the Arbitration Rules of CIETAC[①] take into account the legitimate rights of the parties and give the arbitral tribunal corresponding powers. At the same time, in order to balance the power and obligations of the arbitral tribunal and the parties, corresponding procedural provisions have been made. 1. The Arbitration Rules clearly stipulate the expiry of the time period for producing evidence and the mandatory obligation of the parties to produce evidence within the specified time period. 2. At the same time, it also stipulates the relief procedures for failure to produce evidence within the time period. Where it is really difficult to produce evidence within the specified time period and an application needs to be submitted in advance, and the arbitration tribunal will decide whether or not to agree. The rules only give the arbitral tribunal the power to refuse to admit the evidence produced after the specified time period, but not the power to arbitrarily admit it. 3. As to whether the arbitral tribunal has the power to admit the evidence produced after the specified time period, the Arbitration Rules of CIETAC adopt a conservative attitude, clearly stipulating restrictive conditions and specifying detailed operating procedures. That is, the parties must meet three conditions: first, they must submit a written application for extension ; second, it must be submitted before the expiry period; third, the arbitral tribunal shall make a decision on whether to extend the

---

[①] Article 41 Evidence (2) of the Arbitration Rules of CIETAC stipulates that the arbitral tribunal may specify a time period for the parties to produce evidence and the parties shall produce evidence within the specified time period. The arbitral tribunal may refuse to admit any evidence produced after that time period. If a party experiences difficulties in producing evidence within the specified time period, it may apply for an extension before the end of the period. The arbitral tribunal shall decide whether or not to extend the time period.

time period for producing evidence. At the same time, the Arbitration Rules of CIETAC also clearly stipulate the legal consequences of failure to produce evidence within the specified time period, that is, "the party with the burden of proof shall bear the consequences arising therefrom."

According to the provisions of the Arbitration Rules of CIETAC, if the parties produce evidence late and does not seek relief in strict accordance with the procedures and conditions stipulated in the arbitration rules, it shall bear the legal consequences of failure to produce evidence. In short, the arbitration rules only give the arbitral tribunal the power to refuse to admit the evidence produced after the specified time period, but not the power to admit evidence at will after the specified time period. In the author's opinion, neither the arbitral tribunal, nor the parties or their attorneys, if the evidence is produced after the specified time period and the extension application is not submitted in advance according to the arbitration rules, it should not be admitted based upon a strict interpretation of the arbitration rules.

However, the parties must produce evidence in accordance with the arbitration rules of the selected arbitration institution and local conditions, so as to ensure their initiative and legality in the arbitration proceedings.

2.3 Common Circumstances and Legal Consequences of Evidence Produced after the Expiry of the Time Period in Violation of Arbitration Rules

2.3.1 A Case Study on Typical violations of CIETAC Arbitration Rules concerning Production of Evidence

Firstly, there was no application of extension for producing evidence within the specified time period. Generally, the arbitration tribunal will specify a reasonable time period for producing evidence based on the agreement of both parties. After the oral hearing, the secretary will sort out and print out a "Key Points of the Oral Hearing" and each party will sign as the expiry of the time period for producing evidence. Secondly, although the application for extension was submitted within the specified time period specified by the arbitral tribunal, the stated reasons are not sufficiently comprehensive.Generally speaking, if the parties wish to delay producing the evidence, they should give a clear explanation to specify the name of the evidence, the difficulty of legally collecting evidence within the specified time period and the significant impact of the evidence on the case, so as to obtain the recognition and support of the arbitration tribunal.Thirdly, no objection has been raised to the tribunal's admission of the evidence produced after the expiry of the time period. In arbitration practice, sometimes the arbitral tribunal admits the evidence produced after the expiry of the time period by one party and refuses to admit such evidence produced by the other party without explicit explanation, which violates the arbitration rules that "An arbitrator shall not represent either party, and shall be and remain independent of the parties and treat them equally."①and "Under all circumstances, the arbitral tribunal shall act impartially and fairly and shall afford a reasonable opportunity to both parties to present their case."②While the other party does not raise a timely objection in writing to the abovementioned violation of the arbitration rules.Fourthly, one party fails to timely require the arbitral tribunal to ask the other party to produce evidence. If the evidence that is not produced timely by one party but owned, deliberately concealed by the other party, the party should explicitly request in oral hearing, or make a request in writing, or request the arbitral tribunal to ask the other party to produce such evidence Such a requirement of mandatory disclosure of evidence is very necessary, but many parties neglect to put forward for various reasons.

  For the parties or attorneys, if the above situation occurs, it will often result in the loss of the opportunity to provide evidence and the loss of

---

① Article 24 Duties of Arbitrator of The Arbitration Rules of CIETAC(2015).
② Article 35 Conduct of Hearing of The Arbitration Rules of CIETAC(2015).

favorable conditions to apply for setting aside the arbitration award in the future due to improper handling.

For the arbitral tribunal, in order to ensure the impartiality and transparency of the arbitration procedure, avoid procedural defects and the potential risk of the setting-aside of the arbitration award , the following matters need to be noted. First, there is no explanation. The arbitral tribunal is the main force to ensure the justice of the trial procedure, and arbitration is based on the parties' full trust in the arbitration system and arbitration institutions. Therefore, the arbitral tribunal should fully respect the opinions of the parties in the process of hearing, and make full explanations. Specifically, as for the evidence produced after the expiry of the time period, it is necessary to with consent of both parties specify the expiry of the time period for producing evidence, and clarify the adverse legal consequences of producing evidence after the specified time period, in order to avoid subsequent dissatisfaction of the parties.Third, without making a decision on whether to admit the evidence produced after the specified time period and arbitrarily admit the evidence.According to the Arbitration Rules of CIETAC, if the arbitral tribunal considers that the time period for producing evidence needs to be extended, generally speaking, the arbitral tribunal should make a corresponding decision on the basis of the parties' application and explain it to the parties in a timely and full way through the arbitral institution, rather than arbitrarily admitting the evidence produced after the specified time period without explanation and decision.

If the arbitration tribunal violates the arbitration rules in terms of the time period of producing evidence, there is a risk that the award may be set aside on such legal ground.It is also harmful to the reputation of the institution.

2.3.2 Key Points for Evidence Produced after the Expiry of the Time Period

For the arbitrators, attorneys and parties, when submitting to the arbitration institution, it is necessary to learn and comprehend the provisions on the evidence produced after the expiry of the time period, so as to protect their procedural rights and avoid producing evidence after the expiry of the specified time period and bearing the the corresponding adverse legal consequences.Firstly, the accurate understanding and grasp of arbitration rules shall be always stressed. Secondly, it is necessary to have a understanding of the procedures and conditions of producing evidence after the specified time period. Rules may vary with the arbitration insititutions and legal consequences are diversified., Thirdly, the right to apply shall be exercised strictly in accordance with the conditions, procedures and time period of the rules.Fourthly,sufficient plans and countermeasures shall be made for the decision of the arbitral tribunal on whether to agree to the extension.The countermeasures include: ① As far as possible, the evidence collection work should be complete, comprehensive, solid and sufficient in advance for the arbitration claim, defense or counterclaim. ② Be meticulous, comprehensive and self-consistent in the study and judgment of the case, and strive to avoid the situation of producing evidence after the expiry of the time period. ③ If, according to the development of the situation, new evidence emerges that has a significant impact on the fair arbitration, the parties shall, within the time period specified by the arbitral tribunal, apply to the arbitral tribunal for an extension of producing evidence and state the reasons and the necessity in strict accordance with the law. ④ If one party's application for extension of producing evidence is refused by the arbitral tribunal while the other party's evidence produced after the specified time period is admitted, one party shall argue on the grounds that the arbitral tribunal should give equal arbitration rights to both parties, and request the arbitral tribunal to treat both parties' evidence produced after the specified time period equally.5.If the arbitral tribunal refuses to admit a party's application for extension of producing evidence while accepts such extension the other party appleid for without giving a full and clear explanation to the party in advance, a party may, after the award is rendered, claim that "the composition of the arbitral tribunal or the arbitral procedure violates legal procedure" on the basis of Article 58 (3) of the Arbitration Law and request the court to set aside the arbitration award.6.As for the "Key Points of the Oral Hearing" issued by the arbitration tribunal after the oral hearing, if the parties do not agree with the time period for producing evidence specified by the arbitration tribunal, or do not agree that the arbitration tribunal examine the evidence produced after the oral hearing, you may reserve your right to express your objection clearly on the "Key Points of the Oral Hearing".

III. The Connection Between the Evidence Produced After the Expiry of the Time Period and the Deliberate Concealment of Evidence by the Holder (and Setting Aside the Arbitration Award)

This is a common problem in practice, as mentioned in the previous part of this paper. It is discussed here as a separate issue in order to attract the parties to attach great importance to it and deeply understand and apply it, so as to lay a solid foundation for applying for setting aside the unfavorable arbitration award in the future.According to the Chinese Arbitration Law, if the other party conceals any evidence which can affect the impartiality of the arbitration award, it can be used as the legal reason for setting aside the arbitration award.[①]In practice, the problem often encountered in practice is that the evidence that the party wants to collect is often held by the other party, and the evidence holder refuses to produce the evidence or disclose the evidence, so that it is often difficult for the other party to collect such evidence .However, it does not mean that the evidence-collecting party only has to wait passively. On the contrary, the evidence-collecting party should formulate positive arbitration strategies

---

① Article 58 (5) of the Arbitration Law.

according to the law and arbitration rules, and take comprehensive and prudent countermeasures to safeguard its arbitration rights, and lay the foundation and create conditions for application for setting aside the arbitration award on the grounds that the evidence holder intentionally concealed the evidence in the future.

The evidence produced after the expiry of the time period, more than often, is held by the other party. Due to the lack of mandatory disclosure mechanism in mianland China, under normal circumstances, evidence holders will not disclose or provide evidence against themselves to the arbitral tribunal. For the evidence-collecting party, due to the lack of compulsory relief means, it is often difficult to collect key evidence during the time period specified by the arbitral tribunal. According to the Arbitration Law and judicial interpretation, the system design of setting aside the arbitration award and not enforcing the arbitration award is not only a punitive provision for the intentional concealment of evidence, but also a means of after-action relief for the evidence-collecting party. The parties to arbitration should fully understand and take this provision as an important means to safeguard their own rights and interests.

In the casewhere the evidence cannot be produced, the evidence-collecting party should focus on the three relevant legal provisions respectively providing"produce evidence after the expiry of the time period", "intentional concealment" [1] and "setting aside the arbitration award"[2], and carefully carry out the corresponding professional arrangements.If, within the time period specified by the arbitral tribunal, the party under the burden of proof fails to collect evidence due to the other party's intentional concealment of evidence, it shall, in accordance with the arbitration rules,

---

[1] Article 58 (5) of the Arbitration Law stipulates that the other party has withheld the evidence which is sufficient to affect the impartiality of the arbitration.

[2] Article 58 of the Arbitration Law stipulates that the people's court shall rule to set aside the arbitration award if a collegial panel formed by the people's court verifies upon examination that the award involves one of the circumstances set forth in the preceding paragraph.

submit an "Application for Extension of Evidence" to the arbitral tribunal in time. In the application, the following matters shall be clearly defined: the act of the other party intentionally concealing evidence, the name of the evidence intentionally concealed and the key role of the evidence in the fair examination of the case, the intention to require the other party to produce evidence, and the act of the other party refusing to produce evidence.For each of the above, corresponding evidence should be produced to support and form a closed loop. Although the evidence-collecting party cannot collect evidence within the specified time period, it should clearly submit the application for the extension of producing evidence;If the arbitration tribunal refuses the application and there are circumstances that affect the impartiality of the arbitration, the arrangement of each mentioned above can be used as a legal reason for setting aside the arbitration award in the future.Of course, there are many factors to be considered in the application for applying to set aside the arbitration award, and there are strict restrictions. The key one is to have sufficient evidence to prove whether it has a substantial impact on the rights of the parties, and whether it may have a significant impact on the fair and correct award. The various arrangements of the above links should also be carried out around this point.

IV. How to Correctly Deal with the Arbitral Tribunal's Arbitrary Admission to the Evidence Produced by the Other Party After the Specified Time Period

What the author refers to is not a frequently encountered problem. However, it may to much extent impact the parties' rights in arbitration proceedings. This article will have a in-depth discussion over the aforesaid issue so as to share more informative insights with the parties.

Referring to the judicial practice of Chinese courts, the court considers the subjective aspects of the parties and the degree of correlation between evidence and facts to decide whether to admit. According to the legal provisions and judicial practice in Chinese Mainland's civil procedure, the legal effect of evidence produced after the specified time period is not universal. We often adopt different attitudes according to whether the party is intentional or gross negligence.In judicial practice, if a party refuses to cross-examine evidence on the grounds that the other party has submitted evidence after the specified time period, can the people's court admit the evidence? The Supreme People's Court did not adopt an one-size-fits-all approach, but adopted a differentiated approach.[①]According to the provisions, the people's court's approach shall vary with the subjective fault degree of the parties who produced evidence after the specified time period.Firstly, as for the evidence produced after the expiry of the time period by the party intentionally or negligently, the people's court may decide whether or not to admit it based on whether it is related to the basic facts of the case.Secondly, on the contrary, the people's court shall admit the evidence produced by the parties that is not due to intent or gross negligence.

Reference significance of judicial practice for arbitration shall be highlighted. In civil proceedings, the other party should not simply refuse or abandon the cross-examination of evidence provided by the party after the specified time period. In arbitration, if one party produces evidence after the time period, the other party shall look into whether such conduct has violated the arbitration rules, whether the evidence should be cross-examined in oral hearing, whether the evidence is related to the ba-

---

[①] Article 102 (1) and (2) of the Interpretation on the Application of the Civil Procedure Law of the People's Republic of China stipulates: "The people's court shall not accept evidence produced by a party within the prescribed time limit with intentional or gross negligence.However, if the evidence is related to the basic facts of the case, the people's court shall accept it and give a reprimand or fine in accordance with the provisions of Article 65 and Paragraph 1 of Article 115 of the Civil Procedure Law. The people's court shall accept the evidence provided by the parties within the prescribed time limit without intentional intent or gross negligence, and admonish the parties."

sic facts of the case, and whether the evidence produced after the specified time period has evidential value for the basic facts of the case, and make a correct judgment. For parties in such status, it is important to remember not to simply refuse to cross-examine on the grounds that the other party has produced evidence after the specified time period, but should actively respond to it and cross-examine on the premise of clarifying the above circumstances, in order to avoid bearing adverse legal consequences.

In arbitration proceedings, if a party is confronted with the situation in which the arbitral tribunal admits the evidence produced after the specified time period by the evidence holder, a more prudent strategy is to make a positive response to cross-examination within the time period of cross-examination specified by the arbitral tribunal. However, opinions shall be submitted to the tribubal, stating that cross examination under such circumstances is only conditional with objections clearly raised. For instance, the party shall argue that the arbitration tribunal admit the evidence produced after the time period is against the arbitration rules, requiring that the evidence shall be presented and cross-examined in oral hearing, stressing that this circumstance can be a legal ground for the setting aside the abrbitration award. In this way, the party will seize the initiative on defending its own rights and interests, promoting fair and impartial arbitration by the arbitral tribunal, and forcing the other party to return to the right track of arbitration in accordance with the law.

V. Legislative Proposals on Legal Issues concerning Evidence Produced After the Expiry of the Time Period

Given the complexity and difficulty of legislation, it is suggested that the Chinese arbitration institutions may learn from the experience of their foreign counterparts and introduce mandatory disclosure of evidence into the law-making. Meanwhile, the strengthening of power by the arbitral tribunal shall be in strict compliance and relevant legal provisions. The arbitration tribunal may sign a letter of integrity commitment while exercising the power of the mandatory disclosure so as to maintain the credibility of the arbitrators and the arbitration system.

5.1 Relevant Provisions of International Arbitration Institutions

5.1.1 Hong Kong International Arbitration Centre (HKIAC)

With regard to the system of evidence for arbitration, HKIAC does not have specific rules concerning evidence producted after the expiry of time period. Instead, its arbitration rules just provide generally on whether the arbitral tribunal has the power to refuse or admit the evidence or not. This is an example worthy of reference by mainland arbitration institutions. According to HKIAC Arbitration Rules, firstly, the time period for producing evidence is "in the arbitration process". Secondly, the parties can choose to submit evidence by choice or upon the request of the arbitral tribunal.Thirdly, the arbitral tribual can resuqest the production of evidence at any time Fourthly, HKIAC Arbitration Rules expressly grants the arbitral tribunal the power to "admit or exclude any documents, exhibits or other evidence." [①]

5.1.2 Relevant Provisions of the Arbitration Court of The Arbitration Institute of the Stockholm Chamber of Commerce (SCC)

SCC has made a similar disclosure provision, only emphasizing that " at the request of a party, or exceptionally on its own motion, the Arbitral Tribunal may order a party to produce any documents or other evidence that may be relevant to the case and material to its outcome." [②]

---

① Article 22.3 Evidence and Hearings of Administered Arbitration Rules of HKIAC stipulates: "At any time during the arbitration, the arbitral tribunal may allow or require a party to produce documents,exhibits or other evidence that the arbitral tribunal determines to be relevant to the case and material to its outcome. The arbitral tribunal shall have the power to admit or exclude any documents, exhibits or other evidence."

② Refer to: SCC Article 26 Evidence (1).

5.1.3 Provisions of the American Arbitration Association (AAA)

AAA also has similar provisions as SCC and HKIAC does, but it emphasizes the power and cognitive judgment of the arbitral tribunal, that is, "at any time during the proceedings, the tribunal may order parties to produce other documents, exhibits or other evidence it deems necessary or appropriate."① AAA also provides that the arbitrator or other person authorized by law to subpoena witness or documents may do so upon the request of any party or independently.②

5.1.4 Provisions of the London Court of International Arbitration (LCIA)

LCIA Arbitration Rules stipulates that the Arbitral Tribunal shall have the power,to order any party to produce to the Arbitral Tribunal and to other parties documents or copies of documents in their possession, custody or power which the Arbitral Tribunal decides to be relevant.③

5.2 Suggestions on How to Improve the Evidence Produced after the Expiry of the Time Period

This article suggests that incorporation of the mandatory evidence disclosure system is necessary. However, given the difficulty and procedure of legislative amendment, under the current framework of the arbitration law, by learning from the experience of Hong Kong, Singapore, the United States, London and Stockholm, and taking into account China's national conditions, the arbitration rules should be amended to give the arbitral tribunal the power to force the disclosure of evidence. In this way, it can greatly reduce the difficulty of collecting concealed evidence, improve the efficiency of arbitration, promote the fair arbitration, and enhance the confidence of the parties in the arbitration system.

It is suggested that the arbitration rules clearly stipulate that the arbi-

---

① Article 19.3 of the AAA International Arbitration Rules.
② Article 31 Evidence, the AAA Commercial Arbitration Rules.
③ Article 22 Additional Powers, the LCIA Arbitration Rules.

tral tribunal has no power to admit the evidence produced after the expiry of the time period without the conditions and procedures stipulated in the rules.

It is suggested to clearly stipulate in the arbitration rules that, if the arbitral tribunal considers it necessary and the reasons are sufficient, the evidence produced after the expiry of the time period can be admitted with the consent of both parties. However, equal treatment should be given to both parties, that is, both parties should have equal opportunities to produce evidence. It is suggested to refer to the relevant provisions of the Evidence Guidelines of CIETAC.[①]

It is suggested that it should be clearly stipulated in the arbitration rules that if only one party's evidence produced after the expiry of the time period is admitted while the other party's same request is refused, it shall be regarded as a serious violation of the arbitration rules. At the same time, it is suggested to build a supporting system of integrity of arbitrators and arbitration institutions, and clarify the responsibilities of relevant arbitrators' conduct, so as to continuously improve and mature the arbitration ecosystem.[②]

Regarding the provisions of the evidence produced after the expiry of the time period, the power of the arbitral tribunal should be authorized on the basis of the independence and impartiality of the arbitrators.In order to avoid misconducts that occur in arbitration, maintain the reputation

---

① Article 5 Time Period for the Submission of Evidence of Chapter II. Submission, Taking and Exchange of Evidence of the CIETAC Guidelines on Evidence stipulates: "Where a party has any genuine difficulty in submitting evidence within the stipulated time period, such party may apply to the Tribunal for an extension before the expiry of the time period by filing a written submission setting out the reasons. The Tribunal shall decide whether or not to grant an extension based on the sufficiency of the reasons. Where an extension is granted, the Tribunal shall at the same time consider giving an appropriate extension to the other party for the submission of evidence."

② Refer to Article 32 of the AAA Commercial Arbitration Rules: "All evidence shall be taken in the presence of all of the arbitrators and all of the parties, except where any of the parties is absent,in default, or has waived the right to be present." " All parties shall be afforded an opportunity to examine and respond to such documents or other evidence."

of arbitration, protect the legitimate rights and interests of the parties, and ensure that the arbitration case are as fair and reasonableas possible, it is suggested to refer to the provisions of the CIETAC to handle evidence produced after the expiry of the time period and also adopts the mechanism of the mandatory disclosure of evidence and the relevant arbitrator integrity guarantee system, and work together to promote the continuous development and maturity of China's arbitration ecosystem.